MEDICAL TRANSCRIPTION

BLANCHE ETTINGER, Ed.D.
Bronx Community College
The City University of New York

ALICE G. ETTINGER, RN, MSN, CPNP
University of Medicine and Dentistry of New Jersey
Robert Wood Johnson Medical School

Consulting Editors
SHERI COALSON, CMT
Maric College of Medical Careers

JENNIFER L. MARTIN, CMT
Editor, *MT Monthly*

KATHLEEN OFFMAN, CMT
Henry Ford Community College

Unicorn Books
Distributed by Pustak Mahal

Developmental Editor	Sonja Brown
Copy Editor	Susan Buie
Proofreader	Nancy Sauro
Indexer	Nancy Fulton
Cover Designer	Joan M. Silver
Text Designer	Jules Design
Desktop Publisher	Jules Design

Definitions for medical terms are based on material from the following sources:

Dorland's Pocket Medical Dictionary, 24th ed., W.B. Saunders Company, 1989
Mosby's Pocket Dictionary of Medicine, Nursing, & Allied Health, Second Ed., Mosby-Year Book, Inc., 1994
Stedman's Medical Dictionary, 26th ed., Williams & Wilkins, 1995
Stedman's Electronic Medical Dictionary, V.1.5, Williams & Wilkins, 1995

Reviewer Acknowledgements—The author and publisher wish to thank the following instructors for their helpful suggestions during the development of this book:

ANN BARTON, Riverside Community College, Riverside, California
EILEEN C. CASSIDY, Springfield Technical Community College, Springfield, Massachusetts
LORRIE GEPHARDT, Vatterotte College, Springfield, Missouri
SARA JANE JONES, Nashville State Technical Institute, Nashville, Tennessee
KAREN A. KITTLE, Oakland Community College, Union Hills, Michigan
JERI LOWRY, Indiana Business College, Terre Haute, Indiana
CAROLYN MARKET, Jones College, Jacksonville, Florida
DORIS MAWN, Riverside Community College, Riverside, California
DEBORAH MARERE, Burdan Institute of Health Professions, Totowa, New Jersey

Dedication—For the support of our spouses, Joseph and Larry, in their patience, understanding, and willingness to assist in this endeavor, we are most grateful. —Blanche Ettinger and Alice G. Ettinger

Publishers
UNICORN BOOKS Pvt. Ltd. New Delhi-110002
Reprinted by Permission of EMC/Paradigm Publishing Inc.–USA

Edition : 2016

Administrative Office
J-3/16 (Opp. Happy School), Daryaganj, New Delhi-110002
Ph: 23276539, 23272783, 23272784 • *Fax:* 011-23257790, 23260518
E-mail: unicornbooks@vsnl.com • *Website:* www.pustakmahal.com

Branch Office

MUMBAI: 23-25, Zaoba Wadi (Opp. VIP Showroom), Thakurdwar, Mumbai-400002
Ph: 22010941 • *Fax:* 022-22053387 • *E-mail:* rapidex@bom5.vsnl.net.in

Printed at : Param Offsetters, Okhla, New Delhi-110020

Contents

*This element appears in every chapter.

Preface

The employment outlook for medical transcriptionists is bright—one that will offer many opportunities for success and personal growth. This text has been designed to enable students to master the competencies required to secure an entry-level position in this fast-growing career area.

We have structured this text in a unique format that represents patient care as seen through the eyes of the healthcare provider. Beginning with chapter 2, the chapters are organized by specialty and are presented in the order that is customary for the performance of a physical examination, i.e., cephalocaudal—head to toe. Since the physician generally begins with an assessment of the skin, dermatology is the first specialty addressed. Chapter 1 discusses the opportunities and role of the medical transcriptionist along with the essential knowledge and skills required to perform successfully and gives an overview of the most common medical reports.

Chapter content focuses on a definition of the specialty followed by a summary of the physician's assessment and common diseases, procedures, and drugs. A section of vocabulary lists the difficult words found in the chapter dictation plus many of the terms common to the specialty. As with a typical medical terminology course offered within the medical transcription curriculum, special emphasis is given to learning root words, combining forms, prefixes, and suffixes. Five exercises, including a particularly challenging one on combining word forms, help develop a thorough knowledge of medical terms. A section on grammar, word use, and style reinforces basic language rules and teaches the special guidelines favored by the American Association for Medical Transcription. Exercises require the application of the rules in realistic report excerpts.

Every chapter also features one of the important types of references for medical transcription and a "Pro Tip" on a topic or skill area that is frequently problematic for transcriptionists. This extensive groundwork and preparation facilitates efficient and accurate transcription of the six to eight reports for each chapter. A commonly used medical report is illustrated and featured in every chapter, and succeeding chapters include a sampling of all documents learned previously. A Performance Report provides a log of work completed and an indication of its quality.

An extensive group of appendices provide reference information on terminology, drugs, abbreviations, language rules and AAMT style, state and province abbreviations, laboratory values, and medical symbols. The final appendix provides answers to all intrachapter exercises.

The heart of this medical transcription program is the dictation on tape. To reinforce listening skills and to foster accurate transcription, each of the 100-plus dictated reports begins with a list of the difficult and/or new words specific to the document. Reports are dictated in a variety of voices and with instances of background noise to simulate the medical transcriptionist's situation in the real world. Students who complete the course will be well prepared to accept the challenges of this demanding, but highly rewarding, medical career.

Note: This Indian reprint edition doesn't include the dictation on tapes.

ACKNOWLEDGEMENTS

We wish to thank our many professional colleagues and staff members for their contributions to this text-workbook. The medical correspondence and documents used in this text represent real-world medical reports. Without the support of numerous physicians at the University of Medicine and Dentistry of New Jersey-Robert Wood Johnson Medical School, this text would not have been possible.

Also, special thanks to Dorothy Fox for the tedious job she performed most graciously.

We thank Rosemary Fruehling and Mel Hecker for asking us to write this book and for their confidence in our delivering a professional teaching/learning text.

—Blanche Ettinger
Alice G. Ettinger

CHAPTER

1

The World of Medical Transcription

Medical transcription is one of many growing professions in the healthcare industry. It offers challenge and interest as well as flexible career paths. This specialty is particularly suited to individuals who like to work independently, learn continuously, pay close attention to detail, and produce a perfect product.

OBJECTIVES

- Examine the overall job environment, types of careers, and future opportunities in the field of medical transcription.
- Explain why the medical transcriptionist is a multi-skilled professional by studying the job expectations and performance standards required by industry.
- Evaluate your own aptitude and personal attributes and assess your readiness for careers in medical transcription.
- Describe the purpose and information contained on the most common types of reports transcribed.
- Explore the issues and importance of record confidentiality and release of information.

OVERVIEW OF THE PROFESSION

The word *transcription* is created from two word forms: *trans* and *scriba.* The prefix *trans* means across, beyond, through, so as to change; *scriba* means official writer. From this definition comes the meaning for transcription: to change the spoken word to the written word.

Transcription had its beginnings in early times when few people could read or write and scribes were hired to copy and interpret the spoken word. Their job was considered important since they frequently transcribed legal and sacred orations into written documents that became the rules and principles by which the society governed its members. Their work provides us with a rich heritage of historical records which portrayed life in their era.

The specialty of medical transcription had its beginnings in the early 1900s when medical stenographers became scribes for physicians who originally had maintained all of their own records. These medical stenographers helped lighten the load for busy physicians by manually documenting all of their patient interactions. Because the technology that we have today was not available, medical stenographers frequently had to follow physicians during rounds, frantically trying to hear and record every word for medical record documentation.

The career of medical transcription evolved with the development of dictating equipment during World War 1. Physicians were able to dictate their findings, modes of treatment, and medical reports for transcription without face-to-face contact. Today, with current technology, a medical transcriptionist (MT) may never have contact with any dictators. From local neighborhood hospitals and clinics to transcription services around the world, physicians rely on medical transcriptionists to provide accurate documentation for their patient records. The medical transcriptionist serves as a vital link between the physician and the patient.

EXPLOSIVE GROWTH IN MEDICAL TRANSCRIPTION

The healthcare profession is the second-largest industry in the nation and is projected to grow at a much faster rate than the average for other industries. This is due in part to the increased specialization in medical treatment and to technological advances in the diagnosis and treatment of disease. Many specialty areas in health care are providing job opportunities for qualified individuals.

Current statistics project increases in employment opportunities for several healthcare positions that require the skill of medical transcription.

	1990	*2005*	*Increase*
Medical Assistant	165,000	287,000	73%
Medical Secretary	232,000	390,000	68%
Medical Records Technician	52,000	80,000	54%

Medical transcription as a specialty is also experiencing a phenomenal growth rate for qualified individuals. Although for years, the profession was not well known because it was not central to hands-on patient care, this field is becoming more publicized because of its diversity, benefits, and career opportunities. The need for trained transcriptionists is growing faster than schools or training centers can supply. Recently, several publications have identified the market demand for medical transcriptionists:

- *Home Office Computing* named medical transcription "One of the Top Ten Businesses of the '90s."
- *Business Start-Ups* magazine selected medical transcription as one of the ten start-up businesses for the future.
- *Entrepreneur Magazine* named medical transcription "One of the Top Ten Businesses in 1995."

EMPLOYMENT OPPORTUNITIES

Medical transcription is a field with many possibilities and areas for advancement. As a professional, multi-skilled medical worker, the medical transcriptionist can choose from a variety of employment options. You can work in a hospital transcription or medical records department; or you can work in a radiology, pathology, or emergency department. You might also find employment in a physician's office, medical clinic, professional medical group practice, outpatient clinic, rehabilitation center, medical transcription service, home office, laboratory, psychiatric center, insurance company, medical research center, or other facility (figure 1.1). Medical transcriptionists can work in specialty areas too. You may choose a specialty which is of interest to you or work initially in a hospital setting and learn many different phases of medicine.

In addition to having a wide choice in work environments, medical transcriptionists also have several career options. You can continue your

Figure 1.1
Transcription is possible wherever there is a computer.

education to pursue a management/leadership role. You can become an instructor, service owner, proofreader, or editor. Once you have medical transcription experience, you may opt to become independent. You may want to establish your own company or work at home using your own equipment, including word processor, dictation system, modem, and fax machine.

Whatever route you take, here's some important advice: The more knowledge and skills you acquire relevant to the medical field, the greater your opportunities. There is a common misconception about the degree of difficulty in doing medical transcription. Medical transcription is more than listening to someone's voice and typing what you hear. You have to acquire a great deal of knowledge and experience to do the job well. Recognizing the important role MTs play in patient care and understanding all of the duties that the job entails will help you get a good start in the field.

ROLE OF THE MEDICAL TRANSCRIPTIONIST IN PATIENT CARE

As a medical transcriptionist, you have an important role as a member of the healthcare team. According to the American Association for Medical Transcription (AAMT), the professional organization for medical transcriptionists, an MT is "...a medical language specialist who interprets and transcribes dictation by physicians and other healthcare professionals regarding patient assessment, workup, therapeutic procedures, clinical course, diagnosis, prognosis, etc., in order to document patient care and facilitate delivery of healthcare services." In essence, MTs transfer the physician's spoken words via tape recorder or digital dictation system into typewritten legal documents. These documents describe the historical and factual data about events leading up to and surrounding patient care and treatment, the outcome of the illness or condition, and the details surrounding release from the hospital.

Some of the most commonly transcribed medical documents include office notes, history and physical examinations, consultations, operative reports, correspondence, discharge summaries, pathology and radiology reports, and laboratory reports. Because these documents become the foundation for a patient's health care, the medical transcriptionist's main responsibility is to produce impeccably accurate reports. A medical transcriptionist also may be responsible for record maintenance, i.e., keeping logs of daily work, printing, charting or delivering medical reports, training, providing administrative support, and evaluating equipment.

PERSONAL ATTRIBUTES OF THE MEDICAL TRANSCRIPTIONIST

Successful medical transcriptionists share certain traits which allow them to fulfill their duties. Read the list of characteristics that follows (adapted from an article originally appearing in *MT Monthly*) and check off those that apply to you. Note that many of the attributes relate to skills that you can develop even if you think they do not describe you now.

Medical transcriptionists. . .

- ☐ have an interest in medicine, medical language, and its usage.
- ☐ love words.
- ☐ have an ability to listen closely to what people say.
- ☐ have a talent for hearing and understanding different dialects.
- ☐ enjoy a challenge.
- ☐ are able to maintain a high level of concentration for long periods.
- ☐ love typing/keyboarding.
- ☐ have an interest in computers.
- ☐ have good memory retention skills.
- ☐ have excellent spelling skills (English, foreign, and medical terms).
- ☐ never guess if unsure of the correct spelling.
- ☐ can think creatively.
- ☐ have investigative minds and know how to use references to research and find correct terms.
- ☐ care about quality and accuracy.
- ☐ take pride in a job well done.
- ☐ are self-disciplined, detail-oriented, independent, and are usually perfectionists.
- ☐ perform tasks completely and comprehensively.
- ☐ are dedicated to professional development and enthusiastically committed to learning.
- ☐ love to help others and share knowledge.
- ☐ are not afraid to ask questions, to know when they don't know.
- ☐ have a caring attitude and an interest in patient care from a medical record standpoint.
- ☐ are careful about keeping patient information confidential.

REQUIRED KNOWLEDGE AND SKILLS

Medical transcription requires practical, detailed knowledge of many aspects of health care and healthcare records. It is your job to manage these records correctly, accurately transcribing dictation, often with short turnaround. Your classroom experiences will help you obtain basic entry-level skills to begin your career. On the job you will continue learning and improving your abilities, which should include the following:

- **High-level keyboarding skills.** As a student, you should be able to touch type at least 45 words per minute. Many positions require 60 words per minute or more. Some experienced MTs transcribe up to 78-80+ words per minute.

- **Computer skills, including the ability to operate various software programs.**
- **Ability to operate dictation and transcription equipment.**
- **Basic background knowledge of the healthcare record, including content, purpose, and format; knowledge of confidentiality issues and ethics.**
- **Excellent language skills.** An MT must know how to use punctuation correctly as well as how to apply common rules of grammar.
- **Above-average spelling skills.** Medical reports often contain foreign words as well as medical terminology. MTs must study and learn how to spell prefixes, suffixes, root words, plurals, possessives, abbreviations, and chemical symbols.
- **Understanding of anatomy (body parts) and physiology (body functions) terms.** Operative reports can be very technical. Pathology reports are very detailed, from descriptions seen with the naked eye down to microscopic features of tissues and other specimens. A medical transcriptionist should therefore know the basic structure and function of cells and tissues in all body systems and organs.
- **Knowledge of surgical terms related to equipment, instruments, and anesthesia.** These terms appear regularly in operative reports and procedure summaries.
- **Directional and body plane terms.** Physicians use a group of special terms to refer to sections of the body and to identify parts of organs or systems in terms of their distance from other parts. These terms help pinpoint the location of an injury or disease. Directional terms are derived from visualizing the body standing in an erect position with the arms down at the sides and palms of the hands facing forward. The following term pairs indicate opposite directions in body sections or organs:

anterior or ventral: front of the body	medial: center of the body, toward the midline
posterior or dorsal: back of the body	lateral: away from the midline
proximal: nearest to the point of attachment or orgin	superior or cranial: toward the head
distal: farthest part from the point of attachment or orgin	inferior or caudal: toward the feet

Body, or anatomic, planes refer to imaginary cross-sections of the body. The coronal or frontal plane is a lengthwise division of the body into an anterior (front) half and a posterior (back) half. The sagittal plane also divides the body lengthwise, but into a "right" half and a "left" half. The transverse plane divides the body horizontally into cranial (upper) and caudal (lower) halves.

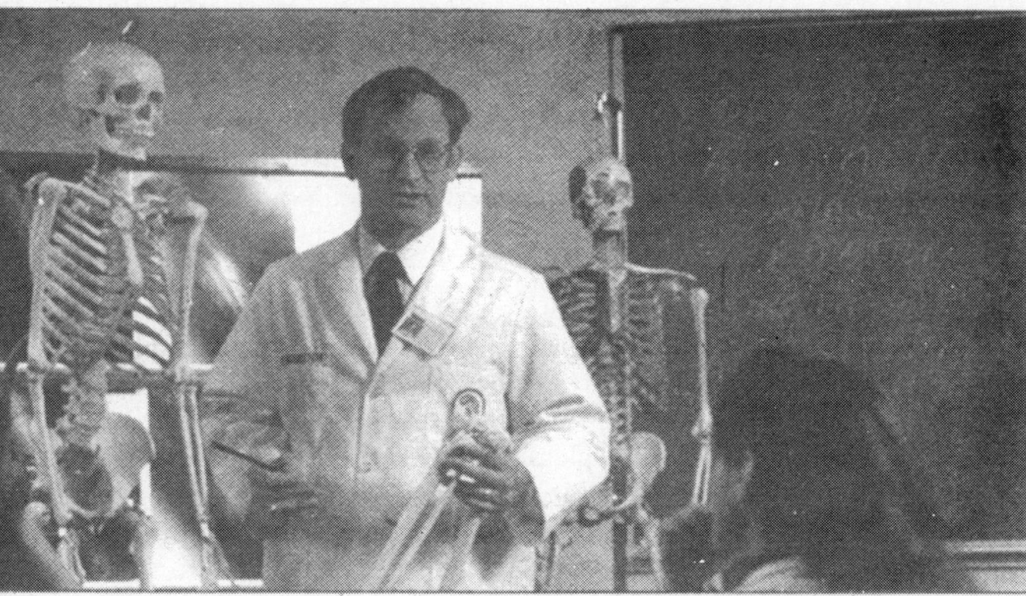

Figure 1.2
Seminars offer opportunities to keep current with industry changes.

- **Background in the common laboratory tests, the significance of the findings, and the expression of their values.**
- **Knowledge of radiology techniques and equipment and terms associated with each.**
- **Drug names and their uses, both brand and generic.**
- **General knowledge of the signs and symptoms of diseases and treatments.**
- **Research skills.** A medical transcriptionist is required to know medical terminology from all fields of medicine. If a term is unfamiliar, an MT should know how to find its meaning and make sure that it fits into the context of the report.

These are just some of the skills you need in order to attain an entry-level position in the field. Because medicine constantly changes, it is important for medical transcriptionists to keep abreast of changes in technologies, breakthroughs in medicine, new drugs, and new techniques. You can do so by attending educational seminars to keep your skills up-to-date (figure 1.2).

GETTING STARTED

If you are not familiar with the process of medical transcription, deciding where to begin can be a bit overwhelming. As with learning any new skill, it is helpful to begin by familiarizing yourself with the steps in the process, the resources and equipment you will need, and how you will use those materials. As you learn, be patient and give yourself time to become comfortable with this unique way of interpreting and communicating medical information.

TRANSCRIPTION EQUIPMENT

Professional MTs use a variety of transcription programs and word processing equipment. Your instructor will explain and demonstrate the particular type of equipment you will use. All transcriber systems, however, have earphones, a foot pedal, and some operational features in common.

Earphones

Your earphones plug into a transcriber, allowing you to hear dictation. Earphones consist of three parts: a chinband, a cord, and a driver. The driver connects the chinband to the cord. With the earpieces in the ears and the chinband near the chin, the cord hangs downward and plugs into the transcriber. This plug may be on the side or on the front of the machine. If you are having trouble hearing with your earphones, one of the first things to check is the earphone cord. It can be worn or cracked and may need replacement.

Earphones are available in a variety of styles. Some have rigid chinbands and others are more pliable. Earpieces also vary from those that fit into the ear snugly, to earpieces padded with sponges, to earpieces that look like small microphones and rest on the inside of the external ear canal. Earphone choice is a matter of personal preference, but whichever earphones you select, you may find that fitting something into the ear for a couple of hours at a time requires some getting used to.

Before you start to play a tape, check the volume and position it at a comfortable range. In situations where you have used the speaker feature to listen to dictation out loud—for example, if you have asked another person to help you decipher a difficult word—remember to turn down the volume after you have finished.

Another point to remember: Earphones collect debris and wax. If they are used by more than one student, they should be sterilized between uses. You may also clean them with rubbing alcohol. Some earpieces unscrew to allow for cleaning from the inside. Use cotton swabs to reach into small areas.

Foot Pedal

The foot pedal allows you to keep your hands free for keyboarding. A foot pedal consists of two parts: the pedal and the cord. Pressing the foot pedal causes the transcriber to play. As soon as you release the pedal with your foot, the machine stops. If you press on the foot pedal and nothing happens, check the cord connection to make sure it is plugged firmly into the transcriber.

Foot pedals are available in a variety of styles. With most models, the center of the foot pedal is the position to press for play; fast forward is on the left; and rewind is on the right. Some foot pedals have only two options: right for play and left for rewind. There is no fast forward on this type of foot pedal.

Look closely at your foot pedal to see which side is which, or test it with your foot. Usually the pedal will have printed instructions on where the positions are. Some models have a knob underneath which allows you to adjust the amount of tension on the foot pedal. Turn your foot pedal over and check to see if it has this extra feature.

Transcriber Features

The transcriber is the device that makes it possible to transform voice recordings into transcript or printed documents. The following features appear on most machines:

ON/OFF button or POWER: This is used to turn the transcriber on and off. Usually there is some type of light to indicate that the power is on. If this light does not come on, check your power source to make sure your machine is plugged in.

INDEX COUNTERS: Some transcribers have an index counter which measures the length of dictation on a cassette. This is a useful tool in finding the correct dictation or in scanning cassettes. The index counter may be an indicator strip and a flashing light or numbers that roll forward or backward as you play the tape. As you fast forward, rewind, stop, or play a tape, the light will move, indicating the minutes of dictation by the numbers on the index counter. You can press the clear button next to the index counter to stop the light from flashing or press the reset button to set the counter to zero.

Some transcribers are set up to "scan" or mark each separate dictation or "seizure." The term "seizure" is coined from the way the report is dictated onto the cassettes. Physicians dictate by telephoning from their office or home to the hospital. They dial a special number that "seizes" the transcribing equipment.

As the tape is scanned, it is being rewound. At the end of every dictation series, you can hear a beep or a blip. At this point, the index counter lights up and marks where the dictation ends for each series on the control strip. When you play the tape, you will be able to see how much more dictation remains. You can tell if you are near the beginning, halfway through, or almost finished.

AUTO PLAYBACK/AUTO REWIND: This feature allows you to replay a word or a string of words. Using an auto backspace button on the bottom of the transcriber, set the adjustment to whatever is comfortable for you. With a digital dictation system, this adjustment may have to be made via a computer system. A little repeat at the beginning is usually helpful by ensuring that you are not missing any words. When you begin transcription, your adjustment may be on or near the maximum amount of replay. Make an effort to lessen the amount of replay as you become more experienced.

SPEAKER: Use the speaker button to listen to dictation out loud or to play the tape for someone to listen to. If your transcriber does not have a SPEAKER button, just remove your headphone cord from the transcriber to activate the speaker feature.

EJECT: The eject button opens the cassette door. Press it to place or remove a cassette.

SPEED CONTROL: You can increase or decrease the speed control while you are learning. Try to match the dictation speed to your transcription speed. The voice should not sound distorted, but natural.

VOLUME CONTROL: Some physicians speak loudly while others are difficult to hear. Increase or decrease the volume to compensate for a louder or softer voice.

TONE: This feature mutes or accentuates consonants (treble/bass) for nasal tones or a stuttering style of dictation.

ERASE: This feature allows you to clear or erase tapes. Be careful with this button to make sure you do not erase dictation before it is transcribed.

Tapes

Standard cassette transcribers play standard audio tapes. There are also microcassette transcribers and minicassette transcribers. When you insert a cassette, make sure the side you wish to play is top side up.

THE TRANSCRIPTION PROCESS

The steps in the transcription process are listed below. As you review the steps, create a mental picture of each one to help you learn the entire sequence:

1. Place all the information and materials you need at your workstation.
2. Position the headset, transcriber, and foot control in the desired location and make sure the components are connected to the unit.
3. Check that the transcription unit is turned on and ready to go.
4. Insert the medium (standard cassette or minicassette).
5. Reset the indicator strip to estimate the length of the document.
6. Adjust the volume and speed controls as necessary.
7. Listen to the instructions (all instructions).
8. Transcribe the dictation.
9. Proofread the document and correct all errors.
10. Print the final document.

USING REFERENCE MATERIALS

One resource that is indispensable for the transcriptionist is a reference library. Although the list of available books is enormous, experienced transcriptionists generally agree that only a few are essential for the beginning transcriptionist.

The following references are types of must-have books that provide general information on medical terminology, language style, drug names, and technical terms. These references are discussed in more detail in chapters 2-13. As you encounter new specialties in your work, you will want to add specialty-specific books to your collection—for example, OB/GYN (obstetrics/gynecology) words, neurology words, or radiology/oncology words.

- **Medical Dictionary.** This book is the medical transcriptionist's primary reference, providing complete definitions of terms listed in alphabetical order. Take time to explore your dictionary, especially the appendices in the back and user's guide in the front. Medical dictionaries also include anatomy charts, which can be helpful sources for terms that sound mumbled. For example, if you know that the dictator is talking about a muscle in the face but you do not recognize even the first sound in the term, looking at the chart may suggest a word that sounds like what the dictator has said.

- **Drug Book.** Your drug book will be your resource that gets the most wear and tear. You can look up drugs by their generic name, trade name, and sometimes indication or usage. This is an excellent source when verifying drug spelling, dosages and indications. Your drug book will often have lab values, abbreviations commonly used in medical orders, chemotherapy regimens, and a list of sound-alike words in the appendices.

- **Medical Style Guide.** This resource provides information on report formats and the use of abbreviations, numbers, capital letters, and punctuation. The standard guide is the *AAMT Book of Style.*

- **Medical Word Book/Medical Phrase Index.** Here you should be able to find just about anything you are looking for—if you have a pretty good idea of how to spell it. If you can make out part of a phrase but not all of it, you can look it up by the word(s) you are able to hear because of the cross-referencing feature. This type of book does not contain definitions.

- **Abbreviations & Acronyms.** You will run into many abbreviations in transcription. Always look up the abbreviation to make sure it is correct and fits into the context of what you are transcribing.

  Tip: If you cannot decipher a word or phrase but can understand some of the syllables, check to see if it is an acronym or abbreviation.

- **Medical Equipment/Surgical Words Book.** This resource lists specific equipment names—especially trade names, e.g., McLean clamp—and surgical terminology that you will not likely find elsewhere, e.g., Lempert incision.

- **Laboratory Word Book.** In this book, you will find laboratory reference range values, eponymic diseases and syndromes and—especially helpful—laboratory test names.

  Tip: If you do not find an answer in one book, go to another. Books on medical equipment words and books of medical phrases have many of the same category entries, but a specific suture, for example, may only be listed in one of them.

- **Eponym Book.** Eponyms are instrument, disease, or procedure names usually derived from the last name of the person who developed the procedure or designed the instrument. An example is *Parkinson's disease.* An eponym reference book lists these names alphabetically.

Additional nonmedical resources that provide essential information include a standard English dictionary and an English language reference manual.

CARDINAL GOALS OF TRANSCRIPTION

With chapter 2, you will begin learning the skills involved in high-quality transcription, including recognizing and understanding medical terminology; proofreading and editing for correct word use and the mechanics of punctuation and capitalization; and keying medical reports in the correct format and style. As you develop your abilities, keep in mind the cardinal goals shared by the best professional medical transcriptionists: accuracy, speed, confidentiality, and ethical behavior.

Accuracy

Unless your document is accurate, a fast typing speed is useless. A medical transcriptionist should always strive for accuracy first and then work toward speed. Learn from your mistakes, ask for help, and apply your own creativity and curiosity as you research answers to questions. Remember that each dictated report becomes a legal document as well as a medical record on which the care and treatment of the patient is based. Because records play such an important role in patient care communication, it is important to correct any errors identified after the report has been transcribed. Each employer has specific procedures and guidelines to correct, change, or add information.

Speed

To get a job, you will need to have high-level keyboarding skills. During your course of study, try to steadily increase your speed. This depends on the integration of two levels of skill: a) keyboarding ability and b) your growing knowledge base. A medical transcriptionist can only key as fast as the dictated word can be heard, spelled correctly, researched, and fit into context. Your instructor may establish speed criteria to meet as you complete this beginning course. Having realistic goals that approximate industry standards can help you focus, evaluate your progress, and improve.

Confidentiality

Confidentiality equals high-quality health care. Medical transcriptionists have both a moral and legal responsibility to keep all patient record information confidential. They must protect the privacy of patients by not discussing patient information with anyone and by making sure that only those people authorized to see a patient's record have access to it. Never give information to a patient's family member or a media representative. Be careful when faxing or delivering reports and do not leave a modem on when you are away from a machine. No identifying information on a patient should leave an MT's place of employment.

Maintaining patient privacy also means that MTs should access chart information only as necessary to provide for the accuracy of the document. Check your hospital or workplace policy for complete confidentiality guidelines. Frequently, an employer will ask a new medical transcription employee to sign a confidentiality agreement. Violation may result in termination or prosecution.

Ethical Behavior

Ethics are moral principles and high standards of personal integrity. Behaving ethically means to conduct oneself in such a manner as to bring dignity and honor to one's profession and person. It means that no matter what is happening in your personal life, you remain objective and expend your best effort with each report. It also means that you respect the dignity of patients and provide considerate care and communication through your work habits so as not to cause a patient harm.

Ethical behavior also means refusing to partake in unethical practices and refusing to conceal them. MTs need to recognize the levels of authority and know when to seek information about proper protocol or procedure.

WORKING WITH MEDICAL RECORDS

A medical record is a permanent compilation of written documents that provide information and insight into a patient's life and health history. Many healthcare professionals contribute reports and other information to this record. Since patient care is multidisciplinary, and order and organization are important in communication, the healthcare industry has developed specific policies, procedures, and guidelines that determine how evaluations and treatments are documented in the medical record.

PROBLEM ORIENTED MEDICAL RECORD

In the 1960s, the healthcare industry developed a record keeping method that has helped standardize information and make it quickly accessible in medical databases. This widely used method, called the problem oriented medical record (POMR), requires the physician or care provider to organize information based on the patient's health problem and a plan to treat it. The record has four sections:

1. **Database:** patient history, physical examination, and test results; with this information, the physician diagnoses the problem and develops a treatment plan.
2. **Problem List:** a numbered list of the patient's problems, which may include a specific diagnosis, a symptom, an abnormal test result, or other health problems.

3. **Initial Plan:** a scheme for resolving each problem. The plan has three parts:
   Diagnostic: orders for specific tests
   Therapeutic: goals for therapy
   Patient education: instructions given to the patient
4. **Progress Notes:** a record of the progress achieved on each problem. The notes are numbered to match each numbered item on the problem list.

   Physicians who do not use the POMR format may use the SOAP format. This acronym stands for kinds of information: Subjective (the patient's description of the problem), Objective (lab test results and other information observed in the physical examination), Assessment (an evaluation of the success of the treatment), and Plan (the choice to continue with or change treatment).

MEDICAL RECORDS CREATED IN THE HOSPITAL

The hospital record is composed of several types of reports, notes, and documents. Here is a list of basic reports that may be contained in the medical record of an inpatient. The eight most common documents (highlighted with an asterisk) are discussed later in the chapter.

SUMMARY SHEET (FACE SHEET)	HISTORY AND PHYSICAL EXAMINATION*
ELECTROCARDIOGRAM/ DIAGNOSTIC REPORTS	PHYSICIAN ORDERS
AUTOPSY REPORT*	PROGRESS (CHART) NOTES*
ANESTHESIA RECORD	MEDICATION RECORD
DISCHARGE SUMMARY*	CONSULTATIONS*
OPERATIVE REPORT*	NURSES' NOTES
AUTHORIZATION FOR TREATMENT	LABORATORY REPORTS
RECOVERY ROOM RECORD	CLOTHING LIST
EMERGENCY ROOM RECORD	RADIOLOGY REPORTS*
PATHOLOGY REPORT*	SOCIAL SERVICE NOTES

How Records Are Used

Each hospital medical record provides information for one admission for one individual patient. Medical records are used to provide:

1) a means of communication for patient treatment and care;
2) justification for insurance and compensation purposes;

3) a means to support research and education, monitoring medical treatments that are successful and those that need improvement;
4) statistics for planning how to best use future resources;
5) objective documentation of care or evidence to protect the legal interests of the hospital, physician, and the patient in a court of law.

Legal Issues Surrounding Medical Records

Although each hospital or physician establishes specific rules and procedures regarding medical records, there are general guidelines for handling patient information. These rules have been developed in the courts through years of litigation.

Retention

The period of retention of medical records is governed by state and local laws. It is typically seven to ten years for original records. Some institutions keep their records indefinitely.

Ownership of Document and Content

Medical records which are created in a healthcare facility are considered to belong to that particular facility as the facility owns the paper on which the record is written. However, the patient owns the information contained in the record. Access to the record is regulated by individual state law.

Release of Information

Medical transcriptionists should not release information related to patient care; however, there are some instances where release of information can be accomplished legally. All requests should be processed according to the institution's release-of-information guidelines with the emphasis on confidentiality. There can be no disclosure to any unauthorized person. If there is any doubt whatsoever about releasing information, the medical transcriptionist should not release the information but rather should refer the request to the proper authority. Security of patient records, both computer records and paper records, is very important.

Medicolegal issues that relate to medical records vary from state to state. On the job, you will need to familiarize yourself with the policy manual or office procedure manual detailing your employer's rules for the release of information. If you have questions, consult your supervisor, your employer, or your employer's legal consultant.

Legal Terms Regarding Release of Information

Here are some terms with which a medical transcriptionist should become familiar:

writ
a written order issued by a court or judicial officer commanding a specified person to perform or refrain from performing a specified act.

subpoena
a writ commanding a specified person to appear in court or else serve a penalty for failure to appear. A subpoena of medical records must be honored because it is a legal document.

subpoena duces tecum
(Latin term "in his possession"): a writ commanding a person to produce in court certain specified documents or evidence.

right of privacy
the right to be let alone and free from unwarranted publicity and to withhold personal information from public scrutiny if so desired.

privileged communication
information that may be disclosed only with the patient's permission.

nonprivileged information
this type of information can be disclosed without the patient's permission and usually relates to admission/discharge, treatment dates, name and address of the patient, and name of the individual who accompanied the patient to the hospital or physician's office.

privileged information
any and all information that can only be disclosed with the patient's permission.

breach of confidential communication
the unauthorized release of patient information.

invasion of the right of privacy
needless investigation into another's personal affairs where there is no valid reason to do so, in a way to cause public embarrassment or humiliation to that person.

libel
a written statement or graphic portrayal made or given to a third party that damages a reputation or subjects a person to ridicule.

slander
a witnessed statement that damages a reputation or subjects a person to ridicule.

defamation
slander or libel.

EIGHT COMMON MEDICAL REPORTS

Whether you work in a clinic, at home, in a physician's office, or in a hospital, most of your dictation will involve a core of eight common reports for which you will need to know the acceptable style and format. This section briefly describes each report and includes a sample of the history and physical report, the core document of the medical record. Subsequent chapters of this book will present detailed formatting information for each of these reports:

History and Physical
Operative Report
Discharge Summary
Chart Note
Consultation Letter or Request
Radiology Report
Pathology Report
Autopsy Report

Four major medical organizations have developed guidelines for preparing and managing medical records:

- American Association for Medical Transcription (AAMT), a nonprofit professional corporation for medical transcriptionists and MT students that administers a certification exam and publishes a medical report style guide as well as a journal for members.
- Joint Commission on Accreditation of Healthcare Organizations (JCAHO), a nongovernmental agency that offers a voluntary healthcare accreditation process for hospitals. Part of the accreditation process

requires compliance with JCAHO's standards for the kinds of information entered into the medical record, the completeness of medical reports, abbreviation systems, and turnaround times for report dictation and transcription.

- American Medical Association (AMA), the professional organization for physicians. This group has developed several medicolegal forms that hospitals use regularly, including a variety of patient consent forms.
- American Health Information Management Association (AHIMA), formerly known as the American Medical Record Association. This organization has developed broad guidelines for the development and distribution of patients' medical record information, including positions on the patient's right of access.

Each chapter of this text features a medical document type and presents the AAMT and JCAHO style, format, and content guidelines for transcribing that document. Follow these guidelines to learn the generally accepted report formats. When you are on the job, however, consider the guidelines a starting point. In all cases, it is the dictator of the report who has the final word on style. Medical transcriptionists must follow their employers' special style preferences.

History and Physical

When a patient enters a healthcare system, the physician or examiner generates a comprehensive document called a history and physical (H&P), which becomes the foundation for the medical record. This two-part report documents the patient's medical history, the immediate problem that prompted the patient to seek help, a social and family history, and the findings of a complete physical exam. The primary purpose of the history and physical is to help the physician determine a diagnosis(es), which provides the basis for the patient's care and treatment.

For the history portion (called "subjective" information since it is supplied by the patient), the examiner interviews the patient, asking first for the reason of the visit (called the "Chief Complaint"). This is followed by questions about childhood illnesses and all previous diseases, surgical procedures, medications, immunizations, and allergies. Also included are questions about parents' and siblings' state of health. Finally, the physician asks the patient questions about all the body systems in a cephalocaudal (head-to-toe) order.

The second part of the report is the complete physical examination (called "objective" information because the physician observes it), which also is conducted in cephalocaudal order. Other objective information includes vital statistics and general appearance.

Concluding the entire report is the physician's impression or diagnosis and a plan of care. Figure 1.3 displays a sample history and physical.

HISTORY AND PHYSICAL

Figure 1.3 Sample history and physical report

PATIENT: Raymond Cheever
DATE: 7/10/XX
HOSPITAL NO: 93-22-17
PHYSICIAN: Harry Washington, MD

CHIEF COMPLAINT: Severe pain in the left hip.

HISTORY OF PRESENT ILLNESS: The patient is a 57-year-old white male who is admitted from the emergency department with hypertension, hyperglycemia, and greater trochanteric bursitis.

The patient has been under treatment for greater trochanteric bursitis with Lortab and Naprosyn. He returns today because of increasing left hip pain.

In the emergency room, he was noted to be significantly hypertensive and hyperglycemic. He is unaware of having a history of either.

ALLERGIES: No medicine allergies.

PRESENT MEDICATIONS
1. Lortab 7.5 mg q.d.
2. Naprosyn 375 mg q.d.

PAST MEDICAL HISTORY: Negative.

SURGICAL HISTORY: Tonsils and adenoids removed in early childhood.

SOCIAL HISTORY: The patient does not smoke at present. He stopped smoking six to seven years ago; he smoked an average of a pack per day for many years. He denies ethanol use. He is married. He has two children who are alive and in good health. He works as a plant manager for a chemical company.

FAMILY HISTORY: Mother is alive and in good health. His father is deceased secondary to complications of black lung and asthma. He has two brothers and one sister. He thinks his sister has a history of hypertension.

(continued)

HISTORY AND PHYSICAL
PATIENT: Raymond Cheever
HOSPITAL NO: 93-22-17
Page 2

REVIEW OF SYSTEMS: A full review of systems was negative. He states that his weight has been stable in the past year. He denies polyuria, polydipsia, or polyphagia.

PHYSICAL EXAMINATION
GENERAL: Well-developed, well-nourished male in no acute distress.
VITAL SIGNS: Blood pressure 200/104. Repeat, after rest and pain medication, was 170/96. The pulse was 72. Respiratory rate was 18 and labored. Patient refused to be weighed at this time because of pain.
HEENT: Pupils were somewhat constricted, but fundi were visualized minimally. No hypertensive retinopathy, exudates, hemorrhages, or papilledema were noted. Oral examination revealed no ulcerations, erosions, or masses.
NECK: Supple, without lymphadenopathy. The carotid upstrokes were brisk and equal bilaterally, without bruits. Thyroid nonpalpable.
CHEST: Chest was clear to auscultation in all fields.
CARDIOVASCULAR: Regular rate and rhythm, without murmurs, thrill, gallop, or click.
ABDOMEN: Abdomen nontender and nondistended, without masses, organomegaly, guarding, tenderness, or rebound.
EXTREMITIES: Without clubbing, cyanosis, or edema. Peripheral pulses were intact, with good upstrokes. Palpation of the left hip did reveal tenderness, although the patient did report it was much improved after analgesia.

LABORATORY DATA: Review of a Chem-7 revealed a blood sugar of 201. His urinalysis revealed greater than 1000 glucose. CBC revealed a hemoglobin of 16.3 and hematocrit of 50. White count was 14.7. Platelets were 291,000. Differential was essentially within normal limits.

IMPRESSION
1. Marked hypertension.
2. Asymptomatic hyperglycemia with glycosuria.
3. Left greater trochanteric bursitis.

(continued)

HISTORY AND PHYSICAL
PATIENT: Raymond Cheever
HOSPITAL NO: 93-22-17
Page 3

PLAN
1. Admit.
2. Orthopedic consultation.
3. Endocrinology consultation.
4. Cardiology consultation.

____

Harry Washington, MD

HW/XX
D: 07/10/XX
T: 07/11/XX

Operative Report

This record describes a surgical or other invasive procedure. Whenever a surgical procedure is done in a hospital, outpatient center, or clinic, an operative report should be recorded in the medical record. The operative report is illustrated and discussed in chapter 4.

Discharge Summary

This report summarizes the reason a patient was admitted to the hospital, a short history and a sequential listing of events and treatment that occurred during the patient's hospitalization, and a final diagnosis(es) upon release from the hospital. See chapter 5 for an illustration and discussion of the discharge summary.

Chart Note

Also called progress notes or office visits, these brief reports document the findings from each examination of the patient. The chart note/office visit is featured in chapter 2.

Consultation Request or Letter

This type of report documents the findings of a specialist requested to see the patient of an attending physician to offer a second opinion. See chapter 3 for an illustration and explanation of the consultation letter.

Radiology Report

These reports describe findings and interpretations from x-rays or special diagnostic studies performed in a radiology department. They list a radiologic diagnosis by the radiologist who reviews the films or test results. The radiology report is featured in chapter 6.

Pathology Report

The pathological report describes disease-related findings from a sample of tissue. This report is illustrated and explained in chapter 7.

Autopsy Report

The autopsy report is also a pathological report requested by the attending physician or a coroner to determine a patient's cause of death. Also called a post-mortem, this report is featured in chapter 13.

STRATEGIES FOR LEARNING

As you learn to transcribe medical documents, you will be integrating the skills of using language correctly; choosing the proper medical terms based on what you hear dictated; applying your knowledge of the mechanics of punctuation, capitalization, abbreviations, and spelling; and formatting medical reports according to healthcare industry standards. Initially, you may experience some frustration dealing with the challenges of this demanding area of study. But those challenges should be balanced with the satisfaction of knowing you will one day play a critical role in an important area of people's lives. As a medical transcriptionist, you will provide essential services and support to physicians and personnel who count on you to communicate medical information. You become a partner in the vital business of caring for people's health.

ISSUES FOR DISCUSSION

1. In the future, transcriptionists may not hear the dictator's voice but instead receive electronic files of reports that the computer "transcribed" from voice input. The following article, reprinted with permission from the publisher of *MT Team Times,* dramatizes this scenario. Read the article; then answer the questions below.
   - How would this scenario change your job as a medical language specialist?
   - How would your job remain the same?

How High-tech is Really High-tech?

The days of couriers dashing about in 5 o'clock traffic to deliver a stat, of MTs leafing through reams of patient census reports for demographic information, and of MT companies and MTs shouldering tremendous telcom costs for re-recording are rapidly coming to an end.

So, just how high-tech could we be with today's technology? Well, consider this scenario. You're an MT working across the country from your company's networking center. An hour prior to starting your scheduled shift, a full day's dictation was transmitted to your hard drive via your company's *intranet.* The digital voice file is completely *encrypted*, secure and confidential at all times. A bridge to the provider's master patient index (*MPI*) provides you up-to-the-minute accurate demographics downloaded directly into the appropriate report formats which pop up on your screen as you move quickly from one report to another. In some cases, reports may have been partially completed by voice recognition or through the use of *point-and-click* templates. Your job is to listen and review the information for accuracy, and when it changes to voice dictation, you switch hats from editor to transcriptionist. The report is completed rapidly, spellchecked for accuracy, and sent on its way once again along the secure intranet with the completed voice file attached to it.

Do you need help with a word or phrase? You access your intranet and utilizing the voice processor and the $89.95 video camera perched above your screen, you seek the assistance of your company's designated mentor for the day. You can always hot key over to the internet and seek the advice of the multitude of word wizards out there in *cyberspace.*

With all your work complete, you can sign out for the day knowing that the reports have already been transmitted through an HL7 interface to the provider's *data repository* or possibly a community health information network (*CHIN*). A caregiver now can create a report with the latest clinical and imaging data accompanied by the voice file and text file of the current and past health information needed to make critical decisions.

Your expertise as a professional medical transcriptionist has directly impacted the decision-making process that guides patient care and determines the all-important patient outcomes.

Congratulations! You are now part of the future of medical transcription and a very important element of the caregiving TEAM.

2. What types of errors in transcribed documents are the most critical from the patient's perspective? From the hospital's perspective? How do you think transcriptionists learn they have made an important error?
3. Think about the job requirements for speed and accuracy. Name two medical situations where a fast turnaround between dictation and transcription may be critical to a patient's care.
4. Review the list of personal attributes needed on the job and then think about what type of employment setting you prefer (home business, clinical, hospital). Which of the personal traits listed are most needed for the job setting you prefer? Evaluate your strengths and weaknesses in each of these areas.
5. The following article, originally published in the June 24, 1996, issue of *Interactive Week,* raises a number of important issues regarding electronic medical records and linked databases of records. Read the article and the questions below. Then formulate your answers and perspectives and be prepared to discuss them in class.
   - Examine the issue of electronic records from the perspective of information services providers. Why do they want the information automated? How do they sell the idea to hospitals and clinics, patients, and insurance agencies? How do they sell their ideas to the legislators? Are they worried about protecting the individual?
   - Explain the importance of the Medical Records Confidentiality Act of 1996. What is the perspective of the privacy advocates? Would the legislation protect the individual?
   - What questions would you ask the committee before they finalized the legislation?
   - Consider the case of Velazquez. Can legislation protect her from information "abuse" in the future? Can the ethics and morals of the reporters or employment companies be legislated?
   - Consider the J&J case and explain why privacy advocates were alarmed by the incident. Suppose the company had been "up-front" with the callers. Do you think it is helpful for people to receive promotional material targeted to their specific problems? Explain your answer.

Keeping Medical Records Cybersafe

Reprinted from *Interactive Week* June 24, 1996

Who has access to your medical records and what they do with them may be the next hot-button issue in cyberspace.

Patients' records are increasingly ending up in electronic storehouses that can be bought and sold at will, according to online watchdogs. And given the history of personal information, it's no longer a question of whether records will be sold, but when.

"There are uses for this information we can't even foresee," says Janlori Goldman, deputy director of the Center for Democracy and Technology, or CDT, in Washington, D.C. "We're moving more and more towards linked networks. Before we start to put these networks in place we need to have rules in place."

To be sure, the push to put records online, or at least on computer, is real. Insurance companies want more data than ever in order to set rates. Hospitals and health care providers increasingly rely on computers to maintain medical records. Even consumers find comfort in knowing that hospitals can access their files instantly in the event they are injured away from home.

All of which raises the issue of safeguards. Companies involved in electronic record keeping say they agree laws are needed to assure privacy, but aren't quite ready to be pinned down the way the CDT would like them to be.

At issue now: a Senate bill that would change radically the way most medical records are kept.

Says Norman Black, spokesman for Equifax, an Atlanta-based information service company best known for its work with credit records: "There are still areas where we have some reservations" about the bill. "We want to continue to work with Sen. [Robert] Bennett [R-Utah] and the privacy community."

Bennett and others will address those reservations in hearings before the Senate Labor and Human Resources Committee later this month when it takes up the proposed Medical Records Confidentiality Act of 1996. The proposed legislation tries to make a crazy quilt of state laws uniform. In its current form, the law would:

- Give people the right to see their medical records, regardless of who held them.
- Limit how much information doctors, employers, insurers and others could disclose.
- Demand that law enforcement produce warrants or subpoenas to gain access to individuals' medical records, provided patients retained their rights to challenge those actions in court.
- Establish penalties for unauthorized disclosure of medical information.
- Forbid researchers to use health data—even when anonymous—without patients' permission.
- Forbid health information services, such as EDS and Equifax, from storing information about individuals without their permission.

Lobbyists offer few specifics about the kind of law they would like to see, but they say the law isn't necessarily germane to all the companies that do what they do. Equifax,

Black says, merely transmits information from one point to another, but maintains no databases on patients.

Even so, the law would forbid them from transmitting those patient records between two parties without first obtaining the patients' go-ahead. And that, Black says, is far too restrictive for Equifax.

"If the Congress can't properly define the difference between a database provider and someone who just transmits data, we've got problems," Black says.

If there's any problem with confidentiality today, it's not necessarily from the doctor's perspective, say backers of the bill. One woman in Springfield, Mass., for instance, went without health insurance for a year and a half because of a computer error at the Medical Information Bureau, a nationwide clearinghouse of medical data used by insurers nationwide.

In another incident, a tabloid reporter disguised himself as a physician to obtain medical records of an actress who, he later reported, had once had venereal disease. In another case, an unknown party obtained the medical records of Congresswoman Nydia Velazquez and publicized a medical history that included a bout with depression and a suicide attempt, nearly upsetting her bid for office.

Perhaps most daunting, though, is the possibility that medical information could be used to push products on an unwary public. Even the Direct Marketing Association, an aggressive advocate of using personal information to sell goods and services, has rejected the outright use of medical records for marketing.

But at least one case gives privacy advocates pause. Johnson & Johnson recently established a toll-free number that incontinent adults could use to learn about treatment of their condition. Thousands of elderly Americans called the number. What J&J didn't tell callers was the company used caller identification services to capture their telephone numbers, then used a reverse directory to find their addresses so it could send them promotional materials. The mere act of calling, says CDT's Goldman, gave the company a database of people with an identifiable medical condition.

CHAPTER

2

Dermatology encompasses the entire integumentary system, which includes the skin, hair, and nails. Because the skin can reflect the general health of the patient, it is the first part of the assessment by the healthcare professional.

Dermatology

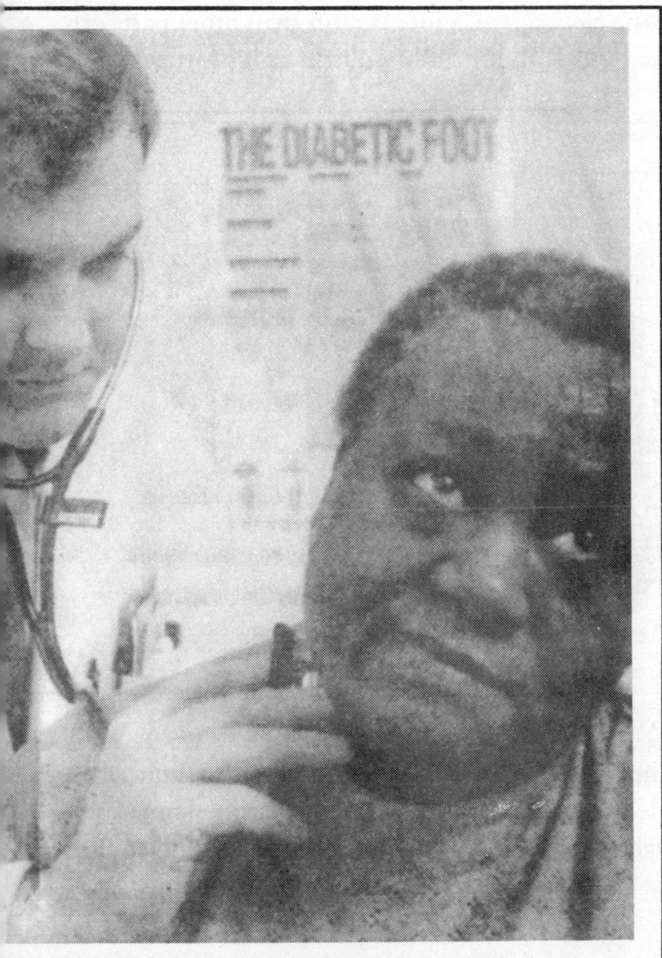

OBJECTIVES

- Use dermatology terms correctly according to the context and purpose of the dictation.
- Select and use appropriate general and specialty reference materials.
- Key dermatology documents of varying complexity and format.
- Transcribe authentic medical dictation requiring concentration and listening skill.
- Edit medical reports to conform with AAMT style guidelines.
- Proofread and correct transcripts to produce error-free documents.

EXPLORING DERMATOLOGY

The skin is the largest organ of the body and is considered the body's first line of defense against organisms. It is an important area of medical concern since approximately 5 to 10 percent of all ambulatory patient visits in the United States are for skin-related complaints.

STRUCTURE AND FUNCTION

The skin forms a barrier between the internal organs and the outside environment. It is rich with various types of sensory nerve endings that constitute the four cutaneous senses: touch pressure (sustained touch), cold, warmth, and pain. It communicates with the external openings of the digestive, respiratory, and urogenital systems through the mucous membranes.

The skin is composed of three layers, or strata: the epidermis, the dermis, and the subcutaneous tissue, as shown in figure 2.1. The epidermis is the external layer of the skin composed of squamous epithelial cells. These cells divide continuously, pushing the older, dead cells closer to the surface and completely replacing them every three to four weeks. The dead cells contain keratin, an insoluble, fibrous protein that helps protect the body. There are different amounts of keratin, which comprises the horny layer of the epidermis, in different areas of the body. The palms of the hands and soles of the feet contain more keratin than other parts of the skin. This extra thickness increases with use and results in callus formation.

Figure 2.1
Anatomic structures of skin

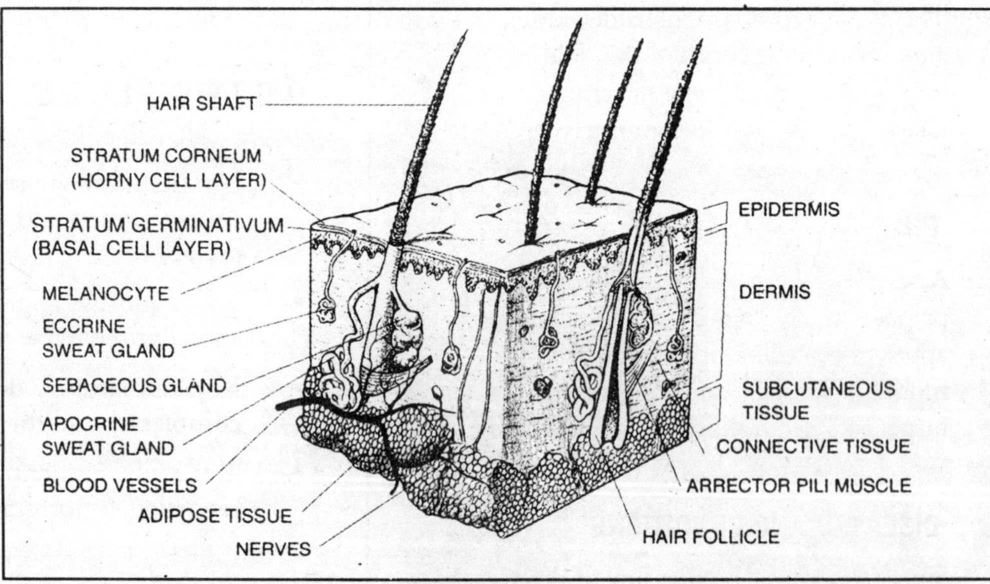

There are cells within the epidermis called melanocytes that produce melanin, the pigment or color of the skin. The more melanin present, the darker the skin color. Melanin can absorb ultraviolet light, protecting the person from the harmful effects of sun exposure. People with lighter skin have an increased risk of sunburn after sun exposure. On the positive side, the ultraviolet rays of sunlight react with chemicals within the skin to convert them into vitamin D, a necessary nutrient, which is absorbed through the skin.

The dermis lies immediately under the epidermis and is composed of collagen and elastic fibers, blood and lymph vessels, nerves, sweat and sebaceous glands, and hair roots.

The subcutaneous layer is composed of adipose, or fat, tissue. This layer is important in the regulation of body temperature and connects the skin to the muscles and bones.

The glands of the skin are within its layers. The sebaceous glands drain an oily secretion into an area between each hair follicle and its hair shaft to make the hair soft and pliable. Sweat glands are found within the skin and are classified into two categories: eccrine and apocrine. Eccrine sweat glands are found all over the body and have ducts that open directly onto the surface of the skin. They secrete a watery fluid in response to warm temperatures and are controlled by the sympathetic nervous system (see chapter 11). Apocrine sweat glands, which become active at puberty, secrete a substance that contains parts of the cells themselves. They produce a milky sweat that is broken down by bacteria and can cause underarm odor. Specialized apocrine sweat glands produce cerumen, the wax found in the ear.

Hair is composed of keratin. It appears all over the body except on the palms and soles. Hair grows from a root within a cavity known as a hair follicle. The follicle is located in the dermis; the hair shaft extends beyond the skin. Hair grows in two phases: a growing phase (anagen) and a resting phase (telogen). About 80 percent of the body's hair follicles on the scalp are in the anagen phase at any one time.

The nails are composed of hardened keratin and overlay the skin. The nail grows from a root within the cuticle, a thin fold of skin at the base of the nail. Nails protect the very sensitive areas of the fingers and toes. Nail growth is relatively slow. Fingernails take about 180 days to completely regenerate; toenails take up to 18 months.

PHYSICAL ASSESSMENT

Assessment of the skin involves the entire body. The physician inspects and palpates the patient's skin, mucous membranes, hair, and nails to determine appearance, color or pigmentation, temperature, and turgor. Turgor includes motility, elasticity, and moisture or dryness. The physician notes vascularity and inspects the skin thoroughly for abnormalities or lesions (figure 2.2).

DISEASES AND CONDITIONS

Since the skin is the first line of defense protecting the inner organs of the body from outside pathogens, early diagnosis and treatment of skin disorders is essential. The most common skin problem is pruritus, or itching, which can indicate either local or systemic problems. Pruritus can cause skin breakdown from the irritation of scratching. Local disorders causing pruritus include allergies to food, medications, soaps, and creams and other topical chemicals. Contact

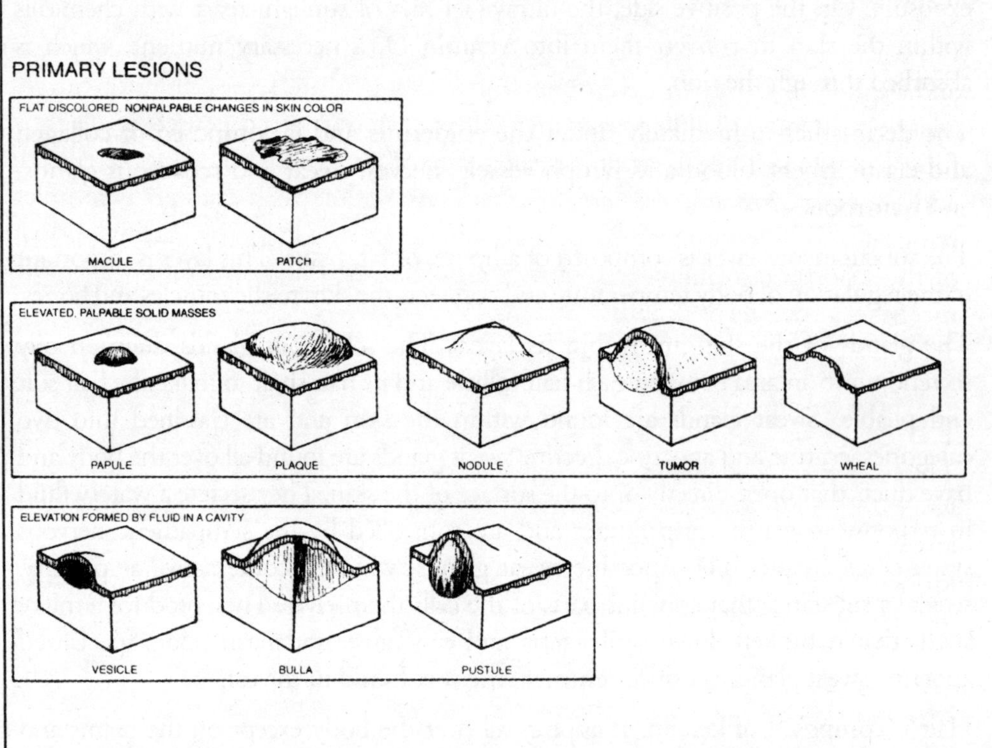

Figure 2.2 Common primary skin lesions

dermatitis, miliaria (prickly heat), dry skin, and poison ivy are some pruritic diseases. It is not always easy to find the cause of pruritus, but it is often necessary to determine the allergen in order to avoid further irritations.

Urticarial and erythematous lesions may be associated with pruritus. Commonly, the varicella (chickenpox) and herpes zoster (shingles) viruses may be associated with itching, redness, burning, and pain. Many of the "childhood" viral illnesses such as measles, rubella, and "fifth disease" display a red rash not usually associated with pruritus.

There are several bacterial, fungal, and yeast infections associated with skin eruptions. Staphylococcus aureus and Streptococcus are common bacteria found on the skin. These organisms can cause skin lesions such as folliculitis, furuncles, carbuncles, bullae, and impetigo. Ringworm is caused by the fungus known as a dermatophyte. Tinea corporis, tinea pedis, tinea manus, tinea cruris, tinea capitis, and tinea unguium are all dermatophyte infections. Candidal rashes are usually found in the groin or other areas where heat and moisture promote growth. People on antibiotic therapy or who are immunocompromised are at increased risk for Candida fungal infections.

Psoriasis is a chronic, noninfectious inflammatory skin disease characterized by an increase in the rate of growth of epidermal cells. It is one of the most common skin diseases although the exact cause is unknown. There may be a combination of genetic and environmental stimuli to precipitate the onset. The immune system, emotional stress, and seasonal and hormonal changes have been implicated in the exacerbation of psoriasis.

COMMON TESTS AND SURGICAL PROCEDURES

Physicians routinely order allergy skin testing such as scratch tests, patch tests, and intradermal tests to determine which allergens are responsible for causing allergic reactions. KOH (potassium hydroxide) preparation is used to diagnose fungal infections, and Tzanck's smear is used to diagnose viral skin vesicles. In addition, the dermatologist performs three types of biopsies: excisional (complete removal of skin lesion), incisional (partial removal of a lesion by cutting out part of the lesion), and punch (removal of a portion of skin containing a lesion by means of a special surgical instrument).

THE VOCABULARY OF DERMATOLOGY

The field of medicine has a specialized language with an enormous vocabulary of words identifying diseases, medical processes and procedures, body structures, and body systems. A prerequisite for working in a healthcare environment is solid knowledge of these medical terms.

This text-workbook uses a systematic approach to enhance your medical vocabulary. In this chapter and those that follow, core medical terms from each specialty are presented for you to learn. In particular, the list includes difficult or unusual words contained in the dictation at the end of the chapter. Some of the terms may apply to more than one medical specialty due to the close interrelationships among body systems.

PRONUNCIATION KEY

Every vocabulary word that may be difficult to pronounce is displayed with a phonetic pronunciation. As is common in dictionaries, the words are broken into syllables (indicated by hyphens), and an accent mark (') indicates which syllable should receive the emphasis when you say the word out loud. Note also that the word's part of speech is included in parentheses—for example, (n) for noun and (adj) for adjective; pl stands for plural. The following letters and letter combinations represent specific sounds in the phonetic pronunciations:

a = the short a as in can
ay = the long a as in cane
ah = a as in father
ai = ai as in fair
ar = ar as in far
aw = a as in fall
e = the short e as in pen
ee = the long e as in me
i = the short i as in pin
I = the long I as in pine
o = the short o as in not
O = the long o as in note
oo = oo as in food
or = or as in for
ow = ow as in cow
oy = oy as in boy
u = the short u as in run
yoo = the long u as in cube
zh = s as in casual

Common Dermatology Drugs

Note: Generic drug names are listed first, followed by a brand-name example (capitalized).

aluminum acetate
Burow's Solution

benzoyl peroxide

clindamycin
Cleocin

clotrimazole & betamethasone
Lotrisone

diphenhydramine hydrochloride
Benadryl

nystatin
Mycostatin Cream

silver sulfadiazine
Silvadene

sulfur and salicylic acid
Aveeno Cleansing Bar

tetracycline hydrochloride

tretinoin, retinoic acid
Refin-A

SUGGESTIONS FOR LEARNING MEDICAL TERMS

Here are suggestions for learning and expanding your vocabulary:

1. Read and study each word for pronunciation and meaning.
2. Write each unfamiliar word from the list below on a notecard, write the definition or a paraphrase of the definition on the back, and draw a simple picture to help you learn the word.
3. Study the pronunciation, spelling, and definition of each word on your notecard, then key each word twice for reinforcement. Check the spelling.
4. Add the terms to your word processor's spell checker.

abrasion
(a-bray'-zhun) (n) scraping away of skin or mucous membrane by friction

abscess
(ab'-ses) (n) a pus-filled cavity, usually because of a localized infection

acne
(ak'-nee) (n) an eruption of papules or pustules on the skin, involving the oil glands

adipose
(ad'-i-pOz) (adj) containing fat

albinism
(al'-bi-nizm/al-bin'-izm) (n) a congenital lack of melanin in the skin, hair, and eyes

allergen
(al'-er-jen) (n) a substance that produces an allergic reaction

alopecia
(al-O-pee'-shee-a) (n) partial or total loss of hair

alopecic
(al-O-pee'-sik) (adj) relating to alopecia

anagen
(an'-a-jen) (n) the actively growing phase of the hair growth cycle

angioedema
(an-jee-O-e-dee'-ma) (n) periodically recurring episodes of noninflammatory swelling

angioma
(an-jee-O'-ma) (n) a swelling or tumor composed primarily of blood vessels; spider, strawberry, cherry angiomas

anhidrosis
(an-hI-drO'-sis) (n) the suppression or absence of perspiration

antecubital
(an-te-kyoo'-bi-tal) (adj) in front of the elbow; often the site for drawing blood

apocrine
(ap'-O-krin) (adj) relating to sweat glands

assessment
(as-ses'-ment) (n) a complete evaluation of the patient; diagnosis

bedsore
(bed'-sor) (n) an infected wound on the skin that occurs at pressure points in patients confined to bed

biopsy
(bI'-op-see) (n) the removal of tissue and/or fluid from the body for microscopic study; the specimen obtained

bullae
(bul'-ee) (n, pl) blisters of the skin containing clear fluid

cafe-au-lait spots
(kaf-ay-O-lay' spots) (n) light brown spots of patchy pigmentation of the skin

callus
(kal'-us) (n) thickened skin which develops at points of pressure or friction; the bony substance which develops around the broken ends of bone during healing

candidal rash
(kan'-di-dal rash) (n) a rash which usually includes itching, a white discharge, peeling, and easy bleeding; caused by the yeastlike fungi Candida; common examples are diaper rash, thrush, and vaginitis

carbuncle
(kar'-bung-kl) (n) subcutaneous, pus-filled interconnecting pockets, caused by staphylococcal infection; eventually discharges through an opening in the skin

caruncle
(kar'-ung-kl) (n) small, fleshy outgrowth

cellulitis
(sel-yoo-lI'-tis) (n) inflammation of the connective tissue caused by infection

cephalocaudal
(sef'-a-lO-caw'-dal) (adj) relating to the axis of the body from the head to the base of the spine

cerumen
(se-roo'-men) (n) earwax

chancre
(shang'-ker) (n) hard sore; the sore that develops at the site of entry of a pathogen

chloasma
(klO-as'-ma) (n) light brown patches on the face and elsewhere; commonly associated with pregnancy

cicatrix
(sik'-a-triks) (n) scar

circumscribed
(ser'-kum-skrIbd) (adj) having a boundary; confined

cirrhosis
(sir-rO'-sis) (n) a degenerative liver disease characterized by damaged cell function and impaired blood flow

collagen
(kol'-a-jen) (n) the protein which forms the tough white fibers of connective tissue, cartilage, and bone

comedo
(kom'-i-dO) (n) in a hair follicle or oil gland, a plug of dead cells and oily secretions; blackhead; comedones (com-i-dO'-neez) (pl)

concussion
(kon-kush'-un) (n) an injury resulting from violent striking or shaking, especially an injury to the brain

confluent
(kon'-floo-ent) (adj) merging together; connecting

contusion
(kon-too'-zhun) (n) a bruise

cryosurgery
(krI'-O-ser-jer-ee) (n) the use of extreme cold to destroy tissue

cuticle
(kyoo'-ti-kl) (n) the edge of thickened skin around the bed of a nail; the sheath surrounding the base of a hair follicle

cyanosis
(cI-a-nO'-sis) (n) bluish cast to the skin and/or mucous membranes due to decreased amount of oxygen in the blood cells

dermabrasion
(der'-ma-bray-zhun) (n) peeling of skin done by a mechanical device with sandpaper or wire brushes

dermatitis
(der-ma-tI'-tis) (n) inflammation of skin often evidenced by itching, redness, and lesions

dermatology
(der-ma-tol'-o-jee) (n) the study of the skin, hair, and nails

dermatophyte
(der'-ma-tO-fIt) (n) a parasitic fungus that causes skin disease

desiccate
(de'-si-kayt) (v) to dry out

diagnosis
(dI-ag-nO'-sis) (n) deciding the nature of a medical condition by examination of the symptoms; diagnoses (pl)

diaphoresis
(dI'-a-fO-ree'-sis) (n) profuse perspiration or sweating

discrete
(dis-kreet') (adj) separate; distinct

ecchymosis
(ek-im-O'-sis) (n) reddish or purplish flat spot on the skin; a bruise; ecchymoses (pl)

eccrine
(ek'-rin) (adj) relating to sweat glands

eczema
(ek'-si-ma/eg'-ze-ma) (n) inflammatory condition of the skin characterized by blisters, redness, and itching

electrodesiccation
(el-ek-trO-de-si-kay'-shun) (n) destruction of tissue by the use of electrical current; fulguration

electrolysis
(el-ek-trol'-i-sis) (n) destruction of a hair follicle by passing an electrical current through it

ephelides
(ef-ee'-lI-deez) (n, pl) freckles

epidermis
(ep-i-der'-mis) (n) the top or outer layer of the skin

epithelial
(ep-i-thee'-lee-al) (adj) relating to or composed of epithelium

epithelium
(ep-i-thee'-lee-um) (n) cell layers covering the outside body surfaces as well as forming the lining of hollow organs (e.g., the bladder) and the passages of the respiratory, digestive, and urinary tracts

erythema
(er-i-thee'-ma) (n) redness of the skin; inflammation

erythema infectiosum
(er-i-thee'-ma in-fek-shee-O'-sum) (n) a mild, infectious disease characterized by an erythematous rash; also called fifth disease

erythematous
(er-i-them'-a-tus/er-i-thee'-ma-tus) (adj) relating to or having erythema

erythrocyte
(e-rith'-rO-sIt) (n) mature red blood cell

erythroderma
(e-rith'-rO-der'-ma) (n) any skin condition associated with unusual redness of the skin

exanthema
(eg-zan-thee'-ma) (n) a disease, such as measles or chickenpox, accompanied by a general rash on the skin, which may have particular characteristics specific to the disease

excisional biopsy
(ek-sizh'-un-al bI'-op-see) (n) surgical removal of a tissue for microscopic examination

excoriation
(eks-kO-ree-ay'-shun) (n) a scratching or scraping injury to the skin

fifth disease
(n) erythema infectiosum; a mild, infectious disease characterized by an erythematous rash

fistula
(fis'-tyoo-la) (n) abnormal opening or channel connecting hollow organs or leading from an internal organ to the outside or a cavity; such as a urinary fistula

follicle
(fol'-i-kl) (n) pouch-like cavity, such as a hair follicle in the skin enclosing a hair

folliculitis
(fol-i-kyoo-lI'-tis) (n) inflammation of the hair follicles

fossa
(fos'-a) (n) channel or shallow depression; fossae (pl)

fulguration
(ful-gyoo-ra'-shun) (n) destruction of tissue by the use of electrical current; electrodessication

furuncle
(fyoo'-rung-kl) (n) a localized, pus-forming infection in a hair follicle or gland

gangrene
(gang'-green) (n) death of cells or tissue due to obstruction of blood supply

gland
(n) organ that secretes one or more substances not needed by the organ itself

glans
(n) the head of the penis; "glans penis"

hemangioma
(he-man'-jee-O'-ma) (n) a congenital benign tumor consisting of a mass of blood vessels

hematology
(hee-ma-tol'-o-jee) (n) the study of blood

herpes zoster
(her'-peez zos'-ter) (n) a viral infection causing inflammation along the path of nerve with associated painful vesicles (blisters), on the skin above; shingles

hirsutism
(hur'-soot-izm) (n) excessive body hair

hyperpigmentation
(hI'-per-pig-men-tay'-shun) (n) darkening of the skin due to excessive pigment in the skin

hypertrophy
(hI-per'-trO-fee) (n) increase in size

impetigo
(im-pe-tI'-gO) (n) a streptococcal or staphylococcal infection of the skin characterized by lesions, usually on the face, which rupture and become covered with a thick yellow crust; highly contagious

incisional biopsy
(in-si'-zhun-al bI'-op-see) (n) removal of part of a lesion for micrscopic examination

incision and drainage
(n) commonly dictated "I and D"; procedure of cutting through an infected lesion and allowing it to drain

integumentary
(in-teg-yoo-men'-ta-ree) (adj) relating to the skin

jaundice
(jawn'-dis) (n) yellowish skin and whites of the eyes

keloid
(kee'-loyd) (n) a mass of scar tissue

keratin
(ker'-a-tin) (n) a tough, fibrous protein in skin, hair, and nails

keratosis
(ker-a-tO'-sis) (n) a condition in which the skin thickens and builds up with excessive keratin

keratotic
(ker-a-tot'-ik) (adj) relating to keratosis

lesion
(lee'-zhun) (n) general term for any visible, circumscribed injury to the skin; such as a wound, sore, rash, or mass

macule
(mak'-yool) (n) a small discolored spot on the skin

maculopapular
(mak-yoo-lO-pap'-yoo-lar) (adj) describing skin lesions that are raised in the center

malformation
(mal-for-may'-shun) (n) abnormal development or structure of the body or a part

melanin
(mel'-a-nin) (n) naturally-occurring dark brown or black pigment found in the hair, skin, and eyes

melanocyte
(mel'-an-O-slt) (n) a cell that produces melanin

melitis
(mee-ll'-tis) (n) inflammation of the cheek

milia
(mil'-ee-a) (n, pl) whiteheads, due to obstruction of the outlet of hair follicles or sweat glands

miliaria
(mil-ee-ay'-ree-a) (n) a skin eruption of small vesicles and papules; heat rash

motility
(mO-til'-i-tee) (n) ability to move spontaneously

mycosis
(ml-kO'-sis) (n) disease caused by a fungus

nevus
(nee'-vus) (n) congenital discoloration of the skin; birthmark or mole; nevi (pl)

obese
(o-bees') (adj) very fat

onycholysis
(on-ee-kol'-i-sis) (n) loosening of the nails from thier beds

papule
(pap'-yool) (n) a small, solid, raised skin lesion

paronychia
(par-O-nik'-ee-a) (n) infected skin around the nail

pathogen
(path'-O-jen) (n) any microorganism or substance capable of producing a disease

pemphigus
(pem'-fi-gus) (n) a distinctive group of diseases marked by successive crops of bullae

perineum
(per-i-nee'-um) (n) the external region between the urethral opening and the anus, including the skin and underlying tissues

peritoneum
(per-i-tO-nee'-um) (n) lining of the abdominal cavity

petechia
(pe-tee'-kee-a/pee-tek'-ee-a) (n, sing.) tiny reddish or purplish flat spot on the skin as a result of a tiny hemorrhage within the skin (usually used in the plural form, petechiae)

petechial
(pee-tee'-kee-al/pee-tek'-ee-al)) (adj) relating to or having petechiae

pigment
(pig'-ment) (n) coloring substance

presents
(pre-sents') (v) appears; shows; displays; the symptoms displayed are the presenting symptoms

pruritic
(pru-ri'-tic) (adj) itching

pruritus
(proo-rl'-tus) (n) itching skin condition

psoriasis
(sO-rl'-a-sis) (n) chronic skin disease in which reddish scaly patches develop

punch biopsy
(punch bl'-op-see) (n) a special instrument is used to take a small cylindrical piece of tissue for microscopic examination

pustular
(pus'-choo-lar) (adj) relating to or having pustules

pustule
(pus'-chool) (n) small pus-containing elevation on the skin

rhinophyma
(rl-nO-fl'-ma) (n) enlargement of the nose

rubella
(roo-bel'-a) (n) a contagious viral disease with fever and a red rash; German measles

scabies
(skay'-beez) (n) contagious rash with intense itching; caused by mites

scrotal
(skrO'-tal) (adj) relating to the scrotum

scrotum
(skrO'-tum) (n) the pouch of skin containing the testes

sebaceous
(see-bay'-shus) (adj) relating to sebum

seborrhea
(seb-O-ree'-a) (n) overactivity of the oil glands of the skin

sebum
(see'-bum) (n) an oily secretion of the oil glands of the skin

Staphylococcus aureus
(staf-il-O-kok'-us awr'-ee-us) (n) a common species of Staphylococcus (a bacteria), present on nasal mucous membranes and skin that causes pus-producing infections

Streptococcus
(strep-tO-kok'-us) (n) a genus of bacteria; many species cause disease in humans

subcutaneous
(sub-kyoo-tay'-nee-us) (adj) under the skin

subjective data
(sub-jek'-tiv day'-tah) (n) information revealed by the patient to the health care provider

telogen
(tel'-O-jen) (n) the resting phase of the hair growth cycle

texture
(teks'-chur) (n) character, structure, and feel of parts of the body

tinea
(tin'-ee-a) (n) fungal infection; such as tinea pedis or athlete's foot

torso
(tor'-sO) (n) trunk of the body

turgor
(ter'-gOr) (n) fullness; the normal resiliency of the skin

Tzanck's smear
(tsangks smeer) (n) a method to help diagnose skin lesions by the miscroscopic examination of material from them

urticaria
(er-ti-kar'-ee-a) (n) hives; an eruption of itching red, raised lesions

urticarial
(er-ti-kar'-ee-al) (adj) relating to or having urticaria

varicella
(var-i-sel'-a) (n) chickenpox; a highly contagious viral disease

vascularity
(vas-kyoo-lar'-i-tee) (n) the blood vessels in a part of the body

vesicle
(ves'-i-kl) (n) blister; small, raised skin lesion containing clear fluid

vitiligo
(vi-ti-lee'-gO) (n) white patches, due to loss of pigment, appearing on the skin

wheal
(hweel) (n) a raised, red circumscribed lesion usually due to an allergic reaction; usually accompanied by intense itching; welt

xanthoma
(zan-thO'-mah) (n) yellowish nodules in or under the skin, especially in the eyelids

ABBREVIATIONS

Bx	biopsy	**HSV-2**	herpes simplex virus Type 2
C&S	culture and sensitivity	**I&D**	incision and drainage
derm.	dermatology	**KOH**	potassium hydroxide
FS	frozen section	**ung.**	ointment
HSV-1	herpes simplex virus Type 1	**UV**	ultraviolet

EXERCISE 2.1: RECOGNIZING LOOK-ALIKES AND SOUND-ALIKES

Below is a list of frequently used words that look alike and/or sound alike. Study the meaning and pronunciation of each set of words, then read each sentence carefully and circle the word in parentheses that correctly completes the meaning.

cirrhosis	disease of the liver
psoriasis	skin condition

patient	(n) an individual who is receiving medical treatment
patient	(adj) behaving calmly

discreet	cautious, careful with speech or behavior
discrete	separate, distinct; "discrete mass"

perianal	around the anus
perinatal	relating to the time shortly before and after birth

glands	organs or groups of cells that produce or secrete substances
glans	head of the penis; "glans penis"

perineum	pelvic floor and associated structures
peritoneum	serous membrane lining the walls of the abdominal and pelvic cavities

miliaria	eruption of vesicles and papules at the sweat glands
malaria	acute blood disease caused from bite of tropical mosquito
milia	white raised "pimple" found on skin of infants

vesical	(adj) relating to a bladder
vesicle	(n) blister

patience	ability to suppress restlessness; to be patient
patients	individuals who are receiving medical treatment
patient's	possessive form of noun patient

wheal	raised, red lesion on the skin
wheel	circular frame of hard material that can turn on an axle (as on a car)

1. We will refer the patient to the dermatologist regarding his (psoriasis, cirrhosis).
2. Due to the patient's (psoriasis, cirrhosis), we need to repeat her liver function tests.
3. It is important to be (discreet, discrete) when transcribing patient care documentation.
4. I noted a few (discreet, discrete) papular lesions on the patient's left arm.
5. On examination of the (perineum, peritoneum), the patient's episiotomy is well healed.
6. A family physician sometimes sees up to 40 (patients, patient's) a day.
7. When transcribing difficult dictation, (patients, patience) is important.
8. He is having some irritations of the foreskin and (glans, glands).
9. Some (vesicles, vesicals) are beginning to form at the burn site.
10. Apparently she is allergic to amoxicillin because she developed pruritic (wheels, wheals) on her trunk a few hours after taking the first dose.

EXERCISE 2.2: MATCHING SOUND AND SPELLING

The numbered list that follows shows the phonetic spelling of hard-to-spell words. Sound out the word, then write the correct spelling in the blank space provided. Each of the words can be found in the glossary or in the drug list in appendix C.

1. er-i-thee'-ma ______________________
2. see-bay'-shus ______________________
3. er-ti-kar'-ee-a ______________________
4. de'-si-kayt ______________________
5. al-O-pee'-shee-a ______________________
6. kon'-floo-ent ______________________
7. pe-tee'-kee-a ______________________
8. kom'-i-dO ______________________
9. per'-i-nee'-um ______________________
10. eks-kO-ree-ay'-shun ______________________
11. an-te-kyoo'-bi-tal ______________________
12. sel-yoo-lI'-tis ______________________
13. ap'-O-krin ______________________
14. sO-rI'-a-sis ______________________
15. ek-im-O'-sis ______________________

EXERCISE 2.3: CHOOSING WORDS FROM CONTEXT

When transcribing dictation, the medical transcriptionist frequently needs to determine the word that correctly completes the sentence based on the situation. From the list of words below, select the term that meaningfully completes each statement.

maculopapular	sebaceous	erythematous
integumentary	pustule	torso
excoriations	pruritic	subcutaneous
comedo	pigment	acne
nevus	perineum	vesicle

1. He has a rash with many ______________, due to constantly scratching the area.
2. The patient is complaining of a ______________ rash and would like a medication to relieve itching.
3. He had a ______________ that opened and drained a clear fluid.
4. The ______________system is the first system noticed when the patient appears in the physician's office.
5. This ______________ on my nose has caused me much embarrassment.
6. The patient has a ______________ rash sprinkled across the nose.
7. The patient has a ______________ that she would like removed from her chin. She states it has been there since birth.
8. The ______________ shows scarring from the episiotomy performed after the birth of her first child.
9. The ______________ glands clog and cause acne.
10. The 16-year-old girl consulted the dermatologist because the over-the-counter medications she used to treat her ______________ were not effective.

EXERCISE 2.4: PAIRING WORDS AND MEANINGS

For each definition provided below, locate the term on the list that best matches the definition. Write the letter of the term in the space provided beside the definition.

A. dermatitis	F. hyperpigmentation	K. erythema
B. petechiae	G. alopecia	L. rhinophyma
C. confluent	H. cafe-au-lait spots	M. I&D
D. wheal	I. cephalocaudal	N. urticaria
E. pruritus	J. ephelides	O. torso

1. patchy light brown spots in pigmentation of skin __________
2. from head to toe __________
3. loss of hair __________
4. redness __________
5. tiny reddish or purplish spots appearing on the skin resulting from tiny hemorrhages __________
6. a raised, red, circumscribed lesion __________
7. merging of tissues, pustules, or lesions __________
8. unusual darkening of the skin __________
9. inflammation of the skin __________
10. trunk of a body __________

EXERCISE 2.5: CREATING TERMS FROM WORD FORMS

In the following exercise, combine prefixes, root words, and suffixes to create medical words that fit the definitions below. Fill in the blanks with the words that you construct. Note that root words appear with a combining vowel (shown as a diagonal slash, then the vowel); prefixes are indicated by a hyphen at the end; and suffixes are shown with a hyphen preceding them. The first word is done for you.

dermat/o	skin	hemat/o	blood
tension	pressure	-trophy	development
erythr/o	red	derm/a	skin
hyper-	above or excessive	-ous	pertaining to
caudal	referring to tail	-logy	study of
cephal/o	head	-ema	condition of
pigmentation	coloring	-brasion	removal
seb/o	oil	-itis	inflammation
-rrhea	discharge	-cyte	cell

1. study of skin, hair, and nails *dermatology*
2. excessive growth __________
3. redness of skin __________
4. peeling of skin with sandpaper __________
5. head to toe __________
6. skin condition associated with abnormal redness of skin __________
7. inflammation of skin __________
8. condition caused by over-activity of the sebaceous glands __________
9. red blood cell __________
10. study of the blood __________

EDITING MEDICAL DOCUMENTS

In this section you will perfect your word use and grammar skills. These skills will help you edit and proofread medical reports for correct language, punctuation, format, and meaning.

REPAIRING SENTENCE FRAGMENTS AND RUN-ON SENTENCES

One of the most common trouble spots in workplace documents such as letters and reports is faulty sentence construction. These problems take the form of either incomplete sentences (sentence fragments) or run-on sentences (two sentences that "run together" without the correct punctuation separating them). To be able to correct fragments and run-ons, you must know what makes a sentence complete. You also must know how to punctuate a sentence so the reader knows where it begins and ends.

What Is a Sentence?

Every complete sentence contains a subject and a verb and expresses a thought. The subject is generally a noun or pronoun, and the verb always expresses some action or state of being (am, was, will be, etc.).

> *Bill worked.*
> s v
>
> *Dr. Brown will see* the patient.
> s v
>
> *You look* tired.
> s v
>
> *The patient* and his *family were informed* of the diagnosis.
> s s v
>
> [compound subject]

Sometimes the subject is implied but not stated. In the following sentence, for example, the subject *you* is understood.

> *Have* a nice day.
> v
>
> *Follow up* with me next week.
> v

Sentence Fragments

A fragment is a group of words that expresses a partial thought and leaves the reader puzzled. It is not a complete sentence.

> WRONG: The patient was instructed that if he develops a fever over 101° or if he has increasing abdominal pain. [This is a long dependent clause. What's missing is important information detailing what the patient should do in these situations.]
>
> CORRECT: The patient was instructed to call the doctor's answering service if he develops a fever over 101° or if he has increasing abdominal pain.

Run-On Sentences

A run-on sentence consists of two sentences that are not separated by punctuation. If the second sentence is closely related, use a semicolon to connect them. Otherwise, key them as two individual sentences, each ending with a period (or a question mark or exclamation mark).

> WRONG: The patient's condition gradually improved on intravenous antibiotic therapy the speech therapist saw the patient in consultation.
>
> CORRECT: The patient's condition gradually improved on intravenous antibiotic therapy. The speech therapist saw the patient in consultation.

Exceptions to the Rules

- Certain sections of medical reports may contain incomplete sentences. For example, a doctor may dictate laboratory values that do not have to be written in sentence form. The physical examination may or may not be in sentence form.

LABORATORY DATA: WBC 5500 with 45 segmented neutrophils, 15 basophils, 5 eosinophils, 17 monocytes.

Heart: Regular rate and rhythm. No murmurs, rubs, or gallops.

- Narrative dictation (for example, the history of present illness) must be in complete sentences. When historical items are placed in a formal list, however, they do not have to be in complete sentences.

PAST MEDICAL HISTORY:
1. Status post coronary artery bypass grafting five years ago.
2. Bilateral hip pain.
3. History of hypertension, under good control on medical therapy.

- Outpatient chart notes are less formal than other types of dictation and may be dictated in clipped sentences. A doctor may dictate without using subjects and articles. These notes should be transcribed as dictated. Such a note might look like this:

Seen for postoperative visit. Doing well. Wound healing, without signs of infection. Sutures removed. Will be seen again in two weeks. May return to work after that time.

EXERCISE 2.6: EDITING FOR CORRECT PUNCTUATION

Read the following sentences and decide if any are run-on sentences or sentence fragments. Create complete sentences by combining groups of words or by changing the punctuation, then key the corrected sentences. Remember that as a transcriptionist, you must remain as true as possible to the original dictation while correcting obvious errors.

1. The patient's wife called 911 and the paramedics arrived some ten minutes later to find the patient in a semiconscious state with an irregular heart rhythm the exact nature of which is unknown.
2. Strict sterile precautions must be taken. Using only autoclaved instruments and adequate skin preparation.
3. Medications Lasix 20 mg per morning Micro-K 10 mEq twice per day Cardizem 30 mg per day Isordil 20 mg twice per day.
4. The patient was extubated and noted to have purulent sputum and purulent urine and blood and urine cultures were positive for Klebsiella pneumoniae therefore the patient was started on gentamicin.
5. The patient was seen in routine follow-up. Six months since the last examination.
6. After informed consent was obtained the patient was brought to the operating room where general anesthesia was established and the lower abdomen was prepared and draped in the usual sterile fashion and an incision made just below the umbilicus.
7. The patient should apply the zinc oxide ointment directly to the lesions as often as needed to cool the burning sensation making sure she washes her hands before and after the application.
8. The patient is a 17-year-old female. A known IV drug abuser. She presents today to the emergency department she has an infected area on her left arm. The area is red and tender.

9. On examination the head shows no deformities the nose and throat are clear the neck has no adenopathy the chest is clear with normal breath sounds the abdomen is soft and nontender extremities are normal skin shows no rash or redness.
10. This 35-year-old Hispanic male presented today with a 1 cm laceration of the right hand at the web space between the middle and ring fingers.

EXERCISE 2.7: PROOFREADING REVIEW

As a medical transcriptionist, you are responsible for producing quality work. One of the most important skills you need to develop is proofreading, which involves checking for all types of mistakes in the document. You must carefully read for accuracy of content, omission of words, consistency of format, English usage, spelling, punctuation, capitalization, word choice, and typographical errors. Read the following report and look for errors in spelling, complete sentences, and punctuation.

> Thank you for referring Kyle Sanderson to me. This baby is truely in pain with scrotal inflammation and excoriation of the perineum. I have instituted Burow soaks to the area q.i.d., with Mycostatin ointment after each soak. If this does not clear the rash I would be concerned about an secondary infection. I would expect to see improvement within 1 week otherwise I feel the baby should be admitted to the hospital and more aggressive antifungal agents be used to clear this rash.

WHERE CAN I FIND THE ANSWER?

As you transcribe dictation, you may hear unfamiliar words or terms. A variety of reference sources are available to help you locate answers to your questions. One of the important types of references for medical transcriptionists is described below. Read the information. If you have access to the reference discussed, explore its capabilities.

MEDICAL REFERENCES: THE AAMT BOOK OF STYLE

The American Association for Medical Transcription (AAMT) publishes the *AAMT Book of Style*, a comprehensive guide to medical report formats and medical language style. The *AAMT Book of Style* covers most of the "How should I..." questions that arise in medical transcription, for example:

How should I transcribe "gravida and para"?

Should I use Arabic or Roman numerals for cranial nerves?

How should I transcribe "milligrams" and "centimeters"?

Exactly what is a Glasgow scale?

When should I use hyphens?

As with any language-centered occupation, there are variations in word treatment from one person to another and from one clinic or hospital to another. There are very successful transcriptionists who deviate from some AAMT standards, and you may occasionally run into situations not addressed in the book. Beginning transcriptionists, however, will find it reassuring to have a comprehensive guide to check whether their developing style closely matches the widely accepted standards of the profession.

TRANSCRIBING DERMATOLOGY DOCUMENTS

In this section your goal is to prepare for the work of transcription by transcribing first from a printed document and then from dictation on tape. The model document that follows illustrates the generally accepted format for the **office note,** the report format featured in this chapter.

BASIC FORMAT: THE OFFICE NOTE

An office note typically describes an office visit and becomes part of the patient's chart. Sometimes the office note may describe a minor procedure performed in the physician's office. These notes are not always written as complete sentences, although physicians frequently use the SOAP (Subjective, Objective, Assessment, Plan) format; as described in chapter 1. The rules of grammar and numeral usage may not be followed precisely. Note that if the report is short, it is acceptable to add a colon after each SOAP heading and key the text on the same line.

PREPARING TO TRANSCRIBE

To prepare for transcribing dictation, key the office note on the next page. You will later key the identical report from tape. Follow these guidelines:

- Study the format and organization of the office note.
- Review the word list presented earlier in this chapter.
- Consult reference books for words or formatting rules that are unfamiliar.
- Proofread your final copy by comparing it to the printed version.

OFFICE NOTE

1" margins → **left justification; no hyphenation**

single-space after colons

PATIENT NAME: Avis Smith
DATE OF VISIT: 3/31/XX **format date as MM/DD/YY**

double-space between headings

CHIEF COMPLAINT
Itching and rash.

double-space

SUBJECTIVE **single-space from heading to following paragraph**
The patient is complaining of itching and a rash which began about three weeks ago, starting on the hands and arms and spreading to the chest and back. Taking Benadryl at bedtime with little relief. Stated that she has tried a new perfume after her shower for the past three or four days.

double-space

OBJECTIVE
VITAL SIGNS: Temperature 98.6°, blood pressure 140/74, weight 185 pounds, height 5 feet 4 inches, heart rate 74, respirations 22.
GENERAL APPEARANCE: Obese. HAIR: Within normal limits.
SKIN: Comedo formations on nose. Several pustular lesions on forehead. Smooth, erythematous rash over neck extending over trunk and back. There is a small hyperpigmented nevus on the right breast. There is a 2 x 3 cm cafe-au-lait spot on the lower back. There are several nevi on the buttocks. On the upper extremities, she has a confluent, erythematous rash extending to fingertips. Wheals with petechiae are noted in the antecubital fossa bilaterally.

double-space

ASSESSMENT
Contact dermatitis, secondary to allergy to perfume.

double-space

PLAN
1. Avoid use of any perfume or perfumed soap.
2. Wash or dry clean all clothing and linens which were exposed to the suspected perfume.
3. Take diphenhydramine (Benadryl) 25 mg q.6h. x 3 days.

1 space after→ number and period or use a tab setting

quadruple-space

____
Julia M. Waters, MD

DR:MT ← **MT stands for transcriptionist's initials; DR stands for dictator's initials**
D: xx/xx/xx
T: xx/xx/xx

1 space after colons

CASES FOR TRANSCRIPTION

In this section you will transcribe medical dictation from tape. Your goal is to produce error-free documents. Read this chapter's Pro Tip (following the case studies) for helpful hints from experienced MTs. Then follow these steps for each dictation:

1. Review the case study and the office note format.
2. Transcribe the dictation, using the process of "listen, stop, key." Listen to a single sentence or phrase (whatever number of words you can mentally retain and repeat to yourself), pause the tape, then key the words. Leave spaces for words you cannot hear or do not understand.
3. Carefully proofread the document and correct as many errors as you can. Use your reference materials to help you identify missing words.
4. Listen to the tape again and correct all remaining errors.

Repeat these steps until you produce an error-free document. Then complete the Performance Report at the end of the chapter, attach it to the top of the transcripts, and submit them to your instructor for evaluation.

CASE STUDY 1: AVIS SMITH

Ms. Avis Smith is a 45-year-old woman who presents with a three-week history of generalized itching and a maculopapular erythematous rash, most prominent on the torso.

Report 2.1: Office Note

CASE STUDY 2: ALBERT ALVAREZ

Mr. Albert Alvarez, a 45-year-old male, was referred to dermatologist Anthony Palmer, MD, by his internist for assessment of several lesions. Although Dr. Palmer found none of the lesions suspicious, he removed them, as they were inflamed.

Report 2.2: Office Note

Transcription Hint

Listen for these terms:
excision
keratotic papules

CASE STUDY 3: KYLE SANDERSON

Ms. Sanderson's 6-month-old infant, Kyle, was referred to Dr. Palmer by the pediatrician for evaluation of a persistent rash on his scalp, behind his ears, and in the diaper area.

Report 2.3: Office Note

Transcription Hints

- Listen for these difficult terms:
  seborrheic (adjective) and seborrhea (noun)
  alopecic (adjective) and alopecia (noun)
  perineum
- PMD means "primary medical doctor." This fairly common medical abbreviation should be transcribed only when it is dictated. Do not change "primary medical doctor" to PMD and do not change "PMD" to primary medical doctor. The same rule applies to other abbreviations such as BP (blood pressure) and ER (emergency room).
- Drug dosages are expressed in Latin abbreviations, for example, q.i.d., which means four times a day, or b.i.d., which means twice a day. The dictator will pronounce the letters rather than saying "four times a day." Transcribe the abbreviation in lowercase letters with periods and no internal spaces. See chapter 9 for more information on capitalization rules.

CASE STUDY 4: RAMON YATES

Ramon Yates, a 45-year-old construction worker, sought medical help after he noticed a small, raised bump in his groin area.

Report 2.4: Office Note

Transcription Hints

- When you hear "injected with point five cee cees of one percent lidocaine with epinephrine," transcribe the amount as 0.5 cc of 1% lidocaine with epinephrine. Note that lidocaine and epinephrine are generic drug names and thus should not be capitalized. Also, see chapter 10 for more information on numbers.
- Silver nitrate is a generic drug name and thus is not capitalized.

CASE STUDY 5: SANDRA MAHONEY

Recently, Ms. Mahoney visited her local clinic to have a mole removed from her forearm.

Report 2.5: Office Note

Transcription Hints

- Mixed numbers (a whole number plus a fraction) should be transcribed in figures, so when you hear "two and a half," key $2^1/_2$.
- Steri-Strips are a brand name and thus should be capitalized. Benzoin is a generic name.

CASE STUDY 6: JOHN SMITH

John Smith is a teenager who was brought to the neighborhood health clinic after his mother noticed a small lump on his scalp while cutting his hair. He had not bumped his head or sustained any other injuries that could have caused the lump to occur.

Report 2.6: Office Note

Transcription Hints

- Listen for these terms:
  parietal
  angioma
- Compound modifiers made up of an adverb or an adjective and a participle, for example, well-defined and oval-shaped, require a hyphen. See chapter 13 for a discussion of compound words.

PRO TIP: TRANSCRIPTION ERGONOMICS

By Kathleen Offman, CMT

Medical transcription is a sedentary occupation. Working at a computer for long periods of time can produce sore muscles, headaches, eyestrain, tension, and fatigue. The good news is that you can arrange your workstation and develop specific habits that will relieve physical and mental stress.

Eyes: Take short, frequent breaks to rest your eyes. The American Optometric Association recommends a 10-minute break for every hour or two spent staring at a computer screen. Or take 30-second microbreaks to focus on distant objects, squeeze your shoulders, stretch your back, and shake your arms. If you wear glasses, tinted lenses may reduce glare from the screen. Move your monitor away from the window or use drapes, blinds, or an antiglare screen. Adjust your contrast and brightness levels to suit your comfort level. Select screen colors that are restful for your eyes. Computer workers blink at one-fifth the normal rate while they are watching the screen, causing dry, scratchy eyes. The solution? Make a conscious effort to blink more often, or moisten your eyes with cool water or a tear substitute (sold at drugstores).

Ears: Prevent ear infections by keeping your earphones clean and not allowing others to use them. Work in a relatively quiet environment and cover printers to reduce noise.

Hands and Wrists: Computers originally were built for speed, not comfort, but as carpal tunnel syndrome and other repetitive motion injuries are becoming a major problem in the workplace, keyboards are being redesigned. A new popular design is the split keyboard, which is slanted to accommodate the natural position of the hands as opposed to a straight, flat keyboard that does not support the wrists. Alternatively, you can purchase a wrist rest. The support provided by this inexpensive device may also alleviate back pain caused by tensing the muscles around the shoulders. Taking frequent breaks and exercising will also help.

Posture: Adjust your workstation to your body. Be creative. Heighten or lower your chair and provide support for your lower back with a lumbar cushion, a rolled up towel, or a small, thin, firm pillow. Use a foot rest such as a footstool. Adjust screen height, the angle of your screen, and the distance between you and your screen. Adjust your table or desk height if possible. Check computer supply catalogs for trays that swing out and offer height options for your keyboard. Make your workstation as comfortable as possible.

Lifestyle Changes: Fatigue and discomfort are major contributors to decreased production and errors. Find an outside activity to relieve tension caused by stress. Eat a varied, nutritious diet, exercise regularly, and get enough sleep to improve your alertness, thinking, and comfort both on and off the job.

ASSESSING TRANSCRIPTION SKILLS

Demonstrate your mastery of the terminology, editing/proofreading, and document transcription skills presented in this chapter by completing the following activities.

USING MEDICAL REFERENCES

Use the appropriate medical reference to locate the correct spelling and part of speech for the words below. (If the reference is not available, use the glossary in this text.) Circle the correct spelling, then write a sentence using the word correctly.

1.	psoriasus	psoriasis	psoriases
2.	impetigo	impettigo	impetigoe
3.	syanosis	cyanosis	sianosus
4.	cicatricks	cickatricks	cicatrix
5.	urticaria	uticaria	urticarea
6.	pruritis	pruritus	puritus
7.	paronychia	peronychia	paronychea
8.	hirsuitism	hirsutism	hirutysm

9. **zanthoma** **xanthoma** **xenthoma**

____

10. **joundice** **jaundyce** **jaundice**

____

MAKING EXPERT DECISIONS

Circle the correct word from the choices in parentheses.

1. The patient fell and sustained a (contusion/concussion) to her elbow.
2. "Mycosis" refers to a (fungal/bacterial/viral) infestation.
3. The patient underwent a skin peel, or (fulguration/dermabrasion/electrolysis), by the dermatologist.
4. The patient had a (KOH/Tzanck's smear) test because a fungal infection was suspected.
5. A, An (excisional/incisional/punch) biopsy was done to completely remove the lesion on the nose.
6. The patient (presence/presents) with symptoms of rubella marked by the (presence/presents) of fever, rash, mild upper respiratory symptoms, enlarged lymph nodes, and pain in the joints.
7. The (macular/papular) rash contained small raised areas that were well circumscribed.
8. The (glands/glans) of the penis showed several verrucous formations.
9. The tumor was composed of several small (discrete/discreet) masses.
10. The (vesicle/vesical) was located on the tip of the fourth digit of the right hand.

TRANSCRIBING PROFESSIONAL DOCUMENTS

Transcribe the document named Assessment 2 from tape. Before you key, review the appropriate report formatting guidelines. Proofread your transcribed document and revise it until you think it is error-free.

PERFORMANCE REPORT

Name____Date ___________

Document	Description	Date Completed	Document Processing Speed (If Available)	Document Appraisal M=Mailable MC=Mailable w/corrections NM=Not Mailable
Report 2.1	Office Note			M MC NM
Report 2.2	Office Note			M MC NM
Report 2.3	Office Note			M MC NM
Report 2.4	Office Note			M MC NM
Report 2.5	Office Note			M MC NM
Report 2.6	Office Note			M MC NM

Comments ____

CHAPTER

3

Ophthalmology is the study and treatment of the eye. The physician who practices ophthalmology is called an ophthalmologist. This term is not to be confused with optometrist and optician. An optometrist tests vision, diagnoses eye problems, and fits people for glasses. An optician is trained to grind lenses and fit glasses after the patient has been examined by the ophthalmologist or optometrist.

Ophthalmology

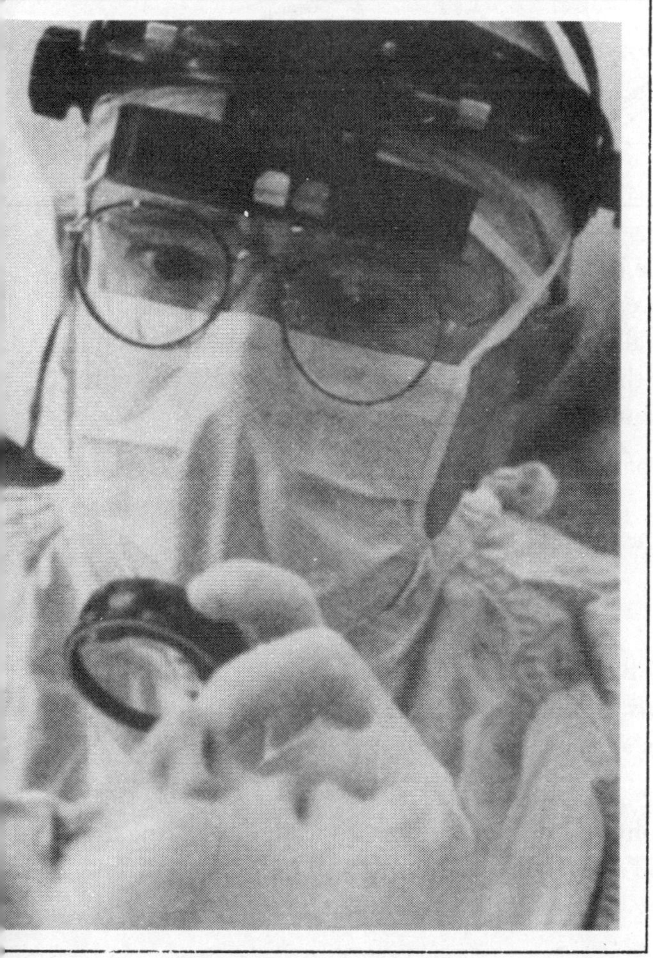

OBJECTIVES

- Use ophthalmology terms correctly according to the context and purpose of the dictation.
- Select and use appropriate general and specialty reference materials.
- Key ophthalmology documents of varying complexity and format.
- Transcribe authentic medical dictation requiring concentration and listening skill.
- Edit medical reports to conform with AAMT style guidelines.
- Proofread and correct transcripts to produce error-free documents.

EXPLORING OPHTHALMOLOGY

The word ophthalmology is derived from a Greek root, *oculus*, for eyeball. This specialty encompasses the study of the eyeball, along with vision, the eyelids, the eye sockets (orbits), and the related parts of the face, brain, sinuses, nose, and throat.

STRUCTURE AND FUNCTION

Working in partnership with the brain, the eye is the organ of sight. Vision is possible when the nervous system converts light rays into nerve impulses, as shown in figure 3.1.

Figure 3.1
Process of vision

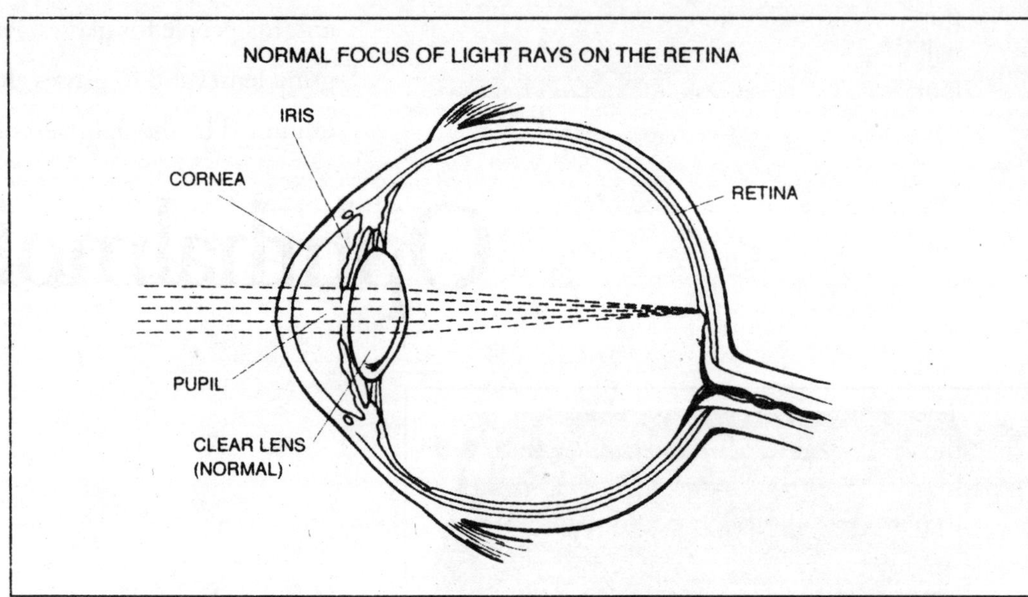

The main parts of the eye include the sclera, cornea, lens, retina, pupil, and iris. The sclera is the "white" of the eye, the outer protective layer of the eyeball. The cornea is the transparent center, allowing light to enter the eye and directing it through the lens to the retina at the back of the eye. The lens focuses the light; the pupil and iris control the amount of light that enters the eye.

Vision occurs when the retinas of both eyes send pictures to the brain, which merges the information into one image. Diplopia, or double vision, occurs when there is failure to merge the images.

PHYSICAL ASSESSMENT

The physician assesses the eye by examining the eyeballs and surrounding structures, including the eyebrows, upper and lower eyelids, and eyelashes. The patient's eyes may reflect feelings such as pain or fear as well as the individual's general health.

After the initial observation, the physician makes a closer inspection by asking the patient to perform certain tasks to reveal facial neuromuscular coordination. The patient's squinting, blinking, raising and lowering of eyebrows, and making faces, such as a grimace, can reveal if there are any neuromuscular problems related to the eyes. These movements test the cranial nerves and are also performed by the neurologist (see chapter 11).

There should be no pain or tenderness on palpation over the forehead, around the eye sockets, or across the lids and eyeballs. The eyeballs should feel firm, round, and bouncy to the touch.

The examination includes the observation of the sclerae, which should be white. Discolored sclerae can indicate jaundice. Very thin, blue-appearing sclerae can occur in some connective tissue disorders. The physician inspects the cornea with a light to determine if there are any irregularities, foreign bodies, or scars. The pupils are inspected for size, equal appearance, and reaction to light. The patient will be asked to look at the examiner's finger about 15 cm from the eyes and then look at a distant object. The pupils should narrow when looking close and widen when looking at a distance.

A Snellen, or "E," chart tests visual acuity. The chart has lines of letters with numbers on the side to represent how far a person can be from the chart to read that line. Therefore, if the patient is seated 20 feet away from the chart and can read the line marked 20 feet, the person is said to have 20/20 vision. That is the distance that a normal eye can read at 20 feet. Testing is also done to determine sight in visual fields, or peripheral vision.

The ophthalmoscope is the instrument used to look at the retina. By observing the veins and arteries directly, the examiner can check for damage associated with hypertension and diabetes. The pupils may be dilated by means of special drops to perform a thorough examination.

DISEASES AND CONDITIONS

The eyelids protect the eyeball; therefore it is important to seek medical attention when there are abnormalities of the eyelid. There can be irritation, inflammation, or infection of the eyelid, including blepharitis, an inflammation of the margins of the lid, and chalazion, a sterile granulomatous inflammation of the meibomian gland. A sty (also spelled stye) is an infection of the lid usually caused by Staphylococcus aureus.

Conjunctivitis is an inflammation of the conjunctiva and can be caused by bacterial, viral, fungal, or parasitic organisms. There is usually hyperemia (redness), discharge, tearing, itching and/or burning, and a feeling of having a foreign body present in the eye.

Trachoma, caused by the organism Chlamydia, is a type of conjunctivitis that affects millions of people. It is rare in the United States, but is endemic to Africa, the Middle East, and Asia. Trachoma is the world's leading cause of blindness. It is very contagious through direct contact with infected individuals or materials they have touched and possibly through insect carriers, but it can be prevented by good hygiene and education. The symptoms of this disease include inflammation, blurred vision, and increasing pain and discomfort. Treatment consists of tetracycline or sulfonamides.

Uveitis is the inflammation of the structures of the uveal tract caused by allergens, bacteria, fungi, viruses, chemicals, or eye trauma. It is characterized by pain, photophobia, blurred vision, and erythema. A physician will prescribe corticosteroid drops to reduce inflammation and proper systemic treatment to treat the underlying cause.

The cornea is the protective membrane at the center of the exterior eye and is important in the refractive system. There are five layers of the cornea (figure 3.2). The nerve fibers in the cornea make it extremely sensitive to pain. Examining the cornea requires a slit lamp that magnifies and lights up the lens, cornea, and iris. A local anesthetic is used to relieve pain during the examination. It may be necessary to use fluorescein staining to outline any epithelial defects.

Corneal abrasions occur from trauma, foreign bodies, including contact lenses,

Figure 3.2
Eyeball

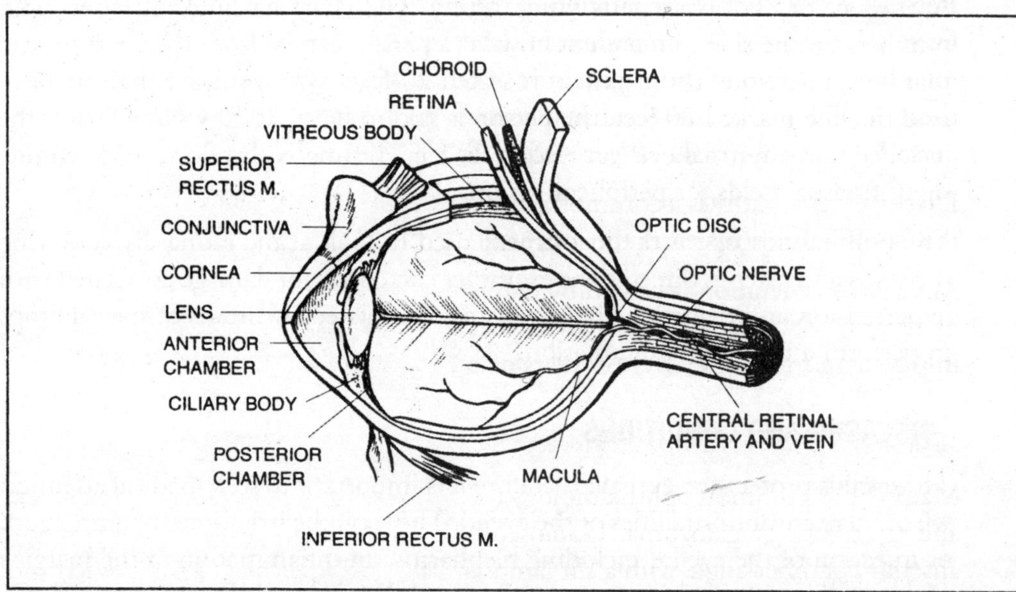

or any defect to the flow of protective tears. Keratitis is an infection of the cornea and can be caused by any organism that has entered the cornea through an abrasion. Because there is easy entry of infectious agents through the eye into the body, patients with severe infectious keratitis are hospitalized and placed on antibiotic therapy.

Keratoconus is a progressive thinning of the cornea that first shows up in puberty and affects women more than men. Vision is distorted, leading to astigmatism and myopia that is difficult to correct even with eyeglasses. Surgery may be necessary to correct this problem.

Corneal transplants are performed using corneas from deceased donors. A circular blade called a trephine is used to incise the cornea. The new cornea is sutured into place. Healing may be slow because of the decreased blood supply of the cornea. A transplant eye bank has been established to make donated corneas available.

Over 2 million persons have been diagnosed with glaucoma in the United States. Glaucoma is one of the leading causes of blindness in the Western world, though blindness is preventable with early diagnosis and management. Glaucoma is characterized by damage to the optic nerve. Primary glaucoma is thought to be hereditary and usually affects both eyes. Secondary glaucoma, or open-angle glaucoma, often affects only one eye and is due to a build-up of pressure inside the eye. Physicians treat glaucoma with drugs that relieve the intraocular pressure (IOP) and restore the normal flow of aqueous humor.

A cataract is a clouding of the crystalline lens. The opaque lens scatters light rather than producing a fine, sharp image. Vision becomes blurred and distorted. While a cataract is usually associated with aging, it can be caused by systemic diseases such as diabetes mellitus, hypoparathyroidism, radiation exposure, or sickle C syndrome.

Retinal detachment is a separation of the neurosensory retina, or rods and cones, from the epithelial, or nourishment, layer of the retina that results in partial or total loss of vision in the affected eye. The most common type of detachment is rhegmatogenous, or a tear-induced detachment, which occurs in 1 out of 10,000 persons between 40 and 70 years old.

Diabetic retinopathy is a common complication of diabetes mellitus. The risk for this complication increases the longer the person has diabetes.

Macular degeneration is caused by damage to the photoreceptor cells in the area of the macula. It may be hereditary and is the leading cause of severe visual impairment for people over 65 years of age.

Common Ophthalmology Drugs

acetylcholine chloride
Miochol

atropine sulfate
Atropair Ophthalmic

cromolyn sodium
Crolom Ophthalmic Drops

cyclopentolate hydrochloride
Cyclogyl

dipivefrin hydrochloride
Propine

idoxuridine
Herplex

naphazoline hydrochloride
Clear Eyes

pilocarpine
Pilocar Ophthalmic

silver nitrate
DeyDrop Ophthalmic Solution

sulfacetamide sodium
Sodium Sulamyd

COMMON TESTS AND SURGICAL PROCEDURES

Many of the common ophthalmology tests and procedures concern the diagnosis and treatment of glaucoma. Gonioscopy, for example, is used to visualize the anterior chamber angle with a slit lamp and a goniolens, a special mirror contact lens. Gonioscopy is necessary to determine if the angle is open or closed in glaucoma. Laser surgery is the primary treatment of glaucoma and other eye disorders. Some of the laser surgical procedures include laser iridotomy, peripheral iridectomy, radial keratotomy, trabeculoplasty, and gonioplasty.

THE VOCABULARY OF OPHTHALMOLOGY

The following word list contains common ophthalmology terms as well as most of the difficult words contained in the dictation at the end of the chapter. Here are suggestion for learning the vocabulary words.

1. Read and study each word for pronunciation and meaning.
2. Write each unfamiliar word from the list below on a notecard, write the definition or a paraphrase of the definition on the back, and draw a simple picture to help you learn the word.
3. Study the pronunciation, spelling, and definition of each word on your notecard, then key each word twice for reinforcement. Check the spelling.
4. Add the correctly spelled terms to your word processor's spell checker.

accommodation
(ah-kom-o-day'-shun) (n) the eye's ability to focus or see

afferent
(af'-er-ent) (adj) inward or toward a center

amblyopia
(am-blee-O'-pee-a) (n) decreased vision in one or both eyes; not correctable

anterior
(an-teer'-ee-or) (adj) front of a part, organ, or structure

astigmatism
(a-stig'-ma-tizm) (n) visual condition in which light rays entering the eye are bent unequally, preventing a sharp focus point on the retina

blepharectomy
(blef-ar-ek'-tO-mee) (n) excision of a lesion of the eyelid

blepharitis
(blef-a-rI'-tis) (n) inflammation of the eyelid

calcification
(kal'-si-fi-kay'-shun) (n) a hardening of tissue resulting from the formation of calcium salts within it

cataract
(kat'-a-rakt) (n) clouding of the lens of the eye, resulting in loss of transparency

chemosis
(kee-mO'-sis) (n) an accumulation of fluid in the eye, causing swelling around the cornea

chemotherapy
(kem-O-thayr'-a-pee/keem'-O-thayr-a-pee) (n) treatment of disease with drugs

choroid
(kO'-royd) (n) a vascular membrane surrounding the eyeball, between the retina and sclera

conjunctiva
(kon-junk-ti'-va) (n) the mucous membrane covering the front of the eyeball and inside the eyelids; conjunctivae (pl)

conjunctivitis
(kon-junk-ti-vI'-tis) (n) inflammation of the conjunctiva

cornea
(kor'-nee-a) (n) the outer, transparent portion of the eye through which light passes to the retina

diplopia
(di-plO'-pee-a) (n) double vision

enucleation
(ee-noo-klee-ay'-shun) (n) removal of a tumor or structure as a whole, as in removal of the eyeball

epiphora
(ee-pif'-O-ra) (n) overflow of tears

esotropia
(es-O-trO'-pee-a) (n) a condition in which one or both eyes appear to turn inward; cross eye(s)

exophthalmos
(ek-sof-thal'-mos) (n) protrusion of the eyeball(s)

exotropia
(ek-sO-trO'-pee-a) (n) outward turning of one eye relative to the other

fundus
(fun'-dus) (n) that part of the interior of the eyeball exposed to view through an ophthalmoscope; fundi (pl)

funduscopic
(fun-dus-skop'-ik) (adj) relating to funduscopy

funduscopy
(fun-dus-kop'-ee) (n) examination of the fundus of the eye using a funduscope; ophthalmoscopy

glaucoma
(glaw-kO'-ma) (n) disease of the eye in which intraocular pressure increases, damaging the optic nerve; can lead to blindness

Goldmann perimeter screen test
(n) assesses patient response when a light comes into view

gonioplasty
(gO-ni-O-plas'-tee) (n) procedure that contracts the peripheral iris to eliminate contact with the trabecular meshwork

gonioscopy
(gO-ni-O'-skOp-ee) (n) procedure that allows viewing of the anterior chamber angle using a slit lamp and a goniolens, a special mirror contact lens

hydrocephalic
(hI-drO-se-fal'-ik) (adj) relating to or having hydrocephalus

hydrocephalus
(hI-drO-sef'-a-lus) (n) increased accumulation of cerebrospinal fluid within the ventricles of the brain

hydrocephaly
(hI-drO-sef'-a-lee) (n) the condition of having hydrocephalus

hyperopia
(hI-per-O'-pee-a) (n) farsightedness

hypertropia
(hI-per-trO'-pee-a) (n) a type of squint in which the eye looks upward

hypotropia
(hI-pO-trO'-pee-a) (n) a type of squint in which the eye looks downward

intraocular pressure
(in-tra-ok'-yoo-lar presh'-er) (n) the pressure of the fluid within the eye

iris
(I'-ris) (n) colored portion of the eye that regulates the amount of light entering through the pupil; irides (ir'-i-deez) (pl)

keratoplasty
(ker'-a-tO-plas'-tee) (n) surgery on the cornea, especially transplant of a cornea

laser iridotomy
(ir-i-dot'-O-mee) (n) cutting some of the fibers of the iris with a laser

macula
(mak'-yoo-la) (n) small discolored spot on the retina or skin

metastasis
(me-tas'-ta-sis) (n) spread of a tumor from its site of origin to distant sites

metastatic
(met-a-stat'-ik) (adj) relating to metastasis

motility
(mO-til'-i-tee) (n) ability to move spontaneously

myopia
(mI-O'-pee-a) (n) nearsightedness

nystagmus
(nis-tag'-mus) (n) involuntary, rhythmic oscillation of the eyeballs

oblique
(ob-leek') (adj) slanting

ophthalmologist
(of-thal-mol'-o-jist) (n) a physician specializing in diseases of the eye

ophthalmoscopy
(of-thal-mos'-ko-pee) (n) procedure used to examine the optic nerve head for color, shape, and vascularization

ophthalmus
(of-thal'-mus) (n) the eye

optic
(op'-tik) (adj) pertaining to the eye or sight

optic chiasm
(op'-tik kI'-azm) (n) the point of crossing of the optic nerves

optometrist
(op-tom'-e-trist) (n) a professional who tests visual acuity and prescribes corrective lenses

osteosarcoma
(os'-tee-O-sar-ko'-ma) (n) a tumor of the bone, usually highly malignant

palsy
(pawl'-zee) (n) an abnormal condition characterized by partial paralysis

papillopathy
(pap-i-lop'-a-thee) (n) the blood supply to the optic disk and retina is obstructed; often producing low-tension glaucoma

peripheral iridectomy
(per-if'-er-al ir-i-dek'- tO-mee) (n) procedure that creates a hole in the iris; used to relieve high intraocular pressure

phacoemulsification
(fak'-O-ee-mul-si-fi-kay'-shun) (n) process that disintegrates a cataract using ultrasonic waves

photophobia
(fO-tO-fO'-bee-a) (n) marked intolerance to light

platelet
(playt'-let) (n) disc-shaped, small cellular element in the blood that is essential for blood clotting

presbyopia
(prez-bee-O'-pee-a) (n) farsightedness associated with aging

prognosis
(prog-nO'-sis) (n) the expected outcome of a disease

pterygium
(ter-ij'-ee-um) (n) web eye; an outward growth of tissue of the eye

ptosis
(tO'-sis) (n) sagging of the upper eyelid

pupil
(pyoo'-pil) (n) the round opening in the center of the iris which opens or closes to adjust to light

pupillary
(pyoo'-pi-layr-ee) (adj) relating to the pupil of the eye

radial keratotomy
(ray'-dee-al ker-ah-tot'-O-mee) (n) incision(s) in the cornea radiating out from the center

radiotherapy
(ray'-dee-O-thayr'-a-pee) (n) the treatment of disease by application of radium, ultraviolet, and other types of radiation

recession
(ree-sesh'-un) (n) the withdrawal of a part from its normal position

rectus
(rec'-tus) (adj) relating to the rectus muscle of the eye

referral
(ree-fer'-al) (n) a physician's sending of a patient to another physician

reflex
(ree'-fleks) (n) an involuntary response to a stimulus

regression
(ree-gresh'-un) (n) returning to an earlier condition

retina
(ret'-i-na) (n) innermost layer of the eyeball that receives images formed by the lens and transmits visual impulses through the optic nerve to the brain; composed of light-sensitive nerves

retinitis pigmentosa
(ret-in-I'-tis) (n) a inflammation of the retina with pigment changes, eventually leading to blindness

retinoblastoma
(ret'-i-nO-blas-tO'-ma) (n) malignant sarcoma or neoplasm of the retina; hereditary and generally occurring in young children

retinopathy
(ret-i-nop'-a-thee) (n) any disorder of the retina without inflammation

retinoscopy
(ret'-i-nos'-ko-pee) (n) light beam test used to detect refractive errors

sclera
(skle'-rah) (n) white of the eye; the tough, outer covering of the eye

sclerostomy
(skle-ros'-tO-mee) (n) surgical formation of an opening in the sclera

scotoma
(skO-tO'-ma) (n) a blind spot; a small area of defective vision

seed
(n) as related to oncology, it is the beginning of a tumor

seeding
(n) the local spreading of immature tumor cells

Seton procedure
(n) placing of a tube in the anterior chamber to drain fulid and decrease the intraocular pressure

slit-lamp
(n) instrument consisting of a microscope and a thin, bright beam of light; used to examine the eye

sphincterotomy
(sfink-tur-ot'-O-mee) (n) procedure that produces cuts in the iris sphincter muscle to allow pupillary enlargement

sporadic
(spO-rad'-ik) (adj) occurring occasionally or in isolated situations

strabismus
(stra-biz'-mus) (n) improper alignment of eyes; crossed eye(s)

sty
(stI) (n) an infection of a marginal gland of the eyelid; stye

tangent screen test
(n) maps the field of vision using a marker

tonometry
(tO-nom'-et-ree) (n) a test that measures intraocular pressure

trabeculectomy
(tra-bek-yoo-lek'-tO-mee) (n) surgical removal of a section of the cornea to decrease intraocular pressure in patients with severe glaucoma

trabeculoplasty
(tra-bek'-yoo-lO-plas'-tee) (n) surgical procedure that decreases intraocular pressure in open-angle glaucoma

unilateral
(yoo-ni-lat'-e-ral) (adj) affecting or occurring on only one side

uveitis
(yoo-vee-I'-tis) (n) inflammation of the uvea, including the choroid and the iris

viable
(vI'-a-bl) (adj) capable of surviving; living

visual acuity
(vizh'-yoo-al a-kyoo'-i-tee) (n) clearness of vision, e.g., 20/20 visual acuity

vitreous humor
(vit'-ree-us hyoo'-mer) (adj) glassy; gelatin-like substance within the eyeball

xanthopsia
(zan-thop'-see-a) (n) yellow vision; a condition in which everything seen appears yellowish

ABBREVIATIONS

ACC	accommodation
AV	arteriovenous
D	diopter (strength of lens in eyeglass prescription)
Em	emmetropia
EOM	extraocular movements
IOL	intraocular lens
IOP	intraocular pressure
L&A	light and accommodation
myop	myopia
OD	right eye; doctor of optometry
OS	left eye
OU	both eyes
PAN	periodic alternating nystagmus or periarteritis nodosa
PAM	potential acuity meter
PERRLA	pupils equal, round, reactive to light and accommodation
REM	rapid eye movement
ST	esotropia
VA	visual acuity
VF	visual field
XT	exotropia

EXERCISE 3.1: RECOGNIZING LOOK-ALIKES AND SOUND-ALIKES

Below is a list of frequently used words that look alike and/or sound alike. Study the meaning and pronunciation of each set of words, then read each sentence carefully and circle the word in parentheses that correctly completes the meaning.

efferent conducting (as a nerve) or progressing away from the center
afferent conducting (as a nerve) or progressing toward the center

hyper - (prefix) more, greater
hypo- (prefix) less, smaller

effluent discharged fecal material
affluent having wealth

macula a small, yellowish spot on the retina at the back of the eye
macule a spot discoloration or thickening of the skin

anterior front
inferior below; lower
posterior back; behind
superior above

metastases plural form of metastasis
metastasis spread of a tumor to different parts of the body
metastasize to invade by metastasis
metastatic relating to metastasis

esotropia	inward turning of the eye	**recession**	withdrawl of part from its normal position
exotropia	outward turning of the eye	**resection**	cutting out part of an organ

fundus	part farthest from the opening	**apprise**	to notify; to tell
fungus	organism	**appraise**	to set a value on; to give an expert judgment of the value or merit of

1. The head is (superior, inferior) to the chest.
2. Your face is located on the (anterior, posterior) part of your body.
3. The legs are (superior, inferior) to the head.
4. The spine is (anterior, posterior) to the chest.
5. Examination of the face revealed a 1 cm (macula, macule) on the cheek.
6. Due to her (hypothyroidism, hyperthyroidism), she requires thyroid supplementation.
7. The patient's (hypotension, hypertension) is under good control on the Calan SR.
8. On ophthalmic exam, the (fundus, fungus) appeared normal.
9. This patient has metastatic colorectal carcinoma with (metastases, metastasis) diagnosed in the liver, lung, and brain.
10. The patient is status post craniotomy for removal of tumor (metastasis, metastatic).

EXERCISE 3.2: MATCHING SOUND AND SPELLING

The numbered list that follows shows the phonetic spelling of hard-to-spell words. Sound out the word, then write the correct spelling in the blank space provided. Each of the words can be found in the glossary or in the drug list in appendix C.

1. kal'-si-fi-kay'-shun ______________________
2. ret'-i-nO-blas-tO'-ma ______________________
3. yoo-ni-lat'-e-ral ______________________
4. pyoo'-pi-layr-ee ______________________
5. ob-leek' ______________________
6. hI-drO-sef'-a-lus ______________________
7. blef'-a-rI'-tis ______________________
8. vit'-ree-us______________________
9. fO-tO-fO'-bee-a ______________________

10. me-tas'-ta-sis ______________________________

11. nis-tag'-mus ______________________________

12. ek-sof-thal'-mos ______________________________

13. os'-tee-O-sar-kO'-ma ______________________________

14. pap-i-lop'-a-thee ______________________________

15. mO-til'-i-tee ______________________________

EXERCISE 3.3: CHOOSING WORDS FROM CONTEXT

When transcribing dictation, the medical transcriptionist frequently needs to determine the word that correctly completes the sentence based on the situation. From the list of words below, select the term that meaningfully completes each statement.

conjunctivitis	retinopathy	diplopia
strabismus	optic	nystagmus
radiotherapy	osteosarcoma	optic chiasm
scotoma	enucleation	epiphora
esotropia		

1. The patient is status post ______________ of the left eye, with a poorly fitted prosthesis in place.
2. The right fundus showed a flame hemorrhage superior to the ______________ nerve.
3. She had an amputation of the right leg below the knee because she was diagnosed with a malignancy called ______________.
4. She describes a blind spot in the right eye; this is most likely a ______________.
5. When you have ______________, your eyes may deviate either toward the nose or to the outside of midline.
6. The patient's allergic ______________ seems to be controlled on the antibiotic eyedrops.
7. It was recommended that Joseph have ______________ treatments to the eye, rather than have an enucleation.
8. A mild form of ______________, where the eye turns inward, can often be corrected with exercises for the eye.
9. The funduscopic exam showed no signs of ______________.
10. The MRI revealed an enhancing lesion surrounding the ______________.

EXERCISE 3.4: PAIRING WORDS AND MEANINGS

For each definition provided below, locate the term on the list that best matches the definition. Write the letter of the term in the space provided beside the definition.

A. pupillary	F. rectus	K. ophthalmus
B. calcification	G. seed	L. amblyopia
C. macula	H. funduscopy	M. nystagmus
D. retinopathy	I. optic	N. retina
E. cornea	J. hydrocephalus	

1. outer portion of eye through which light passes to retina __________
2. pertaining to vision __________
3. pertaining to pupil of eye __________
4. accumulation of cerebrospinal fluid within ventricles of brain __________
5. examination of the base of the eye __________
6. small, yellowish spot on retina __________
7. hardening of tissue resulting from calcium salts __________
8. beginning of a tumor __________
9. disorder of the retina __________
10. a muscle of the eye __________

EXERCISE 3.5: CREATING TERMS FROM WORD FORMS

In the following exercise, combine prefixes, root words, and suffixes to create medical words that fit the definitions below. Fill in the blanks with the words you construct.

conjunctiv/o	mucous membrane lining inner eyeball and eyelids	kerat/o	hard or cornea
		-phobia	excessive fear
hypo	below or deficient	-scopy	examination
ophthalm/o	eye	-itis	inflammation
blephar/o	eyelid	-ectomy	removal
angi/o	vessel	-plasty	surgical repair
hyper	above or excessive	-a	word ending
phot/o	light	-pathy	disease
retina	nerve tissue layer of eye	-tropia	condition of turning

1. disease of the retina ____________
2. type of squint when the eye looks downward ____________
3. inflammation of the membrane lining the inner eyelid and the eyeball ____________
4. excision of a lesion on the eyelid ____________
5. light beam test that detects refractive errors ____________
6. operation to correct defect in eyelids ____________
7. visualizes the optic nerve for color and shape ____________
8. mucous membrane lining the inner surface of the eye ____________
9. inflammation of the eyelid ____________
10. corneal transplant ____________

EDITING MEDICAL DOCUMENTS

In this section you will perfect your word use and grammar skills. These skills will help you edit and proofread medical reports for correct language, punctuation, format, and meaning. The special focus for this chapter is subject-verb agreement.

CREATING SUBJECT-VERB AGREEMENT

The subject and verb of a sentence must match in number and person. Singular verbs require singular subjects, and plural verbs require plural subjects. Use first-person verbs with first-person subjects (I, we), second-person verbs with second-person subjects (you), and third-person verbs with third-person subjects (he, she, it, they).

I am confused.
S V
[singular subject and verb]

You are an excellent student.
S V
[The pronoun *you* can be either singular or plural in meaning, but it always takes a plural verb.]

The patient and her *husband are discussing* the procedure.
S S V
[plural subject and plural verb]

Note: Sometimes subjects can "look" plural, but they function as one unit and are singular in meaning. Be sure you use singular verbs in such cases.

I&D was performed.
S V

[The procedure involves two steps, but together they make up ONE procedure; therefore this subject is singular.]

Pediatrics is her specialty.
S V

[Even though pediatrics has an s, it is the name of a single specialty and therefore requires a singular verb.]

Complicating Factors: Inverted Order Sentences; Intervening Words and Phrases

Inverted order sentences: Sentences are usually written with the subject before the verb. However, sometimes the sentence is inverted, meaning that the verb comes first. This can cause some confusion in achieving subject-verb agreement. Many of these sentences begin with *Here* or *There.*

There *is* no *reason* to delay treatment.
V S

There *was* no *tenderness* to palpation.
V S

Here *are* my *reasons* for declining the position.
V S

Intervening words and phrases: In complicated sentences, first identify the verb and then the subject(s) of that verb. Then be sure you choose a singular verb for a singular subject or a plural verb for a plural subject. Disregard the parts of the sentence that come between the subject and the verb.

A verbal *report* of the biopsies *was requested.*
S V

Resection of the malignant tumors *was carried out.*
S V

The *patient,* along with his family, *is* pleased with the outcome of his surgery.
S V

EXERCISE 3.6: EDITING FOR SUBJECT-VERB AGREEMENT

Read the following discharge summary section and circle the correct verbs from the choices in parentheses. Then key the report using correct subject-verb combinations.

SUBJECTIVE: The patient, a 56-year-old female with multiple medical problems, (present/presents) to the ophthalmology outpatient clinic with 24 hours of tearing and irritation of both eyes. Vision in both eyes (seems/seem) unimpaired. She has no history of allergies or URIs and (does/do) not wear contact lenses.
She has a thick mucous discharge in both eyes, which (causes/cause) the lashes to stick together. She denies any history of trauma to the eyes and no previous history of similar symptoms (is/are) noted.

OBJECTIVE: In each eye the conjunctiva (is/are) grossly inflamed and injected. There (is/are) moderate chemosis and some lid edema. Traces of mucopurulent discharge (is/are) noted on the eyelashes. Examination with Tetracaine and fluorescein (reveals/reveal) no corneal abrasion. Funduscopic and slit-lamp exam (is/are) entirely normal.

ASSESSMENT: Acute bacterial conjunctivitis OU.

PLAN: The patient, with her sister in attendance, (was/were) instructed to use sulfonamide ophthalmic solution two drops OU q.i.d. Techniques of careful handwashing and hygiene (was/were) explained to the patient. The patient will return if her symptoms (does/do) not improve.

EXERCISE 3.7: PROOFREADING REVIEW

Read the following partial report and look for errors in punctuation, spelling, plural vs. singular word forms, run-on sentences, and subject-verb agreement. Circle the errors; then key the report with the errors corrected.

OBJECTIVE: On examination visual aquity at distance was 20/20 in both eyes. The interocular pressure was 20 in both eyes. Motility was strait, with full versions and the pupils was normal. External exam revealed fat pertrusion on the lateral aspect of the upper and lower lids on both eye. There was a firmness on the right eye. The contacts were centered will, with good movement, slit lamp exam revealed a white conjunctiva, with a clear cornia. The lenses had some cortical changes. Dilated funduscopic exam revealed a normal cup-to-disc ratio, with a normal macule, blood vessels, and peripheral retina.

WHERE CAN I FIND THE ANSWER?

As you transcribe dictation, you may hear unfamiliar words or terms. A variety of reference sources are available to help you locate answers to your questions. One of the important types of references for medical transcriptionists is described below. Read the information; then if you have access to the reference discussed, explore its capabilities.

MEDICAL REFERENCES: MEDICAL DICTIONARIES

No medical transcriptionist can survive without a good, up-to-date medical dictionary. A medical dictionary gives pronunciation, word origins, and definitions. It is important to read the definitions of terms to ensure that you are using them correctly. This practice also helps you build your medical vocabulary based on meaning, not just spelling.

There are several popular medical dictionaries. Choose one aimed at medical professionals. The language of medicine changes very rapidly, so it is important that you replace your medical dictionary every five years or so.

When faced with an unfamiliar term, the first thing to decide is what kind of term it is. If it is a specialized term for which you have a specialized reference, such as a surgical or pharmaceutical term, first try that reference book. Use the medical dictionary for anatomic and physiologic terms such as nerves, muscles, syndromes, and bacteria, but not for sutures, dressings, and medication names.

If the term contains an adjective and a noun, for example, Valsalva maneuver, the noun is usually the word to look up. For instance, if you hear *shogrun syndrome*, look in your medical dictionary under *syndrome* and then find *Sjögren* listed alphabetically under that heading. If the term is Latin, the order may be noun-followed-by-adjective, as in *fascia lata*, in which case you would look up *fascia.*

If the term is just one word, remember that different letters or combinations of letters can make certain sounds. The sound of the letter *s* can be made by *s, c, ps*, etc. The sound of *f* can be made by *f* or *ph.*

Don't give up if you don't find a term in the first place you look. If you are looking for some kind of disease and it's not listed under the heading *disease*, try *syndrome*, or *sickness.* Also try your eponyms reference, if appropriate.

TRANSCRIBING OPHTHALMOLOGY DOCUMENTS

In this section your goal is to prepare for the work of transcription by transcribing first from a printed document and then from dictation on tape. The model document that follows illustrates the generally accepted format for the **consultation letter**, the report format featured in this chapter.

BASIC FORMAT: CONSULTATION LETTER/REPORT

The consultation letter is a report that a patient's primary or attending physician requests of a specialist. Dictated in either a letter or report form, this document provides an opinion on a particular problem or diagnosis. The specialist dictates the letter/report and addresses it to the primary physician.

Required Headings/Content

JCAHO guidelines require no special headings; the format varies among institutions. The content includes sections similar to a history and physical, including date of consultation, reason for consultation, present history, past history, physical and laboratory evaluation, and the consultant's impression and recommendations. Physicians often add a phrase such as "thank you for referring this patient to me" at the end of the dictation.

Turnaround Time

For emergency room situations, specialists' consultations are available within approximately 30 minutes; initial consultation through two-way voice communication is acceptable. Consultations should be dictated within 24 hours from the time the request is received by the physician, and the report should be transcribed and on the chart within the next 24 hours. This guideline varies among institutions.

CONSULTATION LETTER

1" margins → **left justification**

Wills Eye Hospital
5849 Garfield Drive
Fort Worth, TX 76555-1223

2 or more line spaces, depending on length of letter

November 29, ____

2 or more line spaces, depending on length of letter

Dr. Albert J. Eisner
Brookfield University Medical School
One University Place
Fort Worth, TX 76104-3223

ds

RE: Lawrence Johnson, Jr.

ds

Dear Al:

ds

We rechecked Lawrence Johnson under anesthesia on November 21. It has been nine months since he completed his course of external beam radiation therapy as management of unilateral sporadic retinoblastoma in the left eye.

ds

On our exam today, our findings remain the same as on our prior exam in August. The tumor is completely regressed, and there is no evidence of viability. There are no new tumors in the left eye. The optic disc is healthy, and there are no signs of radiation retinopathy or papillopathy.

ds

The right eye is perfectly normal, with no evidence of retinoblastoma. Regarding the visual prognosis, because of the macular location of the regressed retinoblastoma, his visual prognosis is very guarded. We will try patching of the right eye in an attempt to stimulate any possible vision in the left eye.

ds

Thank you for allowing us to assist in his care.

ds

Very sincerely yours,

quadruple-space

Richard Sowers, MD

ds

RS/XX

PREPARING TO TRANSCRIBE

To prepare for transcribing dictation, key the consultation letter above. You will later key the identical report from dictation. Follow these guidelines:

- Study the format and organization of the document.
- Review the word list presented earlier in this chapter.
- Consult reference books for words or formatting rules that are unfamiliar.
- Proofread your final copy by comparing it to the printed version.

CASES FOR TRANSCRIPTION

In this section you will transcribe medical dictation from tape. Your goal is to produce error-free documents. Read this chapter's Pto Tip (following the case studies) for helpful hints from experienced MTs. Then follow these steps for each dictation:

1. Prepare to transcribe by reviewing the case study and the appropriate report format.
2. Transcribe the dictation, using the process of "listen, stop, key." Listen to a single sentence or phrase (the maximum number of words you can mentally retain and repeat to yourself), pause the tape, then key the words. Leave spaces for words you cannot hear or do not understand.
3. Carefully proofread the document and correct as many errors as you can. Use your reference materials to help you identify missing words.
4. Listen to the tape again and correct all remaining errors.

Repeat these steps until you produce an error-free document. Then complete the Performance Report at the end of the chapter, attach it to the top of the transcripts, and submit them to your instructor for evaluation.

CASE STUDY 1: LAWRENCE JOHNSON

Lawrence Johnson is an infant who was diagnosed with retinoblastoma by Dr. Richard Sowers at Wills Eye Hospital. He was referred to Dr. Albert J. Eisner at Brookfield University Medical School for followup care. Dr. Eisner sent Lawrence to Dr. Jorge Frieze, a specialist in radiation oncology, for radiotherapy.

Report 3.1: Consultation Letter

Transcription Hints

- Listen for these troublesome terms:
  enucleation
  unilateral sporadic retinoblastoma
- Measurements of tumors are done with metric terms, as in 15 by 15 by 5.9 mm. Transcribe "by" as x with one space before and after. The abbreviation for millimeters requires no period, and the abbreviation should be keyed only once, at the end of the measurement.

Report 3.2: Letter of Referral

Transcription Hint

The word *followup* functions as a noun, an adjective, and a verb. Key the term as one word when used as a noun or adjective and as two words when used as a verb. A hyphenated construction (*follow-up*) is also acceptable for adjective uses, but one word is preferred. In this report, *followup* is used three times as a noun. See chapter 13 for a more complete discussion of compound words.

Report 3.3: Consultation Letter

CASE STUDY 2: RONALD JONES

Ronald Jones is a 21-year-old male diagnosed with osteosarcoma. While hospitalized for administration of chemotherapy, he developed difficulty with his vision, and a specialist in ophthalmology, Dr. Regina Smyth, was called as a consultant to assist with this complication.

Report 3.4: Consultation Report

Transcription Hints

- Listen for these difficult terms:
  metastatic osteosarcoma
  scotoma
- Visual acuity results are dictated as two numbers ("twenty twenty") and transcribed as two numerals separated by a diagonal slash, as in *20/20*.
- The word *re-examine* requires a hyphen since the prefix ends with the first letter of the following word, *examine*.

Report 3.5: Consultation Letter

CASE STUDY 3: RELING QUANG

Reling Quang is a 47-year-old secretary who reports that she has been finding it more diffucult to see her computer screen and that her eyes tire easily. She has never worn glasses, but thinks that it may be necessary now.

Report 3.6: Office Note

Transcription Hint

When transcribing visual acuity test results, separate the abbreviation (for example, OD) and the numbers with a space but no comma. However, include a comma between the results for the right and left eyes, as in *OD 20/20, OS 20/20.*

CASE STUDY 4: ELIZABETH HAMMERS

Elizabeth Hammers is a young woman who has been referred to an ophthalmologist for an opinion about her dimness of vision in the right eye. Although the problem has been present since birth, Elizabeth's primary physician wanted to ensure that no disease process was occurring in the eye.

Report 3.7: Consultation Letter

Transcription Hint

Listen for these difficult terms:
afferent
amblyopic
cup-to-disc ratio
disc edema
dot-and-blot hemorrhage
fluorescein angiogram
ischemia
pupillary
rubeosis

CASE STUDY 5: GLEN BRIAN

Glen Brian is a child who has a disorder of the eye because of increased pressure within the brain. His pediatrician, Dr. Richard Golden, has referred him to Sanford Guterman, MD, Ophthalmologist, for treatment.

Report 3.8: Consultation Letter

Transcription Hint

Listen for these difficult terms:
bimedial rectus resection
esotropia
hydrocephalus
oblique over-action
strabismus

PRO TIP: DISCERNING SIMILAR SOUNDS

By Kathleen Offman, CMT

Many medical terms and drug names sound alike. When attempting to identify a term in a dictation, you may be tripped up because the word is spelled differently than it sounds. Here are a few tips for discerning similar sounds in words that sound alike (with examples of each):

If you hear...	Also consider...	Examples
c	k and g	Kufs disease, guanine
f	ph	phacocyst, farnesol
i (short i as the first or second sound)	e, a, and y	enalapril, indoluria, Restoril
y	j	Jungian analysis
k	c, ch	kaliuresis, chiasm
m	n	modal, nodal, naproxen
n	m, pn, gn, mn, kn, cn	nacreous, macrocyte, pneumonia, gnathic, mnemic, knismogenic, cnemis
s	z, c, ps	zymoscope, ciliary, pseudopsia
t	b, p, pt, ct, v	popliteal, ptosis, vinculum
z	x	Xylocaine, Xanax, xanthiuria, Zaglas ligament
	s	seromuscular, Szent-Gyorgyi reaction

Pro Tip continued on next page

Pro Tip continued from previous page

Whole syllables, not just single letters, are sometimes confused. Here are some alternative spellings for some hard-to-discern word beginnings and endings. Syllables that begin a word are shown with a hyphen at the end. Syllables that end a word are shown with a hyphen before them.

If you hear…	Also consider…
-able	-ible
-air	-are, -aer
-ance	-ence
-ant	-ent
ante-	anti-
-cer	-cre
-cks, -gz	-x
dis-	dys-
-ei	-ie
-ere	-ear, -eir, -ier
fizz-	phys-
hyper-	hypo-
inter-	intra-
-is	-us, -ace, -ice
-le	-tle, -el, -al
ny-	gn-, n-
para-	peri-, pero-
per-	par-, pir-, por-, pur-, pre-, pro-, pru-, pyr-
peri-	para-, pero-
pre-	per-, pra-, pri-, pro-, pru-
si-	psi-, ci-
super-	supra-
-tion	-sion, -cion, -cean, -cian
-tious	-seous, -scious
-ture	-teur
we-	whe-
wi-	whi-
zi-	xy-

ASSESSING TRANSCRIPTION SKILLS

Demonstrate your mastery of the terminology, editing/proofreading, and document transcription skills presented in this chapter by completing the following activities.

USING MEDICAL REFERENCES

Use the appropriate medical reference to locate the correct spelling and additional usage information for the words below. (If the reference is not available, use the glossary in this text.) Circle the correct spelling; then write a sentence using the word correctly.

1. accomodation accommodation acommodation
   ____

2. conjunctivi conjunctiva conjunktiva
   ____

3. retinopathy retanopathy retinopathey
   ____

4. glaucoma glacoma gloucoma
   ____

5. phacoemulsification phacoemulcifikation phakoemulsiphication
   ____

6. tosis ptosis phtosis
   ____

7. nystagmis nistagymus nystagmus
   ____

8. cattaract cataracht cataract
   ____

9. pterygim pterygium terygium

____

10. blepharitis blepharytis blefaritis

____

MAKING EXPERT DECISIONS

Circle the correct word from the choices in parentheses.

1. Examination noted the iris, ciliary body, and choroid to be inflamed; thus, the diagnosis of (conjunctivitis/uveitis) was considered.
2. A physician who specializes in the treatment of disorders of the eyes is called an (ophthalmologist/optometrist).
3. The (anterior/posterior) portion of the sclera becomes the cornea.
4. The (macula/macule) revealed a small, patchy lesion on the surface of the skin.
5. The condition whereby the eyes turn toward the nose is called (esotropia/exotropia); turning the eye toward the temple is called (esotropia/exotropia).
6. Examination of the optic nerve for color, shape, and vascularization was performed during (ophthalmoscopy/funduscopy).
7. The patient had yellow (sclerae or scleras/conjunctivae), so we ran liver function tests.
8. The (pupil/iris) regulates the size of the (pupil/iris).
9. The patient squinted downward, indicating (hypertropia/hypotropia).
10. A (corneal/cataract) transplant was done due to excessive scarring.

TRANSCRIBING PROFESSIONAL DOCUMENTS

Transcribe the document named Assessment 3 from tape. Before you key, review the appropriate document formatting guidelines. Proofread your transcribed document and revise it until you think it is error-free.

PERFORMANCE REPORT

Name______________________________Date __________

Document	Description	Date Completed	Document Processing Speed (If Available)	Document Appraisal M=Mailable MC=Mailable w/corrections NM=Not Mailable
Report 3.1	Consultation Letter			M MC NM
Report 3.2	Letter of Referral			M MC NM
Report 3.3	Consultation Letter			M MC NM
Report 3.4	Consultation Report			M MC NM
Report 3.5	Consultation Letter			M MC NM
Report 3.6	Office Note			M MC NM
Report 3.7	Consultation Letter			M MC NM
Report 3.8	Consultation Letter			M MC NM

Comments ______________________________

C H A P T E R

4

The ears, nose, and throat are important passageways into the body that can be affected by a variety of medical conditions. Otorhinolaryngology, from the Greek for ear ("ous"), nose ("rhis"), and larynx ("larynx"), is the medical speciality that deals with these passageways. Physicians who practice in this area are called otorhinolaryngologists or ENT specialists.

Otorhinolaryngology (ENT)

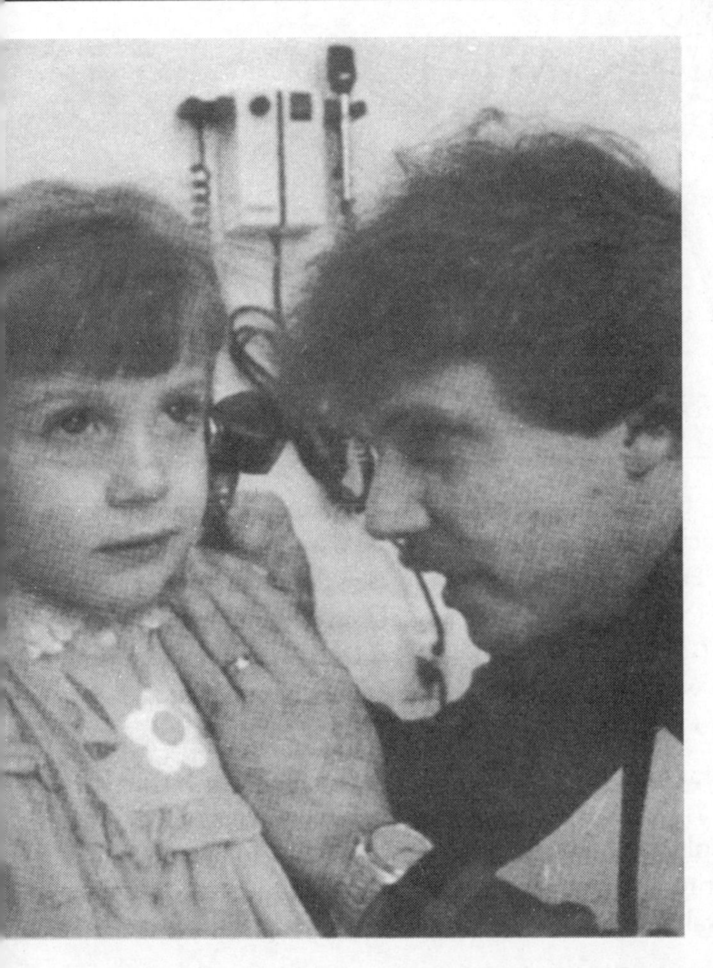

- Use otorhinolaryngology terms correctly according to the context and purpose of the dictation.
- Select and use appropriate general and specialty reference materials.
- Key otorhinolaryngology documents of varying complexity and format.
- Transcribe authentic medical dictation requiring concentration and listening skill.
- Edit medical reports to conform with AAMT style guidelines.
- Proofread and correct transcripts to produce error-free documents.

EXPLORING OTORHINOLARYNGOLOGY (ENT)

The specialty of otorhinolaryngology studies and treats diseases of the ears, nose, and throat. Because many common illnesses affect the ears, nose, and throat, people frequently visit the doctor with complaints of symptoms affecting these areas. In addition, because the ears and nose are so visible and prominent, people often seek corrective treatment of deformities or malformations of these structures.

STRUCTURE AND FUNCTION

The ear is the organ of hearing and equilibrium. It has three parts: the external, middle, and inner ear. Figure 4.1 shows the sections of the ear consisting of the external auricle, or pinna, and the external ear canal. The auricle is designed to collect sound waves from the air and conduct them through the external ear canal into the middle ear.

Figure 4.1
Sections of the ear

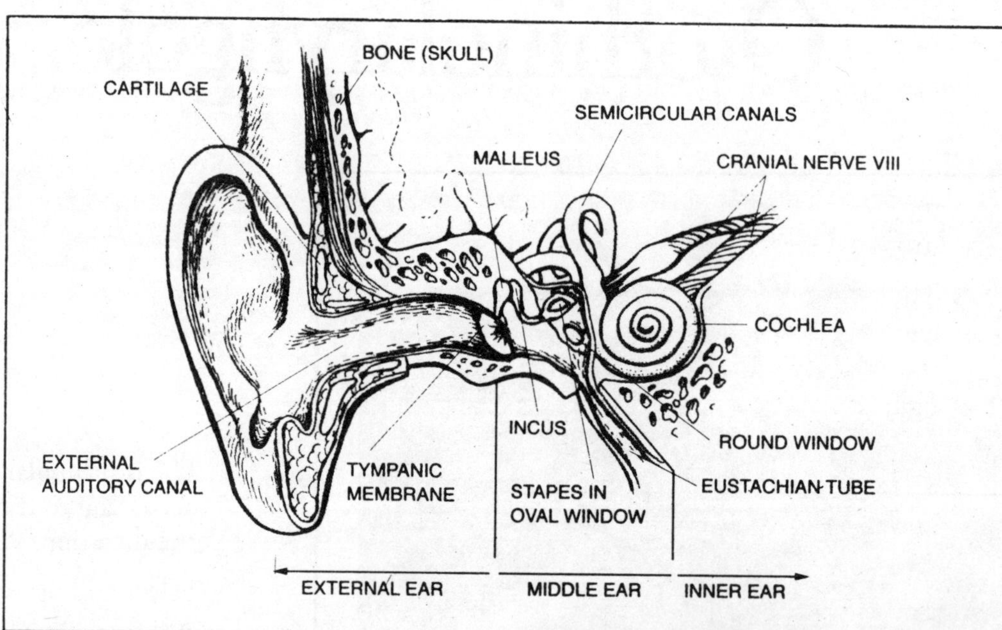

When sound waves enter the ear canal, they strike against the tympanic membrane, or eardrum, which is located at the outer end of the middle ear (also called the tympanic cavity). From the tympanic membrane the sound waves pass through bones called the ossicles. The ossicles include the malleus (hammer), the incus (anvil), and the stapes (stirrup). All of the parts of the ossicular chain (group of three ear bones) must be working properly for the sound-pressure ratio to be in balance and for hearing to be in the normal range.

The structure of the inner ear, or labyrinth, includes the cochlea, the vestibule, and the semicircular canals, as well as the auditory and vestibular receptors of the eighth cranial nerve (the vestibulocochlear nerve—see figure 11.1 in Chapter 11, "Neurology"). The inner ear receives sound waves when the stapes gently pushes on the membrane of the oval window, or fenestra ovalis, forcing fluid to move within the cochlea. This moving fluid stimulates nerve endings on the hairs of Corti within the cochlea. The auditory nerve transmits the neural stimulation to the brain, where it is interpreted as sound.

Cerumen, or ear wax, is a normal byproduct of a healthy ear. It prevents foreign particles from entering the passageway. Cerumen is produced by glands in the middle ear.

The eustachian tube connects the middle ear with the nasal passages and larynx. This tube equalizes the pressure on the two sides of the eardrum.

The nose is an important structure with multiple functions. Besides being the organ of smell, the nose is the passageway for air into the sinuses and the respiratory tract. It assists with the production of sound during speech and is the disposal system for tears. In addition, the mucous membrane within the nose catches inhaled dust and germs and moistens and warms air as it enters the body.

A cartilage called the septum divides the nose into right and left nasal cavities. The lateral wall of the septum contains three bony structures: the inferior, middle, and superior turbinates, or conchae. The nasal cavities open into the frontal, maxillary, ethmoid, and sphenoid sinuses.

Goblet cells, within a mucous membrane covering, continuously secrete mucus. This mucus is moved back into the nasopharynx by the ciliary action of hairs, called vibrissae, within the nasal cavities. The nasal passages also contain sophisticated nervous tissue which detects odors and promotes sneezing to expel irritants.

The larynx, or voice box, is a cartilaginous structure containing the pharynx and the trachea. The principal function of the larynx is vocalization. It contains the epiglottis, the glottis, and the thyroid and cricoid cartilage, as shown in figure 4.2.

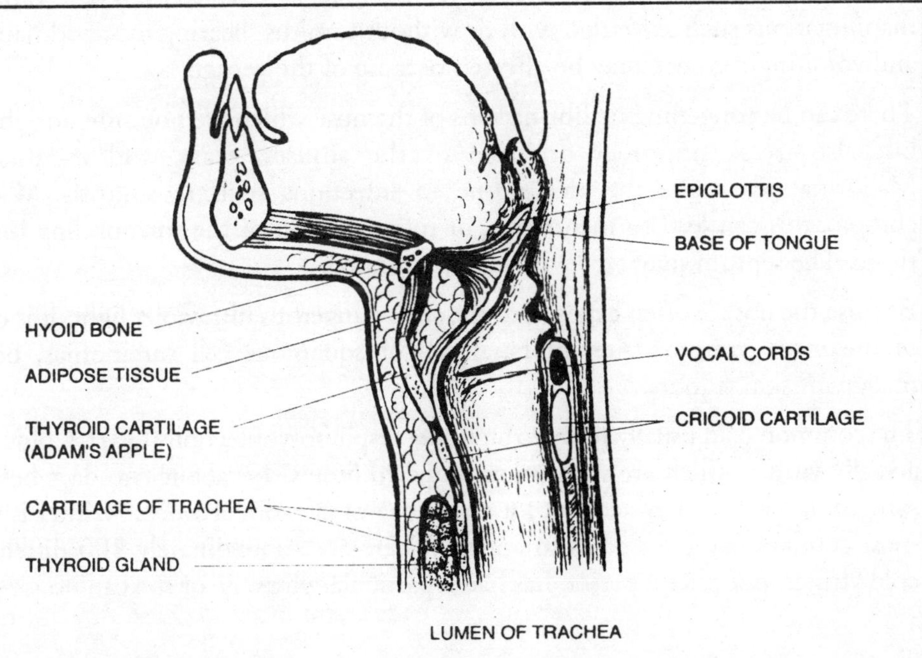

Figure 4.2
Larynx

PHYSICAL ASSESSMENT

The physician assesses the ears, nose, and throat through otoscopy, using an instrument called an otoscope. The otoscope is equipped with a bright light; it illuminates and magnifies internal areas.

During physical examination of the ear, the speculum is inserted into the external auditory meatus. The physician can see a portion of the tympanic membrane and important landmarks: the malleus, the annulus, and Wilde's triangle, which is a triangular area that under normal conditions reflects the otoscope's light. A normal tympanic membrane should be flat or concave and pearly gray in color. It should reflect a good cone of light.

The physician also observes the external areas of the ears, nose, and throat for abnormalities such as low-set ears (which may indicate genetic syndromes), malformations, or discharge.

DISEASES AND CONDITIONS

One of the most common complaints of the ear is otitis media, an inflammation of the middle ear. In children, the eustachian tube is curved in such a manner that it is easy for pathogens to migrate from the nasopharynx. The curve also makes proper drainage of fluid difficult, especially in the presence of an upper respiratory infection (URI). There is pain associated with the increase in fluid and pressure; occasionally the eardrum will rupture and then the fluid will drain.

Abnormalities of the tympanic membrane include injection, bulging, retraction, perforation, or the production of exudate. Ear diseases include otosclerosis, the hardening of the spongy bone surrounding the oval window, which results in hearing loss; cholesteatoma, a tumor in the middle ear; and presbycusis, hearing loss due to the aging process.

Labyrinthitis is an inflammation of the inner ear resulting in vertigo. Mènière's disease is a disturbance of the labyrinth that is characterized by various manifestations such as vertigo with or without tinnitus, hearing loss, and nausea and vomiting. Balance may be affected because of the vertigo.

There can be congenital malformations of the nose which are not only unsightly, but also cause improper drainage of the sinuses, tears, and/or mucus. Malformations make the area prone to infections such as sinusitis. When chronic, this can lead to meningitis, or inflammation of the surrounding brain tissue. The septum may be deviated or perforated.

Because the nose is often exposed to the sun's dangerous ultraviolet light, it is one of the most common sites of basal cell or squamous cell carcinomas, both malignant skin tumors.

The common cold usually refers to an upper respiratory infection (URI). Colds are actually viruses which are shed (transmitted to others) for about two days before symptoms appear. They account for about half of all work absences. Winter is the most common time for colds to appear. There are approximately 100 different cold viruses, but once a person has had a particular virus, he or she can no longer "catch" that cold again. The usual signs and symptoms of a URI are rhinitis, pharyngitis, and laryngitis lasting between 5 to 14 days. Coryza (acute rhinitis) is the term for acute head cold.

Sinusitis occurs as a result of a URI in persons whose nasal passages are obstructed by a deviated septum, hypertrophied turbinates, or other obstructions, preventing fluids and infectious materials from draining. The symptoms include pressure and pain over the affected sinus areas, with or without purulent nasal secretions. Allergens can cause acute sinus infections.

Although pharyngitis is caused by a viral pathogen at least 70 percent of the time, group A Streptococcus is the most common cause of bacterial pharyngitis (strep throat). Symptoms include pain, fever, swollen tonsils with exudate, and enlarged and often tender lymph nodes.

Obstruction of the pharynx can occur from severe allergic reactions, foreign bodies, or epiglottitis, usually caused by Haemophilus influenzae. Epiglottitis can create a partial or complete airway obstruction, leading to a medical emergency. Other common conditions of the upper airway include sleep apnea syndrome, tonsillitis, and chronic cryptic tonsillitis.

Common ENT Drugs

antipyrine and benzocaine (otic analgesic)

beclomethasone dipropionate
Beclovent Oral Inhaler

chloramphenicol (otic)
Chloromycetin

cocaine

fluoride

oxymetazoline

hydrochloride
4-Way Nasal Spray

COMMON TESTS AND SURGICAL PROCEDURES

A patient's hearing at various sound frequencies can be assessed through audiometry, which measures nerve conduction. Other common hearing tests include the Rinne test and the Weber test.

Airway obstructions are cleared in an emergency by means of the Heimlich maneuver, designed to force food or other obstructions from the airway; severe obstructions may require an emergency tracheotomy to create an artificial airway.

Common ENT procedures include tonsillectomies and adenoidectomies, which may be performed in patients who have had recurrent bouts of tonsillitis that have caused enlarged tonsils and adenoids, or where there is hearing loss from frequent infections.

In cancers of the larynx, an ENT specialist may perform a laryngectomy, which can involve partial or complete removal of the organs of the larynx, depending upon the extent of the cancer involved.

ENT also includes numerous constructive or reconstructive surgeries: otoplasty to correct an ear deformity, myringoplasty and tympanoplasty to reconstruct the eardrum, and myringotomy, most common in small children, to place a small tube into the eardrum in order to provide proper drainage of fluid from the middle ear.

Dacryocystorhinostomy is a surgical procedure for creating an opening into the nose for the drainage of tears. Rhinoplasty is the surgical restructuring of the nose, which can be performed for cosmetic reasons or for medical necessity—to improve breathing, for example.

THE VOCABULARY OF OTORHINOLARYNGOLOGY

The following word list contains common otorhinolaryngology words as well as most of the difficult words contained in the dictation at the end of the chapter. Take time to become familiar with these words now, and review them again before you key the medical documents.

Here are suggestions for learning the vocabulary words:

1. Read and study each word for pronunciation and meaning.
2. Write each unfamiliar word from the list below on a notecard, write the definition or a paraphrase of the definition on the back, and draw a simple picture to help you learn the word.
3. Study the pronunciation, spelling, and definition of each word on your notecard, then key each word twice for reinforcement. Check the spelling.
4. Add the correctly spelled terms to your word processor's spell checker.

adenitis
(ad-e-nI'-tis) (n) inflammation of a lymph node or gland

adenoidectomy
(ad'-e-noy-dek'-tO-mee) (n) surgical removal of the adenoids from the nasopharynx

ala nasi
(a'-la nay'-sI) (adj) the outer flare of each nostril; alae nasi (a'-lee) (pl)

allergen
(al'-er-jen) (n) a substance that produces an allergic reaction

amplitude
(am'-pli-tood) (n) the extent of a vibrating or alternating movement or wave from the average to the extreme; a louder sound has a greater amplitude

annulus
(an'-yoo-lus) (n) a circular structure or opening

arytenoid
(ar-i-tee'-noyd) (n) cartilage and muscles of the larynx

audiometry
(aw-dee-om'-e-tree) (n) test used to measure hearing (using an audiometer)

aural
(aw'-ral) (adj) relating to the ear

auricle
(aw'-ri-kl) (n) external ear; pinna

buccal
(buk'-al) (adj) relating to the area inside the cheek

cavernous sinus thrombosis
(kav'-er-nus sI'-nus throm-bO'-sis) (n) a group of symptoms caused by an obstruction in the cavernous intracranial sinus

cerumen
(se-roo'-men) (n) earwax

cholesteatoma
(kO-les-tee-a-tO'-ma) (n) a tumor-like mass of scaly epithelium and cholesterol in the middle ear

ciliary action
(sil'-ee-ar-ee) (n) the lashing movement of a group of cilia, which can produce a current of movement in a fluid

cochlea
(kok'-lee-a) (n) a spiral-shaped cavity in the internal ear

concha
(kon'-ka) (n) a shell-shaped anatomical structure, such as the auricle of the ear; conchae (pl)

conductive deafness
(n) hearing impairment due to obstruction of sound waves; the sound waves are not passed on to the inner ear

coryza
(ko-rI'-za) (n) acute rhinitis; acute head cold; inflammation of the mucous membrane of the nose with sneezing, tearing, and watery nasal discharge

cricoid cartilage
(krI'-koyd) (n) a ring-shaped cartilage in the lower part of the larynx

culture
(kul'-chur) (n) propagation of microorganisms in a solid or liquid medium

dacryocystorhinostomy
(dak'-ree-O-sis'-tO-rI-nos'-tO-mee) (n) a surgical opening to provide drainage between the tear duct and the nasal mucosa

debride
(da-breed'/dee-brId') (v) to remove unhealthy tissue and foreign material to prevent infection and permit healing

distress
(n) trouble; mental or physical suffering

dysphagia
(dis-fay'-jee-a) (n) difficulty swallowing

en bloc
(ahn blok) (adj) as a whole, in one piece

epiglottis
(ep'-I-glot'-is) (n) flap of elastic cartilage at the back of the mouth that covers the opening to the windpipe during swallowing, thereby preventing choking.

epiglottitis
(ep-i-glot-tI'-tis) (n) inflammation of the epiglottis, causing potentially fatal airway obstruction, especially in small children

epistaxis
(ep'-i-stak'-sis) (n) nosebleed

ethmoidal
(eth-moy'-dal) (adj) relating to the ethmoid bone or ethmoid sinus

eustachian tube
(yoo-stay'-shun/yoo-stay'-kee-an) (n) a tube leading from the middle ear to the nasopharynx; thus air pressure is equalized on both sides of the tympanic membrane

excision
(ek-si'-zhun) (n) cutting out; surgical removal of all or part of a lesion, structure, or organ

exudate
(eks'-oo-dayt) (n) any fluid that has oozed out of a tissue, usually due to inflammation or injury

exudative
(eks'-oo-dayt-iv) (adj) relating to exudate

fenestra ovalis
(fe-nes'-tra O-val'-is) (n) an oval opening between the middle ear and the vestibule; closed by the base of the stapes

fixation
(fik-say'-shun) (n) process of securing a part, as by suturing

foramen
(fO-ray'-men) (n) hole or opening, especially in a bone or membrane

gingival
(jin'-ji-val) (adj) relating to the gums

glossopharyngeal neuralgia
(glos'-O-fa-rin'-jee-al noo-ral'-jee-a) (n) a condition of sharp spasmic pain in the throat or palate

helix
(hee'-liks) (n) the folded edge of the external ear

incus
(ing'-kus) (n) the anvil-shaped bone in the middle ear

jugular
(jug'-yoo-lar) (adj) relating to the throat or neck

labial
(lay'-bee-al) (adj) relating to the lips

labyrinth
(lab'-i-rinth) (n) an anatomical structure made up of a complex of cavities, such as the inner ear

labyrinthitis
(lab'-i-rin-thI'-tis) (n) inflammation of the inner ear (labyrinth) or ethmoidal labyrinth (nose)

lacrimation
(lak'-ri-may'-shun) (n) secretion of tears

laryngectomy
(lar'-in-jek'-tO-mee) (n) surgical removal of the larynx

laryngostomy
(lar'-ing-gos'-tO-mee) (n) surgically creating an opening into the larynx

larynx
(lar'-ingks) (n) the voice box, located between the pharynx and the trachea

lucency
(loo'-sen-see) (n) giving off light; being luminous or translucent

lymph
(limf) (n) fluid that bathes the tissues of the body and circulates through lymphatic vessels

malleus
(mal'-ee-us) (n) the largest of the three inner ear bones; club-shaped; attached to the tympanic membrane

mandibular
(man-dib'-yoo-lar) (adj) relating to the lower jaw

mastoiditis
(mas-toy-dI'-tis) (n) inflammation of the mastoid process (part of the temporal bone behind the ear)

maxilla
(mak-sil'-a) (n) the upper jaw

maxillary sinus
(mak'-si-layr-ee sI'-nus) (n) an air cavity in the body of the upper jaw bone; connects with the middle passage (meatus) of the nose

meatus
(mee-ay'-tus) (n) a passage or channel, especially with an external opening

Meniere's disease
(mayn-yairz') (n) a disease of the inner ear with attacks of dizziness, nausea, ringing in the ear, and increasing deafness

meninges
(me-nin'-jeez) (n) membranes covering the brain and spinal cord

meningitis
(men-in-jI'-tis) (n) inflammation of the meninges

mucoperiosteum
(myoo'-kO-per-ee-os'-tee-um) (n) the mucous membrane covering the hard palate at the front of the roof of the mouth

mucosa
(myoo-kO'-sa) (n) mucous membrane

myringitis
(mir-in-jI'-tis) (n) inflammation of the tympanic membrane; tympanitis

myringoplasty
(mi-ring'-gO-plas'-tee) (n) surgical repair of the eardrum

myringotomy
(mir-ing-got'-o-mee) (n) surgical incision into the tympanic membrane

naris
(nay'-ris) (n) nostril; nares (nay'-rees) (pl)

neoadjuvant
(nee-O-ad'-joo-vant) (adj) used in conjunction with other types of therapy

neuroblastoma
(noor'-O-blas-tO'-ma) (n) malignant (cancerous) tumor containing embryonic nerve cells

node
(nOd) (n) a small knot of tissue, distinct from surrounding tissue; a lymph node

orbital cellulitis
(or'-bit-al sel-yoo-lI'-tis) (n) inflammation of tissue around or behind the eye

organism
(or'-ga-nizm) (n) a living plant, animal, or microorganism

orifice
(or'-i-fis) (n) an opening

ossicles
(os-i-kls) (n) small bones, such as the auditory ossicles (the three bones of the inner ear)

ostectomy
(os-tek'-tO-mee) (n) surgical removal of all or part of a bone

otalgia
(Otal'-jeea) (n) earache

otitis externa
(O-tI'-tis eks-ter'-na) (n) inflammation of the external ear

otitis media
(O-tI'-tis mee'-dee-a) (n) inflammation of the middle ear

otorhinolaryngology
(O'-tO-rI'-nO-lar-in-gol'-o-jee) (n) study of the ears, nose, and throat

otosclerosis
(O'-tO-sklee-rO'-sis) (n) a growth of sponge-like bone in the inner ear, eventually leading to deafness

otoscope
(O'-tO-skOp) (n) an instrument for examining the eardrum

palpable
(pal'-pa-bl) (adj) able to be identified by touch

palate
(pal'-at) (n) the roof of one's mouth, composed of the hard palate (front) and the soft palate (back)

pathogen
(path'-O-jen) (n) any microorganism or substance that can cause a disease

periauricular
(per'-ee-aw-rik'-yoo-lar) (adj) around the ear

pharyngitis
(far-in-jI-tis) (n) inflammation of the pharynx

pharynx
(far'-ingks) (n) throat; passageway for air from nasal cavity to larynx, and food from mouth to esophagus

pinna
(pin'-a) (n) the external ear; auricle; pinnae (pin'-ee) (pl)

polyp
(pol'-ip) (n) an outgrowth of tissue from a mucous membrane

presbycusis
(prez'-bee-koo'-sis) (n) the loss of hearing acuity due to aging

pterygoid plate
(ter'-i-goyd) (n) wing-shaped bones at the back of the nasal cavity

purulent
(pyoor'-u-lent) (adj) relating to, containing, or forming pus

rhinitis
(rI-nI'-tis) (n) inflammation of the mucous membrane of the nose

rhinoplasty
(rI'-nO-plas-tee) (n) surgery to correct a defect in the nose or to change its shape

Rinne test
(rin'-ne) (n) also Rinne's (rin'-ez); a hearing test comparing perception of air and bone conduction in one ear with a tuning fork; normally air conduction is more acute

semicircular canals
(sem'-ee-sir'-kyoo-lar ka-nals') (n) three fluid-filled loops in the labyrinth of the inner ear, associated with the body's sense of balance

sensorineural deafness
(sen'-sOr-i-noor'-al) (n) hearing impairment due to nerve disturbance

septum
(sep'-tum) (n) division between two cavities or two masses of tissue, such as the nasal septum; septa (pl)

serous
(seer'-us) (adj) relating to or having a watery consistency

serous otitis media
(seer'-us O-tI'-tis mee'-dee-a) (n) inflammation of the middle ear accompanied by production of a watery fluid (serum)

shotty
(shot'-ee) (adj) having a rubbery type of feel to the touch; as shotty nodes

sinus
(sI'-nus) (n) a passageway or hollow in a bone or other tissue

sinusitis
(sI-nu-sI'-tis) (n) inflammation of the nasal sinuses, occurring as a result of an upper respiratory infection, an allergic response, or a defect of the nose

sleep apnea syndrome
(ap'-nee-a) (n) breathing stops, briefly and periodically, due to partial upper airway obstruction during sleep

speculum
(spek'-yoo-lum) (n) an instrument used for examining the interior of a cavity

sphenoidal sinus
(sfee-noy'-dal) (n) one of two sinuses in the sphenoid bone opening to the nasal cavity

stapes
(stay'-peez) (n) the smallest and innermost of the three auditory bones in the inner ear; stirrup

strep
(n) short form of Streptococcus, a genus of bacteria; many species cause disease in humans

submandibular
(sub-man-dib'-yoo-lar) (adj) under the lower jaw

symphysis
(sim'-fi-sis) (n) joint in which fibrocartilage firmly unites the bones

thyroid
(thI'-royd) (n) a gland in the neck that secretes thyroid hormone

tinnitus
(ti-nI'-tus) (n) noise, such as ringing, in the ears

trachea
(tray'-kee-a) (n) the windpipe

tracheostomy
(tray'-kee-os'-tO-mee) (n) a surgical opening into the trachea

tracheotomy
(tray'-kee-ot'-O-mee) (n) the surgical procedure in which a tracheostomy is created

tragus
(tray'-gus) (n) the small projection of cartilage in front of the external opening to the ear canal

turbinate
(ter'-bi-nayt) (n) one of several thin, spongy, bony plates within the walls of the nasal cavity

tympanic membrane
(tim-pan'-ik) (n) eardrum

tympanoplasty
(tim'-pa-nO-plas-tee) (n) surgical repair of the middle ear

umbo
(um'-bO) (n) the inner surface of the tympanic membrane where it connects with the malleus in the middle ear

unremarkable
(adj) nothing unusual is noted

upper respiratory infection (URI)
(n) an infection of the upper respiratory tract such as the common cold, laryngitis, sinusitis, and tonsillitis

uvula
(yoo'-vyoo-la) (n) small, fleshy mass hanging from the soft palate in the mouth

uvulitis
(yoo-vyoo-lI'-tis) (n) inflammation of the uvula

uvulopalatopharyngoplasty
(yoo'-vyoo-lO-pal'-a-tO-fa-rin'-gO-plas-tee) (n) UPPP for short; a surgical treatment for sleep apnea for patients who cannot tolerate or respond to medical therapies

vertigo
(ver'-tigO) (n) dizziness

vestibulum
(ves-tib'-yoo-lum) (n) the central cavity of the labyrinth in the inner ear, between the cochlea and the semicircular canals

vibrissae
(vI-bris'-a) (n) nose hairs

Weber test
(web'-er) (n) a hearing test performed with a tuning fork placed at points in the middle of the skull to determine where the vibration is heard (not where it is felt)

xerostomia
(zeer-O-stO'-mee-a) (n) dryness of the mouth

ABBREVIATIONS

AC	air conduction
AD	right ear (auris dextra)
AOM	acute otitis media
AS	left ear (auris sinistra)
C&S	culture and sensitivity
db	decibel
EAC	external ear canal
EENT	eyes, ears, nose, throat
ENT	ear, nose, throat
PE tubes	pressure-equalizing tubes
SAR	seasonal allergic rhinitis
T&A	tonsillectomy and adenoidectomy
TM	tympanic membrane
TMJ	temporomandibular joint
UPPP	uvulopalatopharyngoplasty
URI	upper respiratory infection

EXERCISE 4.1: RECOGNIZING LOOK-ALIKES AND SOUND-ALIKES

Below is a list of frequently used words that look alike and/or sound alike. Study the meaning and pronunciation of each set of words, then read each sentence carefully and circle the word in parentheses that correctly completes the meaning.

assistance	aiding, helping
assistants	individuals who give aid and support

aural	pertaining to the ear
oral	pertaining to the mouth

auricle	external ear
oracle	a wise person; a god-like person

dysphagia	difficulty swallowing
dysphasia	difficulty using language due to injury or disease

dysphonia	difficulty in speaking
dysphoria	depression

malleus	a structure in the inner ear
malleolus	a rounded bone on either side of the ankle

osteal	bony or bonelike
ostial	relating to an ostium (a small opening, e.g., eustachian tube)

passed	past tense of verb pass; to move, to accomplish
past	time that has gone by

serious	not joking
serous	resembling serum

shoddy	inferior or imitation goods
shotty	a rubbery type of feel to the touch

subtle	hard to detect
supple	limber

tendinitis or tendonitis	inflammation of a tendon
tinnitus	ringing in the ears

1. (Aural, Oral) examination revealed cerumen in the canal.
2. Examination of the mouth reveals no (aural, oral) lesions.
3. The patient complains of tenderness around the (auricle, oracle).
4. Examination of the neck revealed a few (shotty, shoddy) nodes.
5. I feel great. I (past, passed) my exam!
6. The patient thinks his (tinnitus, tendinitis) and headache symptoms may be associated with his high blood pressure.
7. Examination of the face revealed only (supple, subtle) changes in the pigmentation of the skin.
8. NECK: (Supple, Subtle) without masses.
9. We will be adding three new medical (assistance, assistants) to the staff this month.
10. Could you please give me some (assistance, assistants) in lifting this patient?
11. While the patient was making a (serious, serous) effort to get out of bed, we noticed the (serious, serous) drainage from his ear.
12. The eustachian tube is blocked, the eardrum is retracted, and the (malleolus, malleus) looks shorter and more horizontal.
13. The injury resulted from a rolling bowling ball, which caused a fractured (malleus, malleolus).
14. A sore throat with (dysphagia, dysphasia) made the child uncomfortable with any solid foods.
15. The patient's (osteal, ostial) opening was about 1.2 centimeters.

EXERCISE 4.2: MATCHING SOUND AND SPELLING

The numbered list that follows shows the phonetic spelling of hard-to-spell words. Sound out the word, then write the correct spelling in the blank space provided. Each of the words can be found in the glossary or in the drug list in appendix C.

1. nee-O-ad'-joo-vant ____________________
2. pyoor'-u-lent ____________________
3. yoo-stay'-shun ____________________
4. aw'-ri-kl ____________________
5. fO-ray'-men ____________________
6. per'-ee-aw-rik'-yoo-lar ____________________
7. nay'-ris ____________________
8. ver'-ti-gO ____________________
9. tim-pan'-ik mem'-brayn ____________________
10. sim'-fi-sis ____________________

11. O-tal'-jee-a ______________________________

12. mal'-ee-us ______________________________

13. ti-nI'-tus ______________________________

14. loo'-sen-see ______________________________

15. ep'-i-stak'-sis ______________________________

EXERCISE 4.3: CHOOSING WORDS FROM CONTEXT

When transcribing dictation, the medical transcriptionist frequently needs to determine the word that correctly completes the sentence based on the situation. From the list of words below, select the term that meaningfully completes each statement.

buccal	jugular	otitis
culture	laryngostomy	palpable
ervythematous	mandibular	purulent
excision	mastoiditis	shotty
exudate	node	

1. On examination of the external ear, a periauricular lymph _________ was noted.
2. DIAGNOSIS: Upper respiratory infection, with acute bilateral __________ media.
3. The central line was changed from her right subclavian to her right internal __________.
4. Her throat is slightly red; however, no drainage or ___________ is noted.
5. The patient's throat _________ came back positive for strep.
6. On examination, there was a (an) ___________ mass in the abdomen.
7. The tympanic membrane on the right is ____________ and bulging.
8. The en bloc ____________ to remove the tumor left a large scar.
9. I instructed the patient to call us promptly if she develops any __________ drainage from the wound site.
10. Mr. Johnson had large open sores on his gingiva and ________ cavity on the right side of his mouth.

EXERCISE 4.4: PAIRING WORDS AND MEANINGS

For each definition provided below, locate the term on the list that best matches the definition. Write the letter of the term in the space provided beside the definition.

A. gingival	F. neuroblastoma	J. tracheostomy
B. labial	G. otitis	K. aural
C. mandibular	H. pathogen	L. cerumen
D. mastoiditis	I. periauricular	M. buccal
E. myringotomy		

1. around the ear ____________
2. inflammation of the ear ____________
3. opening created surgically in the trachea ____________
4. relating to the gums ____________
5. relating to the lower jaw ____________
6. substance capable of producing a disease ____________
7. pertaining to the lips ____________
8. infection of the mastoid bones ____________
9. surgical incision into tympanic membrane ____________
10. malignant tumor of nerve cells ____________

EXERCISE 4.5: CREATING TERMS FROM WORD FORMS

In the following exercise, combine prefixes, root words, and suffixes to create medical words that fit the definitions below. Fill in the blanks with the words you construct.

a-	without, absence	-auricular	pertaining to the ear
dys-	difficult	-blastoma	malignant cell/tumor
ex-	out	-cision	to cut
laryng/o-	larynx	-ectomy	removal of body structure
neur/o-	nerve	-gen	to produce
or/o-	mouth	-itis	inflammation or infection
oste/o-	bone	-mandibular	lower jaw
oto-	ear	-pharyng/o	throat
peri-	around	-phonia	voice; sound
rhin-	nose	-stomy	artificial or surgical opening
sub-	beneath, under		

1. loss of voice ______________________
2. difficulty in speaking ______________________
3. to cut out ______________________
4. surgical opening into the larynx ______________________
5. malignant tumor containing nerve cells ______________________
6. surgical excision of a bone ______________________
7. inflammation of the ear ______________________
8. middle of the throat, between roof of mouth and upper edge of epiglottis ______________________
9. surrounding the ear ______________________
10. inflammation of the nasal mucosa ______________________

EDITING MEDICAL DOCUMENTS

In this section you will perfect your word use and grammar skills. These skills will help you edit and proofread medical reports for correct language, punctuation, format, and meaning. The special focus for this chapter is pronoun-antecedent agreement.

CREATING AGREEMENT BETWEEN PRONOUNS AND ANTECEDENTS

Remember that a pronoun takes the place of a noun in a sentence. Words such as *she, he, it, they, us, them, I,* and *you* are pronouns.

Pronouns must agree in person and number with the nouns they represent, which are called antecedents.

The *patient* reports that *his* headaches have been increasing.

The physician dictated the *report* and sent *it* to the transcriptionist.

Transcriptionists know *they* must keep *their* skills sharp.

Holly keeps *her* problems to *herself.*

The pronouns *this, that, these,* and *those* must also agree with the nouns they modify:

this procedure	these procedures
that medication	those medications

The pronouns *them* and *their* are plural forms. Do not use these pronouns for singular meanings. When gender is not known, try to create a sentence that does not require the awkward construction of his/her.

WRONG:	The patient should be asked to empty their bladder prior to the test.
CORRECT:	The patient should be asked to void prior to the test.
WRONG:	If the child completes the assignment, praise them for their efforts.
CORRECT:	Praise children for their efforts in completing their assignments.

A pronoun can represent a subject or an object. That is, the pronoun can be either the performer of an action or the recipient of the action. Subject pronouns are *I, you, he, she, it, we, they.* Object pronouns are *me, you, him, her, it, us, them.*

Most people do not have difficulty achieving pronoun agreement in simple sentences that contain one pronoun in the predicate, e.g., Bill dislikes *me.* However, problems do come about when a sentence contains multiple nouns and pronouns, e.g., Bill dislikes *he/him* and *I/me.* To select the correct pronoun, simplify the sentence by looking only at the verb and the pronoun in question. Your ear should help you make the right choice.

dislikes *he* or *him?*	correct choice: dislikes *him*
dislikes *I* or *me?*	correct choice: dislikes *me*

Bill dislikes *him* and *me.*

Who versus Whom

Use the pronoun *who* for the subject of a verb; use *whom* for the object of a verb.

> *Who* has the first appointment?
> S V
>
> *Whom* did you assign to the emergency room?
> O V S V

In sentences or questions that contain a who/whom dilemma, substitute *he* for *who* and *him* for *whom* and then trust your ear.

> *Who* will deliver these reports? [*He* will deliver these reports].
>
> James will deliver these reports to *whom?* [James will deliver these reports to *him.*]

Myself, Himself, and Other Reflexive Pronouns

Myself, yourselves, herself, etc., are reflexive pronouns, meaning that they must reflect back to a noun or pronoun within that same sentence (*Mikey* wrapped the gift all by *himself.*) Many dictators mistakenly refer to themselves as *myself* instead of me (He was seen by *myself* in the clinic). Do not use a reflexive in a sentence when a simple personal pronoun is appropriate.

> WRONG: The surgery was conducted by Dr. Jones, Dr. Roberts, and *myself.*
>
> CORRECT: The surgery was conducted by Dr. Jones, Dr. Roberts, and *me.*
>
> WRONG: The physician who had a middle ear infection treated *her.*
>
> CORRECT: The physician who had a middle ear infection treated *herself.*

EXERCISE 4.6: EDITING FOR AGREEMENT OF PRONOUNS AND ANTECEDENTS

Read each sentence and circle the pronoun in parentheses that correctly completes the meaning.

1. The patient and (I/me) have discussed the options for treatment.
2. (Whom/who) is my first patient today?
3. I will ask the nurse to arrange for my partner or (I/me) to see the child tomorrow.
4. A patient (who/whom) has a cholesteatoma may present with unilateral hearing loss.
5. The receptionist should always ask a new patient if (he or she/they) brought (his or her/their) records.
6. Do not assume that patients know how (his or her/their) medications are to be taken.
7. Both tympanic membranes were noted to be bulging, and (its/their) color was bright red.
8. This patient, (who/whom) I consider to be reliable, says that he was treated poorly by your department.
9. Please call if Dr. Adams or (I/me) can be of help.
10. A patient with chronic tonsillitis often has to have (their/his or her) throat cultured.

EXERCISE 4.7: PROOFREADING REVIEW

Read the following report and look for errors in format, usage, and spelling. Circle the errors, then key the report with the errors corrected.

CHIEF COMPLAINT: The patient Had been well until about four wks ago when he develloped a runy nose, sore throat, and pain in both ears. He was seen by his peditritian, who gave him an antibiotic for seven days. Two week later the ear pain has not resolved.

PAST MEDICAL HX: Noncontributory.

PHYSICAL EXAMINATION: L TM is injected with whitish exadate. Palpable shoddy L submandibalar lymph nodes and a 2 cm firm periaurcular lymph node. Physical exam is otherwise within normal limits.

WHERE CAN I FIND THE ANSWER?

As you transcribe dictation, you may hear unfamiliar words or terms. A variety of reference sources are available to help you locate answers to your questions. One of the important types of references for medical transcriptionists is described below. Read the information; then if you have access to the reference discussed, explore its capabilities.

MEDICAL REFERENCES: ABBREVIATIONS BOOKS

Healthcare workers use a great many abbreviations and acronyms. Chapters 2-13 of this text feature brief lists of abbreviations common to the specialty featured in each chapter. These lists should be considered a starting point for the numerous abbreviations you will encounter on the job.

Several good abbreviations references are available. When choosing between two (or more), assess the books based on the following factors:

1. Number of entries. Obviously, the more entries a book has, the more likely it is that you will find the abbreviation you are looking for.
2. Copyright date. Which book is most up-to-date? There may not be many differences between a book published in 1994 and one published in 1995, but there may be significant differences between a book published in 1987 and one published in 1997.
3. Price. An expensive book is not necessarily better than a more moderately priced one. You may be paying for a fancy binding rather than better content. Base your decision on the true merits of the book, not just the price tag.

TRANSCRIBING ENT DOCUMENTS

In this section your goal is to prepare for the work of transcription by transcribing first from a printed document and then from dictation on tape. The model document that follows illustrates the generally accepted format for the **operative report,** the report format featured in this chapter.

BASIC FORMAT: THE OPERATIVE REPORT

The operative report is a narrative description of an operation or other invasive procedure. The surgeon or an assistant to the surgeon dictates the report. This type of document is often quite long and detailed. It is likely to be the most technically demanding report a medical transcriptionist will encounter.

Required Headings/Content

Operative reports are variously structured but usually include the preoperative and postoperative diagnoses, the surgeon's name, the title and date of the procedure, the indications for surgery, the anesthesia, the surgical findings, the specimen removed, and the actual description of the surgery, called the procedure. The report usually contains a sponge count and an estimate of blood loss. It typically ends with the patient being taken to the recovery room.

Other headings in the operative report may include the assistant surgeon's name, the name of the anesthesiologist, type of incision, drains used, complications. The operative report may also include information on when an informed consent document was presented by the surgeon and signed by the patient.

Many hospitals break down the operative description into three sections: (1) positioning, prepping and draping, and opening the incision; (2) the internal operation; and (3) the closing.

Turnaround Time

An operative report is dictated or written in the medical record immediately after surgery and ideally transcribed within six hours. This guideline applies to all surgical procedures done in hospitals, outpatient surgical centers, and clinics.

OPERATIVE REPORT

1" top and side margins

Aligning information at tab settings is another acceptable format

NAME: Jane Henry
MEDICAL RECORD #: 7054922
DATE OF SURGERY: 8/18/XX
SURGEON: Jack Einhorn, MD
ASSISTANT: Neil Fischer, MD

ds

No colon since entry for this heading begins on next line

PREOPERATIVE DIAGNOSIS
Mandibular symphysis osteotomy. Open wound at floor of mouth and buccal mucosa.

ds

POSTOPERATIVE DIAGNOSIS
Mandibular symphysis osteotomy. Open wound at floor of mouth and buccal mucosa.

ds

left justification

PROCEDURE
Repair with internal fixation and repair of soft tissue defect.

ds

ANESTHESIA
General.

ds

OPERATIVE INDICATIONS
This is a youngster with a history of neuroblastoma whom I had first seen six months earlier. At that time, the lesion presented as a neck mass, which was biopsied. Subsequent studies showed extensive involvement of the right neck and right cranial base, namely extension into the jugular foramen. The patient received neoadjuvant chemotherapy and is slated for radical en bloc excision today.

ds

OPERATIVE PROCEDURE
Through the mandibular-splitting approach, a radical neck dissection with en bloc resection of the tumor from the cranial base around the jugular foramen was carried out without complication after tracheostomy had been performed. The right floor of the mouth incision, extending from the posterior middle third of the tongue up to the anterior floor of the mouth, was closed with interrupted sutures of Vicryl, with care being taken to maintain a watertight closure.

(continued) **Include this notation on multiple-page reports**

OPERATIVE REPORT
NAME: Jane Henry **Include a header on second and succeeding pages**
MEDICAL RECORD #: 7054922
Page 2
ds

The mandibular symphysis osteotomy was carried out through the socket of the extracted right mandibular central incisor halfway down the vertical height of the symphysis and then stair-stepped to the left and then down across the mandibular border. Care was taken to preserve both mental nerves bilaterally. The horizontal portion of the osteotomy had necessarily coursed through two tooth buds of the permanent dentition, and these were subsequently debrided. An anatomic approximation of the symphysis was carried out and held in place while a 2.0 compression plate made of titanium was applied to the lower rim of the symphysis. Good solid bony union was achieved. The mucosa, both labial and gingival, of the lower lip were then reapproximated with five interrupted sutures of Vicryl. The gingiva was then brought up to the tooth crowns and secured into the mucosa in the anterior floor of the mouth with sutures. These sutures encircled the teeth and created a nice watertight seal, with no exposure of the underlying mandible. The lip was then prepared, and the remainder of the neck closure was carried out by Dr. Fischer.

ds

ESTIMATED BLOOD LOSS
Negligible.
ds

COMPLICATIONS
None.
ds

SPECIMENS
None.

qs

____

Jack C. Einhorn, MD
ds

JCE/XX
D: 8/18/XX
T: 8/18/XX

PREPARING TO TRANSCRIBE

To prepare for transcribing dictation, key the operative report above. You will later key the identical report from dictation. Follow these guidelines:

- Study the format and organization of the report
- Review the word list presented earlier in this chapter.
- Consult reference books for words or formatting rules that are unfamiliar.
- Proofread your final copy by comparing it to the printed version.

CASES FOR TRANSCRIPTION

In this section you will transcribe medical dictation from tape. Your goal is to produce error-free documents. Read this chapter's Pro Tip (following the case studies) for helpful hints from experienced MTs. Then follow these steps for each dictation:

1. Prepare to transcribe by reviewing the case study and the appropriate report format.
2. Transcribe the dictation, leaving spaces for words you cannot hear or do not understand.
3. Carefully proofread the document and correct as many errors as you can. Use your reference materials to help you identify missing words.
4. Listen to the tape again and correct all remaining errors.

Repeat these steps until you produce an error-free document. Then complete the Performance Report at the end of the chapter, attach it to the top of the transcripts, and submit them to your instructor for evaluation.

CASE STUDY 1: MARK RANKIN

Pediatrician Marcus Green, MD, treats 5-year-old Mark Rankin for ear pain. When the antibiotic regimen is unsuccessful, Dr. Green refers Mark to Dr. Joseph Strong, otorhinolaryngologist, for consultation.

Report 4.1: Office Note

Transcription Hints

- CBC stands for complete blood count, a common laboratory test that measures levels of red blood cells, white blood cells, and platelets. The abbreviation for white blood cells, WBC, is frequently dictated letter-by-letter. The measurement unit, cubic millimeters, should be transcribed as mm with a superscript 3.
- Use the abbreviations HGB for hemoglobin results and HCT for hematocrit.
- The shortened forms *polys, lymphs,* and *monos* can be transcribed as dictated.

Report 4.2: Office Note

Transcription Hint

Listen for these difficult words:
exudate (noun) and exudative (adjective)
submandibular
periauricular
mastoiditis
myringotomy

CASE STUDY 2: YARVELLA HARVES

Yarvella Harves is an 11-week-old girl who had been well until a few days ago. She had a neck mass that did not appear to be painful, but it had been growing steadily for several days. The baby was referred to the specialist from the pediatrician's office.

Report 4.3: Consultation Letter

Transcription Hints

- BUMC stands for Brookfield University Medical Center
- Nafcillin is a brand-name drug

CASE STUDY 3: JANE HENRY

Jane Henry is a 2-year-old girl who was diagnosed with a neuroblastoma arising from the floor of the mouth and extending to the neck and lower base of the skull. She has been treated with chemotherapy and is now undergoing surgery to remove any residual tumor. Dr. Einhorn is an otorhinolaryngologist who is performing the surgery with the assistance of a plastic surgeon, Dr. Fischer.

Report 4.4: Operative Report

CASE STUDY 4: JULIA WANG

Fifty-three-year-old Julia Wang is seeing the physician regarding a snoring problem that disrupts her sleep, leaving her feeling chronically tired. She also thinks she may have allergies or a sinus infection because of an annoying drainage into her throat.

Report 4.5: Office Note

Transcription Hints

- Vancenase Nasal Spray and Seldane-D are brand-name drugs.
- Listen for these terms:
  apnea
  somnolence

CASE STUDY 5: CYNTHIA MANCINI

Cynthia Mancini is a 35-year-old woman who was in an automobile accident five years ago. At that time she had a fracture of the septum, causing a deviation. She presents to the surgeon for correction of the nasal obstruction.

Report 4.6: Operative Report

Transcription Hints

- Every operative report must contain a preoperative and postoperative diagnosis, the name of the procedure, the name of the surgeon, and a description of the procedure.
- In many operative reports, the preoperative and postoperative diagnoses are the same. Most hospitals require that the diagnosis be repeated, even if the dictator says "same." Do this efficiently by blocking and copying the item.
- Suture size is dictated as "four O" and should be transcribed as 4-0.

CASE STUDY 6: ROSA VALDEZ

Rosa Valdez is seeking relief for recurring headaches and dizziness, for which she has been treated in the past. This 30-year-old ad agency account manager leads a hectic work life and wants to resolve her medical problem before it worsens and requires her to miss work for an extended period.

Report 4.7: Office Note

Transcription Hints

- The abbreviation PO stands for *postoperative.* In other instances, this abbreviation can stand for *by mouth.*
- Listen for these drug names:
  Bactrim-DS
  Beconase
  Antivert

CASE STUDY 7: SARA VAGTS

Sara Vagts is a 44-year-old woman who has been seen by her primary physician for recurrent sinusitis. A consultation with the ENT specialist results in a recommendation for an ethmoidectomy and a different antibiotic.

Report 4.8: Office Note (Phone Call Note)

Transcription Hints

- Aspergillus is the genus name of a fungi. Aspergillosis is an infection caused by that fungus.
- Listen for these drug names:
  vancomycin
  amphotericin
  Tussionex

PRO TIP: 16 WAYS TO SEARCH FOR UNKNOWN WORDS

Compiled by on-line MTs for MT Daily (www.angelfire.com/mt.2)

1. Listen to the word several times; then listen to the whole sentence.
2. Back the tape up and listen just for the first sound. Consider the possibility that the first letter of the word is silent (like *p* as in *ptosis*).
3. With the first sound of the word in mind, check a dictionary in the specialty.
4. Consider all the possible vowels and vowel combinations.
5. In the context, determine if the word is a medical term, a common term, or a proper name.
6. Look up the word by category, e.g., by disease, syndrome, phenomenon, sign, muscle, bone, nerve, and so forth.
7. Mark the blank and finish the document to see if the word is repeated.
8. Your spell-checker may have a "Look Up" feature that will list similar words from which you can choose.
9. Scan the supplemental dictionary list.
10. Look at other reports of the same kind from that dictator. Use the Find command in Windows applications or the Search command in WordPerfect 5.1.
11. Ask a friend to listen or mark this spot for a proofreader.
12. Take a break and get away from the computer. Come back to listen to the word again.
13. Check the Medline Web Site: http://www2.ncbi.nlm.nih.gov/medline/query_form.html.
14. Post a query to an MT Forum hotline.
15. When you find the word, write it in a dictionary by phonetic first sound so it will be easier to find next time.
16. If you cannot find the word, do not enter a guess. Leave a blank.

ASSESSING TRANSCRIPTION SKILLS

Demonstrate your mastery of the terminology, editing/proofreading, and document transcription skills presented in this chapter by completing the following activities.

USING MEDICAL REFERENCES

Use the appropriate medical reference to locate the correct spelling and additional usage information for the words below. (If the reference is not available, use the glossary in this text.) Circle the correct spelling, then write a sentence using the word correctly.

1.	cerumen	serumen	cerumun
2.	tinitus	tinnitus	tinnitis
3.	aretinoid	aretynoid	arytenoid
4.	labrinthitis	labyrinthitis	labirynthitis
5.	pharyngitis	pharingitis	pharingytis
6.	turbunate	turbinate	terbinate
7.	disphagia	dysphagea	dysphagia
8.	malleus	maleus	malleas

9. buccal buckal bucchal

____

10. epitaxsis epistacsis epistaxis

____

MAKING EXPERT DECISIONS

Circle the correct word from the choices in parentheses.

1. There was a large lesion in the (oral/aural) cavity on the buccal mucosa.
2. There were several (shoddy/shotty) nodes located in the neck.
3. Redness of the external ear canal was noted; (otits media/otitis externa) was diagnosed.
4. There was fluid in the middle ear and recurrent otitis media, so a (tympanoplasty/myringotomy) was performed with insertion of polyethylene tubes.
5. The (osteal/ostial) opening of the eustachian tube was blocked.
6. This (past/passed) year, the patient had PE tubes placed because of chronic infections.
7. It was felt that the patient had (vertigo/tinnitus) when she said she had a sensation of spinning, even when standing still.
8. Placing a tuning fork on the center of the forehead (vertex), a (Rinne/Weber) test was performed.
9. This was a 47-year-old male with basal cell carcinoma located on the right (naris/nares).
10. Using a Zeiss microscope, the middle ear was visualized; the incus was malformed and fused to the head of the (malleus/malleolus).

TRANSCRIBING PROFESSIONAL DOCUMENTS

Transcribe the document named Assessment 4 from tape. Before you key, review the document formatting guidelines. Proofread your transcribed document and revise it until you think it is error-free

PERFORMANCE REPORT

Name____Date __________

Document	Description	Date Completed	Document Processing Speed (If Available)	Document Appraisal M=Mailable MC=Mailable w/corrections NM=Not Mailable
Report 4.1	Office Note			M MC NM
Report 4.2	Office Note			M MC NM
Report 4.3	Consultation Letter			M MC NM
Report 4.4	Operative Report			M MC NM
Report 4.5	Office Note			M MC NM
Report 4.6	Operative Report			M MC NM
Report 4.7	Office Note			M MC NM
Report 4.8	Office Note (Phone Call Note)			M MC NM

Comments ____

CHAPTER

5

Pulmonology, from the Latin for lung ("pulmo"), is the medical specialty that deals with the respiratory system. The respiratory system functions with the circulatory system to transport oxygen and carbon dioxide between the lungs and tissues of the body. The organs of the respiratory system include the nose, mouth, pharynx, epiglottis, esophagus, trachea, lungs, bronchi, bronchioles, and alveoli.

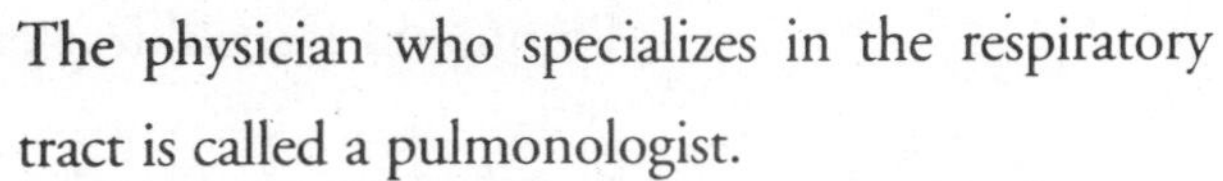

Pulmonology

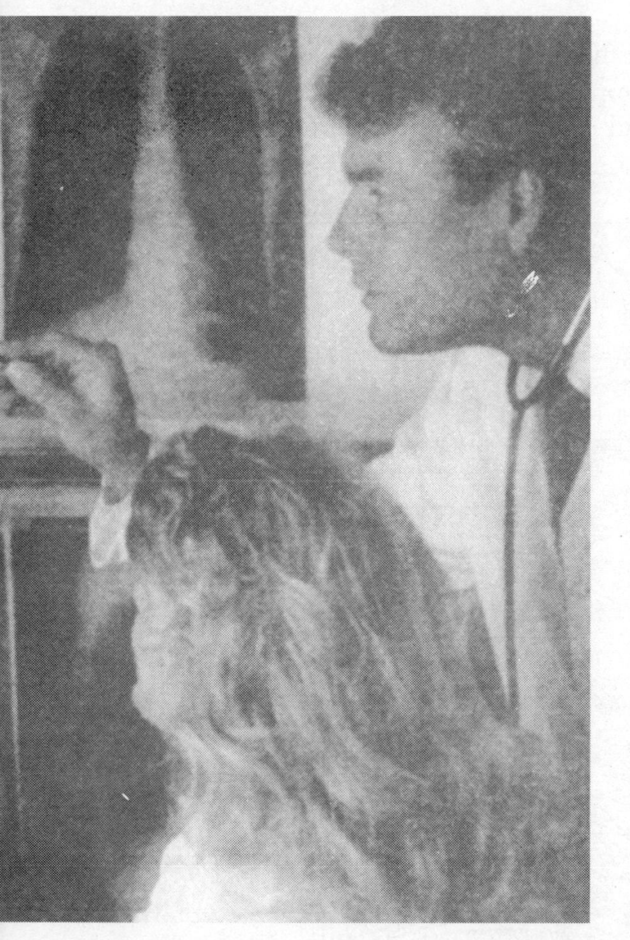

The physician who specializes in the respiratory tract is called a pulmonologist.

OBJECTIVES

- Use pulmonology terms correctly according to the context and purpose of the dictation.
- Select and use appropriate general and specialty reference materials.
- Key pulmonology documents of varying complexity and format.
- Transcribe authentic medical dictation requiring concentration and listening skill.
- Edit medical reports to conform with AAMT style guidelines.
- Proofread and correct transcripts to produce error-free documents.

EXPLORING PULMONOLOGY

Our bodies need oxygen to function properly. The air we breathe, inhaled through the nose and mouth, contains oxygen. The respiratory system uses this oxygen and, in the processs, converts the gas to carbon dioxide. It then eliminates this waste gas from the body. Each step of the respiratory process is essential for good health.

STRUCTURE AND FUNCTION

The central part of the respiratory system is the thorax, which contains the sternum, ribs, the thoracic vertebrae, and the lungs (figure 5.1). The muscles of the respiratory tract are also important. These muscles transfer air by moving the ribs during inspiration and expiration.

Air enters the body through the nose or mouth, then passes through the pharynx and into the trachea, or windpipe. After further warming and filtration of noxious substances, the air passes into the tracheobronchial tree (figure 5.2). This tree, so named because of its branching into the left and right bronchi, is further divided into bronchioles which terminate into air sacs, called alveoli. Adjacent to the alveoli lie tiny capillary beds. These circulatory beds provide exchange of oxygen from the alveoli to the blood and carbon dioxide from the blood to the alveoli.

During the normal respiratory cycle there is an inspiratory phase which requires active muscle movement, and a passive expiratory phase. During inspiration the muscles between the ribs elevate the ribs, increasing the diameter of the chest. At the same time, the diaphragm drops to allow free entry of air. The recoiling of the thoracic cavity expels the air and causes the expiration to occur. In the normal adult, there is a 6–8 cm. expansion during each of the 16–20 cycles per minute.

Figure 5.1
Respiratory system

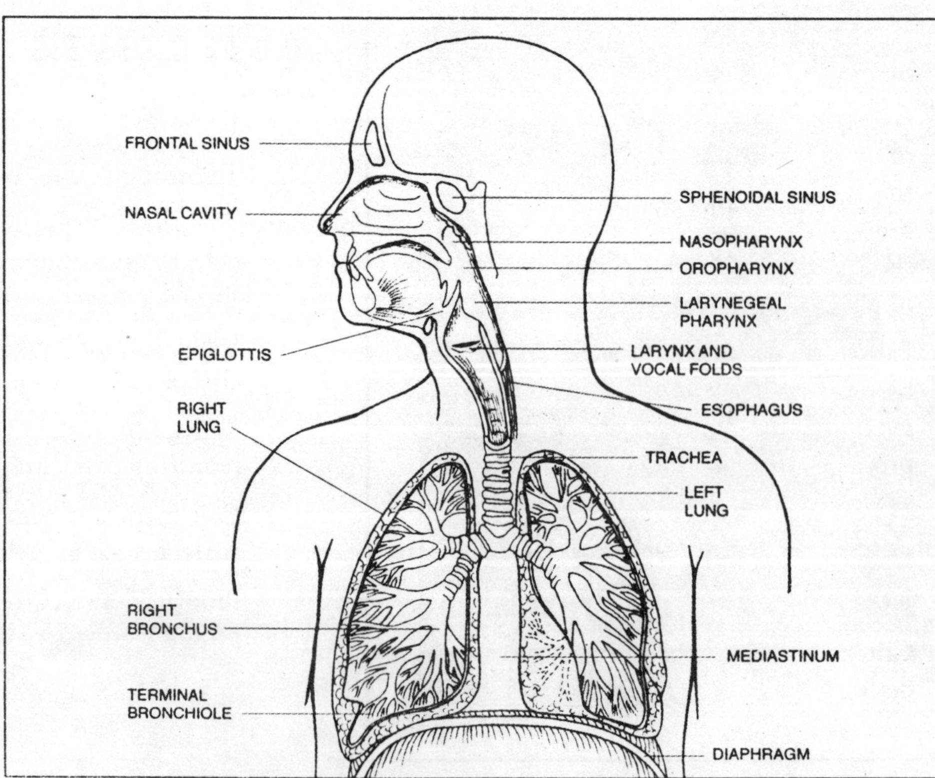

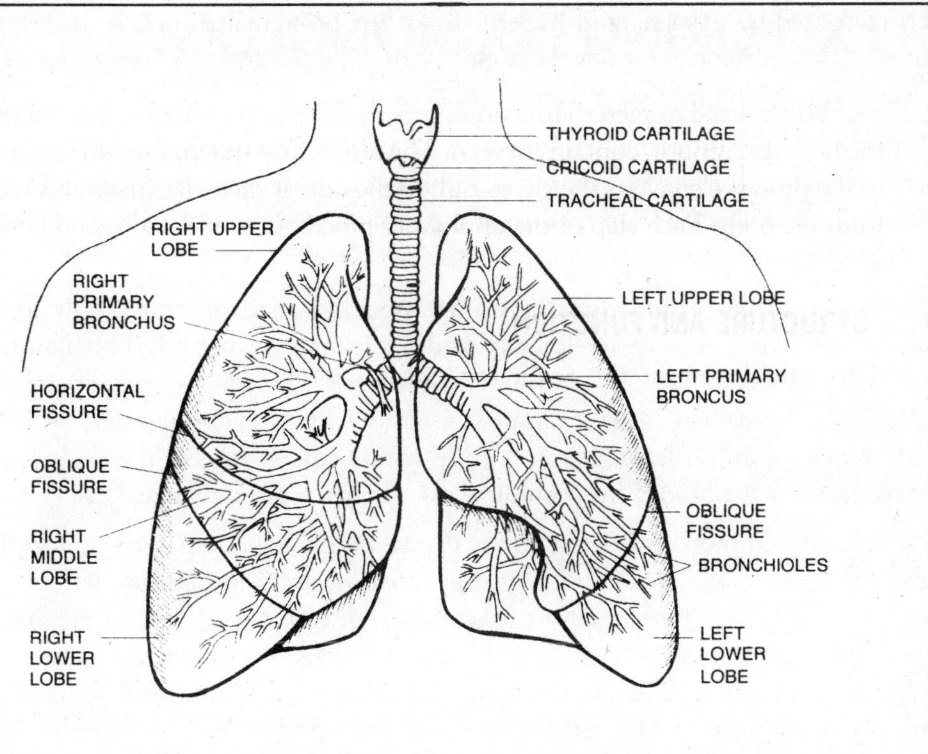

Figure 5.2 Anterior view of trachea, bronchial tree, and lobes of lungs

Respiration is divided into the external and internal processes. External respiration is the exchange of oxygen and carbon dioxide between the person and the environment. Internal respiration takes place on a cellular level, exchanging the oxygen carried on the red blood cells with the carbon dioxide in the tissues. After this exchange takes place both internally and externally, the lungs eliminate the carbon dioxide.

PHYSICAL ASSESSMENT

Assessment begins with visualization of the nose, observing for deviated septum or other abnormalities that would decrease the amount of air entry. Inspection of the chest includes counting the respirations, observing the movement of the chest during inspiration and expiration, and noting the general shape of the thorax and symmetry of expansion. Posture, contour, and movement are important elements in proper air exchange.

Palpation of the back should include feeling for fremitus, the vibrations caused by breathing. A resonant sound should be produced when tapping on the chest over the area of the lungs. Tapping, or percussing, on the ribs and sternum produces a dull sound. On auscultation, the physician listens for breath sounds as well as rattling, wheezing, and snoring-like sounds.

DISEASES AND CONDITIONS

Chronic obstructive pulmonary disease (COPD) or chronic obstructive lung disease (COLD) occurs when there is difficulty with oxygenation. It is

Common Pulmonology Drugs

albuterol
Proventil, Ventolin

aminophylline
Aminophyllin

beclomethasone dipropionate
Vancenase

dobutamine hydrochloride
epinephrine

guaifenesin and dextromethorphan
Robitussin-DM

ipratropium bromide
Atrovent

isoproterenol hydrochloride
Isuprel Hydrochloride

ioratadine
Claritin

pancreatin
Creon, Dizymes

pancrelipase
Cotazym, Pancrease, Zymase

pseudoephedrine sulfate
Sudafed

terfenadine
Seldane

theophylline
Slo-Phyllin, Slobid

triamcinolone acetonide
Azmacort

characterized by dyspnea and hyperplasia of the bronchial tissues. In late stages of this disease, the patient may become very debilitated and require oxygen to be delivered continuously via a nasal cannula or mask.

Inflammation of the bronchi is known as bronchitis. It is usually caused by a viral or bacterial pathogen. Symptoms include cough, usually productive, and chest pain. Bronchiolitis is inflammation of the bronchioles and is usually only found in children.

Emphysema results from chronic asthma, bronchitis, and/or smoking. It occurs when the alveoli lose their elasticity and air is trapped within. This constant expansion leads to the characteristic "barrel chest." During periods of difficult breathing, the patient must remain erect, either sitting up continuously or in an orthopneic position, leaning over a table with arms resting on the surface and extended over the head. This position allows for better air exchange.

Asthma is a common obstructive airway disease producing intermittent attacks that usually are reversible. It is characterized by a narrowing of the airways, resulting in dyspnea, cough, and wheezing in response to various stimuli. An asthma attack may be triggered by known or unknown allergens, or by exercise, an upper respiratory infection (URI), or emotions. Asthma is usually controlled with the use of pharmacologic agents, although severe asthma can lead to chronic lung problems.

Pneumonia is an inflammatory process affecting the tissue of the lung. It is usually caused by infectious organisms. The types of pneumonia are described by the causative agent: bacterial, viral, fungal, or parasitic. Other causes include chemical inhalations or aspiration pneumonia. Manifestations may include cough, with or without sputum production; lethargy; fever; pain in the chest; changes in the respiratory rate; grunting; and nasal flaring. Assessment includes rattling breath sounds, increased tactile fremitus, dullness on percussion, bronchovesicular breath sounds, egophony, and pectoriloquy. A diagnostic evaluation includes physical examination, chest x-ray, sputum culture if productive cough exists, and blood culture if bacteremia is a concern.

Respiratory distress syndrome (RDS) is a series of symptoms found most commonly in premature infants and small children. It is characterized by very rapid breathing, cyanosis, nasal flaring, grunting, and retractions of the muscles between the ribs. Premature infants are at risk because of the immaturity of their lung tissue which has not yet developed surfactant, the substance that the lungs require to expand. Without surfactant, the alveoli collapse and breathing is difficult.

Cystic fibrosis is a hereditary disorder affecting the lungs, pancreas, and digestive system. Thick, viscous mucus is produced, blocking the airway and trapping air in the lungs. Pancreatic enzymes are not produced, causing problems with digestion and fatty, frequent, foul-smelling stools. Presently, lifelong treatment with pancreatic enzyme replacement, respiratory or pulmonary toilet including postural drainage, and antibiotic therapy for frequent associated pneumonia is necessary. The genetic abnormality causing this disease has been discovered and progress is being made to replace the aberrant gene in order to develop a cure for persons affected with cystic fibrosis.

COMMON TESTS AND SURGICAL PROCEDURES

Pulmonary function tests are essential to diagnosing chronic obstructive pulmonary disease and other lung ailments. These breathing tests include measurement of lung volume and the distribution of gases along with diffusion studies.

Another common procedure is bronchoscopy. The bronchoscopy is usually performed with a flexible bronchoscope that allows the physician to see even the small airways and to remove pieces of tissue for biopsy.

Thoracentesis is a surgical procedure to remove fluid from the pleural cavity. Pneumonectomy, or pulmonectomy, is an excision of all lobes of the lung in a single operation.

THE VOCABULARY OF PULMONOLOGY

The following word list contains common pulmonology terms as well as most of the difficult words contained in the dictation at the end of the chapter. Take time to become familiar with these words now, then review them again before you key the medical documents.

Here are suggestions for learning the vocabulary words:

1. Read and study each word for pronunciation and meaning.
2. Write each unfamiliar word from the list below on a notecard, write the definition or a paraphrase of the definition on the back, and draw a simple picture to help you learn the word.
3. Study the pronunciation, spelling, and definition of each word on your notecard, then key each word twice for reinforcement. Check the spelling.
4. Add the correctly spelled terms to your word processor's spell checker.

abscess
(ab'-ses) (n) a pus-filled cavity, usually because of a localized infection

aerosol
(ayr'-O-sol) (n) a liquid or solution dispensed as a fine mist or a product dispensed from a pressurized container as a fine mist

afebrile
(ay-feb'-ril) (adj) without fever

alveolus
(al-vee'-O-lus) (n) air cells of the lungs where the exchange of oxygen and carbon dioxide takes place; alveoli (al-vee'-O-lI) (pl)

anicteric
(an-ik-ter'-ik) (adj) without jaundice or icterus (a yellowing of the skin and whites of the eyes)

asthma
(az'-ma) (n) respiratory disorder with temporary narrowing of the airways, resulting in difficulty in breathing, coughing, gasping, wheezing

atraumatic
(ay-traw-mat'-ik) (adj) without injury or trauma

auscultation
(aws-kul-tay'-shun) (n) act of listening through a stethoscope to sounds from within the body, including lungs, heart, and abdomen

bacteremia
(bak-te-ree'-mee-a) (n) the presence of live bacteria in the blood

bifurcation
(bI-fer-kay'-shun) (n) forking into two branches

bolus
(bO'-lus) (n) masticated (chewed) food or substance that is ready to be swallowed

bronchial
(brong'-kee-al) (adj) relating to the bronchi

bronchiectasis
(brong-kee-ek'-ta-sis) (n) persistent, abnormal widening of the bronchi, with an associated cough and spitting up of mucus

bronchiole
(brong'-kee-Ol) (n) one of the smaller subdivisions of the bronchi

bronchitis
(brong-kI'-tis) (n) inflammation of the bronchi

bronchovesicular
(brong'-kO-ve-sik'-yoo-lar) (adj) relating to the bronchioles and alveoli in the lungs

bronchus
(brong'-kus) (n) the divisions of the trachea leading to the lungs; bronchi (brong'-kI) (pl)

cilium
(sil'-ee-um) (n) a short hairlike extension of a cell surface, capable of lashlike movement, which aids in the movement of unicellular organisms and in the movement of fluids in higher organisms; eyelash; cilia (pl)

cyanosis
(cI-a-nO'-sis) (n) bluish discoloration of the skin and/or mucous membranes due to decreased amount of oxygen in the blood cells

cystic fibrosis
(sis'-tik fI-brO'-sis) (n) an inherited disease, in which the mucus-producing glands become clogged with thick mucus; digestion and respiration are affected

diffuse
(di-fyoos') (adj) spreading, scattered

dorsal
(dOr'-sal) (adj) relating to the back; posterior

dyspnea
(disp-nee'-a) (n) shortness of breath; difficulty in breathing

edema
(e-dee'-ma) (n) excessive accumulation of fluid in tissues, especially just under the skin or in a given cavity

effusion
(e-fyoo'-zhun) (n) escape of fluid into a cavity or tissues; the fluid itself

egophony
(ee-gof'-O-nee) (n) an abnormal voice sound, like the bleating of a goat

electrolyte
(ee-lek'-trO-lIt) (n) an ionized chemical capable of conducting an electric current; the body contains many different electrolytes in specific amounts to keep it functioning properly

epiglottis
(ep'-I-glot'-is) (n) flap of elastic cartilage at the back of the mouth that covers the opening to the windpipe during swallowing, thereby preventing choking.

erythema
(er-i-thee'-ma) (n) redness of the skin

esophagus
(ee-sof'-a-gus) (n) the muscular canal that connects the pharynx and stomach

expectoration
(ek-spek-tO-ray'-shun) (n) expelling by mouth; spitting

expiratory
(ek-spI'-ra-tO'-ree) (adj) relating to expiration, or breathing out air from the lungs

extraocular
(eks-tra-ok'-yoo-lar) (adj) outside the eye

femoral
(fem'-o-ral) (adj) relating to the thigh bone or femur

flaring
(flayr'-ing) (adj) widening of an area, as the nostrils; a spreading area of redness around a lesion

fremitus
(frem'-i-tus) (n) a vibration that can be felt by the hand on the chest

hemoptysis
(hee-mop'-ti-sis) (n) expectoration of blood; spitting or coughing up blood

hemothorax
(hee-mO-thOr'-aks) (n) blood in the chest cavity

hyperemia
(hI-per-ee'-mee-a) (n) increased blood in part of the body, caused by inflammatory response or blockage of blood outflow

hyperplasia
(hI-per-play'-see-a) (n) increase in the number of cells in a tissue or organ resulting in an increase in size (does not include tumor formation)

inspiratory
(in-spI'-ra-tO-ree) (adj) relating to inhalation, drawing air into the lungs

lobectomy
(lOb-ek'-tO-mee) (n) the removal of a lobe from an organ or gland

nasopharynx
(nay'-zO-far'-ingks) (n) open chamber behind the nose and above the palate

nebulization
(neb'-yoo-li-zay'-shun) (n) production of fine particles, such as a spray or mist, from liquid

organomegaly
(Or'-ga-nO-meg'-a-lee) (n) abnormal enlargement of an organ, particularly an organ of the abdominal cavity, such as the liver or spleen

orthopnea
(Or-thop-nee'-a) (n) difficulty in breathing when lying down

pathogen
(path'-O-jen) (n) any microorganism or substance that can cause a disease

pectoriloquy
(pek-tO-ril'-O-kwee) (n) voice sounds transmitted through the pulmonary structures, clearly audible on auscultation

pectus carinatum
(pek'-tus kar-i-nay'-tum) (n) forward protusion of the sternum; pigeon breast

pectus excavatum
(pek'-tus eks-ka-vay'-tum) (n) markedly sunken sternum; funnel breast

percussion
(per-kush'-un) (n) a technique of physical examination in which the sound of fingers or a small tool tapping parts of the body is used to determine position and size of internal organs and to detect the presence of fluid

pharynx
(far'-ingks) (n) throat; passageway for air from nasal cavity to larynx, and food from mouth to esophagus

pleura
(ploor'-a) (n) membrane lining the chest cavity and covering the lungs

pleural
(ploor'-al) (adj) relating to the pleura

pleurisy
(ploor'-I-see) (n) inflammation of the pleura; pleuritis

pneumonia
(noo-mO'-nee-a) (n) inflammation and congestion of the lung, usually due to infection by bacteria or viruses

pneumonitis
(noo-mO-nI'-tis) (n) inflammation of the lungs

pneumothorax
(noo-mO-thor'-aks) (n) abnormal presence of air or gas in the chest cavity

Pseudomonas
(soo-dO-mO'-nas) (n) a genus of bacteria commonly found in soil and water and which may cause infection

rales
(rahls) (n) abnormal sounds, such as rattling or bubbling, heard on auscultation of the lungs

rectal
(rek'-tal) (adj) relating to the rectum, the lower part of the large intestine

regimen
(rej'-I-men) (n) plan of therapy, including drugs

respiration
(res-pi-ray'-shun) (n) inhalation and exhalation; the exchange of gases—oxygen and carbon dioxide—between an organism and the environment

respiratory
(res'-per-a-tOr-ee) (adj) relating to respiration

respiratory distress syndrome
(res'-pi-ra-tOr-ee dis-tres' sin'-drOm) (n) acute lung disease, especially in premature newborn babies, caused by a lack of surfactant in the lung tissue

rhonchus
(rong'-kus) (n) abnormal sound heard on auscultation of the chest, usually during expiration

septum
(sep'-tum) (n) division between two cavities or two masses of tissue; such as nasal septum; septa (pl)

sputum
(spyoo'-tum) (n) spit; expectorated material

sternum
(ster'-num) (n) the breast bone

tachycardia
(tak'-I-kar'-dee-a) (n) rapid heart rate

tachycardiac
(tak'-e-kar'-dee-ak) (adj) relating to or suffering from an abnormally rapid heart rate

tachypnea
(tak-ip-nee'-a) (n) rapid rate of breathing

thorax
(thor'-aks) (n) the chest

thyromegaly
(thI-rO-meg'-a-lee) (n) enlargement of the thyroid gland

tibia
(tib'-ee-a) (n) larger bone of the lower leg; shin bone

tibial
(tib'-ee-al) (adj) relating to the tibia

trachea
(tray'-kee-a) (n) the windpipe

tympanic membrane
(tim-pan'-ik) (n) eardrum

wheezing
(hweez'-ing) (n) breathing with difficulty and with a whistling sound; can be heard aloud and/or on auscultation

ABBREVIATIONS

A&P	auscultation and percussion
ABG	arterial blood gas (gases)
AFB	acid-fast bacilli
AP	anterior posterior
ARDS	acute respiratory distress syndrome
BiPAP	bilevel positive airway pressure
BOOP	bronchiolitis obliterans with organizing pneumonia
CO_2	carbon dioxide
COLD	chronic obstructive lung disease
COPD	chronic obstructive pulmonary disease
CPAP	continuous positive airway pressure
CPR	cardiopulmonary resuscitation
CXR	chest x-ray
DNR	do not resuscitate
IPPB	intermittent positive pressure breathing
IS	incentive spirometry
MDI	metered dose inhaler
O_2	oxygen
PA	posterior anterior
PAP	positive airway pressure
PEEP	positive end expiratory pressure
PND	paroxysmal nocturnal dyspnea
RDS	respiratory distress syndrome
SIDS	sudden infant death syndrome
SMR	submucosal resection
SOB	shortness of breath
TB	tuberculosis
URI	upper respiratory infection
VC	vital capacity

PULMONARY FUNCTION TEST (PFT) ABBREVIATIONS

FEF	forced expiratory flow
FEF25-75	forced midexpiratory flow during the middle half of the FVC
FEV	forced expiratory volume
FEV1	forced expiratory volume in one second
FEV3	forced expiratory volume in three seconds
FVC	forced vital capacity
FVL	flow volume loop
PEF	peak expiratory flow

EXERCISE 5.1: RECOGNIZING LOOK-ALIKES AND SOUND-ALIKES

Below is a list of frequently used words that look alike and/or sound alike. Study the meaning and pronunciation of each set of words, then read each sentence carefully and circle the word in parentheses that correctly completes the meaning.

breath	(n) air taken into the lungs
breathe	(v) to take air into the lungs

coarse	rough; "coarse breath sounds"
course	progress or duration of time

dose	(n) a measure
doze	(v) to nap

expiratory	breathing out from the lungs
inspiratory	breathing into the lungs

loose	(adj) free from anything that restrains
lose	(v) to miss something

loss	(n) something that is missing
lost	(v) past tense of lose
lost	(adj) missing as in "a lost watch"

perfuse	to force blood or other fluid to flow; "toes are well perfused"
profuse	abundant; "the patient had profuse bleeding"

presence	(n) attendance; close proximity
presents	(n) gifts
presents	(v) manner in which the patient appears to the caregiver

afebrile	(adj) without fever
a febrile	(adj) [condition] with fever

viscous	(adj) sticky
viscus	(n) a hollow, multilayered, walled organ such as an organ of the digestive system or the heart

1. The patient is to take three (doses, dozes) of the medication daily.
2. It was unfortunate that she (dosed, dozed) through the lecture.
3. The patient (presence, presents) for follow up of his colitis.
4. On cardiac examination, I detected the (presence, presents) of a systolic murmur.
5. When the patient took a deep breath, I noted (inspiratory, expiratory) wheezing.
6. She is complaining of shortness of (breath, breathe) on exertion.
7. When she exercises, she feels like she cannot (breath, breathe) as easily.
8. We will have her complete her full (course, coarse) of antibiotics.
9. When she cut her finger, she noted (perfuse, profuse) bleeding.
10. The patient was directed to (loose, lose) 10 pounds by her next visit.

EXERCISE 5.2: MATCHING SOUND AND SPELLING

The numbered list that follows shows the phonetic spelling of hard-to-spell words. Sound out the word, then write the correct spelling in the blank space provided. Each of the words can be found in the glossary or in the drug list in appendix C.

1. tak'-i-kar'-dee-a ______
2. ploor'-al ______
3. an-ik-ter'-ik ______
4. thee-of'-i-leen ______
5. brong-kee-ek'-ta-sis ______
6. noo-mO-nI'-tis ______
7. rong'-kus ______
8. aws-kul-tay'-shun ______
9. tak-ip-nee'-a ______
10. thI-rO-meg'-a-lee ______
11. nay'-zO-far'-ingks ______
12. hee-mop'-ti-sis ______
13. di-fyoos' ______
14. tray'-kee-a ______
15. Or'-ga-nO-meg'-a-lee ______

EXERCISE 5.3: CHOOSING WORDS FROM CONTEXT

When transcribing dictation, the medical transcriptionist frequently needs to determine the word that correctly completes the sentence based on the situation. From the list of words below, select the term that meaningfully completes each statement.

afebrile	respiratory distress	tachycardiac
erythema	bolus	diffuse
alveoli	rhonchi	tachypneic
hemoptysis	cyanotic	effusion
auscultation		nebulizer

1. Upon presentation to the emergency room, the patient was in severe ________________, making breathing painful.
2. On ____________ of the lungs, I heard rhonchi and rales.
3. Her fingernails were ________________, indicating that she needed oxygen.
4. Mrs. Smith is ___________ today, with a temperature of 98.6° on exam.
5. The chest x-ray showed improvement in her pleural __________.
6. The patient has had two episodes of __________, when he noticed flecks of blood in his sputum.
7. Although she complains of rapid breathing, she is not __________ on exam.
8. On auscultation, there were _________ heard in the lower lung fields.
9. Jackie has developed a lot of chest congestion over the past 24 hours, with an increase in her wheezing. She has been using her __________ at home but no other medications
10. The patient is _______________, with a heart rate of 160.

EXERCISE 5.4: PAIRING WORDS AND MEANINGS

A. bronchiole	F. hyperemia	K. Ventolin
B. cystic fibrosis	G. pathogen	L. effusion
C. edema	H. Pseudomonas	M. hemothorax
D. epiglottis	I. theophylline	N. trachea
E. esophagus	J. tympanic membrane	

1. a drug resembling caffeine that dilates blood vessels ______________
2. a genus of small, motile bacilli ______________
3. a muscular canal that carries food from the mouth to the stomach ______________
4. one of the smaller divisions of the bronchial tubes ______________
5. a transparent membrane that separates the outer ear ______________
6. abnormal collection of fluid in spaces between cells ______________
7. a disease in which the passageways (including pancreatic and bile ducts, intestine, and bronchi) become clogged with thick mucus ______________
8. cartilage at the back of the mouth cavity that covers the windpipe during swallowing ______________
9. increased blood supply in part of the body ______________
10. a microorganism that can produce disease ______________

EXERCISE 5.5: CREATING TERMS FROM WORD FORMS

In the following exercise, combine prefixes, root words, and suffixes to create medical words that fit the definitions below. Fill in the blanks with the words you construct.

pneum/o or pneumon/o	air or lung	-cythemia	red blood cells
		-ectomy	removal of anatomical structure
bronch/o	airway	-emia	blood condition
pulmon/o	lung	-itis	inflammation or infection
hypo	below or deficient	-ia	condition of
hyper	above or excessive	-capnia	carbon dioxide
thyroid	gland	oxa- or oxy- or oxo-	oxygen
-plasia	formation; growth		

1. excision of the thyroid ______________
2. reduction of oxygen supply to tissue ______________
3. excision of all pulmonary lobes from lung ______________
4. increase in number of cells, enlarging the organ ______________
5. excess of carbon dioxide ______________
6. underdevelopment of organ growth ______________
7. excess of red blood cells ______________
8. excision of entire lung ______________
9. deficiency of carbon dioxide ______________
10. inflammation of the mucosa of the bronchi ______________

EDITING MEDICAL DOCUMENTS

In this section you will perfect your word use and grammar skills. These skills will help you edit and proofread medical reports for correct language, punctuation, format, and meaning. The special focus for this chapter is using commas, semicolons, and colons.

PUNCTUATING WITH COMMAS, SEMICOLONS, AND COLONS

In a spoken conversation, meaning is conveyed through tone of voice, gestures, and pauses. We pause and change the inflection in our voices to clarify meaning. In written language, punctuation marks serve as "road signs" for readers. Punctuation clarifies meaning and prevents confusion.

Commas

To introduce

Use a comma to set off an introductory word or phrase.

> Fortunately, the records were located.
>
> Because he spiked a fever, the patient was not cleared for discharge.
>
> Due to her rapid deterioration, the patient was transferred to the intensive care unit.

TIP: A sentence that is in the natural order (subject followed by verb and modifiers) does not contain an introductory clause and does not need an introductory comma.

> I confirmed the patients' appointments for next week before leaving the office.
>
> Your first-aid kit should be readily accessible in the event of a medical emergency.

When a sentence is out of the natural order (inverted), a comma is needed to help the reader identify the important information of the sentence.

> Before leaving the office, I confirmed the patients' appointments for next week.

In the event of a medical emergency, your first-aid kit should be readily accessible.

Be careful to place introductory phrases close to the word they modify; otherwise your sentence may be grammatically incorrect and/or cause confusion to readers.

UNCLEAR: After pausing the tape, the operative report was completed.

CLEAR: After pausing the tape, he completed the operative report.

To separate

Coordinate conjunctions (*and, but, or, nor, for, so*) join two main clauses into one sentence. Use a comma immediately before the coordinate conjunction. Remember that a main clause contains a subject, verb, and complement and can stand alone. It is also called an independent clause.

The patient was prepared and draped in the usual sterile orthopedic fashion, *and* the tourniquet was inflated to 250 mm Hg.

The patient has had intermittent confusion, *so* the home health nurse was assigned to dispense the patient's medications.

I don't know how long it will last, *but* the patient has stopped smoking.

TIP: If the main clauses are very short, you may omit the comma.

The wound was cleaned and a dressing was applied.

Use a comma to separate items in a series.

The patient's past medical history is significant for coronary artery disease, insulin-dependent diabetes mellitus, and peptic ulcer disease.

Dr. Johnson sees outpatients on Mondays, Wednesdays, and Fridays.

Use a comma between adjectives that equally modify the same noun if the *and* is omitted.

> She is a kind, dedicated nurse. (She is a kind and dedicated nurse).

Do not use a comma between two adjectives if you would not use *and.*

> The patient is an elderly white female. (We would not say she is an elderly *and* white female).

When placing commas, be sure you do not separate the subject from the verb. Even if the subject is several words long, it must not be separated from the verb by a comma.

> WRONG: Patients who are afraid of hospitals and doctors because of past painful experiences, need to be given an extra dose of compassion.
>
> CORRECT: Patients who are afraid of hospitals and doctors because of past painful experiences need to be given an extra dose of compassion.

To enclose

Use commas to set off nonessential or interrupting words or phrases from the rest of the sentence.

> I will graduate, unless I fail my chemistry class, next year.
>
> The dose, at least according to my calculations, is 12.5 mg per hour.

TIP: Think of commas that enclose as parentheses. By enclosing information in commas, you are telling the reader that the information is not vital to the meaning of the sentence.

Semicolons

Semicolons are used in two situations: 1) to join two independent clauses and 2) to separate items in a series that has internal commas.

To join independent clauses

Use a semicolon to join two closely related independent clauses. Note that the clauses could also stand alone as sentences.

> We have given you clear instructions; be sure to follow them explicitly.
>
> The patient has continued to take the medication; however, his condition has not improved.

To separate items in a series with internal commas

Use a semicolon to separate items in a series when one or more of those items contains an internal comma.

> He has written books about antique automobiles, specifically the Model T; sports trivia, his favorite topic; and outdoor cooking.
>
> I have lived in Phoenix, Arizona; Portland, Oregon; and Seattle, Washington.

Colons

Colons are the neon signs of punctuation, alerting the reader to important information. Most commonly, they are used with report headings and in ratios.

After a heading

Use a colon (and one space) after a report heading, but only if the information follows on the same line. Capitalize the first letter after the heading.

> HISTORY: The patient is a .....

To express a ratio

Use a colon to express a ratio. Do not key a space before or after the colon.

> EKG revealed 2:1 block.
>
> Xylocaine with 1:100,000 epinephrine was instilled for local anesthesia.

EXERCISE 5.6: EDITING FOR CORRECT PUNCTUATION

Read the following sentences and add commas, semicolons, or colons where necessary for correct meaning.

1. Since the patient has improved with conservative management we will not consider operative intervention at this time.
2. Our latest project remodeling the waiting room is going to be more expensive than we had planned.
3. Past surgeries include hysterectomy cholecystectomy and appendectomy.
4. Surprisingly the patient's condition improved.
5. Laboratory tests to be ordered include a complete blood count chemistry panel and electrolytes.
6. The risks and benefits of the procedure were explained to the patient and his wife and the patient signed the consent forms.
7. The planned surgery has a very high success rate however I explained to the patient that any surgery has an element of risk.
8. Abdomen is soft no organomegaly is noted.
9. The patient is to return to the emergency department immediately if he develops nausea fever over 100° or dramatically increased pain.
10. The patient has a history of coronary artery disease having undergone an angioplasty.
11. When testing the students should refrain from speaking.
12. After the induction of general anesthesia an endotracheal tube was placed.
13. The wound was then irrigated using normal saline and the deep muscles were closed using chromic sutures.
14. The experimental drug studies were carried out in San Diego California Denver Colorado Minneapolis Minnesota and Atlanta Georgia.
15. The patient is a young female college student.
16. Patients with AIDS who generally are underweight should receive nutritional counseling.
17. Thank you Dr. Smith for seeing this patient in pulmonary consultation.
18. Given the patient's overall debilitated condition and end-stage lung disease he wishes to be made a DNR.

EXERCISE 5.7: PROOFREADING REVIEW

Read the following partial medical report and look for errors in word use, spelling, the use of commas, pronoun and reference agreement, and subject and verb agreement. Also check for complete sentences. Circle the errors, then key the report with the errors corrected.

PHYSICAL EXAMINATION: Plus of 120, respertory rate of 30, temperature of 99° and weight 40.6 kg. She is a thin, pale, adolescence female in mild respiratory distress. Head is normocephalic and a traumatic. Pupil are equal, round and reaction to light. Extraocular movements are full. Sclera are anicteric. Conjunctavae is not injected. Nose is without discharge. No flareing. Her mouth have pink and moist mucosa with no lesions. Her lips are cyanotic. His face has a flush over the cheek bones. Her neck is supply, without palpable limph nodes.

WHERE CAN I FIND THE ANSWER?

As you transcribe dictation, you may hear unfamiliar words or terms. A variety of reference sources are available to help you locate answers to your questions. One of the important types of references for medical transcriptionists is described below. Read the information; then if you have access to the reference discussed, explore its capabilities.

MEDICAL REFERENCES: WORD BOOKS

Unlike dictionaries, word books do not contain definitions or pronunciations; they contain only the correct spelling of words and terms, which, in most cases, is all the transcriptionist needs. Most word books are directed toward a specific field. There is a surgical word book, a pathology word book, a radiology word book, a psychiatry word book, and others. They can range from 200 pages to over 1200 pages.

Which word books should I have?

The types of documents and area of medicine you work with will determine the reference books most useful to you. If you work in a specialty or your dictations contain specialty words, you will want to have word books that cover these areas.

The Medical Word Book by Sheila Sloane contains words for a number of specialities. While not as complete in any one area as a true specialty word book, it is a "mini word book" for specialties, including cardiology, respiratory medicine, urology, plastic surgery, neurology, obstetrics and gynecology, and dermatology.

The Surgical Word Book is devoted to surgical words and terms—catheters, sutures, pins, scopes, valves, as well as anatomic terms. It is comprehensive, listing over 3,000 kinds of forceps and over 1,200 retractors, for example. If you regularly transcribe operative reports, this book is indispensable.

The other specialty word books are based on the same principle. They are devoted to those words, terms, and phrases specific to one branch of medicine. If you need advice about which books to buy, ask some experienced MTs what they use or call AAMT.

TRANSCRIBING PULMONOLOGY DOCUMENTS

In this section your goal is to prepare for the work of transcription by transcribing first from a printed document and then from dictation on tape. The model document that follows illustrates the generally accepted format for the **discharge summary**, the report format featured in this chapter.

BASIC FORMAT: THE DISCHARGE SUMMARY

Sometimes called a dismissal summary or summary of hospitalization, the discharge summary provides a review of the patient's hospitalization, including the reason for entering the hospital, the patient's medical history, and a description of the procedures and treatment performed during the stay.

Required Headings/Content

Headings required by JCAHO include history, course in the hospital, instructions to the patient (disposition), and final diagnosis(es). Physicians may also add history of present illness, family history, social history, physical examination, laboratory data, x-ray findings, and condition on discharge.

The instructions for continuing care can include information on therapy, diet, activity, and medications prescribed for the patient at discharge.

Turnaround Time

Medical records for discharged patients are to be completed within a time period specified by the hospital but not to exceed 30 days. Because subsequent medical care can proceed without the discharge summary, the turnaround time on this report is typically three to seven days, which is longer than for other, more critical chart reports.

DISCHARGE SUMMARY

1" top and side margins

Aligning name, dates, and record numbers is another acceptable format

left justification

PATIENT NAME: **tab** Jaheem Arnold
ADMISSION DATE: **tab** 2/13/XX
DISCHARGE DATE: **tab** 2/20/XX
MEDICAL RECORD #: **tab** 7013920
ds
ADMITTING DIAGNOSIS: Reactive airway disease.
ds
DISCHARGE DIAGNOSIS: Reactive airway disease.
ds
HISTORY OF PRESENT ILLNESS: The patient is a 19-month-old African-American male who had been well until two days prior to admission, when he developed a loose cough. Mother gave him an over-the-counter children's cough remedy several times each day. He was afebrile during this time. During the day, the child had increased difficulty breathing, and wheezing was noted in the late p.m., when the child was brought to the emergency room.

In the emergency room, the child was found to have a fever of 102° F rectally. He was found to be in respiratory distress and was given Ventolin nebulization and admitted.
ds
PHYSICAL EXAMINATION: Physical examination showed a patient sitting in bed with mild respiratory distress. He was alert. Respiratory rate was 40, heart rate was 115, temperature was 102.3°. Right tympanic membrane was slightly erythematous. There was slight nasal flaring. Throat was slightly injected. On auscultation, the lungs were found to have diffuse inspiratory and expiratory wheezes. The heart showed the presence of normal heart sounds with mild tachycardia.
ds
HOSPITAL COURSE: Reactive airway disease. The patient was admitted, started on theophylline, bolused with theophylline 1 mg/kg and subsequently put on a maintenance dose of theophylline. High-flow nebulization was also given p.o. every two hours.

With this management, the patient showed rapid improvement and his respiratory treatments were gradually spaced out so that, subsequently, the patient was changed to oral medication of theophylline. Theophylline levels were monitored during the hospital course.

(continued)

DISCHARGE SUMMARY
PATIENT NAME: Jaheem Arnold
MEDICAL RECORD #: 7013920
Page 2

ds

DISPOSITION: The child was discharged after a one-week hospitalization on theophylline. Condition at time of discharge was improved. Mother was instructed to bring him to our office in one week.

qs

____
Mencer Alcott, MD

ds

MA/XX
D: 2/22/XX
T: 2/25/XX

PREPARING TO TRANSCRIBE

To prepare for transcribing dictation, key the discharge summary above. You will later key the identical report from dictation. Follow these guidelines:

- Study the format and organization of the report.
- Review the word list presented earlier in this chapter.
- Consult reference books for words or formatting rules that are unfamiliar.
- Proofread your final copy by comparing it to the printed version.

CASES FOR TRANSCRIPTION

In this section you will transcribe medical dictation from tape. Your goal is to produce error-free documents. Read this chapter's Pro Tip (following case studies) for helpful hints from experienced MTs. Then follow these steps for each dictation:

1. Prepare to transcribe by reviewing the case study and the model report format.
2. Transcribe the dictation, leaving spaces for words you cannot hear or do not understand.
3. Carefully proofread the document and correct as many errors as you can. Use your reference materials to help you identify missing words.
4. Listen to the tape again and correct all remaining errors.

Repeat these steps until you produce an error-free document. Then complete the Performance Report, attach it to the top of the transcripts, and submit them to your instructor for evaluation.

CASE STUDY 1: JAHEEM ARNOLD

Jaheem Arnold is a 19-month-old African-American male who came to the emergency room (ER) of the hospital at 10 p.m., with a history of cough for two days. He began wheezing and having increased difficulty breathing for one hour prior to coming to the ER.

Report 5.1: Discharge Summary

Transcription Hints

- When the dictator refers to nebulization given "pee oh," transcribe this abbreviation for *by mouth* as p.o.
- Listen for these drug names:
  Ventolin
  theophylline

CASE STUDY 2: CHARLES INGRID

Charles Ingrid is a 4½-year-old male who was diagnosed with cystic fibrosis several months ago. He had a history of frequent colds, with large amounts of thick nasal discharge and thick respiratory sputum. His growth was slow, and his mother noticed that he had very sticky bowel movements. The diagnosis of cystic fibrosis was made after the pediatrician sent him for a sweat test which was positive for the disease. Charles is being admitted to the hospital because of a respiratory tract infection, which is common for persons with cystic fibrosis.

Report 5.2: Physical Examination Section of Discharge Summary

Transcription Hint

PERRL and PERRLA are common abbreviations in the HEENT (head, eyes, ears, nose, and throat) examination. They stand for "pupils equal, round, reactive to light" or "pupils equal, round, reactive to light and accommodation." This means that the pupils are equal in size and round in shape and that they constrict when a light is shined into the eyes. Accommodation refers to the changing shape of the lens in response to the patient focusing on an object across the room and then on an object a foot or two away These abbreviations should be on your list of macros. (See chapter 12.)

Report 5.3: Consultation Letter

Transcription Hints

- Physicians sometimes use the words *regime* and *regimen* interchangeably in dictation. However, *regimen* is the word that is usually intended.

  A regime is a system of government or a social system.

  A regimen is a daily routine, as in a *medication regimen.*

CASE STUDY 3: DENISE SULTAN

Denise Sultan is a 17-year-old girl diagnosed one year ago with Hodgkin's disease. She has been receiving chemotherapy for the past year. She was admitted to the hospital for difficulty breathing. She was diagnosed with pneumonia and had a complicated hospital course.

Report 5.4: Discharge Summary

Transcription Hints

- Blood gases are transcribed using the chemical abbreviations and numbers. The dictator may use the full term (for example, carbon dioxide) for some gases and may pronounce the letters of the abbreviation for others. In this report, the blood gases should be transcribed as pH of 7.5, pCO_2 of 31, pO_2 of 35, CO_2 of 24, and an O_2 saturation of 84.2.
- Listen for these shortened terms for blood cells in the CBC results:
  segs
  lymphs
  monos
  eos
  basos

CASE STUDY 4: JANIS MILLER

Janis Miller is a tour guide and part-time college student who has been feeling ill for about a week. She has had a runny nose along with shortness of breath.

Report 5.5: Office Note

Transcription Hint

Listen for these special terms:
rhinorrhea
Wright peak flow

CASE STUDY 5: RHONDA BENTZ

A third-grader with chronic asthma, Rhonda Bentz is returning for a checkup following treatment for pneumonia.

Report 5.6: Office Note

Transcription Hint

Listen for these pharmaceutical terms:
albuterol inhaler with InspirEase
Azmacort

CASE STUDY 6: JORDAN WHITE

Jordan White is an 11-year-old boy with Hurler's syndrome. Over the past months, he has been hospitalized several times with recurrent bronchitis. On this admission, he will undergo laryngoscopy and bronchoscopy to rule out tracheal granulomas.

Report 5.7: Operative Report

Transcription Hint

Listen for these terms:
arytenoids
cannulate
KTP laser

CASE STUDY 7: THOMAS KALAMARA

Thomas Kalamara is a 17-year-old young man who complained of severe pain on the right side and immediately collapsed. He was rushed to the emergency room. Chest x-ray revealed a collapse of his right lung. He is being taken to the OR for immediate surgery.

Report 5.8: Operative Report

Transcription Hint

Listen for these difficult terms:

pneumothorax	blebs
pneumothoraces	latissimus
Surgiport	2-0 Vicryl
apical	Scarpa's layer
bullous	4-0 Monocryl
emphysematous bullae	

PRO TIP: PROOFREADING METHODS

Compiled by on-line MTs for MT Daily (www.angelfire.com/mt.2)

- **Proofread while Transcribing.** The experienced MT's mind is continuously engaged—listening, keying, checking, listening again, rechecking—to ensure that each moment of dictation is reflected on the screen in accurately keyed words, punctuation, style, and format.

- **Proofread after Transcribing.** Beginners *may* proofread while transcribing but *must* do so after transcribing the entire report. Go back to the beginning, replay the dictation, and fill in any blanks. Print out the document and proofread it again, watching for errors that were not spotted on the screen.

- **Proofread with a Mental Checklist.**

___ **Grammar:** Are all sentences complete where warranted? Are pronouns (he/she/it) used consistently throughout the report? Are verb tenses consistent (is/was, are/were, etc.)?

___ **Mechanics:** Are paragraphs labeled or headed properly? Does the content of the paragraphs fit under the heading given? Are directional terms consistent? Do all dates fall within the admission/discharge dates dictated? Are there any abbreviations in the diagnoses or procedures? Are drug brand names capitalized, and generic names shown in lowercase? Are indentations consistent, and are there no widow/orphan lines? Use your View Page feature to look at the entire page at one time.

___ **Punctuation:** Is all punctuation correct (commas, semicolons, apostrophes, colons, quotation marks, dashes, parentheses, slashes, periods)? Are hyphens used properly?

___ **Spelling:** Have you checked the document with the spell check feature of your word processor? Are there any sound-alike words that the spelling checker won't catch?

- **Proofread from Other Angles:** When you think you have keyed the words correctly, read the report from a new angle: in reverse from the bottom of the report to the top, or "farmer style" from the right side of the page to the left, then from left to right, checking for errors on each pass across the "field."

ASSESSING TRANSCRIPTION SKILLS

Demonstrate your mastery of the terminology, editing/proofreading, and document transcription skills presented in this chapter by completing the following activities.

USING MEDICAL REFERENCES

Use the appropriate medical reference to locate the correct spelling and additional usage information for the words below. (If the reference is not available, use the glossary in this text.) Circle the correct spelling, then write a sentence using the word correctly.

1. pneumothorax pneumothorix pneumothoracs

____

2. broncholes bronchiols bronchioles

____

3. abscess absess abcsess

____

4. theophyllin theophyline theophylline

____

5. pneumonitus pneumanitis pneumonitis

____

6. bronciectasis bronchiectasis bronchiectasus

____

7. thyromegaly thyromagely thyroidmegaly

____

8. bronchitis broncitis bronchitus

____

9. fibrous fibrus fibruos

____

10. diaphram diagphram diaphragm

____

MAKING EXPERT DECISIONS

Circle the correct word from the choices in parentheses.

1. (Inspiratory/Expiratory) wheezing was noted as the patient breathed out.
2. The patient had a ventilation (perfusion/profusion) scan to assess the pulmonary function.
3. The patient reports having difficulty breathing while laying down. She stated that she had two-pillow (orthopnea/dyspnea).
4. Sounds heard on inspiration and expiration were normal indicating (vesicular/vascular) breathing.
5. Lungs revealed good air entry and vesicular breathing. No rales or (course/coarse) rhonchi were heard.
6. Utilizing a stethoscope, the physician performed (auscultation/percussion) of the lung fields.
7. Air exchange takes place in the (bronchi/alveoli).
8. The patient stated that she could not (breath/breathe) through her nose.
9. Only the left lower lobe of the lung was removed during the (pneumonectomy/lobectomy).
10. During the hospital course, this (regime/regimen) was tried and deemed successful.

TRANSCRIBING PROFESSIONAL DOCUMENTS

Transcribe the document named Assessment 5 from tape. Before you key, review the document formatting guidelines. Proofread your transcribed document and revise it until you think it is error-free.

PERFORMANCE REPORT

Name____Date __________

Document	Description	Date Completed	Document Processing Speed (If Available)	Document Appraisal M=Mailable MC=Mailable w/corrections NM=Not Mailable
Report 5.1	Discharge Summary			M MC NM
Report 5.2	Discharge Summary			M MC NM
Report 5.3	Consultation Letter			M MC NM
Report 5.4	Discharge Summary			M MC NM
Report 5.5	Office Note			M MC NM
Report 5.6	Office Note			M MC NM
Report 5.7	Operative Report			M MC NM
Report 5.8	Operative Report			M MC NM

Comments ____

CHAPTER

6

Cardiology is the study of the heart and the blood vessels that carry blood throughout the body. Although cardiovascular diseases are the major cause of death in the United States and many other Western societies, advances in surgical techniques over the past few decades have resulted in a significant decline in the death rate from heart disease. Medical transcriptionists working in cardiology are constantly challenged by the terminology for procedures, new drugs, and technology.

Cardiology

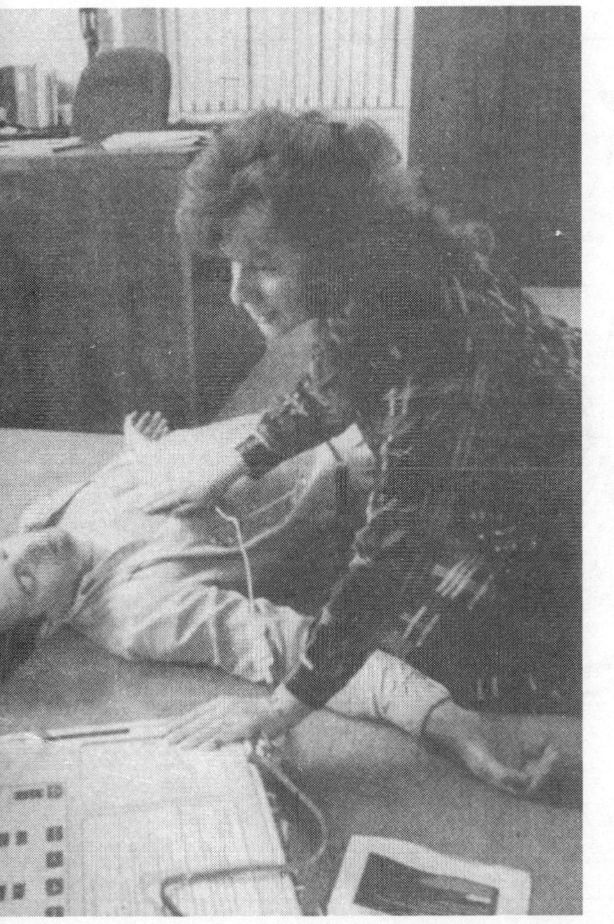

OBJECTIVES

- Use cardiology terms correctly according to the context and purpose of the dictation.
- Select and use appropriate general and specialty reference materials.
- Key cardiology documents of varying complexity and format.
- Transcribe authentic medical dictation requiring concentration and listening skill.
- Edit medical reports to conform with AAMT style guidelines.
- Proofread and correct transcripts to produce error-free documents.

EXPLORING CARDIOLOGY

Cardiology is the study of the heart and the vessels surrounding the heart.The heart is a muscular pump that circulates blood through the body via the pulmonary and systemic circulation. The physician who specializes in this field is the cardiologist. Subspecialists include interventional cardiologists, who assess the function of the heart through invasive and noninvasive procedures, and cardiovascular surgeons, who operate on the heart and its vessels.

STRUCTURE AND FUNCTION

The function of the heart is to pump blood throughout the body. The blood vessels are arranged so that each contraction of the heart pumps blood through the pulmonary circulation and the systemic circulation simultaneously, although each has a distinct purpose.

The heart and great vessels are located between the lungs in the middle of the thoracic rib cage, which is called the mediastinum. The normal heart extends from the second to the fifth intercostal space and from the right sternal border to the left midclavicular line. The heart is shaped like a triangle with the wider portion, called the base, located on the top, and the point, or apex, pointing downward and to the left (figure 6.1).

Figure 6.1
Structure of heart

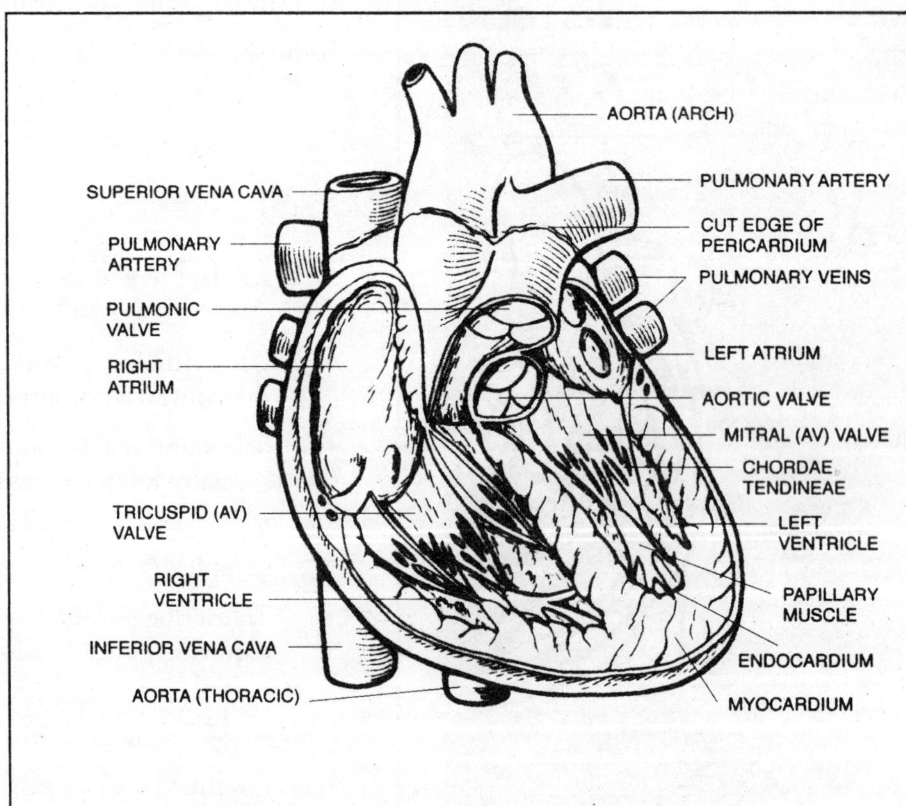

The heart is surrounded by several layers of tissue. The pericardium is a tough, fibrous protective sac that contains pericardial fluid. This fluid facilitates smooth movement of the heart muscle. The myocardium, the muscular wall of the heart, is the tissue that does the actual pumping. The endocardium is the thin membrane of tissue lining the inside of the heart.

The right side of the heart pumps blood into the lungs, and the left side simultaneously pumps blood throughout the body. A wall called the septum separates the two sides. Each side consists of two chambers: an atrium (anteroom), which holds the blood, and a ventricle, which pumps the blood. One-way valves at the entry to each chamber open only in response to pressure gradients in the blood, preventing backflow.

The atrioventricular (AV) valves separate the atria and ventricles. The right AV valve is the tricuspid, and the left AV valve is the bicuspid, or mitral valve. The AV valves open during the heart's filling phase, or diastole. This allows the ventricles to fill with blood. During the systole phase, when the heart pumps blood out of the ventricles, the valves close to prevent regurgitation of blood back into the atria.

The semilunar (SL) valves are located between the ventricles and the arteries. The pulmonic valve is in the right side of the heart, and the aortic valve is in the left side. They open during systole to allow ejection of blood from the heart.

The cardiac cycle, consisting of diastole and systole, is produced in response to an electrical current contained within specialized cells in the sinoatrial (SA) node located near the superior vena cava (figure 6.2). Because the SA node has its own rhythm, it is known as the heart's "pacemaker."

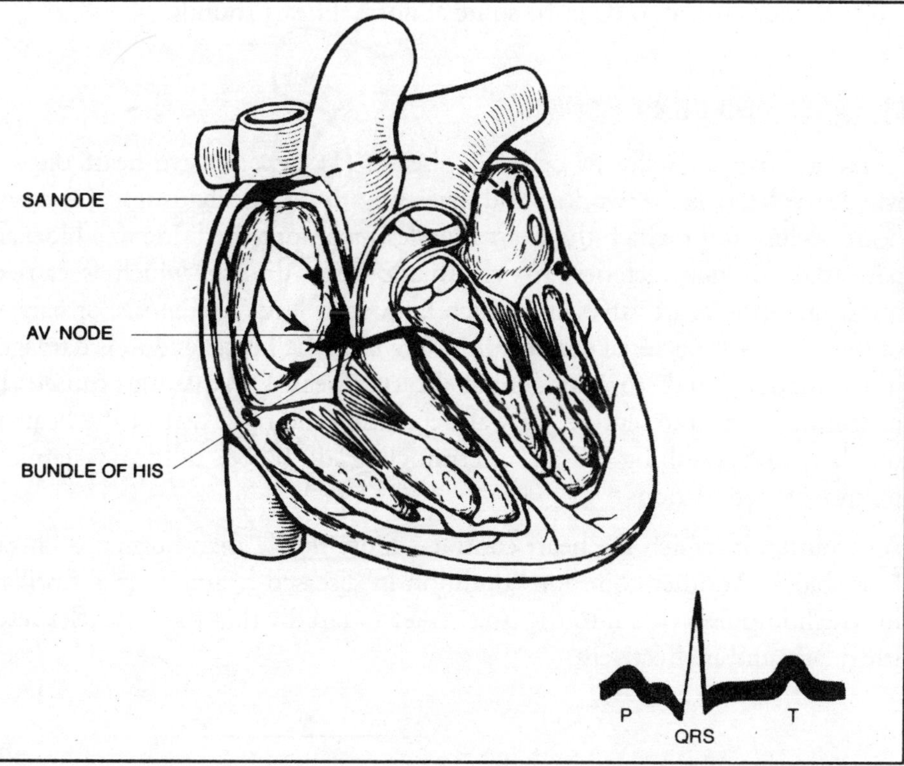

Figure 6.2
Electrical current flow in the heart

During each cardiac cycle, unoxygenated red blood cells are pumped from the right side of the heart into the lungs for oxygenation. Simultaneously, the left side of the heart pumps oxygenated blood into the body. The heart pumps between 4 and 6 liters of blood per minute throughout the body.

Common Cardiology Drugs

amlodipine vesylate
Norvasc

atenolol
Tenormin

benazepril
Lotensin

captopril
Capoten

diazoxide
Hyperstat

digoxin
Lanoxin

diltiazem
Cardizem

dipyridamole
Persantine

enalapril
Vasotec

furosemide
Lasix

heparin
Calciparine

lovastatin
Mevacor

nifedipine
Procardia

nitroglycerin
Nitrostat

pravastatin sodium
Pravachol

quinapril hydrochloride
Accupril

simvastatin
Zocor

triamterene with hydrochlorothiazide
Dyazide

triamterene
Dyrenium

verapamil hydrochloride
Calan, Isoptin

warfarin sodium
Coumadin

PHYSICAL ASSESSMENT

Cardiovascular assessment begins by noting the patient's vital signs. Abnormal respirations, blood pressure, and pulse can indicate heart disease. A bluish color around the lips (circumoral cyanosis) and/or on the nail beds may indicate decreased oxygen. Clubbing of the fingers is a sign of chronic oxygen deficiency. The carotid artery and the jugular veins in the neck reflect of the efficiency of cardiac function. The examiner uses palpation to feel for the pulses and auscultation to listen for bruits or other abnormal sounds.

The examiner may palpate the patient's chest for the point of maximal impulse (PMI). A complete assessment includes auscultation of the heart's sounds in all the "stations": aortic, pulmonic, tricuspid, and mitral valve. The rate and rhythm are noted. The start of systole, caused by the AV valves closing, is noted as S1 and serves as the reference point for the other cardiac sounds. The S2 sound represents the closure of the semilunar valves.

The heart is examined with the patient in different positions to be sure that any murmurs, or abnormal heart sounds are ascertained. The sound of a murmur is described by the intensity in terms of six grades. For example, the physician may dictate the phrase "a grade two over six systolic ejection murmur" (which is transcribed using Roman numerals II and VI). The quality and location of the murmur may be described, and the physician may use words such as gallop, whistle, and musical to describe some abnormal heart sounds.

DISEASES AND CONDITIONS

There are five main forms of heart disease: (1) hypertensive heart disease, in which the heart is overworked and gives way through exhaustion; (2) coronary heart occlusion, in which the heart muscle is malnourished due to a blockage in narrowed coronary arteries; (3) rheumatic heart disease, which is caused by infection of the heart valves and which frequently leads to stenosis, or narrowing of the valves; (4) bacterial endocarditis, in which the heart's action is damaged by inflammation; and (5) congenital heart disease, frequently caused by a malformation in the septum, or wall separating the right half of the heart from the left, and resulting in an intermingling of blood in the systemic and pulmonary circulations.

A condition in which the heart contracts more slowly than normal is known as heart block. Another common condition in diseased hearts is atrial fibrillation, in which impulses pass into the pacemaker so rapidly that the ventricles respond irregularly and ineffectively.

Heart disease can be treated by lifestyle changes (diet and exercise programs and smoking cessation), with drugs, and with surgical procedures.

TESTS AND PROCEDURES

Evaluation of the heart includes a chest x-ray to determine size and position, an electrocardiogram (ECG) to record the conduction system (figure 6.3), and an echocardiogram to record the physiology and pumping status of the heart. Other tests include angiograms, arteriograms, and venograms. Cardiac catheterization provides a visualization of the coronary arteries. A small flexible tube (catheter) is threaded from an arterial access site toward the heart. Dye is injected and the resulting pictures are viewed to determine abnormalities.

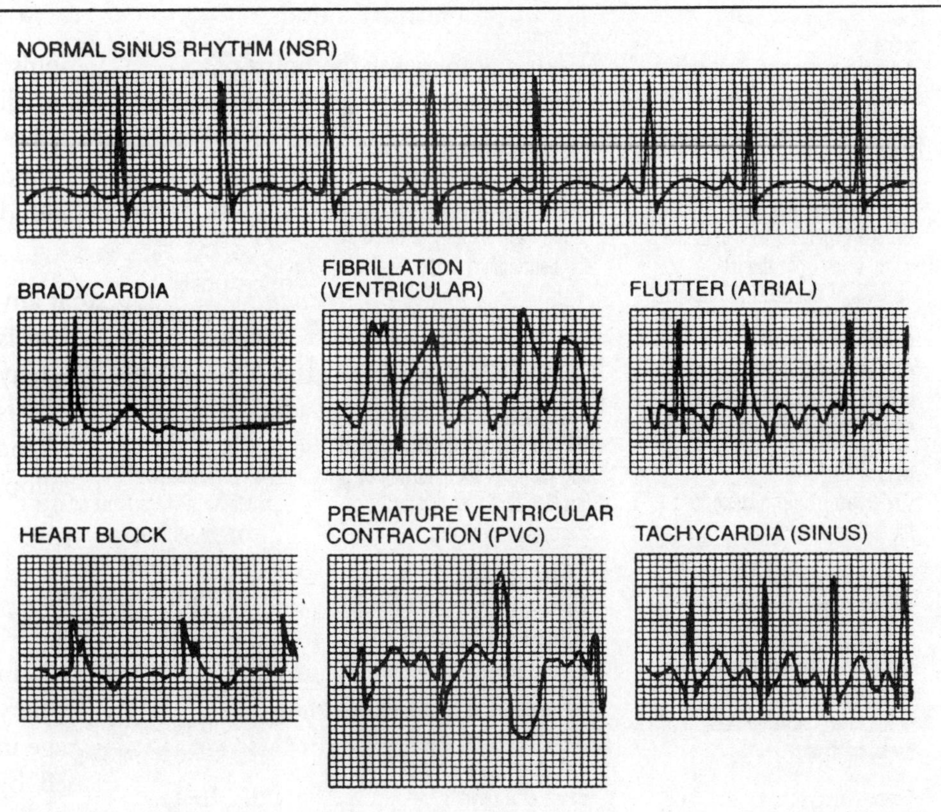

Figure 6.3 Heart rhythms in ECG tests

Drug treatments include enzyme inhibitors, antianginals, antiarrhythmics, anticoagulants, antihypertensives, beta blockers, calcium channel blockers, cardiotonics, and hypolipidemics.

Cardiac surgical procedures include coronary artery bypass surgery; embolectomy, thrombectomy, angioplasty or atherectomy to open or clear blocked arteries; valve replacement surgery; and pacemaker, internal defibrillator devices, and intravascular stent implantations.

THE VOCABULARY OF CARDIOLOGY

The following word list contains common cardiology terms as well as most of the difficult words contained in the dictation at the end of the chapter. Take time to become familiar with these words now, then review them again before you key the medical documents.

Here are suggestions for learning the vocabulary words:

1. Read and study each word for pronunciation and meaning.
2. Write each unfamiliar word from the list below on a notecard, write the definition or a paraphrase of the definition on the back, and draw a simple picture to help you learn the word.
3. Study the pronunciation, spelling, and definition of each word on your notecard, then key each word twice for reinforcement. Check the spelling.
4. Add the correctly spelled terms to your word processor's spell checker.

ambulation
(am-byoo-lay'-shun) (n) walking or moving about

anastomosis
(a-nas'-tO-mO-sis) (n) a natural or surgical connection between two blood vessels, spaces, or organs

aneurysm
(an'-yoo-rizm) (n) bulging out of an arterial wall due to a weakness in the wall

angina pectoris
(an'-ji-na/an-jI'-na pek'-tO-ris) (n) an attack of intense chest pain; also known as stenocardia

angiography
(an-jee-og'-ra-fee) (n) x-ray of blood vessels, usually after injecting a radiopaque substance

aorta
(ay-Or'-ta) (n) the main artery leaving the heart

aortic root
(ay-Or'-tik) (n) the opening of the aorta in the left ventricle of the heart

aortogram
(ay-Or'-tO-gram) (n) x-ray of the aorta after injection of a radiopaque substance

arrhythmia
(a-rith'-mee-a) (n) disturbance of normal rhythm; irregular heart beat

arteriosclerosis
(ar-teer'-ee-O-skler-O'-sis) (n) hardening of the arteries

artery
(ar'-ter-ee) (n) a vessel that carries blood away from the heart to other tissues throughout the body

ascending aorta
(n) the beginning section of the aorta, rising from the left ventricle of the heart to the arch

atherosclerosis
(ath'-er-O-skler-O'-sis) (n) buildup of fatty plaques inside arteries; a type of arteriosclerosis

atrial
(ay'-tree-al) (adj) relating to the atrium

atrioventricular
(ay'-tree-O-ven-trik'-yoo-lar) (adj) relating to both the atria (upper chambers) and the ventricles (lower chambers) in the heart, or blood flow between them

atrioventricular groove
(n) a groove visible on the outside of the heart between the atria and the ventricles

atrium
(ay'-tree-um) (n) one of the two upper chambers of the heart

attenuation
(a-ten-yoo-ay'-shun) (n) process of weakening, such as the potency of a drug or the virulence of a disease-causing germ

caliber
(kal'-i'-ber) (n) diameter of a tube or vessel, such as a blood vessel

capillary
(kap'-I-layr-ee) (n) smallest type of blood vessels

cardiac tamponade
(kar'-dee-ak tam-po-nayd') (n) compression of the venous return to the heart by fluid or blood in the pericardium

cardiomyopathy
(kar'-dee-O-mI-op'-a-thee) (n) disease of the heart muscle

catheter
(kath'-e-ter) (n) a tube inserted into the body for removing or instilling fluids for diagnostic or therapeutic purposes

catheterization
(kath'-e-ter-I-zay'-shun) (n) the insertion of a catheter

circumflex
(ser'-kum-fleks) (adj) bending around; describes anatomical structures that are shaped like an arc of a circle

collaterals
(ko-lat'-er-als) (n) accompanying, as side by side; blood vessels that branch from larger vessels

congestive heart failure
(CHF) (kon-jes'-tiv) (n) condition in which the heart is unable to pump adequate blood to the tissues and organs, often due to myocardial infarction

coronary bypass surgery
(kOr'-o-nayr-ee) (n) vein grafts or other surgical methods are used to carry blood from the aorta to branches of the coronary arteries in order to increase the flow beyond a local obstruction

coronary cusp
(n) one of the triangular parts of a heart valve

cyanosis
(cI-a-nO'-sis) (n) bluish discoloration of the skin and/or mucous membranes due to decreased amount of oxygen in the blood cells

defibrillator
(dee-fib'-ri-lay-ter) (n) an agent, measure, or machine, e.g., an electric shock, that stops fibrillation of the ventricular muscle and restores the normal beat

diaphoresis
(dI'-a-fO-ree'-sis) (n) profuse perspiration or sweating

diaphragm
(dI'-a-fram) (n) the muscle that separates the thoracic (chest) and abdominal cavities

dilatation
(dil-a-tay'-shun) (n) stretching or enlarging; dilation

distal
(dis'tal) (adj) away from a center or point of reference; toward the far end of something

dysfunction
(dis-funk'-shun) (n) abnormal or impaired function

echocardiogram
(ek-O-kar'-dee-O-gram) (n) a

sound-wave image of the heart's size, position, and motion

electrocardiogram
(ee-lek'-trO-kar'-dee-O'-gram) (n) a graphic record of electrical waves within the heart

embolism
(em'-bO-lizm) (n) blockage of a blood vessel by an abnormal object, such as a clot

endocarditis
(en'-dO-kar-dI'-tis) (n) inflammation of the endocardium and/or the heart valves

endocardium
(en-dO-kar'-dee-um) (n) inner lining of the heart

femoral
(fem'-o-ral) (adj) relating to the thigh artery or bone, the femur

gross
(grOs) (adj) visible to the naked eye

hemodynamic
(hee'-mO-dI-nam'-ik) (adj) relating to the mechanics of blood circulation

hemostasis
(hee'-mO-stay-sis/hee-mos'-ta-sis) (n) stopping bleeding either naturally through blood coagulation, mechanically (as with surgical clamps), or chemically (with drugs)

hypokinesis
(hI'-pO-ki-nee'-sis) (n) decreased or slow motor reaction to stimulus

hypoperfusion
(hI'-pO-per-fyoo'-zhun) (n) lower-than-normal passage of a liquid through an organ or body part

infarction
(in-fark'-shun) (n) formation of dead tissue as a result of diminished or stopped blood flow to thé tissue area

inferior
(in-fee'-ree-Or) (adj) lower; below; of lesser value

intimal
(in'-ti-mal) (adj) relating to the innermost lining of a part, especially of a blood vessel; (n) intima

intravenous
(IV) (in'-tra-vee'-nus) (adj) within or by way of a vein

ischemia
(is-kee'-mee-a) (n) decreased blood supply due to obstruction, such as narrowing of the blood vessels

lesion
(lee'-zhun) (n) general term for any visible, circumscribed injury to the skin; such as a wound, sore, rash, or mass

mammary
(mam'-a-ree) (adj) relating to the breast

millicuries
(mil'-i-kyoo'-rees) (n) a unit of radioactivity, abbreviated mc

mitral
(mI'-tral) (adj) relating to the bicuspid or mitral valve of the heart, between the atrium and the ventricle on the left side of the heart

murmur
(mer'-mer) (n) abnormal heart sound

myocardial
(mI-O-kar'-dee-al) (adj) relating to the myocardium, the heart muscle

obtuse
(ob-toos') (adj) dull or blunt; not pointed or acute

occlusion
(o-kloo'-zhun) (n) blockage, such as coronary occlusion

oscilloscope
(o-sil'-O-scOp) (n) an instrument which displays electrical oscillations (waves) on a screen

oximetry
(ok-sim'-e-tree) (n) measuring the amount of oxygen combined with the hemoglobin in a blood sample

pallor
(pal-'or) (n) abnormal paleness of the skin; deficiency of color

palpitations
(pal-pi-tay'-shuns) (n) stronger and more rapid heartbeats as felt by the patient; pounding or throbbing of the heart

parenteral
(pa-ren'-ter-al) (adj) not through the digestive system, such as introduction of nutrients into the veins or under the skin

paroxysmal
(par-ok-siz'-mal) (adj) relating to or recurring in paroxysms (sudden, severe attacks of symptoms or convulsions)

patent
(pa'-tent) (adj) open; unblocked

pedal
(ped'-al or pE'dal) (adj) relating to the foot

pericardial
(per-i-kar'-dee-al) (adj) surrounding the heart; relating to the pericardium

pericardium
(per-i-kar'-dee-um) (n) sac around the heart allowing movement without friction

peripheral vascular disease
(pe-rif'-e-ral vas'-kyoo-lar) (n) any disorder affecting the blood circulatory system, except the heart

phlebitis
(fle-bI'-tis) (n) inflammation of a vein

phlebotomy
(fle-bot'-O-mee) (n) incision into a vein for drawing blood

photon
(fO'-ton) (n) a unit of radiant energy or light intensity

prolapse
(prO-laps') (n) dropping of an organ from its normal position, a sinking down

proximal
(prok'-si-mal) (adj) nearest to a point of reference or center of the body

radiopaque
(ray-dee-O-payk') (adj) opaque to x-rays or other radiation; an injection of a radiopaque dye or substance may be used to visualize areas of the body by x-ray

ramus
(ray'-mus) (n) branch, especially of a nerve or blood vessel

regurgitation
(ree-ger'-ji-tay'-shun) (n) a backward flowing, as a backflow of blood through a defective heart valve or the bringing up of gas or undigested food from the stomach

retrograde
(ret'-rO-grayd) (adj) moving or going backward

rheumatic fever
(roo-mat'-ik fee'-ver) (n) fever following infection with Streptococcus bacteria; may affect the joints, skin, and heart

saphenous vein
(sa-fee'-nus vayn) (n) either of two main veins in the leg that drain blood from the foot

scan
(n) scanning a tissue, organ, or system using a special apparatus that displays and records its image, such as computer tomography (CAT scan); the image so obtained

sheath
(n) structure surrounding an organ, body part, or object

sinus rhythm
(si'-nus rith'-um) (n) normal cardiac rhythm

stenocardia
(sten-O-kar'-dee-a) (n) an attack of intense chest pain; also called angina pectoris

stenosis
(ste-nO'-sis) (n) narrowing or constriction of a passageway or opening, such as a blood vessel

sublingual
(sub-ling'-gwahl) (adj) beneath the tongue

thermodilution
(ther'-mO-di-loo'-shun) (n) method of determining cardiac output; involves injecting a cold liquid into the bloodstream and measuring the temperature change downstream

thrombophlebitis
(throm'-bO-fle-bI'-tis) (n). inflammation of a vein with clot formation (thrombus)

tomographic
(tO-mog'-ra-feek) (adj) referring to an x-ray technique which displays an organ or tissue at a particular depth

vascular
(vas'-kyoo-lar) (adj) relating to the blood vessels

venous
(vee'-nus) (adj) relating to a vein or veins

ventricle
(ven'-tri-kl) (n) either of the two lower chambers of the heart

ventriculogram
(ven-trik'-yoo-lO-gram) (n) an x-ray of the ventricles

ventriculography
(ven-trik-yoo-log'-ra-fee) (n) x-ray visualization of heart ventricles after injection of a radiopaque substance

xiphoid
(zif'-oyd) (adj) referring to the xiphoid process, the cartilage at the lower end of the sternum (breast bone)

ABBREVIATIONS

ACG	angiocardiography
AICA	anterior inferior communicating artery
AS	aortic stenosis
ASD	arterial septal defect
ASHD	arteriosclerotic heart disease
BBB	bundle-branch block
CAD	coronary artery disease
CC	cardiac catheterization
CCU	coronary care unit
CF	circumflex [artery]
CHF	congestive heart failure
CPR	cardiopulmonary resuscitation
CV	cardiovascular
DVT	deep vein thrombosis
ECG or EKG	electrocardiogram
ICA	internal carotid artery
IMA	internal mammary artery
IV	intravenous
LAD	left anterior descending coronary artery
LCA	left coronary artery
LCF	left circumflex
LIMA	left internal mammary artery
LMCA	left main coronary artery
LPA	left pulmonary artery
MCL	midclavicular line
MI	myocardial infarction
MPA	main pulmonary artery
MS	mitral stenosis
MVP	mitral valve prolapse
OM	obtuse marginal [coronary artery]
PA	pulmonary artery
PAT	paroxysmal atrial tachycardia
PDA	posterior descending artery; patent ductus arteriosis
PICA	posterior inferior communicating artery
PMI	point of maximal impulse
PVC	premature ventricular contraction
RCA	right coronary artery
RPA	right pulmonary artery
S-A	sinoatrial node
SFA	superficial femoral artery
VSD	ventricular septal defect

EXERCISE 6.1: RECOGNIZING LOOK-ALIKES AND SOUND-ALIKES

Below is a list of frequently used words that look alike and/or sound alike. Study the meaning and pronunciation of each set of words, then read each sentence carefully and circle the word in parentheses that correctly completes the meaning.

endocardial	within the heart
myocardial	relating to the heart muscle

profuse	(adj) overabundant
perfuse	(v) to spread about

pericardial	surrounding the heart
precordial	in front of the heart

pulse	regular, rhythmic beat
plus	increased by or added to

inter-	between
intra-	within
infra-	below or under

pedal	(adj) relating to the foot
pedal	(n) a foot-operated mechanism
petal	(n) part of a flower

nitrate	a salt of nitric acid; medication
nitrite	a salt of nitrous acid; found on urinalysis

reinjected	injected again
reinfected	to become infected again (as with an organism or pathogen)

palpation	examination by touching
palpitation	rapid or fluttering heartbeat

recent	(adj) not long ago
resent	(v) to be annoyed at

1. The patient's (intraocular, interocular) pressure was within normal limits.
2. A (recent, resent) blood pressure check reveals the patient to be hypertensive.
3. The posterior tibial (pulses, pluses) were 2+/4+.
4. The patient had 1+ (pedal, petal) edema.
5. The patient was given an (injection, infection) of amoxicillin (intramuscularly, intermuscularly).
6. Her urine shows no white cells, trace leukocytes, and positive (nitrates, nitrites).
7. The patient has no tenderness to deep (palpation, palpitation).
8. She is complaining of (palpations, palpitations) after drinking several cups of coffee.
9. His night sweats are so (profuse, perfuse) that he regularly soaks his pajamas.
10. His previous heart surgeries resulted in (pericardial, precordial) adhesions.

EXERCISE 6.2: MATCHING SOUND AND SPELLING

The numbered list that follows shows the phonetic spelling of hard-to-spell words. Sound out the word, then write the correct spelling in the blank space provided. Each of the words can be found in the glossary or in the drug list in appendix C.

1. zif'-oyd ______
2. a-rith'-mee-a ______
3. a-nas'-tO-mO-sis ______
4. ni-fed'-i-peen ______
5. lIs-in'-O-pril ______
6. lO-va-stat'-in ______
7. lee'-zhun ______
8. o-kloo'-zhun ______
9. an'-yoo-rizm ______
10. vee'-nus ______
11. te-ray'-zO-sin ______
12. pal-pi-tay'-shuns ______
13. an-jI'-na ______
14. ver-ap'-a-mil ______
15. cap'-tO-pril ______

EXERCISE 6.3: CHOOSING WORDS FROM CONTEXT

When transcribing dictation, the medical transcriptionist frequently needs to determine the word that correctly completes the sentence based on the situation. From the list of words below, select the term that meaningfully completes each statement.

ambulating	diaphoresis	ischemia
arrhythmia	dilatation	oximetry
artery	hemodynamic	prolapse
attenuation	infarction	proximal
catheter	intravenous	ventricular

1. If the patient had an MI, it means he or she had a myocardial ________________.
2. The patient is ________________ well, with the use of a quad cane.
3. Due to dehydration, we will need to place her on ________________ fluids.
4. The blockage was not in a main ________________.
5. While my father was in the hospital, he was monitored by pulse ________________.
6. The patient's ECG showed left ________________ dysfunction.
7. After the surgery, he needed a transfusion to return him to his usual ________________ state.
8. The patient's mitral valve ________________ meant she needed to take an antibiotic whenever she had dental work done.
9. A vaccine gives you an (a) ________________ of the disease.
10. He needed a Foley ________________ inserted to collect the urine.

EXERCISE 6.4: PAIRING WORDS AND MEANINGS

For each definition provided below, locate the term on the list that best matches the definition. Write the letter of the term in the space provided beside the definition.

A. angiography	F. hypertension	J. ramus
B. aorta	G. ischemia	K. stenosis
C. atrium	H. myocardial	L. thermodilution
D. diaphoresis	I. pericardial	M. ventricle
E. hemostasis		

1. concerning the middle layer of the heart walls ________________
2. branch of a nerve or blood vessel ________________
3. method of cardiac output determination ________________
4. study describing the blood vessels of the heart ________________
5. main trunk of the arterial system ________________
6. decreased blood supply to a given body part ________________
7. abnormal narrowing of a passageway or opening ________________
8. profuse sweating ________________
9. either of the two upper chambers of the heart ________________
10. cessation of bleeding ________________

EXERCISE 6.5: CREATING TERMS FROM WORD FORMS

In the following exercise, combine prefixes, root words, and suffixes to create medical words that fit the definitions below. Fill in the blanks with the words you construct.

a-	no, without	sub-	beneath, under
brady-	slow	tachy-	swift, rapid
cardio-	heart	-cardia/o	heart
circum-	around	-flect/-flex	bend
dia-	through, complete	-function	work, action, operation
dys-	pain, improper, short	-gram	letter, picture, printout
electro-	current, conduction	-lingual	tongue
hemo-	blood, bleeding	-pathy	disease
intra-	within	-pnea	breathing, breath
myo-	muscle	-stasis	stopping, halting
peri-	around, near	-stolic	sent, sending
steno-	compressed	-ventricular	front, ventricle

1. rapid heartbeat ______________________
2. under the tongue ______________________
3. a squeezing pain in the heart ______________________
4. the stopping of bleeding ______________________
5. around the heart ______________________
6. shortness of breath ______________________
7. sending through (blood into heart) ______________________
8. bent around ______________________
9. condition characterized by a slow heartbeat ______________________
10. complete picture ______________________

EDITING MEDICAL DOCUMENTS

In this section you will perfect your word use and grammar skills. These skills will help you edit and proofread medical reports for correct language, punctuation, format, and meaning. The special focus of this chapter's section is the correct use of special punctuation marks.

USING DASHES, QUOTATION MARKS, AND PARENTHESES

Dashes

Use dashes to set off interrupting phrases from the rest of the sentence. They indicate a change in thought or a side comment not essential to the meaning of the sentence. Use them sparingly, especially in any type of formal document.

> Thank you for seeing Mrs. Johnson–especially on such short notice–for evaluation of her chest pain.

Note: Key dashes with no spaces before or after them. Proportional fonts such as New Times Roman, the default for Word 6 and 7 and WordPerfect 6.1 and 7 for Windows, include a special dash character. If you are using a monospaced font such as Courier, create a dash by keying two hyphens.

Quotation Marks

Use quotation marks to surround the exact words someone has spoken. The marks should appear in pairs, with one set at the beginning of the quote and the other at the end. The placement of other punctuation marks with quotes frequently causes confusion.

Always key a period and comma inside the quotation marks.

> The surgeon said, "We will first repair the heart valves and then deal with her coronary artery disease."

> "I cannot tolerate pain," the patient complained, "but I know I need this surgery."

Place a colon or semicolon outside quotation marks.

> These are her "requirements": Arrive on time and attend all sessions.

> He said "thrombophlebitis"; I'm sure of it.

Place a question mark outside the quotation marks if the entire sentence is a question but inside if only the quoted words are a question.

> Was she the physician who said, "No two surgeries are alike"?
>
> "If the pain subsides in two days," she asked, "should I continue taking the medicine?"

History and physical reports may begin with a chief complaint. If the chief complaint is dictated in first person, key it in quotation marks.

> CHIEF COMPLAINT: "I have been throwing up for two days."

If the quoted material is not a complete sentence, do not start the quote with a capital letter (unless the first word is a proper noun or an acronym).

> The patient says his left knee "doesn't feel right."
> [Contractions are acceptable in direct quotes but not in other dictation.]
>
> The patient said he had "some kind of x-ray test" on his back but did not know the name of the study.

Use quotation marks to draw attention to words and phrases or to designate slang, cliches, or nicknames.

> The patient's condition was "touch-and-go" for the first 24 hours but then gradually stabilized.
>
> I saw your patient Richard "Bud" Goodman for evaluation of his hypertension.

Use quotation marks to set off titles of magazine or newspaper articles and chapters of a book. The titles of magazines, newspapers, brochures, and books are placed in italics (in proportional spaced fonts such as Times New Roman) or underlined (in Courier).

> All of our pregnant patients receive the *Eating For Two* brochure.
>
> According to "Guide to a Healthy Heart," an article in the *Health Nuts* magazine, individuals who maintain a low-fat diet and who exercise regularly lower their risk of heart attack.

Parentheses

Use parentheses to enclose side thoughts or words not vital to the main idea of the sentence.

> The sodium level was 131 (normal).
>
> According to the surgery schedule (usually a reliable source), Michelle Brown will be admitted for excisional biopsy tomorrow.

Use parentheses to enclose acronyms or abbreviations.

> Mr. Johnson underwent transurethral resection of the prostate (TURP) on the day of admission.
>
> He will be referred for percutaneous transluminal coronary angioplasty (PTCA) of his right coronary artery lesion.

Use parentheses to enclose numbers when a list is given in paragraph form.

> The past history is remarkable for (1) coronary artery disease treated with PTCA, (2) diabetes mellitus, controlled on insulin therapy, and (3) hypertension, not well controlled.

If parentheses enclose a complete sentence that does not interrupt another sentence, place the period inside the parentheses.

> The risks and benefits of the procedure were explained to the patient, and he opted to proceed. (The signed consent form is on the chart.)

If parentheses enclose an interrupting statement within a sentence, do not place a period inside the parentheses.

> The procedure and its risks (bleeding, infection, possible need for transfusion) were explained to the patient.
>
> His risk factors for coronary artery disease include history of smoking (he quit one year ago), positive family history, and elevated cholesterol level.

EXERCISE 6.6: EDITING FOR CORRECT PUNCTUATION

Read the following sentences from a medical report and add the appropriate special punctuation marks.

1. CHIEF COMPLAINT: I think I'm having a heart attack. [the patient's statement]
2. Gertrude Trudy Schmidt presented to my office today. [Indicate that Trudy is a nickname.]
3. Because her chest pain did not resolve with sublingual nitroglycerin, she was transported to the emergency department by a family member her son.
4. The patient states that his knee doesn't feel right when he walks. [a partial quote]
5. The patient's history has been well documented on previous admissions please see old records.
6. In accordance with his wishes, the patient was made a DNR do not resuscitate.
7. DISCHARGE DIAGNOSIS: Acute bacterial endocarditis, resolving.
8. Please set up an appointment with Dr. Edwards you can get his phone number from my secretary at your earliest convenience.
9. The patient has a history of one chronic obstructive pulmonary disease, two congestive heart failure, and three hypertension.
10. If the infection does not respond to amoxicillin, we may need to call in one of the big guns like cephalexin. [mark the slang phrase]

EXERCISE 6.7: PROOFREADING REVIEW

Read the following report section and look for errors in punctuation, plural vs. singular word forms, subject-verb agreement, complete sentences, pronoun-reference agreement, capitalization, and special punctuation marks such as quotation marks. Circle the errors, then key the report with the errors corrected.

Left heart catheterization and coronary angiography was performed via Judkins Technique using the rite femoral artery. hemodynamic recordings was made in the ascending aorta at rest.

blood samples for oximetry were obtained from the pulmonary artery and ascending aorta. Repeat hemodynamic recordings were made on pull-back. The catheter was then withdrawn and direct pressure was applied to the right femoral artery. Both good hemostasis and petal pluses were obtained. the patient tolerated the procedure well and left the laboratory in satisfactory condition.

WHERE CAN I FIND THE ANSWER?

As you transcribe dictation, you may hear unfamiliar words or terms. A variety of reference sources are available to help you locate answers to your questions. One of the important types of references for medical transcriptionists is described below. Read the information; then if you have access to the reference discussed, explore its capabilities.

MEDICAL REFERENCES: DRUG BOOKS

Every medical transcriptionist needs an up-to-date, complete pharmaceutical reference. There are many drug references, but only a select few contain the information MTs need—the correct spelling and the generic/brand names of 20,000-plus medications. Since pharmaceutical companies place several new drugs on the market each year, it is wise to purchase a book that is geared to the medical professional and updated annually.

Which book should I buy?

The two most common drug references are *The American Drug Index* and the *Physicians' Desk Reference.* Of these, the former is designed specifically for medical transcriptionists.

The American Drug Index resembles a word book in that it provides only the basic information of product name, generic name, possible doses, number of tablets in a bottle, and two or three words about the product's use. The *Physicians' Desk Reference* lists the medication names alphabetically in three sections: by manufacturer, by brand and generic name, and by product category. The fourth section shows pictures of the product ("Product Identification Guide"). The voluminous fifth section contains the product information.

How do I use the book?

Search carefully for drug names to ensure you do not confuse two drugs with similar pronunciations but with radically different uses. For example, Xanax, pronounced "zay-naks," is a common antianxiety drug. Zantac, pronounced "zan-tak," is an antiulcer medication. Drug dosage can sometimes narrow a search. For example, Xanax is available in 0.25, 0.5, 1, and 2 mg tablets, and Zantac is offered in 150 and 300 mg tablets.

What if I still can't find it?

Use the patient's chart, if available, to check prescribed medications. A friendly pharmacist is also a reliable source, but save this person as a last resource. If you do call the druggist, remember to ask if the drug is a brand or generic. Keep a journal or "cheat sheet" of drug names to save time looking up the information in the future. By the time your drug book is a year old, you probably will have penciled in several new medications.

TRANSCRIBING CARDIOLOGY DOCUMENTS

In this section your goal is to prepare for the work of transcription through transcribing first from a printed document and then from dictation on tape. The model document that follows illustrates the generally accepted format for the **radiology report**, the medical document featured in this chapter.

BASIC FORMAT: THE RADIOLOGY REPORT

The radiology report is a description of the findings and interpretations of x-ray procedures. Dictated by a radiologist after reviewing the films or test results, the report can focus on bone and joint films, soft tissue films, or special studies of the internal organs. The major diagnostic procedures include roentgenograms (basic x-rays), CT scans (computerized tomography scans), MRI scans (magnetic resonance imaging scans), nuclear medicine procedures such as thyroid scans and bone scans with an injection or infusion of radioactive contrast, and fluoroscopic examinations.

Required Headings/Content

Standard components include preliminary information, the type of examination performed and area of focus—for example, chest, skull—plus the contrast media used, and the findings or impressions.

Turnaround Time

The usual turnaround time is 12 to 24 hours or even less. However, some hospitals make a voice report available as soon as the radiologist dictates the report.

RADIOLOGY REPORT

1" top and side margins

DEPARTMENT OF RADIOLOGY

use left justification

PATIENT NAME: Jim Andrews
MEDICAL RECORD #: 7093578
DATE: 1/12/XX
DOB: 12/23/56
SEX: Male
ROOM #: 804
REQUESTING PHYSICIAN: Sondra Southward, MD

ds

STRESS THALLIUM SCAN WITH REINJECTION ← **test or x-ray name in all caps**

At the time of peak exercise, 4 mc of thallium-201 chloride was injected intravenously and exercise was continued for at least an additional minute. Single-photon emission computer tomographic study, as well as a planar LAO 45 image, was obtained immediately after exercise. The patient returned at least three hours later and was reinjected with 1 mc of thallium-201 chloride. Thirty minutes later, a single-photon emission computer tomographic exam was obtained. The SPECT studies were reconstructed with images obtained in the short, horizontal, long, and vertical long axes. Comparison was made with standard data base, as well as bull's eye plots. Images were evaluated on film, as well as on the computer console.

ds

Images reveal some mild fixed hypoperfusion of the inferior wall, compared to the rest of the myocardium. This is probable on the basis of diaphragmatic attenuation. Heart appears smaller on stress than it does on redistribution imaging. Findings consistent with normal response to exercise.

ds

Quantitative analysis reveals several inconsistent areas of hypoperfusion. The inferior wall is relatively unremarkable on these plots.

ds

IMPRESSION: NO EVIDENCE FOR STRESS-INDUCED ISCHEMIA.

qs

____

J. Kronin, MD

ds

JK:XX
D: 1/12/XX
T: 1/12/XX

PREPARING TO TRANSCRIBE

To prepare for transcribing dictation, key the radiology report above. You will later key the identical report from tape. Follow these guidelines:

- Study the format and organization of the report.
- Review the word list presented earlier in this chapter.
- Consult reference books for words or formatting rules that are unfamiliar.
- Proofread your final copy by comparing it to the printed version.

CASES FOR TRANSCRIPTION

In this section you will transcribe medical dictation from tape. Your goal is to produce error-free documents. Read this chapter's Pro Tip (following the case studies) for helpful hints from experienced MTs. Then follow these steps for each dictation:

1. Review the case study and the model report formats from this and earlier chapters.
2. Transcribe the dictation, leaving spaces for words you cannot hear or do not understand.
3. Carefully proofread each document and correct as many errors as you can. Use your reference materials to help you identify missing words.
4. Listen to the tape again and correct all remaining errors.

Repeat these steps until you produce an error-free document. Then complete the Performance Report at the end of the chapter, attach it to the top of the transcripts, and submit them to your instructor for evaluation.

CASE STUDY 1: JIM ANDREWS

The patient is a 63-year-old male who was admitted to the Intensive Care Unit with chest pain radiating down to the left hand, diaphoresis, and pallor. His physical examination, blood work, and ECG were within normal limits during a routine checkup two months ago.

Report 6.1: Office Note

Report 6.2: Radiology Report of Stress Thallium Scan

Transcription Hint

Listen for these terms:
thallium-201 chloride
LAO 45 image
SPECT studies

Report 6.3: Consultation Letter

CASE STUDY 2: CHRIS BELTRE

The patient is a 50-year-old male admitted for evaluation of coronary artery disease. His health history included a previous heart attack. During his last admission, the patient had severe chest pain and was diagnosed with acute anterior wall myocardial infarction. A cardiac catheterization showed severe left main coronary artery disease, and subsequent bypass surgery followed by a stress test showed persistent abnormalities at peak exercise. Cardiac catheterization was advised to evaluate the coronary disease and guide further therapy.

Report 6.4: Cardiac Catheterization Lab Report

CASE STUDY 3: JOSHUA WARREN

Twenty-six-year-old Joshua Warren experienced mild chest pains while playing racquetball and subsequently was admitted to the emergency room. A treadmill stress test was ordered to determine the possibility of cardiovascular disease.

Report 6.5 Treadmill Stress Test

Transcription Hint

Use figures for transcribing electrocardiographic chest leads and capital letters for waves and segments. The leads are V_1 through V_6 and aVL, aVR, and aVF. (It is also acceptable to transcribe the L, R, and F as subscript letters.) Waves include P, Q, R, S, T, and U and their combinations.

CASE STUDY 4: BABY GIRL SMITH

This female infant was born prematurely at approximately $24\frac{1}{2}$ weeks gestation. Cardiovascular surgeons will perform a ductus arteriosus ligation to stabilize the baby's heart function.

Report 6.6 Operative Report

CASE STUDY 5: JUNICE MONROE

Junice Monroe is a 65-year-old woman who presented with symptoms of congestive heart failure and lung collapse. A CT scan and echocardiogram revealed a cardiac tumor, which surgeons will remove.

Report 6.7 Operative Report

Transcription Hint

Listen for these difficult terms:
atelectasis
pedicle
trilobulated
pacifico
foramen ovale
autologous
pledgeted

CASE STUDY 6: LOUIS FRAMPTON

This 65-year-old man has a history of atherosclerosis and suffered a heart attack three years ago. He presented to the ER with chest pain, profuse sweating, and shortness of breath, which his nitroglycerin tablets had failed to relieve.

Report 6.8 Discharge Summary

Transcription Hint

Listen for these new laboratory and pharmaceutical terms:
SMA-20
BUN 21
Isordil
Slow-K
Dalmane
Lasix

PRO TIP: EDITING AND MAKING CORRECTIONS

By Kathleen Offman, CMT

Editing while transcribing can range from making simple to complex choices. Some simple editing includes adding punctuation, making a word singular when it is dictated as plural, or correcting subject-verb agreement, such as changing *was* to *were*. More complex editing requires knowing the difference between glaring inaccuracies and technically correct, but perhaps poorly stated, information.

So how do you decide if it is prudent to make a few changes to the content of a dictation? Here is a rule of thumb: If the dictation *makes sense,* leave it as is. The physician alone knows all the details of the case and most likely wants to convey the information in the manner presented. On the other hand, if the dictation is missing an obvious piece of information that you can verify as correct, or if slight rephrasing would make muddled content clearer, you may carefully edit in these situations.

On the job, you can ask for help if you are unsure of a statement's accuracy. Never guess. Ask someone with good transcription habits and someone whose judgment you value. But if another person listens to the dictation and suggests what to key, remember that ultimately you are responsible for the content of the report you transcribe. Concentrate on providing accurate, clear, complete reports, and consider instructor guidelines, hospital or department policy, and physician preference. If you still cannot make a decision, leave a blank space.

Situations Requiring Editing

Experienced transcriptionists identify the following inaccuracies in word use as acceptable to edit:

- **Tense:** Physicians frequently change tense from present to past while dictating. Choose a tense and use it consistently.
- **Articles *a* and *an*:** Use *a* before words beginning with a consonant sound; use *an* before words beginning with a vowel or vowel sound.
- **Prepositions:** Use a more accurate preposition when warranted. For example, change *into* to *in* in the following statement: "An incision was made into the artery."
- **Forms of a word:** Improve awkward phrasing in dictation. For example, change *refilling* to *refill* in the following statement:"He will need a *refilling* of his medications."
- **Made-up words:** Physicians sometimes coin words ("nonremarkable," for example) or combine words that are difficult to verify. Use your dictionary and the context to make the correct choice.

ASSESSING TRANSCRIPTION SKILLS

Demonstrate your mastery of the terminology, editing/proofreading, and document transcription skills presented in this chapter by completing the following activities.

USING MEDICAL REFERENCES

Use the appropriate medical reference to locate the correct spelling and additional usage information for the words below. (If the reference is not available, use the glossary in this text.) Circle the correct spelling, then write a sentence using the word correctly.

1. benazepril benazipril benazaprel

   ____

2. Cardezen Cardizim Cardizem

   ____

3. Acupril Accuprill Accupril

   ____

4. anurism aneurysm anurysm

   ____

5. arrhythmia arrythmea arythmea

   ____

6. parenteral parentaral parenterel

   ____

7. paroxismal paroxysmal peroxsymal

   ____

8.	reumatic	rheumatic	rhuematic
9.	xiphioid	xipoid	xiphoid
10.	Coumidin	Coumadin	Cumadin

MAKING EXPERT DECISIONS

Circle the correct word from the choices in parentheses.

1. During the physical examination, the physician performed (auscultation/oscillation/oscitation/osculation) and percussion to hear the chest sounds.
2. Mr. Yoshida's blood pressure was 200/90, indicating (hypertension/hypertensin/hypotension).
3. Mrs. Lockhard's blood pressure was 90/60, indicating (hypertension/hypertensin/hypotension).
4. The cardiac catheterization showed that, though major vessels were obstructed, there was sufficient (canalization/cannulation/recanalization/rechannelization) that medical therapy, rather than bypass, could be tried.
5. After angioplasty, the patient's vessel restenosed, so a (canalization/cannulation/recanalization/rechannelization) was done.
6. (Canalization/Cannulation/Recanalization/Rechannelization) was done via the femoral artery with a JL4 guiding catheter.
7. There was diffuse inflammation of the (pericardium/precordium/pericardial/precordial) and congestive heart failure.
8. The patient complains of (pericardium/precordium/pericardial/precordial) chest pain.
9. An (osteal/ostial) lesion was noted near the takeoff of the posterior descending artery from the right coronary artery.
10. The ECG showed irregular rhythm, and the patient complained of (palpations/palpitations/papillations).

TRANSCRIBING PROFESSIONAL DOCUMENTS

Transcribe the document named Assessment 6 from tape. Before you key, review the document formatting guidelines. Proofread your transcribed document and revise it until you think it is error-free.

PERFORMANCE REPORT

Name____ Date __________

Document	Description	Date Completed	Document Processing Speed (If Available)	Document Appraisal M=Mailable MC=Mailable w/corrections NM=Not Mailable
Report 6.1	Office Note			M MC NM
Report 6.2	Radiology Report			M MC NM
Report 6.3	Consultation Letter			M MC NM
Report 6.4	Lab Report			M MC NM
Report 6.5	Treadmill Stress Test			M MC NM
Report 6.6	Operative Report			M MC NM
Report 6.7	Operative Report			M MC NM
Report 6.8	Discharge Summary			M MC NM

Comments ____

____

____

____

____

CHAPTER

7

Gastroenterology is the study of the digestive tract, liver, and pancreas. The digestive tract, also called the alimentary canal or gastrointestinal (GI) tract, is similar to a tube with openings at both ends. It includes the mouth, pharynx, esophagus, stomach, and small and large intestines. It also incorporates accessory organs: the salivary glands, teeth, liver, gallbladder, pan-

Gastroenterology

creas, and appendix. The physician who specializes in the GI tract is called a gastroenterologist. A rectosigmoid specialist (proctologist) studies diseases of the lower end of the digestive tract.

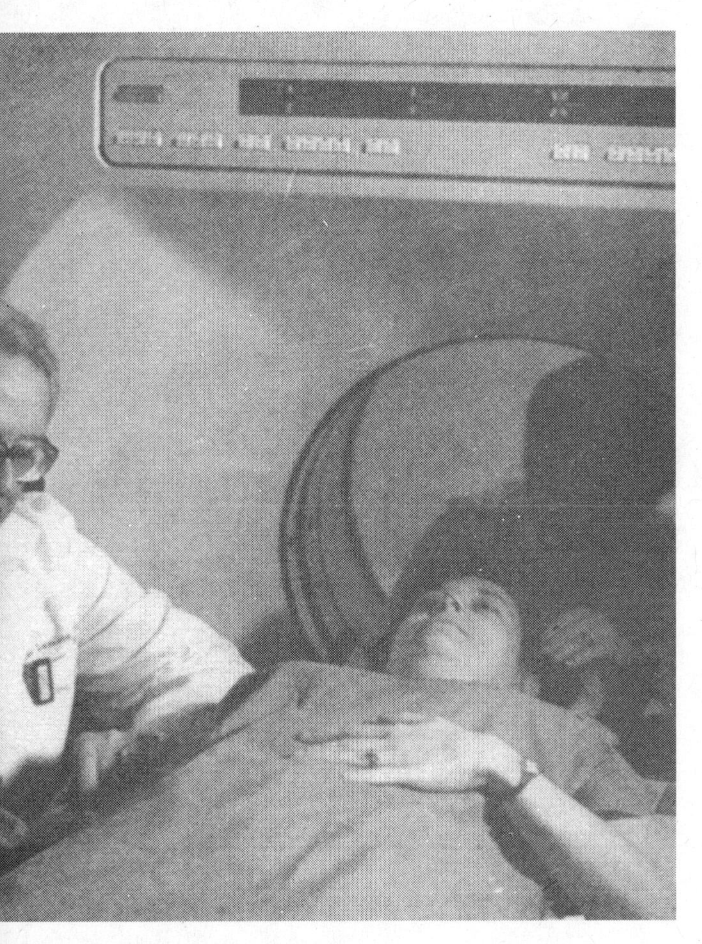

OBJECTIVES

- Use gastroenterology terms correctly according to the context and purpose of the dictation.
- Select and use appropriate general and specialty reference materials.
- Key gastroenterology documents of varying complexity and format.
- Transcribe authentic medical dictation requiring concentration and listening skill.
- Edit medical reports to conform with AAMT style guidelines.
- Proofread and correct transcripts to produce error-free documents.

EXPLORING GASTROENTEROLOGY

Digestion, absorption, and elimination are the processes of the gastrointestinal tract. This complex system feeds the cells of the body, providing energy for cell functions. As with the other systems of the body, the digestive system involves several organs and interacts with other body systems to carry out its vital functions.

STRUCTURE AND FUNCTION

The mouth is the first organ of digestion (figure 7.1). Food enters the body through the mouth, and the teeth masticate or chew to break the food into small particles. The salivary glands (parotid, submaxillary, and sublingual) located in the mouth secrete digestive juices and salivary enzymes at the rate of about 1.5 liters per day. These substances begin the digestion process. As the food is swallowed, it passes through the pharynx into the esophagus by an involuntary process that causes the epiglottis to cover the tracheal opening. This prevents the aspiration of food into the airways. Esophageal peristalsis, or rhythmic muscle movements, cause the food to move down the esophagus, passing the esophageal sphincter (or cardiac sphincter), and into the stomach. In order to prevent reflux into the esophagus, this sphincter closes tightly when the food enters the stomach. The stomach lining contains many villi, or hairlike projections, that help move the food.

Figure 7.1
Digestive system

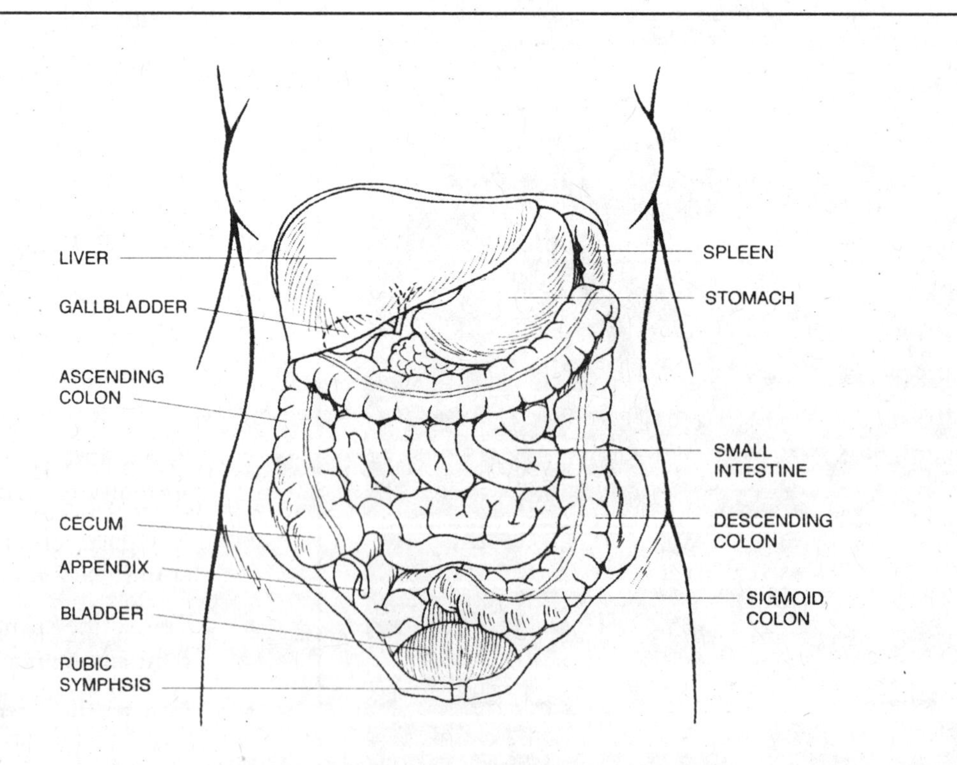

In the stomach, hydrochloric acid is secreted by the gastric gland to further decompose the food particles. This highly acidic fluid is produced at the rate of about 2.5 liters per day. Pepsin is secreted to begin the digestion of proteins. Additionally, intrinsic factor is produced and aids in the absorption of vitamin B_{12} in the ileum.

The pyloric sphincter acts as a two-way valve moving small, digested particles toward the small intestine and preventing large particles from entering too soon to allow proper absorption of nutrients. In the small intestine, the duodenum continues the digestive processes. There are several hormones and other regulators that control the secretions of the digestive system. Alkaline digestive juices flow into the intestine from the pancreas and neutralize the acid contents. Other digestive enzymes produced in the pancreas continue to break down the food. Trypsin, amylase, and lipase assist in the digestion of proteins, starches, and fats respectively. The intestinal glands secrete mucus which coats the lining of the intestine and protects it from erosion by the acidic juices.

Bile is secreted by the liver and stored in the gallbladder. When needed, the bile salts, cholesterol, and lecithin contained in the bile emulsify fatty substances into products that can be absorbed by the small intestine. At this point, peristalsis (the contractions of the intestine) causes the contents of the small intestine to be propelled into the colon.

Bacteria present in the large intestine play an important role in digestion, assisting with the absorption of bile salts and the further breakdown of waste products. Escherichia coli, or E. coli, is one of the most common bacteria that normally occur in the intestines.

The final step of digestion is moving the waste material out of the body. As peristalsis propels waste products through the small intestine, the ileocecal valve opens, allowing some contents to enter the colon. Once waste has moved past the ileocecal valve, the valve closes to prevent the products from moving back into the small intestine. As the waste fills the colon and reaches the rectum, the rectum expands until there is an urge to defecate. The movement of waste from the rectum and out of the body can take up to three days, a period that allows for the resorption of fluid and electrolytes.

Stool, or feces, contains undigested foodstuffs, bacteria, water, and inorganic matter. The characteristic brown color is produced as bile is broken down by bacteria within the intestine. The fecal odor is caused by chemicals produced during digestion. The gastrointestinal tract contains gas from swallowed air and the action of intestinal bacteria. Gas expelled through the mouth is called a belch, burp, or eructation; gas expelled from the anus is called flatus.

PHYSICAL ASSESSMENT

Obtaining an accurate, complete patient history is probably the most important technique for the examiner. The patient is asked to describe any problems, starting from the mouth and teeth, and ending with a description of bowel habits. Diet and eating habits can suggest routines that could lead to the

Common Gastroenterology Drugs

calcium carbonate
Alka-Mints, Mylanta, Os-Cal, Rolaids, Tums

calcium chloride
Cal Plus

cascara sagrada

cimetidine
Tagamet

diphenoxylate and atropine
Lomotil

docusate and casanthranol
PeriColace

famotidine
Pepsid

hyoscyamine, atropine, scopolamine & phenobarbital
Donnatal

nizatidine
Axid

omeprazole
Prilosec

ranitidine hydrochloride
Zantac

senna
Senokot

improper functioning of the GI organs. The mouth is inspected for proper moisture, teeth alignment, and any deviations in the structures. Next, the examiner may auscultate the abdomen from the epigastric area down to the suprapubic, using a stethoscope and dividing the abdomen into four sections called quadrants (see the abbreviations at the end of the vocabulary list). Each quadrant is examined since different sounds might be heard in different areas. The physician then percusses (taps) all four quadrants, listening for the different sounds from the gas-filled mid-abdomen versus the denser spleen and liver. Lastly, the examiner palpates the abdomen from the suprapubic area up to the ribs, watching the patient for signs of pain, tenderness, or rebound tenderness, and palpating for masses, adenopathy, or organomegaly. Although it is customary to perform palpation before auscultation with other systems of the body, this is reversed in the examination of the abdomen since palpation could change the sound and pattern of gas within the intestine, and this could have an influence on the results of the examination.

DISEASES AND CONDITIONS

Because the GI tract encompasses so many organs and structures, the number of diseases affecting this region is extensive. Each area has its common maladies, as summarized in table 7.1 below and as illustrated in figure 7.2:

Area of GI Tract	Common Diseases
mouth and pharynx	candidiasis (thrush, moniliasis), herpetic stomatitis (Most illnesses are treated by the ENT specialist.)
esophagus	ulcers, infections, hiatal hernia, diverticula, cancer, gastroesophageal reflux disease, Schatzke's ring, strictures
stomach	gastric ulcers, tumors, gastritis, cancer
duodenum	cancer, ulcers
liver	hepatitis, syphilis, tuberculosis, fungal infections, leptospirosis, abscesses, tumors, parasites, cirrhosis, cancer
gallbladder	gallstones
pancreas	acute and chronic pancreatitis, benign pseudocysts, malignant tumors
small intestine	tumors, Crohn's disease, regional enteritis, terminal ileitis, cancer, hernia, appendicitis
colon	cancer, polyps, diverticular disease, ulcerative colitis, Crohn's disease, irritable bowel syndrome
rectum	hemorrhoids, cancer

Table 7.1
Common diseases of the GI tract

COMMON TESTS AND SURGICAL PROCEDURES

Many of the diagnostic procedures in gastroenterology center on the use of the endoscope and its variations. The endoscope is a flexible tube with fiberoptics, which allows the physician to look inside the esophagus, stomach, and other areas of the GI tract. Some of the common studies include gastroscopy (stomach), exploratory laparoscopy (intestinal tract), and colonoscopy and flexible sigmoidoscopy (colon). Other important tests include x-rays using barium (commonly called a GI series), computed tomography (CT scans), abdominal ultrasound, insertion of a PEG tube, and Whipple's operation (removal of all or part of the pancreas and duodenum). A hemorrhoidectomy is the surgical removal of hemorrhoids; an appendectomy is the surgical removal of the appendix.

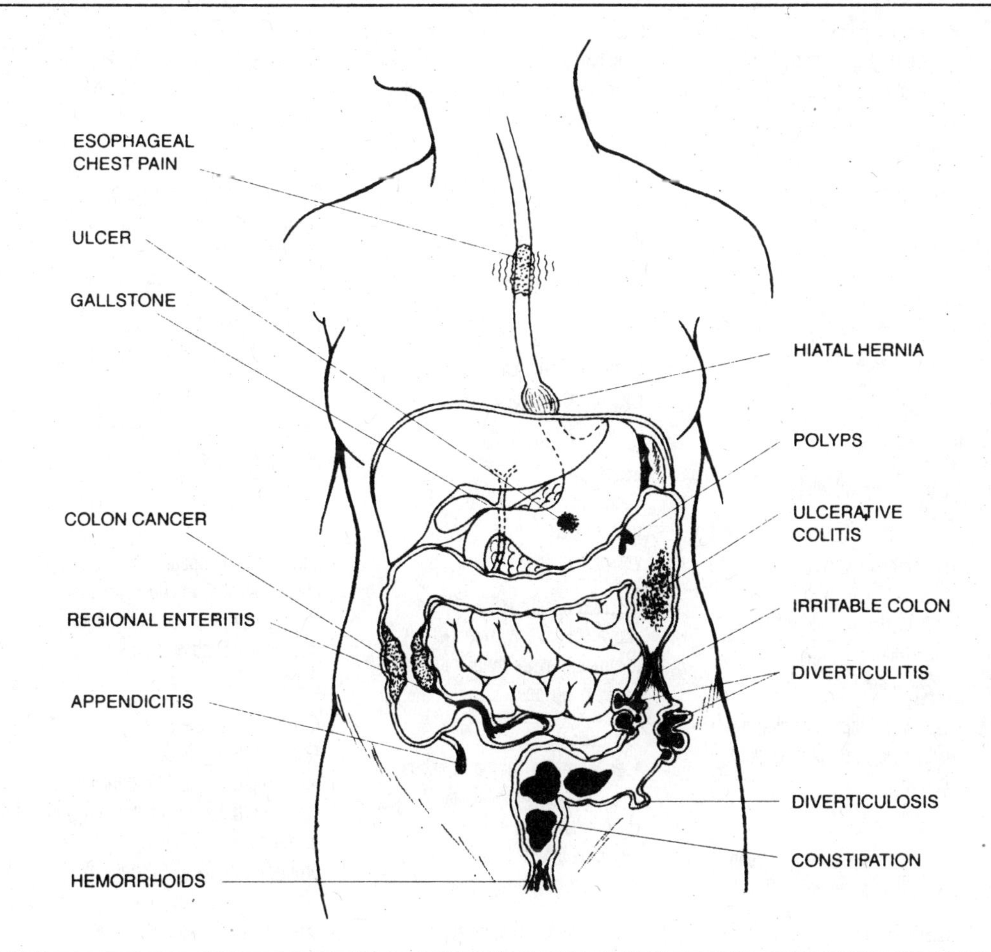

Figure 7.2 Common diseases and their locations in the digestive tract

THE VOCABULARY OF GASTROENTEROLOGY

The following word list contains common gastroenterology terms as well as most of the difficult words you will hear in the dictation at the end of the chapter. Take time to become familiar with these words now, then review them again before you key the medical documents.

Here are suggestions for learning the vocabulary words:

1. Read and study each word for pronunciation and meaning.
2. Write each unfamiliar word from the list below on a notecard, write the definition or a paraphrase of the definition on the back, and draw a simple picture to help you learn the word.
3. Study the pronunciation, spelling, and definition of each word on your notecard, then key each word twice for reinforcement. Check the spelling.
4. Add the correctly spelled terms to your word processor's spell checker.

abdomen
(ab-dO'-men) (n) that part of the body between the chest and the pelvis (the lower part of the trunk of the body)

adenocarcinoma
(ad'-en-O-kar'-si-nO'-ma) (n) malignant tumor of epithelial cells arising from the glandular structures which are a part of most organs of the body

adenopathy
(ad-e-nop'-a-thee) (n) swelling or enlargement of the lymph nodes

adipose
(ad'-i-pOz) (adj) fatty

albumin
(al-byoo'-min) (n) a type of simple protein, varieties of which are widely distributed throughout the tissues and fluids

alimentary canal
(al-i-men'-ter-ee ka'-nal') (n) gastrointestinal tract; tubelike structure through which food passes and is digested and absorbed

anesthesia
(an'-es-thee'-zee-a) (n) absence of sensation, especially pain; usually applied to the medical technique of reducing or eliminating a person's sensation of pain to enable surgery to be performed

anesthetic
(an'-es-thet'-ik) (n) the medications used to produce anesthesia

angiodysplasia
(an'-jee-O-dis-play'-zee-a) (n) degenerative stretching or enlarging of the blood vessels in an organ

anorexia
(an-O-rek'-see-a) (n) loss of appetite

antiemetic
(an'-ti-em-et'-ik) (n) pharmacologic agent used to decrease nausea and/or vomiting

aphagia
(a-fay'-jee-a) (n) inability to swallow

aphthous stomatitis
(af'-thus stO-ma-tI'-tis) (n) small ulcers of the mucous membrane of the mouth

benign
(bee-nIn') (adj) describing a mild illness or a nonmalignant tumor

bile
(bIl) (n) a thick, yellow-green-brown fluid secreted by the liver

bilirubin
(bil-i-roo'-bin) (n) a red bile pigment, formed from hemoglobin during normal and abnormal destruction of erythrocytes

biopsy
(bI'-op-see) (n) removal of a small amount of tissue and/or fluid from the body for microscopic examination; the specimen obtained

bulimia
(boo-lim'-ee-a) (n) a chronic disorder involving repeated and secretive bouts of binge eating followed by self-induced vomiting, use of laxatives, or vigorous exercise in order to prevent weight gain

cachexia
(ka-kek'-see-a) (n) a general weight loss and wasting occurring in the course of a chronic disease or emotional disturbance

caliber
(kal'-i'-ber) (n) diameter of a tube or vessel; e.g., a blood vessel

cauterization
(kaw-ter-i-zay'-shun) (n) destroying tissue by burning for medical reasons

cecum
(see'-kum) (n) any part ending in a cul-de-sac; specifically the closed, pocket-like beginning of the large intestine in the lower right part of the abdomen

cholangiography
(kO-lan-jee-og'-ra-fee) (n) x-ray examination of the bile ducts

cholecystectomy
(kO'-lee-sis-tek'-tO-mee) (n) excision of the gallbladder

cholecystitis
(kO'-lee-sis-tI-tis) (n) inflammation or irritation of gallbladder, usually caused by the presence of gallstones

choledocholithiasis
(kO-led'-O-kO-lith-I'-a-sis) (n) presence of calculi (stones) in the common bile duct

cholelithiasis
(kO'-lee-lith-I'-a-sis) (n) presence of gallstones (calculi) in the gallbladder

cirrhosis
(si'-rO'-sis) (n) a chronic, degenerative disease of the liver

cirrhotic
(sir-rot'-ik) (adj) relating to or having cirrhosis

colostomy
(kO-los'-to-mee) (n) surgical creation of an opening in the abdominal wall to allow material to pass from the bowel through that opening rather than through the anus

Crohn's disease
(krOnz) (n) chronic inflammatory condition affecting the colon and/or terminal part of the small intestine and producing frequent episodes of diarrhea, abdominal pain, nausea, fever, weakness, and weight loss

cyst
(sist) (n) a bladder or an abnormal sac containing gas, fluid, or a semisolid material

cystic
(sis'-tik) (adj) relating to a cyst

cystic duct
(n) the duct of the gallbladder which unites with the hepatic duct from the liver to form the bile duct

dehydration
(dee-hI-dray'-shun) (n) extreme loss of water from the body tissues

digital
(dij'-i-tal) (adj) relating to or resembling a finger or toe

distention
(dis-ten'-shun) (n) the state of being stretched out or inflated

diverticulosis
(dI'-ver-tik-yoo-lO'-sis) (n) presence of diverticula (pouches) in the intestinal tract

dyspepsia
(dis-pep'-see-a) (n) imperfect digestion

dysphagia
(dis-fay'-jee-a) (n) difficulty swallowing

emetic
(e-met'-ik) (n) pharmacologic agent used to induce vomiting and eliminate toxic substances

epiploic
(ep'-i-plO'-ik) (adj) relating to the omentum, a fold of peritoneum attached to the stomach and connecting it with the adjacent organs

epithelial
(ep-i-thee'-lee-al) (adj) relating to or consisting of epithelium

epithelium
(ep-i-thee'-lee-um) (n) cell layers covering the outside body surfaces as well as forming the lining of hollow organs (e.g., the bladder) and the passages of the respiratory, digestive, and urinary tracts

eructation
(ee-ruk-tay'-shun) (n) belching

esophagus
(ee-sof'-a-gus) (n) the muscular canal that connects the pharynx and stomach

extravasation
(eks-trav'-a-say'-shun) (n) a leakage of fluid (e.g., blood) to the tissues outside the vessel normally containing it, which may occur in injuries, burns, and allergic reactions

fissure
(fish'-ur) (n) a deep furrow, cleft, or slit; e.g., in the liver, lungs, ligaments, brain, or teeth

fistula
(fis'-tyoo-la) (n) abnormal opening or channel connecting two internal organs or leading from an internal organ to the outside; e.g., urinary fistula

flatulence
(flat'-yoo-lens) (n) presence of an excessive amount of gas in the stomach and intestines

flexure
(flek'-sher) (n) a bend, as in an organ or structure

gallbladder
(gawl'-blad'-er) (n) pear-shaped organ that is located on the lower surface of the liver and is a reservoir for bile until discharged through the cystic duct

gastritis
(gas-trI'-tis) (n) inflammation of the gastric (stomach) mucosa

gastroenteritis
(gas'-trO-en-ter-I'-tis) (n) inflammation of the gastric mucosa and intestine

gingiva
(jin'-ji-va) (n) the gum; the tissue that attaches the teeth to the jaws

hematemesis
(hee-ma-tem'-e-sis) (n) vomiting of blood

hematochezia
(hee'-ma-tO-kee'-zee-a) (n) passage of bloody stools

hemorrhoid
(hem'-a-royd) (n) varicose vein of anal opening

hemostasis
(hee'-mO-stay-sis/hee-mos'-ta-sis) (n) cessation of bleeding either naturally through the blood coagulation process, mechanically (with surgical clamps), or chemically (with drugs)

hemostatic
(hee'-mO-stat'-ik) (adj) relating to procedure, device, or substance that stops flow of blood

hepatitis
(hep-a-tI'-tis) (n) acute or chronic inflammation of the liver

hepatoduodenal
(hep'-at-O-doo-O-dee'-nal) (adj) referring to the portion of the lesser omentum (fold of peritoneal tissue attaching and supporting the stomach and adjacent organs) between the liver and the duodenum

hernia
(her'-nee-a) (n) protrusion of an organ or part of an organ or other structure through the muscle wall of the cavity that normally contains it

homeostasis
(hO'-mee-O-stay'-sis) (n) equilibrium in the body with respect to various functions (e.g., temperature, heart rate) and to the chemical compositions of the fluids and tissues

hyperemesis
(hI-per-em'-e-sis) (n) excessive vomiting

hyperemia
(hI-per-ee'-mee-a) (n) increased blood in part of the body, caused by inflammatory response or blockage of blood outflow

hyperemic
(hI-per-ee'-mik) (adj) showing hyperemia

ileostomy
(il'-ee-os'-tO-mee) (n) surgical formation of an opening of the ileum (distal portion of the small intestine) onto the abdominal wall through which feces pass

ileum
(il'-ee-um) (n) the third portion of the small intestine, about 12 feet in length, extending from the junction with the jejunum to the ileocecal opening

ilium
(il'-ee-um) (n) the broad, flaring portion of the hip bone

ileus
(il'-ee-us) (n) obstruction of the intestines

infraumbilical
(in'-fra-um-bil'-i-kal) (adj) below the umbilicus (navel)

intestine
(in-tes'-tin) (n) the portion of the alimentary canal extending from the pyloric opening of the stomach to the anus (opening of the rectum)

intussusception
(in'-tus-su-sep'-shun) (n) taking up or receiving one part within another, especially the infolding of one segment of the intestine within another

lamina
(lam'-i-na) (n) thin membrane or plate-like structure, such as the two parts of a vertebra that join to hold the spinous process of the vertebra over the spinal cord (pl laminae)

laminar
(lam'-i-nar) (adj) relating to lamina

laparoscope
(lap'-a-rO-skOp) (n) a device for observing the inside of an organ or cavity

lateral
(lat'-er-al) (adj) relating to a side, away from the center plane; e.g., cheeks are lateral to the nose

leukocyte
(loo'-kO-sIt) (n) white blood cell

leukoplakia
(loo-kO-play'-kee-a) (n) a precancerous change in a mucous membrane, such as the mouth or tongue

ligament
(lig'-a-ment) (n) band of fibrous connective tissue that binds joints together and connects bones and cartilage

lobe
(lOb) (n) rounded part of an organ, separated from other parts of the organ by connective tissue or fissures

lumen
(loo'-men) (n) cavity, canal, or channel within an organ or tube; the space inside a structure

lymph
(limf) (n) a thin fluid that

lymph
(limf) (n) a thin fluid that bathes the tissues of the body, circulates through lymph vessels, is filtered in lymph nodes, and enters the blood stream through the thoracic duct

lymphatic
(lim-fat'-ik) (adj) relating to lymph

lymphoid
(lim'-foyd) (adj) resembling lymph or relating to the lymphatic system

lymphoma
(lim-fO'-ma) (n) a general term for various types of tumors of the lymphatic system

malaise
(ma-layz') (n) an indefinite feeling of weakness or being unwell; uneasiness, often the first sign of illness

malignancy
(ma-lig'-nan-see) (n) a cancer that is invasive and spreading

mastication
(mas-ti-kay'-shun) (n) process of chewing food

melena
(me-lee'-na) (n) passage of dark, tarry stool

mucosal
(myoo-kO'-sal) (adj) concerning any mucous membrane

mucous
(myoo'-kus) (adj) having the nature of or resembling mucus

mucus
(myoo'-kus) (n) viscous (sticky, gummy) secretions of mucous membranes and glands

nausea
(naw'-zee-a/naw'-zha) (n) inclination to vomit

nauseous
(naw'-zee-us/naw'-shus) (adj) causing nausea or feeling nausea

nodular
(nod'-yoo-lar) (adj) small, firm, and knotty

obstipation
(ob-sti-pay'-shun) (n) severe constipation

opacification
(O-pas'-i-fi-kay-shun) (n) clouding or loss of transparency, especially of the cornea or lens of the eye

organomegaly
(Or'-ga-nO-meg'-a-lee) (n) abnormal enlargement of an organ, particularly an organ of the abdonimal cavity, such as the liver or spleen

palpable
(pal'-pa-bl) (adj) perceivable by touch

palpation
(pal-pay'-shun) (n) technique of examination in which the examiner feels the firmness, texture, size, shape, or location of body parts

pancreas
(pan'-kree-as) (n) gland lying behind the stomach

parasite
(par'-a-slt) (n) an organism that lives on or in another and draws its nourishment therefrom

percutaneous
(per-kyoo-tay'-nee-us) (adj) through the skin

perforation
(per-fO-ray'-shun) (n) abnormal opening or hole in a hollow organ

peristalsis
(per-i-stal'-sis) (n) the movement of the intestine or other tubular structure, characterized by waves of alternate circular contraction and relaxation of the tube by which the contents are propelled onward

peritoneum
(per-i-tO-nee'-um) (n) lining of the abdominal cavity

pharynx
(far'-ingks) (n) throat; passageway for air from nasal cavity or larynx, and food from mouth to esophagus

pneumoperitoneum
(noo'-mO-per-i-ton-ee'-um) (n) presence of air or gas in the chest cavity

polyp
(pol'-ip) (n) a general descriptive term used with reference to any mass of tissue that bulges or projects outward or upward from the normal surface level

proximal
(prok'-si-mal) (adj) nearest to a point of reference

pyrosis
(pl-rO'-sis) (n) heartburn

reflux
(ree'-fluks) (n) abnormal backflow, as sometimes occurs with fluids in the esophagus or other body parts

regurgitation
(ree-gur-ji-tay'-shun) (n) the return of gas or small amounts of food from the stomach

salivary gland
(sal'-i-vayr-ee) (n) a gland that secretes saliva into the mouth

sigmoid colon
(sig'-moyd kO'-lon) (n) that part of the colon extending from the end of the descending colon to the rectum

sigmoidoscopy
(sig'-moy-dos'-ko-pee) (n) the inspection of the rectum and colon

sphincter
(sfingk'-ter) (n) a muscle that encircles a duct, tube, or opening in such a way that its contraction constricts the opening

sterile
(ster'-il) (adj) free from living microorganisms

supine
(soo-pln') (adj) lying on the back

suprapubic
(soo-pra-pyoo'-bik) (adj) above the pubic arch

tachycardia
(tak'-e-kar'-dee-a) (n) an abnormally rapid heart rate

tachycardiac
(tak'-e-kar'-dee-ak) (adj) relating to or suffering from an abnormally rapid heart rate

tracheostomy
(tray-kee-os'-tO-mee) (n) a surgically created opening into the trachea (windpipe)

transmural
(trans-myoo'-ral) (adj) relating to the entire thickness of the wall of an organ

trocar
(trO'-kar) (n) sharply pointed surgical instrument used for aspiration or removal of fluids from cavities

ulcerative colitis
(ul'-ser-a-tiv kO-ll'-tis) (n) a chronic disease characterized by ulcers in the colon and rectum

ultrasound
(ul'-tra-sownd) (n) sound waves at very high frequencies used in the technique of obtaining images for diagnostic purposes

villi
(vil'-l) (n) many tiny projections, occurring over the mucous membrane of the small intestine that functions in the absorption of nutrients and fluids; villus (sing)

villous
(vil'-us) (adj) relating to villi

ABBREVIATIONS

a.c.	before meals	LLQ	left lower quadrant
BaE or BE	barium enema	LRQ	lower right quadrant
BCM	below costal margin	LUQ	left upper quadrant
BM	bowel movement (bone marrow in oncology)	n.p.o.	nothing by mouth
		p.c.	after meals
EGD	esophagogastroduodenoscopy	p.p.	postprandial (after eating)
FBS	fasting blood sugar	RLQ	right lower quadrant
GB	gallbladder	RUQ	right upper quadrant
GERD	gastroesophageal reflux disease	TPN	total parenteral nutrition
GI	gastrointestinal	UGI	upper gastrointestinal
HAL	hyperalimentation	ULQ	upper left quadrant
HCl	hydrochloric acid	URQ	upper right quadrant
IVC	intravenous cholangiography		

EXERCISE 7.1: RECOGNIZING LOOK-ALIKES AND SOUND-ALIKES

Below is a list of frequently used words that look alike and/or sound alike. Study the meaning and pronunciation of each set of words, then read each sentence carefully and circle the word in parentheses that correctly completes the meaning.

anesthesia	the loss of sensation of pain
anesthetic	the substance used to produce anesthesia

cite	(v) to quote or mention
sight	(n) vision, view
site	(n) location in the body

luminal	(adj) pertaining to a lumen (cavity a channel) within an organ or tube
Luminal	trade name for anticonvulsant and sedative phenobarbital

mucous	(adj) having the nature of or resembling mucus
mucus	(n) viscous (sticky, gummy) secretions of mucous membranes and glands

hemostasis	cessation of bleeding
hemostatic	pertaining to procedure, device, or substance that stops flow of blood
homeostasis	steady state in the internal environment of the body

ileum	the last part of the small intestine, between the jejunum and the large intestine
ileus	obstruction of the intestines
ilium	superior portion of the hipbone

dysphagia	difficulty swallowing
dysphasia	difficulty speaking

reflux	abnormal backflow of fluid
reflex	involuntary reaction or return

1. After adequate (anesthesia, anesthetic) was documented, the cyst was incised.
2. Local (anesthesia, anesthetic) consisting of 1% lidocaine with epinephrine was infiltrated into the chest region.
3. After sutures were placed, good (hemostasis, homeostasis) was documented.
4. Colonoscopy was normal to the terminal (ileum, ilium).
5. The patient is to call if he develops yellow or green (mucus, mucous).
6. The (mucus, mucous) membranes are injected, with clear rhinorrhea.
7. I (cited, sighted) to the patient several reasons for quitting smoking.
8. The excision (cite, site) showed good healing.
9. Due to her (dysphagia, dysphasia) she has had little food intake over the past 24 hours.
10. Due to an (ileum, ileus) the patient was placed on total parenteral nutrition.

EXERCISE 7.2: MATCHING SOUND AND SPELLING

The numbered list that follows shows the phonetic spelling of hard-to-spell words. Sound out the word, then write the correct spelling in the blank space provided. Each of the words can be found in the glossary or in the drug list in appendix C.

1. sir-rO'-sis ____________________
2. a-fay'-jee-a ____________________
3. ee-ruk-tay'-shun ____________________
4. pol'-ip ____________________
5. al-byoo'-min ____________________
6. af'-thus stO-ma-tI'-tis ____________________
7. in'-tus-su-sep'-shun ____________________
8. me-lee'-na ____________________
9. sfingk'-ter ____________________
10. ka-kek'-see-a ____________________
11. me-layz' ____________________
12. flek'-sher ____________________
13. hee-ma-tem'-e-sis ____________________
14. bil-i-roo'-bin ____________________
15. dI'-ver-tik-yoo-lO'-sis ____________________
16. il'-ee-um ____________________

EXERCISE 7.3: CHOOSING WORDS FROM CONTEXT

When transcribing dictation, the medical transcriptionist frequently needs to determine the word that correctly completes the sentence based on the situation. From the list of words below, select the term that meaningfully completes each statement.

biopsy	palpable	hyperemesis
laparoscope	dehydration	hernia
cauterization	salivary glands	benign
malignancy	hyperemic	supine
Crohn's disease		

1. It was necessary to __________ the nodule to determine if it was malignant.
2. The homeless man was brought into the emergency room suffering from ______________. He was started on IV fluids.
3. They found Mrs. Arnold lying ____________ on her bed.
4. The patient had no _________ lymph nodes.
5. Mr. Johnson had a biopsy of the intestine which confirmed the diagnosis of ___________________.
6. Her tonsils are enlarged and mildly _____________.
7. A ______________ was passed through the abdominal wall to examine the peritoneal cavity.
8. If it is suspected that you have a _________________, a biopsy may be performed.
9. _________________ was used during the procedure to prevent excess bleeding.
10. There was a swelling on the face, particularly about the cheeks, which led to the diagnosis of obstruction of the _______________________.

EXERCISE 7.4: PAIRING WORDS AND MEANINGS

For each definition provided below, locate the term on the list that best matches the definition. Write the letter of the term in the space provided beside the definition.

A. adenocarcinoma	F. epithelium	J. tachycardia
B. adipose	G. extravasation	K. tracheostomy
C. cholecystectomy	H. lymph	L. lymphoma
D. cirrhosis	I. pancreas	M. gallbladder
E. colostomy		

1. cell layers that cover the outside body surfaces and line the hollow organs ______
2. a leakage of fluid from a vessel to the tissues outside it ______
3. an abnormally rapid heart rate ______
4. gland lying behind the stomach ______
5. surgical creation of an opening in the abdominal wall ______
6. excision of a gallbladder ______
7. a chronic disease of the liver ______
8. malignant tumor of a gland ______
9. fatty tissue ______
10. a thin fluid that bathes the tissues of the body and is filtered in the lymph nodes before entering the blood stream ______

EXERCISE 7.5: CREATING TERMS FROM WORD FORMS

In the following exercise, combine prefixes, root words, and suffixes to create medical words that fit the definitions below. Fill in the blanks with the words you construct.

stomat/o	mouth	cyst/o	bladder
dys-	poor or bad; painful	enter/o	small intestine
parotid	glands by the ear	chol/e	bile
aden/o	glands	hemat/o	blood
gloss/o	tongue	hepat/o	liver
carcin/o	cancer	-oma	tumor
per-	throughout, completely	-itis	inflammation
-emesis	vomiting	peptic	digestion
cutaneous	skin	-blast	immature cell

1. through the skin ______
2. cancerous tumor ______
3. inflammation of the gallbladder ______
4. mumps (inflammation of the parotid gland) ______ ______
5. swelling, redness, and pain in the mouth ______
6. malignant tumor in the glands ______
7. inflammation of the tongue ______
8. vomiting of blood ______
9. imperfection of digestion ______
10. maligant tumor in the liver ______

EDITING MEDICAL DOCUMENTS

In this section you will perfect your word use and grammar skills. These skills will help you edit and proofread medical reports for correct language, punctuation, format, and meaning. The special focus for this chapter is the correct use and placement of modifiers.

USING MODIFIERS TO ACHIEVE CORRECT MEANING

Modifiers are words, phrases, and clauses that describe or tell more about another word, phrase, or clause. Good transcriptionists pay careful attention to the placement of modifiers to ensure clear meaning of sentences.

Related Words Should Be Placed Together

Place modifiers as close as possible to the words being modified.

UNCLEAR: Examination at that time of the esophagus was negative. [What is "that time of the esophagus"?]

CLEAR: Examination of the esophagus at that time was negative.

Many transcription "bloopers" are caused by misplaced or dangling modifiers, particularly prepositional phrases or phrases beginning with *ing* words. These phrases are adjective phrases that modify a noun. Miscommunication occurs when the phrase is not placed next to the noun it modifies.

WRONG: The bleeder was clamped with a hemostat, *hoping to achieve hemostasis.* [The phrase *hoping to achieve hemostasis* is an adjective phrase that refers to the surgeon—not to the bleeder, as is suggested in this sentence construction.]

CORRECT: The bleeder was clamped with a hemostat *in the hope of achieving hemostasis.*

OR: *Hoping to achieve hemostasis*, the *surgeon* clamped the bleeder with a hemostat.

WRONG: Withdrawing the instrument, polyps were encountered in the transverse colon.
[Are the polyps withdrawing the instrument?]

CORRECT: Withdrawing the instrument, I encountered polyps in the transverse colon.

Note: Be very careful when altering dictation. Reserve rewording for instances when the dictation is not clear because of the misplacement or misuse of a modifier. If you must edit, always use the dictator's original words for terms, procedures, instruments, and diseases. Too much editing can be considered tampering.

EXERCISE 7.6: EDITING FOR PLACEMENT OF MODIFIERS

Revise and key the following dictated sentences to show the correct use and placement of modifiers.

1. The patient was referred to a gastroenterologist who, because of increasing complaints of esophageal reflux, ordered an upper GI.
2. In the left lateral Sims position, the doctor performed the rectal examination.
3. When three weeks post appendectomy, she called about her husband's inflamed incision.
4. X-ray this morning of the chest revealed moderate clearing of the infiltrate.
5. After improving on antibiotic therapy, surgery was deferred.
6. At 225 pounds, her doctor instructed her to eat smaller meals and to exercise more often.
7. A curved incision was made just above the umbilicus of 3 cm.
8. Feeling very nauseous, the nurse handed the patient an emesis basin.
9. With a family history of colon polyps, screening colonoscopy will be carried out every two years.
10. The doctor arranged for Mr. Smith's admission. Had he notified the insurance company, reimbursement would have been greater.

EXERCISE 7.7: PROOFREADING REVIEW

Read the following report section and circle errors in format, usage, punctuation, capitalization, spelling, and mechanics. Then key the report with the errors corrected.

OPERATIVE PROCEDURE The patient was placed on the operating table in the supine position. After satisfactory induction of general anesthesia, the abdomenal wall was prepared and drapped in the usual sterile fashion. Pneumoperitoneum was installed through a small infraumbilical excision and a Veress needle.
Disection of the hepato-duodenal ligament was then commenced with identification of the cistic artery and the cystic duck.
Earlier in the procedure a percutaneous liver biopsy was preformed to the right lobe of the liver, using a True-Cut needle under direct vision. No bleeding was found from this sight later in the operation.
The abdomen was now copiously irritated through the lateral ports. The ports were now removed under direct vision.

WHERE CAN I FIND THE ANSWER?

As you transcribe dictation, you may hear unfamiliar words or terms. A variety of reference sources are available to help you locate answers to your questions. One of the important types of references for medical transcriptionists is described below. Read the information; then if you have access to the reference discussed, explore its capabilities.

MEDICAL REFERENCES: CHOOSING AN EPONYMS BOOK

Eponyms are adjectives taken from a surname and used to describe diseases, instruments, procedures, and so on. They are a tribute of sorts to the person who developed the procedure, first had the disease, or designed the instrument. *Parkinson's* disease, *Foley* catheter, and *Valsalva* maneuver are all examples of eponyms.

How should I look for eponyms?

You can find most of these terms by looking up the noun that accompanies the eponymic adjective—looking up *disease,* not *Parkinson's,* in the medical dictionary or looking up *catheter,* not *Foley,* in your surgical book. Another weapon in your arsenal should be an eponyms reference book. The entries are listed alphabetically by the *adjective,* not the noun. So in an eponyms book, you would look up *Foley,* not *catheter.*

A good eponyms reference book can be very helpful to a medical transcriptionist. The book lists all manner of eponymic diseases, syndromes, operations, instruments, positions, stains, tests, reflexes, and so on. Brief definitions for diseases, syndromes, and operations are included to ensure correctness. Instruments, stains, and such are listed only alphabetically.

Which one should I buy?

Your choices for an eponyms reference are more limited than for other medical references. The following books are representative of the group:

Dictionary of Medical Eponyms, published by The Parthenon Publishing Group.
Medical Abbreviations and Eponyms, published by the W.B. Saunders Company. This book contains abbreviations *and* eponyms, making it two reference books in one.

TRANSCRIBING GASTROENTEROLOGY DOCUMENTS

In this section your goal is to prepare for the work of transcription by transcribing first from a printed document and then from dictation on tape. The model document that follows illustrates the generally accepted format for the **pathology report**, the medical document featured in this chapter.

BASIC FORMAT: THE PATHOLOGY REPORT

The pathology report is a diagnostic report describing the pathological or disease-related findings of a tissue sample taken during surgery, a biopsy, a special procedure, or an autopsy. Dictated by a pathologist, the report may also be called a biopsy report.

Required Headings/Content

Although the wording of headings may vary among institutions, the following content categories are included in all pathology reports: name of specimen submitted, macroscopic (gross) findings, microscopic findings, remarks, and diagnosis(es). The central information in a pathology report includes the gross findings (the appearance of the specimen before it is prepared for microscopic study), the microscopic findings (cell- and blood-related), and the pathological diagnosis. Frequently, the gross descriptions of all the surgical specimens are dictated, transcribed, and given to the pathologist, who then dictates the microscopic descriptions. Once the microscopic descriptions are transcribed, the complete pathology reports are submitted to the pathologist for signature. Note that the pathology report is not the same as a laboratory report. The pathology report focuses on disease findings usually limited to tissue, while laboratory data usually concern body fluids.

Turnaround Time

The expected turnaround time for a pathology report is generally 12 to 24 hours. However, in cases where a malignancy is suspected, the pathologist may render an opinion based on a frozen section of the specimen even before the patient is sutured, since more extensive surgery may be required.

PATHOLOGY REPORT

1" top and side margins

use left justification

PATIENT: Johnson, Sara
MR #: 7904532
SPECIMEN #: 30240
ROOM #: 931
SEX: Female
DATE OF BIRTH: 11/04/43
PHYSICIAN: Binger, A
PROCEDURE: ABDOMINAL RESECTION
PROCEDURE DATE: 8/10/XX

ds

CLINICAL DIAGNOSIS: CARCINOMA OF RECTUM

ds

CLINICAL HISTORY: UNSTATED

ds

GROSS DESCRIPTION
The specimen is received in three portions.

ds

Portion one is stated to be "colon" and consists of a portion of large intestine, measuring 28.0 cm in length and 6.0 cm in greatest diameter. The serosal surface is reddish tan, smooth and glistening with attached epiploic adipose tissue. The mucosal surface is tan-red, smooth and glistening with normal folds. At 0.5 cm from one surgical margin, there is a flat, fungating, ulcerated mass which occupies more than two-thirds of the circumference of the lumen and measures 6.5 x 3.5 cm in greatest diameter. Grossly, the tumor invades the serosal surface in the central portion. The surgical margin close to the tumor is inked. Representative sections of the tumor are submitted in three cassettes. Cassette A contains the surgical margin close to the tumor submitted in CM; surgical margin far from tumor submitted in FM; random sections in R, nodes close to tumor submitted in CN; nodes far from tumor submitted in FN.

ds

Portion two is stated to be "proximal ring" and consists of a ring of tan-pink soft tissue, measuring 1.5 x 1.4 x 0.5 cm, which has attached staples. The stapled portion of the specimen is removed, and the remainder of the specimen is submitted in cassette B.

ds

Portion three is stated to be "distal ring" and consists of a fragment of pinkish

(continued)

PATHOLOGY REPORT
PATIENT: Johnson, Sara
MR #: 7904532

tan, soft tissue, measuring 2.3 x 1.4 x 0.3 cm, and has some attached staples. The stapled portion is removed, and the remainder of the specimen is submitted in cassette C.

ds

DIAGNOSES (GROSS AND MICROSCOPIC)

A: Colon resection—infiltrating, moderately differentiated
indent adenocarcinoma with transmural invasion into pericolonic fat.
-- No tumor seen in proximal and distal margins of resection.

ds

-- Nine lymph nodes isolated, no tumor seen.

ds

-- Based on the available histologic information, the tumor is classified as T3, N0, MX.

B: Proximal ring, segment—segment of large bowel with no evidence of malignancy.

C: Distal ring, segment—segment of large bowel with no evidence of malignancy.

qs

____

PATHOLOGIST: NURI BANO, MD

ds

NB/XX
D: 8/10/XX
T: 8/11/XX

PREPARING TO TRANSCRIBE

To prepare for transcribing dictation, key the pathology report above. You will later key the identical report from dictation. Follow these guidelines:

- Study the format and organization of the report.
- Review the word list presented earlier in this chapter.
- Consult reference books for words or formatting rules that are unfamiliar.
- Proofread your final copy by comparing it to the printed version.

CASES FOR TRANSCRIPTION

In this section you will transcribe medical dictation from tape. Your goal is to produce error-free documents. Read this chapter's Pro Tip (following the case studies) for helpful hints from experienced MTs. Then follow these steps for each dictation:

1. Prepare to transcribe by reviewing the case study and the appropriate model report format.
2. Transcribe the dictation, leaving spaces for words you cannot hear or do not understand.
3. Carefully proofread each document and correct as many errors as you can. Use your reference materials to help you identify missing words.
4. Listen to the tape again and correct all remaining errors.

Repeat these steps until you produce an error-free document. Then complete the Performance Report, attach it to the top of the transcripts, and submit them to your instructor for evaluation.

CASE STUDY 1: JAMES WELTON

James Welton is a 34-year-old man who had eaten dinner and later complained of pain in his right side. He was nauseated and vomited several times during the evening and eventually was taken to the emergency room.

Report 7.1: Operative Report

Transcription Hint

Listen for these special terms:
Veress needle
Tru-Cut needle

Report 7.2: Consultation Letter

Transcription Hint

Listen for these special terms:
Demerol
D5W 0.45 NS (space between W and 0 and between 5 and N)

CASE STUDY 2: SARA JOHNSON

Sara Johnson is a 51-year-old woman who saw her physician after several weeks of intermittent constipation, abdominal distention, and bloody stools.

Report 7.3: Pathology Report

Report 7.4: Consultation Letter

Transcription Hint

This report includes a tumor classification based on the TNM system described in the chapter overview. The classification should be transcribed as T3, N0, MX.

CASE STUDY 3: JONATHAN PRINCE

Jonathan Prince is an 18-year-old young man who was diagnosed with Crohn's disease one year prior to surgery. He had been doing well until last week when he began having intractable diarrhea, which required hospitalization for dehydration. He was given a presurgical barium enema and then sent to the operating room for a colostomy.

Report 7.5: X-Ray Report of Barium Enema

Transcription Hint

Listen for the following new term:
gastrografin enema

Report 7.6: Pathology Report of Colostomy Procedure

Transcription Hints

- Transcribe the letter designations for specimen portions in capitals (A, B, etc.) and the labels in quotation marks, for example, "15 cm ileostomy."
- In the gross description section, treat each portion description as a separate paragraph.

CASE STUDY 4: DAVID DRONEN

David Dronen is a 52-year-old man who has been evaluated in the emergency room for severe abdominal pain.

Report 7.7: Flexible Sigmoidoscopy

CASE STUDY 5: MARY GONZALES

Mary Gonzales is a 64-year-old woman with a long history of anemia. She was admitted to the hospital for tests to determine the cause of chest pain and dark, tarry stools.

Report 7.8: Discharge Summary

Transcription Hint

Listen for these new words:
guaiac-negative
Prilosec
Xanax

PRO TIP: DEALING WITH CLIPPED SENTENCES

By Kathleen Offman, CMT

For a novice medical transcriptionist, acceptable sentence structure can be a confusing matter. Individual dictation styles are usually unique, varying from very formal, to informal, to unconventional. Each physician may use many recurring phrases and terms that reflect his or her speech patterns when transcribing medical documents. It is important to try to retain as much of the physician's dictating style as possible.

Given that medical language tends to be condensed whenever possible, a physician's style may seem terse, compressed, sometimes inconsistent, and sometimes confusing. In addition, some phrases that are perfectly acceptable and understandable in a medical context may seem illogical to the layperson. Knowing when a phrase is acceptable comes with experience and familiarity with medical jargon. Always adhere to departmental guidelines or physician preference when making a decision about acceptable sentence structure. If there are no guidelines, use the following tips to help you decide how to treat a clipped sentence.

What is the definition of a clipped sentence?
A clipped sentence is very brief. It consists of only a noun and a verb, or sometimes, just a verb.

When is a clipped sentence acceptable?

1. When it is the physician's style and preference to dictate in clipped sentences for most of the report.
2. In the physical examination part of a medical report.
3. In the laboratory data section of a medical report.
4. In the review of systems portion of a medical report.

When is a clipped sentence not acceptable?

1. When it is not dictated. Never clip sentences yourself.
2. When the physician's style is mostly complete sentences.

If the physical exam, lab data, and review of systems portion of the report have clipped sentences, how do you handle the other portions of the report?

1. If sentences in the other portions of the report are complete, then key them as such.
2. If the physician dictates clipped sentences in the other portions of the report, it is okay to transcribe the entire report in a clipped style.

How do you determine what to use if there is a mix in the report itself?
If there is a mix, try to assess what is used in the majority of the report. If the majority of the sentences are clipped, it is okay to type the entire report in this style. If the physician mostly used complete sentences, extend the few or occasional clipped sentences into complete sentences by adding "was" or "were" or prepositions. Most importantly, be consistent and make sure your sentences make sense and do not change the original meaning or intent.

ASSESSING TRANSCRIPTION SKILLS

Demonstrate your mastery of the terminology, editing/proofreading, and document transcription skills presented in this chapter by completing the following activities.

USING MEDICAL REFERENCES

Use the appropriate medical reference to locate the correct spelling and additional usage information for the words below. (If the reference is not available, use the glossary in this text.) Circle the correct spelling, then write a sentence using the word correctly.

1.	intusussception	intususception	intussusception
2.	guaiac	guiaic	guaic
3	cachectic	cacechtic	cackhetic
4.	cirhossis	cirrhosis	cirhosis
5.	herniorhapy	herniorraphy	herniorrhaphy
6.	cholelithiasis	colelithiasis	cholelithisis
7.	diverticulae	diverticuli	diverticula
8.	hematochezia	hematachezia	hematocezia

9. tenismus tenesmus tenesmis

____

10. candydiasis candidiosis candidiasis

____

MAKING EXPERT DECISIONS

Circle the correct word from the choices in parentheses.

1. The patient had a hiatal hernia with esophageal (reflux/reflex).
2. The (mucous/mucus) membrane around the stomal opening was inflamed.
3. There was pain and tenderness in the area of the (parotid/carotid) gland.
4. The (acidic/acetic/ascitic) fluid was drained from the abdomen, which relieved a great deal of pressure.
5. Multiple (diverticulum/diverticula) were found along the wall of the colon.
6. Hyperactive bowel sounds were heard upon (percussion/auscultation) of the abdomen.
7. The patient had been suffering from inflammatory (bowel/bile) disease for two years now.
8. On endoscopic examination, the (ileum/ilium) was found to be normal.
9. Colonoscopic exam revealed a large tumor of the colonic mucosa and on pathological exam, this was found to be a (villus/villous/villi) adenoma.
10. The patient began to (wretch/retch) soon after eating dinner.

TRANSCRIBING PROFESSIONAL DOCUMENTS

Transcribe the document named Assessment 7 from tape. Before you key, review the appropriate report formatting guidelines. Proofread your transcribed document and revise it until you think it is error-free.

PERFORMANCE REPORT

Name____ ____Date ____________

Document	Description	Date Completed	Document Processing Speed (If Available)	Document Appraisal M=Mailable MC=Mailable w/corrections NM=Not Mailable
Report 7.1	Operative Report			M MC NM
Report 7.2	Consultation Letter			M MC NM
Report 7.3	Pathology Report			M MC NM
Report 7.4	Consultation Letter			M MC NM
Report 7.5	X-Ray Report			M MC NM
Report 7.6	Pathology Report			M MC NM
Report 7.7	Flexible Sigmoidoscopy Report			M MC NM
Report 7.8	Discharge Summary			M MC NM

Comments ____

C H A P T E R

8

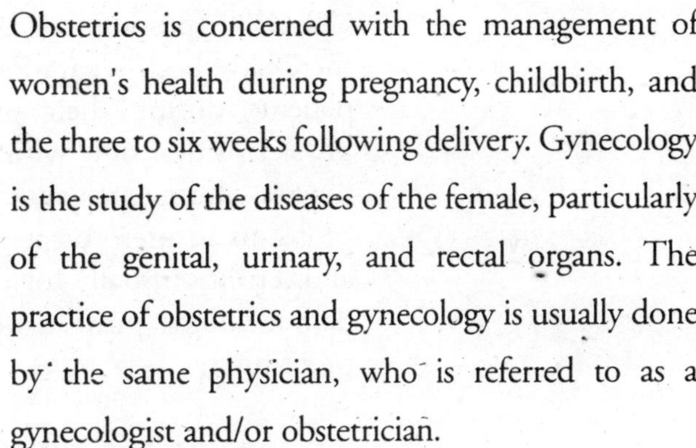

Obstetrics is concerned with the management of women's health during pregnancy, childbirth, and the three to six weeks following delivery. Gynecology is the study of the diseases of the female, particularly of the genital, urinary, and rectal organs. The practice of obstetrics and gynecology is usually done by the same physician, who is referred to as a gynecologist and/or obstetrician.

Obstetrics and Gynecology

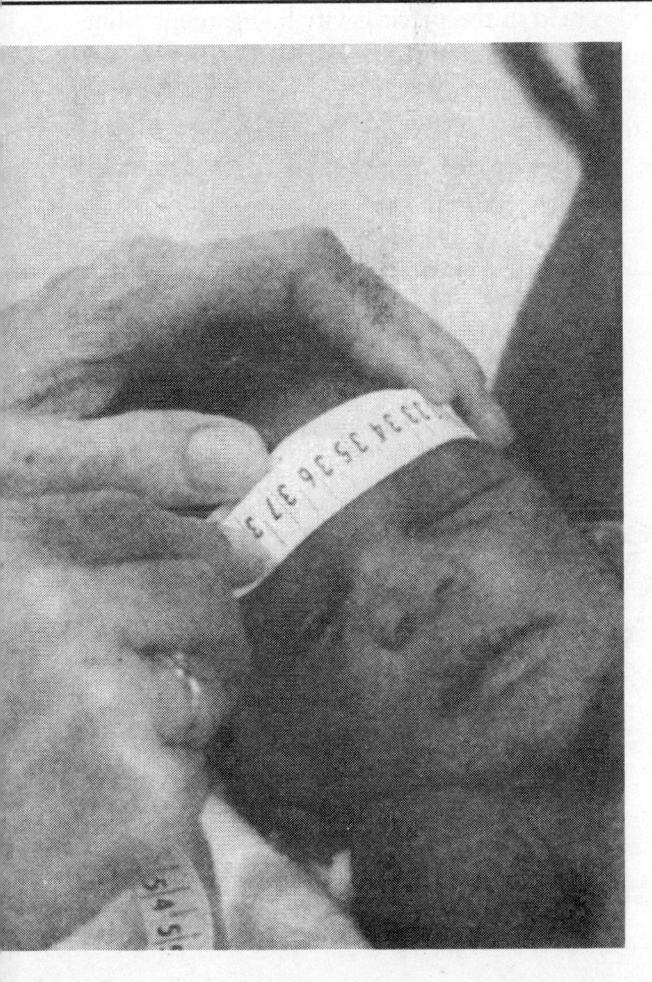

OBJECTIVES

- Use obstetrics and gynecology terms correctly according to the context and purpose of the dictation.
- Select and use appropriate general and specialty reference materials.
- Key obstetrics and gynecology documents of varying complexity and format.
- Transcribe authentic medical dictation requiring concentration and listening skill.
- Edit medical reports to conform with AAMT style guidelines.
- Proofread and correct transcripts to produce error-free documents.

EXPLORING OBSTETRICS AND GYNECOLOGY

The joint specialty of obstetrics and gynecology has an acronym for its name: OB-GYN (pronounced letter by letter, O-B-G-Y-N, or as O-B-Gin). Recently, there have been separations in this specialty. There are physicians who only see patients during their prenatal, antenatal, and parturition periods. Other physicians deal only with high-risk pregnancies, that is, with women who have illnesses during pregnancy or who have fetuses that are considered at risk for problems in utero or at parturition. Other specialties include nurse-midwifery and fertility (usually for infertility). Some family and general practitioners also deliver babies, provide well-women exams, and perform gynecologic/obstetric procedures.

STRUCTURE AND FUNCTION

The female is born with a lifetime supply of eggs, or ova. These 30,000 to 40,000 eggs exist in an undeveloped form within the ovaries, which are almond-shaped glands located in the pelvic cavity on either side of the uterus (figure 8.1). The uterus is a pear-shaped muscular organ that has a narrow neck called the cervix, a body or corpus, and the fundus, which is the uppermost part. The uterus is surrounded by the peritoneum and is held in the pelvic cavity by ligaments. The cornua is the upper lateral portion of the uterus from which the oviducts or fallopian tubes extend. The fallopian tubes are called the adnexa. The lumen of these tubes is contiguous with the uterine cavity. At the distal end of each fallopian tube is the fundibulum, which is broad and funnel-like. At the end of this part is an arm-like structure called the fimbria.

Figure 8.1
Uterus and related structures

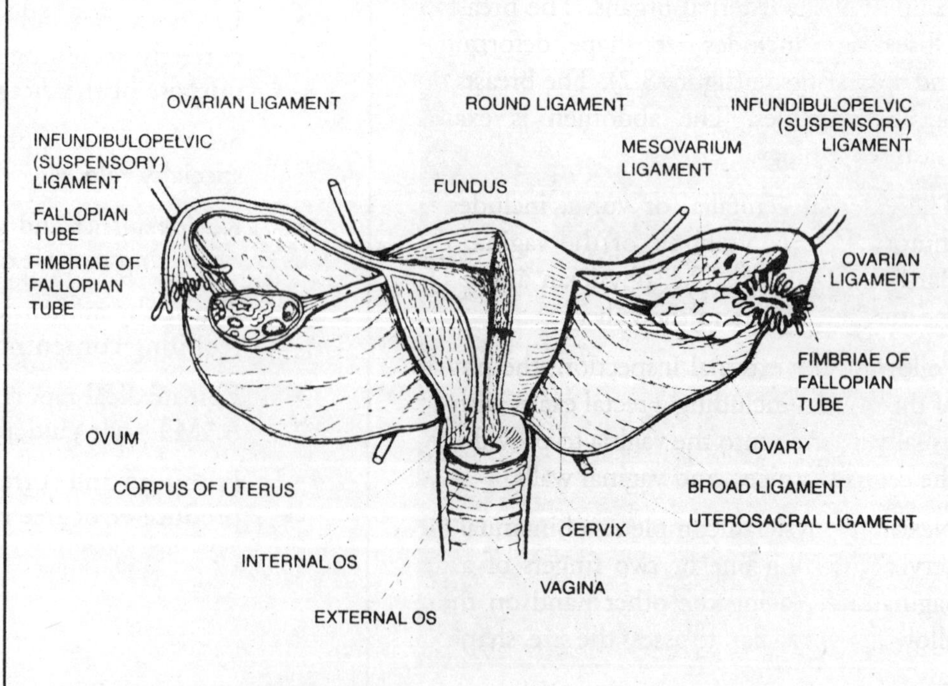

At puberty, hormones cause the ova to ripen and mature into a graafian follicle, a type of cyst that enlarges until it reaches the surface of the ovary. This is the beginning of the follicular phase of the menstrual cycle. The surface of the ovary ruptures, releasing an egg, or oocyte, into the pelvic cavity. The fimbriae sweep the oocyte into the fallopian tube.

The discharge of the oocyte from the ovary is referred to as ovulation, which may be associated with some pain, called mittelschmerz, in the lower groin area and some vaginal discharge. This is the luteal phase. If the oocyte is met by a spermatozoon, the male reproductive cell, conception takes place, usually occurring within the fallopian tubes. The cells of the graafian follicle become yellow and are referred to as the corpus luteum which helps prepare the uterus for the fertilized egg.

If conception does not occur, the ovum disintegrates and together with the upper layer of the endometrium of the uterus, is sloughed through the cervix and vagina. This blood flow is called menstruation and occurs approximately every 28 days during the reproductive life of the woman. Ovulation occurs about midway between menstrual periods.

The menstrual cycle occurs in response to the stimulation of hormones. Follicle stimulating hormone (FSH) and luteinizing hormone (LH) are released by the pituitary gland located in the brain (see chapter 11). Estrogen and progesterone are hormones released by the follicle to prepare the uterus to receive the egg. This cycle continues until the woman reaches menopause, (average age is about 50 years). At this time the hormone production diminishes, causing atrophy of the genital organs, breast changes, loss in bone density, and vascular changes.

PHYSICAL ASSESSMENT

The physician begins the assessment of the female reproductive system by examining the external organs. The breasts are the first part of the assessment. Observation includes size, shape, deformities, markings (such as nevi), nipples, and areolar tissue (figure 8.2). The breasts are then palpated for texture, masses, or abnormalities. The abdomen is examined as described in Chapter 7, Gastroenterology.

The external genitalia, or vulva, includes the mon pubis, labia majora, labia minora, clitoris, vestibule of the vagina, the Skene's or vestibular glands, and Bartholin's glands. The physician inspects the genitalia, noting the urinary meatus, the anus, and the vulva.

Following the external inspection, the physician performs a digital examination of the organs, including a rectal exam with a stool swab for blood. A speculum is usually inserted into the vagina to provide a wider opening for the visual exam of the cervix, fornices, and vaginal walls.

Next, the physician completes a bimanual ("two hands") exam of the vagina and cervix, inserting one or two fingers of a gloved and lubricated hand into the vagina and placing the other hand on the patient's abdomen. This procedure allows the physician to assess the size, shape, and position of the uterus along with any masses or tenderness.

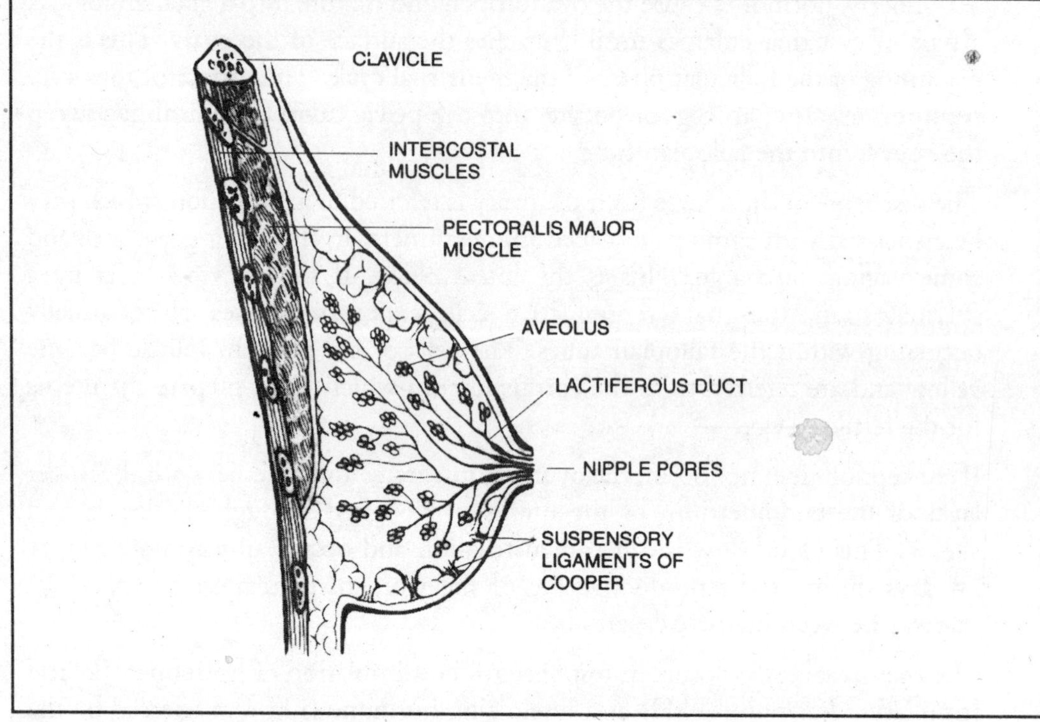

Figure 8.2 Structure of the female breast

DISEASES AND CONDITIONS

Along with cancers of the breast, uterus, ovaries, and cervix, common diseases of the female reproductive system include endometriosis, pelvic inflammatory disease, and sexually transmitted diseases.

Endometriosis is a benign condition in which there is aberrant uterine tissue growing outside the uterine wall. Symptoms associated with endometriosis include extreme menstrual pain, abnormal bleeding, infertility, and dyspareunia. Surgery and/or hormonal therapy to cause atrophy of the endometrium may be necessary to treat endometriosis.

Pelvic inflammatory disease (PID) is an inflammatory condition of the pelvic cavity that may be localized or spread throughout the reproductive organs. Also called acute salpingitis, the disease is usually caused by a bacterial agent such as gonococci or staphylococci and results in vaginal discharge, pain, and tenderness. PID is treated with the appropriate antibiotic therapy.

Human papillomavirus (HPV) is a sexually transmitted disease (STD) that is associated with small growths on the genitalia. Certain types of HPV are associated with increased risk of cervical cancer; therefore, frequent Pap smears are indicated. Other STDs include gonorrhea, syphilis, Chlamydia, and herpes.

COMMON TESTS AND SURGICAL PROCEDURES

The most common test performed during the gynecologic examination is the Papanicolaou (Pap) smear, which is a cytologic test that can detect cervical cancer. When the test was first developed, findings were classified in the following categories:

- Class I: Absence of atypical or abnormal cells
- Class II: Atypical cytology, usually cervical inflammation, but no evidence of malignancy
- Class III: Cytology suggestive of, but not conclusive for, malignancy
- Class IV: Cytology strongly suggestive of malignancy
- Class V: Cytology conclusive for malignancy

In the past decade, a National Cancer Institute-sponsored workshop developed a standardized system for reporting Pap smears that has generally replaced the older classification system. Called The Bethesda System (TBS), the new system is based on narrative reporting of descriptive diagnoses using clinically relevant cell findings. Physicians may incorporate within the narrative reporting a classification subsystem called the CIN system, which includes the following categories (CIN stands for cervical intraepithelial neoplasia, also called dysplasia, which are precancerous lesions):

- CIN-1: mild dysplasia
- CIN-2: moderate dysplasia
- CIN-3: severe dysplasia

Colposcopy is a procedure that is performed when there is an abnormal Pap smear other than Class V. The colposcope is inserted into the cervix allowing visualization of the abnormal tissue. Biopsies are taken to provide more tissue for diagnosis. Cone biopsy is performed for the removal of premalignant cells. The patient has an excision of an inverted cone of tissue from the cervix.

Dilatation and curettage (D&C) is a surgical procedure performed to obtain endometrial or endocervical tissue for cytologic examination and to control abnormal uterine bleeding. The cervix is dilated and a curette is used to obtain uterine scrapings.

Hysterectomy is the surgical procedure to remove the cervix and uterus. A hysterectomy with removal of the fallopian tubes and ovaries is known as a total hysterectomy with bilateral salpingo-oophorectomy (TAH, if done abdominally /BSO).

C-section (cesarean section) is the surgical delivery of a baby. This type of delivery accounts for approximately 20 to 25 percent of all deliveries and is carried out in cases of ineffective labor, fetal distress, breech presentations, multiple births, and infections in the mother.

Mastectomy is the surgical removal of a breast, usually because of a cancerous tumor. The removal of only the tumor and minimal surrounding tissue is called a lumpectomy.

Common Obstetrics and Gynecology Drugs

desogestrel & ethinyl estradiol
OrthoSept

estradiol
Estrace, Estraderm

estrogens, conjugated
Premarin

levonorgestrel & ethinyl estradiol
Triphasil-21

medroxyprogesterone acetate
Provera

norethindrone/mestranol
Ortho-Novum

THE VOCABULARY OF OBSTETRICS AND GYNECOLOGY

The following word list contains common obstetrics and gynecology terms as well as most of the difficult words you will hear in the dictation at the end of the chapter. Take time to become familiar with these words now, then review them again before you key the medical documents.

Here are suggestions for learning the vocabulary words:

1. Read and study each word for pronunciation and meaning.
2. Write each unfamiliar word from the list below on a notecard, write the definition or a paraphrase of the definition on the back, and draw a simple picture to help you learn the word.
3. Study the pronunciation, spelling, and definition of each word on your notecard, then key each word twice for reinforcement. Check the spelling.
4. Add the correctly spelled terms to your word processor's spell checker.

adenopathy
(ad-e-nop'-a-thee) (n) swelling or enlargement of any gland, especially the lymph nodes

adipose
(ad'-i-pOz) (adj) containing fat

adnexal
(ad-nek'-sal) (adj) relating to appendages or accessory parts of an organ

adrenarche
(ad'-ren-ar-kee) (n) the beginning of hormonal activity that leads up to puberty and the associated sexual development

amenorrhea
(a-men-O-ree'-a) (n) stoppage or absence of menses

amniocentesis
(am'-nee-O-sen-tee'-sis) (n) taking a sample of amniotic fluid

anovulation
(an-ov-yoo-lay'-shun) (n) absence of egg production or release from the ovary

anovulatory
(an-ov'-yoo-la-tOr-ee) (adj) not accompanied by production of or discharge of an ovum (egg) or suppressing ovulation

anteflexion
(an-te-flek'-shun) (n) the abnormal position of an organ that is bent forward over itself

Apgar score
(n) scoring system to assess newborn's physical condition

biopsy
(bI'-op-see) (n) the sampling of tissue and/or fluid from the body for microscopic study; the specimen obtained

Braxton Hicks sign
(n) irregular contractions of the uterus after the first trimester of pregnancy

breech presentation
(n) fetal position in which the feet or buttocks appear first in the birth canal

calcification
(kal'-si-fi-kay'-shun) (n) a hardening of tissue resulting from the formation of calcium salts within it

carcinoma
(kar-si-nO'-ma) (n) a malignant growth of epithelial cells

centimeter
(sen'-ti-mee-ter) (n) unit of measurement; one hundredth of a meter; approximately 0.4 inches

cervical
(ser'-vi-kal) (adj) relating to a neck, or cervix, especially the neck (cervix) of the uterus

cervix
(ser'-viks) (n) the neck or part of an organ resembling a neck, such as the cervix of the uterus

chromosome
(krO'-mO-sOm) (n) the structure in the cell nucleus that transmits genetic information; consists of a double strand of DNA in the form of a helix; there are normally 46 in humans

colostrum
(kO-los'-trum) (n) the first milk secreted after childbirth

colposcopy
(kol-pos'-ko-pee) (n) examination of the tissues of the vagina and cervix with a lighted instrument that magnifies the cells

condyloma
(kon-di-lO'-ma) (n) warty growths in the genital area

curettage
(kyoo-re-tahzh) (n) surgical scraping or cleaning, usually of the interior of a cavity or tract, for removal or sampling of tissue

cyanosis
(cI-a-nO'-sis) (n) condition in which the skin and/or mucous membranes turn blue due to decreased amount of oxygen in the blood cells

dysgerminoma
(dis-jer-mi-nO'-ma) (n) a rare cancerous ovarian tumor

dysmenorrhea
(dis-men-Or-ee'-a) (n) painful menstruation

dyspareunia
(dis-pa-roo'-nee-a) (n) painful sexual intercourse

ectopic pregnancy
(ek-top'-ik) (n) pregnancy in which a fertilized ovum is implanted outside the uterus, often in a fallopian tube

edema
(e-dee'-ma) (n) excessive accumulation of fluid in tissues, especially just under the skin or in a given cavity

emesis
(em'-e-sis) (n) retching; throwing up

endometrium
(en'-dO-mee'-tree-um) (n) lining of the womb, composed of three layers and shed during menstruation

engorged
(en-gOrjd') (adj) filled to the limit of expansion

episiotomy
(e-piz-ee-ot'-O-mee) (n) incision of perineum to facilitate delivery and prevent laceration (jagged tear)

estradiol
(es-tra-dI'-ol) (n) a hormone produced by the ovary; often used to treat menopausal symptoms

eversion
(ee-vur'-zhun) (n) turning out or inside out

excrescence
(eks-kres'-ens) (n) abnormal projection or outgrowth; such as a wart

fallopian tubes
(fa-lO'-pee-an) (n) passageways from ovaries to uterus

fetal distress
(fee'-tal) (n) life-threatening condition affecting the fetus

fundus
(fun'-dus) (n) the bottom or base of an organ; the part farthest from the opening; fundi (pl)

genital
(jen'-i-tal) (adj) relating to reproduction or the organs of reproduction

genitalia
(jen'-i-tay'-lee-a) (n) male or female reproductive organs, especially the external ones

gestation
(jes-tay'-shun) (n) the intrauterine development of an infant; pregnancy

gonorrhea
(gon-O-ree'-a) a contagious disease usually affecting the genitourinary tract; transmitted chiefly by sexual intercourse

Graafian follicle
(graf'-ee-an) (n) a mature follicle on the ovary in which an oocyte matures and is released at ovulation

gravida
(grav'-i-da) (n) a pregnant woman; may be used in combination with a number or prefix to indicate the number of pregnancies and their outcome

homeostasis
(hO'-mee-O-stay'-sis/hO'-mee-os'-ta-sis) (n) equilibrium in the internal environment of the body, such as temperature and electrolytic balance

hypermenorrhea
(hI'-per-men-O-ree'-a) (n) lengthy or heavy menses; menorrhagia

hypomenorrhea
(hI'-pO-men-O-ree'-a) (n) decreased menses

hysterectomy
(his-ter-ek'-tO-mee) (n) surgical removal of the uterus

immunohistochemistry
(im'-yoo-nO-his'-tO-kem'-is-tree) (n) special techniques used on cells to identify certain characteristics, especially the presence of specific antigens

infundibulopelvic
(in-fun-dib'-yoo-lO-pel'-vik) (adj) relating to or located in the infundibulum (the end of the fallopian tube farthest from the uterus) and the pelvis

in situ
(in sI'-too) (adj, adv) in position; at the original location, or site

intraductal
(adj) inside a duct

introitus
(in-trO'-i-tus) (n) an opening or entrance into a canal or cavity, such as the vagina

inversion
(in-vur'-shun) (n) reversal of position, as upside down or inside out

knuckle
(nuk'-l) (n) a finger joint; an abnormal kink or loop

laparotomy
(lap-a-rot'-O-mee) (n) a surgical procedure in which an incision is made into the abdominal wall

leiomyoma
(lI'-O-mI-O'-ma) (n) tumor in smooth muscle tissue

leukemia
(loo-kee'-mee-a) (n) production of abnormal white blood cells; a type of cancer of the blood

lochia
(lO'-kee-a) (n) vaginal discharge occurring after childbirth

loop
(n) a curve or bend forming a complete or almost complete oval or circle

loupe
(loop) (n) a magnifying lens

lymphatic
(lim-fat'-ik) (adj) relating to or resembling lymph or lymph nodes

lymphocyte
(lim'-fO-sIt) (n) white blood cell that produces antibodies

lymphocytic
(lim-fO-sit'-ik) (adj) relating to or characteristic of lymphocytes

mammogram
(mam'-O-gram) (n) x-ray of the breast

mediolateral
(mee'-dee-O-lat'-er-al) (adj) relating to the middle and side of a structure

menarche
(me-nar'-kee) (n) the initial menstrual period

menometrorrhagia
(men'-O-mee-trO-ray'-jee-a) (n) excessive menstrual bleeding or bleeding between menstrual periods

menopause
(men'-O-pawz) (n) the end of a woman's reproductive period of life and cessation of menses

menorrhagia
(men-O-ray'-jee-a) (n) prolonged or heavy menses; hypermenorrhea

menorrhalgia
(men-O-ral'-jee-a) (n) painful menstruation or pelvic pain accompanying menstruation

menses
(men'-seez) (n) monthly flow of bloody fluid from the uterus

menstruation
(men-stroo-ay'-shun) (n) the discharge of a bloody fluid from the uterus at regular intervals during the life of a woman from puberty to menopause

mesosalpinx
(mez'-O-sal'-pinks) (n) free end of the broad ligament which supports the fallopian tubes

metrorrhagia
(mee-trO-ray'-jee-a) (n) bleeding from the uterus between menstrual periods

multipara
(mul-tip'-a-ra) (n) a woman who has given birth to two or more children

nodule
(nod'-yool) (n) a small mass, distinct from surrounding tissue

nuchal
(noo-kal) (adj) relating to the nape or back of the neck

nulligravida
(nul-i-grav'-i-da) (n) a woman who has never been pregnant

oligomenorrhea
(ol'-i-gO-men-O-ree'-a) (n) infrequent or very light menstrual bleeding

omental
(O-men'-tal) (adj) relating to the omentum

omentum
(O-men'-tum) (n) fold of peritoneal tissue attaching to and supporting the stomach and intestines

oophorectomy
(O-of-Or-ek'-tO-mee) (n) surgical removal of one or both ovaries

organomegaly
(Or'-ga-nO-meg'-a-lee) (n) abnormal enlargement of an organ, particularly an organ of the abdominal cavity, such as the liver or spleen

palpate
(pal'-payt) (v) to examine by touch; to feel

para
(par'-a) (n) a woman who has given birth to one or more children; the term may be used in combination with a number or prefix to indicate how many times a woman has given birth

pelvic
(pel'-vik) (adj) relating to or located near the pelvis

pendulous
(pen'-ju-lus) (adj) loosely hanging

perineum
(per'-i-nee'-um) (n) the external region between the urethral opening and the anus, including the skin and underlying tissues

peritoneal
(per'-i-tO-nee'-al) (adj) relating to the peritoneum

peritoneum
(per-i-tO-nee'-um) (n) lining of the abdominal cavity

polycystic
(pol-ee-sis'-tik) (adj) having or consisting of many cysts

primipara
(prE-mip'-ah-ra) (n) a woman who has had one pregnancy that produced a living infant

pyelogram
(pī'-el-Ō-gram) (n) x-ray of the kidney and ureters; usually a radiopaque dye is injected into the patient to show the outline of the kidney and associated structures

rectovaginal
(rek'-tŌ-vaj'-i-nal) (adj) relating or located near the rectum and vagina

retraction
(ree-trak'-shun) (n) the act of pulling back

sac
(sak) (n) pouch

sonometer
(son-Ō-mee'-ter) (n) a bell-shaped instrument used to measure hearing

supine
(soo-pīn') (adj) lying on the back

Tanner staging
(n) method of indicating the sexual development of a child or adolescent

thelarche
(thee-lar'-kee) (n) the beginning of breast development in girls

thyroid
(thī'-royd) (n) a gland in the neck that secretes thyroid hormone

thyromegaly
(thī-rŌ-meg'-a-lee) (n) enlargement of the thyroid gland

uterine
(yoo'-ter-in/yoo'-ter-īn) (adj) relating to the uterus (the female reproductive organ where the fertilized egg develops before birth; the womb)

vertex
(ver'-teks) (n) the crown or top of the head

vortex
(vŌr'-teks) (n) whirlpool; resembling a whirlpool

vulva
(vul'-va) (n) external female genital organs; vulvae (pl)

vulvar
(vul'-var) (adj) relating to the vulva

xeromammogram
(zeer'-Ō-mam'-o-gram) (n) type of x-ray of the breast

ABBREVIATIONS

AB, Ab	abortion
AIDS	acquired immune deficiency syndrome
BTL	bilateral tubal ligation (sterilization by cutting or cauterizing the fallopian tubes)
BBT	basal body temperature
BSO	bilateral salpingo-oophorectomy (removal of both ovaries and fallopian tubes)
CPD	cephalopelvic disproportion
CS, C-section	cesarean section
D&C	dilatation (or dilation) and curettage (instrumental expansion of the cervix and scraping of the uterine cavity)
DOB	date of birth
DUB	dysfunctional uterine bleeding
EDC	estimated date of confinement
FEKG	fetal electrocardiogram
FHR	fetal heart rate
FHT	fetal heart tones
FSH	follicle-stimulating hormone
FTND	full term normal delivery
FTNSVD	full term, normal spontaneous vaginal delivery
GC	gonorrhea
GYN	gynecology
HCG	human chorionic gonadotropin
HIV	human immunodeficiency virus
HRT	hormone replacement therapy
HSG	hysterosalpingography
IUD	intrauterine device
LH	luteinizing hormone
LMP	last menstrual period
NB	newborn
OB	obstetrics
PID	pelvic inflammatory disease
PMP	previous menstrual period
TAH	total abdominal hysterectomy
TAH/BSO	total abdominal hysterectomy with bilateral salpingo-oophorectomy
UC	uterine contractions
VH	vaginal hysterectomy
VBAC	vaginal birth after cesarean section

EXERCISE 8.1: RECOGNIZING LOOK-ALIKES AND SOUND-ALIKES

Below is a list of frequently used words that look alike and/or sound alike. Study the meaning and pronunciation of each set of words, then read each sentence carefully and circle the word in parentheses that correctly completes the meaning.

thorough complete, meticulous
through nonstop, straight, finished

continuous ceaseless; uninterrupted in time
continual regular or frequent

menometrorrhagia irregular or excessive bleeding during menses and between menses
menopause cessation of reproductive period of life and cessation of menses for at least one year

menorrhagia prolonged or heavy menses
menorrhalgia painful menstruation or pelvic pain accompanying menstruation

elicit (v) to bring out
illicit (adj) illegal

decent (adj) appropriate, conforming to acceptable behavior
descent (n) downward movement, lowering

eminent prominent, famous, standing out
imminent about to occur

amenorrhea absence of menses for three months or more
dysmenorrhea painful menstruation
oligomenorrhea infrequent or scant menstrual bleeding
hypermenorrhea prolonged or heavy menses
hypomenorrhea diminished menses

1. The patient denies use of (elicit, illicit) drugs.
2. Palpation of the area did not (elicit, illicit) pain.
3. She had a (continual, continuous) menstruation that lasted more than four weeks.
4. The patient seemed anxious to get (thorough, through) the physical examination.
5. The (descent, decent) of the laparoscope into the suprapubic area proceeded with minimal discomfort to the patient.
6. The patient states she has (amenorrhea, dysmenorrhea) with menses but Advil usually controls the pain.
7. Hypermenorrhea and (menorrhalgia, menorrhagia) mean the same thing.

8. Noting that the birth of the baby seemed (imminent, eminent), the nurse paged the obstetrician.
9. Dysmenorrhea and (menorrhalgia, menorrhagia) mean the same thing.
10. The end of one's reproductive life phase is called (menses, menopause).

EXERCISE 8.2: MATCHING SOUND AND SPELLING

The numbered list that follows shows the phonetic spelling of hard-to-spell words. Sound out the word, then write the correct spelling in the blank space provided. Each of the words can be found in the glossary or in the drug list in appendix C.

1. e-piz-ee-ot'-O-mee ________________
2. kol-pos'-ko-pee ________________
3. krO'-mO-sOm ________________
4. a-men-O-ree'-a ________________
5. kon-di-lO'-ma ________________
6. graf'-ee-an ________________
7. jes-tay'-shun ________________
8. his-ter-ek'-tO-mee ________________
9. kyoo'-re-tahzh' ________________
10. in-sI'-too ________________
11. mul-tip'-a-ra ________________
12. gon-O-ree'-a ________________
13. men'-O-ray'-jee-a ________________
14. ol'-i-gO-men-O-ree'-a ________________
15. per'-i-nee'-um ________________

EXERCISE 8.3: CHOOSING WORDS FROM CONTEXT

When transcribing dictation, the medical transcriptionist frequently needs to determine the word that correctly completes the sentence based on the situation. From the list of words below, select the term that meaningfully completes each statement.

carcinoma	menses	uterine
lymphocyte	gravida	para
dysmenorrhea	peritoneum	hypomenorrhea
mammogram	introitus	menopause
genital		

1. The ________________ showed she had a small, pea-sized mass in the right breast.
2. Mrs. Jones states she has severe cramping at the time of her ______________.
3. She had condyloma on her external __________ area.
4. The ____________ is found at the entrance of the vagina.
5. Her blood count revealed an increased _____________ count, possibly indicating a viral infection.
6. The patient states that ibuprofen relieves the __________ during her menstrual periods.
7. The hysterectomy was performed after the biopsy revealed a ______________.
8. Mrs. Green is a (an) _______________2, para 1 and presents to the birthing center today in active labor.
9. The ________________contractions increased steadily until the baby was delivered.
10. After the tumor was removed from the abdominal wall, the _______________ was washed.

EXERCISE 8.4: PAIRING WORDS AND MEANINGS

For each definition provided below, locate the term on the list that best matches the definition. Write the letter of the term in the space provided beside the definition.

A. calcification	F. adrenarche	J. oophorectomy
B. edema	G. dysgerminoma	K. dysmenorrhea
C. menarche	H. anovulation	L. hysterectomy
D. nulligravida	I. menses	M. amenorrhea
E. oligomenorrhea		

1. absence of egg release from ovary ______
2. malignant neoplasm of the ovary ______
3. changes that occur at puberty ______
4. surgical removal of an ovary ______
5. a hardening of tissue from formation of calcium ______
6. painful menstruation ______
7. excessive amount of fluid in body tissues ______
8. first menstrual period ______
9. a woman who has never conceived a child ______
10. monthly flow of blood from the uterus ______

EXERCISE 8.5: CREATING TERMS FROM WORD FORMS

In the following exercise, combine prefixes, root words, and suffixes to create medical words that fit the definitions below. Fill in the blanks with the words you construct.

hepat/o	liver	germin	germinal tissue
mast/o	breast	son-o	sound waves
thyr/o	thyroid	-megaly	enlargement
dys-	difficult, painful	-rrhea	flow, discharge
lei/o	smooth	-itis	inflammation
my/o	muscle	-oma	tumor
men/o	month	-gram	record
mamm/o	breast	-ectomy	cutting out, removal
oophor/o	ovary	mast-	breast
salping/o	tube	organ/o	liver, spleen

1. removal of fallopian tubes ______
2. very large thyroid gland ______
3. inflammation of the ovary ______
4. menstruation ______
5. tumor of smooth muscle tissue ______
6. rare ovarian malignant tumor, that causes pain ______
7. x-ray of breast ______
8. benign tumor in the uterus ______
9. removal of ovaries ______

10. abnormally large liver ______________________
11. removal of breast ______________________
12. ultrasound image/record ______________________

EDITING MEDICAL DOCUMENTS

In this section you will perfect your word use and grammar skills. These skills will help you edit and proofread medical reports for correct language, punctuation, format, and meaning. The special focus for this chapter is plural and singular word forms.

FORMING PLURALS

Chapter 2 reviewed the guidelines for creating agreement between subjects and verbs. The guidelines are based on the principle that plural subjects require plural verbs and singular subjects require singular verbs. Since nouns and pronouns function as subjects of sentences, it is important to know the general rules for creating the plural forms of medical terms.

Generally, most nouns are made plural by adding *s* or *es* to the singular form. The same rules usually apply to nouns in medical reports. However, many medical words and terms are of Latin and Greek origin; therefore they do not follow the English rules. For example, the plural form of *diagnosis* is not *diagnosises.* Consult a medical dictionary when necessary.

As you become more familiar with the medical language, forming and/or recognizing plural forms will become easier. The following rules for making plural forms will be helpful:

1. If the singular form ends in *a*, make the plural by adding *e.* (vertebra–vertebrae).
2. If the singular form ends in *um,* change the *um* to *a.* (diverticulum–diverticula).
3. If the singular form ends in *us*, change the *us* to *i.* (fungus–fungi).
4. If the singular form ends in *is*, change the *is* to *es.* (diagnosis–diagnoses).
5. If the singular form ends in *ax* or *ix*, change the *x* to *ces.* (thorax–thoraces; cervix–cervices).
6. If the singular form ends in *ex*, change the *ex* to *ices.* (index–indices).
7. If the singular form ends in *nx*, change the *x* to *ges.* (pharynx–pharynges).
8. If the singular form ends in *en*, change the *en* to *ina.* (lumen–lumina).
9. If the singular form ends in *on,* change the *on* to *a.* (phenomenon–phenomena).
10. If the singular form ends in *ma*, add *ta.* (condyloma–condylomata). Note that it is also acceptable to form plurals of these words just by adding *s.* (carcinoma–carcinomas).

EXERCISE 8.6A: EDITING FOR CORRECT PLURAL FORMS

Write the appropriate plural form on the blank line after each word.

1. fossa ________________
2. prognosis ________________
3. appendix ________________
4. labium ________________
5. datum ________________
6. salpinx ________________
7. uterus ________________
8. ovum ________________
9. criterion ________________
10. foramen ________________

Other Plural Forms

- Very few plural forms contain an apostrophe, so do not be tempted to add one when keying a plural unless you are certain it is correct.
- Some words have only a singular or plural form. The word *adnexa* means appendages or auxiliary parts (plural), usually referring to the fallopian tubes and ovaries. So if you heard "right and left adnexa nontender" in a report of a pelvic examination, you would transcribe *adnexa,* not *adnexae* or *adnexi* because there are no such words. Also, the words *feces, genitalia, menses, scabies, tongs,* and *tweezers* are always plural in use. On the other hand, the words *circulation, vision, ascites,* and *herpes* are singular in meaning. *Biceps, forceps, scissors*, and *series* are the same whether the meaning is singular or plural.

TRANSCRIPTION TIP: Always consider the context of the dictation when choosing the singular or plural form of a noun. For instance, if you hear "conjunctiva clear," you would transcribe this in plural form (unless the patient only has one eye or the eye exams are being dictated individually).

Abbreviations

- Add *s* (no apostrophe) after all uppercase abbreviations.

  Serial ECG*s* revealed no changes.

  CBC*s* over the last six months have been abnormal.

- Add s to abbreviated forms such as *poly* or *seg* (polys, segs).

  White count was 5500 with 67 seg*s*, 7 mono*s*, 2 eo*s*.

Numbers: Add *s* without an apostrophe unless the number is only one digit.

> She had her appendix removed in her 20*s*.
>
> Doctors have made many advances in the 1990*s*.
>
> 8'*s* and 9'*s* on Apgar scores are common.

Abbreviated units of measure: Do not put an *s* on the end of an abbreviated unit of measure, no matter how large the value is, e.g., 1 mg or 1,000,000 mg.

> We removed 200 cc of fluid from the patient's peritoneal cavity.
>
> The incision measured 6 cm.

EXERCISE 8.6B: EDITING FOR CORRECT PLURAL FORMS

From the choices given, write the correct plural form for each word.

1. Colonoscopy revealed multiple (diverticulum/diverticula) in the ascending colon. ______
2. Hysterosalpingogram showed right (hydrosalpinx/hydrosalpinges). ______
3. Her history of intolerance to cold led to the diagnosis of Raynaud's (phenomenon/phenomena). ______
4. She was treated with ampicillin 500 (mg/mgs) q.i.d. times ten days. ______
5. Delivery of the infant was achieved using (forcep/forceps). ______
6. James was told by his doctor that he had a (herpe/herpes) infection. ______
7. Examination of her cervix revealed the presence of different (fungus/fungi). ______
8. Babinskis/Babinski's were negative. ______
9. Serial (CBC/CBCs/CBC's) were obtained. ______
10. (Ascitis/Ascites) is a common condition in people with liver disease. ______

EXERCISE 8.7: PROOFREADING REVIEW

Read the following report sections and circle errors in punctuation, spelling, plural forms, subject-verb agreement, complete sentences, and the placement of modifiers. Then key the report with the errors corrected.

Bilateral mammograms were preformed using film scream technique and compared to previous xeromammograms from June 1992 and February 1993. There appears to be a small and smoothly marginated oval shaped nodular in the upper quadrant of the right breast. Not as clearly visualised on the previous xeromammograms.

Increased density is again seen in the upper outer quadrants bilaterally, unchanged and consistent with fibroglandular tissue. Neither breasts demonstrates evidence of architectural distortion, clustered microcalcifications, skin thickening or retraction.

The patient was placed on the operating table in the supine position under satisfactory general endotracheal anesthesias. A #14 foley cathether was inserted. The abdomen was then prepped with betadine scrub and solution and was drapped in the usual sterile manner.

WHERE CAN I FIND THE ANSWER?

As you transcribe dictation, you may hear unfamiliar words or terms. A variety of reference sources are available to help you locate answers to your questions. One of the important types of references for medical transcriptionists is described below. Read the information; then if you have access to the reference discussed, explore its capabilities.

MEDICAL REFERENCES: GRAMMAR BOOKS

The medical transcriptionist must know proper punctuation and grammar. Although some physicians will dictate punctuation, most rely on the transcriptionist to appropriately punctuate reports. This is a big responsibility. Meaning can be lost or distorted with improper or missing punctuation.

Most beginning MTs are not grammar experts. However, with a little effort, you can acquire a basic background in punctuation and grammar and apply that knowledge in your transcription.

In addition to mastering grammar basics, you should have a grammar reference at your fingertips to answer questions on the fine points of style—issues you do not encounter on a daily basis or questions the *AAMT Book of Style* does not cover. This text includes some basic information on common grammar and punctuation questions, but these guidelines are not intended to replace a grammar reference book.

(continued on next page)

Which one is best for me?

There are many different grammar reference books available. Some are organized alphabetically, others are organized by broad categories such as punctuation or numbers with subcategories. Some reference manuals include exercises so that you can practice the guidelines and rules. Think about your skills and decide which features you require. Do you fit into one of the following categories?

Category A: I am confident of my grammar and punctuation abilities.

Category B: I am a little shaky in grammar and punctuation.

Category C: A wave of nausea overtakes me when I think about grammar and punctuation.

If you are in category A, a concise reference manual is probably your best choice. Suggested titles include *Rules for Writers* by Diana Hacker, *The Paradigm Reference Manual* published by EMC/Paradigm Publishing, or *The Little-Brown Book.*

If you are in category B or C, you may consider a study-type book. Two choices include *Good Grief, Good Grammar* by Dianna Booher and *The Paradigm Reference Manual* plus its accompanying workbook, published by EMC/Paradigm Publishing.

TRANSCRIBING OBSTETRICS AND GYNECOLOGY DOCUMENTS

In this section your goal is to prepare for the work of transcription through transcribing first from a printed document and then from dictation on tape. The model document that follows illustrates the generally accepted format for the **labor and delivery report**, the medical report featured in this chapter.

BASIC FORMAT: THE LABOR AND DELIVERY REPORT

As its title suggests, the labor and delivery report summarizes the procedures used in the delivery of a baby. Although most are brief reports, those describing a delivery that requires the physician's surgical intervention—for example, delivery by forceps—can be as extensive as an operative report.

Required Headings/Content

Although no specific headings are required, the labor and delivery report includes headings similar to those in an operative report. Usually dictated are the preoperative and postoperative diagnoses, the title and date of the procedure, the indications for the procedure, and the actual description of the procedure.

Turnaround Time

Generally, labor and delivery reports should be transcribed within 24 hours after dictation. However, this guideline varies among hospitals.

LABOR AND DELIVERY REPORT

1" top and side margins → **left justification**

PATIENT NAME: Jung-Ah Wang
DATE: 10/21/XX

ds

PREOPERATIVE DIAGNOSIS: Arrest of descent.

ds

POSTOPERATIVE DIAGNOSIS: Single viable female infant.

ds

OPERATION PERFORMED: Indicated low forceps delivery.

ds

INDICATIONS: This is a 33-year-old gravida 1, para 0 who pushed greater than two hours and then consented to epidural anesthesia. She pushed for one more hour and pushed the baby to +2 station and consented for assisted vaginal delivery.

ds

PROCEDURE: After adequate epidural anesthesia, the patient was placed in stirrups and was prepared and draped in the usual sterile fashion. The cervix was again examined and noted to be completely dilated, completely effaced. The pelvis was noted to be adequate. The estimated fetal weight was approximately 8 pounds. Position of the infant was noted to be right occiput posterior. The station was noted to be +2.

ds

The bladder was drained with a red Robinson catheter. Simpson forceps were then soaked in Betadine solution and the posterior blade was carefully placed, with the opposite hand protecting the vaginal side wall. The same procedure was repeated on the opposite site. Correct blade placement was then verified times two. A midline episiotomy was then performed. With adequate maternal expulsive efforts, a viable female infant was delivered over a midline episiotomy. A vigorous cry was noted on the perineum. Inspection of the infant noted correct blade placement. The baby was bulb suctioned on the perineum and passed off to the awaiting pediatricians, given Apgar scores of 9 and 10. Weight of the infant was 3762 grams. Cord pH was obtained; arterial 7.29, venous 7.33.

ds

The vagina was inspected for lacerations and there were none. The cervix and rectum were intact. The midline episiotomy was then reapproximated with 2-0

(continued)

LABOR AND DELIVERY REPORT
PATIENT NAME: Jung-Ah Wang
Page 2
ds

Vicryl suture. The placenta was easily removed, followed by vigorous fundal massage, and intravenous Pitocin was given. Uterine tone was noted to be firm. There were no complications. After delivery of the infant at 0234, both mother and infant were doing well.

qs

____

Alexandra Mateo, MD
ds
AM:XX
D: 10/21/XX
T: 10/22/XX

PREPARING TO TRANSCRIBE

To prepare for transcribing dictations, key the labor and delivery report above. You will later key the identical report from dictation. Follow these guidelines:

- Study the format and organization of each report.
- Review the word list presented earlier in this chapter.
- Consult reference books for words or formatting rules that are unfamiliar.
- Proofread your final copy by comparing it to the printed version.

CASES FOR TRANSCRIPTION

In this section you will transcribe medical dictation from tape. Your goal is to produce error-free documents. Read this chapter's Pro Tip (following the case studies) for helpful hints from experienced MTs. Then follow these steps for each dictation:

1. Prepare to transcribe by reviewing the case study and the model report formats from this and earlier chapters.
2. Transcribe the dictation, leaving spaces for words you cannot hear or do not understand.
3. Carefully proofread each document and correct as many errors as you can. Use your reference materials to help you identify missing words.
4. Listen to the tape again and correct all remaining errors.

Repeat these steps until you produce an error-free document. Then complete the Performance Report, attach it to the top of the transcripts, and submit them to your instructor for evaluation.

CASE STUDY 1: FELICIA STALLWARD

Felicia Stallward is a 25-year-old woman who had leukemia as a young child and presently complains of irregular menstruation. She is seen by the gynecologist.

Report 8.1: Consultation Letter

Transcription Hint

Listen for these new abbreviations:
TSH (thyroid-stimulating hormone)
DHEAS (dehydroepiandrosterone sulfate)

CASE STUDY 2: ROSEMARY BARNES

Rosemary Barnes discovered a lump in her left breast when she was performing her monthly breast self-examination. She was seen in the gynecologist's office immediately. She was sent to the surgeon for examination and excision of the mass.

Report 8.2: Pathology Report

CASE STUDY 3: IRENE REMONA

Irene Remona is a 51-year-old woman who had a routine mammography as part of her annual checkup at the gynecologist. Her checkup was completely within normal limits. Her mammogram results follow.

Report 8.3: Radiology Report

CASE STUDY 4: JUNG-AH WANG

Jung-ah Wang is a 33-year-old woman who was admitted to the hospital to deliver her first child. She has had an unproductive labor and has agreed to an assisted vaginal delivery with forceps.

Report 8.4: Labor and Delivery Report

Transcription Hints

- Gravida refers to the number of times a woman has been pregnant. Para indicates the number of deliveries after the 20th week of gestation. A woman who has been pregnant five times (two term infants, one premature infant, one abortion, and one miscarriage) may be described in several different ways, all of which are acceptable:

  "The patient is gravida five, para three." (transcribed gravida 5, para 3)

  "The patient is G five, P three." (transcribed G5, P3)

  "The patient is gravida five, para three, aborta two." (transcribed gravida 5, para 3, aborta 2)

  "The patient is G five, P three, AB two [or A two]." (transcribed G5, P3, AB 2[or A2])

  The physician may also use TPAL terminology, listing numbers in an order that correlates with the following designations: T = term infants, P = premature infants, A = abortions or miscarriages, L = living children

  Thus if the dictator says, "The patient is gravida five, para two one two three" OR "obstetric history two one two three," you would key: The patient is gravida 5, para 2-1-2-3 OR Obstetric history: 2-1-2-3.

- Some physicians use the military style for expressing time. For example, in this report, the dictator notes that the infant was delivered at "zero two thirty-four," which means 2:34 a.m., and which should be transcribed as 0234. See chapter 10 for more information on transcribing time expressions.

CASE STUDY 5: MARY EWING

Mary Ewing is an 18-year-old female who has experienced intermittent abdominal pain for several weeks. She was seen by her physician; and, at that time, there were no significant findings. Three weeks ago, she found that her waist had significantly increased in size. She also had continued abdominal pain and had some vomiting for the past several days. She returned to her physician who palpated a mass in the lower abdomen and referred her to the surgeon.

Report 8.5: Operative Report

CASE STUDY 6: GENA MARTIN

Gena Martin is a 21-year-old woman who was admitted to the hospital in labor with her first child. When tests indicated fetal distress, Gena agreed to undergo a cesarean section.

Report 8.6: Operative Report

Transcription Hint

Listen for these new terms:
DeLee suctioned
Vancomycin

CASE STUDY 7: MARTA VALDEZ

Marta Valdez is a 22-year-old woman who is pregnant with twins. With her previous pregnancy, she developed cervical dilation at 20 weeks of gestation, which required cervical cerclage. Her obstetrician has recommended cervical cerclage with this pregnancy to prevent premature labor and delivery.

Report 8.7: Operative Report

Transcription Hints

- Physicians may use clock terminology to indicate areas on a circular surface. In this report, for example, the dictator describes the placement of a 5 mm Mersilene band at the "six o'clock position" and the "two o'clock" position of the cervix. Transcribe these expressions using figures and the word "o'clock" (6 o'clock and 2 o'clock).
- Listen for these terms:
  Unasyn
  Indocin
  Sims elevator
  amnion
  Trendelenburg position

CASE STUDY 8: AMY BATAGLIA

Amy Bataglia is a 21-year-old pregnant woman who was admitted to the hospital in labor. She has received her prenatal care in the medical center's OB clinic and is known to have a breech malpresentation with oligohydramnios. In consultation with her physician, she has agreed to a cesarean section.

Report 8.8: Operative Report

Transcription Hint

Listen for these terms:
Pfannenstiel incision
Kocher clamp
Metzenbaum scissors
Mauriceau-Smellie-Veit maneuver

PRO TIP: DEALING WITH SLANG & QUESTIONABLE COMMENTS

By Kathleen Offman, CMT

On the job, it is generally appropriate to delete vulgar terms, personal or angry remarks, or inflammatory comments from a medical report. Slang terms referring to patients, employees, other health professionals, allied health staff members, or management should not appear in the medical record. Fortunately, these occurrences are rare. But MTs will encounter questionable language uses that require careful judgement.

Physicians are sometimes stressed when dictating. They may make comments not meant for the record or engage in soliloquy. Evaluate these situations carefully. Here are some examples:

- In dictating a discharge summary, a physician indicated that the patient was noncompliant, uncooperative, and refused all treatment. He dictated a patient's remark that contained an obscenity. He wanted the remark put in quotations, and the MT complied. In this instance, it was important to include the information in the record as documentation for the sequence of events should the situation result in litigation. The remarks he made were relevant to the content of the case and patient care.
- In the extremities section of a history and physical report, a physician dictated in an off-hand manner that the patient was wearing new, unwashed jeans. The MT could not determine whether or not to include this comment; however, a later section in the report indicated that the patient had bluish skin. It became apparent that the physician was documenting that the cause may have been from the dye in the jeans and not cyanosis! The MT's careful reading helped shape an educated decision.

Comments Usually Acceptable to Include in a Report

- Comments about missing laboratory data or any results of a procedure are usually acceptable. For example, if the physician notes, "Lab results are not on the chart at this time," this is okay to document.
- Also acceptable are comments about poor prep, for example, on a colonoscopy. This should be documented as it will affect the outcome of the procedure.
- Unprescribed drugs or an overdose of a drug administered should be documented in the patient record if dictated, as this may affect subsequent treatment.

Guidelines for Making Decisions on Questionable Comments

- Note the language the physician uses. Is it factual, sensible, objective, and relevent to the case and patient care? If so, this information can be included in the report.
- Note the tone of the physician. Is it angry, sarcastic, or impatient? Words spoken in these tones may need to be edited out or questioned. Check with your supervisor before including these in the report. Other departments that may be involved in these issues may be Risk Management or Health Information Management. Never exceed the limits of your authority on these matters. Consult the experts.

ASSESSING TRANSCRIPTION SKILLS

Demonstrate your mastery of the terminology, editing/proofreading, and document transcription skills presented in this chapter by completing the following activities.

USING MEDICAL REFERENCES

Use the appropriate medical reference to locate the correct spelling and additional usage information for the words below. (If the reference is not available, use the glossary in this text.) Circle the correct spelling; then write a sentence using the word correctly.

1.	colpscopy	colposcopy	colpuscopy
2.	adnexi	adnexa	adnexae
3.	falopian	faloppian	fallopian
4.	dilatation	dialatation	dilitation
5.	condyloma	chondyloma	condaloma
6.	oophorectomy	oopherectomy	ophorectomy
7.	ceaserean	caesarean	cesarean
8.	genetalia	gentalia	genitalia

9. cytalogy cytology cytologey

____

10. obsterics obstetrics obsetrics

____

MAKING EXPERT DECISIONS

Circle the correct word from the choices in parentheses.

1. After delivery, umbilical (cord/chord) blood samples were obtained and submitted for testing.
2. The baby was delivered from the (vertex/vortex) position after a lengthy labor period.
3. During the prenatal examination, it was determined that the baby was in a transverse (lay/lie).
4. There was one (loop/loupe) of (cord/chord) wrapped around the baby's neck.
5. The amniotic (sac/sack) was ruptured artificially when the patient was at 3 cm, revealing meconium-stained fluid.
6. During her pregnancy, the patient achieved a 20-lb (weight/wait) gain.
7. The (culdoscope/colposcope) was introduced through the posterior vaginal wall and the rectovaginal pouch was visualized.
8. (Descent/Decent) of the baby's head into the birth canal was in progress.
9. Labor progressed rapidly and it was felt delivery was (imminent/eminent).
10. The placental cord contained the normal (compliment/complement) of three vessels.

TRANSCRIBING PROFESSIONAL DOCUMENTS

Transcribe the document named Assessment 8 from tape. Before you key, review the report formatting guidelines. Proofread your transcribed document and revise it until you think it is error-free.

PERFORMANCE REPORT

Name______________________________ Date __________

Document	Description	Date Completed	Document Processing Speed (If Available)	Document Appraisal M=Mailable MC=Mailable w/corrections NM=Not Mailable
Report 8.1	Consultation Letter			M MC NM
Report 8.2	Pathology Report			M MC NM
Report 8.3	Radiology Report			M MC NM
Report 8.4	Labor and Delivery Report			M MC NM
Report 8.5	Operative Report			M MC NM
Report 8.6	Operative Report			M MC NM
Report 8.7	Operative Report			M MC NM
Report 8.8	Operative Report			M MC NM

Comments ______________________________

CHAPTER

9

Urology is the study of the urinary tract in both sexes and the genital tract in the male. Nephrology is the science related to the structure and function of the kidney. Because the systems are interdependent, the specialties are often considered together in medical studies. The subspecialists concerned with the urinary system are the urologist and the nephrologist.

Urology and Nephrology

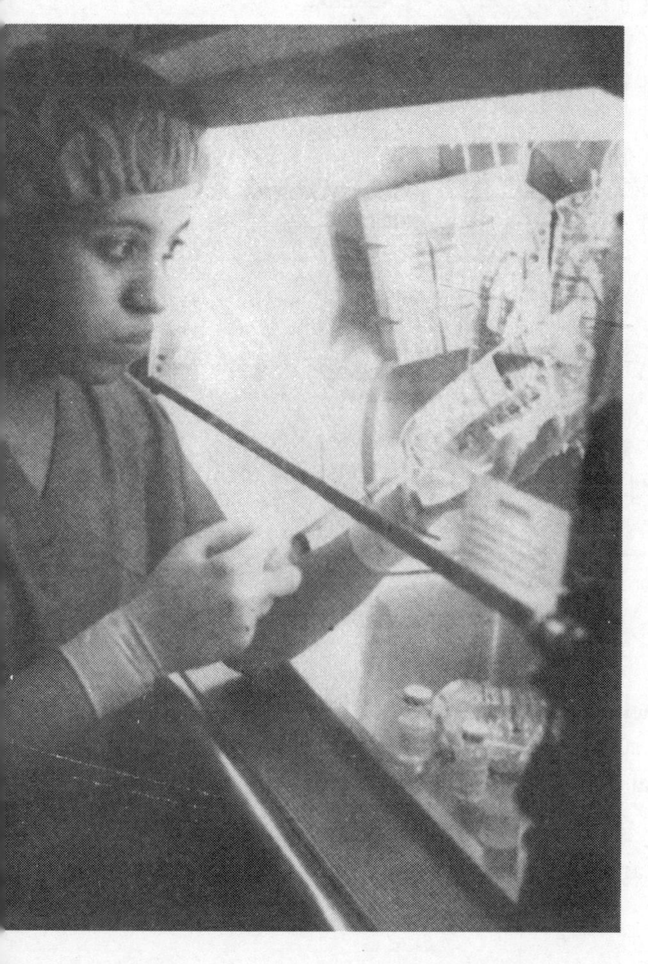

OBJECTIVES

- Use urology and nephrology terms correctly according to the context and purpose of the dictation.
- Select and use appropriate general and specialty reference materials.
- Key urology and nephrology documents of varying complexity and format.
- Transcribe authentic medical dictation requiring concentration and listening skill.
- Edit medical reports to conform with AAMT style guidelines.
- Proofread and correct transcripts to produce error-free documents.

EXPLORING UROLOGY AND NEPHROLOGY

The urinary system consists of those organs that produce urine and eliminate it from the body: the kidneys, ureters, bladder, and urethra figure 9.1). The body must have a proper balance of fluids and electrolytes to sustain life. Electrolytes are charged particles that make up the fluid portion of cells and intracellular, extracellular, and intravascular compartments. The urinary system regulates the fluid and electrolyte balance within the body by filtration, reabsorption, and secretion. The kidneys help maintain the balance by excreting about 1–2 liters of fluid per day and 6–8 grams of salt.

The urinary system is also responsible for transporting and excreting chemical and metabolic wastes from the body. Although there are other avenues by which the body eliminates wastes, such as sweat and stool, urine is the primary end product of the body's metabolism.

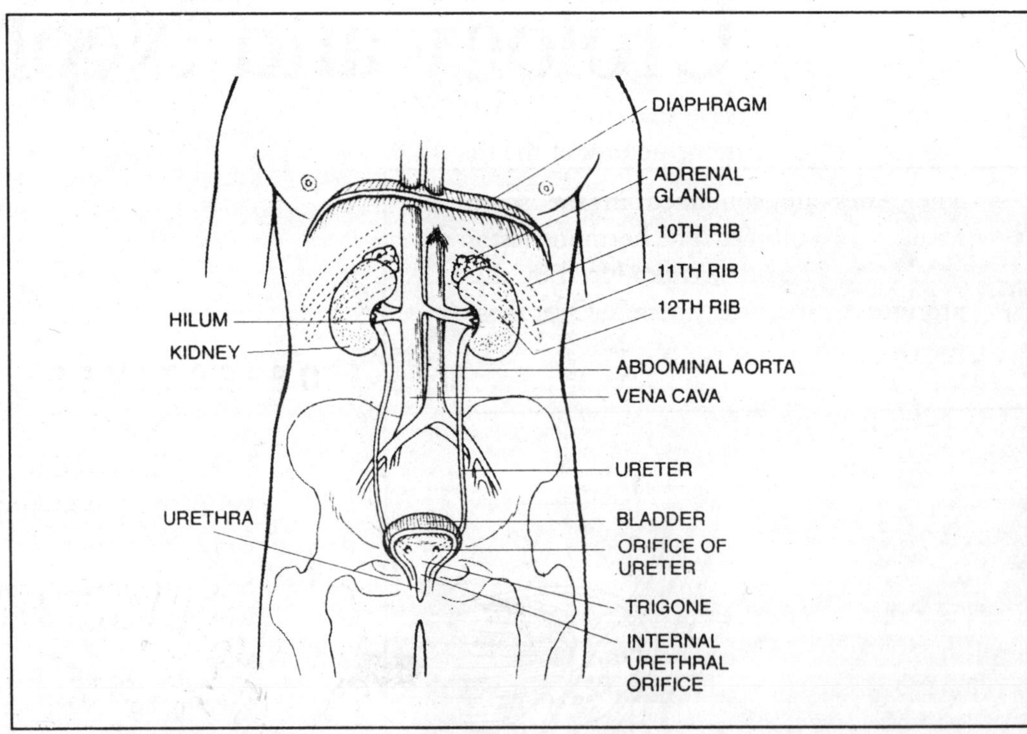

Figure 9.1 Urinary system structures

STRUCTURE AND FUNCTION

The body houses two kidneys, each a few centimeters to the right and left of the thoracic vertebrae. A thin capsule surrounds each kidney to protect and separate it from the abdominal cavity. A renal artery and renal vein provide the blood supply.

The outer portion of the kidney is called the cortex; the inner portion is called the medulla. Within the kidney are approximately one million nephrons, which do the actual work of the kidney. Bowman's capsule surrounds the glomerulus, which contains capillaries composed of endothelial cells and basement membrane. The tubule is divided into four parts: a proximal tubule, the loop of Henle, a distal tubule, and a collecting tubule.

As blood flows through the glomerulus, fluid filters out through the walls of the glomerular capillary tufts. This filtrate is composed primarily of water and electrolytes. Some of the substances are selectively reabsorbed into the blood and the rest continues to travel through the tubule. The remaining fluid that reaches the kidney pelvis is urine.

From the renal pelvis, the urine travels through the ureters and into the bladder by peristaltic waves occurring about one to five times per minute. The bladder is lined with smooth muscle which adapts to the slow filling and does not usually produce the sensation to void until there is approximately 200 to 300 ml of urine. The external urethral sphincter is a muscle that is under voluntary control, which is learned in early childhood. When there is a desire to urinate, the sphincter is relaxed. This allows the bladder muscles to contract and expel urine through the urethra and out the urinary meatus.

Men usually are seen by the urologist for problems with the urogenital system, which includes the male sexual organs. While male sexual dysfunction may be treated by the urologist, male infertility may be managed by infertility specialists. Figure 9.2 depicts the structures of the male anatomy.

The testes are contained in the scrotum. They are made of coils called seminiferous tubules. The hormone testosterone, responsible for male secondary sexual characteristics, is produced by the testes. The seminiferous tubules also produce spermatozoa (sperm). Over these tubules is the epididymis where sperm migrate and mature.

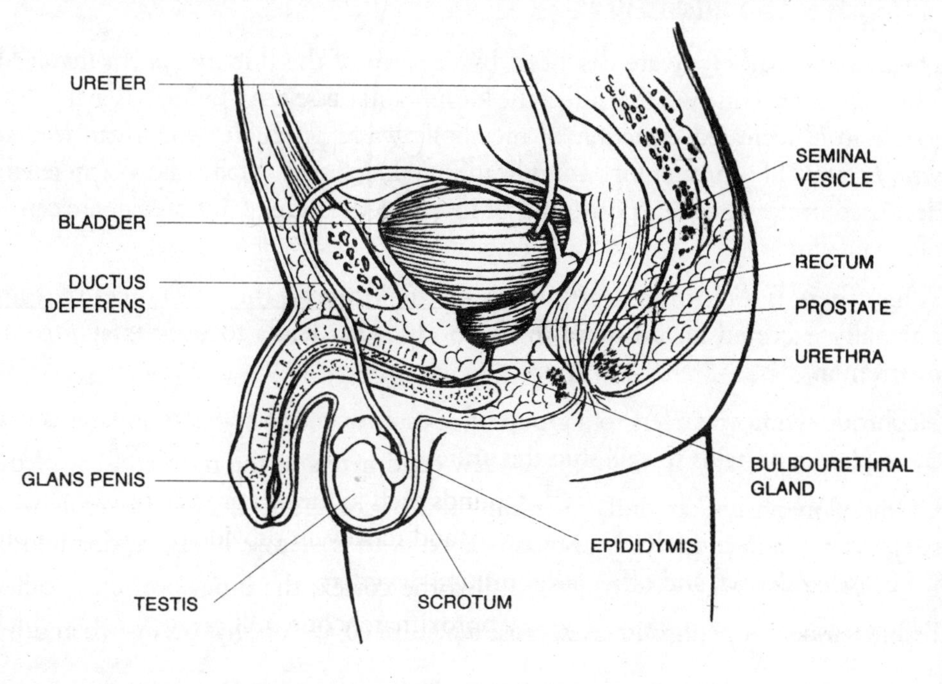

Figure 9.2
Male urogenital system

Urology and Nephrology Drugs

acetazolamide
Diamox

allopurinol
Zyloprim

benazepril
Lotensin

calcitonin
Calcimar, Osteocalcin

calcitriol
Rocaltrol, Calcijex

epoetin alfa
Epogen, Procrit

potassium chloride
K-Dur

spironolactone with hydrochlorothiazide
Aldactazide

terazosin hydrochloride
Hytrin

When the penis is stimulated, it fills with blood and becomes erect. Sperm travels from the epididymis through the vas deferens by smooth muscle contractions. The sperm mixes with fluid secreted by the prostate gland, located at the base of the bladder. This alkaline substance, called semen, protects the sperm from the acidic environment of the male urethra and the female vagina. During ejaculation, semen passes through the urethra. The sphincter at the base of the bladder closes during ejaculation to prevent urine from exiting and semen from entering the bladder.

PHYSICAL ASSESSMENT

Assessment of the urinary system is done by evaluating the patient's medical history and laboratory findings. The physical examination usually is secondary. The examiner asks about the color, odor, frequency, amount, and circumstances under which urine is produced. A urine sample obtained in one of the following ways provides important information:

- For urinalysis, the patient voids into a clean container. The specimen provides general characteristics of the urine and allows the physician to rule out problems.
- For clean-catch urine, the urinary meatus is cleaned with an antiseptic. The urine is collected midstream in a sterile container and then viewed through the microscope to determine the number and type of bacteria present. A clean-catch specimen is collected when the patient has complaints that suggest a urinary tract infection.
- For a catheterized specimen, a sterile, flexible tube, or catheter, is inserted through the meatus into the bladder. Urine is collected in a sterile receptacle for culture.

DISEASES AND CONDITIONS

Diseases and pathology are described by the area of the urinary system involved. There are several diseases that affect the kidney and cause renal failure. Renal failure results in a decreased excretion of metabolic waste products, which can lead to serious and life-threatening complications. Decreased blood flow (prerenal), decreased urinary output (postrenal), or injury to the kidney (intrarenal) are causes of renal failure.

When there is a chronic dysfunction of the kidneys, the substances that are normally excreted accumulate in the body. This leads to uremic syndrome or uremia.

Nephrotic syndrome refers to a group of diseases of the glomerular apparatus that cause plasma proteins to spill into the urine.

Glomerulonephritis, an inflammation of the glomeruli, is often a result of a streptococcal infection. It is also associated with systemic lupus erythematosus (SLE), scleroderma, and other autoimmune disorders.

Kidney stones, or nephrolithiases, cause a painful condition that occurs when urine salts are solidified and cannot be dissolved. When these salts, or stones, lodge in the urinary structures, painful spasms called renal colic occur. Urine may accumulate in the kidney, leading to hydronephrosis. If the stones cannot be passed, the physician may perform lithotripsy using a laser to break down the calculi.

COMMON TESTS AND SURGICAL PROCEDURES

Urea is one of the end products of protein metabolism. Other components are creatinine, phosphates, sulfates, and uric acid. These substances can be measured in the blood, giving an indication of the functioning of the kidneys. A creatinine clearance is a measurement of the urine concentration of creatinine which indicates the glomerular filtration rate (GFR). The GFR is obtained by using a formula which measures the urine concentration in a volume of urine collected over a specific time and dividing that by the plasma concentration of the creatinine. This means that the patient must provide urine and blood samples to obtain the GFR result. A more exact method to determine the filtration rate is through a nuclear scan, or nuclear GFR.

Blood urea nitrogen (BUN) is a blood test that measures the blood level of urea. In kidney disease, the BUN results will be elevated, indicating the kidneys' inability to excrete urea properly.

Orchidopexy is a surgical procedure performed to correct an undescended testicle.

THE VOCABULARY OF UROLOGY AND NEPHROLOGY

The following word list contains common ophthalmology terms as well as most of the difficult words contained in the dictation at the end of the chapter. Here are suggestion for learning the vocabulary words.

1. Read and study each word for pronunciation and meaning.
2. Write each unfamiliar word from the list below on a notecard, write the definition or a paraphrase of the definition on the back, and draw a simple picture to help you learn the word.
3. Study the pronunciation, spelling, and definition of each word on your notecard, then key each word twice for reinforcement. Check the spelling.
4. Add the correctly spelled terms to your word processor's spell checker.

biliary
(bil'-ee-ayr-ee) (adj) relating to bile or the gallbladder and its ducts

biopsy
(bI'-op-see) (n) the removal of tissue and/or fluid from the body for microscopic examination; the specimen obtained

bulbar
(bul'-bar) (adj) bulb-shaped or relating to the medulla oblongata in the brain

calculus
(kal'-kyoo-lus) (n) stone; a hard stone-like mass formed in the body; calculi (pl)

catheter
(kath'-e-ter) (n) a tube inserted into the body for removing or instilling fluids for diagnostic or therapeutic purposes

cystitis
(sis-tI'-tis) (n) inflammation of the urinary bladder

cystoscopy
(sis-tos'-ko-pee) (n) examination of the inside of the urinary bladder with a lighted instrument inserted through the urethra

cystostomy
(sis-tos'-tO-mee) (n) surgical creation of an opening in the bladder

dilation
(dI-lay'-shun) (n) expansion of an organ or vessel

dysuria
(dis-yoo'-ree-a) (n) difficult or painful urination

edema
(e-dee'-ma) (n) excessive accumulation of fluid in tissues, especially just under the skin or in a given cavity

edematous
(e-dem'-a-tus) (adj) having edema

electron
(ee-lek'-tron) (n) a subatomic particle with a negative charge

endocapillary
(en'-dO-cap'-i-layr-ee) (n) within one of the tiny blood vessels

endoscope
(en'-dO-skOp) (n) a lighted instrument for examining the inside of a body cavity or organ

enuresis
(en-yoo-ree'-sis) (n) bed-wetting; involuntary urination, especially at night in bed

epididymis
(ep-i-did'-i-mis) (n) one of a pair of long coiled ducts in the scrotum; they carry and store spermatozoa between the testes and ductus deferens

epithelial
(ep-i-thee'-lee-al) (adj) relating to or composed of epithelium

epithelium
(ep-i-thee'-lee-um) (n) cell layers covering the outside body surfaces as well as forming the lining of hollow organs (such as the bladder) and the passages of the respiratory, digestive, and urinary tracts

extrahepatic
(eks-tra-he-pat'-ik) (adj) unrelated to or located outside the liver

fascia
(fash'-ee-a) (n) a thin layer of fibrous connective tissue that supports soft organs and covers structures such as muscles; fasciae (pl)

fetoprotein
(fee-tO-prO'-teen) (n) antigen (substance or organism that produces an antibody) naturally present in the fetus and sometimes present in adults with certain cancers

fossa
(fos'-a) (n) channel or shallow depression; fossae (pl)

genital
(jen'-i-tal) (adj) relating to reproduction or the organs of reproduction

genitalia
(jen'-i-tay'-lee-a) (n) the genitals; male or female reproductive organs, especially the external ones

glomerulus
(glO-mayr'-yoo-lus) (n) a cluster of capillaries at the beginning of each nephron (the functional unit of the kidney); glomeruli (pl)

hematuria
(hee-ma-too'-ree-a) (n) presence of blood in the urine

hemorrhagic
(hem-O-raj'-ik) (adj) relating to or experiencing a hemorrhage

hyperplasia
(hI-per-play'-see-a) (n) increase in size of a tissue or organ due to an increase in the number of cells (not including tumor formation)

hyperplastic
(hI-per-plas'-tik) (adj) relating to hyperplasia

idiopathic
(id'-ee-O-path'-ik) (adj) of unknown cause; describes a disease for which no identifiable cause can be determined

idiopathy
(id-ee-op'-a-thee) (n) any disease of unknown cause

interstitial
(in-ter-stish'-al) (adj) relating to or located in the space between tissues, such as interstitial fluid

kidneys
(kid'-neez) (n) a pair of bean-shaped organs near the spinal column that filter blood and produce urine

levator
(le-vay'-ter/le-vay'-tOr) (n) muscle that lifts or raises the body part it is attached to

lithotomy
(li-thot'-O-mee) (n) surgical removal of a stone, especially from the urinary tract

lithotripsy
(lith'-O-trip-see) (n) procedure using a laser to break apart stones (calculi)

lumen
(loo'-men) (n) cavity, canal, or channel within an organ or tube; lumina or lumens (pl)

lymphadenitis
(lim'-fad'-e-nI'-tis) (n) inflammation of one or more lymph nodes

lymphadenopathy
(lim-fad-e-nop'-a-thee) (n) any disorder of lymph nodes or of the lymphatic system

meatus
(mee-ay'-tus) (n) a passage or channel, especially with an external opening

microscopy
(mI-kros'-kO-pee) (n) use of a microscope to magnify and examine objects

mucosa
(myoo-kO'-sa) (n) mucous membrane

neoplasm
(nee'-O-plazm) (n) any abnormal growth of tissue, usually malignant; tumor

nephrectomy
(ne-frek'-tO-mee) (n) surgical removal of a kidney

nephrolithiasis
(nef'-rO-li-thI'-a-sis) (n) presence of stones (calculi) in the kidney(s)

nephrolithotomy
(nef'-rO-li-thot'-O-mee) (n) surgical incision into a kidney to remove stones (calculi)

nephron
(nef'-ron) (n) the functional unit of the kidney that filters the blood

nephrostomy
(ne-fros'-tO-mee) (n) surgical creation of an opening in the kidney for drainage

nocturia
(nok-too'-ree-a) (n) frequent urination during the night

nodular
(nod'-yoo-lar) (adj) containing or resembling nodules; having small, firm, knotty masses

obturator
(ob'-too-ray-tor) (n) device or body structure that closes up or covers an opening

orchidopexy
(Or-ki-dop'-eks-ee) (n) surgical procedure in which an undescended testicle is sutured into place

orchiectomy
(Or-kee-ek'-tO-mee) (n) surgical removal of one or both testes

orchiocele
(Or'-kee-O-seel) (n) scrotal hernia; tumor of a testis

pendulous
(pen'-ju-lus) (adj) loosely hanging

perineum
(per'-i-nee'-um) (n) the external region between the vagina and the anus in women and between the scrotum and the anus in men

polyuria
(pol-ee-yoo'-ree-a) (n) excessive urinary output

prostate gland
(pros'-tayt) (n) a gland located at the base of the bladder and surrounding the beginning of the urethra in the male

prostatic
(pros-tat'-ik) (adj) relating to the prostate gland

proteinaceous
(prO'-tee-nay'-shus/prO'-tee-i-nay'-shus) (adj) relating to or resembling proteins

proteinuria
(prO-tee-noo'-ree-a) (n) presence of abnormally large amounts of protein in the urine

proximal
(prok'-si-mal) (adj) nearest to a point of reference or center of the body

renal failure
(ree'-nal) (n) inability of the kidneys to function

rhabdomyosarcoma
(rab'-dO-mI'-O-sar-kO'-ma) (n) highly malignant tumor developing from striated muscle cells

sonography
(so-nog'-ra-fi) (n) ultrasonography; use of high frequency sound waves to produce an image of an organ or tissue

steroid
(steer'-oyd) (n) any of a large number of similar chemical substances, either natural or synthetic; many are hormones; produced mainly in the adrenal cortex and gonads

stress incontinence
(stres in-kon'-ti-nens) (n) inability to retain urine under tension, such as sneezing or coughing

suprapubic
(soo-pra-pyoo'-bik) (adj) above the pubic bones

transperineal
(adj) across or through the perineal region between the urethral opening and the anus, including the skin and underlying tissues

transurethral
(trans-yoo-ree'-thral) (adj) through the urethra, such as a surgical procedure

ureter
(yoo-ree'-ter/yoo'-ree-ter) (n) either of a pair of tubes that carry urine from the kidney to the urinary bladder

ureteral
(yoo-ree'-te-ral) (adj) relating to the ureters

urethra
(yoo-ree'-thra) (n) a tube that drains urine from the bladder to the outside

urethroscopy
(yoo-ree-thros'-ko-pee) (n) an examination of the inside of the urethra with a urethroscope, a lighted instrument

vesical
(ves'-i-kul) (adj) referring to the bladder or gallbladder

vesicle
(ves'-i-kl) (n) blister; small, raised skin lesion containing clear fluid

viscera
(vis'-er-a) (n) main internal organs within the trunk of the body, especially those in the abdominal cavity

visceral
(vis'-er-al) (adj) relating to or located near the viscera

visualization
(n) the act of viewing an object, especially the picture of a body structure as obtained by x-ray study

ABBREVIATIONS

AGN	acute glomerulonephritis
ATN	acute tubular necrosis
BPH	benign prostatic hypertrophy
BUN	blood urea nitrogen (lab test)
CVA	costovertebral angle
cysto	cystoscopy
ESWL	extracorporeal shock-wave lithotripsy
GFR	glomerular filtration rate
GU	genitourinary
I&O	intake and output
IVP	intravenous pyelogram
KUB	kidneys, ureters, bladder (x-ray)
PD	peritoneal dialysis
PE	physical exam
RP	retrograde pyelogram
SLE	systemic lupus erythematosus
TUR; TURP	transurethral resection (prostatectomy)
UA; U/A	urinalysis
UTI	urinary tract infection
VDRL	Venereal Disease Research Laboratory (test for syphilis)

EXERCISE 9.1: RECOGNIZING LOOK-ALIKES AND SOUND-ALIKES

Below is a list of frequently used words that look alike and/or sound alike. Study the meaning and pronunciation of each set of words, then read each sentence carefully and circle the word in parentheses that correctly completes the meaning.

addition	counting, increase
edition	issue of a publication

dilatation	synonym of dilation
dilation	expansion of an organ or vessel
dilution	a substance that has been diluted (liquid has been added)

do	to perform
due	owing

farther	(adv) refers to physical distance
further	(adv) additional, extra, greater
further	(v) to advance, to help
father	(n) male parent

hole	opening
whole	total, complete

seen	noticed, viewed
scene	sight, background, display of emotion

states	(n) government units of land
states	(v) expresses, says
status	(n) rank, condition

to	toward, through
too	also, additionally
two	numerical unit, a pair

1. A tracheostomy establishes a (hole, whole) into the trachea.
2. Are you going to the medical conference with them (to, too, two)?
3. He lives (further, farther) from the hospital than I do.
4. If you have (further, farther) questions about the medical procedure, please call.
5. The ambulance arrived on the (scene, seen) within a few minutes.
6. The lesion was (to, too, two) small to be seen by the naked eye.
7. The patient is (states, status) post hysterectomy.
8. We went (to, too, two) the anatomy lecture yesterday.
9. With the (addition, edition) of hydrochlorothiazide, her blood pressure is now under good control.
10. The pupils were (dilated, diluted) on exam.

EXERCISE 9.2: MATCHING SOUND AND SPELLING

The numbered list that follows shows the phonetic spelling of hard-to-spell words. Sound out the word, then write the correct spelling in the blank space provided. Each of the words can be found in the glossary or in the drug list in appendix C.

1. dis-yoo'-ree-a ____________________
2. pol-ee-yoo'-ree-a ____________________
3. lim-fad'-e-nI'-tis ____________________
4. nok-too'-ree-a ____________________
5. rab'-dO-mI'-O-sar-kO'-ma ____________________
6. prO'-tee-noo'-ree-a ____________________
7. nef'-rO-li-thot'-O-mee ____________________
8. ep-i-did'-i-mis ____________________
9. Or-kee-ek'-tO-mee ____________________
10. kal'-kyoo-lus ____________________
11. prO'-tee-nay'-shus ____________________
12. ep-i-thee'-lee-um ____________________
13. ne-fros'-tO-mee ____________________
14. Or'-kee-O-seel ____________________
15. pros'-tayt ____________________

EXERCISE 9.3: CHOOSING WORDS FROM CONTEXT

When transcribing dictation, the medical transcriptionist frequently needs to determine the word that correctly completes the sentence based on the situation. From the list of words below, select the term that meaningfully completes each statement.

catheter	genitalia	steroid
pendulous	renal failure	neoplasm
endoscope	hematuria	vesicle
proximal		

1. When we saw Mr. Johnson in our office, his exam revealed a blood pressure of 210/100, ascites, and pitting pedal edema. He was admitted to the hospital immediately with the diagnosis of impending ________________.
2. The ________ was inserted, and the urinary collection totaled only 50 cc in the first hour.
3. Breast exam revealed ____________ breasts, probably accounting for the patient's upper back pain.
4. The IV catheter was placed _____________ to the antecubital fossa.
5. There was an oozing __________ on the abdomen where the incision had been made.
6. It was decided to place Mr. Arnold on ____________ therapy to decrease the allergic reaction.
7. After the Foley catheter was removed, the patient had a small amount of gross ______________, which cleared with the next void.
8. In our differential diagnosis, we considered an infectious process versus a (an) _________.
9. Pelvic exam revealed normal female _____________.
10. During the procedure, the __________ was repositioned several times to obtain different views.

EXERCISE 9.4: PAIRING WORDS AND MEANINGS

For each definition provided below, locate the term on the list that best matches the definition. Write the letter of the term in the space provided beside the definition.

A. edema
B. epididymis
C. fascia
D. idiopathic
E. perineum
F. proteinuria
G. sonography
H. suprapubic
I. transurethral
J. viscera

1. pertains to an operation performed through the urethra ____________
2. region between the urethral opening and the anus ____________
3. presence of large amounts of protein in the urine ____________
4. abnormal collection of fluid in spaces between cells ____________
5. fibrous connective tissue that supports soft organs ____________
6. a pair of long, tightly coiled ducts that carries sperm ____________
7. a disease for which no cause can be determined ____________
8. main internal organs within body cavities ____________
9. use of ultrasound to produce an image ____________
10. the area above the pubis ____________

EXERCISE 9.5: CREATING TERMS FROM WORD FORMS

In the following exercise, combine prefixes, root words, and suffixes to create medical words that fit the definitions below. Fill in the blanks with the words you construct.

intra-	inside	-itis	inflammation
extra-	outside	-ectomy	removal, incision
lymph/o	clear, thin fluid	nephr/o	kidney
path/o	disease	cyst/o	bladder or sac
ur/o	urine	orchi/o	testicle
aden/o	gland	hepat/o	liver
hem/o	blood	noct	night
dys-	painful	-ia	condition of
-ic	pertaining to		

1. removal of the kidneys ____________________
2. difficult, painful urination____________________
3. related to the liver ____________________
4. blood in the urine ____________________
5. disease of the lymph glands____________________
6. urination during the night ____________________
7. excessive urea in the blood ____________________
8. removal of a testicle____________________
9. inflammation of the kidney____________________

0. outside of the liver ____________________

EDITING MEDICAL DOCUMENTS

In this section you will perfect your word use and grammar skills. These skills will help you edit and proofread medical reports for correct language, punctuation, format, and meaning. The special focus of this chapter is the rules of capitalization.

USING CAPITALS CORRECTLY

Capitalization is a signal writers can use to tell the reader that what is capitalized is important or specialized. However, the overuse of capitals diminishes their effect and may confuse rather than help the reader. Transcriptionists need to know the basic rules of capitalization and how and when to apply them.

Proper Nouns

- Capitalize formal names of persons, places, and organizations.

  John A. Smith, MD — Mayo Clinic

  Coronado Hospital, San Diego — the American Cancer Society

- Capitalize languages and races. Do not capitalize skin color (black, white).

  French

  Caucasian

  Mexican-American

- Capitalize days of the week, months, and holidays, but not seasons.

  Thursday, May 28

  Independence Day

  spring 1997

- Capitalize trade or brand names, but do not capitalize generic drugs.

  Amoxil — amoxicillin

  Cardizem — diltiazem

  Xeroform dressing

- Capitalize a job title only when it precedes a name and is used as that person's title. Do not capitalize the title when it replaces or renames the person.

  Director of Education Maria Jaeb will read the announcement.

  [The job title precedes the name.]

  Maria Jaeb, education director, will read the announcement. [*Maria Jaeb* identifies the person being discussed, and *education director* gives further information about (or renames) Maria.]

- Capitalize the genus but not the species of bacteria.

  Clostridium difficile

  Streptococcus aureus

- Do not capitalize hospital department names.

intensive care unit	operating room
emergency department	neurology service

Abbreviations

- Do not capitalize Latin abbreviations that deal with drug dosage (b.i.d., a.c., p.o.). According to the AAMT, the correct form for Latin abbreviations is lowercase with periods between each letter.

h.s.	at bedtime	q.4h.	every four hours
a.m.	morning	q.d.	once a day
a.c.	before meals or food	q.12h.	every twelve hours
t.i.d.	three times a day	p.o.	by mouth
q.	every	p.m.	afternoon or evening
q.i.d.	four times a day	b.i.d.	twice a day

- Some hospitals direct their MTs to capitalize the abbreviation NPO, which stands for *nil per os* (nothing by mouth). They want the term capitalized because it is very important information. If the term goes unnoticed in a patient's record, there could be life-threatening consequences. However, in this instance, as with other style issues, follow your employer's preference.

Acronyms

Acronyms are abbreviations formed using the initial letters of words or phrases. No periods are required.

ASHD	atherosclerotic / arteriosclerotic heart disease	LVD	left ventricular dysfunction
LAO	left anterior oblique	CHF	congestive heart failure
		MI	myocardial infarction

Eponyms

Eponyms are adjectives created from proper nouns. The terms usually derive from the name of the person who identified the disease, developed the protocol, or designed the instrument. The eponym itself, but not the noun, is capitalized.

Alzheimer's disease
Bruce protocol
Foley catheter
Gram stain

Note that *Parkinson's disease* is capitalized, but *parkinsonian* is not.

The patient exhibited symptoms of Parkinson's disease.

The patient's symptoms were parkinsonian.

Drug Allergies

Some hospitals require the capitalization of all letters of a drug name listed under an allergies heading. This format attracts the reader's attention.

The patient is allergic to MORPHINE, which causes a rash.

Document Elements

- Capitalize the first letter of a formal list.

DISCHARGE INSTRUCTIONS
- Activities ad lib.
- Diet as tolerated.
- Followup will be in one week in my office.

MEDICATIONS
1. Aspirin one a day.
2. Hydrochlorothiazide 50 mg p.o. q.d.

- Capitalize headings and the first word after a heading.

HEENT: Pupils, equal, round, reactive to light.

HISTORY OF PRESENT ILLNESS: The patient presents…

FAMILY HISTORY: Noncontributory.

EXERCISE 9.6: EDITING FOR CORRECT CAPITALIZATION

Read the following partial discharge summary and circle all capitalization errors. Then key the summary with the errors corrected.

History of present illness: willie dayton is a 55-year-old african-american who speaks french and chinese, presenting with a chief complaint of chest pain. he has been having mild chest pain since early autumn, but it has been increasing recently, especially over the holidays. he has been taking dyazide for blood pressure and also uses ibuprofen occasionally. On Sunday, new year's day, he called his insurance company and was referred to south side hospital.

the patient presented to the emergency department for evaluation and was noted to have t wave inversions on his ecg. chest x-ray showed no pneumonia or pulmonary edema. he was given nitroglycerin sublingually times two, with resolution of his chest pain. cpk was shown to be elevated, and cardiology was called to evaluate this patient and assume his care. The patient was admitted to the intensive care unit at 0300.

past medical history: the patient has a diagnosis of early parkinson's disease and is treated by a neurologist for this.

allergies: sulfa (hives)

physical examination
vital signs: blood pressure 110/95, pulse 75, respirations 18.
heent: normocephalic, atraumatic, pupils equal, round, reactive to light and accommodation. fundi clear, no av nicking. ears, nose, and throat clear.
neck: supple, no jvd, no lymphadenopathy.
chest: clear to percussion and auscultation
heart: s1 and s2 normal. there was a grade 2/6 systolic ejection murmur heard best at the left lower sternal border.
abdomen: supple. no organomegaly or rebound tenderness.
genitalia: deferred.
extremities: no clubbing, cyanosis, or edema.
hospital course: the patient was taken to the cardiac catheterization laboratory on the morning of admission. This study revealed no areas of stenosis of the coronary arterial system.

(continued)

the patient was given nitroglycerin sublingually p.r.n. chest pain and was given procardia for his hypertension. His ecg normalized, and on Tuesday he was subjected to a treadmill exercise test using the modified bruce protocol. this test was interpreted by the cardiologist as showing no signs of ischemia.

the patient was discharged in excellent condition, to follow up in one week with dr. smith at the south bay regional cardiac center.

discharge medications
1. procardia 10 mg q.d.
2. aspirin one per day.
3. nitroglycerin sublingual p.r.n. chest pain.

EXERCISE 9.7: PROOFREADING REVIEW

Read the following partial report and look for errors in capitalization, word use, punctuation, spelling, meaning, and format. Key the report with the errors corrected.

S: 56-year-old middle eastern male who is seen in follow up for a elevated PSA, recent pylonephritis and microscopic hematuria. He has been referred to urology and will see them in 2 weeks. Today, he says he has occasional mild burning with urination but the disuria has overall improved. He denies any flake or abdominal pain, nausea or vomiting.

O: Routine laboratory was done at his last visit. His PSA was 14.3. He says that in the past his highest PSA was 6, and that was roughly six months ago. He had a transureteral resection of the prostrate in 1992. Other laboratories: A CBC showed a platelet count of 124,000. Hemoglobin 14.9. MCV 92. Chemistry profile within normal limits, including renal function.

A:
1. Resolved pyelonephritis.
2. Elevated PSA with a patient history of benign prostatic hypotrophy raises the question of possible prostate cancer.

P:
1. Will give another 7-day course of Bactrim to insure that the urinary track infection is resolved by the time of his Urology appointment in two weeks.
2. Patient is to call if he has any worsening of his symptoms.

WHERE CAN I FIND THE ANSWER?

As you transcribe dictation, you may hear unfamiliar words or terms. A variety of reference sources are available to help you locate answers to your questions. One of the important types of references for medical transcriptionists is described below. Read the information. If you have access to the reference discussed, explore its capabilities.

MEDICAL REFERENCES: STANDARD ENGLISH DICTIONARY

Every MT needs a good collegiate English dictionary—not the pocket paperback kind, not the crossword puzzle kind, but a big, current, complete English dictionary. Although you may not use this reference as frequently as you use medical references, periodically you will need to locate the correct spelling of nonmedical words. It is a frustrating and humbling experience to have worked very hard on a medical report only to have it returned because of nonmedical errors.

How do I use it?

The dictionary lists words alphabetically in boldface type. Each of these main entries includes the word's pronunciation, part of speech, etymology (root words in the language from which the word originated), and definition.

When you look up a word, check the pronunciation as well as the definition. This ensures that you are choosing the correct word by its sound and by its meaning. Once you are confident you have selected the right word, make sure you use the correct form for your sentence. For example, if the sentence calls for a verb, use the verb form of the root word:

> I will advise the patient to have surgery.
> [*advice* is the noun; *advise* is the verb]

This attention to accuracy is part of developing your medical transcription skills. It is really about paying attention to detail and not making careless mistakes.

TRANSCRIBING UROLOGY AND NEPHROLOGY DOCUMENTS

In this section your goal is to prepare for the work of transcription by transcribing first from a printed document and then from dictation on tape. The model document that follows illustrates the generally accepted format for a **history and physical**, the medical report featured in this chapter.

BASIC FORMAT: THE HISTORY AND PHYSICAL

When a patient enters a healthcare system, the physician or examiner generates a comprehensive document called a history and physical (H&P). This report focuses on the patient's medical and social history and the illness or complaint that prompted the person to seek medical attention. The primary purpose of the history and physical is to provide the information the physician needs to make a diagnosis and choose the appropriate care and treatment for the patient. The MT transcribes the H&P to provide a written documentation for the chart.

Required Headings/Content

As the title of the report suggests, there are two main sections: 1) a complete history, including the current medical problem; and 2) the results of the physical examination performed by the physician. For the entire report, the Joint Commission on the Accreditation of Healthcare Organizations (JCAHO) requires these headings: Chief Complaint, History of Present Illness, Review of Systems, Physical Examination, and Impression or Admitting Diagnosis(es). Individual hospitals and physicians, however, may expand the headings beyond these basic requirements. Medical transcriptionists need to be aware of the specific format the employer prefers.

History

In the history section of the report, several variations or subheadings are possible, including details of present illness, past medical history, social history, surgical history, operations, habits, and risk factors. Despite the variety of subheadings, most physicians follow the same order when dictating the report, including more or less information depending on the complexity of the patient's complaint.

Chief Complaint: The healthcare provider frequently documents the actual words used by the patient in describing the subjective data. This information may be called the Chief Complaint (CC) or History of Present Illness (HPI). Or, the physician may dictate both headings, using a brief summary statement for the Chief Complaint and a longer explanation under History of Present Illness. Also included may be objective data, organized through review of available clinical information such as vital signs, measurements, laboratory tests, x-ray findings, and so on, which have been performed before admission and for which results are known.

Past History: This section begins by listing the patient's childhood illnesses and includes all past medical history with reference to diseases, illnesses, surgical procedures, accidents, medications, immunizations, and allergies (each topic is often indented as a subheading and keyed in capital letters). A history of pregnancies and deliveries is recorded for a female. Social history is another subheading that may be included. This subsection describes social habits such as alcohol use, smoking history, occupation, recreational interests, home environment, marital status, and sexual history. This information helps the interviewer develop an understanding of the patient as an individual and as a member of a family and a community.

Family History: Information on the health of the patient's parents, siblings, and grandparents may follow as a separate section. This data can point to the possibility of genetic traits or diseases.

Review of Systems: This section is a question-and-answer review of all the body systems conducted by the healthcare provider. The review is in cephalocaudal order–from head to foot.

- SKIN: Lesions, rashes, discolorations, itching, moles, eruptions
- HAIR: Texture, distribution, scalp problems
- HEENT: (Head, Ears, Eyes, Nose, Throat)
  Head: Headaches, dizziness

Eyes: Visual problems, glaucoma, conjunctivitis, discharge, use of glasses
Ears: Earaches, hearing loss, discharge, dizziness, fainting, ringing in the ears, pain
Nose: Discharges, sense of smell, colds, allergies, nosebleeds
Mouth and Throat: Condition of teeth, dental history, difficulty in swallowing, hoarseness, tonsillectomy

- NECK: Thyroid, movement of neck
- RESPIRATORY: Shortness of breath, cough with or without production of sputum or blood
- HEART: Increased heart rate, angina, or chest pain
- GASTROINTESTINAL: Appetite, indigestion, difficulty swallowing, vomiting, changes in weight, stool history, jaundice, gallbladder problems
- GENITOURINARY: Pain on urination, blood in urine, frequency, incontinence, urgency, sexually transmitted diseases
- GYNECOLOGIC: Menarche, menstrual history, discharges, contraceptive use, obstetric history, painful menses
- MUSCULOSKELETAL: Pain, stiffness, limitation of movement, fractures
- NEUROLOGICAL: Headaches, dizziness, fainting, pain, paralysis, difficulty walking, convulsions, emotional state

Physical

A complete physical exam (PE) is usually performed after the history is recorded. This is arranged in cephalocaudal order, beginning with the visible areas of the body. Four basic procedures are included in the exam:

1) Inspection: looking at the body
2) Palpation: feeling various parts and organs
3) Percussion: listening to the sounds produced when a particular region is tapped using the hands or a small hammerlike tool
4) Auscultation: listening to body sounds

After noting general appearance, height, weight, age, race, nutritional state, and possibly emotional status (euphoric, lethargic, distracted, alert, oriented, agitated, flat affect), the physician dictates vital signs and then a description of findings on the rest of the body, similar to those described above in "Review of Systems."

A final section in the history and physical is the impression or diagnosis (may be called differential or admitting), which lists many possibilities to explore or rule out. The plan of care is often dictated as a numbered list, written in order of most important to least, or as a random list. It will include recommendations for further studies and treatment and followup.

Turnaround Time

The history and physical examination should be completed, dictated, and transcribed within the first 24 hours of admission as an inpatient. If a complete exam has been performed within 30 days before admission, such as in a physician's office, a copy of this report is placed in the patient's medical record and—in some hospitals—no new exam is required (provided no changes have occurred or provided changes that have occurred are noted in the medical record at the time of admission).

HISTORY AND PHYSICAL

PATIENT: Raymond Cheever
DATE: 7/10/XX
HOSPITAL NO: 93-22-17
PHYSICIAN: Harry Washington, MD
ds
CHIEF COMPLAINT: Severe pain in the left hip.
ds
HISTORY OF PRESENT ILLNESS: The patient is a 57-year-old white male who is admitted from the emergency department with hypertension, hyperglycemia, and greater trochanteric bursitis. The patient has been under treatment for greater trochanteric bursitis with Lortab and Naprosyn. He returns today because of increasing left hip pain. In the emergency room, he was noted to be significantly hypertensive and hyperglycemic. He is unaware of having a history of either.

ALLERGIES: No known allergies.

PRESENT MEDICATIONS
1. Lortab 7.5 mg q.d.
2. Naprosyn 375 mg q.d.

PAST MEDICAL HISTORY: Negative.

SURGICAL HISTORY: Tonsils and adenoids removed in early childhood.

SOCIAL HISTORY: The patient does not smoke at present. He stopped smoking six to seven years ago; he smoked an average of a pack per day for many years. He denies ethanol use. He is married. He has two children who are alive and in good health. He works as a plant manager for a chemical company.

FAMILY HISTORY: His mother is alive and in good health. His father is deceased secondary to complications of black lung and asthma. He has two brothers and one sister. He thinks his sister has a history of hypertension.

REVIEW OF SYSTEMS: A full review of systems was negative. He states that his weight has been stable in the past year. He denies polyuria, polydypsia, or polyphagia.

(continued)

HISTORY AND PHYSICAL
PATIENT: Raymond Cheever
HOSPITAL NO.: 93-22-17
Page 2

ds

PHYSICAL EXAMINATION
GENERAL: Well-developed, well-nourished male in no acute distress.

ds

VITAL SIGNS: Blood pressure 200/104. Repeat, after rest and pain medication, was 170/96. The pulse was 72. Respiratory rate was 18 and labored. Patient refused to be weighed at this time because of pain.
HEENT: Pupils were somewhat constricted, but fundi were visualized minimally. No hypertensive retinopathy, exudates, hemorrhages, or papilledema were noted. Oral examination revealed no ulcerations, erosions, or masses.
NECK: Supple, without lymphadenopathy. The carotid upstrokes were brisk and equal bilaterally, without bruits. Thyroid nonpalpable.
CHEST: Chest was clear to auscultation in all fields.
CARDIOVASCULAR: Regular rate and rhythm, without murmurs, thrill, gallop, or click.
ABDOMEN: Abdomen nontender, nondistended, without masses, organomegaly, guarding, tenderness, or rebound.
EXTREMITIES: No clubbing, cyanosis, or edema. Peripheral pulses were intact, with good upstrokes. Palpation of the left hip did reveal tenderness, although the patient did report it was much improved after analgesia.

LABORATORY DATA: Review of the Chem-7 revealed a blood sugar of 201. His urinalysis revealed greater than 1000 glucose. CBC revealed a hemoglobin of 16.3 and hematocrit of 50. White count was 14.7. Platelets were 291,000. Differential was essentially within normal limits.

IMPRESSION
1. Marked hypertension.
2. Asymptomatic hyperglycœmia with glycosuria.
3. Left greater trochanteric bursitis.

PLAN
1. Admit.
2. Orthopedic consultation.
3. Endocrinology consultation.
4. Cardiology consultation.

(continued)

HISTORY AND PHYSICAL
PATIENT: Raymond Cheever
HOSPITAL NO.: 93-22-17
Page 3

qs

____

Harry Washington, MD
ds
HW/XX
D: 07/10/XX
T: 07/11/XX

PREPARING TO TRANSCRIBE

To prepare for transcribing dictation, key the history and physical report above. You will later key the identical report from tape. Follow these guidelines:

- Study the format and organization of each report.
- Review the word list presented earlier in this chapter.
- Consult reference books for words or formatting rules that are unfamiliar.
- Proofread your final copy by comparing it to the printed version.

CASES FOR TRANSCRIPTION

In this section you will transcribe medical dictation from tape. Your goal is to produce error-free documents. Read this chapter's Pro Tip (following the case studies) for helpful hints from experienced MTs. Then follow these steps for each dictation:

1. Prepare to transcribe by reviewing the case study and the model report formats from this and earlier chapters.
2. Transcribe the dictation, leaving spaces for words you cannot hear or do not understand.
3. Carefully proofread each document and correct as many errors as you can. Use your reference materials to help you identify missing words.
4. Listen to the tape again and correct all remaining errors.

Repeat these steps until you produce an error-free document. Then complete the Performance Report, attach it to the top of the transcripts, and submit them to your instructor for evaluation.

CASE STUDY 1: ALICE CASTANZA

Alice Castanza is a 5-year-old child whose mother noticed that her pants were fitting tightly at the waist. When she was in the bathtub, her mother also noticed that her stomach appeared to be larger than usual. Alice had no complaints of pain, but her mother took her to the pediatrician, who was able to palpate an abdominal mass. She was sent for x-rays, lab work, and other tests. A surgical procedure was performed to remove a tumor and the right kidney to which it was attached. Alice was diagnosed with a Wilms' tumor, a malignant tumor of the kidney, treated by surgery and chemotherapy.

Report 9.1: Radiology Report

Transcription Hint

Listen for these new words:
echogenicity
intrahepatic
extrahepatic

CASE STUDY 2: MELISSA PERLMAN

Melissa Perlman is a 3½-year-old child who was healthy until June of (last year) when she developed tonsillitis. The throat culture was negative for strep. In July, her mother noted that her diapers were not wet for one whole day and she was edematous. She was taken to the pediatrician and, after testing, was diagnosed with renal failure.

Report 9.2: Pathology Report

Transcription Hint

Listen for these new words:
hypercellularity
PAS (physician will dictate individual letters)
pseudocrescents
proteinaceous
glomerulosclerosis

CASE STUDY 3: JONATHAN BLONDELL

Jonathan Blondell is a 35-year-old male who was having difficulty voiding for about two weeks. He saw his internist, who diagnosed a urinary tract infection. After treatment for several days, Jonathan continued to have pain on urination and blood in the urine. He was referred to the urologist for further evaluation.

Report 9.3: Operative Report

Transcription Hint

Listen for these instrument names:
Vim-Silverman needle
#20 French two-way tube
#24 French three-way catheter with 5 cc balloon

CASE STUDY 4: RAYMOND CHEEVER

Raymond Cheever is a 57-year-old male who is admitted from the emergency department with hypertension, hyperglycemia, and greater trochanteric bursitis. He came to the emergency department because of increasing left hip pain and was unaware of his hypertension and hyperglycemia.

Report 9.4: History and Physical

CASE STUDY 5: DENNIS CHANG

Dennis Chang is a 9-month-old male who was well until two weeks ago when his parents noticed that his left testicle was enlarged. The pediatrician referred the Changs to Dr. Roland Browne, a urologist, who scheduled a biopsy.

Report 9.5: Consultation Letter

Transcription Hint

The results for the alpha fetoprotein test should be transcribed as 1652.5 (N: <9.0), and the beta subunit HCG should be transcribed using symbols and abbreviations, as follows: <2.0 MIU/ml.

CASE STUDY 6: WILLIAM BOOTH

William Booth has an appointment for his annual physical. Since he lives in an out-state area and was once treated by this urologist for a prostate problem, he continues to have his annual check-up with the urologist.

Report 9.6: History and Physical

CASE STUDY 7: MARC BARIO

Marc Bario is a 32-year-old male who was admitted through the emergency department with a history of six hours of acute ureteral colic on the right side. Subsequent testing revealed a large stone in his right ureter.

Report 9.7: History and Physical

Transcription Hint

Listen for these special terms:
ureterovesical junction
JV distention

CASE STUDY 8: SANDRA DAVIS

Sandra Davis is a 78-year-old woman who was recently hospitalized for a herpes infection. Two days after she was discharged, she was brought to the emergency room with a possible stroke and subsequently was admitted to the hospital for tests and treatment.

Report 9.8: Discharge Summary

Transcription Hints

- This report includes an exception to the hyphenation rule for the prefix *non.* If this prefix appears with a hyphenated compound adjective (insulin-dependent), add a hyphen after the prefix (non-insulin-dependent diabetes mellitus) to clarify meaning. Without a hyphen, the prefix appears to apply only to the word *insulin.* When the hyphen is included, the reader understands that non applies to the entire compound adjective *insulin-dependent.*
- Listen for these disease and drug terms:
  bilateral ureteral lithiasis
  clindamycin
  ceftazidime
  Diltiazem-CD
  Nephro-Vite
  DSS

PRO TIP: DEALING WITH HEAVY ACCENTS

Adapted, with permission, from *MT Daily's* home page (www.angelfire.com/mt.2)

Reports dictated by physicians with accents may be difficult to understand, especially when you are new to transcription and are just learning medical terms. With practice, however, you will soon be able to decipher the sometimes unusual pronunciations of a nonnative speaker. In particular, you may hear different word endings or extra sounds at the ends of words. The degree of difficulty in transcribing will depend on the heaviness or thickness of the accent.

Avoid the trap of second-guessing physicians who speak English as a second language. Redesigning their dictation according to what you think it should include would be considered tampering. Edit obvious errors, following general guidelines for editing medical documents. Always try to retain the physician's basic style.

Hints for Deciphering Difficult Dictation

If you have to stop and listen again more than three times in the first couple of sentences, try these tips:

- Listen to the dictation once from beginning to end, transcribing all the words you can without stopping or playing the tape again.
- For every word you don't know, key an asterisk (*); for every phrase, key a double asterisk (**); and for every sentence, key a triple asterisk (***).
- Go through a second time. You will be surprised at how many words, phrases, and sentences you will be able to fill in. This is because it takes time to get into the rhythm of some speech patterns and accents, to determine the flow of words and the way they are pronounced. Or, perhaps the physician may dictate the same word a little clearer later in the report. You can use this second "go through" as an opportunity to correct sentence structure and grammar. (If you use WordPerfect, you can jump from blank to blank using the Find and Replace feature for the asterisks.)
- Keep a record of words or phrases you did not understand or transcribed incorrectly. Refer to this when you think you are unsure of what you are hearing.
- Save copies of past reports that may help you decipher what the physician is saying on subsequent similar reports.

ASSESSING TRANSCRIPTION SKILLS

Demonstrate your mastery of the terminology, editing/proofreading, and document transcription skills presented in this chapter by completing the following activities.

USING MEDICAL REFERENCES

Use the appropriate medical reference to locate the correct spelling and additional usage information for the words below. (If the reference is not available, use the glossary in this text.) Circle the correct spelling; then write a sentence using the word correctly.

1.	epididymis	epidydimis	epididymus
2.	ideopathic	idiopathec	idiopathic
3.	rhabdomyosarcoma	rabdomyocarcoma	rhabdomysarcoma
4.	fulgeration	fulguration	folguration
5.	meatus	meaetos	meatis
6.	nephrolithiesis	nephrolithiasis	neprolithiasis
7.	glomerular	glamerular	glumerular
8.	dysuria	disuria	dysurea

9.	cystoscopy	cystascopy	cystoscapy
10.	orchectomy	orchictomy	orchiectomy

MAKING EXPERT DECISIONS

Circle the correct word from the choices in parentheses.

1. The bladder neck was inspected beginning distally after (ureteral/urethral) dilatation.
2. There was 3+ bacteria noted on microscopic exam and the patient was started on antibiotics after a specimen was obtained for (CNS/C&S)
3. A contracture of the (vesical/vesicle) neck was noted.
4. At the end of the cystoscopy, both ureters were seen to be (refluxing/effluxing/reflexing) clear urine from both sides.
5. (Testis/Testes) were descended bilaterally.
6. The main function of the urinary (track/tract) consists of production and elimination of urine.
7. The patient was started on a (regimen/regiment/regime) of diet, activity, and medication.
8. With the (addition/edition) of Bactrim-DS, the patient's UTI subsided.
9. Upon visualization, there were (to/too/two) patent ureters.
10. Examination revealed the (prostrate/prostate) to be normal in size and benign in consistency.

TRANSCRIBING PROFESSIONAL DOCUMENTS

Transcribe the document named Assessment 9 from tape. Before you key, review the appropriate report formatting guidelines. Proofread your transcribed document and revise it until you think it is error-free.

PERFORMANCE REPORT

Name____ Date ____________

Document	Description	Date Completed	Document Processing Speed (If Available)	Document Appraisal M=Mailable MC=Mailable w/corrections NM=Not Mailable
Report 9.1	Radiology Report			M MC NM
Report 9.2	Operative Report			M MC NM
Report 9.3	Operative Report			M MC NM
Report 9.4	History and Physical			M MC NM
Report 9.5	Consultation Letter			M MC NM
Report 9.6	History and Physical			M MC NM
Report 9.7	History and Physical			M MC NM
Report 9.8	Discharge Summary			M MC NM

Comments ____

CHAPTER

10

Orthopedics (also spelled orthopaedics) is the field of medicine concerned with diseases, injuries, and deformities of the musculoskeletal system, which includes the joints, muscles, and the fibrous connective tissue surrounding the bones and joints. Specialists in orthopedic medicine are orthopedists, who may also be skilled orthopedic surgeons. Because the volume of skeletal system problems is

Orthopedics

so large, orthopedic surgeons usually further specialize in one anatomic area such as hip, knee, shoulder, foot, hand, or spine.

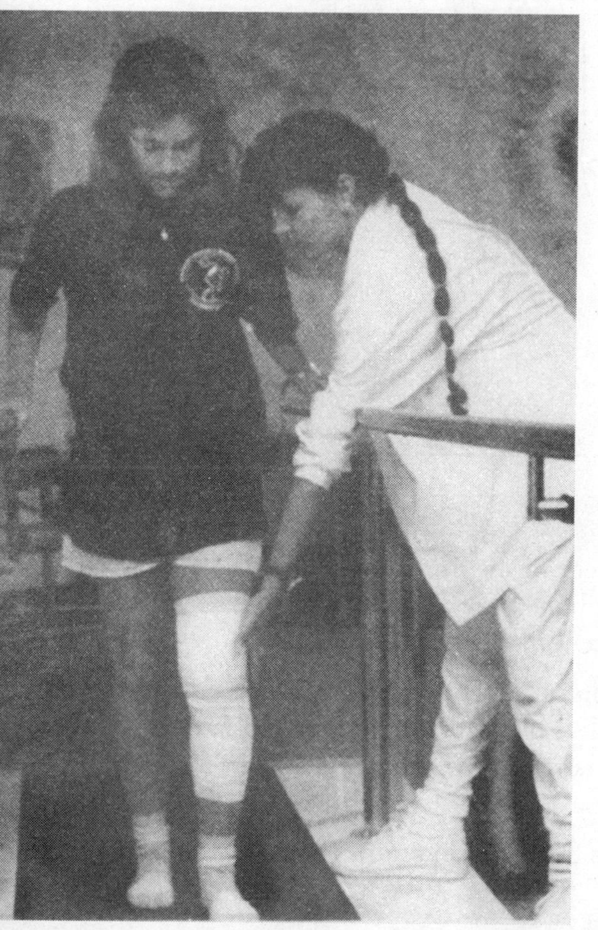

OBJECTIVES

- Use orthopedics terms correctly according to the context and purpose of the dictation.
- Select and use appropriate general and specialty reference materials.
- Key orthopedics documents of varying complexity and format.
- Transcribe authentic medical dictation requiring concentration and listening skill.
- Edit medical reports to conform with AAMT style guidelines.
- Proofread and correct transcripts to produce error-free documents.

EXPLORING ORTHOPEDICS

The musculoskeletal system (figure 10.1) enables the body to move. It also provides support and protection for body organs. The bone marrow has the equally important responsibility of producing blood cells, a process called hematopoiesis. Bones are responsible for storing calcium and phosphorus. There are approximately 216 bones in the human body.

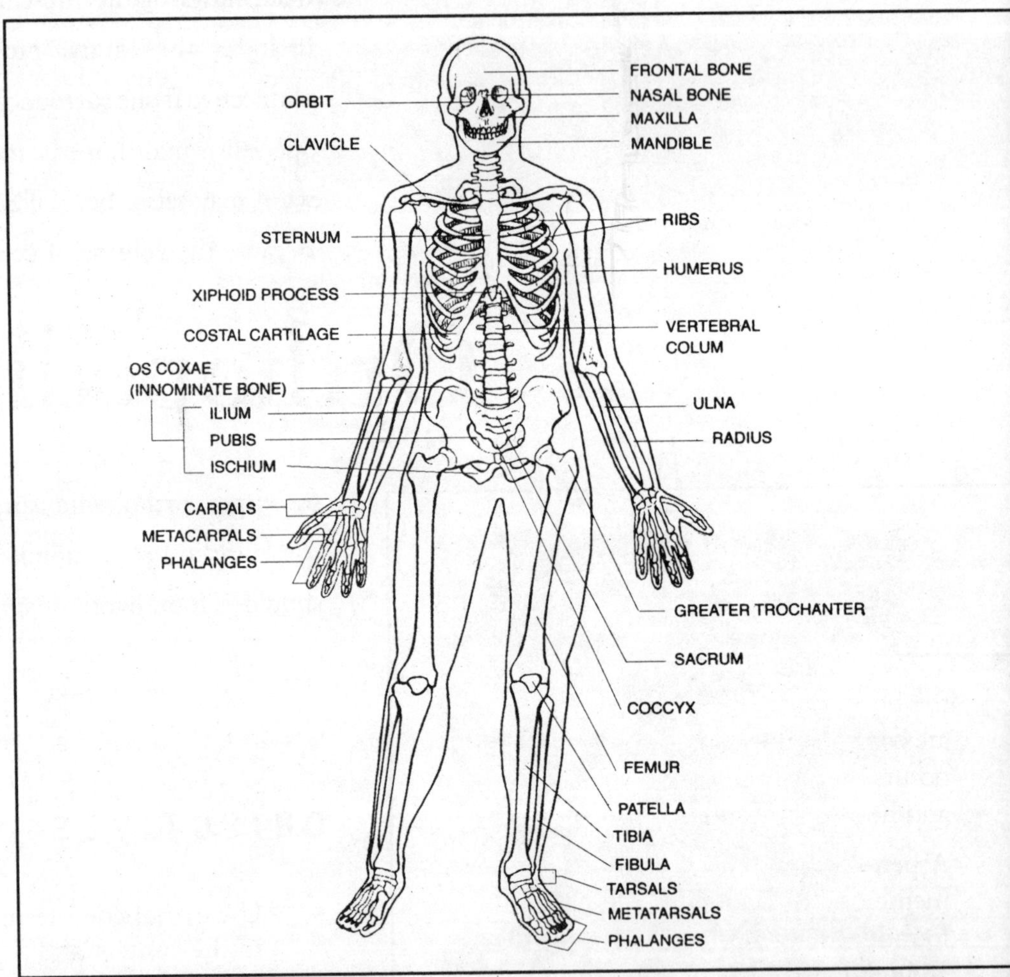

Figure 10.1 Skeletal system

STRUCTURE AND FUNCTION

Bone is the major tissue component of the musculoskeletal system. A complex type of calcified connective tissue, bone is made up of approximately 95 percent organic material and about 5 percent inorganic minerals.

The center of the bone is the medullary cavity, which contains the bone marrow (figure 10.2). The marrow looks like blood that has gritty and fatty particles in it. All bones of the body contain marrow. However, blood cells are formed mostly in the long, large, flat bones.

An extensive vascular system feeds the bones and moves blood cells in and out of

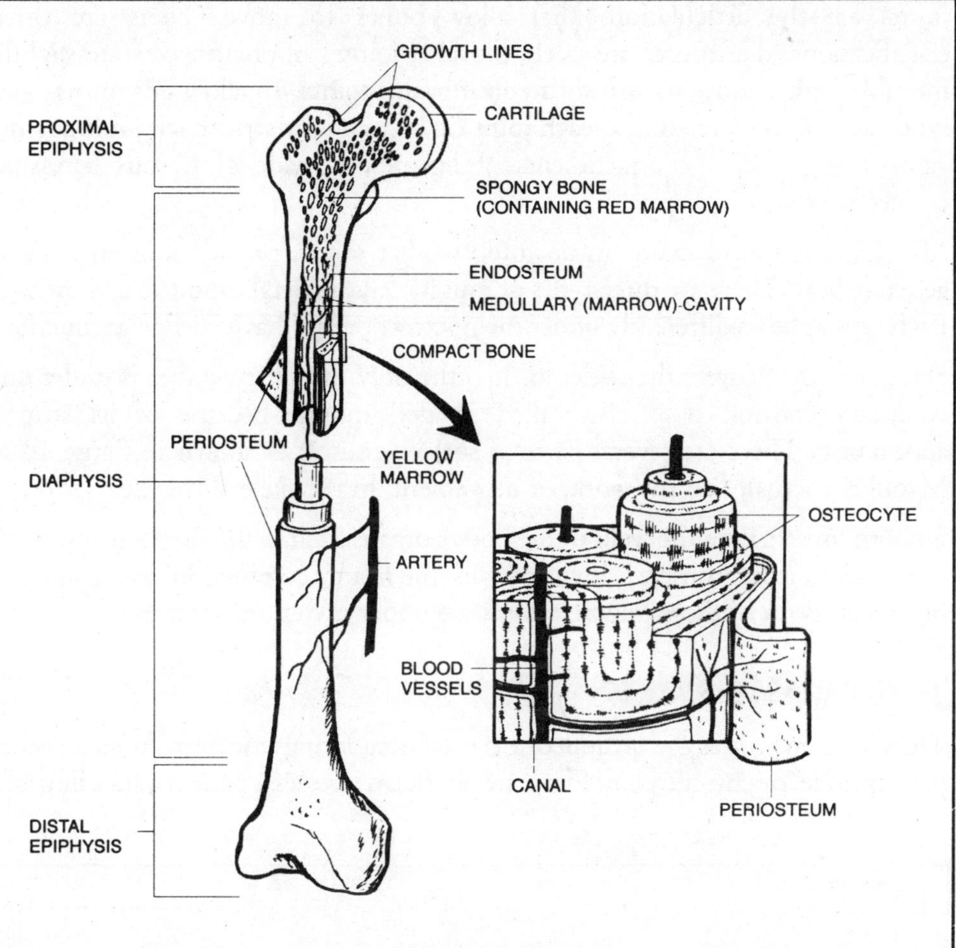

Figure 10.2 Cross-section of long bone

the bone marrow. Osteocytes, the small living cells contained within the bone, are continually cycling through bone formation and bone destruction. This cycle occurs throughout the life of a healthy individual in response to physical pressure and hormonal stimuli.

A periosteal layer of cells forms the covering of bone. This is a dense, fibrous membrane that contains the nerves, blood, and lymph vessels. Osteoblasts are found in the periosteum, which is the attachment point for muscles, ligaments, and tendons.

A long bone is divided into the distal and proximal epiphyses (singular: epiphysis) on each end, and the diaphysis, the shaft or long section. The epiphyses are formed of spongy bone necessary to maintain growth, while the diaphysis is composed of compact bone that provides support. The articular cartilage on the end of the epiphyses provides the cushioning effect in the joints.

Flat bones provide protection for internal organs and wide surfaces for muscle attachment. The skull bones and sternum are flat bones. Short bones have a core of spongy or cancellous bone, surrounded by a layer of compact tissue. These bones are small and have an irregular shape, as in the wrists and phalanges. The irregular bones such as the vertebrae and bones of the ear do not fit into any one category.

Joints are the articulations that allow bones to move. There are three classifications: diarthroses are freely movable joints, amphiarthroses are slightly movable joints, and synarthroses are immovable joints. To allow free movement, synovial fluid is secreted into each joint cavity as a lubricant. Each joint capsule gains strength by the attachments of ligaments, made of fibrous bands of connective tissue.

Muscles function to maintain posture, stabilize joints, provide movement, and generate heat. There are three types of muscle cells: skeletal, smooth, and cardiac. Each type appears differently under the microscope and has a particular function.

Skeletal muscle covers the skeleton. It is the only muscle type that is under our voluntary control. It is also called striated muscle because of its striped appearance. There are several parts of skeletal muscle as shown in figure 10.3. Myofibrils actually do the work, or movement, in the skeletal muscle.

Smooth muscle lines the walls of the body's organs such as the stomach and small intestines. Cardiac muscle is involved with the heart's conduction system and the heartbeat. Both of these muscle groups are under involuntary control.

PHYSICAL ASSESSMENT

The patient who sees the orthopedist is usually suffering from a fracture, an acute pain episode, or chronic pain. First, the physician assesses a patient's standing and

Figure 10.3
Cross-section of skeletal muscle

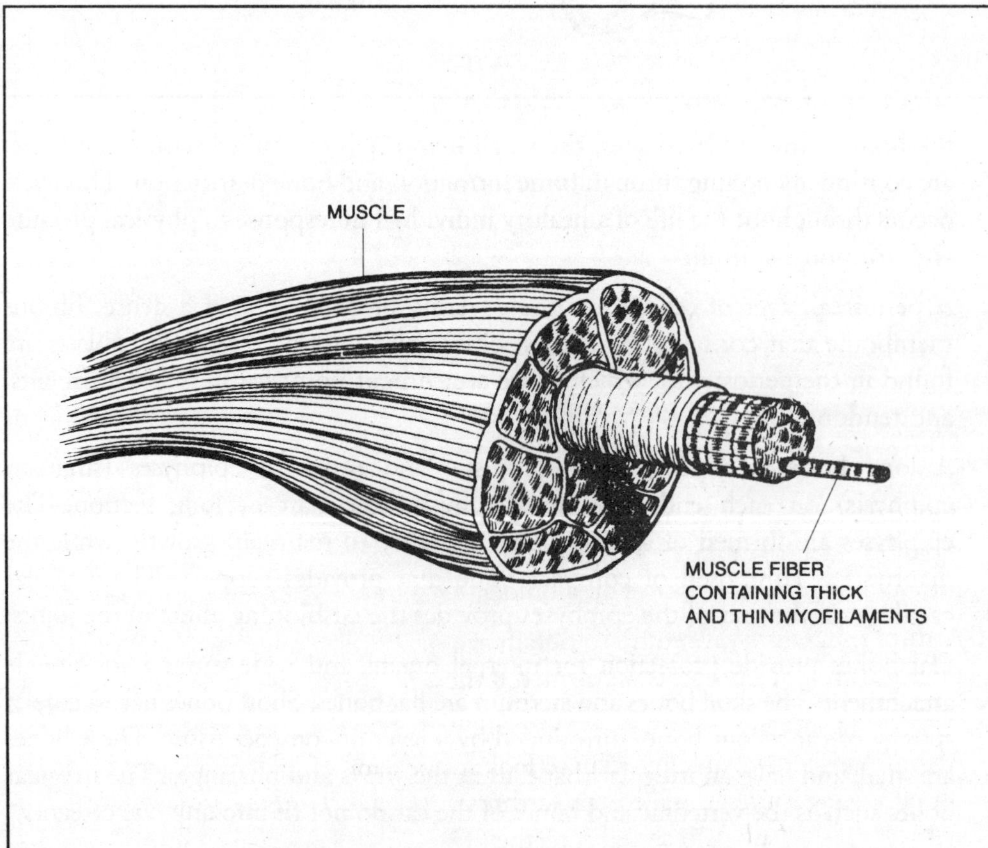

walking movements. Noted at this time are posture, movement of the extremities, and any signs of pain (facial grimace is the giveaway). The orthopedist will ask about the history of the pain, the beginning of the pain, any precipitating events, and injuries. Information about activities, sports, sleeping habits, and lifestyle also will be noted in the medical record.

The examination will include full range of motion activities and strength assessment for each muscle group. Obvious malformations such as scoliosis or kyphosis will be noted. Asymmetry may be an indication of an abnormality. Because of the interrelationship of the nervous system with the musculoskeletal system, the physician will test reflexes, gait, and other areas.

Common Orthopedics Drugs

acetylsalicylic acid (ASA)
Anacin, Bufferin, Bayer

diclofenac sodium
Voltaren

etodolac
Lodine

hydrocodone and acetaminophen
Lortab

ibuprofen
Advil, Motrin, PediaProfen

indomethacin
Indocin

nabumetone
Relafen

oxaprozin
Daypro

oxycodone hydrochloride and acetaminophen
Percocet, Roxicet, Tylox

propoxyphene
Darvon

DISEASES, CONDITIONS, AND INJURIES

For young people, a bone fracture may precipitate the first visit to the orthopedist. Inflammatory joint diseases or stress injuries are likely reasons for older adults to seek medical help from an orthopedist. Osteoarthritis, for example, is a degenerative disease characterized by pain, swelling, and a loss of flexibility in the area where cartilage is worn away. It affects mostly weight-bearing joints and is the main reason for total hip joint replacement surgery.

Osteoporosis, or fragile bones, is a common disease in older women. Caused by the loss of bone mass, osteoporosis results in porous and brittle bones that break easily.

Another frequent disorder is herniated intervertebral discs (also spelled disks), which occur most often in patients between 20 and 45 years of age and more commonly in men. Some 90 percent of intervertebral herniations occur in one of two spinal interspaces, the areas experiencing the greatest amount of motion.

A common work-related orthopedic injury is carpal tunnel syndrome, which results from abnormal pressure on the median nerve passing through the wrist to the hand. Carpal tunnel syndrome is one of many repetitive stress injuries produced by years of continually repeated joint motions (for example, keyboarding).

COMMON TESTS AND SURGICAL PROCEDURES

Other than surgery to repair bone fractures, the most common procedures in orthopedics are probably x-rays and various kinds of computerized scans. Closed reduction refers to the repair of a fracture by manipulation, casting or cast application, and splinting. Open reduction is done when the area is surgically repaired. Arthrography is a radiograph taken after injection of a radiopaque dye into a joint such as the knee or shoulder. The x-ray outlines the joint.

Arthrocentesis is a procedure to obtain synovial fluid for examination under the microscope. Usually this is performed if there is a suspected pathogen causing an infection.

Arthroscopy allows the physician to look inside a joint, most frequently the knee, using an instrument called an arthroscope. When there is an injury, an arthroscopic needle is inserted into the area. The area is viewed and a biopsy is taken if necessary.

THE VOCABULARY OF ORTHOPEDICS

The following word list contains common orthopedics words as well as most of the difficult words contained in the dictation at the end of the chapter. Take time to become familiar with these words now, then review them again before you key the medical documents.

Here are suggestions for learning the vocabulary words:

1. Read and study each word for pronunciation and meaning.
2. Write each unfamiliar word from the list below on a notecard, write the definition or a paraphrase of the definition on the back, and draw a simple picture to help you learn the word.
3. Study the pronunciation, spelling, and definition of each word on your notecard, then key each word twice for reinforcement.
4. Add the correctly spelled terms to your word processor's spell checker.

abduction
(ab-duk'-shun) (n) movement of a leg or arm away from the middle of the body

adduction
(ad-duk'-shun) (n) movement of a leg or arm toward the middle of the body

ankylosis
(ang'-ki-lO'-sis) (n) stiffening or rigidity of a joint either as a result of a disease process or from surgery

ankylotic
(ang-ki-lot'-ik) (adj) relating to or having ankylosis

apophyseal
(a-pO-fiz'-ee-al) (adj) relating to or having an apophysis

apophysis
(a-pof'-i-sis) (n) a projection or outgrowth of a bone

arteritis
(ar'-tur-I'-tis) (n) inflammation of one or more arteries

arthralgia
(ar-thral'-jee-a) (n) joint pain

arthritis
(ar-thrI'-tis) (n) inflammation of one or more joints

arthroplasty
(ar'-thrO-plas-tee) (n) surgical repair of a joint; creation of a new joint

articulation
(ar-tik-yoo-lay'-shun) (n) the connecting of bones as a joint

asepsis
(a-sep'-sis) (n) lack of germs; a state of sterility; methods used to create or maintain a sterile environment

aseptic
(a-sep'-tik/ay-sep'-tik) (adj) sterile; being without infection or contamination

calcaneus
(kal-kay'-nee-us) (n) heel bone; calcanei (kal-kay'-nee-I) (pl)

callous
(kal'-us) (adj) pertaining to or resembling callus

callus
(kal'-us) (n) thickened skin that develops at points of pressure or friction; the bony deposit which develops around the broken ends of bone during healing

carpal tunnel
(kar'-pul tun'-nul) (n) where the median nerve and flexor tendons pass through the wrist

cervical
(ser'-vi-kal) (adj) relating to a neck or cervix

chondral
(kon'-drul) (adj) relating to cartilage

chondritis
(kon-drI'-tis) (n) inflammation of cartilage

chondromalacia
(kon'-drO-ma-lay'-shee-a) (n) softening of cartilage

claudication
(klaw'-di-ka'-shun) (n) limping; painful cramps in calf of leg due to poor blood circulation

clavicle
(klav'-i-kl) (n) clavicula; collar bone

clavicula
(kla-vik'-yoo-la) (n) clavicle; collar bone

condyle
(kon'-dil) (n) the rounded projecting end of a bone where ligaments are attached

crepitus
(krep'-i-tus) (n) grating sound or vibration made by movement of fractured bones (bone fragments); crepitation

dactylomegaly
(dak-til-O-meg'-a-lee) (n) abnormal enlargement of one or more fingers or toes

degenerative
(di-jen'-er-a-tiv) (adj) relating to or causing deterioration or worsening of a condition

diaphysis
(dI-af'-i-sis) (n) shaft of a long bone

edema
(e-dee'-ma) (n) excessive accumulation of fluid in tissues, especially just under the skin or in a given cavity

edematous
(e-dem'-a-tus) (adj) having edema

epiphyseal
(ep-i-fiz'-ee-al) (adj) relating to an epiphysis

epiphysis
(e-pif'-i-sis) (n) end of a long bone, separated by cartilage from the shaft until the bone stops growing when the shaft and end are joined

eversion
(ee-vur'-zhun) (n) turning out or inside out

facial
(fay'-shul) (adj) relating to the face

fascia
(fash'-ee-a) (n) fibrous connective tissue that supports soft organs and encloses structures such as muscles; fasciae (pl)

fascial
(fash'-ee-al) (adj) relating to fascia

femoral
(fem'-o-ral) (adj) relating to the thigh bone or femur

foramen
(fO-ray'-men) (n) hole or opening, especially in a bone or membrane

fracture
(frak'-chur) (v) to break; (n) a broken bone

hemarthrosis
(hee'-mar-thrO'-sis/hem'-ar-thrO'-sis) (n) accumulation of blood in a joint

humerus
(hyoo'-mer-us) (n) the long bone of the upper arm

ischium
(is'-kee-um/ish'-ee-um) (n) bone upon which body rests when sitting; fuses with the ilium and pubis to form the

pelvis; ischia (is'-kee-a) (pl)

kyphosis
(kI-fO'-sis) (n) abnormal curving of the spine causing a hunchback

lipping
(lip'-ing) (n) excessive growth in a liplike shape at the edge of a bone

lordosis
(lOr-dO'-sis) (n) abnormal curving of the spine causing a swayback

malleolus
(ma-lee'-O-lus) (n) either of the two bumplike projections on each side of the ankle; malleoli (pl)

metatarsal
(met'-a-tar'-sal) (adj) relating to a metatarsus; (n) a metatarsal bone

metatarsus
(met'-a-tar'-sus) (n) any of the five long bones of the foot between the ankle and the toes

necrosis
(ne-krO'-sis) (n) death of some or all of the cells in a tissue

necrotic
(ne-krot'-ik) (adj) relating to or undergoing necrosis

neural
(noo'-ral) (adj) relating to nerves or the nervous system

odontoid process
(O-don'-toyd pros'-es) (n) the toothlike projection from the upper surface of the second cervical vertebra on which the head rotates

osseous
(os'-ee-us) (adj) bony; resembling bone; osteal

osteal
(os'-tee-ul) (adj) bony; resembling bone; osseous

ostealgia
(os-tee-al'-jee-a) (n) pain in a bone

osteophyte
(os'-tee-O-fIt) (n) a bony outgrowth; projection or bone spur

osteoporosis
(os-tee-O-pO-rO'-sis) (n) abnormal loss of bone tissue, causing fragile bones that fracture easily

ostial
(os'-tee-ul) (adj) relating to any opening (ostium)

parietal
(pa-rI'-e-tal) (adj) relating to the walls of a body cavity

plantar
(plan'-tar) (adj) relating to the undersurface (sole) of the foot

prosthesis
(pros-thee'-sis) (n) artificial replacement for a diseased or missing part of the body, such as artificial limbs; prostheses (pl)

radiograph
(ray'-dee-O-graf) (n) an image produced through exposure to x-rays

residual
(re-zid'-yoo-al) (adj) related to a residue which is left behind

rheumatoid
(roo'-ma-toyd) (adj) resembling rheumatism, with pain, inflammation, and deformity of the joints

rigidity
(rijid'-i-tee) (n) stiffness; inflexibility

scoliosis
(skO-lee-O'-sis) (n) abnormal curvature of the spine to one side

spondylitis
(spon-di-lI'-tis) (n) inflammation of one or more vertebrae

sprain
(n) injury to a joint by overstretching the ligaments; (v) to injure a joint and sometimes the nearby ligaments or tendons

strain
(n) injury, usually to muscle, caused by overstretching or overuse; (v) to injure muscles by overstretching or overuse

synovial fluid
(si-nO'-vee-al floo'-id) (n) protective lubricating fluid around joints

tibia
(tib'-ee-a) (n) the larger bone of the lower leg; shin bone

transverse
(trans-vers') (adj) at right angles to the long axis of the body or an organ; crosswise; side to side

trochanter (trO-kan'-ter) (n) one of the projections at the upper end of the femur (thigh bone)

ABBREVIATIONS

AE	above the elbow (amputation)
AK	above the knee (amputation)
AP	anterioposterior
AROM	active range of motion
BE	below the elbow (amputation)
BK	below the knee (amputation)
C-1, etc.	cervical vertebrae
CDH	congenital dislocation of the hip
DIP joint	distal interphalangeal joint
DJD	degenerative joint disease
EMG	electromyography
fx	fracture
HD	hip disarticulation
HNP	herniated nucleus pulposus (disc)
HP	hemipelvectomy
ID	internal development (ortho)
IS	intracostal space
KD	knee disarticulation
L-1, etc.	lumbar vertebrae
MCP joint	metacarpophalangeal joint
OA	osteoarthritis
ortho	orthopedics
PIP joint	proximal interphalangeal joint
PROM	passive range of motion
ROJM	range of joint motion
S-1, etc.	sacral vertebrae
SD	shoulder disarticulation
T-1, etc.	thoracic vertebrae
TENS	transcutaneous electric nerve stimulation
THA	total hip arthroplasty

EXERCISE 10.1: RECOGNIZING LOOK-ALIKES AND SOUND-ALIKES

The following list includes frequently used words that look alike and/or sound alike. Study the meaning and pronunciation of each set of words, then read each sentence carefully and circle the word in parentheses that correctly completes the meaning.

affect	(n) emotional or psychological disposition
affect	(v) to influence or alter
affective	(adj) pertaining to emotions
effect	(n) result
effect	(v) to bring about, accomplish
effective	(adj) producing the desired result

checkup	(n) an examination of the health of an individual
check up	(v) to investigate

ostial	(adj) relating to an orifice
osteal	(adj) bony

accept	(v) to take
except	(prep) other than; with exclusion of
except	(v) to leave out

sprain	(v) to injure a joint
sprain	(n) traumatic injury to a joint
strain	(v) to injure a muscle
strain	(n) injury to a muscle

weak	(adj) feeble, delicate
week	(n) a period of seven successive days

off	(adj) gone, absent
off	(adv) apart, away, below
of	(prep) indicating possession or origin

1. She complains of feeling (weak, week) and tired.
2. She has had flu symptoms for approximately one (weak, week).
3. The medication (affected, effected) her bladder control.
4. As the patient was gradually tapered (off of, off, of) steroids, his strength returned.
5. The new medication was (affective, effective) in reducing inflammation.
6. The patient acknowledged the instruction and (accepted, excepted) the plan.
7. Mr. Braccia's pain was diagnosed as originating in the (ostial, osteal) tissue of the hip.
8. The patient displayed a flat (effect, affect).
9. During her gymnastics class, the patient jumped off the balance beam and (strained, sprained) her ankle.
10. The skin exam was unremarkable (accept, except) for a small lesion on the left cheek.

EXERCISE 10.2: MATCHING SOUND AND SPELLING

The numbered list that follows shows the phonetic spelling of hard-to-spell words. Sound out the word, then write the correct spelling in the blank space provided. Each of the words can be found in the glossary or in the drug list in appendix C.

1. os'-ee-us ______________________
2. kon'-drO-ma-lay'-shee-a ______________________
3. kal-kay'-nee-us ______________________
4. krep'-i-tus ______________________
5. trO-kan'-ter ______________________
6. ang-ki-lO'-sis ______________________
7. kI-fO'-sis ______________________
8. kla-vik'-yoo-la ______________________
9. dI-af'-i-sis ______________________
10. kon-drI'-tis ______________________
11. pa-rI'-e-tal ______________________
12. os'-tee-O-fIt ______________________
13. is'-kee-um/is'-shee-um ______________________
14. skO-lee-O'-sis ______________________
15. hyoo'-mer-us ______________________
16. dak'-til-O-meg'-a-lee ______________________
17. ang-ki-lot'-ik ______________________
18. spon-di-lI'-tis ______________________
19. roo'-ma-toyd ______________________
20. os-tee-al'-jee-a ______________________

EXERCISE 10.3: CHOOSING WORDS FROM CONTEXT

When transcribing dictation, the medical transcriptionist frequently needs to determine the word that correctly completes the sentence based on the situation. From the list of words below, select the term that meaningfully completes each statement.

aseptic	chondritis	edematous
neural	degenerative	residual
kyphosis	radiograph	necrosis
cervical	crepitus	tibia
prosthesis		

1. It was necessary for Mr. Jones to have a ____________ after the amputation.
2. The ______________ of the chest showed pneumonia.
3. Although there was considerable necrosis of the tumor after the chemotherapy, there was some ____________ tumor remaining.
4. The boy suffered a fractured __________ after he fell off his bicycle.
5. The legs were ____________ because the woman was in heart failure.
6. The pain was in the ____________ region of the back.
7. When he opened the sterile package, he used a(n) ________ technique.
8. He had _____________ of the thoracic spine, which caused pain when he stood too long.
9. The pathology report showed ________ tissue taken from the brain.
10. After the radiation treatments, there was considerable _________ at the tumor site.

EXERCISE 10.4: PAIRING WORDS AND MEANINGS

For each definition provided below, locate the term on the list that best matches the definition. Write the letter of the term in the space provided beside the definition.

A. apophysis	E. fascia	H. odontoid process
B. epiphysis	F. malleolus	I. osteoporosis
C. femoral	G. metatarsus	J. synovial sarcoma
D. foramen		

1. a bone of the foot ____________
2. a malignant tumor ____________
3. loss of bone tissue ____________
4. a small projection or outgrowth on a bone ____________
5. toothlike projection that serves as pivot point when head turns ____________
6. end portion of a long bone ____________
7. a hole or opening in a bone or membrane ____________
8. fibrous, connective tissue that supports small organs ____________
9. a bumplike projection on the ankle bone ____________
10. pertaining to the thigh bone ____________

EXERCISE 10.5: CREATING TERMS FROM WORD FORMS

In the following exercise, combine prefixes, root words, and suffixes to create medical words that fit the definitions below. Fill in the blanks with the words you construct.

dia-	through	-itis	inflammation
epi-	on, in addition to	kyph/o	humped
lord/o	bent	-osis	condition
meta-	change, beyond	physis	bone portion; growth
myel/o	bone marrow or spinal cord	phyte	outgrowth
necro/o	death	spondyl/o	vertebra
oste/o	bone	tarsus	instep of foot
por/o	cavity, passage		

1. abnormal loss of bone tissue ____________
2. end of long bone, secondary bone ____________
3. inflammation of vertebra ____________
4. cell tissue death ____________
5. convexity of spine; sway back ____________
6. inflammation of bone and marrow ____________
7. bone between ankle and toes ____________
8. inflammation of spinal cord ____________
9. shaft of long bone ____________
10. hunchback, curved spine ____________
11. growth zone of long bone ____________
12. bony outgrowth ____________

EDITING MEDICAL DOCUMENTS

In this section you will perfect your language and grammar skills. These skills help you edit and proofread medical reports for correct word use, punctuation, capitalization, format, and meaning. The special focus for this chapter is using numbers and figures correctly.

USING NUMBERS IN WORD OR FIGURE FORM

Numbers are written in figures or words, depending on the situation. As a basic rule, spell out numbers up to and including ten. Use figures for numbers above ten.

> The patient will be seen again in three weeks.
>
> About 50 doctors attended the meeting.

Exceptions to the basic rule are discussed below.

First Word of a Sentence

Spell out numbers that are the first word of a sentence.

> Twelve years ago the patient had a stroke.
>
> Two of the lymph nodes were positive.

Large numbers spelled out at the beginning of a sentence may slow down the reader. Instead, rewrite the sentence so the number appears in a different location.

> WORDY. Forty-three thousand five hundred was his highest white count.
>
> BETTER His highest white count was 43,500.

Units of Measurement and Lab Values

Use figures when indicating quantity with a unit of measurement or with lab values.

> Three 1-liter solutions were used.
>
> The surgeon made two 5-cm incisions.
>
> Results of the PSA revealed a mild elevation of 4.1 ug/L.

Similar Types of Data

When numbers in a sentence describe the same kind of data, express them in the same style regardless of their size.

> There were 65 lymphocytes, 2 monocytes, and 5 eosinophils.
>
> Today the doctor saw 15 patients in the office and 5 in the hospital.
>
> Pathology revealed two positive lymph nodes from the left groin and one positive node from the right.

Dates

Use figures for short-form dates with slashes and for the day of a month. A day that precedes a month should be expressed in ordinal numbers (numbers expressing place or position as in first, second, third).

> He has an appointment for 3/29/97.
>
> Please arrange for surgery to be performed on October 3.
>
> We have continued to follow this patient on the 5th of each month.

The military and international style for expressing dates reverses the day and month, with no commas in between. Follow this format if your client or employer prefers.

> The patient was admitted on 10 April 1996.

Age

Express ages and other vital statistics in figures.

> She is a 21-year-old, well-developed, well-nourished white female. Height 5 feet 6 inches, weight 130 pounds, blood pressure 110/70, pulse 74, respirations 18. [Note that common nonmetric units of measurement (feet, inches, pounds) are spelled out.]

Time

Use figures to express times of day. No zeros are required when the time falls on the hour.

> The patient will be seen at 2 p.m.
>
> Surgery is scheduled for 7 a.m.
>
> The patient expired at 11:45 p.m.

Many medical facilities follow the military style of expressing time. Military time uses no colons, and instead of starting over at 12 noon, the clock continues to count to 2400 (stated as "twenty-four hundred hours"). If this confuses you, simply subtract 1200 to get "civilian" time, for example, 2350 - 1200 = 1150 p.m. Note the following dictated sentences and the times intended.

> The infant was delivered at fourteen forty-five. [2:45 p.m.]
>
> The last dose was given at zero three twenty. [3:20 a.m.]

Anatomic position may be dictated using a clock-face orientation (o'clock). Use figures in these expressions.

> A suspicious mass was noted at the 3 o'clock position on the left breast.
>
> The lesion appears at 12 o'clock on the right cheek.

Money

Use figures to express amounts of money. Do not include zeros in even dollar amounts.

> The patient has a $5 copay. [Not $5.00]

Measurements, Mathematical Expressions, and Symbols

Use figures for measurements and ratios and in expressions involving symbols and abbreviations.

> The mass on the head of the pancreas measured 2 x 3 cm. [Note that the unit of measurement is expressed only once.]

The patient's height is 5 feet 6 inches and her weight is 135 pounds.

The incision was closed with 3-0 Prolene.

The baby's rectal temperature was 103°.

The patient has 20/50 vision in the right eye and 20/70 in the left eye.

The solution was diluted 1:50. [no space before or after the colon]

Pulses were 2+.

Express vertebral levels using a capital C, T (or D), L, or S followed by an arabic numeral, as in T2. Do not use a hyphen. Do not superscript or subscript the numeral.

Use a hyphen to express the interevertebral space (space between two vertebrae), as in L5-S1 or L2-L3.

Decimals

Use figures to express decimals. If a decimal less than 1 is dictated, transcribe a zero before the decimal, even if it is not dictated. When whole numbers are dictated, do not add a decimal point and zero.

DICTATED:	The patient takes digoxin point 125 mg q.d.
TRANSCRIBED:	The patient takes digoxin 0.125 mg q.d.
INCORRECT:	She was given 5.0 mg of Valium.
CORRECT:	She was given 5 mg of Valium.

When a metric measurement is dictated as a fraction, convert the fraction to a decimal. Common fractions and decimal equivalents include the following: 1/4 = 0.25, 1/2 = 0.5, and 3/4 = 0.75.

INCORRECT:	Local anesthesia was achieved using 1/2 percent Xylocaine.
CORRECT:	Local anesthesia was achieved using 0.5% Xylocaine.

When a physician dictates a fraction in a general, nontechnical form, use words to express the fraction.

INCORRECT:	The upper 1/2 of the esophagus appeared normal.
CORRECT:	The upper one-half of the esophagus appeared normal.
INCORRECT:	The distal 2/3 of the esophagus revealed no abnormalities.
CORRECT:	The distal two-thirds of the esophagus revealed no abnormalities.

EXERCISE 10.6: EDITING FOR CORRECT USE OF NUMBERS

Edit the following discharge summary for the correct use of numbers. Circle the correct number expressions from the choices in parentheses, then key the report with the errors corrected.

DISCHARGE SUMMARY

PATIENT: Juarez, Juan
MR#: 12-34-56
DATE OF ADMISSION: (April 4 19XX; 4/4/XX)
DATE OF DISCHARGE: (April 6 19 XX; 4/6/XX)

DISCHARGE DIAGNOSIS: Herniated nucleus pulposus, (L-5-S-1; L5-S1).

OPERATION PERFORMED: Right partial (L-4; L4) hemilaminectomy with excision of herniated disc

HISTORY: This is a (fifty; 50)-year-old Hispanic male who presented with a (four; 4)-month history of progressive low back pain. Over the past (one; 1) month he has had worsening symptoms and now has numbness, tingling, and pain radiating down his right leg.

PAST MEDICAL HISTORY: His history is significant for (two; 2) episodes of pneumonia (five; 5) years ago, and he has chronic asthma.

SOCIAL HISTORY: The patient smokes (one; 1) pack of cigarettes per day and has done so for the past (20; twenty) years. He drinks (2 6-packs; two six-packs; two 6-packs; 2 six-packs) of beer per week.

ADMISSION MEDICATIONS
1. Theo-Dur (three hundred milligrams; 300 milligrams; 300 mg) (tid; t.i.d.; TID).
2. Proventil inhaler (two; 2) puffs (q12h; q. 12 h.; q.12h.)

DRUG ALLERGIES: CODEINE, which causes a rash.

PHYSICAL EXAMINATION
GENERAL APPEARANCE: This is a slightly obese Hispanic male appearing slightly older than his stated age of (50-years; fifty-years; 50 years).
VITAL SIGNS: Blood pressure (one hundred twenty over sixty; 120 over 60; 120/60), pulse (eighty; 80) and regular, respirations (twelve; 12), temperature (ninety-eight degrees; 98°).
HEENT: Pupils equal and reactive to light. The left tympanic membrane was (one plus/1+) injected. Nares were patent bilaterally.
NECK: Right shotty supraclavicular lymph node approximately (2, two) cm in size. Trachea midline.
LUNGS: Clear to percussion and auscultation.
HEART: Auscultation revealed a grade (two over six; 2 over 6; 2/6) systolic ejection murmur. PMI is at the (fifth; 5th) intercostal space.

(continued)

DISCHARGE SUMMARY
PATIENT: Juarez, Juan
MR#: 12-34-56
Page 2

ABDOMEN: Slightly obese, (one plus; 1 plus; 1+) tenderness in the epigastrium. Bowel sounds were present, no hepatosplenomegaly.
SPINE: Negative CVA tenderness. There was (two plus; 2+) tenderness in the (L-4-L-5; L4-L5) area. Straight leg raising was negative on the left, positive on the right at (forty-five; 45) degrees.
EXTREMITIES: No clubbing, cyanosis, or edema. Distal pulses were good.
NEUROLOGIC: Cranial nerves (two through twelve; II-XII; 2-12) were intact. The patient was alert and oriented (times three; x3).

LABORATORY DATA: Admission CBC revealed WBC of (5,800; 5800) with (seventy-one; 71) polys, (two; 2) bands, (one; 1) eosinophil and (twenty-six; 26) lymphs. Hemoglobin was (thirteen; 13), hematocrit (thirty-nine percent; 39%; 39 percent). BUN was (eight; 8), creatinine (point nine; .9; 0.9).

HOSPITAL COURSE: Lumbar myelogram on day of admission revealed significant disc herniation at the (L-4-L-5; L4-L5) level. The patient was taken to the operating room, where right hemilaminectomy was performed.

Postoperatively the patient had a temperature spike to (101°; one-hundred one degrees) and was started on Ancef. He had no further temperature elevations and his chest x-ray remained clear. He had good resolution of his symptoms.

The patient was discharged to home to be followed in clinic in (five; 5) days. Instructions were given for no heavy lifting. It was suggested that a (thirty, 30)-minute walk be taken daily.

DISCHARGE MEDICATIONS
1. Vicodin (one; 1) p.o. (q.3-4h.; q. three to four hours) p.r.n. pain.
2. Theo-Dur and Proventil as previously.

NS/XX
D: 1/8/XX
T: 1/10/XX

EXERCISE 10.7: PROOFREADING REVIEW

Read the following report section and look for errors in punctuation, plural vs. singular word forms, subject-verb agreement, complete sentences, and the use of numbers. Circle the errors, then key the document with the errors corrected.

DATE OF ADMISSION: August 5/XX

Jonathan is states post rite baloney amputation for synoviale sarcoma he is without complaints and is ambulating with his below knee prosthesis quiet well. His abdomen is soft and non-tender. there are no mass. The incisor is well heeled. The right thigh skin graph sight is clean. Their is no palpable mass and there is no open wound. If he experiences pain, he is to take one Vicodin p.o. q four to six hours.

WHERE CAN I FIND THE ANSWER?

As you transcribe dictation, you may hear unfamiliar words or terms. A variety of reference sources are available to help you locate answers to your questions. One of the important types of references for medical transcriptionists is described below. Read the information; then if you have access to the reference discussed, explore its capabilities.

MEDICAL REFERENCES: ELECTRONIC MEDICAL DICTIONARIES

Some of the popular medical dictionaries are available in electronic form. Because this type of dictionary can be accessed from within a word processing program, it can save the medical transcriptionist considerable time. Electronic dictionaries typically contain all the information that is included in the printed version. Entries are organized as they are in the book. For example, each entry appears first as a headword, followed by the word's pronunciation, the etymology, or history, of the word, and then the definition.

Search Features

Besides quick access, the other major benefit of an electronic medical dictionary is the ability to search its entire database of words almost instantly. Most programs allow you to enter a word from the keyboard and press a key or click a mouse button to search for a match. Even if you have spelled the word incorrectly, the dictionary will try to find a match and will list several choices for your consideration.

Thesaurus

Another time-saving component often included in some electronic dictionaries is a thesaurus. This option allows you to enter partial words a letter at a time. With each letter you add, the program displays a list of words beginning with those letters. This feature is especially helpful for those occasions when you may know only the first few letters of a medical term.

TRANSCRIBING ORTHOPEDICS DOCUMENTS

In this section your goal is to prepare for the work of transcription by transcribing first from a printed document and then from dictation on tape. The model document that follows illustrates the generally accepted format for the **emergency room note,** the medical document featured in this chapter.

BASIC FORMAT: THE EMERGENCY ROOM NOTE

Because emergency room cases can range from simple injuries to life-threatening traumas, ER reports can likewise vary from short chart notes to lengthy, complex reports. The latter may include the results of laboratory studies, x-ray films, and ECGs, along with operative procedures and the results from detailed physical examinations. Common procedures in the emergency room include endotracheal intubation, insertion of chest tubes and nasogastric tubes, catheterization of the bladder, placement of central venous catheters, and suturing of wounds.

Transcribing emergency room reports presents challenges usually not encountered with other medical specialties. For example, sometimes a dictation may be incomplete or interrupted because the physician may have been handling several complex cases, including some that were life-threatening. This factor may also lead to inconsistencies in the dictation, which should be pointed out to the physician for correction.

Required Headings/Content

JCAHO mandates no specific headings. However, reports typically include chief complaint, history of present illness, primary physician, physical examination, diagnosis, treatment plan, and condition at discharge. JCAHO does require ER physicians to record the patient's time of arrival, time seen by the physician, and the time of discharge or transfer. Sometimes the physician dictates these times; otherwise, the information is included in another part of the medical record.

Turnaround Time

Rapid turnaround is required for ER reports since frequently the patient is admitted to the hospital and the information is vital for continued treatment. The ideal turnaround time is one to two hours, although critical cases may require that transcription is completed within an hour of dictation.

EMERGENCY DEPARTMENT REPORT

1-inch margins
left justification

PATIENT: Alex Cavara
MR#: 510-879-21
DATE SEEN: 9/5/XX

HISTORY: This 27-year-old Hispanic male was admitted today following a motor vehicle accident.

The patient was the unrestrained driver of a vehicle which struck a tree at approximately 40 miles per hour. The patient had a momentary loss of consciousness and appeared confused at the scene. He complained of immediate head and neck pain. Paramedics transported the victim in full spine precautions.

PHYSICAL EXAMINATION: On examination the patient noted pain in the right arm with left lateral flexion-rotation-compression maneuvers to the neck. There was profound hematoma along the course of the sternocleidomastoid muscle. Cervical flexion-extension maneuvers were limited. There was gross crepitus on palpation of the spinous processes of C-5, C-6, and C-7.

Double-space between sections and between parapraphs within sections

The patient had a 5 x 8 cm hematoma of the left forehead and several small facial lacerations. The pupils were slow to respond but equal and round. The teeth were not broken. There were no intraoral lacerations. Pharynx was clear.

The lungs were clear to auscultation, and the heart showed regular rate and rhythm and no murmurs. The abdomen was mildly tender diffusely but without signs of splenic or hepatic trauma.

There was an obvious spiral oblique fracture of the right humeral shaft with marked malangulation and shortening. Distal pulses were intact and the fingers were warm and well perfused.

IMPRESSION: Major polytrauma and major skeletal injuries secondary to motor vehicle accident.

TREATMENT PLAN: The patient will be admitted to the orthopedic surgical unit and taken immediately to surgery for internal fixation of his fractures. His hemodynamic status will be carefully monitored over the next few hours. Chest x-ray and labs will be followed serially.

(continued)

EMERGENCY DEPARTMENT REPORT
PATIENT: Alex Cavara
MR#: 510-879-21
Page 2

CONDITION ON DISCHARGE: The patient is hemodynamically stable at the present time.

____
Jill McKensie, MD

JM/XX
D: 9/5/XX
T: 9/5/XX

PREPARING TO TRANSCRIBE

To prepare for transcribing dictation, key the emergency room note above. You will later key the identical report from tape. Follow these guidelines:

- Study the format and organization of the report.
- Review the word list presented earlier in this chapter.
- Consult reference books for words or formatting rules that are unfamiliar.
- Proofread your final copy by comparing it to the printed version.

CASES FOR TRANSCRIPTION

In this section you will transcribe medical dictation from tape. Your goal is to produce error-free documents. Read this chapter's Pro Tip (following the case studies) for helpful hints from experienced MTs. Then follow these steps for each dictation:

1. Prepare to transcribe by reviewing the case study and the model report formats from this and earlier chapters.
2. Transcribe the dictation, leaving spaces for words you cannot hear or do not understand.
3. Carefully proofread each document and correct as many errors as you can. Use your reference materials to help you identify missing words.
4. Listen to the tape again and correct all remaining errors.

Repeat these steps until you produce an error-free document. Then complete the Performance Report at the end of the chapter, attach it to the top of the transcripts, and submit them to your instructor for evaluation.

CASE STUDY 1: ROBERTA FLAGNER

Roberta Flagner is a 51-year-old woman who was complaining of back pain, particularly around the upper spine, radiating toward the left arm from the shoulder blade. She went to see her physician, Joseph White, M.D., who referred her to an orthopedist, Samuel Larchmont, M.D.

Report 10.1: Radiology Report

Transcription Hint

To find the name of a joint, muscle, ligament, tendon, or bone, look first under the noun (joint, muscle, ligament, and so on). This also applies to surgical terms as there are many specialized names for the screws, nails, plates, and wires used to repair fractures.

Report 10.2: Consultation Letter

CASE STUDY 2: STEVE GATLIN

Steve Gatlin is a 28-year-old man who cut his left index finger with a carving knife and came to the emergency room for treatment.

Report 10.3: Emergency Room Note

CASE STUDY 3: ARLENE ELVIN

Mrs. Arlene Elvin was walking through the Brookfield Natural History Museum when she tripped on a slanted floor board and twisted her foot. She felt immediate pain and was assisted by her husband and the security guard to a seat. The museum nurse brought a wheelchair, and ice was applied. Mrs. Elvin was taken to the Brookfield Emergency Room where she was diagnosed with a fracture of the foot.

Report 10.4: Radiology Report

Report 10.5: Discharge Summary

Transcription Hint

Listen for a reference to another physician, Dr. Levendowski.

CASE STUDY 4: ALEX CAVARA

Alex Cavara is a 27-year-old man who was brought to the emergency room by ambulance following a car accident in which he ran into a tree while driving approximately 40 miles per hour. He suffered a momentary loss of consciousness and complained of immediate head and neck pain.

Report 10.6: Emergency Room Note

Transcription Hints

- The term *flexion-rotation-compression maneuvers* requires hyphens, as shown.
- Listen for these new terms:
  sternocleidomastoid muscle
  malangulation

CASE STUDY 5: IVY HAINES

Ivy Haines is a 72-year-old woman with a history of chronic, progressive left hip pain for the past 25 years. She has been admitted to the hospital for left total hip arthroplasty.

Report 10.7: History and Physical

CASE STUDY 6: JANE STANLEY

Jane Stanley is a 36-year-old woman with a history of juvenile rheumatoid arthritis. In 1990 she had a bilateral total knee replacement with good results. In the past few years, however, she has experienced increasing left hip pain and was recently admitted to the hospital for a left total hip replacement.

Report 10.8: Discharge Summary

PRO TIP: CREATIVE RESEARCH TECHNIQUES (Nonmedical Terms)

By Kathleen Offman, CMT

Every medical report records a life event that becomes part of the patient's permanent medical record. The transcriptionist must ensure that the names, places, and elements associated with these life events are spelled accurately. The following sentences gleaned from authentic dictation illustrate the kinds of nonmedical words that may not appear in a spell checking program and thus may require special research to verify the spelling:

- The specimen had the consistency of Jell-O™.
- While fighting, the patient was hit with nunchuks.
- The patient was skiing and hit a mogul.
- Hot slag flew into a patient's ear.
- The child had swallowed a Lee™ Press-On Nail.
- The patient ate chicken at Donatelli's before coming to the emergency room with severe vomiting.
- The patient recently returned from a trip to Wiesbaden, Germany.

There are a number of sources you will find useful as you transcribe medical documents and encounter unique and hard-to-spell words and names.

Research Sources

- English dictionary—always a first choice for many unfamiliar words.
- International dictionary or encyclopedia—these are somewhat expensive (can cost up to $100) but can be valuable in locating words not found in smaller dictionaries.
- Telephone books—local phone books are an excellent reference for verifying unfamiliar company names and locations, for example, places of employment, schools the patient may be attending, and other healthcare facilities. Phone books also are a good source for verifying the spelling of ethnic names.
- *American Hospital Association Guide to the Health Care Field* (AHA Guide). Frequently, a patient may have been treated previously at an out-of-state hospital. This guide can help you find the correct spelling of hospitals across the country.
- *Proper Noun Speller* by Diana Gregory, published by QuikRef Publishing—offers over 15,000 entries including business, politics, sports, and brand names.
- A book of American slang.
- Current magazines–these can help verify brand names of popular products such as cigarettes and names of celebrities (sometimes referred to in psychiatric reports).

Specific Sources for Physician Names

- *American Medical Association Membership Directory*—listings available by county for physician names, addresses, and specialties.
- Insurance company lists of participating physicians—many times these are sent to employees contemplating which health plan to use.
- Local hospital telephone directories—these are usually available for the asking. Keeping several area hospital directories available can narrow your search criteria if the hospital name is known before the physician's name is dictated.
- Hospital libraries—if you work in a hospital, you should have access to a hospital library, which offers all kinds of sources. Check the *American Medical Directory*, a geographical register of physicians. You can also research other medical and nonmedical terms in the library.

ASSESSING TRANSCRIPTION SKILLS

Demonstrate your mastery of the terminology, editing/proofreading, and document transcription skills presented in this chapter by completing the following activities.

USING MEDICAL REFERENCES

Use the appropriate medical reference to locate the correct spelling and additional usage information for the words below. (If the reference is not available, use the glossary in this text.) Circle the correct spelling, then write a sentence using the word correctly.

1. acetabulem acetabulum ascetabulum

____

2. humerous humeres humerus

____

3. hematopoiesis hematapoiesis hematopoisis

____

4. perosteum periosteum periostium

____

5. epiphysis epiphisys epiphises

____

6. hemearthrosis hemarthrosus hemarthrosis

____

7. calcaneus calcaneas calcuneas

____

8. trocanter trochanter trochantor

____

9.	ischium	ishium	ischeum
	______		
10.	chondromalacia	condromalacia	chondromalacea
	______		

MAKING EXPERT DECISIONS

Circle the correct word from the choices in parentheses.

1. Sterilization was (effected/affected) using Hibiclens followed by an alcoholic wash of the area.
2. There was a hard (callus/calus) noted on her heel.
3. The new equipment will be able to determine (osteal/ostial) density in women at risk for osteoporosis.
4. The patient was taken to the operating suite where an (open reduction/open deduction) and internal fixation were performed.
5. A preliminary (plain/plane) film of the abdomen revealed distended loops of bowel.
6. The patient had hypertension and arthritis and was taking nonsteroidal anti-inflammatory medication for the (later/latter).
7. The slip and fall was (humerus/humorous) when it happened, but upon discovery of a fractured (humerus/humorous), my friend apologized for laughing.
8. The doctor said he thought some ligamentous fibers were ruptured, but he thought my (sprain/strain) would heal nicely.
9. The physician's assistant had the patient (adduct/abduct) his foot by pushing against the assistant's hands, thereby testing for muscle strength.
10. The patient had a stroke last year with a residual of left (fascial/facial) weakness.

TRANSCRIBING PROFESSIONAL DOCUMENTS

Transcribe the document named Assessment 10 from tape. Before you key, review the document formatting guidelines. Proofread your transcribed document and revise it until you think it is error-free.

PERFORMANCE REPORT

Name____Date ___________

Document	Description	Date Completed	Document Processing Speed (If Available)	Document Appraisal M=Mailable MC=Mailable w/corrections NM=Not Mailable
Report 10.1	Radiology Report			M MC NM
Report 10.2	Consultation Letter			M MC NM
Report 10.3	Emergency Room Note			M MC NM
Report 10.4	Radiology Report			M MC NM
Report 10.5	Discharge Summary			M MC NM
Report 10.6	Emergency Room Note			M MC NM
Report 10.7	History and Physical			M MC NM
Report 10.8	Discharge Summary			M MC NM

Comments ____

____

____

____

____

C H A P T E R

11

Neurology is the study of the nervous system, the body's communication network. The organs of the nervous system consist of the brain, the spinal cord, and nerves. The physician who treats diseases of the nervous system is the neurologist. A neurosurgeon performs surgery on organs of the nervous system.

Neurology

OBJECTIVES

- Use neurology terms correctly according to the context and purpose of the dictation.
- Select and use appropriate general and specialty reference materials.
- Key neurology documents of varying complexity and format.
- Transcribe authentic medical dictation requiring concentration and listening skill.
- Edit medical reports to conform with AAMT style guidelines.
- Proofread and correct transcripts to produce error-free documents.

EXPLORING NEUROLOGY

The nervous system is probably the most complicated system in the human body. Think of it as the body's Internet, an information superhighway that activates and controls all bodily functions and receives and processes stimuli from the outside world. The most powerful computers in the world cannot match the complexity of the human brain and the supporting components of the nervous system.

STRUCTURE AND FUNCTION

The human nervous system is divided into the central nervous system (CNS), which includes the brain and spinal cord, and the peripheral nervous system (PNS), which connects the spinal cord to the nerve, sensory, and muscle fibers (figure 11.1). The PNS is further divided into the somatic nervous system (SNS) and autonomic nervous system (ANS). The somatic nervous system is under the voluntary control of the individual. It innervates nerves that control voluntary muscle movement.

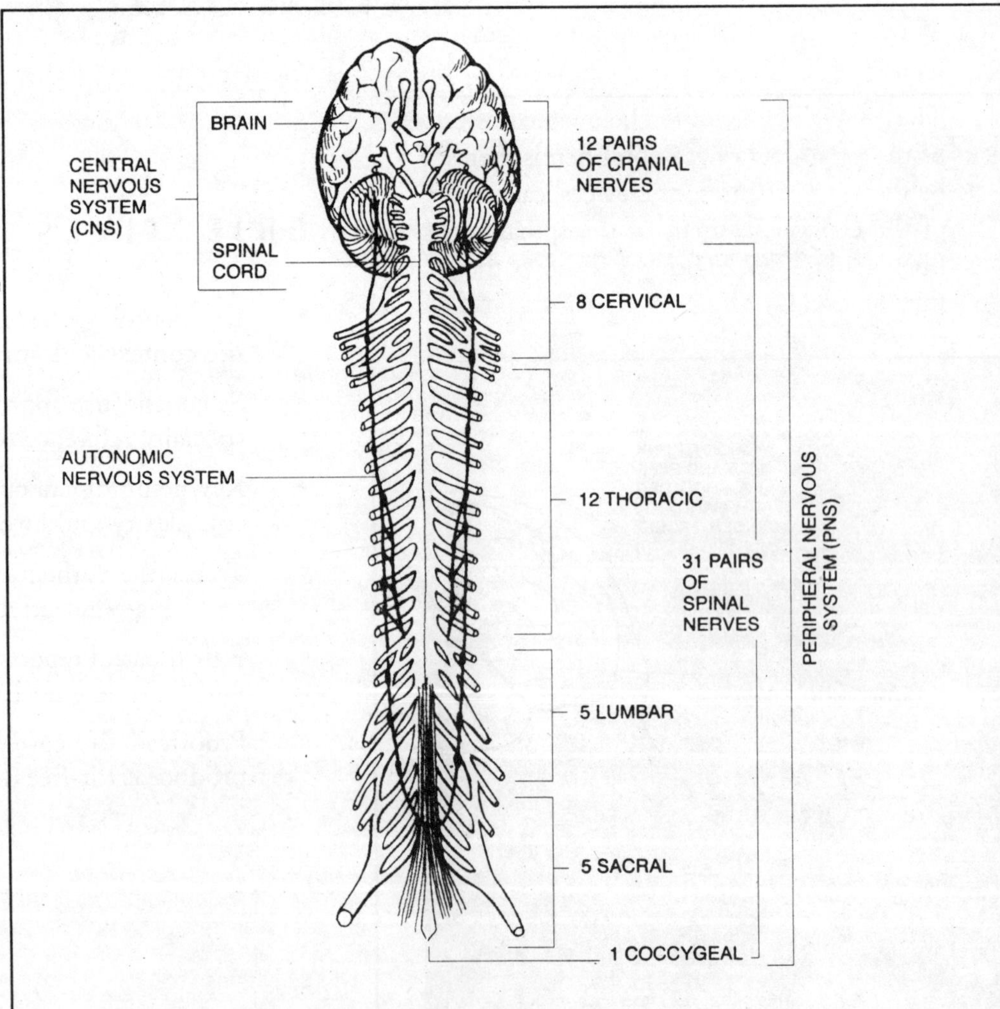

Figure 11.1 Spinal cord, lower brain, and spinal nerves

The autonomic nervous system produces the involuntary actions of the body such as the heartbeat and digestion. There are two subdivisions of the ANS: the sympathetic and parasympathetic nervous systems, which function as opposites. The hormones norepinephrine and acetylcholine, also opposites, mediate these responses. Most notably these two are responsible for the "fight or flight" response. At the first sign of fear, the sympathetic nerve fibers prepare the body to fight and move quickly by increasing the heart rate, constricting peripheral blood vessels to move more blood to the heart and skeletal muscles, dilating the pupils for better vision, slowing down peristalsis, and increasing secretions to produce more sugar for energy. The parasympathetic nervous system, by contrast, includes the nerves that function during quiet, nonstressful times.

The brain sends feedback to the endocrine system, which responds with the appropriate hormones. This combined system is known as the neuroendocrine system. The cerebrum is the portion of the brain that generates thought through the cerebral cortex, which is the gray matter. Folds, or gyri, on the surface of the brain increase the amount of gray matter that can fit inside the skull. The brain is divided into the left and right sides. The left brain, which controls muscles on the right side of the body, is involved with reasoning and language, as required for science and math. The right brain, which controls the muscles on the left side of the body, is responsible for imagination, insight, and artistic and musical abilities.

The cerebellum is located below the posterior portion of the cerebrum. It consists of the right and left cerebral hemispheres. The hemispheres are further divided by the brain's fissures, or crevices, called sulci. The brain stem is the continuation of the cervical segment of the spinal cord, which consists of bundles of nerve fibers and nuclei. Figure 11.2 shows the sections of the brain and the functions they control.

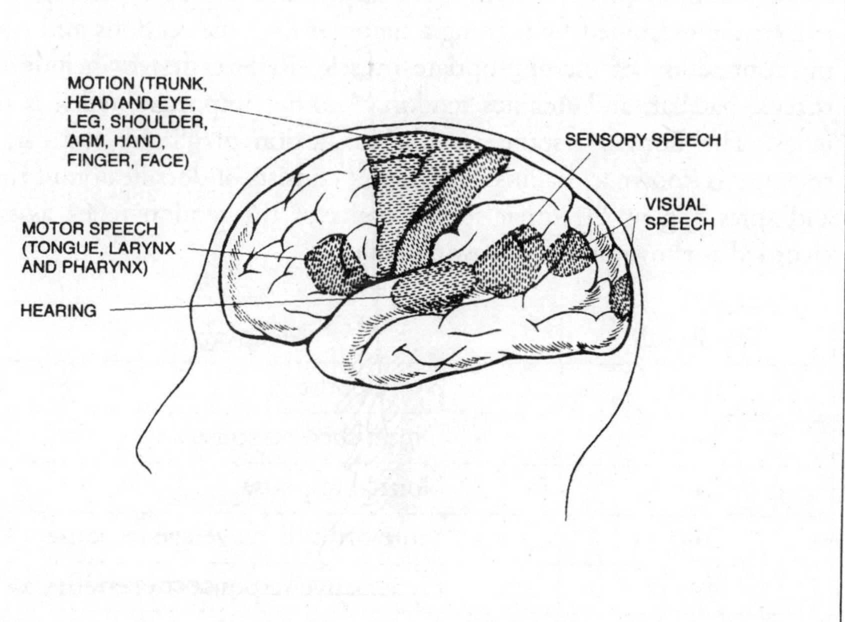

Figure 11.2 Brain sections and their functions

The neuron is the basic structural cell of the nervous system. Another class of cells called the neuroglia are supporting cells. The parts of a neuron include the soma (body), dendrites (branches leading toward the center of the soma), and an axon (a branch leading away from the soma). The soma contains the DNA for the cell. The dendrite is a tree-like area that receives signals from other neurons and sensory cells. The axon transmits signals away from the cell body and passes these signals to other neurons. Many of the axons are surrounded by a myelin sheath that protects the axon and accelerates impulses through it.

Communication between two neurons occurs when an electrical signal is converted into a chemical signal. This signal crosses a synapse, a minuscule space, where a neurotransmitter (a chemical) permits transmission at nearly unfathomable speed.

PHYSICAL ASSESSMENT

Neurologic diseases have presenting symptoms ranging from paralysis, numbness, shaking, and weakness to gait disturbances, recurring headaches, seizures, and passing out. Using both direct and indirect methods, the physician tests cerebral and cerebellar function, cranial nerves, motor and sensory systems, and reflexes.

First, if the patient has use of all of the senses, can answer questions accurately, can coordinate muscle movements, and is oriented to time (time of day, date, season, year), person (identification of self, family, and friends), and place (location, city, and state), there is appropriate cerebral and cerebellar function.

Motor and sensory deficits are another level of the assessment. Weakness, paralysis, or atrophy of muscles are indicators of motor nerve impairment. Sensory nerves are tested by feel (touch and gentle pinpricks), temperature (heat, cold), vibration perception in a few areas, and position (limb position). The reflexes are examined by tapping a hammer over the tendons and watching for the contraction of the appropriate muscle. Reflexes tested include the biceps, triceps, patellar, and Achilles tendon. Another important reflex is the plantar reflex. The normal response is plantar flexion of all the toes; an abnormal response is known as Babinski's sign and consists of dorsiflexion of the great toe and spreading of the other toes. Results of the tendon reflex assessment are recorded as shown in the following table:

Table 11.1 Tendon reflex assessment

Test Result	Meaning
0	No response
1+	Diminished response
2+	Normal response
3+	More brisk than average response
4+	Hyperactive response (hyperreflexia)

The patient's state of consciousness is assessed in a range from alert to comatose. The affect, or mood, is described using words such as hyperactive, euphoric, hostile, agitated, or flat. A general assessment of intellect involves asking the patient to perform simple mathematical calculations, define familiar vocabulary, and describe recent, intermediate, and remote, or past, events (a test of memory).

A patient's behavior is evaluated by assessing the state of dress, appropriateness of language, gestures, facial expressions, and attentiveness to the examiner. Speech is an important part of the neurologic examination. It shows coordination of thought and muscle movements and function of the cranial nerves.

The cerebellum is the center for balance and muscle coordination. There are several tests that the physician uses to assess this function. Balance is tested by observing gait. If there is any abnormality, a cerebellar disorder is suggested. The Romberg is a test for sensory equilibrium. A positive Romberg test means the patient loses balance with eyes closed and feet together.

The finger-to-nose test assesses coordination by checking for "past-pointing" in which the patient brings the fingertip beyond the nose. The physician will test for muscle strength and range of motion and observe for involuntary body movements such as tics, twitches, and tremors.

Common Neurology Drugs

alprazolam
Xanax

amantadine hydrochloride
Symadine, Symmetrel

amitriptyline hydrochloride
Elavil

buspirone
Buspar

carbamazepine
Tegretol

clonazepam
Klonopin

diazepam
Valium

fluoxetine hydrochloride
Prozac

flurazepam hydrochloride
Dalmane

imipramine
Tofranil

lorazepam
Ativan

paroxetine hydrochloride
Paxil

phenytoin
Dilantin

sertraline hydrochloride
Zoloft

zolpidem tartrate
Ambien

PHYSICAL ASSESSMENT

Cerebrovascular disease accounts for the majority of patients treated by neurologists. This group of diseases includes cerebral arteriosclerosis, cerebral atherosclerosis, aneurysm, thrombosis, and embolism. Another major disease is a cerebrovascular accident (CVA), commonly known as a stroke. All these disorders are caused by mild to severe interruption of blood flow to the brain.

Another important disease class is demyelinating disease, which affects the nerve coverings. Multiple sclerosis is perhaps the best-known example of this type of disease.

Peripheral neuropathy is a disease category encompassing diseases of the peripheral nerves. In the United States the primary cause of peripheral neuropathy is diabetes mellitus. Worldwide, a common cause is leprosy.

Brain tumors, both malignant and benign, are another frequent neurological affliction. Cancerous tumors either destroy or compress brain tissue and vary in aggressiveness. The most common brain tumors are tumors that have spread from another area, usually the breast or lung. Spinal cord tumors may be benign or malignant and occur one-tenth as frequently as brain tumors.

Degenerative disc disease is another common ailment treated by neurologists. Herniated discs may cause pressure on a nerve, resulting in arm, trunk, or leg pain.

Alzheimer's disease results from structural changes in the brain, the exact cause of which is unknown. Patients experience a gradual loss of cognitive function that ends with total disability and death.

COMMON TESTS AND SURGICAL PROCEDURES

Many procedures give insight into the nervous system without requiring surgery. Magnetic resonance imaging (MRI) is used extensively to visualize the brain or spinal cord. A contrast medium, usually gadolinium, is used to enhance or outline the structures. The computerized axial tomography (CT or CAT) scan provides section views of structures.

Cerebral angiography provides visualization of the vascular system using a radiopaque dye introduced through the carotid or vertebral artery.

Electroencephalography (EEG) produces a graphic recording of the electrical activities of the brain, similar to an electrocardiogram (ECG) for the heart. Electrodes are placed on the scalp to detect and record brain impulses. This test assists in the diagnosis of epilepsy.

Myelography produces an x-ray picture of the spinal cord after injection of a radiopaque dye.

Lumbar puncture (LP), or spinal tap, is performed by inserting a small gauge needle between the vertebrae into the spinal canal. This test is used to measure the pressure within the spinal canal and to withdraw cerebrospinal fluid (CSF) for examination under the microscope. Medications can be injected directly into the CSF through the needle.

Stereotactic surgery is a method of locating a precise area of the brain using a three-dimensional measurement. This operation is performed by a highly skilled neurosurgeon. Laminectomy can be performed by a neurosurgeon or an orthopedic surgeon. It involves excision of a portion of the vertebral body to relieve pressure on spinal nerves.

Trephination is performed by making a burr hole into the skull to decrease intracranial pressure.

THE VOCABULARY OF NEUROLOGY

The following word list contains common neurology words as well as most of the difficult words contained in the dictation at the end of the chapter. Take time to become familiar with these words now, then review them again before you key the medical documents.

Here are suggestions for learning the vocabulary words:

1. Read and study each word for pronunciation and meaning.
2. Write each unfamiliar word from the list below on a notecard, write the definition or a paraphrase of the definition on the back, and draw a simple picture to help you learn the word.
3. Study the pronunciation, spelling, and definition of each word on your notecard, then key each word twice for reinforcement. Check the spelling.
4. Add the correctly spelled terms to your word processor's spell checker.

agnosia
(ag-nO'-see-a) (n) unable to perceive or recognize sensory stimuli

agraphia
(a-graf'-ee-a) (n) impairment of the ability to write

akinesis
(ay-ki-nee'-sis/ay-kI-nee'-sis) (n) absence or loss of the power of voluntary motion; partial or incomplete paralysis

amnesia
(am-nee'-zee-a) (n) a disturbance of long-term memory; total or partial inability to recall past experiences

angiography
(an-jee-og'-ra-fee) (n) an x-ray taken after a radiopaque dye is given to visualize the vessels

aphasia
(a-fay'-zee-a) (n) difficulty with use and understanding of words

aphonia
(a-fO'-nee-a) (n) loss of the voice as a result of disease or injury

arachnoid
(a-rak'-noyd) (n) the middle of the three membranes covering the brain; it is a delicate fibrous membrane, resembling a cobweb

astereognosis
(a-steer'-ee-og-nO'-sis) (n) loss of the ability to judge the form of an object by touch

ataxia
(a-tak'-see-a) (n) muscular incoordination

atrophy
(at'-rO-fee) (n) a decrease in size of a part or organ; a wasting away of tissue as a result of disuse, radiation therapy, surgery, disease

aura
(aw'-ra) (n) a sensation, as of light or warmth, that may precede an attack of migraine or a seizure

auscultation
(aws-kul-tay'-shun) (n) act of listening through a stethoscope to body sounds, including lungs, heart, and abdomen

axial
(ak'-see-al) (adj) situated in or relating to an axis

Babinski's reflex
(bab-in'-skeez ree'-fleks) (n) an extension or moving of the big toe upward or toward the head, with the other toes fanned out and extended

Brudzinski's sign
(n) in meningitis, if a leg is passively flexed, a similar movement occurs in the other leg; if the neck is passively flexed, the legs also flex

causalgia
(kaw-zal'-jee-a) (n) persistent severe burning sensation of the skin, usually following injury of a sensory nerve

central nervous system (CNS)
(n) portion of the nervous system consisting of the brain and spinal cord

cephalalgia
(sef'-al-al'-jee-a) (n) headache

cerebellar
(ser-e-bel'-ar) (adj) relating to the cerebellum, the part of the brain concerned with the coordination and control of voluntary muscular activity

cerebrospinal
(ser'-e-brO-spI-nal/se-ree'-brO-spI-nal) (adj) relating to the brain and spinal cord

cerebrovascular
(ser'-e-brO-vas'-kyoo-lar) (adj) relating to the blood vessels of the brain, especially to pathological changes

Chvostek's sign
(khvosh'-teks) (n) an abnormal spasm of facial muscles when the facial nerve is tapped lightly

concussion
(kon-kush'-un) (n) an injury of a soft structure, as the brain, resulting from a blow or violent shaking

cortex
(kOr'-teks) (n) an outer part of an organ, such as the brain

cortical
(kOr'-ti-kal) (adj) relating to a cortex

cranium
(kray'-nee-um) (n) the bony skull that holds the brain

cyanosis
(sI-a-nO'-sis) (n) bluish discoloration of the skin and mucous membranes, occurring when the oxygen in the blood is sharply diminished, as in carbon monoxide poisoning

decompression
(dee'-kom-presh-un) (n) removal of bone to relieve pressure

dementia
(dee-men'-shee-a) (n) a general mental deterioration due to organic or psychological factors

dura mater
(doo'-ra may'-ter/mah'-ter) (n) the outermost of the three membranes surrounding the brain and spinal cord; it is tough and fibrous

echolalia
(ek-O-lay'-lee-a) (n) involuntary repetition of a word or sentence just spoken by another person

electrophoresis
(ee-lek-trO-fO-ree'-sis) (n) the movement of charged suspended particles through a liquid medium in response to changes in an electric field; for example, a hemoglobin electrophoresis measures the types of hemoglobin in the blood

encephalopathy
(en-sef'-a-lop'-a-thee) (n) disease or dysfunction of the brain

epilepsy
(ep'-i-lep'-see) (n) convulsive disorder

epileptiform
(ep-i-lep'-ti-fOrm) (adj) having the form of epilepsy

exotropia
(ek-sO-trO'-pee-a) (n) outward turning of one eye relative to the other

extraocular
(eks-tra-ok'-yoo-lar) (adj) outside the eye

fissures
(fish'-urz) (n) deep grooves in the brain

fundus
(fun'-dus) (n) that part of the interior of the eyeball exposed to view through the ophthalmoscope (pl. fundi)

funduscopic
(fun-dus-skop'-ik) (adj) the examination of the ocular fundus with an ophthalmoscope

gadolinium
(gad-O-lin'-ee-um) (n) a rare earth metallic element

ganglion
(gang'-glee-on) (n) a group of nerve cell bodies located in the peripheral nervous system

Glasgow coma scale
(glas'-gO/glaz'-gO) (n) a clinical scale to assess impaired consciousness; assessment includes motor responsiveness, verbal performance, and eye opening

glove-stocking anesthesia
(n) glove or gauntlet anesthesia is loss of sensation in the hand; stocking anesthesia is loss of sensation in the area covered by a stocking

hematocrit
(hee'-ma-tO-krit, hem'-a-tO-krit) (n) a measure of the packed cell volume of red cells

hemifocal
(hem-i-fO'-kal) (adj) refers to half of the body; usually a type of seizure

hemiparesis
(hem-ee-pa-ree'-sis, hem-ee-par'-e-sis) (n) muscular weakness of one half of the body

hemoglobin
(hee-mO-glO'-bin) (n) the iron-containing pigment of the red blood cells

hippocampus
(hip-O-kam'-pus) (n) structure within the brain

hydrocephalus
(hI-drO-sef'-a-lus) (n) an excessive accumulation of fluid in the brain

hyperreflexia
(hI'-pur-re-flek'-see-a) (n) condition in which deep tendon reflexes are abnormally strong

hypometabolism
(hI'-pO-me-tab'-O-lizm) (n) lowered metabolism

ictal
(ik'-tal) (adj) referring to immediate onset

icteric
(ik-ter'-ik) pertaining to the effects of jaundice

interictal
(in-ter-ik'-tal) (adj) between seizures

ischemia
(is-kee'-mee-a) (n) decreased blood supply due to obstruction, such as narrowing of the blood vessels

lethargy
(leth'-ar-jee) (n) state of sluggishness, stupor, unresponsiveness

medulla oblongata
(me-dool'-a ob-long-gah'-ta) (n) the lowest part of the brain, connecting to the spinal cord; contains the cardiac, vasomotor, and respiratory centers of the brain

meninges
(me-nin'-jeez) (n) membranes covering the brain and spinal cord

meningitis
(men-in-jI'-tis) (n) inflammation of the membranes of the brain or spinal cord

meningocele
(me-ning'-gO-seel) (n) protrusion of the brain or spinal cord through a defect in the skull or spinal column

mesial
(mee'-zee-al; mes'-ee-al) (adj) situated toward the midline of the body or the central part of an organ or tissue (also called medial)

myasthenia gravis
(mI-as-thee'-nee-a grav'-is) (n) a chronic progressive muscular weakness, beginning usually in the face and throat, due to a defect in the conduction of nerve impulses

nausea
(naw'-zee-a, naw'-zha) (n) an inclination to vomit

neuralgia
(noo-ral'-jee-a) (n) pain of a severe, throbbing, or stabbing character along the course of a nerve

neurapraxia
(noor-a-prak'-see-a) (n) loss of conduction in a nerve without structural degeneration

neurasthenia
(noor-as-thee'-nee-a) (n) an ill-defined condition, commonly accompanying or following depression, characterized by vague fatigue believed to be brought on by psychological factors

neurilemma
(noor-i-lem'-a) (n) a cell that enfolds one or more axons of the peripheral nervous system

neuron
(noor'-on) (n) nerve cell; neurocyte; the morphological and functional unit of the nervous system, consisting of the nerve cell body, the dendrites, and the axon

neuropathy
(noo-rop'-a-thee) (n) disorder affecting the cranial or spinal nerves

nystagmus
(nis-tag'-mus) (n) involuntary, rhythmic oscillation of the eyeballs

palsy
(pawl'-zee) (n) an abnormal condition characterized by partial paralysis

parietal
(pa-rI'-e-tal) (adj) relating to the inner walls of a body cavity; a section (lobe) of the brain

peripheral
(per-if'-er-al) nervous system (n) portion of nervous system that connects the CNS to other body parts

petit mal
(pe-tee' mahl) (n) a brief blackout of consciousness with only minor rhythmic movements, seen especially in children, recurring daily

phonation
(fO-nay'-shun) (n) process of uttering vocal sounds

pia mater
(pI'-a may'-ter/pee'-a mah'-ter) (n) the innermost of the three membranes surrounding the brain and spinal cord; it carries a rich supply of blood vessels

pineal gland
(pin'-ee-al) (n) small, cone-shaped gland in the brain thought to secrete melatonin

pituitary gland
(pi-too'-i-tayr-ee) (n) an unpaired compound gland suspended from the base of the hypothalamus

plantar
(plan'-tar) (adj) relating to the undersurface (sole) of the foot; a reflex

plexus
(plek'-sus) (n) a network of intersecting nerves and blood vessels or of lymphatic vessels

postictal
(pOst-ik'-tal) (adj) relating to the period following a seizure

proprioception
(prO'-pree-O-sep'-shun) (n) sensation due to receiving stimuli from muscles, tendons, or other internal tissues

proton
(prO'-ton) (n) a positively charged particle that is a fundamental component of the nucleus of all atoms; used in radiotherapy

psychosomatic
(sI'-kO-sO-mat-ik) (adj) relating to the influence of the mind upon the functions of the body

quadriparesis
(kwod-ri-pa-ree'-sis) (n) paralysis of both arms and both legs

radiculopathy
(ra-dik'-yoo-lop'-a-thee) (n) disease of the spinal nerve roots

reticulocyte
(re-tik'-yoo-lO-sIt) (n) a red blood cell containing a network of granules or filaments representing an immature stage in development

retina
(ret'-i-na) (n) a 10-layered, delicate nervous tissue membrane of the eye that receives images of external objects and transmits visual impulses through the optic nerve to the brain

sagittal
(saj'-i-tal) (adj) relating to a line from front to back in the middle of an organ or the body

sciatica
(sI-at'-i-ka) (n) pain in the lower back and hip radiating down the back of the thigh into the leg, usually due to herniated lumbar disk

sickle cell anemia
(sik'-l sel a-nee'-mee-a) (n) hereditary blood disease in which abnormal hemoglobin causes red blood cells to become sickle-shaped, fragile and nonfunctional, leading to many acute and chronic complications

subdural hematoma
(sub-doo'-ral hee-ma-tO'-ma/hem-a-tO'-ma) (n) an accumulation of blood under the dura mater surrounding the brain

syncopal
(sin'-kO-pal) (adj) relating to fainting

syncope
(sin'-ko-pee) (n) fainting

thecal
(thee'-kal) (adj) referring to a covering or enclosure

thrombosis
(throm-bO'-sis) (n) condition in which a blood clot forms within a blood vessel

uvula
(yoo'-vyoo-la) (n) small, fleshy mass hanging from the soft palate in the mouth

ventricle
(ven'-tri-kl) (n) either of the two lower chambers of the heart; areas of the brain that produce and drain cerebrospinal fluid (CSF)

ABBREVIATIONS

ALS	amyotrophic lateral sclerosis	EEG	electroencephalogram or electroencephalography
ANS	autonomic nervous system	HNP	herniated nucleus pulposus
CAT or CT	computerized axial tomography	LP	lumbar puncture
CNS	central nervous system	MRI	magnetic resonance imaging
CP	cerebral palsy	MS	multiple sclerosis
CSF	cerebrospinal fluid	PNS	peripheral nervous system
CVA	cerebrovascular accident	SNS	somatic nervous system
DTR	deep tendon reflexes	TIA	transient ischemic attack

EXERCISE 11.1: RECOGNIZING LOOK-ALIKES AND SOUND-ALIKES

Below is a list of frequently used words that look alike and/or sound alike. Study the meaning and pronunciation of each set of words, then read each sentence carefully and circle the word in parentheses that correctly completes the meaning.

workup (n) an intensive diagnostic study
work up (v) to produce by mental or physical work

clinch (v) confirm, ensure
clench (n) fist, vice
clench (v) clasp, clutch

conscience (n) the sense of right and wrong
conscious (adj) aware

pair (n) two, couple
pare (v) peel, scrape
pear (n) fruit

radicle (n) a nerve or vessel branch that joins others to form larger vessels or nerves
radical (adj) aimed at the origin of a disease or condition; complete, as in surgical excision

there (adv) in that place
their (possessive pronoun) belonging to
they're (contraction) they are

crisis (n, sing) turning point
crises (n, pl) turning points

hemifacial half of the face
hemifocal refers to half of the body; usually a seizure

recession the withdrawal of a part from its normal position
resection the cutting out of a portion of an organ

regression a return to an earlier condition
repression restraint
remission partial or total disappearance of a disease

1. Because he did not take good care of his teeth, he now has (recession, regression, repression) of the gums.
2. He is suffering jaw pain because of frequent teeth (clenching, clinching).
3. Within two hours of surgery, the patient became (conscience, conscious).
4. I used a (pair, pare, pear) of tweezers to remove the splinter.
5. The surgeon had to (pair, pare, pear) the nerve from the bone.
6. She is suffering from situational depression precipitated by several (crisis, crises) in her life.
7. After experiencing severe trauma to the lower spine, the patient underwent (radicle, radical) surgery.
8. (Their, There, They're) children are both in college now.
9. The patient frequently suffered (hemifacial, hemifocal) seizures.
10. We are thankful his leukemia is now in (regression, remission, repression).

EXERCISE 11.2: MATCHING SOUND AND SPELLING

The numbered list that follows shows the phonetic spelling of hard-to-spell words. Sound out the word, then write the correct spelling in the blank space provided. Each of the words can be found in the glossary or in the drug list in appendix C.

1. sin'-ko-pee ______
2. ra-dik'-yoo-lop'-a-thee ______
3. naw'-zee-a ______
4. noor'-on ______
5. me-nin'-jeez ______
6. noor-as-thee'-nee-a ______
7. a-fay'-zee-a ______
8. noo-ral'-jee-a ______
9. pe-tee'-mahl ______
10. sI'-kO-sO-mat'-ik ______
11. me-ning'-gO-seel ______
12. pi-too'-i-tayr-ee ______
13. ser'-e-brO-spI-nal ______
14. a-tak'-see-a ______

EXERCISE 11.3: CHOOSING WORDS FROM CONTEXT

When transcribing dictation, the medical transcriptionist frequently needs to determine the word that correctly completes the sentence based on the situation. From the list of words below, select the term that meaningfully completes each statement.

atrophy	cerebrovascular	plantar
hemiparesis	parietal	funduscopic
cerebellar examination	cranium	ventricle
interictal		

1. The brain is found within the ____________________.
2. There was marked ________________________ after the stroke.
3. The ____________________ section of the brain was effected by the cerebrovascular accident.
4. The neurologic exam was normal, including ___________ flexion, a negative Babinski sign.
5. Increased intracranial pressure can be visualized by ____________ examination with the ophthalmoscope.
6. ____________________________ is best performed by having the patient walk down the hallway to see if there is any ataxia.
7. The radiation therapy caused a small amount of______________ of the parietal area of the brain.
8. Between seizures, the woman had a (an) ___________________ period where she slept for a few minutes.
9. There was a blockage of the right ________________ in the brain caused by a cystic lesion, most likely benign.
10. The 72-year-old man had a (an) _____________________ accident which caused him to have left-sided hemiparesis.

EXERCISE 11.4: PAIRING WORDS AND MEANINGS

For each definition provided below, select the term on the list that best matches the definition. Write the letter of the term in the space provided beside the definition.

A. adenopathy	E. hemifocal palsy	H. sagittal
B. cerebrovascular	F. icteric	I. thrombosis
C. cyanosis	G. retina	J. uvula
D. epileptiform		

1. an abnormal condition characterized by paralysis, aphasia, or amnesia __________
2. the plane from front to back in the middle of an organ or body __________
3. small structure hanging from soft palate in mouth __________
4. formation of a blood clot within a blood vessel __________
5. enlarged lymph nodes __________
6. bluish discoloration of skin resulting from diminished supply of oxygen in blood __________
7. having the form of epilepsy __________
8. pertaining to jaundice __________
9. pertaining to blood vessels of brain __________
10. membrane of the eye that receives images and transmits visual impulses through the optic nerve to the brain __________

EXERCISE 11.5: CREATING TERMS FROM WORD FORMS

In the following exercise, combine prefixes, root words, and suffixes to create medical words that fit the definitions below. Fill in the blanks with the words you construct.

hemi-	half, slight	-lepsy	seizure
inter-	between	poly-	two or more, many
myel/o	bone marrow	-paresis	minor paralysis
post-	after	-itis	inflammation
mening/o	membrane	-plegia	paralysis
somi	body, body of a cell	neur	nerves
encephal/o	brain	path/o	disease
para-	beside, beyond	ictal	immediate onset, as in a stroke

1. partial paralysis ______________________________
2. inflammation of brain tissue ______________________________
3. a sleep disorder ______________________________
4. paralysis of the lower extremeties ______________________________
5. between seizures ______________________________
6. inflammation of the membrane(s) of the brain or spinal cord ______________________________
7. inflammation of large number of nerves ______________________________
8. following a seizure ______________________________
9. paralysis on one side ______________________________
10. disease of spinal cord ______________________________

EDITING MEDICAL DOCUMENTS

In this section you will perfect your word use and grammar skills. These skills will help you edit and proofread medical reports for correct language, punctuation, format, and meaning. The special focus for this chapter is abbreviations.

USING ABBREVIATIONS CORRECTLY

Abbreviations are selected letters of a longer word or phrase. Abbreviations save space and may speed up communication, but they can also cause confusion and misinterpretation.

As you learned in chapter 1, your medical transcription library should include an abbreviations reference. Keep context in mind as you search for abbreviations to ensure that the extended form you choose is the appropriate term.

Generally, transcribe abbreviations in full capital letters without punctuation and without spaces between the letters. Short forms, such as *segs* for *segmented neutrophils* or *lymphs* for *lymphocytes,* are transcribed as dictated.

To Abbreviate or Not to Abbreviate

In medical reports, there are some areas in which abbreviations are not used even if they are dictated. Do not use abbreviations in any impression, assessment, admitting or discharge diagnosis, or preoperative or postoperative diagnosis. Do not use abbreviations in the title of the procedure for an operative report.

> DICTATED:
> ADMITTING DIAGNOSIS: S/P CVA.
>
> TRANSCRIBED:
> ADMITTING DIAGNOSIS: Status post cerebrovascular accident.

DICTATED:

PROCEDURE PERFORMED: ORIF, right hip fracture.

TRANSCRIBED:

PROCEDURE PERFORMED: Open reduction and internal fixation, right hip fracture.

Do not abbreviate any medical term that is dictated in full except for metric units of measure (milligrams, milliliters) preceded by a number (for example, transcribe 5 mg, *not* 5 milligrams). Metric units of measure most often appear in laboratory results and drug dosages.

Units of Measure

Use abbreviations when a numeric quantity precedes metric units of measure. Do not add *s* or *'s*.

DICTATED:	Ampicillin five hundred milligrams
TRANSCRIBED:	Ampicillin 500 mg
DO NOT USE:	Ampicillin 500 mg.; or 500 mgs; or 500 mgs.

Spell out common nonmetric units of measure, like foot, inch, ounce, and so on, except in tables. Do not use an apostrophe or quotation marks to indicate feet or inches except in tables.

The child's height was 4 feet 2 inches.

The infant weighed 8 pounds 8$^1/_2$ ounces

A 5-inch incision was made.

Punctuation with Abbreviations

Usually, no punctuation is used with abbreviations. The exception is the group of Latin abbreviations that deal with medication administration. These are always keyed in lowercase with periods in between (for example, b.i.d.; p.r.n.; q.12h.).

If more than one Latin abbreviation is dictated together, put a space between the two abbreviations (Zantac 150 mg p.o. b.i.d.).

DICTATED:	She takes Valium five milligrams p-o-b-i-d-p-r-n anxiety.
TRANSCRIBED:	She takes Valium 5 mg p.o. b.i.d. p.r.n. anxiety.

Plural Abbreviations

Abbreviations in capital letters do not require an apostrophe before the *s* (for example, WBCs, ECGs). Add an *s* to short forms for laboratory terms (for example, lymphs, monos, segs).

Abbreviations That Have Multiple Meanings

Do not guess. If an abbreviation with multiple meanings is dictated—for example, PT, you may or may not be able to determine the intended meaning based on the context of the report. To figure out the meaning, read the rest of the report to see if the full term has been dictated elsewhere, or look at the patient's record if you have easy access to it. If you are unsuccessful, leave the term in abbreviated form, even in a diagnosis. It is better to leave an abbreviated form that knowledgeable people will be able to interpret than to transcribe a full term that is incorrect.

If the abbreviation itself is not clear (CVP? CPT? CCP?), try the same methods as above. Again, do not guess. It is better to leave a blank than to guess incorrectly.

Shorthand Dictation

Physicians sometimes use a verbal "shorthand" for certain words or expressions that appear regularly in medical reports. For example, the terms *discharged, discontinued,* and *identified* may be dictated as "dee seed" [DC'd] and "i deed" [ID'd]. The terms should be transcribed in full:

DICTATED:	Streptococcus was ID'd on blood culture.
TRANSCRIBED:	Streptococcus was identified on blood culture.
DICTATED:	The patient was DC'd from the hospital today.
TRANSCRIBED:	The patient was discharged from the hospital today.
DICTATED:	Physical therapy was DC'd because the patient complained of severe pain.
TRANSCRIBED:	Physical therapy was discontinued because the patient complained of severe pain.

EXERCISE 11.6: IDENTIFYING ABBREVIATIONS

Use your abbreviations references, if available, to find the appropriate extended forms. Otherwise, use the abbreviations appendix at the end of the book. Then key the report with the abbreviations spelled out.

1. The patient was diagnosed with ALS, a degenerative neurologic disease commonly known as Lou Gehrig's disease.
2. Because of her symptoms of left hemiparesis and confusion, Mrs. Smith was believed to have suffered a CVA.
3. An EEG, a test showing the electrical activity of the brain, was performed to rule out seizure disorder.
4. HEENT: PERRLA. Extraocular movements intact.
5. The patient suffers from weakness, paresthesias, and speech disturbances secondary to MS, a degenerative neurologic disorder.
6. The patient is alert and oriented, in NAD, resting comfortably.
7. The patient is NPO in preparation for surgery; do not serve him breakfast.
8. The infant's PKU test was positive, so he will require a diet very low in phenylalanine to prevent mental retardation.
9. The patient has had several episodes of TIAs with neurologic deficits.
10. Myelogram revealed HNP at the L3-L4 level, with a significant disc protrusion.

EXERCISE 11.7: PROOFREADING REVIEW

Read the following emergency department note and look for errors in punctuation, word use, capitalization, spelling, and abbreviations. Then key the report with all errors corrected.

DOB: 3/29/56

ADMISSION DIAGNOSIS: LOC, drug OD.

HPI: The patient is a 40 y.o. female who was found blue in the face and unconscious by family this a.m. This occurred approximately 10 to 15 minutes after she had injected a line of heroin IV. Reportedly her son started CPR and she gasped for breath. Fire department arrived and administered Narcan.

The patient now complains of headache. She reports that she has not used heroin for several months. The family reports that she does heroin 4-5 x/week.

PMH: Seizure disorder, epilepsy since childhood. IVDA x 10 yrs.

MEDICATIONS: Percocet for migraine HAs, Dilantin, and Phenobarbital.

ALLERGIES: NKDA.

PHYSICAL EXAMINATION: A WDWN Caucasian female in NAD, awake, alert, oriented. HEENT: PERRLA; EOMI. Speech clear, respirations unlabored. Lungs clear to P&A. Heart: RRR. She follows instructions appropriately and moves all extremities. DTRs are symmetric.

ER COURSE: The patient was examined as above. She will be observed for another hour, and if she maintains her present level of consciousness, plan to DC to home with appropriate instructions.

ASSESSMENT: Heroin overdose.

PLAN: The patient is to be referred to the mental health unit for addiction counseling. She should continue with her Dilantin and Phenobarb and follow-up with her family M.D.

WHERE CAN I FIND THE ANSWER?

As you transcribe dictation, you may hear unfamiliar words or terms. A variety of reference sources are available to help you locate answers to your questions. One of the important types of references for medical transcriptionists is described below. Read the information; then if you have access to the reference discussed, explore its capabilities.

MEDICAL REFERENCES: MEDICAL SPELL CHECKERS

Many professional medical transcriptionists would not consider working without an electronic spell checking program. These can save you time and help to ensure accuracy. A variety of spell checkers are available for DOS-, Windows-, and MAC-based computers.

Electronic medical spell checkers include the entire range of medical words in their databases, from standard medical specialty terms to the names of instruments, procedures, and drugs. One of the more popular spell checkers includes both trade and generic drug names and will check not only for the correct spelling but also for capitalization.

Medical spell checkers can also be linked to your word processor's existing spell checker dictionary and can be customized according to your personal preferences. For example, you can choose an option that tells the spell checker to skip over single letters or words with numbers. You can also personalize the spell checker by adding words that you have trouble remembering.

TRANSCRIBING NEUROLOGY DOCUMENTS

In this section your goal is to prepare for the work of a transcriptionist by transcribing first from a printed document and then from dictation on tape. The model document that follows illustrates the generally accepted format for the **neuropsychological evaluation,** the medical document featured in this chapter.

BASIC FORMAT: THE NEUROPSYCHOLOGICAL EVALUATION

Neuropsychological evaluations or reports contain information on patients seen in a clinic or hospital setting. A psychologist dictates the report. The purpose of the report is to document a psychiatric patient's history, mental status, assessment, and previous treatment to assist with planning care and treatment. The language on these reports includes terms related to neuropsychological development, human behavior, and treatment.

Required Headings/Content

Typically, the information is provided in narrative format. Content includes a history of the present illness followed by the findings of both physical and neurological examinations. The dictator may omit report headings. Sometimes, only neurological information is included, along with the results of specific developmental and neurological tests.

Turnaround Time

If the patient is admitted to a hospital, the report is usually dictated and transcribed within the first 24 hours of admission, In clinic settings, the report may be dictated and transcribed within 48 hours.

NEUROPSYCHOLOGICAL EVALUATION

1-inch margins and left justification

RE: Rightman, Aaron
DOB: 8/30/90
DOV: 7/10/XX

double-space

Aaron Rightman, age 7 years 10 months, was seen for a pediatric neurological assessment on July 10. The parents were the informants. The reason for this visit was for a "second opinion." Aaron has been diagnosed as having a learning disability with an attention deficit disorder.

At 2 years of age it was noted that Aaron had articulation difficulties and delayed expressive language. He was given speech therapy. At 3 years of age he was placed in a preschool program for the handicapped. He had no problems socially and began to do well. At that time the school recommended that he attend a regular nursery school. Aaron was enrolled in the synagogue nursery school at the age of 4. He soon developed encopresis. The parents characterized Aaron's school experiences as being "a disaster." He began to exhibit poor attention, anger, and hostility. When he reached the age of 5, he was placed in a day school, which was also attended by his friends from nursery school. By this time he was "already viewed as a bad child by the other children."

Aaron recently completed second grade at the day school. There he received tutoring on a one-to-one basis. He was also seen by a learning disability expert twice a week. He had speech and language therapy one-half hour per week. He is still reading below grade level.

In March, Aaron had a neurobehavioral evaluation. It was noted that Aaron was "functioning within the High Average range perceptually and in the Very Superior range verbally." However, there was a 22-point disparity between his verbal and nonverbal abilities. He did best when he "was able to communicate verbally." His cognitive strengths included "word fluency and word knowledge, practical knowledge, common sense, and paper/pencil skills. Cognitive weaknesses included shifting of mental set, visual discrimination, visual searching, nonverbal deductive reasoning, and analysis/synthesis." The evaluators thought that Aaron did have an attention deficit hyperactive disorder syndrome and they noticed that he was a child with "poor phonological awareness, was unable to process certain sounds quickly enough, and encountered problems holding language sounds in short-term memory and manipulating them in active working memory. It is hard for him to break

(continued)

NEUROPSYCHOLOGICAL EVALUATION
RE: Rightman, Aaron
Page 2

words down into their component sounds and reblend them or try to substitute a new sound for an existing one in a word."

Family history reveals that the father has reading problems. A paternal uncle has ADD. A paternal cousin is in a special education class and is said to have a learning disability and ADD. The mother's cousin has ADD. There is no family history of tics or obsessive compulsive habits. There are three siblings—a 12-year-old and a 4-year-old are doing well. Daniel, who is 10, has mild learning difficulties and ADHD symptoms.

Aaron entered the examining room while his parents waited outside. He appeared to be anxious about the exam since there were three other observers in the room with me. Initially, he was very subdued and almost sad. However, he answered questions appropriately and showed no evidence of an activity disturbance. He is poorly oriented to left and right on himself and in space. When he copied geometric forms, he exhibited visual/motor integration difficulties, putting "ears" on the diamond figure. When he was given the Boder test for dyslexia, he had marked trouble spelling words which are in his sight vocabulary. From the screening test, he seemed to me to have a combination of dyseidetic-dysphonetic difficulties.

His height of 130 cm was in the 80th percentile; his weight of 26.6 kg was in the 60th percentile, and his head circumference of 52 cm was in the 50th percentile.

Head and neck were benign. Lungs were clear to percussion and auscultation. Heart—regular sinus rhythm, no murmurs. Abdomen—soft and nontender, liver and spleen not palpable. Genitalia—testes in scrotal sac. Tanner I. Skin revealed mild ichthyosis over the dorsum of his legs. Skeletal was negative. There were no dysmorphic features.

On neurological exam, Aaron's head was of normal shape. He had a single whorl on the right. He tracked well. He did have difficulty with rapidly moving his tongue from side to side. He could not isolate the tongue movement from movement of his jaw. The remainder of the cranial nerves were normal. Visual fields by confrontation were normal. Vision and hearing

(continued)

NEUROPSYCHOLOGICAL EVALUATION
RE: Rightman, Aaron
Page 3

were grossly normal. The tone of his muscles was normal. Fine and gross coordination was normal. Deep tendon reflexes were physiologic. Plantars were flexor. There was no clonus. He had some immature overflow phenomenon and a slightly positive Prechtl sign. He is right-handed. He held a pencil well.

In summary, Aaron has many symptoms of minimal cerebral dysfunction, which is probably on a genetic basis. These symptoms include: (1) a learning disability, primarily involving reading, which grossly appears to be the dyseidetic-dyskinetic type, (2) an attention deficit hyperactivity disorder, which is responding well to Dexedrine, (3) a vocal tic, which may be a precursor to developing Tourette syndrome, and (4) immature motor signs, as noted on the Prechtl and overflow phenomenon. I think that Aaron's regression six months ago may reflect overt depression, which may still be present.

Therapeutically speaking, I think the parents are doing everything possible to help this young man. There is no question that he belongs in a psychotherapeutic relationship. I am assuming that the tricyclic antidepressant is being given for his depressive symptoms. (The parents think that this is helping.) The Dexedrine is effective for the ADHD symptoms. Personally, if his weight loss continues, I would suggest not using the sustained release form but, rather, giving him a dose in the morning, at noon, and at 4 p.m., and this should be given before meals.

I told the parents that they should not put too much stress on Aaron's academic learning, but look for activities where he might be successful, which would make him feel good about himself.

I also told them that I would discuss Aaron's case with Dr. Balla, a research educator who is utilizing a specific therapy for children who have problems with auditory processing. I promised to send the reports of the neuropsychological evaluation and my reports to Dr. Balla to see if she would be interested in seeing Aaron.

qs

____

Lawrence Trent, MD
Professor of Pediatrics

(continued)

NEUROPSYCHOLOGICAL EVALUATION
RE: Rightman, Aaron
Page 4

ds

LTT/XX

ds

C: Dr. L. Balla

ds

D: 7/11/XX
T: 7/12/XX

PREPARING TO TRANSCRIBE

To prepare for transcribing dictation, key the neuropsychological evaluation above. You will later key the identical report from tape. Follow these guidelines:

- Study the format and organization of the report.
- Review the word list presented earlier in this chapter.
- Consult reference books for words or formatting rules that are unfamiliar.
- Proofread your final copy by comparing it to the printed version.

CASES FOR TRANSCRIPTION

In this section you will transcribe medical dictation from tape. Your goal is to produce error-free documents. Read this chapter's Pro Tip (following the case studies) for helpful hints from experienced MTs. Then follow these steps for each dictation:

1. Prepare to transcribe by reviewing the case study and the model report formats from this and earlier chapters.
2. Transcribe the dictation, leaving spaces for words you cannot hear or do not understand.
3. Carefully proofread each document and correct as many errors as you can. Use your reference materials to help you identify missing words.
4. Listen to the tape again and correct all remaining errors.

Repeat these steps until you produce an error-free document. Then complete the Performance Report at the end of the chapter, attach it to the top of the transcripts, and submit them to your instructor for evaluation.

CASE STUDY 1: BRIAN BRENDON

Brian Brendon is a 31-year-old gentleman who was diagnosed with a pineal region tumor one year prior to this visit. He had suffered dizzy spells, difficulty walking, and headaches for a month prior to his diagnosis. He was referred to Dr. Stone, who placed a ventricular shunt in the right ventricle to relieve the increased pressure caused by the tumor. He was then treated with chemotherapy and cranial irradiation. He is having an MRI of the brain as a follow-up study at the completion of his therapy.

Report 11.1: MRI Brain Scan

CASE STUDY 2: MICHELLE KUVELL

Michelle Kuvell is a 7-year-old girl diagnosed with a brain tumor arising in the brainstem. She has been treated with radiation therapy and chemotherapy. She is visiting the neurologist for continuing followup in the office.

Report 11.2: Consultation Letter

Transcription Hint

The radiation therapy dosages should be transcribed at 120 cGy and 6480 Gy.

CASE STUDY 3: MICHAEL WRIGHT

Michael Wright is a 40-year-old male with a history of complex partial seizures for the past 23 years. Although he is taking Dilantin and Mysoline, his seizures have occurred more frequently in recent months. He was admitted to the hospital for evaluation and subsequently underwent a left anterior temporal lobectomy.

Report 11.3: Discharge Summary

Transcription Hint

Listen for these terms and drug names:
semiology
Vicodin
Decadron taper

CASE STUDY 4: AARON RIGHTMAN

Seven-year-old Aaron Rightman has been diagnosed previously as having a learning disability with an attention deficit disorder. His parents have requested an evaluation and a second opinion by Dr. Lawrence Trent.

Report 11.4: Neuropsychological Evaluation

Transcription Hint

Listen for these abbreviations and terms:
ADD (attention deficit disorder)
ADHD (attention deficit hyperactivity disorder)
Boder test
dyseidetic-dysphonetic difficulties
encopresis
whorl
clonus
Prechtl sign
Tourette syndrome

CASE STUDY 5: JOSEPH DRINKOWSKI

Joe Drinkowski is a 21-year-old man who has been experiencing episodes of involuntary contractions of his right arm followed by involuntary "shaking" of his legs. There are no other symptoms of seizures.

Report 11.5: History and Physical

Transcription Hint

Listen for these terms:
pronator drift
proprioception

CASE STUDY 6: TANISHA WILDER

Tanisha Wilder is a 14-year-old child who has a history of sickle cell anemia. She has had multiple admissions for sickle cell crises and other complications related to sickle cell. She was admitted to the hospital with a history of confusion, lethargy, and inability to speak clearly.

Report 11.6: Discharge Summary

Transcription Hints

- Listen for these terms and drug names:
  Pen Vee-K
  Hib and Pneumovax vaccine
  reticulocyte
- Note that a primary physician name is supplied in the patient information section, but another physician has dictated the report.

CASE STUDY 7: BRYAN CHARLES

Bryan Charles is a 5-year-old boy who has been diagnosed with a recurring primary brain sarcoma. He has had chemotherapy, a bone marrow transplant, and radiation therapy following surgery. His parents brought him to the Institute for the Study of Child Development for a neuropsychological evaluation.

Report 11.7 Neuropsychological Evaluation

Transcription Hint

Test results for the Stanford-Binet Intelligence Scale should be transcribed in columnar form. List the subtests in the first column, the SAS (Standard Age Score) in the second column, and the percentile rank in the third column. The test includes four subtests (verbal reasoning, abstract/visual reasoning, quantitative reasoning, and short-term memory) and a composite score. Each subtest is further divided into parts, the names of which should be indented.

PRO TIP: STRESS RELIEVERS

By Kathleen Offman, CMT

Medical transcription can be very rewarding. The field is full of benefits, but this career also has its daily stressors that will not fully affect you until you are on the job. Fortunately, each stressor has an effective solution.

Stressor #1: A Heavy Workload
The shortage of transcriptionists often creates a workload that may seem overwhelming to the newcomer or even the experienced transcriptionist. MTs can turn their thoughts around and see the heavy workload as job security.

Stressor #2: Demanding Pace
Some employers may place unrealistic demands on the transcriptionist. Ideally, the MT has a say in the development of the standards, and the standards are based on average characters keyed over a period of time. AAMT has resolved that the standard unit of measure for medical transcription is the character (all letters, numbers, symbols, and function keys including, but not limited to, the space bar, carriage return, underscore, all characters contained within a macro, headers, and footers). They propose a standard equal to 65 characters per line. However, some institutions measure productivity by total minutes of dictation.

Stressor #3: Emphasis on Quality
While an employer's emphasis on quality is desirable, it can frustrate experienced high producers who feel they are carrying a majority of the workload in the department when others with less experience transcribe a little slower. Some employers have created incentive programs to solve this problem. These programs have both benefits and drawbacks. The benefit is that more work gets done and high producers are compensated for their efforts. The drawback is that sometimes quantity rules over quality, and employees are reluctant to help one another. A best-case scenario is an hourly rate of pay with payment per line or character produced over and above the maximum standard with ongoing quality checks.

Stressor #4: Improper Equipment
Outdated or malfunctioning equipment, along with inadequate reference material, can also cause stress. If you are self-employed, the solution is to invest in proper equipment. If you work in an office or hospital, notify your supervisor of equipment problems.

Stressor # 5: Inadequate Training
Not knowing proper punctuation, not having adequate typing skills or lacking medical terminology background can all cause a great deal of stress. Study hard, and ask a lot of questions, both of your instructor/trainer and those you work with. In this field, it is important to foster good working relationships with your co-workers. They can help you a great deal.

ASSESSING TRANSCRIPTION SKILLS

Demonstrate your mastery of the terminology, editing/proofreading, and document transcription skills presented in this chapter by completing the following activities.

USING MEDICAL REFERENCES

Use the appropriate medical reference to locate the correct spelling and additional usage information for the words below. (If the reference is not available, use the glossary in this text.) Circle the correct spelling, then write a sentence using the word correctly.

1. neurapathy nueropathy neuropathy

   ____

2. neuropraxia neuroproxia neurapraxia

   ____

3. hyereflexia hyperreflexia hyperefflexia

   ____

4. neurilemma neurolemma neuralemma

   ____

5. nuron neuron nueron

   ____

6. sciatica scyatica sciattica

   ____

7. Babinsky Babinskey Babinski

   ____

8. meninges meningies menenges

   ____

9. proprioception propriaception proprioseption

10. quadraparesis quadreparesis quadriparesis

MAKING EXPERT DECISIONS

Circle the correct word from the choices in parentheses.

1. The patient fell asleep for 15 minutes after the seizure, when he was in a (an) (ictal/postictal/interictal) state.
2. The patient was alert and (conscious/conscience) at the time of my examination.
3. At discharge, the physicians recommended nursing home placement, but the family said (they/their/they're) willing to provide care for the patient.
4. The skin graft healed, but the plastic surgeon wants to (pair/pare/pear) down the surface after the swelling goes down.
5. The smallest branch of a nerve is called a (radical/radicle).
6. The dura mater is on top (off/of) the arachnoid.
7. "I was never more embarrassed," said the transcriptionist in training, "than when I transcribed (fecal/thecal)sac, rather than (fecal/thecal) sac, on the pathology report."
8. The thumb and fingers had good (apposition/opposition) when placed tip to tip.
9. An (incision/excision) was made into the subcutaneous tissue.
10. The patient stopped taking her medications and started to (recess/regress/repress), going back to a time when she felt safe and secure.

TRANSCRIBING PROFESSIONAL DOCUMENTS

Transcribe the document named Assessment 11 from tape. Before you key, review the appropriate document formatting guidelines. Proofread your transcribed document and revise it until you think it is error-free.

PERFORMANCE REPORT

Name______________________________ Date __________

Document	Description	Date Completed	Document Processing Speed (If Available)	Document Appraisal M=Mailable MC=Mailable w/corrections NM=Not Mailable
Report 11.1	MRI Brain Scan			M MC NM
Report 11.2	Consultation Letter			M MC NM
Report 11.3	Discharge Summary			M MC NM
Report 11.4	Neuropsychological Evaluation			M MC NM
Report 11.5	History and Physical			M MC NM
Report 11.6	Discharge Summary			M MC NM
Report 11.7	Neuropsychological Evaluation			M MC NM

Comments ______________________________

CHAPTER

12

Hematology is the field of medicine devoted to diagnosing and treating diseases of the blood and blood-forming tissues. Oncology is the study and treatment of all kinds of cancers. Since many blood-related diseases are malignancies and since the blood is the means by which many cancers spread, the subspecialties of hematology and oncology are often combined in one practice. The

Hematology-Oncology

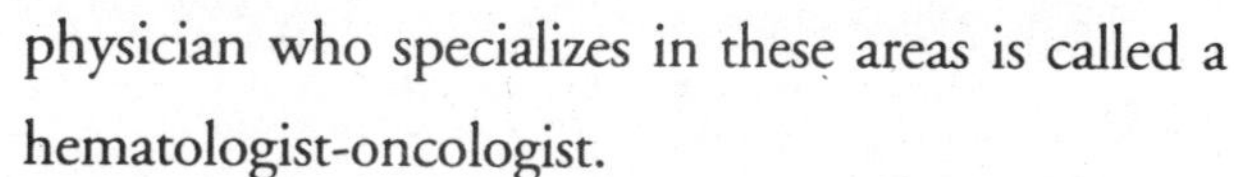

physician who specializes in these areas is called a hematologist-oncologist.

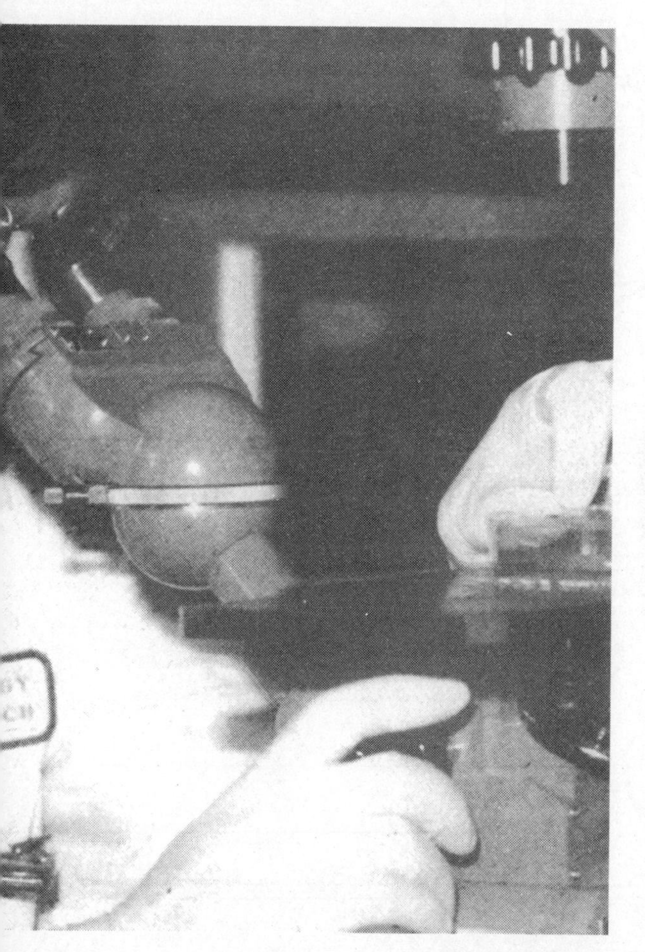

OBJECTIVES

- Use hematology-oncology terms correctly according to the context and purpose of the dictation.
- Select and use appropriate general and specialty reference materials.
- Key hematology-oncology documents of varying complexity and format.
- Transcribe authentic medical dictation requiring concentration and listening skill.
- Edit medical reports to conform with AAMT style guidelines.
- Proofread and correct transcripts to produce error-free documents.

EXPLORING HEMATOLOGY-ONCOLOGY

The word *hematology* derives from the Greek word *haima,* for blood. The term *cancer* was first used by the Greek physician Hippocrates as a metaphor for the spreading tendency of the disease. He compared metastases to the tentacles of a crab, which is Latin for *cancer.* Cancer is indeed frightening because of the destruction it causes within the body. Though life-threatening, many adult cancers and more than 70 percent of pediatric cancers are curable today.

STRUCTURE AND FUNCTION

Blood cells are produced in the red bone marrow in a process called hematopoiesis. Figure 12.1 shows the location of bone marrow in the spongy bone, which is found in the ends of some long bones. Children have more red bone marrow than do adults. Once an individual reaches full growth and development, much of the red marrow is converted to an inactive tissue called yellow marrow.

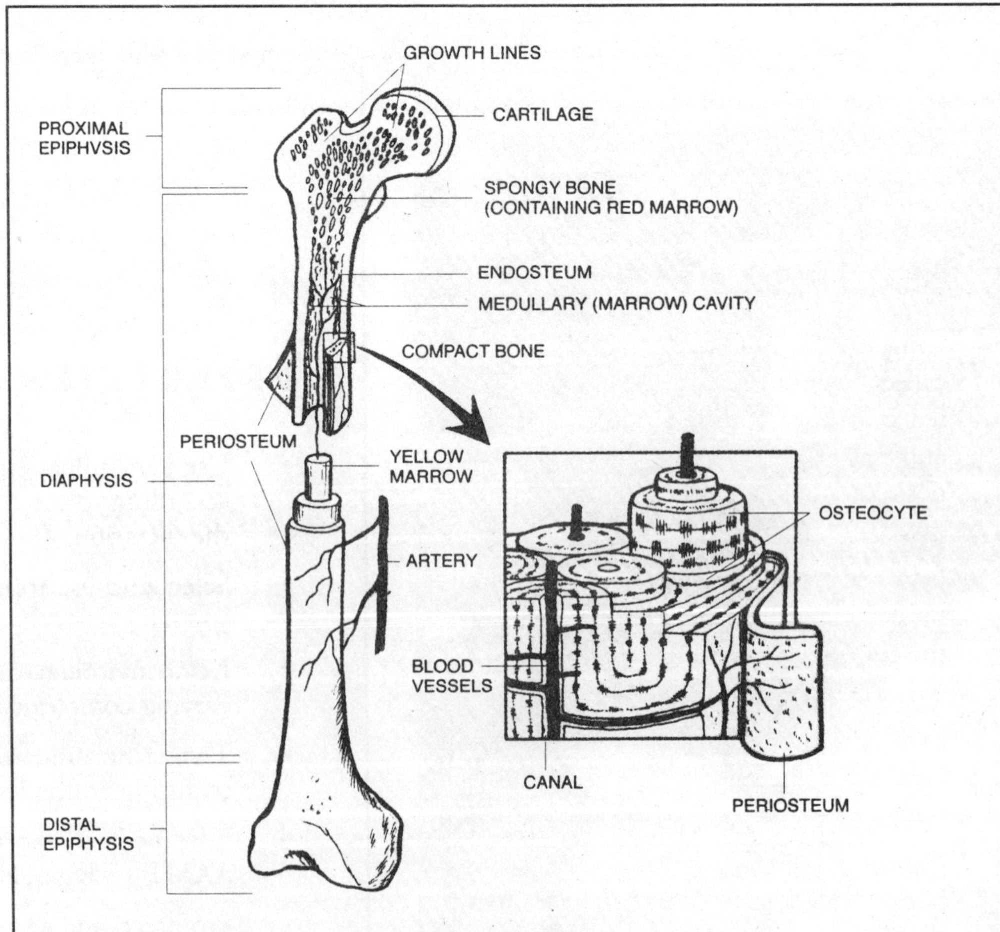

Figure 12.1 Hematopoiesis within the bone marrow

The major kinds of blood cells are white blood cells, red blood cells, and platelets. These cells are suspended in the plasma portion of blood, which also contains proteins such as albumin, immunoglobulins, and fibrinogens. Blood cells provide a vehicle for the transport of nutrients, gases, hormones, electrolytes, and cellular waste products. Table 12.1 lists blood cells by their type and function.

CELL TYPE	FUNCTION
Red blood cells (RBCs)	Carry oxygen to cells
White blood cells (WBCs)	Fight invading substances such as bacteria and viruses
Neutrophils	Set up immune defenses
Eosinophils	Defend against parasites and allergic responses
Basophils	Involved in inflammatory response
Lymphocytes	Produce antibodies (B) Creates cellular immunity (T)
Monocytes	Set up immune defenses
Platelets	Promote blood clotting after injury

Table 12.1 Types of blood cells

The membranes of red blood cells contain a variety of antigens called agglutinogens. The presence or absence of these antigens is a major factor in blood typing. Blood typing is done to determine an individual's specific blood type, which is inherited from both parents. If a person is given a blood transfusion of an incompatible blood type, a dangerous hemolytic transfusion reaction could occur.

There are four major blood types: A, B, AB, and O. Individuals whose red cells carry only one antigen, A, are considered type A; those whose red cells carry antigen B are categorized as type B; and individuals carrying neither antigen are called group O. A small group of people have type AB blood, which means their red cells have both the A and B antigens. Red blood cells may also carry Rh antigens (D, C, E, e, and c). People who carry the D antigen are called Rh-positive. Those who do not are called Rh-negative.

Plasma protein factors in the blood, which work to provide the delicate balance between proper blood clotting and anticlotting, contribute to hemostasis (the proper balance among chemicals in body fluids and tissues). Any abnormality in the clotting cascade, or pathway, can cause problems with clot formation.

The lymph system works with the blood system to protect the body and remove by-products of cellular processes. Encompassing a network of lymph nodes and vessels plus the spleen, thymus, and tonsils, the lymph system drains fluids from body tissues, particularly waste products, and carries them into the blood.

Cancer is a disease resulting from excessive cell division. Normally, all cells of the body divide and replace themselves in a carefully controlled process. In cancers, the process is disturbed and cell division continues past its normal point. Cancer cells usually do not carry out their intended function. Instead, they eventually invade and overtake normal cells and prevent normal function. There are three main methods for cancer cells to metastasize: 1) by direct extension to surrounding structures; 2) through the lymphatic system; or 3) via the blood system, which is called hematogenous spread.

PHYSICAL ASSESSMENT

The patient who presents to the hematology-oncology (heme-onc) specialist is nervous, upset, and often quite ill. The referring physician may have already ordered blood tests that have suggested a blood dyscrasia, hemoglobinopathy, or cancer. Prior x-rays and/or scans may have indicated the possibility of a solid tumor. Sometimes specific symptoms send the person to the hematologist-oncologist. A detailed review of systems and a complete physical examination are essential to planning the patient's care.

HEMATOLOGIC DISEASES AND CONDITIONS

Hemophilia is an inherited autosomal disorder that causes bleeding because of the lack of certain clotting factors in the blood.

Sickle cell anemia and thalassemias are inherited hemoglobinopathies that stem from an absence of a globin chain on the red blood cell. Globin chains are named with the letters of the Greek alphabet.

Immune thrombocytopenic purpura (ITP) is characterized by petechiae and ecchymoses as a result of a low platelet count. It is believed that ITP results from a viral organism that has caused the immune system to turn against itself (autoimmune) and coat the platelet cell with an antigen. The body makes antibodies against these antigens, causing the platelets to be destroyed.

Thrombosis is the formation of clots inside the blood vessels rather than in the normal extravascular pathway. Several different kinds of thromboses can occur, including cerebral, coronary, placental, and compression, to name a few. They typically are the result of injury to a vessel wall or reduced blood circulation.

There are several red cell abnormalities that cause hemolysis. These include osmotic fragility, hereditary spherocytosis, and a deficiency of the glucose-6-phosphate dehydrogenase (G6PD) enzyme.

ONCOLOGIC DISEASES AND CONDITIONS

Cancers are classified into two major categories, hematologic tumors and solid tumors. Hematologic tumors involve the blood-forming organs and include lymphomas, leukemias, and multiple myeloma. Solid tumors include sarcomas and carcinomas. Sarcoma describes cancers of the connective tissues, such as muscle, blood vessels, and bone. Carcinomas are subdivided into adenocarcinomas (originating in surface linings of the glands) and squamous cell, or epidermoid, carcinomas (originating in epithelium of a nonglandular nature, such as the surface of the skin or the membranes of the respiratory tract).

Some 90 percent of cancers are solid tumors; 10 percent are hematologic tumors. The leading causes of cancer deaths in adults are lung cancer, colorectal cancer, prostate cancer, and breast cancer. In children, the most prevalent type of cancer is leukemia.

COMMON TESTS, SURGICAL PROCEDURES, AND TREATMENT REGIMENS

Methods for treating cancers depend on the specific type of cancer. For solid tumors, the staging or classification is most important for prognosis and treatment. Several classification systems are used, depending on the body area affected. For example, Dukes' staging is used for colon cancer, and Jewett's staging is used for bladder cancer. The TNM system is the most widely used classification and involves three components and subcategories:

T (T1–T4)	Extent of the primary tumor
N (N0–N3)	Extent of regional lymph node involvement
M (M0–M1)	Presence or absence of distant metastasis

Solid tumors are removed surgically if the tumor is resectable. For hematologic cancers, chemotherapy is usually the first treatment of choice. Another widely used treatment is radiation therapy, which involves directing a radiation beam toward the cancer to rearrange the cellular DNA and kill the cell.

The word *chemotherapy* means chemical therapy and can refer to any pharmacologic agent. However, the term usually refers to the chemical treatment of cancer. Chemotherapeutic agents kill rapidly dividing cells including cancer cells, hair cells, cells of the mucous membranes, and blood cells. The toxicities and side effects associated with chemotherapeutic agents are due to the destruction of the normal cells in these areas. These agents are usually given in combinations and are named with acronyms. The following list includes some of the most common chemotherapy treatment regimens:

ABV	Adriamycin, bleomycin, vinblastine
CAF	cyclophosphamide, Adriamycin, 5-fluorouracil
CAV	cyclophosphamide, Adriamycin, vincristine
CHOP	cyclophosphamide, hydroxyldaunorubicin, Oncovin, prednisone
COD	cyclophosphamide, Oncovin, DTIC
CytaBOM	cytarabine, bleomycin, Oncovin, methotrexate
DCTER	("doctor") dexamethasone, cytosine arabinoside, thioguanine, etoposide, rubidomycin
DECAL	daunomycin, etoposide, cyclophosphamide, Ara-C, L-asparaginase

Common Hematology-Oncology Drugs

albumin human
Albuminar

aminocaproic acid
Amicar

antihemophilic factor, human
Hemofil, HumateP, KoateHP

asparaginase
Elspar

azathioprine
Imuran

bleomycin sulfate
Blenoxane

busulfan
Myleran

carboplatin
Paraplatin

carmustine
BiCNU

chlorambucil
Leukeran

cisplatin
Platinol

cyclophosphamide
Cytoxan, Neosar

cytarabine hydrochloride (AraC)
CytosarU

dacarbazine
DTICDome

dactinomycin (actinomycinD)
Cosmegen

daunorubicin hydrochloride (daunomycin)
Cerubidine

deferoxamine mesylate
Desferal

desmopressin acetate
DDAVP

doxorubicin hydrochloride
Adriamycin

continued on next page

Common Hematology-Oncology Drugs

epoetin alfa
Epogen, Procrit

etoposide
VePesid

factor IX complex (human)
Konyne, Profilnine, Proplex

filgrastim (rhGCSF)
Neupogen

flucytosine (5–FC, 5–flurocytosine)
Ancobon

fludarabine phosphate (FAMP, FaraAMP)
Fludara

fluorouracil (5–fluorouracil, 5–FU)
Adrucil

hydroxyurea
Hydrea

ifosfamide
Ifex

interferon alfa2a
RoferonA

FAM	5–fluorouracil, Adriamycin, mitomycin C
HiDAC	("high dak") high dose Ara-C
MACOPB	("May-cop–B") methotrexate, Adriamycin, cyclophosphamide, Oncovin, prednisone, bleomycin
MOPP	mechlorethamine, Oncovin, prednisone, procarbazine
ProMACE	prednisone, methotrexate, Adriamycin, cytarabine, etoposide,
VAD	vincristine, Adriamycin, dexamethasone

Researchers the world over continue to try to find a cure for all cancers. Scientists are experimenting with recombinant DNA technology and interferon therapies as well as studying the influence of the mind-body connection, or neuropsychoimmunology. Despite great advances in the treatment of cancer, early detection is still the best weapon against this dreaded disease. Recommended periodic screening methods include breast self-exam (BSE), mammography, prostate exam, and sigmoidoscopy. In addition, certain markers in the blood can predict persons at risk for specific cancers. Those with known genetic risks should be watched closely for the earliest signs of cancer.

THE VOCABULARY OF HEMATOLOGY-ONCOLOGY

The following word list contains common hematology-oncology words as well as most of the difficult words contained in the dictation at the end of the chapter. Take time to become familiar with these words now; then review them later before you key the medical documents.

Here are suggestions for learning the vocabulary words:

1. Read and study each word for pronunciation and meaning.
2. Write each unfamiliar word from the list below on a notecard, write the definition or a paraphrase of the definition on the back, and draw a simple picture to help you learn the word.
3. Study the pronunciation, spelling, and definition of each word on your notecard, then key each word twice for reinforcement. Check the spelling.
4. Add the terms to your word processor's spell checker.

additive
(ad'-i-tiv) (n) a substance which is added in small quantities to improve the qualities of the original

adenopathy
(ad-e-nop'-a-thee) (n) swelling or enlargement of any gland, especially the lymph nodes

agglutination
(a-gloo-ti-nay'-shun) (n) the process in which cells group or clump together, especially as a response to a specific antibody; commonly used in blood typing

allogenic
(al-O-jen'-ik) (adj) describing tissues or cell types that are from different individuals belonging to the same species; describing individuals of the same species

anaphylactic
(an'-a-fi-lak'-tik) (adj) describing an allergic hypersensitivity reaction of the body to a substance

apoptosis
(ap-O-tO'-sis/ap'-op-tO'-sis) (n) a cell fragmenting into pieces which are phagocytosed by other cells

autologous
(aw-tol'-o-gus) (adj) describing a transplantation where the tissue graft is taken from the same individual receiving it

beta subunit
(bay'-ta) (n) glycoprotein hormone containing two different polypeptide subunits designated as alpha and beta chains

bilateral
(bI-lat'-er-al) (adj) affecting or relating to two sides

capillary fragility
(kap'-i-layr-ee) (n) used in a test to determine the presence of vitamin C deficiency or thrombocytopenia; pressure is applied to the arm, and then the number of petechiae (representing broken capillaries) in a small area are counted

carcinoma
(kar-si-nO'-ma) (n) a malignant tumor of epithelial cells

cellular
(sel'-yoo-lar) (adj) composed of or derived from cells

cellular immunity
(n) immunity which is based on the T cells recognizing the antigen itself, rather than the presence of an antibody; cell-mediated immunity

chromic
(krO'-mik) (adj) relating to or containing chromium, such as chromic acid

coagulation
(kO-ag-yoo-lay'-shun) (n) process of blood clotting

ecchymosis
(ek-im-O'-sis) (n) reddish or purplish flat spot on the skin; a bruise; ecchymoses (pl)

embryo
(em'-bree-O) (n) in humans, the developing prenatal child from conception to the end of the second month

embryonal
(em'-bree-O-nal) (adj) relating to an embryo; in an early stage of development

eosinophil
(ee-O-sin'-O-fil) (n) a type of white blood cell readily stained with eosin

erythrocyte
(e-rith'-rO-sIt) (n) mature red blood cell

fetoprotein
(fee-tO-prO'-teen) (n) antigen (substance or organism that produces an antibody) naturally present in the fetus and sometimes present in adults with certain cancers

fibrinogen
(fi-brin'-O-jen) (n) a substance in the blood plasma that can be converted into fibrin to produce blood clotting

follicle
(fol'-i-kl) (n) pouch-like cavity, such as a hair follicle in the skin enclosing a hair; Graafian follicle

fundus
(fun'-dus) (n) the bottom or base of an organ; the part farthest from the opening

gallium
(gal'-ee-um) (n) a rare metal; a gallium scan after an infusion of gallium provides a better view of lymphatic tissue

granuloma
(gran-yoo-lO'-ma) (n) a mass of tissue consisting of many newly growing capillaries formed during the healing process; growth may be due to injury, infection, or inflammation

hemangioma
(he-man'-jee-O'-ma) (n) a congenital benign tumor consisting of a mass of blood vessels

hemophilia
(hee-mO-fil'-ee-a) (n) an inherited blood disorder in males characterized by a defect in the clotting process due to a lack of one or more of the clotting factors

hemorrhage
(hem'-o-rij) (n) loss of a large amount of blood quickly, either externally or internally

hyperdiploid
(hI'-per-dip'-loyd) (n) an individual organism or cell that has one or more extra chromosomes; (adj) relating to such an individual or cell

inguinal
(ing'-gwi-nal) (adj) relating to or located in the groin area (where the abdomen and thighs join)

karyotype
(kar'-ee-O-tIp) (n) chromosomal makeup of a cell; often displayed as chromosome pairs arranged by size

laparotomy
(lap-a-rot'-O-mee) (n) a surgical procedure in which an incision is made into the abdominal wall

leukemia
(loo-kee'-mee-a) (n) production of abnormal white blood cells; a type of cancer of the blood

lumbar
(lum'-bar) (n) relating to the lower back, between the ribs and pelvis

lymphadenitis
(lim'-fad'-e-nI'-tis) (n) inflammation of one or more lymph nodes

lymphadenopathy
(lim-fad-e-nop'-a-thee) (n) any disorder of lymph nodes or of the lymphatic system

lymphatic
(lim-fat'-ik) (adj) relating to or resembling lymph or lymph nodes

lymphoblastic
(lim-fO-blas'-tik) (adj) relating to or resembling lymphoblasts, immature white blood cells

lymphocyte
(lim'-fO-sIt) (n) white blood cell that produces antibodies

mediastinal
(mee'-dee-as-tI'-nal) (adj) relating to the space in the chest cavity between the lungs that contains the heart, aorta, esophagus, trachea, and thymus

metastasis
(me-tas'-ta-sis) (n) spread of a tumor from its site of origin to distant sites

morphology
(mOr-fol'-O-jee) (n) the shape and structure of an organism or body part

necrosis
(ne-krO'-sis) (n) death of some or all of the cells in a tissue

neutrophil
(noo'-trO-fil/noo'-trO-fIl) (n) the most common type of mature white blood cell; its primary function is phagocytosis; granular leukocyte

orchiectomy
(Or-kee-ek'-tO-mee) (n) surgical removal of one or both testes

organomegaly
(Or'-ga-nO-meg'-a-lee) (n) abnormal enlargement of an organ, particularly an organ of the abdominal cavity, such as the liver or spleen

palliative
(pal'-ee-a-tiv) (adj) describes a treatment that minimizes symptoms but does not cure the disease

parenchyma
(pa-reng'-ki-ma) (n) the functional or specific tissue of an organ, not including supporting or connective tissue

pelvis
(pel'-vis) (n) the bones in the lower portion of the trunk of the body; the bones between the spine and legs

petechial
(pee-tee'-kee-al/pee-tek'-ee-al)) (adj) relating to or having petechiae, tiny reddish or purplish spots on the skin from broken capillaries

phagocytosis
(fag'-O-sI-tO'-sis) (n) the process in which a cell engulfs and destroys bacteria, foreign particles, cellular debris, and other cells

platelet
(playt'-let) (n) disc-shaped, small cellular element in the blood that is essential for blood clotting

poikilocytosis
(poy'-ki-lO-sI-tO'-sis) (n) having poikolocytes (abnormal and irregularly shaped red blood cells) in the blood

porphyrins
(pOr'-fi-rinz) (n) a group of pigmented compounds essential to life; for example, hemoglobin contains the heme porphyrin

pruritus
(proo-rI'-tus) (n) itching skin condition

purpura
(pur'-poo-ra) (n) any of several bleeding disorders in which the escape of blood into tissues below the skin causes reddish or purplish spots

roentgenology
(rent'-gen-ol'-o-jee) (n) the study of the use of roentgen rays (x-rays) for diagnosis and therapy

scirrhous
(skir'-us) (adj) describing or resembling a hard, fibrous, malignant tumor

sclerosis
(skle-rO'-sis) (n) condition characterized by hardening of a tissue or organ, resulting from inflammation and mineral deposits

scrotal
(skrO'-tal) (adj) relating to the scrotum

scrotum
(skrO'-tum) (n) the pouch of skin containing the testes, the male reproductive glands

sequela
(see-kwel'-a) (n) an abnormal condition resulting from a disease; sequelae (see-kwel'-ee) (pl)

serous
(seer'-us) (adj) relating to or having a watery consistency

sessile
(ses'-il) (adj) attached directly at the base; not on a stalk

sonography
(so-nog'-ra-fi) (n) ultrasonography; use of high frequency sound waves to produce an image of an organ or tissue

splenectomy
(sple-nek'-tO-mee) (n) surgical removal of the spleen

squamous
(skway'-mus) (adj) scaly; covered with or consisting of scales

staphylococcemia
(staf'-i-lO-kok-see'-mee-a) (n) the presence of staphylococci (bacterial microorganisms) in the blood

suppuration
(sup'-yu-ray'-shun) (n) the production or discharge of pus

testicular
(tes-tik'-yoo-lar) (adj) relating to the testes, the male reproductive glands

thrombocytopenia
(throm'-bO-sI-tO-pee'-nee-a) (n) an abnormal decrease in platelets in the blood, resulting in bleeding and easy bruising

thrombocytopenic
(throm'-bO-sI-tO-pee'-nik) (adj) relating to thrombocytopenia

tumor
(too'-mor) (n) abnormal mass of tissue; neoplasm

yolk sac
(yOk sak) (n) a membranous sac surrounding the food yolk in the embryo

ABBREVIATIONS

HEMATOLOGY

AFP	alpha-fetoprotein (tumor marker for liver and germ cells)
AHF	antihemophilic factor VIII
AHG	antihemophilic globulin factor VIII
ANC	absolute neutrophil count
baso	basophil
CA-125	ovarian carcinoma antigen (tumor marker for ovary)
CBC	complete blood count
CEA	carcinoembryonic antigen (tumor marker for colon, lung, breast, others)
diff	differential
eosin/eos	eosinophil
ESR	erythrocyte sedimentation rate
hCG	human chorionic gonadotropin (tumor marker for germ cells)
HCT, Hct	hematocrit
HGB, Hgb	hemoglobin
ITP	idiopathic thrombocytopenic purpura
LDH	lactic dehydrogenase (tumor marker germ cell and lymphoma)
lymphs	lymphocytes
MCH	mean corpuscular hemoglobin
MCHC	mean corpuscular hemoglobin concentration
MCV	mean corpuscular volume
mono	monocyte
plts or PLT	platelets
PMN	polymorphonuclear neutrophil
polys	polymorphonuclear neutrophils
PSA	prostate specific antigen (tumor marker for prostate)
PT	prothrombin time
PTT	partial thromboplastin time
RBC	red blood cell
sed rate	sedimentation rate
segs	segmented neutrophils
WBC	white blood cell

ONCOLOGY

AFP	alpha-fetoprotein
ALL	acute lymphoblastic leukemia
AML	acute myelogenous leukemia
ANLL	acute nonlymphoblastic leukemia
APL, APML	acute promyelocytic leukemia
BCE	basal cell epithelioma
BM	bone marrow (or bowel movement)
BMA	bone marrow aspiration
BMT	bone marrow transplant
BSE	breast self-exam
bx	biopsy
CA	cancer, carcinoma
cGy	centigray
CLL	chronic lymphoblastic leukemia
CML	chronic myelogenous leukemia
DES	diethylstilbestrol
Gy	gray
HD	Hodgkin's disease
RT	radiation therapy
TNM	tumor, nodes, metastasis (refers to tumor staging)

EXERCISE 12.1: RECOGNIZING LOOK-ALIKES AND SOUND-ALIKES

The following is a list of frequenly used words that look alike and/or sound alike. Study the meaning and pronunciation of each set of words, then read each sentence carefully and circle the word in parentheses that correctly completes the meaning.

knot	(n) lump, bump; measurement of nautical speed
naught	(adj) zero
not	a negative response

radical	(adj) going to the root of the cause
radicle	(n) small root of a nerve or vessel
free radical	(n) an atom or group of atoms carrying an unpaired electron and no charge

acidic	(adj) acid-forming
acetic	(adj) pertaining to acetic acid or vinegar
ascitic	(adj) watery, albumin- and glucose-containing

anergy	(n) impaired ability to react to certain antigens
energy	(n) capacity to do work

advice	(n) opinion given
advise	(v) to counsel, to give advice

basal	(adj) basic, elemental, forming the base
basil	(n) herb used in cooking

generic	(adj) nonspecific, nontrademark
genetic	(adj) hereditary

prostate	(n) male gland
prostrate	(adj) lying face down

for	(prep) as; to
fore	(adj) front; near
four	(adj) the number "4"

presence	(n) attendance
presents	(n) gifts
presents	(v) displays, appears

1. I (advised, adviced) the patient to return in one week.
2. Medical papers always use the (genetic, generic) name for drugs.
3. The patient (presents, presence) with a two-week history of headaches.
4. I gave the patient (advice, advise) regarding proper diet and exercise.
5. The pathology report states that the lesion is a (basal, basil) cell carcinoma.
6. The patient appears depressed and is complaining of lack of (anergy, energy) and insomnia.
7. The patient had breast cancer, requiring a (radical, radicle) mastectomy.
8. The patient was cautioned regarding greasy, spicy, and (acidic, acetic) foods.
9. The (prostate, prostrate) was smooth and without nodules.
10. When the ambulance arrived, she was found (prostate, prostrate) on her bathroom floor.

EXERCISE 12.2: MATCHING SOUND AND SPELLING

The numbered list that follows shows the phonetic spelling of hard-to-spell words. Sound out the word, then write the correct spelling in the blank space provided. Each of the words can be found in the glossary or in the drug list in appendix C.

1. ek-i-m-O'-sis __________
2. fag'-O-sI-tO'-sis __________
3. ses'-il __________
4. pal'-ee-a-tiv __________
5. lim-fat'-ik __________
6. me-tas'-ta-sis __________
7. rent'-gen-ol'-o-jee __________
8. loo-kee'-mee-a __________
9. a-gloo-ti-nay'-shun __________
10. skir'-us __________
11. hem'-o-rij __________
12. skway'-mus __________
13. lim'-fO-sIt __________
14. krO'-mik __________
15. staf'-i-lO-kok'-see'-mee-a __________

EXERCISE 12.3: CHOOSING WORDS FROM CONTEXT

When transcribing dictation, the medical transcriptionist frequently needs to determine the word that correctly completes the sentence based on the situation. From the list of words below, select the term that meaningfully completes each statement.

carcinoma	embryo	platelet
lymphadenopathy	pelvis	lumbar
ecchymoses	leukemia	sclerosis
parenchyma		

1. The most common childhood malignancy is ______________.
2. The patient had a low ______________count, which caused him to bleed profusely after the phlebotomy.
3. Mr. Smith had a hepatic ______________, which required chemotherapy.
4. There was ______________ of the vein after the chemotherapeutic agent infiltrated at the infusion site.
5. After the ______________puncture, Johnny had to lie down for about an hour.
6. Drinking alcohol, using drugs, and smoking during pregnancy are dangerous to the forming ______________.
7. There were ______________all over the child's body, leading to the diagnosis of immune thrombocytopenic purpura (ITP).
8. The ______________ of the left kidney was invaded by the tumor.
9. The physical examination of the child with leukemia revealed cervical______________.
10. The tumor was invading the ______________, requiring removal of the adjacent hip.

EXERCISE 12.4: PAIRING WORDS AND MEANINGS

For each definition provided below, locate the term on the list that best matches the definition. Write the letter of the term in the space provided beside the definition.

A. ecchymosis	E. lymphocytes	H. orchiectomy
B. gallium	F. necrosis	I. phagocytosis
C. hemophilia	G. neutrophils	J. thrombocytopenia
D. laparotomy		

1. white blood cell ______________
2. the process by which certain cells destroy microorganisms ______________
3. surgical excision of a testicle ______________
4. bruise; purplish spot from accumulation of blood under skin ______________
5. a condition with diminished number of platelets, resulting in bleeding and bruising ______________
6. a rare metal ______________
7. a disorder characterized by excessive bleeding and occurring only in males ______________

8. surgical procedure in which an incision is made in abdominal wall ____________
9. death of some or all of the cells in a tissue ____________
10. leukocytes that increase in the presence of infection ____________

EXERCISE 12.5: CREATING TERMS FROM WORD FORMS

In the following exercise, combine prefixes, root words, and suffixes to create medical words that fit the definitions below. Fill in the blanks with the words you construct.

reticul/o	net	-philia	attraction for
macro	big	-oma	tumor
micro	small	-logy	study of
immun/o	safe, protected against	-plasia	growth; formation
phag/o	eating, swallowing	-osis	increase or condition
papilla	nipple-like	cyt/o	cell
basal	base	thromb/o	clot
an-	without, no		

1. no growth ____________
2. network of cells, occuring during active blood regeneration ____________
3. cell clotting ____________
4. benign, nipple-like tumor ____________
5. blood cell that functions as an anticoagulant ____________
6. neutral stain of white blood cell that fights bacteria ____________
7. study of cells ____________
8. ingestion/digestion of cells, bacteria ____________
9. study of immune system ____________
10. abnormally large cells ____________

EDITING MEDICAL DOCUMENTS

In this section you will perfect your word use and grammar skills. These skills will help you edit and proofread medical reports for correct language, punctuation, format, and meaning. The special focus of this chapter's section is apostrophes.

USING APOSTROPHES CORRECTLY

Apostrophes are used to denote omitted letters in contractions, to express a year or decade, to show possession, and to form some plurals.

Contractions

Use contracted forms in medical reports only in a direct quote; otherwise, write out the words.

> DICTATED: I don't feel the patient is improving.
>
> TRANSCRIBED: I do not feel the patient is improving.
>
> DICTATED: The patient said, "I don't feel I'm improving."
>
> TRANSCRIBED: The patient said, "I don't feel I'm improving."

Remember that *it's* means *it is,* while the word *its* is a singular possessive pronoun. Because *it's* is a contraction, do not use it in a medical report.

> The central venous line was placed and *its* ports were flushed with saline.
>
> It is important that the bandages be changed every two hours.

Whose is a relative pronoun that can function in various ways, including as a connector between a subordinate clause and a main clause. *Who's* is a contraction for the two words *who is.* Note the differences in use:

She is a physician whose research is widely regarded as the best in the field.

[*whose* connects the subordinate clause with the main clause]

> It is not important who's speaking at the conference, as long as the field of candidates is carefully selected.
>
> [*who's* stands for *who is*]

Years

When a single year is expressed without the century, precede it with an apostrophe ('97). Use an apostrophe preceding expressions of decades of the century (in the '90s), but not when referring to decades of a patient's life (in his 50s).

Possessive Forms

Apostrophes indicate ownership, either literally or figuratively. When the noun is singular, add an *'s* to create the possessive.

> SINGULAR: The *patient's* laboratory tests were normal.
> [one patient, his tests]
>
> SINGULAR: He will be seen in one *day's* time.
> [the time belonging to one day]
>
> PLURAL: I went to the laboratory to retrieve my *patients'* tests.
> [more than one patient and more than one test]

Some singular nouns (Mr. Harris) become difficult to pronounce when you add *'s* because the addition makes an extra syllable. In this case, add only an apostrophe to show possession.

> Mrs. *Billings'* condition is stable.

When a possessive is an abbreviation, use *'s* just as you would with a singular word.

> The *HMO's* policies are clear.

Add only an apostrophe to express the possessive of plural nouns that end in *s*.

> PLURAL: The *physicians'* opinions were varied.
> [more than one physician]
>
> PLURAL: All of the AIDS *patients'* study results were compiled.
> [more than one patient, their results]

Add *'s* to plural nouns that do not end in *s* to make them possessive.

> The conference dealt with *children's* issues.

Use *'s* after the last word in a hyphenated compound term.

> Her *mother-in-law's* health was failing.
>
> Her *daughters-in-laws'* schedules were conflicting.
> [the schedules of both daughters-in-law]

The AAMT style guidelines state not to use *'s* with eponymic terms (Alzheimer disease, not Alzheimer's disease). However, this has not been widely accepted. Therefore, defer to the wishes of your client or employer. It should be noted, though, that eponymic surgical terms generally do not require *'s*. Without the apostrophe, *As* could be read as the word *as*.

Plurals

In some instances, *'s* forms plurals that are not possessives. For example, use *'s* to form plurals of single letters or numbers.

> Three *A's,* two *B's,* and two *C's.*
>
> Mind your *p's* and *q's.*
>
> He rates his pain as mostly *1's* and *2's* on a scale of 1-10.

However, do not use an apostrophe to form the plural of capital letter abbreviations or numbers of two characters or more.

> Serial *EKGs* showed no change.
>
> Her hematocrits have been in the high *30s.*

Plural nouns that act as descriptive terms in the name of a company or organization may or may not require an apostrophe. Determine the organization's preference and follow their usage.

> *Childrens* Hospital, or *Children's* Hospital.

EXERCISE 12.6: EDITING FOR CORRECT APOSTROPHE USE

Circle the letter beside each correctly written sentence below. Some items may have more than one correct answer.

1. (a) Its important to rule out malignancy in this case.
   (b) It's important to rule out malignancy in this case.
   (c) It is important to rule out malignancy in this case.

2. (a) CBC's have continued to show decreased hemoglobin and hematocrit.
   (b) CBCs have continued to show decreased hemoglobin and hematocrit.
   (c) CBCS have continued to show decreased hemoglobin and hematocrit.

3. (a) The CMT's knowledge was evident in her reports.
   (b) The CMTs knowledge was evident in her reports.
   (c) The CMTs' knowledge was evident in her reports.

4. (a) The physician who's patients' records were transferred is Dr. Che.
   (b) The physician whose patients records were transferred is Dr. Che.
   (c) The physician whose patients' records were transferred is Dr. Che.

5. (a) The patients CD4s have been decreasing.
   (b) The patient's CD4's have been decreasing.
   (c) The patient's CD4s have been decreasing.

6. (a) I don't think she will respond to more aggressive therapy.
   (b) I do not think she will respond to more aggressive therapy.
   (c) I dont think she will respond to more aggressive therapy.

7. (a) The patient whose family just arrived was discharged from the hospital today.
   (b) The patient who's family just arrived was discharged from the hospital today.

8. (a) He had an appendectomy in his '40s.
   (b) He had an appendectomy in his 40s.
   (c) He had an appendectomy in his 40's.

9. (a) She was first diagnosed with lupus in the late 80s.
   (b) She was first diagnosed with lupus in the late '80s.
   (c) She was first diagnosed with lupus in the late '80's.

10. (a) She will be followed up in two days time.
    (b) She will be followed up in two day's time.
    (c) She will be followed up in two days' time.

11. (a) Her son-in-laws all came to visit her.
    (b) Her sons-in-law's all came to visit her.
    (c) Her sons-in-law all came to visit her.

12. (a) Mr. Simmons's condition is stable.
    (b) Mr. Simmon's condition is stable.
    (c) Mr. Simmons' condition is stable.

EXERCISE 12.7: PROOFREADING REVIEW

Read the following partial report and look for errors in form, meaning, capitalization, word choice, punctuation, and spelling. Circle the errors, then key the report with the errors corrected.

Charlotte is a 30 yr old women who first noted a fullness in the right lower anterior cervical region in the late winter. It had gradually groin in size. In early March she was treated with a one week course of erythromycin with out response. the mass 'bothered" her slightly but it was not painful. Their has been no change in her usually good appetite her weight has remained staple.

The outside radiographic studies were reviewed with the radiologist The chest x-ray reveals a relatively small anterior mediastinal mass (approximately 1/4 of the chest diameter). The chest CT scan conforms the presents of the mediastinal mass, without pulmonary parenchymal involvement.

WHERE CAN I FIND THE ANSWER?

As you transcribe dictation, you may hear unfamiliar words or terms. A variety of reference sources are available to help you locate answers to your questions. One of the important types of references for medical transcriptionists is described below. Read the information; if you have access to the reference discussed, explore its capabilities.

MEDICAL REFERENCES: PRODUCTIVITY PROGRAMS

Many professional MTs purchase productivity software to boost their transcription speed and accuracy. These programs use macros that instantly expand keyed abbreviations or the first few letters of a word into complete words, saving keystrokes and thus time.

A macro is a word processing file containing recorded commands for a series of tasks. For example, a macro can contain the keystrokes to reproduce instantly a report format, a sentence, or just a single medical term. Each macro is assigned a short name. When you key that name, the software immediately creates the text or, in the case of report formats, the headings in the style defined by the macro.

Commercial productivity programs contain macros for frequently used words and phrases. Typically, the programs require no memorizing of the abbreviations. As soon as the first few letters of the word are keyed, the program displays a list of word choices. In addition, you can customize the macro list by adding your own favorites.

Experienced transcriptionists report impressive speed improvements of 60 to 70 percent by using productivity software. Before you purchase a program, however, you may want to research the effectiveness of the software choices via the medical transcription forums on the Internet (see the addresses listed in the Medical References section in chapter 13).

TRANSCRIBING HEMATOLOGY-ONCOLOGY DOCUMENTS

In this section your goal is to prepare for the work of a transcriptionist by transcribing first from a printed document and then from dictation on tape. The model document that follows illustrates a general format for an **outpatient visit,** the report format featured in this chapter.

BASIC FORMAT: THE OUTPATIENT VISIT

The outpatient visit report is a medical document similar in content to a brief history and physical or a chart note.

Required Headings/Content

No specific headings are required in the outpatient visit report. The report usually begins with the patient's diagnosis and includes a brief history of the illness, the results of a physical examination, results of laboratory tests, the physician's impression and treatment plan, including lab tests scheduled for subsequent visits, and referrals to other physicians. The format varies considerably from clinic to clinic, since this report is one of the more recent document types in the medical industry.

Turnaround Time

The outpatient visit report is generally transcribed within 48 hours after dictation.

OUTPATIENT VISIT

1-inch margins and left justification

PATIENT NAME: Connors, Elizabeth
DATE: (current date)
double-space between all sections
DIAGNOSIS
Immune thrombocytopenic purpura (ITP)

INTERVAL HISTORY
Elizabeth was well until three weeks ago when she had a viral URI. She had fevers to 101°. Yesterday, mother noted a "red rash" on her back and legs and many bruises. She was referred by Dr. Sanderson for evaluation.

PHYSICAL EXAMINATION
VITALS: Temperature 98.7°, blood pressure 98/56, weight 22 kg.
GENERAL: The patient appears very well.
SKIN: Petechial rash on arms, back, and thighs. Several large ecchymoses over legs, arms, and abdomen.
HEENT: Within normal limits.
FUNDI: Within normal limits.
NODES: Several small shotty nodes in submandibular chain.
CHEST: Clear.
HEART: Within normal limits, no murmur.
ABDOMEN: Soft, no palpable masses.
LIVER: Not palpable.
SPLEEN: Not palpable.
GU: Within normal limits.
EXT: Within normal limits.
NEURO: Grossly intact.

LABORATORY DATA
WBC: 6500 ,
HGB/HCT: 12.3/37.1
PLTS: 34,000
SEGS/BANDS: 52/0
EOS/BASOS: 3/2
LYMPHS/ATYP: 43/0
ANC: 3380

(continued)

PATIENT NAME: Connors, Elizabeth
Page 2

IMPRESSION
Immune thrombocytopenic purpura.

THERAPY
Will repeat counts tomorrow. If platelets are rising, will continue to watch. If decreasing, will hospitalize for a three-day course of IVIG.

REFERRALS
None at present.

RETURN TO CLINIC
(1 day after current date).

LAB/PROCEDURES (NEXT VISIT)
Counts.

qs

____

Sandford J. Arnold, MD
ds
SA/XX
ds
C: Lawrence C. Cohen, MD
ds
D: (two days before transcription date)
T: (current date)

PREPARING TO TRANSCRIBE

To prepare for transcribing dictation, key the outpatient visit report above. You will later key the identical report from tape. Follow these guidelines:

- Study the format and organization of the model report.
- Review the word list presented earlier in this chapter.
- Consult reference books for words or formatting rules that are unfamiliar.
- Proofread your final copy by comparing it to the printed version.

CASES FOR TRANSCRIPTION

In this section you will transcribe medical dictation from tape. Your goal is to produce error-free documents. Read this chapter's Pro Tip (following the case studies) for helpful hints from experienced MTs. Then follow these steps for each dictation:

1. Prepare to transcribe by reviewing the case study and the model report format.
2. Transcribe the dictation, leaving spaces for words you cannot hear or do not understand.
3. Carefully proofread the document and correct as many errors as you can. Use your reference materials to help you identify missing words.
4. Listen to the tape again and correct all remaining errors.

Repeat these steps until you produce an error-free document. Then complete the Performance Report at the end of the chapter, attach it to the top of the transcripts, and submit them to your instructor for evaluation.

CASE STUDY 1: ELIZABETH CONNORS

Elizabeth Connors is a 5-year-old who was well until three weeks ago when she developed a cold with a fever. She recovered in about a week. Yesterday, her mother noticed that her back and legs were covered with tiny red dots that appeared to be a rash. She also had several large bruises on her body. Her mother brought Elizabeth to the pediatrician, who sent her to the Hematology Outpatient Clinic.

Report 12.1: Outpatient Visit Report

CASE STUDY 2: STEPHANIE AARON

Stephanie Aaron is an 11-year-old who was diagnosed with acute lymphoblastic leukemia (ALL). She completed a 2½-year regimen of chemotherapy and is doing very well off all therapy for one year.

Report 12.2: Chart Summary

Transcription Hints

- No special format exists for a chart summary. It is normally a narrative report of one or several paragraphs summarizing the patient's history and treatment. List the patient's name at the top, along with the current date. Key the first paragraph a double-space below the date.
- Listen for these drug terms:
  FAB L1 morphology
  cALLa
  vincristine
  intrathecal
  methotrexate
  PEG-L-asparaginase
  BFM regimen

CASE STUDY 3: NETTIE BRANDISE

Nettie Brandise is a 24-year-old young woman who was diagnosed with leukemia five years ago. She was treated with radiation, chemotherapy, and a bone marrow transplant (BMT) and is doing well off all therapy. She is seen at the Brookfield Oncology Group for followup every three months.

Report 12.3: Outpatient Visit Report

CASE STUDY 4: LINDA EASTMAN

Linda Eastman is a 65-year-old woman who had a right radical mastectomy three years ago. She presented to urgent care with fever, chills, abdominal pain, and bloody diarrhea, which had been occurring over the previous two days. She was transported by ambulance to the hospital for further evaluation and treatment.

Report 12.4: History and Physical

CASE STUDY 5: CHARLOTTE TRENT

Charlotte Trent is a 30-year-old woman who noticed that she had a lump on her neck. It caused her no pain so she did not see her physician until it grew bigger. Her internist sent her to the surgeon for a biopsy, which showed Hodgkin's disease. She was then referred to the oncologist for further workup and treatment.

Report 12.5: Consultation Letter

Report 12.6: Pathology Report

Transcription Hint

Listen for this cell type name:
Reed-Sternberg

CASE STUDY 6: ROBERT HUDSON

Robert Hudson is a 35-year-old man with a history of sickle cell anemia. He has been hospitalized several times to receive intravenous fluids, blood transfusions, and pain medications. Recently, he had a flu-like illness and subsequently presented to the ER with severe pain in the lower left leg.

Report 12.7: History and Physical

CASE STUDY 7: BELINDA KOTTKE

Belinda Kottke is a 57-year-old woman with colorectal cancer that has metastasized to the liver, lung, and brain. She underwent a craniotomy for resection of a brain lesion that was identified on a CT scan.

Report 12.8: Discharge Summary

Transcription Hint

Listen for this drug term:
Pepcid

PRO TIP: CREATING MACROS

By Sheri Coalson, CMT

Macros are powerful tools for the medical transcriptionist. If you create macros for terms, acronyms, measurements, and formats common within each discipline, you can expect to save hundreds of hours annually.

You can choose from several commercial macro programs on the market, or you can build your own macro library within WordPerfect or Word. If you build your own library, be sure to create a file that lists all the macro names. Once you start creating and using macros, you will be surprised at how much they help you.

When to Create a Macro

If you find yourself transcribing the same phrase or sentence over and over, create a macro for it. For example, the sentence "The area was prepared and draped in the usual sterile fashion" appears in probably 90 percent of all operative reports. You can save considerable time and ensure accuracy by creating a macro for the sentence.

Choosing Names for Macros

Call a macro anything you like, as long as it is short and you are likely to remember it. Even if you keep a log of your macros, try to memorize as many as possible. Here are some examples of macro names:

COPD = chronic obstructive pulmonary disease

PERRLA = Pupils equal, round, reactive to light and accommodation.

Using Capitals or Lowercase Letters

If a macro is a sentence or the first word is a proper noun, then the macro should begin with a capital letter. Otherwise, use capitals only if the words or abbreviation is capitalized in normal use. However, you can still run a macro that starts with the wrong case letter. For instance, if you have a macro for chronic obstructive pulmonary disease but you need Chronic obstructive pulmonary disease, key the capital C. Then (with no space in between) run the macro COPD. Your result should look like this: Cchronic obstructive pulmonary disease. When you run your spell checker, the checker will stop on Cchronic, allowing you to delete the lowercase c.

Learning to use macros is not simply about acquiring a word processing skill. It is about learning to work efficiently and accurately, producing the highest quality reports in the shortest possible time.

ASSESSING TRANSCRIPTION SKILLS

Demonstrate your mastery of the terminology, editing/proofreading, and document transcription skills presented in this chapter by completing the following activities.

USING MEDICAL REFERENCES

Use the appropriate medical reference to locate the correct spelling and additional usage information for the words below. (If the reference is not available, use the glossary in this text.) Circle the correct spelling; then write a sentence using the word correctly.

1. reontgenogram roentgenogram roentgenagram

____

2. hemorrages hemorhages hemorrhages

____

3. scirrhous schirrhous scirhous

____

4. adjuviant adjuvent adjuvant

____

5. metastesis metastassis metastasis

____

6. leucocytes leukocytes luekocytes

____

7. karyotype kariotype caryotype

____

8. poikylocytosis poiklocytosis poikilocytosis

____

9. paliative palliative palleative

____

10. mammeogram mammogram mammagram

____

MAKING EXPERT DECISIONS

Circle the correct word from the choices in parentheses.

1. As the patient was 94, the family did not want treatment or invasive procedures done, and the patient was given (palliative/adjuvant) treatment only.
2. DIAGNOSIS: (Basal/Basil) cell carcinoma of the skin of the cheek.
3. This 3-month-old Caucasian male (presence/presents) to the Eagle County Medical Center in the arms of his mother, who rushed the patient here saying the patient is having trouble breathing.
4. Contrast material was injected through the T-tube, and the right hepatic (radicle/radical) was outlined.
5. The patient stated that she could not (breathe/breath) through her nostrils.
6. The mass was (aberrant/apparent) in the left upper outer quadrant of the breast.
7. The patient's symptoms were brought to the (for/fore/four) upon careful questioning during the history and physical.
8. A (cor/core/corps) of bone marrow was obtained on biopsy to rule out aplastic anemia.
9. A tumor was suspected when a mass was felt in the abdomen, but on further testing, this was found to be a (gr3/grade 3) carcinoma.
10. When considering a course of therapy, it is important to use a group of drugs that work together, not as (agonists/antagonists).

TRANSCRIBING PROFESSIONAL DOCUMENTS

Transcribe the document named Assessment 12 from tape. Before you key, review the appropriate document formatting guidelines. Proofread your transcribed document and revise it until you think it is error-free.

PERFORMANCE REPORT

Name ______________________________ Date ____________

Document	Description	Date Completed	Document Processing Speed (If Available)	Document Appraisal M=Mailable MC=Mailable w/corrections NM=Not Mailable
Report 12:1	Outpatient Visit Report			M MC NM
Report 12:2	Chart Summary			M MC NM
Report 12:3	Outpatient Visit Report			M MC NM
Report 12:4	History and Physical			M MC NM
Report 6:5	Consultation Letter			M MC NM
Report 6:6	Pathology Report			M MC NM
Report 12:7	History and Physical			M MC NM
Report 12:8	Discharge Summary			M MC NM

Comments ______________________________

CHAPTER

13

The field of immunology includes the study and treatment of allergies and infectious diseases. The specialist in this field of medical practice is called an allergist/immunologist. Both allergies and infectious diseases are the products of the body's immune response to environmental and biological stimuli. Infectious agents that can cause disease in the human host are called pathogens. Foreign

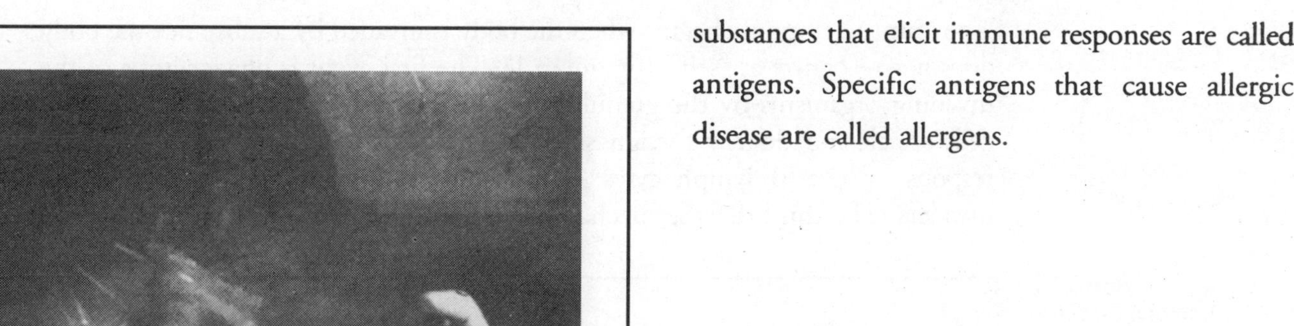

Immunology

substances that elicit immune responses are called antigens. Specific antigens that cause allergic disease are called allergens.

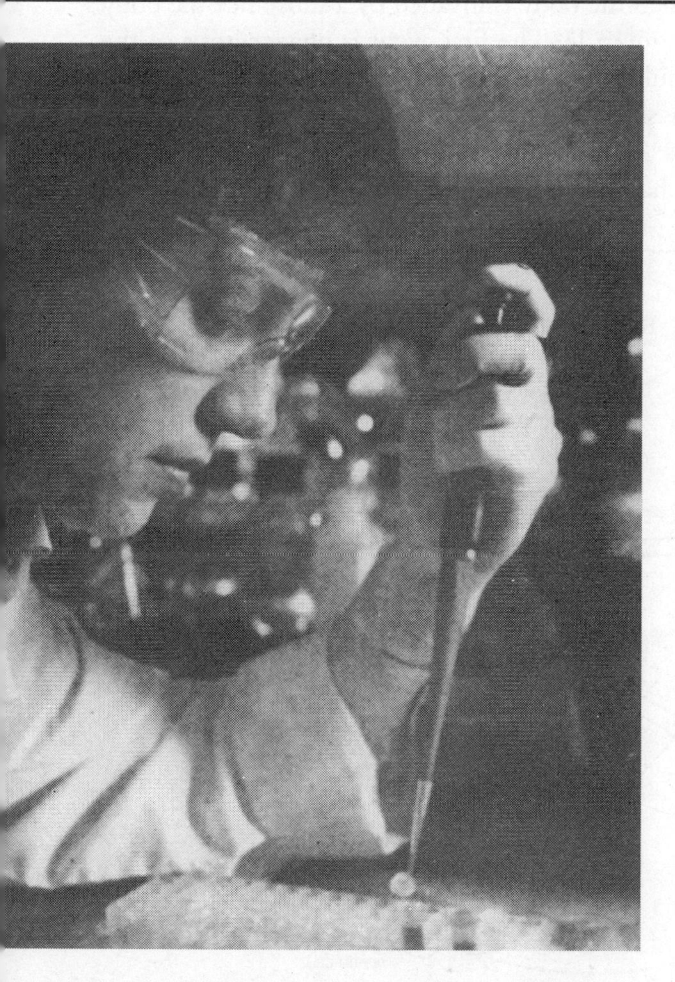

OBJECTIVES

- Use immunology terms correctly according to the context and purpose of the dictation.
- Select and use appropriate general and specialty reference materials.
- Key immunology documents of varying complexity and format.
- Transcribe authentic medical dictation requiring concentration and listening skill.
- Edit medical reports to conform with AAMT style guidelines.
- Proofread and correct transcripts to produce error-free documents.

EXPLORING IMMUNOLOGY

With the emergence of acquired immunodeficiency syndrome (AIDS) in the 1980s, both the medical profession and the public have focused enormous attention on the functioning of the immune system. Breakthroughs in the treatment of immune system disorders are occurring so quickly that medical support personnel, including medical transcriptionists, must make an extra effort to remain knowledgeable about changes and news in this specialty.

STRUCTURE AND FUNCTION

Immunity refers to the healthy body's response to foreign substances or organisms. There are two types of immunity: natural immunity, which is present at birth, and acquired immunity, which is specific and develops after birth. Natural immunity provides the body with the ability to recognize "self" from "nonself." The intact skin and mucous membranes are important barriers that are part of natural immunity. The hairs in the nose, the cilia of the respiratory tract, the gastric juices, and other internal mechanisms help to protect the internal body from invading pathogens. Acquired immunity develops as a result of exposure to disease (active immunity) or through immunization (passive acquired immunity). The white blood cells assist in both types of immunity.

The immune response begins when the body is invaded by a substance the body does not recognize as "self" (figure 13.1). The first event is phagocytosis of the invading organisms by the granulocytes and macrophages. These white blood cells attack and destroy foreign substances. Next is the humoral or antibody response where B lymphocytes manufacture specific antibodies against the invaders. The third defense mechanism is cellular and involves T lymphocytes,

Figure 13.1
Immune response

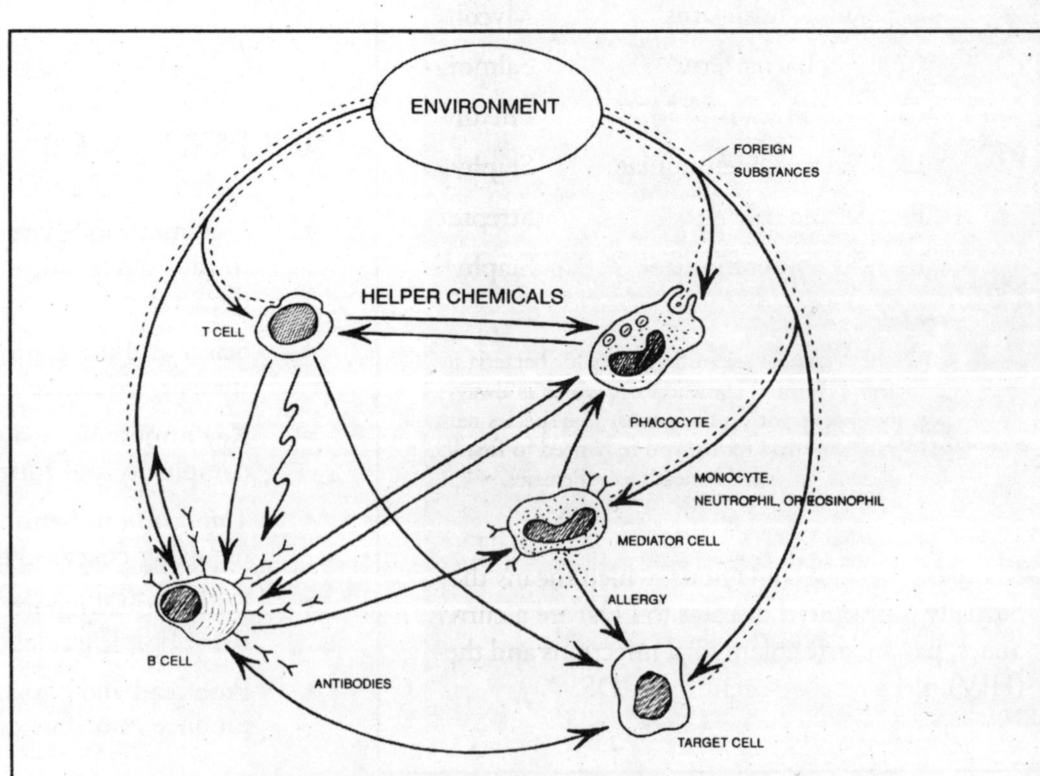

which produce cytotoxic substances to kill the organisms.

The body also produces biologic response modifiers (BRMs) such as interferons, whose complete function is only just being recognized. Cytokines are BRMs that regulate the growth and function of other cells within the immune system. These substances are being investigated for their therapeutic potential as antiviral, anticancer, and acquired immunodeficiency syndrome (AIDS) treatments.

PHYSICAL ASSESSMENT

Because early symptoms of infectious disease may be nonspecific, the physician must listen very carefully to the history given by the patient. The general health of the person may indicate the ability to fight off serious infections. The very young, the elderly, persons with chronic diseases, and persons who are receiving immunosuppressive agents are more susceptible to infection. The physical examination should be complete and include cultures from any secretion that may contain infectious organisms.

DISEASES AND CONDITIONS

Diseases affecting the immune system can be grouped into five broad categories: infections, allergies, autoimmune disorders, diseases associated with organ transplant, and malignancies.

Infectious disease is any disease that is caused by the growth of a pathogenic organism in the body. There are hundreds of organisms capable of causing disease in humans. The following list includes a few of the most commonly found pathogens.

Aspergillus fumigatus*	Mycobacterium avium
Campylobacter fetus	Salmonella choleraesuia
Candida albicans	Pneumocystis carinii
Diplococcus pneumoniae	Staphylococcus aureus
Escherichia coli	Streptococcus pneumoniae
Klebsiella pneumoniae	Staphylococcus viridans
Legionella	

*Note that these scientific names for bacteria include two words. The first is the genus (group) classification, which is always capitalized. The second word is the species within the genus. The species name is never capitalized. When looking up these terms, you may need to first locate the genus name. Species names will be listed beneath as subentries.

Many diseases are contagious, which means they can be passed to other persons. Sexually transmitted diseases (STDs) are a current health problem in the United States, particularly chlamydial infections and the human immunodeficiency virus (HIV), the causative agent for AIDS.

Infections spread through a series of events that include a causative agent, a reservoir, a portal of exit, a mode of transmission, a mode of entry, and a susceptible host. All of these must be present. If any one element is missing, the series is interrupted and the spread of infection is halted.

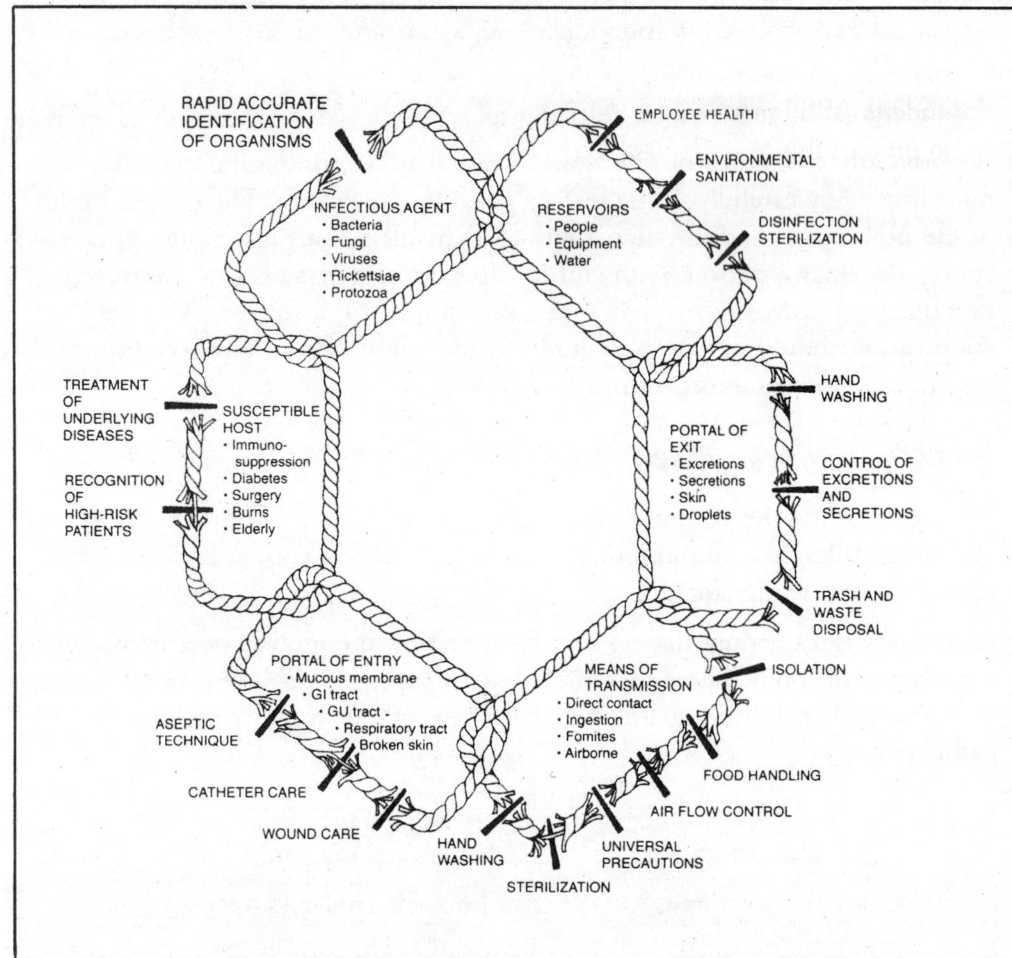

Figure 13.2 Interventions that halt the transmission of infections

The most common method of stopping the spread of infectious agents is to stop the mode of transmission (figure 13.2). Handwashing is the single most important step to stopping the spread of infections. In addition, immunizations are available to prevent certain diseases from spreading. Smallpox and polio have been successfully eliminated in the United States because of a vigorous immunization program.

Allergic reactions result from a hyperactive response to an allergen. Allergens include any substance that produces an allergic response. Examples include inhalants such as dust, perfumes, and pollens; foods such as chocolate, eggs, wheat, and strawberries; drugs such as antibiotics; and contact substances such as wool, chemicals, animals, and plants. In sensitive individuals, the immune system produces antibodies that attack these specialized antigens. Histamine released by the damaged cells will cause symptoms such as runny eyes, sneezing, itching, and a rash. In nonsensitive persons, no significant effects occur.

Common Immunology Drugs

acyclovir
Zovirax

amoxicillin
Amoxil, Trimox

amoxicillin and clavulanic acid
Augmentin

amphotericin B
Fungizone

ampicillin
Omnipen, Polycillin

azithromycin
Zithromax

cefaclor
Ceclor

cefadroxil monohydrate
Duricef

cefazolin sodium
Ancef, Kefzol, Zolicef

cefixime
Suprax

cefotaxime sodium
Claforan

cefotetan disodium
Cefotan

cefoxitin sodium
Mefoxin

cefpodoxime proxetil
Vantin

Continued on next page

Autoimmune diseases are disorders resulting from an overactive response to self-antigens, those molecules native to a person's body that the immune system uses to identify "self" components. Examples of autoimmune diseases include rheumatoid arthritis, multiple sclerosis, myasthenia gravis, Graves' disease, and systemic lupus erythematosus (SLE).

An excessive reaction to antigens from a different person is the cause of organ transplant disorders, which result in the rejection of grafted tissue. Patients who undergo a kidney, liver, or heart transplant must take antirejection drugs to try to prevent this.

COMMON TESTS AND PROCEDURES

Specific blood and specimen tests can help in the diagnosis of allergy and infectious disease. It is also possible to test for immune status through very sophisticated blood tests looking at lymphocyte subsets, particularly helper and suppressor lymphocytes, natural killer cells, and immunoglobulins.

Cultures of urine, blood, sputum, bronchial aspirates, and wounds can help determine pathogenic organisms. Stool cultures can reveal the presence of ova and parasites. After a specimen is collected, it is grown on a culture medium and then tested to determine which antibiotics can kill it. This is called the sensitivity.

cefprozil
Cefzil

ceftazidime
Fortaz

ceftriaxone sodium
Rocephin

cefuroxime
Ceftin

cephalexin monohydrate
Keflex

cephalothin sodium
Keflin

cephapirin sodium
Cefadyl

chloroquine phosphate
Aralen phosphate

ciprofloxacin hydrochloride
Cipro

clarithromycin
Biaxin

clotrimazole
Gyne-Lotrimin, Mycelex, Mycelex Troches

cyclosporine
Sandimmune

erythromycin
E.E.S., E-Mycin, Ery-Tab

ethambutol hydrochloride
Nyambutol

fluconazole
Diflucan

gentamicin
Garamycin

griseofulvin
Fulvicin

hydroxyzine
Vistaril

imipenem/cilastatin
Primaxin

immune globulin, IV
Gamimune N, Gammagard, Sandoglobulin

penicillin V potassium
Veetids

trimethoprim sulfamethoxazole
Bactrim, Cotrim, Septra

THE VOCABULARY OF IMMUNOLOGY

The following word list contains common immunology words as well as most of the difficult words contained in the dictation at the end of the chapter. Take time to become familiar with these words now, then review them later before you key the medical documents.

Here are suggestions for learning the vocabulary words:

1. Read and study each word for pronunciation and meaning.
2. Write each unfamiliar word from the list below on a notecard, write the definition or a paraphrase of the definition on the back, and draw a simple picture to help you learn the word.
3. Study the pronunciation, spelling, and definition of each word on your notecard, then key each word twice for reinforcement. Check the spelling.
4. Add the correctly spelled term to your word processor's spell checker.

aerosolized
(ayr'-O-sol-Izd) (adj) describing a solution that is dispensed in the form of a mist

allergen
(al'-er-jen) (n) a substance that produces an allergic reaction

antibody
(an'-tee-bod-ee) (n) an immunoglobulin produced as an immune response to a specific antigen

antigen
(an'-ti-jen) (n) a substance that causes the formation of an antibody which will react specifically to the antigen to neutralize, destroy, or weaken it

asthma
(az'-ma) (n) respiratory disorder with temporary narrowing of the airways, resulting in difficulty in breathing, coughing, gasping, wheezing

autoimmune disease
(aw-tO-i-myoon') (n) any disorder in which the body's immune responses produce antibodies that destroy the body's own tissues

B cell
(n) a type of lymphocyte; produces immunoglobulin antibodies in response to antigens

bronchitis
(brong-kI'-tis) (n) inflammation of the bronchi

communicable
(ko-myoon'-i-ka-bl) (adj) contagious; capable of being spread with direct or indirect contact

costal
(kos'-tal) (adj) relating to or located near a rib; the costal margin is the area at the lower end of the rib cage

cytokines
(sI'-tO-kIns) (n) proteins that are not antibodies but are released on contact with a specific antigen as an immune response

cytomegalovirus
(sI-tO-meg'-a-lO-vI'-rus) (n) CMV; one of a group of large-cell, species-specific herpes-type viruses with a wide variety of disease effects

enterovirus
(en'-ter-O-vI'-rus) (n) a group of viruses that multiply in the gastrointestinal tract but may cause various diseases, such as polio

Grave's disease
(n) one type of hyperthyroidism

heparin
(hep'-a-rin) (n) a naturally occurring anticoagulant (a substance which prevents or slows the clotting of blood)

hepatosplenomegaly
(hep'-a-tO-splee-nO-meg'-a-lee) (n) enlargement of the liver and spleen

histiocyte
(his'-tee-O-sIt) (n) a phagocyte present in connective tissue

hypergammaglobulinemia
(hI'-per-gam-a-glob'-yoo-li-nee'-mee-a) (n) excessive amount of gamma globulins in the blood

immune system
(i-myoon') (n) complex interactions that protect the body from pathogenic organisms and other foreign invaders

immunity
(i-myoo'-ni-tee) (n) one's resistance to disease

immunodeficiency
(im'-yoo-nO-dee-fish'-en-see) (n) some part of the body's immune system is inadequate; therefore, the person has decreased resistance to infectious diseases

immunoglobulin
(im'-yoo-nO-glob'-yoo-lin) (n) antibody protein

immunology
(im-yoo-nol'-O-jee) (n) study of the body's response to foreign invasion, such as bacteria or viruses, and allergies

inoculation
(i-nok-yoo-lay'-shun) (n) the introduction of pathogenic organisms or antigens into the body in order to increase immunity by stimulating the production of antibodies

intercostal
(in-ter-kos'-tal) (adj) relating to or located between the ribs

in vitro
(in vee'-trO) (adj, adv) literally, in glass; outside the living organism and in an artificial environment, such as a test tube

in vivo
(in vee'-vO) (adj, adv) literally, in the living body

isoagglutination
(I'-sO-a-gloo-ti-nay'-shun) (n) process in which antibodies (agglutinins) occurring naturally in blood cause clumping of red blood cells of a different group carrying a corresponding antigen (isoagglutinogen)

Kupffer's cells
(koop'-ferz) (n) phagocytes present in the liver

lymphocyte
(lim'-fO-sIt) (n) white blood cell that produces antibodies

lymphopenia
(lim-fO-pee'-nee-a) (n) a decrease in the number of lymphocytes in the blood

macrophage
(mak'-rO-fayj) (n) any phagocytic cell, such as histiocytes and Kupffer's cells

neutropenia
(noo-trO-pee'-nee-a) (n) a decrease in the number of neutrophils in the blood

neutrophil
(noo'-trO-fil/noo'-trO-fIl) (n) the most common type of mature white blood cell; its primary function is phagocytosis; granular leukocyte

opportunistic infection
(n) a disease caused by normally harmless microorganisms when the body's resistance to disease is impaired

otitis
(O-tI'-tis) (n) inflammation of the ear

Parvovirus
(par'-vO-vI-rus) (n) a genus of viruses; strain B19 can cause anemia in humans

pathogen
(path'-O-jen) (n) any microorganism or substance that can cause a disease

phagocyte
(fag'-O-sIt/fAg'O-sIt) (n) a cell able to engulf and destroy bacteria, foreign particles, cellular debris, and other cells

phagocytosis
(fag'-O-sI-tO'-sis) (n) the process in which a cell engulfs and destroys bacteria, foreign particles, cellular debris, and other cells

Pneumocystis carinii
(noo-mO-sis'-tis ka-rI'-nee-I) (n) a tiny parasite which causes Pneumocystis carinii pneumonia (PCP) in individuals with impaired immune systems

pompholyx
(pom'-fO-liks) (n) a skin eruption primarily on the hands and feet; may be accompanied by excessive sweating

prophylaxis
(prO-fi-lak'-sis) (n) prevention of disease or its spread

protease
(prO'-tee-ays) an enzyme that breaks down proteins

protease inhibitor
(n) an agent that inhibits (prevents or slows down) the release of protease

pyrexia
(pI-rek'-see-a) (n) fever

sinusitis
(sI-nu-sI'-tis) (n) inflammation of the nasal sinuses, occurring as a result of an upper respiratory infection, an allergic response, or a defect of the nose

steroid
(steer'-oyd) (n) any of a large number of similar chemical substances, either natural or synthetic; many are hormones; produced mainly in the adrenal cortex and gonads

substernal
(sub-ster'-nal) (adj) situated beneath the sternum (breast bone)

systemic lupus erythematosus
(sis-tem'-ik loo'-pus er-i-them'-a-tO-sis/er-i-thee'-ma-tO-sis) (n) a chronic disease with inflammatory symptoms in various systems of the body; characteristics of the disease and the systems involved may vary widely

T cell
(n) a type of lymphocyte; responsible for cell-mediated immunity

thrush
(n) infection with the fungus Candida, causing white patches in the mouth and throat

titer
(tI'-ter) (n) strength or concentration of a solution; a unit of measurement usually expressed as a ratio that indicates the minimum concentration of an antibody before losing its power to react to a specific antigen

toxoplasmosis
(tok'-sO-plaz-mO'-sis) (n) disease caused by a protozoan parasite

virus
(vI'-rus) (n) an organism or the infection caused by the organism; the organism is much smaller than bacteria; it depends completely on the host and is unaffected by common antibiotics

Western blot
(n) a laboratory test to detect the presence of antibodies to specific antigens in the blood

ABBREVIATIONS

AFB	acid-fast bacilli
AIDS	acquired immunodeficiency syndrome; caused by HIV
CMV	cytomegalovirus; one of a group of large species-specific herpes-type viruses with a wide variety of disease effects
DPT	diptheria, pertussis, tetanus immunization
EBV	Epstein-Barr virus
ELISA	enzyme-linked immunoabsorbent assay (test to determine the amount of a given chemical in a mixture); test for AIDS
FUO	fever of unknown origin
GC	gonorrhea
HIV	human immunodeficiency virus; causes deterioration of the immune system
PCP	Pneumocystis carinii pneumonia
PID	pelvic inflammatory disease
SLE	systemic lupus erythematosus
STD	sexually transmitted disease
strep	streptococcus
TB	tuberculosis
URI	upper respiratory infection
VD	venereal disease

EXERCISE 13.1: RECOGNIZING LOOK-ALIKES AND SOUND-ALIKES

The following is a list of frequently used words that look alike and/or sound alike. Study the meaning and pronunciation of each set of words, then read each sentence carefully and circle the word in parentheses that correctly completes the meaning.

coarse	(adj) composed of large particles; harsh or rough in tone
course	(n) direction, path

except	(v) to eliminate, to exclude
except	(prep) barring, excluding
accept	(v) to receive, to welcome

in vitro	(adj) in a test tube
in vivo	(adj) in the living body

costal	(adj) relating to a rib
coastal	(adj) relating to area where land and sea meet

dose	(n) dosage, prescription
doze	(v) to nap or to snooze

weight	(n) heaviness, load
wait	(v) to remain, to stay
wait	(n) a delay

allergen	(n) antigen that causes an allergy
antigen	(n) substance causing formation of antibodies

1. After years of infertility, the couple opted for (in vitro, in vivo) fertilization.
2. The patient tolerated every antibiotic in the treatment regimen (except, accept) Ceclor.
3. After taking her sleep medication, she was able to (dose, doze) intermittently.
4. Tests identified the (allergen, antigen) responsible for his itching, watery eyes.
5. She suffered a minor fracture in the (costal, coastal) area of the upper left quadrant.
6. The patient was unable to (except, accept) the limitations imposed by his illness.
7. The hip is a major (weight-, wait-) bearing joint.
8. The treatment (course, coarse) for non-Hodgkin's lymphoma is radiation and chemotherapy.
9. After years of careful research, scientists isolated the pathogen in a (costal, coastal) region of the South.
10. All anti-rejection drugs (accept, except) one produced severe reactions in the transplant patient.

EXERCISE 13.2: MATCHING SOUND AND SPELLING

The numbered list that follows shows the phonetic spelling of hard-to-spell words. Sound out the word, then write the correct spelling in the blank space provided. Each of the words can be found in the glossary or in the drug list in appendix C.

1. noo'-trO-fil ______
2. path'-O-jen ______
3. prO-fi-lak'-sis ______
4. fag'-O-sIt ______
5. pI-rek'-see-a ______
6. ko-myoon'-i-ka-bl ______
7. i-myoo'-ni-tee ______
8. tI'-ter ______
9. lim-fO-pee'-nee-a ______
10. sef'-a-klor ______

EXERCISE 13.3: CHOOSING WORDS FROM CONTEXT

When transcribing dictation, the medical transcriptionist frequently needs to determine the word that correctly completes the sentence based on the situation. From the list of words below, select the term that meaningfully completes each statement.

aerosolized	costal margin	in vitro
neutrophil count	sinusitis	titer
antigens	immunodeficiency	allergens
prophylaxis	substernal	

1. It is necessary for children with sickle cell disease to take penicillin daily as ______ against life-threatening infection.
2. When examining the abdomen, the physician percusses and palpates around the ______ for the liver and spleen.
3. New drug therapies are tested ______ in the laboratory before being used in vivo.

4. Mr. Rogers had a severe frontal headache. This is often a sign of an infection called ____________________.
5. Joanne caught many colds and viruses; therefore her doctor was performing laboratory tests to rule out an/a ____________ disorder.
6. When you have a low ____________________, you are susceptible to many bacterial infections.
7. The varicella ____________________ was 1:32, indicating a past exposure to chicken pox.
8. If you have allergies, it is often necessary to determine which ____________ cause the allergy.
9. Whenever John took a deep breath, he had ______________ pain.
10. When you have asthma, it is often necessary to have the medications ____________________ through a nebulizer in order for them to reach deep into the lungs.

EXERCISE 13.4: PAIRING WORDS AND MEANINGS

For each definition provided below, locate the term on the list that best matches the definition. Write the letter of the term in the space provided beside the definition.

A. bronchitis	E. immune system	H. oral thrush
B. cytomegalovirus	F. immunoglobulins	I. steroid
C. enterovirus	G. neutropenia	J. immunology
D. hypergamma-globulinemia		

1. fungal infection of the mouth ____________
2. antibodies produced in lymph tissues ____________
3. body processes and organs that produce the interactions to protect the body from pathogens and other invaders ____________
4. inflammation of the mucous membranes of the bronchial tubes ____________
5. a virus that multiplies in the intestinal tract ____________
6. abnormally low number of white blood cells in the blood ____________
7. study of the body's response to foreign invasion ____________
8. excessive amount of gamma globulins in the blood ____________
9. a herpes-type virus that produces large cells and causes illness ____________
10. a hormonal substance ____________

EXERCISE 13.5: CREATING TERMS FROM WORD FORMS

In the following exercise, combine prefixes, root words, and suffixes to create medical words that fit the definitions below. Fill in the blanks with the words you construct.

immun/o	safe, protected	-genesis	beginning
globulin	protein	-emia	in the blood
auto-	oneself	virus	organism
ox/o	oxygen	-itis	inflammation
bacteri/o	bacteria	lymph/o	clear tissue fluid
-megaly	oversized	phag/o	eating, swallowing
path/o	disease	-oma	tumor
enter/o	small intestine	splen/o	spleen
ot/o	ear	hem/o	blood
bronch/o	bronchus	aden/o	gland
cyt/o	cell		

1. infection of one or more bronchi ______________________
2. protein that protects [the body] ______________________
3. enlarged spleen ______________________
4. imflammation of the lymph nodes ______________________
5. self-protected ______________________
6. viral intestinal organism ______________________
7. bacteria in the blood ______________________
8. ear infection ______________________
9. oxygen-carrying protein in the erythrocytes ______________________
10. large-cell virus with disease effects ______________________

EDITING MEDICAL DOCUMENTS

In this section you will perfect your word use and grammar skills. These skills will help you edit and proofread medical reports for correct language, punctuation, format, and meaning. The special focus of this chapter's section is hyphenation.

USING HYPHENS CORRECTLY

Hyphens are commonly used to form compound adjectives, nouns, and verbs. In these cases, hyphens help readers understand that a combination of words has a single meaning and function in the sentence, as in the phrase *24-year-old patient.* Hyphens are also occasionally used to connect prefixes to root words, especially when an unhyphenated spelling may confuse the reader. Finally, hyphens are used in fractions and in certain medical technical terms such as L1-L2.

Using hyphens to create compounds can be complicated because so many variables are involved and because the construction of a compound may change as it becomes widely used. For these reasons, you should always consult a current dictionary when you question the spelling of a compound word. The rules below provide general guidelines.

Compound Adjectives

Compound adjectives are two or more words that work together to modify the same noun *(follow-up visit, once-in-a-lifetime opportunity, gram-negative bacteria).* Use a hyphen to connect the words that form a compound adjective:

> The patient is a 24-year-old female. [The adjective *24-year-old* modifies female].

> Lymphocytes are bacteria-fighting white blood cells. [The adjective *bacteria-fighting* modifies blood cells.]

> She is a well-developed, well-nourished infant. [The adjectives *well-developed* and *well-nourished* modify infant].

When the compound adjective appears *after* the word it modifies, do not hyphenate the words:

> The infant is well developed and well nourished.

Do not hyphenate adverb-adjective combinations because the meaning is usually clear without a hyphen. You can identify these combinations by checking if the first word ends in *ly,* which means it is an adverb. In the phrase, *a slowly enlarging lesion,* for example, *slowly* is not an adjective but an adverb, so the modifying phrase is not hyphenated.

Compound adjectives using the prefixes *self-* or *all-,* or the suffix *-free* should always be hyphenated, whether or not they precede a noun.

self-esteem	all-encompassing	symptom-free
self-limiting	all-inclusive	pain-free

Note: You may decide to rewrite a sentence to omit some of the hyphenated words. Do this cautiously and only when absolutely necessary.

DICTATED:	The patient has a 2-pack-per-day-times-30-year cigarette-smoking history.
TRANSCRIBED:	The patient smoked two packs of cigarettes per day for 30 years.

Prefixes and Suffixes

Do not hyphenate words with the prefix *non-* unless the root word is an eponym. Do not hyphenate words with the prefix *extra-* unless the word can be easily misread.

nonsteroidal	anti-inflammatory drugs
nonnarcotic	antibiotic
non-Hodgkin or non-Hodgkin's (lymphoma)	extra-large
nontender	extradural
antiemetic	extrapapillary
	extra-apical

Do not use a hyphen with the prefixes *anti-, bi-, tri-, uni-, co-, infra-, inter-, intra-, mid-, mini-, multi-, pseudo-, sub-, super-, supra-, ultra-, out-, over-, ante-, semi-, un-, non-, pre-, post-, pro-, trans-,* and *re-* unless the word that follows begins with the same vowel that ends the prefix.

Do not hyphenate words with the suffix *-like* unless the first word is an eponym, ends in *l* or a vowel, or has more than three syllables.

flu-like	slitlike
plate-like	Raynaud-like

Hyphenate words with the prefix *ex-* when *ex-* means former. Otherwise do not hyphenate.

ex-husband	excision
ex-president	expression
ex-patient	exogenous

Hyphenate words that would be misread without a hyphen. If the lack of a hyphen makes a word difficult to interpret, hyphenate the word.

re-cover (to cover again, not to return to normal)	non-neoplastic
re-create (to make again, not to play)	pre-clotting

Some words are so commonly used together that they are read as a unit without hyphenation. A few examples are listed below. Check your dictionary when in doubt, since there are no firm guidelines.

arterial blood gas	blood pressure readings
deep tendon reflex	exercise tolerance test
jugular venous distention	left upper lobe
low back pain	normal sinus rhythm
status post cellulitis	red cell count

Suspended Hyphens

Suspended hyphens connect two or more prefixes or adjectives to the same term. Use a suspended hyphen after each prefix or word in the series.

full- and split-thickness skin grafts

2- and 3-cm lengths

Specific Words

The verb, adjective, and noun variations of the words *follow up* are each treated differently and can cause confusion if not transcribed correctly.

verb:	The patient will *follow up* with me next week.
adjective:	He will have a *follow-up* chest film to document resolution of his pneumonia. (Note: AAMT suggests one word, although both treatments are acceptable.)
noun:	*Followup* will be with her primary physician.

Other Uses of the Hyphen

Hyphenate fractions expressed in words.

> The lower one-third of the right lung was removed.
>
> Three-fourths of my patients are nonsmokers.

Use a hyphen to express the space between two vertebrae.

> C4-C5
> L5-S1

Use hyphens with most suture sizes. Include the number symbol (#) if the physician dictates the word *number.*

DICTATED:	The fascia was reapproximated with three oh Vicryl.
TRANSCRIBED:	The fascia was reapproximated with 3-0 Vicryl.
DICTATED:	The skin was closed with number seven Ethibond.
TRANSCRIBED:	The skin was closed with #7 Ethibond.

Use a hyphen in place of the words *to* and *through* in numeric and alphabetic ranges.

> The child brought to the emergency room appeared to be 2-3 years old.

EXERCISE 13.6: EDITING FOR CORRECT USE OF HYPHENS

Edit the following clinic summary, placing hyphens where needed. Also correct those words written as two words that should be written as one word. Then key the report with the correct hyphenation and word format.

HISTORY: This 30 year old white male reported to clinic today for routine follow up, with diagnosis of HIV disease.

He was initially diagnosed in mid August 1993. Additional diagnoses include major depression, chronic serous otitis media, chronic active hepatitis, low back pain, and headaches.

Since his previous examination, the patient has continued to have active medical problems. With regard to his HIV infection, the patient continues to have a decreasing CD4 count. He is followed by a physician in Los Angeles, and his most recent CD4 count was an absolute value of 250. The patient notes a 10 to 12 week history of increasing night sweats. The patient at present is on no anti retro viral therapy, having discontinued AZT therapy two months ago.

The patient also had a long recovery complicated by infection following a scar revision of his lower lip earlier this year. He also continues to be followed for his diagnosis of chronic active hepatitis. He also is followed for chronic depression, for which he is treated with Zoloft therapy. The patient continues to be affected by right sided migraine like headaches, for which he had a recent CT scan which was negative for any intra cranial pathology.

FAMILY HISTORY: Non contributory.

SOCIAL HISTORY: The patient continues to work but on a part time basis. He works at home using his computer. He is a non drinker. He was a one pack per day smoker until two years ago, when he stopped.

PHYSICAL EXAMINATION: He is a slightly ill appearing white male who just turned 30 years old. VITAL SIGNS: Temp. 97.6° F, P 80, R 20, BP 140/80. HEENT: Pupils equal and reactive. Extra ocular movements are intact. NECK: Mild supraclavicular adenopathy. No jugular venous distention. LUNGS: Mild end expiratory wheezes, worse on the left. HEART: Regular rate and rhythm. PMI is in the 5th left inter costal space at mid clavicular line. ABDOMEN: Soft, non tender on the left with some mild right sided pain. Liver span is two finger breadths below the costal margin. Back reveals mild tenderness at the L4 L5 level. No costo vertebral angle tenderness. GENITALIA:

(cintinued)

Normal male phallus with descended testes bilaterally. Rectal exam reveals normal anal sphincter tone with a few mild external and internal hemorrhoids. Pulses, including brachio radialis, femoral, popliteal, and dorsalis pedis, normal.

LABORATORY DATA: White blood cell count is 4.1, hematocrit 45.5, hemoglobin 15.6, platelet count 181,000. Differential shows 52% segs, 34% lymphocytes, 12% monocytes, 2% eosinophils. The urinalysis revealed 1 to 2 white cells per high power field, otherwise normal. The liver function tests are normal. The CD4 count is 210 with a CD4 percentage of 15%. Intradermal skin testing reveals the patient to be anergic. VDRL is nonreactive.

DIAGNOSES
1. Human immuno deficiency virus infection.
2. Chronic hepatitis B.
3. History of major depression.
4. Migraine like headaches.
5. History of chronic middle ear infections.

PLAN: The patient will follow up in six months for clinic visit and repeat labs. We have discussed appropriate short and long term goals for this patient. He will continue to work part time, as he enjoys this and is having no difficulty performing his job related activities.

EXERCISE 13.7: PROOFREADING REVIEW

Read the following partial report and look for errors in form, meaning, capitalization, word choice, punctuation, and spelling. Circle the errors, then key the report with the errors corrected.

This is a nown severe asthmatic patient who has been admitted on numerus occasions. She developed her asthma approximately 2 years ago. She was well up until a weak prior to addmission when she developed a cold which caused her to be a short of breath and conjested. The conjestion continued, and he gave herself some infections of Adrenalin.

Physical examination at the time of admission revealed a lady in moderate distress there were wheezes, rails and ronchi throughout all lung fields. Their were some substernal and intracostal retractions. the throat was somwhat inflammed. The rest of the physical examination at the time of admission was entirely within normal limits.

WHERE CAN I FIND THE ANSWER?

As you transcribe dictation, you may hear unfamiliar words or terms. A variety of reference sources are available to help you locate answers to your questions. One of the important types of references for medical transcriptionists is described below. Read the information; if you have access to the reference discussed, explore its capabilities.

MEDICAL REFERENCES: ON-LINE RESOURCES

On the Internet you can find reference information and chat forums that will help you become more knowledgeable on the job. With a Web browser, you can search for information on any topic that interests you, including medical specialties, new drugs, transcription products, and directories of physician names.

Medical transcriptionists have created a lively and mutually supportive on-line community where you can find others who have similar interests and questions. For example, within a chat forum an MT may pose a question about the use of hyphens. Or, someone else might ask for help finding the spelling of certain terms or physicians' names. Over the Internet, you can get advice and information from hundreds of working medical transcriptionists quickly and easily. Be careful, however, about accepting information as correct unless you can verify it in a reference source.

Listed below are examples of commercial on-line services that serve as gathering spots for MTs.

Note that addresses may change and new groups may become available as others are discontinued.

- **America On-Line (AOL):** Look under EXCHANGE on the Careers bulletin board. AOL subscribers can also access a medical dictionary via the Reference Desk or Health Channel, or by entering the keyword: MEDICAL DICTIONARY.
- **CompuServe:** Go to WORK, then look under the Medical Transcription topic for the Work-at-Home forum.
- **Genie:** Look on the Medical bulletin board under the Medical Transcription category.
- **Prodigy:** Look on the Careers bulletin board under the Medical Transcription topic.

You may access several Internet newsgroups from the above commercial on-line services or from local FREENET services. You'll find some of the busiest home pages at these addresses:

- **MT Daily:** www.angelfire.com
- **Keeping Abreast of Medical Transcription:** www.wwma.com/kamt
- **MT Monthly:** www.mtmonthly.com
- **MT Newsgroup:** Look for the USENET group under sci.med.transcription.
- **American Association for Medical Transcription (AAMT):** http://www.aamt.org E-mail: aamt@sna.com

TRANSCRIBING IMMUNOLOGY DOCUMENTS

In this section your goal is to prepare for the work of transcription by transcribing first from a printed document and then from dictation on tape. The model document that follows illustrates the generally accepted format for the **autopsy report,** the report format featured in this chapter.

BASIC FORMAT: THE AUTOPSY REPORT

When a patient dies unexpectedly or if the cause of death is uncertain or needs clarification, the attending physician requests an autopsy report. Persons who die at home unexpectedly also will have an autopsy. These specialized pathology reports vary in length and scope. For example, the report may focus on test results for a single organ. Or, if the autopsy concerns a crime victim, the report may detail the results of an extensive examination and studies of all body systems. Often, the autopsy report includes a cover letter that summarizes the results of the postmortem examination.

Required Headings/Content

At a minimum, the autopsy report includes these categories:

- Authorization for the procedure
- Date of examination
- Name of the person performing the autopsy
- Names of the managing and consulting physicians
- Summary of the patient's clinical status and any details known to have contributed to the death
- Description of the body and all organs and cavities examined
- Preliminary report based on the gross examination (exam before tissues are removed)
- List of photos and studies completed
- List of microscopic studies
- Diagnosis based on the gross exam and lab studies

The report must be signed by the pathologist in compliance with hospital policy and state and federal regulations.

Turnaround Time

In a hospital setting, the autopsy report should be completed within 90 days of the patient's death. However, for a criminal investigation, the turnaround time is rapid.

AUTOPSY REPORT (COVER LETTER)

use letter formatting guidelines

Date

Elgar Lewis, MD
Department of Pediatrics
University Medical School
Fort Worth, TX 78095-1509

Dear Dr. Lewis:

The postmortem examination performed on your patient, Rebecca Arnold, resulted in the following findings:

I. Acute lymphoblastic leukemia, widely disseminated, including bone marrow, spleen, liver, kidneys, lungs, lymph nodes, and other visceral organs.
II. Hemophagocytosis and intravascular coagulopathy within the bone marrow, spleen, liver, and kidneys.
III. Bleeding diathesis (clinical thrombocytopenia)
    A. Massive hemorrhage with hematoma formation in pelvic and lower abdominal retroperitoneal space.
    B. Punctate petechiae within the ascending aorta, heart, and gastrointestinal tract.
    C. Petechiae, with ecchymoses, both extremities.

Based on the above findings, the cause of death is attributed to massive retroperitoneal bleeding with thrombocytopenia (29,000) arising from intravascular coagulopathy and hemophagocytosis-platelet phagocytosis, in a patient with acute lymphoblastic leukemia.

Marvin L. Smith, MD
Pathologist

MS/XX
D: (4 days before today's date)
T: (today's date)

AUTOPSY REPORT

1-inch margins
left justification

AUTOPSY #: A-4832
NAME: Arnold, Rebecca
MR # 0329415

double-space between sections

This 4-year-old white female was admitted with bruises of a two-week duration, fever of one week, and nose bleeding of one day.

On admission hemoglobin was 5.8, platelets 29,000, WBC 30,200 with 85% lymphoblasts. Acute lymphoblastic leukemia with L1 FAB classification was diagnosed after a bone marrow aspiration and biopsy were performed. She received allopurinol for hyperuricemia with a uric acid of 11.9 mg/dl (normal: 2.6-7.0). She was started on Vancomycin for fevers. She was transfused single-donor platelets, but experienced a hypersensitivity reaction with chills, intercostal retractions, and nasal flaring with perioral cyanosis. Although the cyanosis improved and the respiratory distress improved, she developed active bleeding from the bone marrow aspiration site.

Shortly thereafter, the patient passed away, two days after her admission.

EXTERNAL EXAMINATION: The body is that of a well-developed, moderately nourished, pale female child. The body measures 85 cm from crown to heel, and weighs 15 kg. The facies are normal. The head is covered by a lot of hair. The eyes are of normal size. There are no epicanthic folds. The external ears show normal cartilaginous development; they are in their normal set location. The external auditory canals are patent. The nasal passages are patent. The posterior choanal canal can be probed. The nasal bridge is normal. The tongue is of normal size, and teeth are present. The tongue is free of ulcers and exudate. The palate is normal. There is no peripheral lymphadenopathy. The chest is symmetrical. The abdomen is slightly distended. Muscle development is normal. The genitalia are those of a normal female child. The urethral meatus is patent. The clitoris is not hypertrophied. The anus is patent. The back shows no scoliosis or kyphosis. There are five normally formed digits on the hands and feet which are free of edema and cyanosis. The palm lines are examined and are not unusual. The nails are developed. The skin shows pallor, petechiae, and ecchymoses.

(continued)

AUTOPSY #: A-4832
NAME: Arnold, Rebecca
MR #: 0329415
Page 2

INTERNAL EXAMINATION: The body is opened through the usual y-shaped incision. Subcutaneous fat is 0.5 cm thick. The umbilicus is removed en bloc with a wide skin margin.

ABDOMINAL CAVITY: The peritoneal cavity contains 50 cc of straw-colored, serosanguinous fluid. The abdominal and pelvic organs are in their normal position. The kidneys are normally located.

THORACIC CAVITY: The great veins are flat. Each pleural space contains 20 ml of clear fluid which is not cultured. No adhesions are found.

PERICARDIAL CAVITY: The pericardium is opened and contains no excess fluid. No adhesions are found. A blood culture is taken.

ORGAN DESCRIPTION
CARDIOVASCULAR SYSTEM **single-space between subsections**
HEART: The apex consists of the right/left ventricle. The aorta and pulmonary artery arise in their normal relation to one another. The pulmonary veins enter the left atrium and no anomalous veins are noted. The heart is opened along the normal blood flow channels. No abnormal valves are noted. The auricular appendage contains no clots or vegetations. The endocardium of the right atrium is of normal thickness. The septum primum covers the foramen ovale adequately and cannot be probed. The tricuspid valve consists of three normal, thin leaflets. The right ventricle shows its usual trabecular muscles: the cristae supraventricularis and outflow tract are normal. The pulmonary valve consists of three cusps without thickening. The pulmonary artery cannot be opened into the aorta. The main pulmonary artery measures 4.1 cm in circumference. The right and left pulmonary arteries are identified. The left atrium receives two pulmonary veins from each lung. The endocardium of the left atrium is thin. The mitral valve contains two normal leaflets, inserted by normal thin chordae tendineae onto the two papillary muscles. The mitral valve is continuous with the aortic valve. The outflow tract of the left ventricle is normal: the aortic valve contains three normal cusps. The myocardium of the left ventricle is mildly hypertrophied.

(continued)

AUTOPSY #: A-4832
NAME: Arnold, Rebecca
MR # 0329415
Page 3

The left coronary artery arises from the left coronary cusps, and the right from the right. These pursue their usual course.
MEASUREMENTS

OPEN CIRCUMFERENCE:	Tricuspid 6.2 cm	Mitral 4.8 cm
	Pulmonic 4.1 cm	Aortic 3.5 cm
THICKNESS:	Right Ventricle 0.25 cm	Left Ventricle 1 cm

AORTA AND GREAT VESSELS: The aorta arises from the left ventricle, gives rise to three normal branches, and descends along the left side of the vertebral column.
VEINS: The inferior vena cava, superior vena cava, renal veins, and hepatic vein are patent. The splenic vein, inferior mesenteric, superior mesenteric, and portal veins are patent.

RESPIRATORY SYSTEM: The larynx and trachea are free of webs, mucous plugs, foreign bodies, edema, and mucosal ulcerations.
LUNGS: The heart and lungs together weigh 310 gm. The pleural surfaces are pale. The bronchial tree is free of mucous plugs and exudate. The pulmonary parenchyma shows consolidation after dissection. The pulmonary arterial tree is free of thromboemboli.

GASTROINTESTINAL SYSTEM: The oral cavity and esophagus are free of fibrinopurulent membranes, vesiculoulcerations, and other lesions. There is no tracheoesophageal fistula, enteric duplication, stenosis, atresia, webs, or diverticula. The stomach is well-rugated and free of ulcers. The mesentery is normally rotated. The small intestine is collapsed. The duodenum, jejunum, ileum, and colon are intact and free of serosal and mucosal lesions. The cecum and appendix are in the right lower quadrant. The colon is normally attached to the posterior abdominal wall. No atresias are noted.
LIVER: The liver weighs 600 gm. The capsule is transparent. The liver parenchyma is a normal brown-red and cuts with increased resistance. The lobular pattern is normal.
GALLBLADDER AND BILIARY TREE: The gallbladder contains green bile. Bile stones are absent. The mucosa is green. Bile can be expressed from the gallbladder into the duodenum. The common duct and right and left hepatic ducts are present.

(continued)

AUTOPSY #: A-4832
NAME: Arnold, Rebecca
MR #: 0329415
Page 4

PANCREAS: The pancreas is cut longitudinally, and the pancreatic duct is visualized. The lobular pattern is normal. No necrosis is noted.
GENITOURINARY SYSTEM: The kidneys weigh 150 gm together and are left attached to the pelvic organs and aorta. The renal veins are opened and contain no thrombi. The renal arteries are normal. The kidneys show normal lobulations. The capsules strip easily revealing a smooth, surface. On cut surface, the corticomedullary junction is sharp. The parenchyma does not bulge from the cut surface. The pyramids and papillae are normal. Pelves are smooth, and ureters arise from these and enter the urinary bladder normally at the trigone. The bladder wall is not hypertrophied. The urethra is opened, and no posterior urethral valves are noted. The uterus is normally formed. The ovaries are unremarkable. The fallopian tubes are of average and uniform width.

HEMOLYMPHATIC SYSTEM
SPLEEN: The spleen weighs 145 gm. The capsular surface is translucent and contains no wrinkling, exudates, or fibrosis. Cut surface is red and deep purple-brown, and consistency is mushy.
LYMPH NODES: The lymph nodes from the cervical, periaortic, peripancreatic, axillary, and inguinal areas are generally swollen.
THYMUS: The thymus weighs 6 gm.
BONE MARROW: The marrow is red, moist, and ample.

ENDOCRINE SYSTEM
THYROID: The red-brown thyroid is normally placed in relation to the larynx. The weight of the bilateral lobes of thyroid is 4 gm.
ADRENALS: The adrenals together weigh 6 gm; cut surface shows a normal fetal and adult cortex.

MUSCULOSKELETAL SYSTEM
BONE: Two ribs are taken and bisected. The cartilage, epiphysis, and metaphysis are normal.
SKELETAL MUSCLES: Skeletal muscles are grossly normal.
JOINTS: The joints are not remarkable.
CRANIAL CAVITY: The reflected scalp shows no evidence of contusion, hematoma, or other lesion. The calvarium and bones at the base of the skull are not remarkable.

(continued)

AUTOPSY #: A-4832
NAME: Arnold, Rebecca
MR #: 0329415
Page 5

No fractures or other injuries are present. The dura mater and pia arachnoid and associated spaces are normal in appearance. They are without hemorrhage or evidence of inflammation. The weight of the brain is 1280 gm. The cerebral hemispheres are symmetrical and normal in appearance. Cut sections of the brain show symmetry and essentially normal structures throughout. The circle of Willis and other intracranial vessels are normal. The pituitary gland is grossly normal. The pineal gland is present.

SPINAL CORD AND VERTEBRAL COLUMN: Spinal cord and vertebral column are intact.

FINDINGS

I. RESPIRATORY SYSTEM: All lobes of lungs show leukemic cell infiltration around the bronchioles or blood vessels. There is edematous fluid accumulated in air spaces of the left lower lobe.

II. CARDIOVASCULAR SYSTEM: Leukemic cell infiltration with scattered aggregates in subepicardial adipose tissue is seen. Myocardium and endocardium are not remarkable.

III. GASTROINTESTINAL SYSTEM
LIVER: Shows extensive leukemic cell infiltration within all portal areas, but the hepatic architecture is well preserved. No bile stasis is seen. There was a proliferation of histiocytes with ingested platelets. Red blood cells in dilated sinusoids are seen, which is consistent with hemophagocytic syndrome. Atypical leukemic cells are seen infiltrated in the gastrointestinal mucosa and submucosa.

IV. GENITOURINARY SYSTEM
KIDNEYS: Bilateral kidneys show leukemic cell infiltration in the interstitium. Hemophagocytic syndrome is seen with erythrophagocytosis or platelet phagocytosis in the renal tubules.

ADNEXA: Adnexa including uterus, ovaries, and fallopian tubes show leukemic cell infiltration. Retroperitoneum parametrium show hemorrhage admixed with a few atypical cells.

URINARY BLADDER: Shows hematoma formation.

(continued)

AUTOPSY #: A-4832
NAME: Arnold, Rebecca
MR#: 0329415
Page 6

V. HEMATOLOGICAL SYSTEM
SPLEEN: Shows extensive leukemic cell infiltration with congestion and hemorrhage. Hemophagocytosis is seen, also.

BONE MARROW: Shows leukemic cell infiltration with hemophagocytosis.

VI. LYMPHATIC SYSTEM: All lymph nodes reveal atypical leukemic cell infiltration.

VII. ENDOCRINE SYSTEM: Thymus, adrenal glands, thyroid, and pancreas all show leukemic cell infiltration.

____
Marvin L. Smith, MD

MS/XX
D: (4 days before today's date)
T: (today's date)

PREPARING TO TRANSCRIBE

To prepare for transcribing dictation, key the cover letter for the autopsy report above. You will later key the cover letter and autopsy report from tape as separate reports. Follow these guidelines:

- Study the format and organization of the cover letter.
- Review the word list presented earlier in this chapter.
- Consult reference books for words or formatting rules that are unfamiliar.
- Proof your final copy by comparing it to the printed version.

CASES FOR TRANSCRIPTION

In this section you will transcribe medical dictation from tape. Your goal is to produce error-free documents. Read this chapter's Pro Tip (following the case studies) for helpful hints from experienced MTs. Then follow these steps for each dictation:

1. Prepare to transcribe by reviewing the case study and the model report formats from this and earlier chapters.
2. Transcribe the dictation, leaving spaces for words you cannot hear or do not understand.
3. Carefully proofread each document and correct as many errors as you can. Use your reference materials to help you identify missing words.
4. Listen to the tape again and correct all remaining errors.

Repeat these steps until you produce an error-free document. Then complete the Performance Report at the end of the chapter, attach it to the top of the transcripts, and submit them to your instructor for evaluation.

CASE STUDY 1: JUNE PRINGLE

June Pringle is a 38-year-old woman who is a severe asthmatic and suffers from chronic sinus problems. She has been to many physicians for treatment of her problems and is on chronic steroid therapy. She is referred to the immunologist for evaluation.

Report 13.1: Discharge Summary

Transcription Hint

Listen for the following drug terms:
adrenalin
Sus-Phrine
aminophylline (Note that the brand name, Aminophyllin, sounds very similar and is spelled similarly, so you will need to determine if the physician intended to specify the generic or the brand name. In this case, use the generic name.)
Solu-Cortef
Slo-Phyllin
prednisone

Report 13.2: Consultation Letter

Transcription Hints

- Listen for the following drug and laboratory terms:
  Alupent
  immunoglobulins G, A, and M (transcribed as IgG, IgA, and IgM; each is sometimes dictated as the abbreviation)
- Transcribe the blood typing terms (anti-A and anti-B) with a lowercase "a" in "anti" and uppercase letters for the antigens A and B.

CASE STUDY 2: RIZA PRINCE

Riza Prince is a 15-month-old female who was born to a known HIV-positive mother. She has had several admissions to the hospital since birth and has been referred to the Pediatric AIDS Center in Fort Worth for treatment of AIDS.

Report 13.3: Chart Summary

Transcription Hints

- Listen for the following abbreviations:

FTNSVD	full-term, normal spontaneous vaginal delivery
ANC	absolute neutrophil count
PCP	Pneumocystis carinii
LFTs	liver function tests

- Listen for these drug and disease terms:
  hypergammaglobulinemia, Bactrim, pentamidine

Report 13.4: Consultation Letter

CASE STUDY 3: REBECCA ARNOLD

Rebecca Arnold is a 4-year-old girl who was admitted to the hospital with a fever, nose bleed, and bruises that had been present for two weeks. She was diagnosed with acute lymphoblastic leukemia and was treated with allopurinol, Vancomycin, and platelet transfusions. Two days after her admission, she died, and an autopsy was performed to confirm the cause of death.

Report 13.5: Autopsy Report (Cover Letter)

Report 13.6: Autopsy Report

CASE STUDY 4: COURTNEY BAIRD

Report 13.7: History and Physical

CASE STUDY 5: JOSH HENRY

Josh Henry is a 26-year-old man whose 2-year-old daughter was recently diagnosed with chickenpox. Mr. Henry presented to the emergency department with a fever and a vesicular rash covering his body. He was diagnosed with chickenpox, treated with Tylenol and Benadryl, and sent home. However, due to domestic problems, he returned to the hospital and was placed in isolation until the chickenpox lesions crusted.

Report 13.8: Discharge Summary

PRO TIP: RELAXATION TECHNIQUES

By Mary Morken, CMT

Take a few minutes to relax before transcribing a new report. Imagine yourself:

- Feeling fresh and alert as you begin working.
- Respecting the work of preparing healthcare records as worthy and valuable.
- Feeling the freedom of working individually, while being a part of a large team surrounding the patient with healing care.
- Carefully arranging each item needed to begin—software loaded, transcriber set correctly, books handy.
- Feeling well equipped to do excellent work.
- Feeling confident and ready to follow the doctor's voice, understanding every tone and turn, with every sound, syllable, and emphasis sounding familiar and meaningful.
- Identifying the doctor's voice quickly, locating the correctly spelled name.
- Pausing to note the spelling of the patient's name, watching for clear indication of male or female.
- Feeling prepared to deal with any obstacles that arise with equipment or vocabulary.
- Handling interruptions, such as problems that can be set aside.
- Developing a log of notes to keep oriented, jotting down any thoughts that will be needed later.
- Listening to understand the diagnosis(es) of the patient, noting whether left or right directions are mentioned.
- Keying steadily and accurately, in perfect tune with what you are hearing, turning the sounds into script.
- Setting the stage of the document carefully, gaining momentum and progressing smoothly and accurately.
- Staying alert to quickly catch any errors the physician may make along the way, confidently yet judiciously editing, while keeping true to the dictator's style.
- Meeting each new word with curiosity, locating it on a word list or book, noting the meaning, committing it to memory, and knowing it will be easier to remember next time.
- Scanning the document, checking for accuracy and completeness, easily spotting words or formats that need to be changed, and swiftly naming the document to store it in just the right place for printing or delivery.
- Resting a moment while preparing for the next dictator, taking a deep breath, relaxing, and feeling ready to begin again.

ASSESSING TRANSCRIPTION SKILLS

Demonstrate your mastery of the terminology, editing/proofreading, and document transcription skills presented in this chapter by completing the following activities.

USING MEDICAL REFERENCES

Use the appropriate medical reference to locate the correct spelling and additional usage information for the words below. (If the reference is not available, use the glossary in this text.) Circle the correct spelling, then write a sentence using the word correctly.

1.	phagocytosis	phagocytosus	phagoscytosis
2.	azithromycin	azythramiacin	azithrimiacyn
3.	prophylaxcis	prophylaxis	prophalaxis
4.	pyrexia	pryrexia	pyrechsea
5.	isoaglutination	isoagluttination	isoagglutination
6.	nuetropenia	neutrapenia	neutropenia
7.	hyprgammaglobulinemia	hypergamaglobulinemia	hypergammaglobulinemia
8.	streptococcus	streptococus	streptacoccus

9. immunodeficeincy immminodeficiency immunodeficiency

____

10. citukynes cytokines cytakynnes

____

MAKING EXPERT DECISIONS

Circle the correct word from the choices in parentheses.

1. A stool sample was obtained to test for (O&P/ONP).
2. The C3 (complement/compliment) was 33 with a reference range of 80-180.
3. Two units of (packed/pact) red blood cells were given to the patient after surgery.
4. After the exam was over, the patient stated, "Oh, by the way, I've been having rectal bleeding, but (its/it's) nothing really."
5. The CD4 cell count of 250 cells/mm3 (lead/led) to treatment with indinavir plus zidovudine.
6. Obtaining a culture and sensitivity of the urine (preceded/proceeded) the start of antibiotic treatment.
7. The patient had a tendency to (dose/doze) when visiting friends and had a history of sleep apnea, so she was advised to make an appointment with the sleep study clinic.
8. Because of the patient's severely immune-compromised state, a prophylactic (course/coarse) of treatment was recommended to prevent Pneumocystis carinii.
9. The patient was given AZT and would have continued on this course, (except/accept) that he developed severe neutropenia.
10. The patient discussed her fears to her physician, (who's/whose) advice was to contact a support group.

TRANSCRIBING PROFESSIONAL DOCUMENTS

Transcribe the document named Assessment 13 from tape. Before you key, review the appropriate formatting guidelines. Proofread your transcribed document and revise it until you think it is error-free.

PERFORMANCE REPORT

Name ______________________________ Date __________

Document	Description	Date Completed	Document Processing Speed (If Available)	Document Appraisal M=Mailable MC=Mailable w/corrections NM=Not Mailable
Report 13.1	Discharge Summary			M MC NM
Report 13.2	Consultation Letter			M MC NM
Report 13.3	Chart Summary			M MC NM
Report 13.4	Consultation Letter			M MC NM
Report 13.5	Autopsy Report			M MC NM
Report 13.6	Autopsy Report			M MC NM
Report 13.7	History and Physical			M MC NM
Report 13.8	Discharge Summary			M MC NM

Comments ______________________________

____

____

____

____

APPENDIX A

Glossary

abdomen
(ab-dO'-men) (n) that part of the body between the chest and the pelvis (the lower part of the trunk of the body)

abduction
(ab-duk'-shun) (n) movement of a leg or arm away from the middle of the body

abrasion
(a-bray'-zhun) (n) scraping away of skin or mucous membrane by friction

abscess
(ab'-ses) (n) a pus-filled cavity, usually because of a localized infection

accommodation
(ah-kom-o-day'-shun) (n) the eye's ability to focus or see

acne
(ak'-nee) (n) an eruption of papules or pustules on the skin, involving the oil glands

additive
(ad'-i-tiv) (n) a substance which is added in small quantities to improve the qualities of the original

adduction
(ad-duk'-shun) (n) movement of a leg or arm toward the middle of the body

adenitis
(ad-e-nI'-tis) (n) inflammation of a lymph node or gland

adenocarcinoma
(ad'-en-O-kar'-si-nO'-ma) (n) malignant tumor arising from epithelial cells of glands

adenoidectomy
(ad'-e-noy-dek'-tO-mee) (n) surgical removal of the adenoids from the nasopharynx

adenopathy
(ad-e-nop'-a-thee) (n) swelling or enlargement of any gland, especially the lymph nodes

adipose
(ad'-i-pOz) (adj) containing fat

adjuvant
(ad'-joo-vant) (adj) helpful; assisting the main ingredient

adnexal
(ad-nek'-sal) (adj) relating to appendages or accessory parts of an organ

adrenarche
(ad'-ren-ar-kee) (n) changes occurring at puberty due to hormones secreted from the adrenal gland

aerosol
(ayr'-O-sol) (n) a liquid or solution dispensed as a fine mist or a product dispensed from a pressurized container as a fine mist

aerosolized
(ayr'-O-sol-Izd) (adj) describing a solution that is dispensed in the form of a mist

afebrile
(ay-feb'-ril) (adj) without fever

afferent
(af'-er-ent) (adj) inward or toward a center

agglutination
(a-gloo-ti-nay'-shun) (n) the process in which cells group or clump together, especially as a response to a specific antibody; commonly used in blood typing

agnosia
(ag-nO'-see-a) (n) loss of the ability to recognize familiar objects

agraphia
(a-graf'-ee-a) (n) loss or impairment of the ability to write

akinesis
(ay-ki-nee'-sis/ay-kI-nee'-sis) (n) loss of the ability to move voluntarily; partial or incomplete paralysis

ala nasi
(a'-la nay'-sI) (adj) the outer flare of each nostril; alae nasi (a'-lee) (pl)

albinism
(al'-bi-nizm/al-bin'-izm) (n) a congenital lack of pigment in the skin, hair, and eyes

albumin
(al-byoo'-min) (n) a protein; widely distributed throughout the body

alimentary canal
(al-i-men'-ter-ee ka'-nal') (n) gastrointestinal tract; tubelike structure through which food passes, is digested and absorbed, and wastes are excreted

allergen
(al'-er-jen) (n) a substance that produces an allergic reaction

allogenic
(al-O-jen'-ik) (adj) describing tissues or cell types that are from different individuals belonging to the same species; describing individuals of the same species

alopecia
(al-O-pee'-shee-a) (n) total or partial loss of hair

alopecic
(al-O-pee'-sik) (adj) relating to alopecia

alveolus
(al-vee'-O-lus) (n) air cells of the lungs where the exchange of oxygen and carbon dioxide takes place; alveoli (al-vee'-O-lI) (pl)

amblyopia
(am-blee-O'-pee-a) (n) decreased vision in one or both eyes; not correctable

ambulation
(am-byoo-lay'-shun) (n) walking or moving about

amenorrhea
(a-men-O-ree'-a) (n) stoppage or absence of menses

amnesia
(am-nee'-zee-a) (n) loss of memory; total or partial inability to recall the past

amniocentesis
(am'-nee-O-sen-tee'-sis) (n) taking a sample of amniotic fluid

amplitude
(am'-pli-tood) (n) the extent of a vibrating or alternating movement or wave from the average to the extreme; a louder sound has a greater amplitude

anagen
(an'-a-jen) (n) the actively growing phase of the hair growth cycle

anaphylactic
(an'-a-fi-lak'-tik) (adj) describing an allergic hypersensitivity reaction of the body to a substance

anastomosis
(a-nas'-tO-mO-sis) (n) a natural or surgical connection between two blood vessels, spaces, or organs

anesthesia
(an'-es-thee'-zee-a) (n) absence of sensation, especially pain; usually applied to the medical technique of reducing or eliminating a person's sensation of pain so surgery can be performed

anesthetic
(an'-es-thet'-ik) (n) the medications used to produce anesthesia

aneurysm
(an'-yoo-rizm) (n) bulging out of an arterial wall due to a weakness in the wall

angina pectoris
(an'-ji-na/an-jI'-na pek'-tO-ris) (n) an attack of intense chest pain; also known as stenocardia

angiodysplasia
(an'-jee-O-dis-play'-zee-a) (n) degenerative stretching or enlarging of the blood vessels in an organ

angioedema
(an-jee-O-e-dee'-ma) (n) periodically recurring episodes of noninflammatory swelling

angiography
(an-jee-og'-ra-fee) (n) x-ray of blood vessels, usually after injecting a radiopaque substance

angioma
(an-jee-O'-ma) (n) a swelling or tumor composed primarily of blood vessels; spider, strawberry, cherry angiomas

anhidrosis
(an-hI-drO'-sis) (n) the suppression or absence of perspiration

anicteric
(an-ik-ter'-ik) (adj) without jaundice or icterus (a yellowing of the skin and whites of the eyes)

ankylosis
(ang'-ki-lO'-sis) (n) stiffening or rigidity of a joint

ankylotic
(ang-ki-lot'-ik) (adj) relating to or having ankylosis

annulus
(an'-yoo-lus) (n) a circular structure or opening

anorexia
(an-O-rek'-see-a) (n) loss of appetite

anovulation
(an-ov-yoo-lay'-shun) (n) absence of egg production or release from the ovary

anovulatory
(an-ov'-yoo-la-tOr-ee) (adj) not accompanied by production of or discharge of an ovum (egg) or suppressing ovulation

antecubital
(an-te-kyoo'-bi-tal) (adj) in front of the elbow; often the site for drawing blood

anteflexion
(an-te-flek'-shun) (n) the abnormal position of an organ that is bent forward over itself

anterior
(an-teer'-ee-or) (adj) front of a part, organ, or structure

antibody
(an'-tee-bod-ee) (n) an immunoglobulin produced as an immune response to a specific antigen

antiemetic
(an'-ti-em-et'-ik) (n) a remedy (drug or procedure) that prevents or controls nausea and/or vomiting

antigen
(an'-ti-jen) (n) a substance that causes the formation of an antibody which will react specifically to the antigen to neutralize, destroy, or weaken it

aorta
(ay-Or'-ta) (n) the main artery leaving the heart

aortic root
(ay-Or'-tik) (n) the opening of the aorta in the left ventricle of the heart

aortogram
(ay-Or'-tO-gram) (n) x-ray of the aorta after injection of a radiopaque substance

Apgar score
(n) scoring system to assess newborn's physical condition

aphagia
(a-fay'-jee-a) (n) inability to swallow

aphasia
(a-fay'-zee-a) (n) difficulty with use and understanding of written and spoken words

aphonia
(a-fO'-nee-a) (n) loss of the voice

aphthous stomatitis
(af'-thus stO-ma-tI'-tis) (n) small ulcers of the mucous membrane of the mouth; canker sores

apocrine
(ap'-O-krin) (adj) relating to sweat glands

apophyseal
(a-pO-fiz'-ee-al) (adj) relating to or having an apophysis

apophysis
(a-pof'-i-sis) (n) a projection or outgrowth of a bone

apoptosis
(ap-O-tO'-sis/ap'-op-tO'-sis) (n) a cell fragmenting into pieces which are phagocytosed by other cells

apposition
(ap-O-zi'-shun) (n) fitting together; side by side or close by in position

arachnoid
(a-rak'-noyd) (adj) the middle of the three membranes covering the brain, between the dura mater and the pia mater; resembles a cobweb

arytenoid
(ar-i-tee'-noyd) (n) cartilage and muscles of the larynx

arrhythmia
(a-rith'-mee-a) (n) disturbance of normal rhythm; irregular heart beat

arteriosclerosis
(ar-teer'-ee-O-skler-O'-sis) (n) hardening of the arteries

arteritis
(ar'-tur-I'-tis) (n) inflammation of one or more arteries

artery
(ar'-ter-ee) (n) a vessel that carries blood away from the heart to other tissues throughout the body

arthralgia
(ar-thral'-jee-a) (n) joint pain

arthritis
(ar-thrI'-tis) (n) inflammation of one or more joints

arthroplasty
(ar'-thrO-plas-tee) (n) surgical repair of a joint; creation of a new joint

articulation
(ar-tik-yoo-lay'-shun) (n) the way the bones are joined; joints

ascending aorta
(n) the beginning section of the aorta, rising from the left ventricle of the heart to the arch

asepsis
(a-sep'-sis) (n) germs are absent; a state of sterility; methods used to create or maintain a sterile environment

aseptic
(a-sep'-tik/ay-sep'-tik) (adj) sterile; being without infection or contamination

assessment
(as-ses'-ment) (n) to make a complete evaluation of the patient; diagnosis

astereognosis
(a-steer'-og-nO-sis) (n) loss of the ability to identify objects by touch

asthma
(az'-ma) (n) respiratory disorder with temporary narrowing of the airways, resulting in difficulty in breathing, coughing, gasping, wheezing

astigmatism
(a-stig'-ma-tizm) (n) visual condition in which light rays entering the eye are bent unequally, preventing a sharp focus point on the retina

ataxia
(a-tak'-see-a) (n) impaired muscular coordination

atherosclerosis
(ath'-er-O-skler-O'-sis) (n) buildup of fatty plaques inside arteries; a type of arteriosclerosis

atraumatic
(ay-traw-mat'-ik) (adj) without injury or trauma

atrial
(ay'-tree-al) (adj) relating to the atrium

atrioventricular
(ay'-tree-O-ven-trik'-yoo-lar) (adj) relating to both the atria and the ventricles (the upper and lower chambers of the heart, respectively), or bloodflow between them

atrioventricular groove
(n) a groove visible on the outside of the heart between the atria and the ventricles

atrium
(ay'-tree-um) (n) one of the two upper chambers of the heart

atrophy (at'-rO-fee) (n) a decrease in size of a part or organ; wasting away of tissue

attenuation
(a-ten-yoo-ay'-shun) (n) process of weakening, such as the potency of a drug or the virulence of a disease-causing germ

audiometry
(aw-dee-om'-e-tree) (n) test used to measure hearing (using an audiometer)

aura
(aw'-ra) (n) peculiar sensations, as of lights or dizziness, that may precede a migraine or seizure

aural
(aw'-ral) (adj) relating to the ear

auricle
(aw'-ri-kl) (n) external ear; pinna

auscultation
(aws-kul-tay'-shun) (n) act of listening through a stethoscope to sounds from within the body, including lungs, heart, and abdomen

autoimmune disease
(aw-tO-i-myoon') (n) any disorder in which the body's immune responses produce antibodies that destroy the body's own tissues

autologous
(aw-tol'-o-gus) (adj) describing a transplantation where the tissue graft is taken from the same individual receiving it

axial
(ak'-see-al) (adj) situated along or relating to an axis

B cell
(n) a type of lymphocyte; produces immunoglobulin antibodies in response to antigens

Babinski's reflex
(bab-in'-skeez ree'-fleks) (n) an abnormal reflex; when the side of the sole of the foot is firmly stroked, the big toe moves upward and the other toes fan out and extend

bacteremia
(bak-te-ree'-mee-a) (n) the presence of live bacteria in the blood

bedsore
(bed'-sor) (n) an infected wound on the skin that occurs at pressure points in patients confined to bed

benign
(bee-nIn') (adj) describing a mild illness or a nonmalignant tumor

beta subunit
(bay'-ta) (n) glycoprotein hormone containing two different polypeptide subunits designated as alpha and beta chains

bifurcation
(bI-fer-kay'-shun) (n) forking into two branches

bilateral
(bI-lat'-er-al) (adj) affecting or relating to two sides

bile
(bIl) (n) a thick, yellow-greenish fluid secreted by the liver; aids in the digestion of fats

biliary
(bil'-ee-ayr-ee) (adj) relating to bile or the gallbladder and its ducts

bilirubin
(bil-i-roo'-bin) (n) a reddish or yellowish bile pigment, found in bile and gallstones

biopsy
(bI'-op-see) (n) the removal of tissue and/or fluid from the body for microscopic examination; the specimen obtained

blepharectomy
(blef-ar-ek'-tO-mee) (n) excision of a lesion of the eyelid

blepharitis
(blef-a-rI'-tis) (n) inflammation of the eyelid

bolus
(bO'-lus) (n) masticated (chewed) food or substance that is ready to be swallowed

Braxton Hicks sign
(n) irregular contractions of the uterus throughout pregnancy

breech presentation
(n) presentation of the fetal buttocks at birth

bronchial
(brong'-kee-al) (adj) relating to the bronchi

bronchiectasis
(brong-kee-ek'-ta-sis) (n) persistent, abnormal widening of the bronchi, with an associated cough and spitting up of mucus

bronchiole
(brong'-kee-Ol) (n) one of the smaller subdivisions of the bronchi

bronchitis
(brong-kI'-tis) (n) inflammation of the bronchi

bronchovesicular
(brong'-kO-ve-sik'-yoo-lar) (adj) relating to the bronchioles and alveoli in the lungs

bronchus
(brong'-kus) (n) the divisions of the trachea leading to the lungs; bronchi (brong'-kI) (pl)

Brudzinski's sign
(n) in meningitis, if one leg is passively flexed, the other leg also flexes; if the neck is passively flexed, the legs also flex

buccal
(buk'-al) (adj) relating to the area inside the cheek

bulbar
(bul'-bar) (adj) bulb-shaped or relating to the medulla oblongata in the brain

bulimia
(boo-lim'-ee-a) (n) insatiable appetite

bullae
(bul'-ee) (n, pl) blisters of the skin containing clear fluid

cachexia
(ka-kek'-see-a) (n) weight loss and weakness occurring in the later stages of an illness or starvation

cafe-au-lait spots
(kaf-ay-O-lay' spots) (n) light brown spots of patchy pigmentation of the skin

calcaneus
(kal-kay'-nee-us) (n) heel bone; calcanei (kal-kay'-nee-I) (pl)

calcification
(kal'-si-fi-kay'-shun) (n) a hardening of tissue resulting from the formation of calcium salts within it

calculus
(kal'-kyoo-lus) (n) stone; a hard stone-like mass formed in the body; calculi (pl)

caliber
(kal'-i'-ber) (n) diameter of a tube or vessel, such as a blood vessel

callous
(kal'-us) (adj) relating to or resembling callus

callus
(kal'-us) (n) thickened skin which develops at points of pressure or friction; the bony deposit which develops around the broken ends of bone during healing

candidal rash
(kan'-di-dal rash) (n) a rash which usually includes itching, a white discharge, peeling, and easy bleeding; caused by the yeastlike fungi Candida; common examples are diaper rash, thrush, and vaginitis

capillary
(kap'-i-layr-ee) (n) the tiniest of blood vessels, connecting arteries with veins

capillary fragility
(kap'-i-layr-ee) (n) used in a test to determine the presence of vitamin C deficiency or thrombocytopenia; pressure is applied to the arm, and then the number of petechiae (representing broken capillaries) in a small area are counted

carbuncle
(kar'-bung-kl) (n) subcutaneous, pus-filled interconnecting pockets, caused by staphylococcal infection; eventually discharges through an opening in the skin

carcinoma
(kar-si-nO'-ma) (n) a malignant tumor of epithelial cells

cardiac tamponade
(kar'-dee-ak tam-po-nayd') (n) compression of the heart by fluid or blood in the pericardium

cardiomyopathy
(kar'-dee-O-mI-op'-a-thee) (n) disease of the heart muscle

carpal tunnel
(kar'-pul tun'-nul) (n) where the median nerve and flexor tendons pass through the wrist

caruncle
(kar'-ung-kl) (n) small, fleshy outgrowth

cataract
(kat'-a-rakt) (n) clouding of the lens of the eye, resulting in loss of transparency

catheter
(kath'-e-ter) (n) a tube inserted into the body for removing or instilling fluids for diagnostic or therapeutic purposes

catheterization
(kath'-e-ter-I-zay'-shun) (n) the insertion of a catheter

causalgia
(kaw-zal'-jee-a) (n) constant severe burning pain of the skin, usually due to injury of a sensory nerve

cauterization
(kaw-ter-i-zay'-shun) (n) destroying tissue by burning with heat or chemicals for medical reasons

cavernous sinus thrombosis
(kav'-er-nus sI'-nus throm-bO'-sis) (n) a group of symptoms caused by an obstruction in the cavernous intracranial sinus

cecum
(see'-kum) (n) the first part of the large intestine

cellular
(sel'-yoo-lar) (adj) composed of or derived from cells

cellular immunity
(n) immunity which is based on the T cells recognizing the antigen itself, rather than the presence of an antibody; cell-mediated immunity

cellulitis
(sel-yoo-lI'-tis) (n) inflammation of the connective tissue caused by infection

centimeter
(sen'-ti-mee-ter) (n) unit of measurement; one hundreth of a meter; approximately 0.4 inches

central nervous system
(CNS) (n) the part of the nervous system consisting of the brain and spinal cord

cephalalgia
(sef'-al-al'-jee-a) (n) headache

cephalocaudal
(sef'-a-lO-caw'-dal) (adj) relating to the axis of the body from the head to the base of the spine

cerebellar
(ser-e-bel'-ar) (adj) relating to the cerebellum, the part of the brain that coordinates and controls voluntary muscular activity

cerebrospinal
(ser'-e-brO-spI-nal/se-ree'-brO-spI-nal) (adj) relating to the brain and spinal cord

cerebrovascular
(ser'-e-brO-vas'-kyoo-lar) (adj) relating to the blood vessels of the brain

cerumen
(se-roo'-men) (n) earwax

cervical
(ser'-vi-kal) (adj) relating to a neck, or cervix, especially the neck (cervix) of the uterus

cervix
(ser'-viks) (n) the neck or part of an organ resembling a neck, such as the cervix of the uterus

chancre
(shang'-ker) (n) hard sore; the sore that develops at the site of entry of a pathogen

chemosis
(kee-mO'-sis) (n) an accumulation of fluid in the eye, causing swelling around the cornea

chemotherapy
(kem-O-thayr'-a-pee/keem'-O-thayr-a-pee) (n) treatment of disease with drugs

chloasma
(klO-as'-ma) (n) light brown patches on the face and elsewhere; commonly associated with pregnancy

cholangiography
(kO-lan-jee-og'-ra-fee) (n) x-ray technique to examine the bile ducts after ingesting or injecting a radiopaque substance

cholecystectomy
(kO'-lee-sis-tek'-tO-mee) (n) surgical removal of the gallbladder

cholecystitis
(kO'-lee-sis-tI-tis) (n) inflammation of the gallbladder

choledocholithiasis
(kO-led'-O-kO-lith-I'-a-sis) (n) presence of stones (calculi) in the common bile duct

cholelithiasis
(kO'-lee-lith-I'-a-sis) (n) presence of stones (calculi) in the gallbladder

cholesteatoma
(kO-les-tee-a-tO'-ma) (n) a tumor-like mass of scaly epithelium and cholesterol in the middle ear

chondral
(kon'-drul) (adj) relating to cartilage

chondritis
(kon-drI'-tis) (n) inflammation of cartilage

chondromalacia
(kon'-drO-ma-lay'-shee-a) (n) softening of cartilage

choroid
(kO'-royd) (n) a vascular membrane surrounding the eyeball, between the retina and sclera

chromic
(krO'-mik) (adj) relating to or containing chromium, such as chromic acid

chromosome
(krO'-mO-sOm) (n) the structure in the cell nucleus that transmits genetic information; consists of a double strand of DNA in the form of a helix; there are normally 46 in humans

Chvostek's sign
(khvosh'-teks) (n) an abnormal spasm of facial muscles when the facial nerve is tapped lightly just in front of the ear

cicatrix
(sik'-a-triks) (n) scar

ciliary action
(sil'-ee-ar-ee) (n) the lashing movement of a group of cilia, which can produce a current of movement in a fluid

cilium
(sil'-ee-um) (n) a short hairlike extension of a cell surface, capable of lashlike movement, which aids in the movement of unicellular organisms and in the movement of fluids in higher organisms; eyelash; cilia (pl)

circumflex
(ser'-kum-fleks) (adj) bending around; describes anatomical structures that are shaped like an arc of a circle

circumscribed
(ser'-kum-skrIbd) (adj) having a boundary; confined

cirrhosis
(sir-rO'-sis) (n) a chronic, degenerative disease of the liver

cirrhotic
(sir-rot'-ik) (adj) relating to or having cirrhosis

claudication
(klaw'-di-ka'-shun) (n) limping; painful cramps in calf of leg caused by poor blood circulation

clavicle
(klav'-i-kl) (n) clavicula; collar bone; a doubly curved long bone that forms part of the shoulder girdle

clavicula
(kla-vik'-yoo-la) (n) clavicle; collar bone

coagulation
(kO-ag-yoo-lay'-shun) (n) process of blood clotting

cochlea
(kok'-lee-a) (n) a spiral-shaped cavity in the internal ear

collagen
(kol'-a-jen) (n) the protein which forms the tough white fibers of connective tissue, cartilage, and bone

collaterals
(ko-lat'-er-als) (n) accompanying, as side by side; blood vessels that branch from larger vessels

colostomy
(kO-los'-to-mee) (n) surgical creation of an opening in the abdominal wall to allow material to pass from the bowel through that opening rather than through the anus

colostrum
(kO-los'-trum) (n) the first milk secreted after childbirth

colposcopy
(kol-pos'-ko-pee) (n) examination of the tissues of the vagina and cervix with a lighted instrument that magnifies the cells

comedo
(kom'-i-dO) (n) in a hair follicle or oil gland, a plug of dead cells and oily secretions; blackhead; comedones (com-i-dO'-neez) (pl)

communicable
(ko-myoon'-i-ka-bl) (adj) contagious; capable of being spread with direct or indirect contact

concha
(kon'-ka) (n) a shell-shaped anatomical structure, such as the auricle of the ear; conchae (pl)

concussion
(kon-kush'-un) (n) an injury resulting from violent striking or shaking, especially an injury to the brain

conductive deafness
(n) hearing impairment due to obstruction of sound waves; the sound waves are not passed on to the inner ear

condyle
(kon'-dil) (n) the rounded projecting end of a bone where ligaments are attached

condyloma
(kon-di-lO'-ma) (n) warty growths in the genital area

confluent
(kon'-floo-ent) (adj) merging together; connecting

congestive heart failure
(CHF) (kon-jes'-tiv) (n) condition in which the heart is unable to pump adequate blood to the tissues and organs, often due to myocardial infarction

conjunctiva
(kon-junk-ti'-va) (n) the mucous membrane covering the front of the eyeball and inside the eyelids; conjunctivae (pl)

conjunctivitis
(kon-junk-ti-vI'-tis) (n) inflammation of the conjunctiva

contusion
(kon-too'-zhun) (n) a bruise

cornea
(kor'-nee-a) (n) the outer, transparent portion of the eye through which light passes to the retina

coronary bypass surgery
(kOr'-o-nayr-ee) (n) vein grafts or other surgical methods are used to carry blood from the aorta to branches of the coronary arteries in order to increase the flow beyond a local obstruction

coronary cusp
(n) one of the triangular parts of a heart valve; point of the crown of a tooth

cortex
(kOr'-teks) (n) the outer part of an organ (the inner part is the medulla)

cortical
(kOr'-ti-kal) (adj) relating to or situated in the cortex of an organ

coryza
(ko-rI'-za) (n) acute rhinitis; acute head cold; inflammation of the mucous membrane of the nose with sneezing, tearing, and watery nasal discharge

costal
(kos'-tal) (adj) relating to or located near a rib; the costal margin is the area at the lower end of the rib cage

cranium
(kray'-nee-um) (n) the bones of the skull that contain the brain

crepitus
(krep'-i-tus) (n) grating sound or vibration made by movement of fractured bones (bone fragments); crepitation

cricoid cartilage
(krI'-koyd) (n) a ring-shaped cartilage in the lower part of the larynx

Crohn's disease
(krOnz) (n) chronic inflammatory condition affecting the colon and/or terminal part of the small intestine and producing frequent episodes of diarrhea, abdominal pain, nausea, fever, weakness, and weight loss

cryosurgery
(krI'-O-ser-jer-ee) (n) the use of extreme cold to destroy tissue

culture
(kul'-chur) (n) propagation of microorganisms in a solid or liquid medium

curettage
(kyoo-re-tahzh) (n) surgical scraping or cleaning, usually of the interior of a cavity or tract, for removal or sampling of tissue

cuticle
(kyoo'-ti-kl) (n) the edge of thickened skin surrounding the bed of a nail; the sheath surrounding the base of a hair follicle

cyanosis
(cI-a-nO'-sis) (n) bluish discoloration of the skin and/or mucous membranes due to decreased amount of oxygen in the blood cells

cyst
(sist) (n) a sac containing gas, fluid, or a semisolid material

cystic
(sis'-tik) (adj) relating to a cyst or having cysts

cystic duct
(n) the duct of the gallbladder which unites with the hepatic duct from the liver to form the bile duct

cystic fibrosis
(sis'-tik fI-brO'-sis) (n) an inherited disease, in which the mucus-producing glands become clogged with thick mucus; digestion and respiration are affected

cystitis
(sis-tI'-tis) (n) inflammation of the urinary bladder

cystoscopy
(sis-tos'-ko-pee) (n) examination of the inside of the urinary bladder with a lighted instrument inserted through the urethra

cystostomy
(sis-tos'-tO-mee) (n) surgical creation of an opening in the bladder

cytokines
(sI'-tO-kIns) (n) proteins that are not antibodies but are released on contact with a specific antigen as an immune response

cytomegalovirus
(sI-tO-meg'-a-lO-vI'-rus) (n) CMV; one of a group of large species-specific herpes-type viruses with a wide variety of disease effects

dacryocystorhinostomy
(dak'-ree-O-sis'-tO-rI-nos'-tO-mee) (n) a surgical opening to provide drainage between the tear duct and the nasal mucosa

dactylomegaly
(dak'-til-O-meg'-a-lee) (n) abnormal enlargement of one or more fingers or toes

debride
(da-breed'/dee-brId') (v) to remove unhealthy tissue and foreign material to prevent infection and permit healing

decompression
(dee'-kom-presh-un) (n) relieving pressure

defibrillator
(dee-fib'-ri-lay-ter) (n) something (such as an electric shock) that stops fibrillation (uncoordinated contractions; twitching) of the heart muscle and restores the normal beat

degenerative
(di-jen'-er-a-tiv) (adj) relating to or causing deterioration or worsening of a condition

dehydration
(dee-hI-dray'-shun) (n) loss of water

dementia
(dee-men'-shee-a) (n) deterioration of mental abilities

dermabrasion
(der'-ma-bray-zhun) (n) peeling of skin done by a mechanical device with sandpaper or wire brushes

dermatitis
(der-ma-tI'-tis) (n) inflammation of skin often evidenced by itching, redness, and lesions

dermatology
(der-ma-tol'-o-jee) (n) the study of the skin, hair, and nails

dermatophyte
(der'-ma-tO-fIt) (n) a parasitic fungus that causes skin disease

desiccate
(des'-i-kayt) (v) to dry out

diagnosis
(dI-ag-nO'-sis) (n) deciding the nature of a medical condition by examination of the symptoms; diagnoses (pl)

diaphoresis
(dI'-a-fO-ree'-sis) (n) profuse perspiration or sweating

diaphragm
(dI'-a-fram) (n) the muscle that separates the thoracic (chest) and abdominal cavities

diaphysis
(dI-af'-i-sis) (n) shaft of a long bone

diffuse
(di-fyoos') (adj) spreading, scattered

digital
(dij'-i-tal) (adj) relating to or similar to a finger or toe

dilatation
(dil-a-tay'-shun) (n) stretching or enlarging; dilation

dilation
(dI-lay'-shun) (n) stretching or enlarging; dilatation

diplopia
(di-plO'-pee-a) (n) double vision

discrete
(dis-kreet') (adj) separate; distinct

distal
(dis'tal) (adj) away from a center or point of reference; toward the far end of something

distention
(dis-ten'-shun) (n) being stretched out or inflated

distress
(n) trouble; mental or physical suffering

diverticulosis
(dI'-ver-tik-yoo-lO'-sis) (n) presence of diverticula (pouches) in the intestinal tract

dorsal
(dOr'-sal) (adj) relating to the back; posterior

dura mater
(doo'-ra may'-ter/mah'-ter) (n) the tough, fibrous, and outermost of the three membranes surrounding the brain and spinal cord; the other two are the arachnoid and the pia mater

dysfunction
(dis-funk'-shun) (n) abnormal or impaired function

dysgerminoma
(dis-jer-mi-nO'-ma) (n) a rare malignant tumor of the ovary

dysmenorrhea
(dis-men-Or-ee'-a) (n) painful menstruation; menorrhagia

dyspareunia
(dis-pa-roo'-nee-a) (n) painful sexual intercourse

dyspepsia
(dis-pep'-see-a) (n) indigestion; "upset stomach"

dysphagia
(dis-fay'-jee-a) (n) difficulty swallowing

dyspnea
(disp-nee'-a) (n) shortness of breath; difficulty in breathing

dysuria
(dis-yoo'-ree-a) (n) difficult or painful urination

ecchymosis
(ek-im-O'-sis) (n) reddish or purplish flat spot on the skin; a bruise; ecchymoses (pl)

eccrine
(ek'-rin) (adj) relating to sweat glands

echocardiogram
(ek-O-kar'-dee-O-gram) (n) a record of the heart obtained by ultrasonography

echolalia
(ek-O-lay'-lee-a) (n) involuntary and automatic repetition of words or phrases spoken by another person

ectopic pregnancy
(ek-top'-ik) (n) fertilized ovum is implanted outside the uterine cavity, as in a fallopian tube

eczema
(ek'-si-ma/eg'-zee-ma) (n) inflammatory condition of the skin characterized by blisters, redness, and itching

edema
(e-dee'-ma) (n) excessive accumulation of fluid in tissues, especially just under the skin or in a given cavity

edematous
(e-dem'-a-tus) (adj) having edema

effusion
(e-fyoo'-zhun) (n) escape of fluid into a cavity or tissues; the fluid itself

egophony
(ee-gof'-O-nee) (n) an abnormal voice sound, like the bleating of a goat

electrocardiogram
(ee-lek'-trO-kar'-dee-O'-gram) (n) a graphic record of electrical waves within the heart

electrodesiccation
(el-ek-trO-de-si-kay'-shun) (n) destruction of tissue by the use of electrical current; fulguration

electrolysis
(el-ek-trol'-i-sis) (n) destruction of a hair follicle by passing an electrical current through it

electrolyte
(ee-lek'-trO-lIt) (n) an ionized chemical capable of conducting an electric current; the body contains many different electrolytes in specific amounts to keep it functioning properly

electron
(ee-lek'-tron) (n) a subatomic particle with a negative charge

electrophoresis
(ee-lek-trO-fO-ree'-sis) (n) a technique to identify specific substances by separating them with an electric field; for example, a hemoglobin electrophoresis identifies the types of hemoglobin in the blood

embolism
(em'-bO-lizm) (n) blockage of a blood vessel by an abnormal object, such as a clot

embryo
(em'-bree-O) (n) in humans, the developing prenatal child from conception to the end of the second month

embryonal
(em'-bree-O-nal) (adj) relating to an embryo; in an early stage of development

emesis
(em'-e-sis) (n) vomiting

emetic
(e-met'-ik) (n) substance that causes vomiting

en bloc
(ahn blok) (adj) as a whole, in one piece

encephalopathy
(en-sef'-a-lop'-a-thee) (n) disease or disorder of the brain

endocapillary
(en'-dO-cap'-i-layr-ee) (n) within one of the tiny blood vessels

endocarditis
(en'-dO-kar-dI'-tis) (n) inflammation of the endocardium and/or the heart valves

endocardium
(en-dO-kar'-dee-um) (n) inner lining of the heart

endometrium
(en'-dO-mee'-tree-um) (n) mucous membrane lining the uterus; shed during menstruation

endoscope
(en'-dO-skOp) (n) a lighted instrument for examining the inside of a body cavity or organ

engorged
(en-gOrjd') (adj) filled to the limit of expansion

enterovirus
(en'-ter-O-vI'-rus) (n) a group of viruses that multiply in the gastrointestinal tract but may cause various diseases, such as polio

enucleation
(ee-noo-klee-ay'-shun) (n) removal of a tumor or structure as a whole, as in removal of the eyeball

enuresis
(en-yoo-ree'-sis) (n) bed-wetting; involuntary urination, especially at night in bed

eosinophil
(ee-O-sin'-O-fil) (n) a type of white blood cell readily stained with eosin

ephelides
(ef-ee'-lI-deez) (n, pl) freckles

epidermis
(ep-i-der'-mis) (n) the top or outer layer of the skin

epididymis
(ep-i-did'-i-mis) (n) one of a pair of long coiled ducts in the scrotum; they carry and store spermatozoa between the testes and ductus deferens

epiglottis
(ep'-I-glot'-is) (n) flap of elastic cartilage at the back of the mouth that covers the opening to the windpipe during swallowing, thereby preventing choking.

epiglottitis
(ep-i-glot-tI'-tis) (n) inflammation of the epiglottis, causing potentially fatal airway obstruction, especially in small children

epilepsy
(ep'-i-lep'-see) (n) disorders characterized by convulsive seizures

epileptiform
(ep-i-lep'-ti-fOrm) (adj) similar to epilepsy

epiphora
(ee-pif'-O-ra) (n) overflow of tears

epiphyseal
(ep-i-fiz'-ee-al) (adj) relating to an epiphysis

epiphysis
(e-pif'-i-sis) (n) end of a long bone, separated by cartilage from the shaft until the bone stops growing when the shaft and end are joined

epiploic
(ep'-i-plO'-ik) (adj) relating to the omentum, a fold of peritoneum attached to the stomach and connecting it with the adjacent organs

episiotomy
(e-piz-ee-ot'-O-mee) (n) incision of perineum to facilitate delivery and prevent laceration (jagged tear)

epistaxis
(ep'-i-stak'-sis) (n) nosebleed

epithelial
(ep-i-thee'-lee-al) (adj) relating to or composed of epithelium

epithelium
(ep-i-thee'-lee-um) (n) cell layers covering the outside body surfaces as well as forming the lining of hollow organs (such as the bladder) and the passages of the respiratory, digestive, and urinary tracts

eructation
(ee-ruk-tay'-shun) (n) belching

erythema
(er-i-thee'-ma) (n) redness of the skin; inflammation

erythema infectiosum
(er-i-thee'-ma in-fek-shee-O'-sum) (n) a mild, infectious disease causing an erythematous rash; also called fifth disease

erythematous
(er-i-them'-a-tus/er-i-thee'-ma-tus) (adj) relating to or having erythema

erythrocyte
(e-rith'-rO-slt) (n) mature red blood cell

erythroderma
(e-rith'-rO-der'-ma) (n) any skin condition associated with unusual redness of the skin

esophagus
(ee-sof'-a-gus) (n) the muscular canal that connects the pharynx and stomach

esotropia
(es-O-trO'-pee-a) (n) a condition in which one or both eyes appear to turn inward; cross eye(s)

estradiol
(es-tra-dI'-ol) (n) a hormone produced by the ovary; often used to treat menopausal symptoms

ethmoidal
(eth-moy'-dal) (adj) relating to the ethmoid bone or ethmoid sinus

eustachian tube
(yoo-stay'-shun/yoo-stay'-kee-an) (n) a tube leading from the middle ear to the nasopharynx; thus air pressure is equalized on both sides of the tympanic membrane

eversion
(ee-vur'-zhun) (n) turning out or inside out

exanthema
(eg-zan-thee'-ma) (n) a disease, such as measles or chickenpox, accompanied by a general rash on the skin, which may have particular characteristics specific to the disease

excision
(ek-si'-zhun) (n) cutting out; surgical removal of all or part of a lesion, structure, or organ

excisional biopsy
(ek-si'-zhun-al bI'-op-see) (n) surgical removal of an entire lesion for microscopic examination

excoriation
(ekskO-ree-ay'-shun) (n) a scratching or scraping injury to the skin

excrescence
(eks-kres'-ens) (n) abnormal projection or outgrowth; such as a wart

exophthalmos
(ek-sof-thal'-mos) (n) protrusion of the eyeball(s)

exotropia
(ek-sO-trO'-pee-a) (n) outward turning of one eye relative to the other

expectoration
(ek-spek-tO-ray'-shun) (n) expelling by mouth; spitting

expiratory
(ek-spI'-ra-tO'-ree) (adj) relating to expiration, or breathing out air from the lungs

extrahepatic
(eks-tra-he-pat'-ik) (adj) unrelated to or located outside the liver

extraocular
(eks-tra-ok'-yoo-lar) (adj) outside the eye

extravasation
(eks-trav'-a-say'-shun) (n) a leakage of fluid (such as blood) to the tissues outside the structure normally containing it, which may occur in injuries, burns, and allergic reactions

exudate
(eks'-oo-dayt) (n) any fluid that has oozed out of a tissue, usually due to inflammation or injury

exudative
(eks'-oo-dayt-iv) (adj) relating to exudate

facial
(fay'-shul) (adj) relating to the face

fallopian tubes
(fa-lO'-pee-an) (n) passageways from ovary to uterus

fascia
(fash'-ee-a) (n) fibrous connective tissue that supports soft organs and encloses structures such as muscles; fasciae (pl)

fascial
(fash'-ee-al) (adj) relating to fascia

femoral
(fem'-o-ral) (adj) relating to the thigh bone or femur

fenestra ovalis
(fe-nes'-tra O-val'-is) (n) an oval opening between the middle ear and the vestibule; closed by the base of the stapes

fetal distress
(fee'-tal) (n) life-threatening condition affecting the fetus

fetoprotein
(fee-tO-prO'-teen) (n) antigen (substance or organism that produces an antibody) naturally present in the fetus and sometimes present in adults with certain cancers

fibrinogen
(fi-brin'-O-jen) (n) a substance in the blood plasma that can be converted into fibrin to produce blood clotting

fifth disease
(n) erythema infectiosum; a mild, infectious disease causing an erythematous rash

fissure
(fish'-ur) (n) a cleft or slit on the surface of an organ; a crack in the skin

fistula
(fis'-tyoo-la) (n) abnormal opening or channel connecting hollow organs or leading from an internal organ to the outside or a cavity; such as a urinary fistula

fixation
(fik-say'-shun) (n) process of securing a part, as by suturing

flaring
(flayr'-ing) (adj) widening of an area, as the nostrils; a spreading area of redness around a lesion

flatulence
(flat'-yoo-lens) (n) gas in the stomach and intestines

flexure
(flek'-sher) (n) a normal bend, as in a body part

follicle
(fol'-i-kl) (n) pouch-like cavity, such as a hair follicle in the skin enclosing a hair; Graafian follicle

folliculitis
(fol-i-kyoo-lI'-tis) (n) inflammation of the hair follicles

foramen
(fO-ray'-men) (n) hole or opening, especially in a bone or membrane

fossa
(fos'-a) (n) channel or shallow depression; fossae (pl)

fracture
(frak'-chur) (v) to break; (n) a broken bone

fremitus
(frem'-i-tus) (n) a vibration that can be felt by the hand on the chest

fulguration
(ful-gyoo-ra'-shun) (n) destruction of tissue by the use of electrical current; electrodessication

fundus
(fun'-dus) (n) the bottom or base of an organ; the part farthest from the opening; that part of the interior of the eyeball exposed to view through the ophthalmoscope; fundi (pl)

funduscopic
(fun-dus-skop'-ik) (adj) relating to funduscopy

funduscopy
(fun-dus-kop'-ee) (n) examination of the fundus of the eye using a funduscope; ophthalmoscopy

furuncle
(fyoo'-rung-kl) (n) a localized, pus-forming infection in a hair follicle or gland

gadolinium
(gad-O-lin'-ee-um) (n) a magnetic metallic element

gallbladder
(gawl'-blad'-er) (n) sac under the liver which stores bile

gallium
(gal'-ee-um) (n) a rare metal; a gallium scan after an infusion of gallium provides a better view of lymphatic tissue

ganglion
(gang'-glee-on) (n) a group of nerve cells located in the peripheral nervous system

gangrene
(gang'-green) (n) death of cells or tissue due to obstruction of blood supply

gastritis
(gas-trI'-tis) (n) inflammation of the stomach lining

gastroenteritis
(gas'-trO-en-ter-I'-tis) (n) inflammation of the linings of the stomach and intestines

genital
(jen'-i-tal) (adj) relating to reproduction or the organs of reproduction

genitalia
(jen'-i-tay'-lee-a) (n) the genitals; male or female reproductive organs, especially the external ones

gestation
(jes-tay'-shun) (n) the intrauterine development of an infant; pregnancy

gingiva
(jin'-ji-va) (n) the gum; the tissue that attaches the teeth to the jaws

gingival
(jin'-ji-val) (adj) relating to the gums

gland
(n) organ that secretes one or more substances not needed by the organ itself

glans
(n) the head of the penis; "glans penis"

Glasgow coma scale
(glas'-gO/glaz'-gO) (n) a clinical scale measuring a patient's level of consciousness; the assessment includes motor responsiveness, verbal performance, and eye opening

glaucoma
(glaw-kO'-ma) (n) disease of the eye in which intraocular pressure increases, damaging the optic nerve; can lead to blindness

globulicidal
(glob'-yoo-li-sI'-dal) (adj) destructive to the blood cells, especially the red blood cells

glomerulus
(glO-mayr'-yoo-lus) (n) a cluster of capillaries at the beginning of each nephron (the functional unit of the kidney); glomeruli (pl)

glossopharyngeal neuralgia
(glos'-O-fa-rin'-jee-al noo-ral'-jee-a) (n) a condition of sharp spasmic pain in the throat or palate

glove-stocking anesthesia
(n) glove anesthesia is loss of sensation in the hand; stocking anesthesia is loss of sensation in the foot and lower leg

Goldmann perimeter screen test
(n) assesses patient response when a light comes into view

gonioplasty
(gO-ni-O-plas'-tee) (n) procedure that contracts the peripheral iris to eliminate contact with the trabecular meshwork

gonioscopy
(gO-ni-O'-skOp-ee) (n) procedure that allows viewing of the anterior chamber angle using a slit lamp and a goniolens, a special mirror contact lens

gonorrhea
(gon-O-ree'-a) a contagious disease usually affecting the genitourinary tract; transmitted chiefly by sexual intercourse

Graafian follicle
(graf'-ee-an) (n) a mature follicle on the ovary in which an oocyte matures and is released at ovulation

granuloma
(gran-yoo-lO'-ma) (n) a mass of tissue consisting of many newly growing capillaries formed during the healing process; growth may be due to injury, infection, or inflammation

Grave's disease
(n) one type of hyperthyroidism

gravida
(grav'-i-da) (n) a pregnant woman; may be used in combination with a number or prefix to indicate how many pregnancies a woman has had

gross
(grOs) (adj) visible to the naked eye

helix
(hee'-liks) (n) the folded edge of the external ear

hemangioma
(he-man'-jee-O'-ma) (n) a congenital benign tumor consisting of a mass of blood vessels

hemarthrosis
(hee'-mar-thrO'-sis/hem'-ar-thrO'-sis) (n) accumulation of blood in a joint

hematemesis
(hee-ma-tem'-e-sis) (n) vomiting of blood

hematochezia
(hee'-ma-tO-kee'-zee-a) (n) presence of blood in the stools

hematocrit
(hee'-ma-tO-krit/hem'-a-tO-krit) (n) the proportional volume of packed red blood cells to the total volume of the blood sample

hematology
(hee-ma-tol'-o-jee) (n) the study of blood

hematuria
(hee-ma-too'-ree-a) (n) presence of blood in the urine

hemifocal
(hem-i-fO'-kal) (adj) refers to half of the body; usually a type of seizure

hemiparesis
(hem-ee-pa-ree'-sis/hem-ee-par'-e-sis) (n) muscular weakness or partial paralysis of one half of the body

hemodynamic
(hee'-mO-dI-nam'-ik) (adj) relating to the mechanics of blood circulation

hemoglobin
(hee-mO-glO'-bin) (n) the iron-containing pigment of the red blood cells that carries oxygen

hemophilia
(hee-mO-fil'-ee-a) (n) an inherited blood disorder in males characterized by a defect in the clotting process due to a lack of one or more of the clotting factors

hemoptysis
(hee-mop'-ti-sis) (n) expectoration of blood; spitting or coughing up blood

hemorrhage
(hem'-o-rij) (n) loss of a large amount of blood quickly, either externally or internally

hemorrhagic
(hem-O-raj'-ik) (adj) relating to or experiencing a hemorrhage

hemorrhoids
(hem'-a-royd) (n) painful, swollen veins at or near the anus

hemostasis
(hee'-mO-stay-sis/hee-mos'-ta-sis) (n) stopping bleeding either naturally through blood coagulation, mechanically (as with surgical clamps), or chemically (with drugs)

hemostatic
(hee'-mO-stat'-ik) (adj) relating to an agent that stops the flow of blood

hemothorax
(hee-mO-thOr'-aks) (n) blood in the chest cavity

heparin
(hep'-a-rin) (n) a naturally occurring anticoagulant (a substance which prevents or slows the clotting of blood)

hepatitis
(hep-a-tI'-tis) (n) acute or chronic inflammation of the liver

hepatoduodenal
(hep'-at-O-doo-O-dee'-nal) (adj) relating to the liver and duodenum (the first part of the small intestine)

hepatosplenomegaly
(hep'-a-tO-splee-nO-meg'-a-lee) (n) enlargement of the liver and spleen

hernia
(her'-nee-a) (n) bulging out of an organ or part of an organ or other structure through a weakness in the adjacent muscle wall

herpes zoster
(her'-peez zos'-ter) (n) a viral infection causing inflammation along the path of a nerve with associated painful vesicles (blisters) on the skin above; shingles

hippocampus
(hip-O-kam'-pus) (n) structure within the brain

hirsutism
(hur'-soot-izm) (n) excessive body hair

histiocyte
(his'-tee-O-sIt) (n) a phagocyte present in connective tissue

homeostasis
(hO'-mee-O-stay'-sis/hO'-mee-os'-ta-sis) (n) equilibrium in the internal environment of the body, such as temperature and electrolytic balance

humerus
(hyoo'-mer-us) (n) the long bone of the upper arm

hydrocephalic
(hI-drO-se-fal'-ik) (adj) relating to or having hydrocephalus

hydrocephalus
(hI-drO-sef'-a-lus) (n) increased accumulation of cerebrospinal fluid within the ventricles of the brain

hydrocephaly
(hI-drO-sef'-a-lee) (n) the condition of having hydrocephalus

hyperdiploid
(hI'-per-dip'-loyd) (n) an individual organism or cell that has one or more extra chromosomes; (adj) relating to such an individual or cell

hyperemesis
(hI-per-em'-e-sis) (n) excessive vomiting

hyperemia
(hI-per-ee'-mee-a) (n) increased blood in part of the body, caused by inflammatory response or blockage of blood outflow

hyperemic
(hI-per-ee'-mik) (adj) showing hyperemia

hypergammaglobulinemia
(hI'-per-gam-a-glob'-yoo-li-nee'-mee-a) (n) excessive amount of gamma globulins in the blood

hypermenorrhea
(hI'-per-men-O-ree'-a) (n) prolonged or heavy menses; menorrhagia

hyperopia
(hI-per-O'-pee-a) (n) farsightedness

hyperpigmentation
(hI'-per-pig-men-tay'-shun) (n) darkening of the skin due to excessive pigment in the skin

hyperplasia
(hI-per-play'-see-a) (n) increase in size of a tissue or organ due to an increase in the number of cells (not including tumor formation)

hyperplastic
(hI-per-plas'-tik) (adj) relating to hyperplasia

hyperreflexia
(hI'-pur-re-flek'-see-a) (n) condition in which the deep tendon reflexes are unusually strong

hypertension
(hI'-per-ten'-shun) (n) high blood pressure

hypertrophy
(hI-per'-trO-fee) (n) increase in size

hypertropia
(hI-per-trO'-pee-a) (n) a type of squint in which the eye looks upward

hypokinesis
(hI'-pO-ki-nee'-sis) (n) decreased or slow motor reaction to stimulus

hypomenorrhea
(hI'-pO-men-O-ree'-a) (n) diminished menses

hypometabolism
(hI'-pO-me-tab'-O-lizm) (n) lowered metabolism

hypoperfusion
(hI'-pO-per-fyoo'-zhun) (n) lower-than-normal passage of a liquid through an organ or body part

hypotropia
(hI-pO-trO'-pee-a) (n) a type of squint in which the eye looks downward

hysterectomy
(his-ter-ek'-tO-mee) (n) surgical removal of the uterus

ictal
(ik'-tal) (adj) referring to immediate onset

icteric
(ik-ter'-ik) (adj) relating to the effects of jaundice

idiopathic
(id'-ee-O-path'-ik) (adj) of unknown cause; describes a disease for which no identifiable cause can be determined

idiopathy
(id-ee-op'-a-thee) (n) an idiopathic disease

ileostomy
(il'-ee-os'-tO-mee) (n) surgical creation of an opening into the ileum through which feces can be passed

ileum
(il'-ee-um) (n) the third and last part of the small intestine, about 12 feet long

ileus
(il'-ee-us) (n) obstruction of the intestines

ilium
(il'-ee-um) (n) the wide upper part of the hip bone

immune system
(i-myoon') (n) complex interactions that protect the body from pathogenic organisms and other foreign invaders

immunity
(i-myoo'-ni-tee) (n) one's resistance to disease

immunodeficiency
(im'-yoo-nO-dee-fish'-en-see) (n) some part of the body's immune system is inadequate; therefore, the person has decreased resistance to infectious diseases

immunoglobulin
(im'-yoo-nO-glob'-yoo-lin) (n) antibody protein

immunohistochemistry
(im'-yoo-nO-his'-tO-kem'-is-tree) (n) special techniques used on cells to identify certain characteristics, especially the presence of specific antigens

immunology
(im-yoo-nol'-O-jee) (n) study of the body's response to foreign invasion, such as bacteria or viruses, and allergies

impetigo
(im-pe-tI'-gO) (n) a streptococcal or staphylococcal infection of the skin characterized by lesions, usually on the face, which rupture and become covered with a thick yellow crust; highly contagious

incision
(in-si'-zhun) (n) cutting into; the wound made by a sharp instrument

incisional biopsy
(in-si'-zhun-al bI'-op-see) (n) removal of part of a lesion for micrscopic examination

incision and drainage
(n) commonly dictated "I and D"; procedure of cutting through an infected lesion and allowing it to drain

incus
(ing'-kus) (n) the anvil-shaped bone in the middle ear

infarction
(in-fark'-shun) (n) formation of dead tissue as a result of diminished or stopped blood flow to the tissue area

inferior
(in-fee'-ree-Or) (adj) lower; below; of lesser value

infraumbilical
(in'-fra-um-bil'-i-kal) (adj) below the umbilicus (navel)

infundibulopelvic
(in-fun-dib'-yoo-lO-pel'-vik) (adj) relating to or located in the infundibulum (the end of the fallopian tube farthest from the uterus) and the pelvis

inguinal
(ing'-gwi-nal) (adj) relating to or located in the groin area (where the abdomen and thighs join)

inoculation
(i-nok-yoo-lay'-shun) (n) the introduction of pathogenic organisms or antigens into the body in order to increase immunity by stimulating the production of antibodies

in situ
(in sI'-too) (adj, adv) in position; at the original site

inspiratory
(in-spI'-ra-tO-ree) (adj) relating to inhalation, drawing air into the lungs

integumentary
(in-teg-yoo-men'-ta-ree) (adj) relating to the skin

intercostal
(in-ter-kos'-tal) (adj) relating to or located between the ribs

interictal
(in-ter-ik'-tal) (adj) between seizures

interstitial
(in-ter-stish'-al) (adj) relating to or located in the space between tissues, such as interstitial fluid

intestine
(in-tes'-tin) (n) the digestive tract between the stomach and the anus (the opening of the rectum)

intimal
(in'-ti-mal) (adj) relating to the innermost lining of a part, especially of a blood vessel

intraductal
(adj) inside a duct

intraocular pressure
(in-tra-ok'-yoo-lar presh'-er) (n) the pressure of the fluid within the eye

intravenous
(IV) (in'-tra-vee'-nus) (adj) within or by way of a vein

introitus
(in-trO'-i-tus) (n) an opening or entrance into a canal or cavity, such as the vagina

intussusception
(in'-tus-su-sep'-shun) (n) a portion of an intestine sliding into an adjacent portion, causing obstruction

inversion
(in-vur'-shun) (n) reversal of position, as upside down or inside out

in vitro
(in vee'-trO) (adj, adv) literally, in glass; outside the living organism and in an artificial environment, such as a test tube

in vivo
(in vee'-vO) (adj, adv) literally, in the living body

iris
(I'-ris) (n) colored portion of the eye that regulates the amount of light entering through the pupil; irides (ir'-i-deez) (pl)

ischemia
(is-kee'-mee-a) (n) decreased blood supply due to obstruction, such as narrowing of the blood vessels

ischium
(is'-kee-um/is'-shee-um) (n) bone upon which body rests when sitting; fuses with the ilium and pubis to form the pelvis; ischia (is'-kee-a) (pl)

isoagglutination
(I'-sO-a-gloo-ti-nay'-shun) (n) process in which antibodies (agglutinins) occurring naturally in blood cause clumping of red blood cells of a different group carrying a corresponding antigen (isoagglutinogen)

jaundice
(jawn'-dis) (n) yellowish skin and whites of the eyes

jugular
(jug'-yoo-lar) (adj) relating to the throat or neck

karyotype
(kar'-ee-O-tIp) (n) chromosomal makeup of a cell; often displayed as chromosome pairs arranged by size

keloid
(kee'-loyd) (n) a mass of scar tissue

keratin
(ker'-a-tin) (n) a tough, fibrous protein in skin, hair, and nails

keratoplasty
(ker'-a-tO-plas'-tee) (n) surgery on the cornea, especially transplant of a cornea

keratosis
(ker-a-tO'-sis) (n) a condition in which the skin thickens and builds up with excessive keratin

keratotic
(ker-a-tot'-ik) (adj) relating to keratosis

kidneys
(kid'-neez) (n) a pair of bean-shaped organs near the spinal column that filter blood and produce urine

knuckle
(nuk'-l) (n) a joint of a finger; an abnormal kink or loop

Kupffer's cells
(koop'-ferz) (n) phagocytes present in the liver

kyphosis
(kI-fO'-sis) (n) abnormal curvature of the spine; hunchback

labial
(lay'-bee-al) (adj) relating to the lips

labyrinth
(lab'-i-rinth) (n) an anatomical structure made up of a complex of cavities, such as the inner ear

labyrinthitis
(lab'-i-rin-thI'-tis) (n) inflammation of the inner ear (labyrinth) or ethmoidal labyrinth (nose)

lacrimation
(lak'-ri-may'-shun) (n) secretion of tears

lamina
(lam'-i-na) (n) thin membrane or plate-like structure; layer; laminae (pl)

laminar
(lam'-i-nar) (adj) relating to lamina; layered

laparoscope
(lap'-a-rO-skOp) (n) a device for observing the inside of an organ or cavity through a small surgical incision

laparotomy
(lap-a-rot'-O-mee) (n) a surgical procedure in which an incision is made into the abdominal wall

laryngectomy
(lar'-in-jek'-tO-mee) (n) surgical removal of the larynx

laryngostomy
(lar'-ing-gos'-tO-mee) (n) surgically creating an opening into the larynx

larynx
(lar'-ingks) (n) the voice box, located between the pharynx and the trachea

laser iridotomy
(ir-i-dot'-O-mee) (n) cutting some of the fibers of the iris with a laser

lateral
(lat'-er-al) (adj) to the side, away from the center

leiomyoma
(lI'-O-mI-O'-ma) (n) tumor in smooth muscle tissue

lesion
(lee'-zhun) (n) general term for any visible, circumscribed injury to the skin; such as a wound, sore, rash, or mass

lethargy
(leth'-ar-jee) (n) state of sluggishness, stupor, unresponsiveness

leukemia
(loo-kee'-mee-a) (n) production of abnormal white blood cells; a type of cancer of the blood

leukocyte
(loo'-kO-sIt) (n) white blood cell

leukoplakia
(loo-kO-play'-kee-a) (n) a white thickened patch on a mucous membrane

levator
(le-vay'-ter/le-vay'-tOr) (n) muscle that lifts or raises the body part it is attached to

ligament
(lig'-a-ment) (n) band of fibrous connective tissue connecting joints, bones and cartilage, or supporting organs

lipping
(lip'-ing) (n) excessive growth in a liplike shape at the edge of a bone

lithotomy
(li-thot'-O-mee) (n) surgical removal of a stone, especially from the urinary tract

lithotripsy
(lith'-O-trip-see) (n) procedure using a laser to break apart stones (calculi)

lobe
(lOb) (n) rounded part of an organ, separated from other parts of the organ by connective tissue or fissures

lobectomy
(lOb-ek'-tO-mee) (n) the removal of a lobe from an organ or gland

lochia
(lO'-kee-a) (n) vaginal discharge occurring after childbirth

loop
(n) a curve or bend forming a complete or almost complete oval or circle

lordosis
(lOr-dO'-sis) (n) abnormal curvature of the spine; swayback

loupe
(loop) (n) a magnifying lens

lucency
(loo'-sen-see) (n) giving off light; being luminous or translucent

lumbar
(lum'-bar) (n) relating to the lower back, between the ribs and pelvis

lumen
(loo'-men) (n) cavity, canal, or channel within an organ or tube; lumina or lumens (pl)

lymph
(limf) (n) fluid that bathes the tissues of the body and circulates through lymphatic vessels

lymphadenitis
(lim'-fad'-e-nI'-tis) (n) inflammation of one or more lymph nodes

lymphadenopathy
(lim-fad-e-nop'-a-thee) (n) any disorder of lymph nodes or of the lymphatic system

lymphatic
(lim-fat'-ik) (adj) relating to or resembling lymph or lymph nodes

lymphoblastic
(lim-fO-blas'-tik) (adj) relating to or resembling lymphoblasts, immature white blood cells

lymphocyte
(lim'-fO-sIt) (n) white blood cell that produces antibodies

lymphocytic
(lim-fO-sit'-ik) (adj) relating to or characteristic of lymphocytes

lymphoid
(lim'-foyd) (adj) resembling or relating to lymph or the lymphatic system

lymphoma
(lim-fO'-ma) (n) a general term for tumors of the lymphatic system

lymphopenia
(lim-fO-pee'-nee-a) (n) a decrease in the number of lymphocytes in the blood

macrophage
(mak'-rO-fayj) (n) any phagocytic cell, such as histiocytes and Kupffer's cells

macula
(mak'-yoo-la) (n) small discolored spot on the retina or skin; macule

macule
(mak'-yool) (n) a small discolored spot on the skin or retina; macula

maculopapular
(mak-yoo-lO-pap'-yoo-lar) (adj) describing skin lesions that are raised in the center

malaise
(ma-layz') (n) an indefinite feeling of weakness or being unwell; uneasiness, often the first sign of illness

malformation
(mal-for-may'-shun) (n) abnormal development or structure of the body or a part

malignancy
(ma-lig'-nan-see) (n) a cancer that is invasive and spreading

malleolus
(ma-lee'-O-lus) (n) either of the two bumplike projections on each side of the ankle; malleoli (pl)

malleus
(mal'-ee-us) (n) the largest of the three inner ear bones; club-shaped; attached to the tympanic membrane

mammary
(mam'-a-ree) (adj) relating to the breast

mammogram
(mam'-O-gram) (n) x-ray of the breast

mandibular
(man-dib'-yoo-lar) (adj) relating to the lower jaw

mastication
(mas-ti-kay'-shun) (n) chewing food

mastoiditis
(mas-toy-dI'-tis) (n) inflammation of the mastoid process (part of the temporal bone behind the ear)

maxilla
(mak-sil'-a) (n) the upper jaw

maxillary sinus
(mak'-si-layr-ee sI'-nus) (n) an air cavity in the body of the upper jaw bone; connects with the middle passage (meatus) of the nose

meatus
(mee-ay'-tus) (n) a passage or channel, especially with an external opening

mediastinal
(mee'-dee-as-tI'-nal) (adj) relating to the space in the chest cavity between the lungs that contains the heart, aorta, esophagus, trachea, and thymus

mediolateral
(mee'-dee-O-lat'-er-al) (adj) relating to the middle and side of a structure

medulla oblongata
(me-dool'-a ob-long-gah'-ta) (n) the lowest part of the brain, connecting to the spinal cord; contains the cardiac, vasomotor, and respiratory centers of the brain

melanin
(mel'-a-nin) (n) naturally occurring dark brown or black pigment found in the hair, skin, and eyes

melanocyte
(mel'-an-O-sIt) (n) a cell that produces melanin

melena
(me-lee'-na) (n) abnormal dark, tarry stools, due to the presence of blood from the upper gastrointestinal tract

melitis
(mee-lI'-tis) (n) inflammation of the cheek

menarche
(me-nar'-kee) (n) the initial menstrual period

Meniere's disease
(mayn-yairz') (n) a disease of the inner ear with attacks of dizziness, nausea, ringing in the ear, and increasing deafness

meninges
(me-nin'-jeez) (n) membranes covering the brain and spinal cord

meningitis
(men-in-jI'-tis) (n) inflammation of the meninges

meningocele
(me-ning'-gO-seel) (n) protrusion of a part of the membrane covering the brain or spinal cord through a defect in the skull or spinal column

menometrorrhagia
(men'-O-mee-trO-ray'-jee-a) (n) excessive menstrual bleeding or bleeding between menstrual periods

menopause
(men'-O-pawz) (n) the end of a woman's reproductive period of life and cessation of menses

menorrhagia
(men-O-ray'-jee-a) (n) prolonged or heavy menses; hypermenorrhea

menorrhalgia
(men-O-ral'-jee-a) (n) painful menstruation or pelvic pain accompanying menstruation; dysmenorrhea

menses
(men'-seez) (n) monthly flow of bloody fluid from the uterus

menstruation
(men-stroo-ay'-shun) (n) the periodic discharge of a bloody fluid from the uterus occurring at more or less regular intervals during the life of a woman from puberty to menopause

mesial
(mee'-zee-al/mes'-ee-al) (adj) relating to or located near the middle; medial

mesosalpinx
(mez'-O-sal'-pinks) (n) free end of the broad ligament which supports the fallopian tubes

metastasis
(me-tas'-ta-sis) (n) spread of a tumor from its site of origin to distant sites

metastatic
(met-a-stat'-ik) (adj) relating to metastasis

metatarsal
(met'-a-tar'-sal) (adj) relating to a metatarsus; (n) a metatarsal bone

metatarsus
(met'-a-tar'-sus) (n) any of the five long bones of the foot, between the ankle and the toes

metrorrhagia
(mee-trO-ray'-jee-a) (n) bleeding from the uterus between menstrual periods

microscopy
(mI-kros'-kO-pee) (n) use of a microscope to magnify and examine objects

milia
(mil'-ee-a) (n, pl) whiteheads; caused by obstruction of the outlet of hair follicles or sweat glands

miliaria
(mil-ee-ay'-ree-a) (n) a skin eruption of small vesicles and papules; heat rash

millicuries
(mil'-i-kyoo'-rees) (n) a unit of radioactivity, abbreviated mc

mitral
(mI'-tral) (adj) relating to the bicuspid or mitral valve of the heart, between the atrium and the ventricle on the left side of the heart

morphology
(mOr-fol'-O-jee) (n) the shape and structure of an organism or body part

motility
(mO-til'-i-tee) (n) ability to move spontaneously

mucoperiosteum
(myoo'-kO-per-ee-os'-tee-um) (n) the mucous membrane covering the hard palate at the front of the roof of the mouth

mucosa
(myoo-kO'-sa) (n) mucous membrane

mucosal
(myoo-kO'-sal) (adj) relating to any mucous membrane(s)

mucous
(myoo'-kus) (adj) relating to or resembling mucus

mucus
(myoo'-kus) (n) viscous (sticky, gummy) secretions of mucous membranes and glands

multipara
(mul-tip'-a-ra) (n) a woman who has given birth to two or more children

murmur
(mer'-mer) (n) abnormal heart sound

myasthenia gravis
(mI-as-thee'-nee-a grav'-is) (n) a disease characterized by progressive muscular weakness, usually beginning in the face, due to a defect in the conduction of nerve impulses

mycosis
(mI-kO'-sis) (n) disease caused by a fungus

myocardial
(mI-O-kar'-dee-al) (adj) relating to the myocardium, the heart muscle

myopia
(mI-O'-pee-a) (n) nearsightedness

myringitis
(mir-in-jI'-tis) (n) inflammation of the tympanic membrane; tympanitis

myringoplasty
(mi-ring'-gO-plas'-tee) (n) surgical repair of the eardrum

myringotomy
(mir-ing-got'-o-mee) (n) surgical incision into the tympanic membrane

naris
(nay'-ris) (n) nostril; nares (nay'-rees) (pl)

nasopharynx
(nay'-zO-far'-ingks) (n) open chamber behind the nose and above the palate

nausea
(naw'-zee-a; naw'-zha) (n) inclination to vomit

nauseous
(naw'-zee-us/naw'-shus) (adj) causing nausea or feeling nausea

nebulization
(neb'-yoo-li-zay'-shun) (n) production of fine particles, such as a spray or mist, from liquid

necrosis
(ne-krO'-sis) (n) death of some or all of the cells in a tissue

necrotic
(ne-krot'-ik) (adj) relating to or undergoing necrosis

neoadjuvant
(nee-O-ad'-joo-vant) (adj) used in conjunction with other types of therapy

neoplasm
(nee'-O-plazm) (n) any abnormal growth of tissue, usually malignant; tumor

nephrectomy
(ne-frek'-tO-mee) (n) surgical removal of a kidney

nephrolithiasis
(nef'-rO-li-thI'-a-sis) (n) presence of stones (calculi) in the kidney(s)

nephrolithotomy
(nef'-rO-li-thot'-O-mee) (n) surgical incision into a kidney to remove stones (calculi)

nephron
(nef'-ron) (n) the functional unit of the kidney that filters the blood

nephrostomy
(ne-fros'-tO-mee) (n) surgical creation of an opening in the kidney for drainage

neural
(noo'-ral) (adj) relating to nerves or the nervous system

neuralgia
(noo-ral'-jee-a) (n) acute pain along a nerve pathway

neurapraxia
(noor-a-prak'-see-a) (n) temporary disruption of nerve conduction, usually due to injury

neurasthenia
(noor-as-thee'-nee-a) (n) nervous exhaustion; a vague disorder with fatigue and weakness but no apparent physical cause, often occurring after depression

neurilemma
(noor-i-lem'-a) (n) a cell or cells surrounding one or more axons in the peripheral nervous system; neurolemma

neuroblastoma
(noor'-O-blas-tO'-ma) (n) malignant (cancerous) tumor containing embryonic nerve cells

neuron
(noor'-on) (n) nerve cell; neurocyte; the basic unit of the nervous system; consists of the nerve cell body, dendrites, and axon

neuropathy
(noo-rop'-a-thee) (n) disease or disorder affecting the nervous system, especially the central nervous system

neutropenia
(noo-trO-pee'-nee-a) (n) a decrease in the number of neutrophils in the blood

neutrophil
(noo'-trO-fil/noo'-trO-fIl) (n) the most common type of mature white blood cell; its primary function is phagocytosis; granular leukocyte

nevus
(nee'-vus) (n) congenital discoloration of the skin; birthmark or mole; nevi (pl)

nocturia
(nok-too'-ree-a) (n) frequent urination during the night

node
(nOd) (n) a small knot of tissue, distinct from surrounding tissue; a lymph node

nodular
(nod'-yoo-lar) (adj) containing or resembling nodules; having small, firm, knotty masses

nodule
(nod'-yool) (n) a small mass, distinct from surrounding tissue; a small node

nuchal
(noo-kal) (adj) relating to the nape or back of the neck

nulligravida
(nul-i-grav'-i-da) (n) a woman who has never been pregnant

nystagmus
(nis-tag'-mus) (n) involuntary, back-and-forth movement of the eyeballs

obese
(o-bees') (adj) very fat

oblique
(ob-leek') (adj) slanting

obstipation
(ob-sti-pay'-shun) (n) constipation due to intestinal obstruction

obturator
(ob'-too-ray-tor) (n) device or body structure that closes up or covers an opening

obtuse
(ob-toos') (adj) dull or blunt; not pointed or acute

occlusion
(o-kloo'-zhun) (n) blockage, such as coronary occlusion

odontoid process
(O-don'-toyd pros'-es) (n) the toothlike projection from the upper surface of the second cervical vertebra on which the head rotates

oligomenorrhea
(ol'-i-gO-men-O-ree'-a) (n) infrequent or scant menstrual bleeding

omental
(O-men'-tal) (adj) relating to the omentum

omentum
(O-men'-tum) (n) fold of peritoneal tissue attaching to and supporting the stomach and intestines

onycholysis
(on-ee-kol'-i-sis) (n) loosening of the nails from their beds

oophorectomy
(O-of-Or-ek'-tO-mee) (n) surgical removal of one or both ovaries

opacification
(O-pas'-i-fi-kay-shun) (n) clouding or loss of transparency, especially of the cornea or lens of the eye

ophthalmologist
(of-thal-mol'-o-jist) (n) a physician specializing in diseases of the eye

ophthalmoscopy
(of-thal-mos'-ko-pee) (n) procedure used to examine the optic nerve head for color, shape, and vascularization

ophthalmus
(of-thal'-mus) (n) the eye

opportunistic infection
(n) a disease caused by normally harmless microorganisms when the body's resistance to disease is impaired

opposition
(op-O-zi'-shun) (n) opposite or against in position

optic
(op'-tik) (adj) pertaining to the eye or sight

optic chiasm
(op'-tik kI'-azm) (n) the point of crossing of the optic nerves

optometrist
(op-tom'-e-trist) (n) a professional who tests visual acuity and prescribes corrective lenses

orbital cellulitis
(or'-bit-al sel-yoo-lI'-tis) (n) inflammation of tissue around or behind the eye

orchiectomy
(Or-kee-ek'-tO-mee) (n) surgical removal of one or both testes

orchiocele
(Or'-kee-O-seel) (n) scrotal hernia; tumor of a testis

organism
(or'-ga-nizm) (n) a living plant, animal, or microorganism

organomegaly
(Or'-ga-nO-meg'-a-lee) (n) abnormal enlargement of an organ, particularly an organ of the abdominal cavity, such as the liver or spleen

orifice
(or'-i-fis) (n) an opening

orthopnea
(Or-thop-nee'-a) (n) difficulty in breathing when lying down

oscilloscope
(o-sil'-O-scOp) (n) an instrument which displays electrical oscillations (waves) on a screen

osseous
(os'-ee-us) (adj) bony; resembling bone; osteal

ossicles
(os-i-kls) (n) small bones, such as the auditory ossicles (the three bones of the inner ear)

osteal
(os'-tee-ul) (adj) bony; resembling bone; osseous

ostealgia
(os-tee-al'-jee-a) (n) pain in a bone

ostectomy
(os-tek'-tO-mee) (n) surgical removal of all or part of a bone

osteophyte
(os'-tee-O-fIt) (n) a bony outgrowth; projection or bone spur

osteoporosis
(os-tee-O-pO-rO'-sis) (n) abnormal loss of bone tissue, causing fragile bones that fracture easily

osteosarcoma
(os'-tee-O-sar-ko'-ma) (n) a tumor of the bone, usually highly malignant

ostial
(os'-tee-ul) (adj) relating to any opening (ostium)

otalgia
(O-tal'-jee-a) (n) earache

otitis
(O-tI'-tis) (n) inflammation of the ear

otitis externa
(O-tI'-tis eks-ter'-na) (n) inflammation of the external ear

otitis media
(O-tI'-tis mee'-dee-a) (n) inflammation of the middle ear

otorhinolaryngology
(O'-tO-rI'-nO-lar-in-gol'-o-jee) (n) study of the ears, nose, and throat

otosclerosis
(O'-tO-sklee-rO'-sis) (n) a growth of sponge-like bone in the inner ear, eventually leading to deafness

otoscope
(O'-tO-skOp) (n) an instrument for examining the eardrum

oximetry
(ok-sim'-e-tree) (n) measuring the amount of oxygen combined with the hemoglobin in a blood sample

palate
(pal'-at) (n) the roof of one's mouth, composed of the hard palate (front) and the soft palate (back)

palliative
(pal'-ee-a-tiv) (adj) describes a treatment that minimizes symptoms but does not cure the disease

pallor
(pal-'or) (n) abnormal paleness of the skin; deficiency of color

palpable
(pal'-pa-bl) (adj) able to be identified by touch

palpate
(pal'-payt) (v) examine by touch; feel

palpation
(pal-pay'-shun) (n) examination by feeling body parts

palpitations
(pal-pi-tay'-shuns) (n) stronger and more rapid heartbeats as felt by the patient; pounding or throbbing of the heart

palsy
(pawl'-zee) (n) partial paralysis; tremor of a body part

pancreas
(pan'-kree-as) (n) gland lying behind the stomach which secretes digestive enzymes and insulin

papillopathy
(pap-i-lop'-a-thee) (n) the blood supply to the optic disk and retina is obstructed; often producing low-tension glaucoma

papule
(pap'-yool) (n) a small, solid, raised skin lesion

para
(par'-a) (n) a woman who has given birth to one or more children; the term may be used in combination with a number or prefix to indicate how many times a woman has given birth

parasite
(par'-a-sIt) (n) an organism that lives on or in another organism and depends on it for nourishment

parenchyma
(pa-reng'-ki-ma) (n) the functional or specific tissue of an organ, not including supporting or connective tissue

parenteral
(pa-ren'-ter-al) (adj) not through the digestive system, such as introduction of nutrients into the veins or under the skin

parietal
(pa-rI'-e-tal) (adj) relating to the walls of a body cavity; a section (lobe) of the brain

paronychia
(par-O-nik'-ee-a) (n) infected skin around the nail

paroxysmal
(par-ok-siz'-mal) (adj) relating to or recurring in paroxysms (sudden, severe attacks of symptoms or convulsions)

Parvovirus
(par'-vO-vI-rus) (n) a genus of viruses; strain B19 can cause anemia in humans

patent (pa'-tent) (adj) open; unblocked

pathogen
(path'-O-jen) (n) any microorganism or substance that can cause a disease

pectoriloquy
(pek-tO-ril'-O-kwee) (n) voice sounds transmitted through the pulmonary structures, clearly audible on auscultation

pectus carinatum
(pek'-tus kar-i-nay'-tum) (n) forward protusion of the sternum; pigeon breast

pectus excavatum
(pek'-tus eks-ka-vay'-tum) (n) markedly sunken sternum; funnel breast

pedal
(ped'-al) (adj) relating to the foot

pelvic
(pel'-vik) (adj) relating to or located near the pelvis

pelvis
(pel'-vis) (n) the bones in the lower portion of the trunk of the body; the bones between the spine and legs

pemphigus
(pem'-fi-gus) (n) a distinctive group of diseases marked by successive crops of bullae

pendulous
(pen'-ju-lus) (adj) loosely hanging

percussion
(per-kush'-un) (n) a technique of physical examination in which the sound of fingers or a small tool tapping parts of the body is used to determine position and size of internal organs and to detect the presence of fluid

percutaneous
(per-kyoo-tay'-nee-us) (adj) through the skin

perforation
(per-fO-ray'-shun) (n) abnormal opening or hole

periauricular
(per'-ee-aw-rik'-yoo-lar) (adj) around the ear

pericardial
(per-i-kar'-dee-al) (adj) surrounding the heart; relating to the pericardium

pericardium
(per-i-kar'-dee-um) (n) sac around the heart allowing movement without friction

perineum
(per'-i-nee'-um) (n) the external region between the urethral opening and the anus, including the skin and underlying tissues

peripheral iridectomy
(per-if'-er-al ir-i-dek'- tO-mee) (n) procedure that creates a hole in the iris; used to relieve high intraocular pressure

peripheral nervous system
(PNS) (per-if'-er-al) (n) the part of the nervous system other than the brain and spinal cord

peripheral vascular disease
(pe-rif'-e-ral vas'-kyoo-lar) (n) any disorder affecting the blood circulatory system, except the heart

peristalsis
(per-i-stal'-sis) (n) waves of contraction and relaxation of the intestine, moving the contents onward

peritoneal
(per'-i-tO-nee'-al) (adj) relating to the peritoneum

peritoneum
(per-i-tO-nee'-um) (n) lining of the abdominal cavity

petechia
(pe-tee'-kee-a/pee-tek'-ee-a) (n) tiny reddish or purplish flat spot on the skin as a result of a tiny hemorrhage within the skin (usually used in the plural form, petechiae)

petechial
(pee-tee'-kee-al/pee-tek'-ee-al)) (adj) relating to or having petechiae

petit mal
(pe-tee' mahl) (n) a mild epileptic seizure with momentary loss of consciousness and sometimes minor twitching; especially seen in children

phacoemulsification
(fak'-O-ee-mul-si-fi-kay'-shun) (n) process that disintegrates a cataract using ultrasonic waves

phagocyte
(fag'-O-sIt) (n) a cell able to engulf and destroy bacteria, foreign particles, cellular debris, and other cells

phagocytosis
(fag'-O-sI-tO'-sis) (n) the process in which a cell engulfs and destroys bacteria, foreign particles, cellular debris, and other cells

pharyngitis
(far-in-jI-tis) (n) inflammation of the pharynx

pharynx
(far'-ingks) (n) throat; passageway for air from nasal cavity to larynx, and food from mouth to esophagus

phlebitis
(fle-bI'-tis) (n) inflammation of a vein

phlebotomy
(fle-bot'-O-mee) (n) incision into a vein for drawing blood

phonation
(fO-nay'-shun) (n) making sounds by using the vocal cords

photon
(fO'-ton) (n) a unit of radiant energy or light intensity

photophobia
(fO-tO-fO'-bee-a) (n) marked intolerance to light

pia mater
(pI'-a may'-ter/pee'-a mah'-ter) (n) the innermost of the three membranes surrounding the brain and spinal cord, carrying a rich supply of blood vessels; the other two are the arachnoid and the dura mater

pigment
(pig'-ment) (n) coloring substance

pineal gland
(pin'-ee-al) (n) pea-sized, cone-shaped gland in the brain which secretes melatonin

pinna
(pin'-a) (n) the external ear; auricle; pinnae (pin'-ee) (pl)

pituitary gland
(pi-too'-i-tayr-ee) (n) a small gland suspended from the base of the hypothalamus; secretes several different hormones; controls many vital functions either directly or indirectly by controlling other glands

plantar
(plan'-tar) (adj) relating to the undersurface (sole) of the foot

platelet
(playt'-let) (n) disc-shaped, small cellular element in the blood that is essential for blood clotting

pleura
(ploor'-a) (n) membrane lining the chest cavity and covering the lungs

pleural
(ploor'-al) (adj) relating to the pleura

pleurisy
(ploor'-I-see) (n) inflammation of the pleura; pleuritis

plexus
(plek'-sus) (n) a network of intersecting nerves, blood vessels, or lymphatic vessels

Pneumocystis carinii
(noo-mO-sis'-tis ka-rI'-nee-I) (n) a tiny parasite which causes Pneumocystis carinii pneumonia (PCP) in individuals with impaired immune systems

pneumonia
(noo-mO'-nee-a) (n) inflammation and congestion of the lung, usually due to infection by bacteria or viruses

pneumonitis
(noo-mO-nI'-tis) (n) inflammation of the lungs

pneumoperitoneum
(noo'-mO-per-i-ton-ee'-um) (n) presence of air or gas in the chest cavity

pneumothorax
(noo-mO-thor'-aks) (n) abnormal presence of air or gas in the chest cavity

poikilocytosis
(poy'-ki-lO-sI-tO'-sis) (n) having poikolocytes (abnormal and irregularly shaped red blood cells) in the blood

polycystic
(pol-ee-sis'-tik) (adj) having or consisting of many cysts

polyp
(pol'-ip) (n) an outgrowth of tissue from a mucous membrane

polyuria
(pol-ee-yoo'-ree-a) (n) excessive urinary output

pompholyx
(pom'-fO-liks) (n) a skin eruption primarily on the hands and feet; may be accompanied by excessive sweating

porphyrins
(pOr'-fi-rinz) (n) a group of pigmented compounds essential to life; for example, hemoglobin contains the heme porphyrin

postictal
(pOst-ik'-tal) (adj) relating to the period following a seizure

presbycusis
(prez'-bee-koo'-sis) (n) the loss of hearing acuity due to aging

presbyopia
(prez-bee-O'-pee-a) (n) farsightedness associated with aging

presents
(pre-sents') (v) appears; shows; displays; the symptoms displayed are the presenting symptoms

prognosis
(prog-nO'-sis) (n) the expected outcome of a disease

prolapse
(prO-laps') (n) dropping of an organ from its normal position, such as the uterus into the vagina

prophylaxis
(prO-fi-lak'-sis) (n) prevention of disease or its spread

proprioception
(prO'-pree-O-sep'-shun) (n) sensations due to receiving stimuli from muscles, tendons, or other internal tissues, especially regarding body position and movement

prostate gland
(pros'-tayt) (n) situated at the base of the bladder, surrounding the beginning of the urethra in the male

prostatic
(pros-tat'-ik) (adj) relating to the prostate gland

prosthesis
(pros-thee'-sis) (n) artificial replacement for a diseased or missing part of the body, such as artificial limbs; prostheses (pl)

protease
(prO'-tee-ays) an enzyme that breaks down proteins

protease inhibitor
(n) an agent that inhibits (prevents or slows down) the release of protease

proteinaceous
(prO'-tee-nay'-shus/prO'-tee-i-nay'-shus) (adj) relating to or resembling proteins

proteinuria
(prO-tee-noo'-ree-a) (n) presence of abnormally large amounts of protein in the urine

proton
(prO'-ton) (n) a subatomic particle with a positive charge

proximal
(prok'-si-mal) (adj) nearest to a point of reference or center of the body

pruritic
(pru-ri'-tic) (adj) itching

pruritus
(proo-rI'-tus) (n) itching skin condition

Pseudomonas
(soo-dO-mO'-nas) (n) a genus of bacteria commonly found in soil and water and which may cause infection

psoriasis
(sO-rI'-a-sis) (n) chronic skin disease in which reddish scaly patches develop

psychosomatic
(sI'-kO-sO-mat'-ik) (adj) relating to the influence of the mind on the body; relating to physical ailments without physical causes

pterygium
(ter-ij'-ee-um) (n) web eye; an outward growth of tissue of the eye

pterygoid plate
(ter'-i-goyd) (n) wing-shaped bones at the back of the nasal cavity

ptosis
(tO'-sis) (n) sagging of the upper eyelid

punch biopsy
(punch bI'-op-see) (n) a special instrument is used to take a small cylindrical piece of tissue for microscopic examination

pupil
(pyoo'-pil) (n) the round opening in the center of the iris which opens or closes to adjust to light

pupillary
(pyoo'-pi-layr-ee) (adj) relating to the pupil of the eye

purpura
(pur'-poo-ra) (n) any of several bleeding disorders in which the escape of blood into tissues below the skin causes reddish or purplish spots

purulent
(pyoor'-u-lent) (adj) relating to, containing, or forming pus

pustular
(pus'-choo-lar) (adj) relating to or having pustules

pustule
(pus'-chool) (n) small pus-containing elevation on the skin

pyelogram
(pI'-el-O-gram) (n) x-ray of the kidney and ureters; usually a radiopaque dye is injected into the patient to show the outline of the kidney and associated structures

pyrexia
(pI-rek'-see-a) (n) fever

pyrosis
(pI-rO'-sis) (n) heartburn, caused by reflux of stomach contents into the esophagus

quadriparesis
(kwa'-dri-pa-ree-sis) (n) weakness or paralysis of both arms and legs

radial keratotomy
(ray'-dee-al ker-ah-tot'-O-mee) (n) incision(s) in the cornea radiating out from the center

radiculopathy
(ra-dik'-yoo-lop'-a-thee) (n) disease of nerve roots

radiograph
(ray'-dee-O-graf) (n) an image produced through exposure to x-rays; roentgenogram

radiopaque
(ray-dee-O-payk') (adj) opaque to x-rays or other radiation; an injection of a radiopaque dye or substance may be used to visualize areas of the body by x-ray

radiotherapy
(ray'-dee-O-thayr'-a-pee) (n) the treatment of disease by application of radium, ultraviolet, and other types of radiation

rales
(rahls) (n) abnormal sounds, such as rattling or bubbling, heard on auscultation of the lungs

ramus
(ray'-mus) (n) branch, especially of a nerve or blood vessel

recession
(ree-sesh'-un) (n) the withdrawal of a part from its normal position

rectal
(rek'-tal) (adj) relating to the rectum, the lower part of the large intestine

rectovaginal
(rek'-tO-vaj'-i-nal) (adj) relating or located near the rectum and vagina

rectus
(rec'-tus) (adj) relating to the rectus muscle of the eye

referral
(ree-fer'-al) (n) when a physician sends a patient to another physician

reflex
(ree'-fleks) (n) an involuntary response to a stimulus

reflux
(ree'-fluks) (n) abnormal backflow

regimen
(rej'-I-men) (n) plan of therapy, including drugs

regression
(ree-gresh'-un) (n) returning to an earlier condition

regurgitation
(ree-ger'-ji-tay'-shun) (n) a backward flowing, as a backflow of blood through a defective heart valve or the bringing up of gas or undigested food from the stomach

renal failure
(ree'-nal) (n) inability of the kidneys to function

residual
(re-zid'-yoo-al) (adj) related to a residue which is left behind

respiration
(res-pi-ray'-shun) (n) inhalation and exhalation; the exchange of gases—oxygen and carbon dioxide—between an organism and the environment

respiratory
(res'-per-a-tOr-ee) (adj) relating to respiration

respiratory distress syndrome
(res'-pi-ra-tOr-ee dis-tres' sin'-drOm) (n) acute lung disease, especially in premature newborn babies, caused by a lack of surfactant in the lung tissue

reticulocyte
(re-tik'-yoo-lO-sIt) (n) an immature red blood cell

retina
(ret'-i-na) (n) innermost layer of the eyeball that receives images formed by the lens and transmits visual impulses through the optic nerve to the brain; composed of light-sensitive nerves

retinitis pigmentosa
(ret-in-I'-tis) (n) a inflammation of the retina with pigment changes, eventually leading to blindness

retinoblastoma
(ret'-i-nO-blas-tO'-ma) (n) malignant sarcoma or neoplasm of the retina; hereditary and generally occurring in young children

retinopathy
(ret-i-nop'-a-thee) (n) any disorder of the retina without inflammation

retinoscopy
(ret'-i-nos'-ko-pee) (n) light beam test used to detect refractive errors

retraction
(ree-trak'-shun) (n) drawing back

retrograde
(ret'-rO-grayd) (adj) moving or going backward

rhabdomyosarcoma
(rab'-dO-mI'-O-sar-kO'-ma) (n) highly malignant tumor developing from striated muscle cells

rheumatic fever
(roo-mat'-ik fee'-ver) (n) fever following infection with Streptococcus bacteria; may affect the joints, skin, and heart

rheumatoid
(roo'-ma-toyd) (adj) resembling rheumatism, with pain, inflammation, and deformity of the joints

rhinitis
(rI-nI'-tis) (n) inflammation of the mucous membrane of the nose

rhinophyma
(rI-nO-fI'-ma) (n) enlargement of the nose

rhinoplasty
(rI'-nO-plas-tee) (n) surgery to correct a defect in the nose or to change its shape

rhonchus
(rong'-kus) (n) abnormal sound heard on auscultation of the chest, usually during expiration

rigidity
(ri-jid'-i-tee) (n) stiffness; inflexibility

Rinne test
(rin'-ne) (n) also Rinne's (rin'-ez); a hearing test comparing perception of air and bone conduction in one ear with a tuning fork; normally air conduction is more acute

roentgenogram
(rent'-gen-O-gram) (n) a type of x-ray using a film or plate sensitive to roentgen rays (x-rays); radiogram

roentgenology
(rent'-gen-ol'-o-jee) (n) the study of the use of roentgen rays (x-rays) for diagnosis and therapy

rubella
(roo-bel'-a) (n) a contagious viral disease with fever and a red rash; German measles

sac
(sak) (n) pouch

sagittal
(saj'-i-tal) (adj) relating to a line from front to back in the middle of an organ or the body

salivary gland
(sal'-i-vayr-ee) (n) one of the glands that secrete saliva into the mouth

saphenous vein
(sa-fee'-nus vayn) (n) either of two main veins in the leg that drain blood from the foot

scabies
(skay'-beez) (n) contagious rash with intense itching; caused by mites

scan
(n) scanning a tissue, organ, or system using a special apparatus that displays and records its image, such as computer tomography (CAT scan); the image so obtained

sciatica
(sI-at'-i-ka) (n) acute pain following the pathway of the sciatic nerve; radiates from the hip, down the back of the thigh, and into the lower leg

scirrhous
(skir'-us) (adj) describing or resembling a hard, fibrous, malignant tumor

sclera
(skle'-rah) (n) white of the eye; the tough, outer covering of the eye

sclerosis
(skle-rO'-sis) (n) condition characterized by hardening of a tissue or organ, resulting from inflammation and mineral deposits

sclerostomy
(skle-ros'-tO-mee) (n) surgical formation of an opening in the sclera

scoliosis
(skO-lee-O'-sis) (n) abnormal curvature of the spine to one side

scotoma
(skO-tO'-ma) (n) a blind spot; a small area of defective vision

scrotal
(skrO'-tal) (adj) relating to the scrotum

scrotum
(skrO'-tum) (n) the pouch of skin containing the testes, the male reproductive glands

sebaceous
(see-bay'-shus) (adj) relating to sebum

seborrhea
(seb-O-ree'-a) (n) overactivity of the oil glands of the skin

sebum
(see'-bum) (n) an oily secretion of the oil glands of the skin

seed
(n) as related to oncology, it is the beginning of a tumor

seeding
(n) the local spreading of immature tumor cells

semicircular canals
(sem'-ee-sir'-kyoo-lar ka-nals') (n) three fluid-filled loops in the labyrinth of the inner ear, associated with the body's sense of balance

sensorineural deafness
(sen'-sOr-i-noor'-al) (n) hearing impairment due to nerve disturbance

septum
(sep'-tum) (n) division between two cavities or two masses of tissue, such as the nasal septum; septa (pl)

sequela
(see-kwel'-a) (n) an abnormal condition resulting from a disease; sequelae (see-kwel'-ee) (pl)

serous
(seer'-us) (adj) relating to or having a watery consistency

serous otitis media
(seer'-us O-tI'-tis mee'-dee-a) (n) inflammation of the middle ear accompanied by production of a watery fluid (serum)

sessile
(ses'-il) (adj) attached directly at the base; not on a stalk

Seton procedure
(n) placing a tube in the anterior chamber to drain fluid and decrease the intraocular pressure

sheath
(n) structure surrounding an organ, body part, or object

shotty
(shot'-ee) (adj) having a rubbery type of feel to the touch; as shotty nodes

sickle cell anemia
(sik'-l sel a-nee'-mee-a) (n) hereditary blood disease in which abnormal hemoglobin causes red blood cells to become sickle-shaped, fragile, and nonfunctional, leading to many acute and chronic complications

sigmoid colon
(sig'-moyd kO'-lon) (n) the last part of the colon (large intestine) before the rectum

sigmoidoscopy
(sig'-moy-dos'-ko-pee) (n) the inspection of the rectum and colon

sinus
(sI'-nus) (n) a passageway or hollow in a bone or other tissue

sinusitis
(sI-nu-sI'-tis) (n) inflammation of the nasal sinuses, occurring as a result of an upper respiratory infection, an allergic response, or a defect of the nose

sinus rhythm
(si'-nus rith'-um) (n) normal cardiac rhythm

sleep apnea syndrome
(ap'-nee-a) (n) breathing stops, briefly and periodically, due to partial upper airway obstruction during sleep

slit-lamp
(n) instrument consisting of a microscope and a thin, bright beam of light; used to examine the eye

sonography
(so-nog'-ra-fi) (n) ultrasonography; use of high frequency sound waves to produce an image of an organ or tissue

sonometer
(son-O-mee'-ter) (n) a bell-shaped instrument used to measure hearing

speculum
(spek'-yoo-lum) (n) an instrument used for examining the interior of a cavity

sphenoidal sinus
(sfee-noy'-dal) (n) one of two sinuses in the sphenoid bone opening to the nasal cavity

sphincter
(sfingk'-ter) (n) a muscle that encircles a duct or opening and controls its opening and closing

sphincterotomy
(sfink-tur-ot'-O-mee) (n) procedure that produces cuts in the iris sphincter muscle to allow pupillary enlargement

splenectomy
(sple-nek'-tO-mee) (n) surgical removal of the spleen

spondylitis
(spon-di-lI'-tis) (n) inflammation of one or more vertebrae

sporadic
(spO-rad'-ik) (adj) occurring occasionally or in isolated situations

sprain
(n) injurv to a joint by overstretching the ligaments; (v) to injure a joint and sometimes the nearby ligaments or tendons

sputum
(spyoo'-tum) (n) spit; expectorated material

squamous
(skway'-mus) (adj) scaly; covered with or consisting of scales

stapes
(stay'-peez) (n) the smallest and innermost of the three auditory bones in the inner ear; stirrup

staphylococcemia
(staf'-i-lO-kok-see'-mee-a) (n) the presence of staphylococci (bacterial microorganisms) in the blood

Staphylococcus aureus
(staf-il-O-kok'-us awr'-ee-us) (n) a common species of Staphylococcus (a bacteria), present on nasal mucous membranes and skin and causes pus-producing infections

stenocardia
(sten-O-kar'-dee-a) (n) an attack of intense chest pain; also called angina pectoris

stenosis
(ste-nO'-sis) (n) narrowing or constriction of a passageway or opening, such as a blood vessel

sterile
(ster'-il) (adj) free from living microorganisms

sternum
(ster'-num) (n) the breast bone

steroid
(steer'-oyd) (n) any of a large number of similar chemical substances, either natural or synthetic; many are hormones; produced mainly in the adrenal cortex and gonads

strabismus
(stra-biz'-mus) (n) improper alignment of eyes; cross eye(s)

strain
(n) injury, usually to muscle, caused by overstretching or overuse; (v) to injure muscles by overstretching or overuse

strep
(n) short form of Streptococcus

Streptococcus
(strep-tO-kok'-us) (n) a genus of bacteria; many species cause disease in humans

stress incontinence
(stres in-kon'-ti-nens) (n) inability to retain urine under tension, such as sneezing or coughing

sty
(stI) (n) an infection of a marginal gland of the eyelid; stye

subcutaneous
(sub-kyoo-tay'-nee-us) (adj) under the skin

subdural hematoma
(sub-doo'-ral hee-ma-tO'-ma/hem-a-tO'-ma) (n) an accumulation of blood under the dura mater surrounding the brain

subjective data
(sub-jek'-tiv day'-tah) (n) information revealed by the patient to the healthcare provider

sublingual
(sub-ling'-gwahl) (adj) beneath the tongue

submandibular
(subman-dib'-yoo-lar) (adj) under the lower jaw

substernal
(sub-ster'-nal) (adj) situated beneath the sternum (breast bone)

supine
(soo-pIn') (adj) lying on the back

suppuration
(sup'-yu-ray'-shun) (n) the production or discharge of pus

suprapubic
(soo-pra-pyoo'-bik) (adj) above the pubic bones

symphysis
(sim'-fi-sis) (n) joint in which fibrocartilage firmly unites the bones

syncopal
(sin'-kO-pal) (adj) relating to fainting

syncope
(sin'-ko-pee) (n) fainting

synovial fluid
(si-nO'-vee-al floo'-id) (n) protective lubricating fluid around joints

systemic lupus erythematosus
(sis-tem'-ik loo'-pus er-i-them'-a-tO-sis/er-i-thee'-ma-tO-sis) (n) a chronic disease with inflammatory symptoms in various systems of the body; characteristics of the disease and the systems involved may vary widely

T cell
(n) a type of lymphocyte; responsible for cell-mediated immunity

tachycardia
(tak'-I-kar'-dee-a) (n) rapid heart rate

tachycardiac
(tak'-e-kar'-dee-ak) (adj) relating to or suffering from an abnormally rapid heart rate

tachypnea
(tak-ip-nee'-a) (n) rapid rate of breathing

tangent screen test
(n) maps the field of vision using a marker

Tanner staging
(n) method of indicating the sexual development of a person

telogen
(tel'-O-jen) (n) the resting phase of the hair growth cycle

testicular
(tes-tik'-yoo-lar) (adj) relating to the testes, the male reproductive glands

texture
(teks'-chur) (n) character, structure, and feel of parts of the body

thecal
(thee'-kal) (adj) relating to an enveloping sheath or capsule

thelarche
(thee-lar'-kee) (n) the beginning of breast development in girls

thermodilution
(ther'-mO-di-loo'-shun) (n) method of determining cardiac output; involves injecting a cold liquid into the bloodstream and measuring the temperature change downstream

thorax
(thor'-aks) (n) the chest

thrombocytopenia
(throm'-bO-sI-tO-pee'-nee-a) (n) an abnormal decrease in platelets in the blood, resulting in bleeding and easy bruising

thrombocytopenic
(throm'-bO-sI-tO-pee'-nik) (adj) relating to thrombocytopenia

thrombophlebitis
(throm'-bO-fle-bI'-tis) (n) inflammation of a vein with clot formation (thrombus)

thrombosis
(throm-bO'-sis) (n) formation of a blood clot in a blood vessel

thrush
(n) infection with the fungus Candida, causing white patches in the mouth and throat

thyroid
(thI'-royd) (n) a gland in the neck that secretes thyroid hormone

thyromegaly
(thI-rO-meg'-a-lee) (n) enlargement of the thyroid gland

tibia
(tib'-ee-a) (n) the larger bone of the lower leg; shin bone

tibial
(tib'-ee-al) (adj) relating to the tibia

tinea
(tin'-ee-a) (n) fungal infection; such as tinea pedis or athlete's foot

tinnitus
(ti-nI'-tus) (n) noise, such as ringing, in the ears

titer
(tI'-ter) (n) strength or concentration of a solution; a unit of measurement usually expressed as a ratio that indicates the minimum concentration of an antibody before losing its power to react to a specific antigen

tomographic
(tO-mog'-ra-feek) (adj) referring to x-ray technique which displays an organ or tissue at a particular depth

tonometry
(tO-nom'-et-ree) (n) a test that measures intraocular pressure

torso
(tor'-sO) (n) trunk of the body

toxoplasmosis
(tok'-sO-plaz-mO'-sis) (n) disease caused by a protozoan parasite

trabeculectomy
(tra-bek-yoo-lek'-tO-mee) (n) surgical removal of a section of the cornea to decrease intraocular pressure in patients with severe glaucoma

trabeculoplasty
(tra-bek'-yoo-lO-plas'-tee) (n) surgical procedure that decreases intraocular pressure in open-angle glaucoma

trachea
(tray'-kee-a) (n) the windpipe

tracheostomy
(tray'-kee-os'-tO-mee) (n) a surgical opening into the trachea

tracheotomy
(tray'-kee-ot'-O-mee) (n) the surgical procedure in which a tracheostomy is created

tragus
(tray'-gus) (n) the small projection of cartilage in front of the external opening to the ear canal

transmural
(trans-myoo'-ral) (adj) through the wall of an organ or other hollow structure

transperineal
(adj) across or through the perineal region between the urethral opening and the anus, including the skin and underlying tissues

transurethral
(trans-yoo-ree'-thral) (adj) through the urethra, such as a surgical procedure

transverse
(trans-vers') (adj) at right angles to the long axis of the body or an organ; crosswise; side to side

trocar
(trO'-kar) (n) sharply pointed surgical instrument used to provide a tube through which fluids can be instilled or removed

trochanter
(trO-kan'-ter) (n) one of the projections at the upper end of the femur (thigh bone)

tumor
(too'-mor) (n) abnormal mass of tissue; neoplasm

turbinate
(ter'-bi-nayt) (n) one of several thin, spongy, bony plates within the walls of the nasal cavity

turgor
(ter'-gOr) (n) fullness; the normal resiliency of the skin

tympanic membrane
(tim-pan'-ik) (n) eardrum

tympanoplasty
(tim'-pa-nO-plas-tee) (n) surgical repair of the middle ear

Tzanck's smear
(tsangks smeer) (n) a method to help diagnose skin lesions by the miscroscopic examination of material from them

ulcerative colitis
(ul'-ser-a-tiv kO-lI'-tis) (n) a chronic disease characterized by ulcers in the colon and rectum

ultrasound
(ul'-tra-sownd) (n) sound waves at very high frequencies used in the technique of ultrasonography to aid diagnosis

umbo
(um'-bO) (n) the inner surface of the tympanic membrane where it connects with the malleus in the middle ear

unilateral
(yoo-ni-lat'-e-ral) (adj) affecting or occurring on only one side

unremarkable
(adj) nothing unusual is noted

upper respiratory infection
(URI) (n) an infection of the upper respiratory tract such as the common cold, laryngitis, sinusitis, and tonsillitis

ureter
(yoo-ree'-ter/yoo'-ree-ter) (n) either of a pair of tubes that carry urine from the kidney to the urinary bladder

ureteral
(yoo-ree'-te-ral) (adj) relating to the ureters

urethra
(yoo-ree'-thra) (n) a tube that drains urine from the bladder to the outside

urethroscopy
(yoo-ree-thros'-ko-pee) (n) an examination of the inside of the urethra with a urethroscope, a lighted instrument

urticaria
(er-ti-kar'-ee-a) (n) hives; an eruption of itching red, raised lesions

urticarial
(er-ti-kar'-ee-al) (adj) relating to or having urticaria

uterine
(yoo'-ter-in/yoo'-ter-In) (adj) relating to the uterus (the female reproductive organ where the fertilized egg develops before birth; the womb)

uveitis
(yoo-vee-I'-tis) (n) inflammation of the uvea, including the choroid and the iris

uvula
(yoo'-vyoo-la) (n) small, fleshy structure hanging from the soft palate in the mouth

uvulitis
(yoo-vyoo-lI'-tis) (n) inflammation of the uvula

uvulopalatopharyngoplasty
(yoo'-vyoo-lO-pal'-a-tO-fa-rin'-gO-plas-tee) (n) UPPP for short; a surgical treatment for sleep apnea for patients who cannot tolerate or respond to medical therapies

varicella
(var-i-sel'-a) (n) chickenpox; a highly contagious viral disease

vascular
(vas'-kyoo-lar) (adj) relating to the blood vessels

vascularity
(vas-kyoo-lar'-i-tee) (n) the blood vessels in a part of the body

venous
(vee'-nus) (adj) relating to a vein or veins

ventricle
(ven'-tri-kl) (n) either of the two lower chambers of the heart; areas of the brain that produce and drain cerebral spinal fluid (CSF)

ventriculogram
(ven-trik'-yoo-lO-gram) (n) an x-ray of the ventricles

ventriculography
(ven-trik-yoo-log'-ra-fee) (n) x-ray visualization of heart ventricles after injection of a radiopaque substance

verrucous
(ve-roo'-kOs) (adj) having warts or resembling a wart

vertex
(ver'-teks) (n) the crown or top of the head

vertigo
(ver'-tigO) (n) dizziness

vesical
(ves'-i-kl) (adj) relating to the gallbladder or urinary bladder

vesicle
(ves'-i-kl) (n) blister; small, raised skin lesion containing clear fluid

vestibulum
(ves-tib'-yoo-lum) (n) the central cavity of the labyrinth in the inner ear, between the cochlea and the semicircular canals

viable
(vI'-a-bl) (adj) capable of surviving; living

vibrissae
(vI-bris'-a) (n) nose hairs

villi
(vil'-I) (n) many tiny projections from the surface of a mucous membrane; villus (sing)

villous
(vil'-us) (adj) relating to or having villi

virus
(vI'-rus) (n) an organism or the infection caused by the organism; the organism is much smaller than bacteria; it depends completely on the host and is unaffected by common antibiotics

viscera
(vis'-er-a) (n) main internal organs within the trunk of the body, especially those in the abdominal cavity

visceral
(vis'-er-al) (adj) relating to or located near the viscera

visual acuity
(vizh'-yoo-al a-kyoo'-i-tee) (n) clearness of vision, such as 20/20 visual acuity

visualization
(n) the act of viewing an object, especially the picture of a body structure as obtained by x-ray study

vitiligo
(vi-ti-lee'-gO) (n) white patches, due to loss of pigment, appearing on the skin

vitreous humor
(vit'-ree-us hyoo'-mer) (adj) glassy; gelatin-like substance within the eyeball

vortex
(vOr'-teks) (n) whirlpool; resembling a whirlpool

vulva
(vul'-va) (n) external female genital organs; vulvae (pl)

vulvar
(vul'-var) (adj) relating to the vulva

Weber test
(web'-er) (n) a hearing test performed with a tuning fork placed at points in the middle of the skull to determine where the vibration is heard (not where it is felt)

Western blot
(n) a laboratory test to detect the presence of antibodies to specific antigens in the blood

wheal
(hweel) (n) a raised, red circumscribed lesion usually due to an allergic reaction; usually accompanied by intense itching; welt

wheezing
(hweez'-ing) (n) breathing with difficulty and with a whistling sound; can be heard aloud and/or on auscultation

xanthoma
(zan-thO'-mah) (n) yellowish nodules in or under the skin, especially in the eyelids

xanthopsia
(zan-thop'-see-a) (n) yellow vision; a condition in which everything seen appears yellowish

xeromammogram
(zeer'-O-mam'-o-gram) (n) type of x-ray of the breast

xerostomia
(zeer-O-stO'-mee-a) (n) dryness of the mouth

xiphoid
(zif'-oyd) (adj) refers to the xiphoid process, the cartilage at the lower end of the sternum (breast bone)

yolk sac
(yOk sak) (n) a membranous sac surrounding the food yolk in the embryo

Editing Reference Guide

REPAIRING SENTENCE FRAGMENTS AND RUN-ON SENTENCES

One of the most common trouble spots in workplace documents such as letters and reports is faulty sentence construction. These problems take the form of either incomplete sentences (sentence fragments) or run-on sentences (two sentences that "run together" without the correct punctuation separating them). To be able to correct fragments and run-ons, you must know what makes a sentence complete. You also must know how to punctuate a sentence so the reader knows where it begins and ends.

Every complete sentence contains a subject and a verb and expresses a thought. The subject is generally a noun or pronoun, and the verb always expresses some action or state of being (am, was, will be, etc.). Sometimes the subject is implied but not stated.

Sentence fragments
A fragment is a group of words that expresses a partial thought and leaves the reader puzzled. It is not a complete sentence.

Run-on sentences
A run-on sentence consists of two sentences that are not separated by punctuation. If the second sentence is closely related, use a semicolon to connect them. Otherwise, key them as two individual sentences, each ending with a period (or a question mark or exclamation mark).

Exceptions to the rules

Certain sections of medical reports may contain incomplete sentences. For example, a doctor may dictate laboratory values that do not have to be written in sentence form. The physical examination may or may not be in sentence form.

Narrative dictation (e.g., the history of present illness) must be in complete sentences. When historical items are placed in a formal list, however, they do not have to be in complete sentences.

Outpatient chart notes are less formal than other types of dictation and may be dictated in clipped sentences. A doctor may dictate without using subjects and articles. These notes should be transcribed as dictated.

CREATING SUBJECT-VERB AGREEMENT

The subject and verb of a sentence must match in number and person. Singular verbs require singular subjects, and plural verbs require plural subjects. Use first-person verbs with first-person subjects (I, we), second-person verbs with second-person subjects (you), and third-person verbs with third-person subjects (he, she, it, they).

Note: Sometimes subjects can "look" plural, but they function as one unit and are singular in meaning. Be sure you use singular verbs in such cases.

Complicating factors: inverted order sentences; intervening words and phrases
Inverted order sentences: Sentences are usually written with the subject before the verb. However, sometimes the sentence is inverted, meaning that the verb comes first. This can cause some confusion in achieving subject-verb agreement. Many of these sentences begin with Here or There.

Intervening words and phrases: In complicated sentences, first identify the verb and then the subject(s) of that verb. Then be sure you choose a singular verb for a singular subject or a plural verb for a plural subject. Disregard the parts of the sentence that come between the subject and the verb.

Creating Agreement between Pronouns and Antecedents
Remember that a pronoun takes the place of a noun in a sentence. Words such as she, he, it, they, us, them, I, and you are pronouns. Pronouns must agree in person and number with the nouns they represent, which are called antecedents. The pronouns this, that, these, and those must also agree with the nouns they modify.

The pronouns them and their are plural forms. Do not use them for singular meanings. When gender is not known, try to create a sentence that does not require the awkward construction of his/her.

A pronoun can represent a subject or an object. That is, the pronoun can be either the performer of an action or the recipient of the action. Subject pronouns are I, you, he, she, it, we, they. Object pronouns are me, you, him, her, it, us, them.

Most people do not have difficulty achieving pronoun agreement in simple sentences that contain one pronoun in the predicate, e.g., Bill dislikes me. However, problems do come about when a sentence contains multiple nouns and pronouns, e.g., Bill dislikes he/him and I/me. To select the correct pronoun, simplify the sentence by looking only at the verb and the pronoun in question. Your ear should help you make the right choice.

Who versus whom
Use the pronoun who for the subject of a verb; use whom for the object of a verb. In sentences or questions that contain a who/whom dilemma, substitute he for who and him for whom and then trust your ear.

Myself, himself, etc.
Myself, yourselves, herself, etc. are reflexive pronouns, meaning that they must reflect back to a noun or pronoun within that same sentence (Mikey wrapped the gift all by himself.) Many dictators mistakenly refer to themselves as myself instead of me (He was seen by myself in the clinic). Do not use a reflexive in a sentence when a simple personal pronoun is appropriate.

PUNCTUATING WITH COMMAS

In a spoken conversation, meaning is conveyed through tone of voice, gestures, and pauses. We pause and change the inflection in our voices to clarify meaning. In written language, punctuation marks serve as "road signs" for readers. Punctuation clarifies meaning and prevents confusion.

To introduce
Use a comma to set off an introductory word or phrase. A sentence that is in the natural order (subject followed by verb and modifiers) does not contain an introductory clause and does not need an introductory comma. When a sentence is out of the natural order (inverted), a comma is needed to help the reader identify the important information of the sentence. Be careful to place introductory phrases close to the word they modify; otherwise your sentence may be grammatically incorrect and/or cause confusion to readers.

To separate
Coordinate conjunctions (and, but, or, nor, for, so) join two main clauses into one sentence. Use a comma immediately before the coordinate conjunction. Remember that a main clause contains a subject, verb, and complement and can stand alone. If the main clauses are very short, you may omit the comma.

Use a comma to separate items in a series.

Use a comma between adjectives that equally modify the same noun if the and is omitted.

Do not use a comma between two adjectives if you would not use and.

When placing commas, be sure you do not separate the subject from the verb. Even if the subject is long and drawn out, it must not be separated from the verb by a comma.

To enclose
Use commas to set off nonessential or interrupting words or phrases from the rest of the sentence. Think of commas that enclose as parentheses. By enclosing information in commas, you are telling the reader that the information is not vital to the meaning of the sentence.

USING DASHES, QUOTATION MARKS, AND PARENTHESES

Dashes
Use dashes to set off interrupting phrases from the rest of the sentence. They indicate a change in thought or a side comment not essential to the meaning of the sentence. Use them sparingly, especially in any type of formal document.

Note: Key dashes with no spaces before or after them. Proportional fonts such as New Times Roman, the default for Word 6 and 7 and WordPerfect 6.1 and 7 for Windows, include a special dash character. If you are using a monospaced font such as Courier, create a dash by keying two hyphens.

Quotation marks
Use quotation marks to surround the exact words someone has spoken. The marks should appear in pairs, with one set at the beginning of the quote and the other at the end. The placement of other punctuation marks with quotes frequently causes confusion.

Always key a period and comma inside the quotation marks.

Place a colon or semicolon outside quotation marks.

Place a question mark outside the quotation marks if the entire sentence is a question but inside if only the quoted words are a question.

History and physical reports may begin with a chief complaint. If the chief complaint is dictated in first person, key it in quotation marks. If the quoted material is not a complete sentence, do not start the quote with a capital letter (unless the first word is a proper noun or an acronym).

Use quotation marks to draw attention to words and phrases or to designate slang, cliches, or nicknames.

Use quotation marks to set off titles of magazine or newspaper articles and chapters of a book. The titles of magazines, newspapers, brochures, and books are placed in italics (in proportional spaced fonts such as New Times Roman) or underlined (in Courier).

Parentheses
Use parentheses to enclose side thoughts or words not vital to the main idea of the sentence.

Use parentheses to enclose acronyms or abbreviations.

Use parentheses to enclose numbers when a list is given in paragraph form.

If parentheses enclose a complete sentence that does not interrupt another sentence, place the period inside the parentheses.

If parentheses enclose an interrupting statement within a sentence, do not place a period inside the parentheses.

USING MODIFIERS TO ACHIEVE CORRECT MEANING

Modifiers are words, phrases, and clauses that describe or tell more about another word, phrase, or clause. Good transcriptionists pay careful attention to the placement of modifiers to ensure clear meaning of sentences.

Related words should be placed together.
Place modifiers as close as possible to the words being modified. Many transcription "bloopers" are caused by misplaced or dangling modifiers, particularly prepositional phrases or phrases beginning with ing words. These phrases are adjective phrases that modify a noun. Miscommunication occurs when the phrase is not placed next to the noun it modifies.

Note: Be very careful when altering dictation. The fact that you like a certain sentence turned around or reworded is not enough to merit changing the dictation. Reserve rewording for instances when the dictation is not clear because of the misplacement or misuse of a modifier. If you must edit, always try to use the dictator's original words for terms, procedures, instruments, and diseases. Too much editing can be considered tampering.

FORMING PLURALS

Chapter 2 reviewed the guidelines for creating agreement between subjects and verbs. The guidelines are based on the principle that plural subjects require plural verbs and singular subjects require singular verbs. Since nouns and pronouns function as subjects of sentences, it is important to know the general rules for creating the plural forms of medical terms.

Generally, most nouns are pluralized by adding s or es to the singular form. The same rules usually apply to nouns in medical reports. However, many medical words and terms are of Latin and Greek origin; therefore they do not follow the English rules. For example, diagnosis is not pluralized as diagnosises, nucleus as nucleuses, or diverticulum as diverticulums. Consult a medical dictionary when necessary.

As you become more familiar with the medical language, forming and/or recognizing plural forms will become easier. The following rules for making plural forms will be helpful:

1. If the singular form ends in a, make the plural by adding e. (vertebra—vertebrae).
2. If the singular form ends in um, change the um to a. (diverticulum—diverticula).
3. If the singular form ends in us, change the us to i. (fungus—fungi).
4. If the singular form ends in is, change the is to es. (diagnosis—diagnoses).
5. If the singular form ends in ax or ix, change the x to ces. (thorax—thoraces; cervix—cervices).
6. If the singular form ends in ex, change the ex to ices. (index—indices).
7. If the singular form ends in nx, change the x to ges. (pharynx—pharynges).
8. If the singular form ends in en, change the en to ina. (lumen—lumina).
9. If the singular form ends in on, change the on to a. (phenomenon—phenomena).
10. If the singular form ends in ma, add ta. (condyloma—condylomata). Note that it is also acceptable to form plurals of these words just by adding s. (carcinoma—carcinomas).

USING CAPITALS CORRECTLY

Capitalization is a signal writers can use to tell the reader that what is capitalized is important or specialized. However, the overuse of capitals diminishes their effect and may confuse rather than help the reader. Transcriptionists need to know the basic rules of capitalization and how and when to apply them.

Proper nouns
Capitalize formal names of persons, places, and organizations.

Capitalize languages and races. Do not capitalize skin color (black, white)

Capitalize days of the week, months, and holidays, but not seasons.

Capitalize trade names, but do not capitalize generic drugs.

Capitalize a job title only when it precedes a name and is used as that person's title. Do not capitalize the title when it replaces or renames the person.

Capitalize the genus but not the species of bacteria.

Do not capitalize hospital department names.

Abbreviations
Do not capitalize Latin abbreviations that deal with drug dosage (b.i.d., a.c., p.o.). According to the AAMT, the correct form for Latin abbreviations is lowercase with periods between each letter.

Capitalize the abbreviation NPO, which stands for nil per os (nothing by mouth). NPO is generally capitalized because it is very important information. If the term goes unnoticed in a patient's record, there could be life-threatening consequences.

Acronyms
Acronyms are abbreviations formed using the initial letters of words or phrases. No periods are required.

Eponyms
Eponyms are adjectives created from proper nouns. The terms usually derive from the name of the person who identified the disease, developed the protocol, or designed the instrument. The eponym itself, but not the noun, is capitalized.

Drug allergies
Capitalize all letters of a drug name listed under an allergies heading. This is very important information that must attract attention.

Document elements
Capitalize the first letter of a formal list.

Capitalize headings and the first word after a heading.

USING NUMBERS IN WORD OR FIGURE FORM

Numbers are written in figures or words, depending on the situation. As a basic rule, spell out numbers up to and including ten. Use figures for numbers above ten. Exceptions to the basic rule are discussed below.

First word of a sentence
Spell out numbers that are the first word of a sentence.

Large numbers spelled out may slow down the reader. Instead, rewrite the sentence so the number appears in a different location.

Units of measurement and lab values
Use figures when indicating quantity with a unit of measurement or with lab values.

Similar types of data
When numbers in a sentence describe the same kind of data, express them in the same style regardless of their size.

Dates
Use figures for short-form dates with slashes and for the day of a month. A day that precedes a month should be expressed in ordinal numbers (numbers expressing place or position as in first, second, third).

The military and international style for expressing dates reverses the day and month, with no commas in between. Follow this format if your client or employer prefers.

Age
Express ages and other vital statistics in figures.

Time
Use figures to express times of day. No zeros are required when the time falls on the hour.

Many medical facilities follow the military style of expressing time. Military time uses no colons, and instead of starting over at 12 noon, the clock continues to count to 2400 (stated as "twenty-four hundred hours"). If this confuses you, simply subtract 1200 to get "civilian" time, for example, 2350 - 1200 = 1150 p.m.

Anatomic position may be dictated using a clock-face orientation (o'clock). Use figures in these expressions.

Money
Use figures to express amounts of money. Do not include zeros in even dollar amounts.

Measurements, mathematical expressions, and symbols
Use figures for measurements and ratios and in expressions involving symbols and abbreviations.

Decimals
Use figures to express decimals. If a decimal less than 1 is dictated, transcribe a zero before the decimal, even if it is not dictated. When whole numbers are dictated, do not add a decimal point and zero.

When a metric measurement is dictated as a fraction, convert the fraction to a decimal. Common fractions and decimal equivalents include the following: 1/4 = .25, Ω = 0.5, and 3/4 = .75.

When a physician dictates a fraction in a general, nontechnical form, use words to express the fraction.

USING ABBREVIATIONS CORRECTLY

Abbreviations are selected letters of a longer word or phrase. Abbreviations save space and may speed up communication, but they can also cause confusion and misinterpretation.

As you learned in chapter 1, your medical transcription library should include an abbreviations reference. Keep context in mind as you search for abbreviations to ensure that the extended form you choose is the appropriate term.

Generally, transcribe abbreviations in full capital letters without punctuation and without spaces between the letters. Short forms, such as segs for segmented neutrophils or lymphs for lymphocytes, are transcribed as dictated.

To abbreviate or not to abbreviate

In medical reports, there are some areas in which abbreviations are not used even if they are dictated. Do not use abbreviations in any impression, assessment, admitting or discharge diagnosis, or preoperative or postoperative diagnosis. Do not use abbreviations in the title of the procedure for an operative report.

Do not abbreviate any medical term that is dictated in full except for metric units of measure (milligrams, milliliters) preceded by a number (for example, transcribe 5 mg, not 5 milligrams). Metric units of measure most often appear in laboratory results and drug dosages.

Units of measure

Use abbreviations when a numeric quantity precedes metric units of measure. Do not add s or 's.
Spell out common nonmetric units of measure, like foot, inch, ounce, and so on, except in tables. Do not use an apostrophe or quotation marks to indicate feet or inches except in tables.

Punctuation with abbreviations

Usually, no punctuation is used with abbreviations. The exception is the group of Latin abbreviations that deal with medication administration. These are always keyed in lowercase with periods in between (for example, b.i.d.; p.r.n.; q.12h.).

If more than one Latin abbreviation is dictated together, put a space between the two abbreviations (Zantac 150 mg p.o. b.i.d.).

Plural abbreviations

Abbreviations in capital letters do not require an apostrophe before the s (for example, WBCs, ECGs). Add an s to short forms for laboratory terms (for example, lymphs, monos, segs).

Abbreviations that have multiple meanings

Do not guess. If an abbreviation with multiple meanings is dictatedófor example, PT, you may or may not be able to determine the intended meaning based on the context of the report. To figure out the meaning, read the rest of the report to see if the full term has been dictated elsewhere, or look at the patient's record if you have easy access to it. If you are unsuccessful, leave the term in abbreviated form, even in a diagnosis. It is better to leave an abbreviated form that knowledgeable people will be able to interpret than to transcribe a full term that is incorrect.

If the abbreviation itself is not clear (CVP? CPT? CCP?), try the same methods as above. Again, do not guess. It is better to leave a blank than to guess incorrectly.

USING HYPHENS CORRECTLY

Hyphens are commonly used to form compound adjectives, nouns, and verbs. In these cases, hyphens help readers understand that a combination of words has a single meaning and function in the sentence, as in the phrase 24-year-old patient. Hyphens are also used occasionally to connect prefixes to root words, especially when an unhyphenated spelling may confuse the reader. Finally, hyphens are used in fractions and in certain medical technical terms such as L1-L2.

Using hyphens to create compounds can be complicated because so many variables are involved and because the construction of a compound may change as it becomes widely used. For these reasons, you should always consult a current dictionary when you question the spelling of a compound word. The rules below provide general guidelines.

Compound adjectives

Compound adjectives are two or more words that work together to modify the same noun (follow-up visit, once-in-a-lifetime opportunity, gram-negative bacteria). Use a hyphen to connect the words that form a compound adjective:

When the compound adjective no longer functions as a single modifier, do not hyphenate the words.

Do not hyphenate adverb-adjective combinations because the meaning is usually clear without a hyphen. You can identify these combinations by checking if the first word ends in ly, which means it is an adverb. In the phrase, a slowly enlarging lesion, for example, slowly is not an adjective but an adverb, so the modifying phrase is not hyphenated.

Compound adjectives using the prefixes self- or all-, or the suffixes -free should always be hyphenated, whether or not they precede a noun.

Note: You may decide to rewrite a sentence to omit some of the hyphenated words. Do this cautiously and only when absolutely necessary.

Prefixes and suffixes
Do not hyphenate words with the prefix non- unless the root word is an eponym. Do not hyphenate words with the prefix anti- or extra- unless the word can be easily misread.

Do not use a hyphen with the prefixes bi, tri, uni, co, infra, inter, intra, mid, mini, multi, pseudo, sub, super, supra, ultra, out, over, ante, anti, semi, un, non pre, post pro, trans, and re unless the word that follows begins with the same vowel that ends the prefix.

Do not hyphenate words with the suffix -like unless the first word is an eponym, ends in l or a vowel, or has more than three syllables.

Hyphenate words with the prefix ex- when ex- means former. Otherwise do not hyphenate.

Hyphenate words that would be misread without a hyphen. If the lack of a hyphen makes a word difficult to interpret, hyphenate the word.

Some words are so commonly used together that they are read as a unit. Check your dictionary when in doubt, since there are no firm guidelines.

Suspended hyphens
Suspended hyphens connect two or more prefixes or adjectives to the same term. Use a suspended hyphen after each prefix or word in the series.

Specific words
Follow up, follow-up, followup

verb: The patient will follow up with me next week.
adjective: He will have a follow-up chest film to document resolution of his pneumonia. (Note: AAMT suggests one word, although both treatments are acceptable.)
noun: Followup will be with her primary physician.

Other uses of the hyphen
Hyphenate fractions expressed in words.

Use a hyphen to express the space between two vertebrae.

Use hyphens with most suture sizes. Include the symbol # if number is dictated.

Use a hyphen in place of the words to and through in numeric and alphabetic ranges.

USING APOSTROPHES CORRECTLY

Apostrophes are used to denote omitted letters in contractions, to show possession, and to form some plurals.

Contractions
Use contracted forms in medical reports only in a direct quote; otherwise, write out the word.

Extend abbreviations that contain apostrophes.

Years
When a single year is expressed without the century, precede it with an apostrophe ('97). Use an apostrophe preceding expressions of decades of the century (in the '90s), but not when referring to decades of a patient's life (in his 50s).

Possessive forms
Apostrophes indicate ownership, either literally or figuratively. Placement of the apostrophe depends on whether the word is singular or plural.

Some singular nouns (Mr. Harris) become difficult to pronounce when you add 's because the addition makes an extra syllable. In this case, add only an apostrophe to show possession.

Plural nouns: Plural nouns that end in s require only an apostrophe.

Possessives with abbreviations: Use 's the same as you would with a word.

Plurals: Use 's to form plurals of single letters or numbers, but do not use an apostrophe to form the plural of capital letter abbreviations or numbers of two characters or more.

Add 's to plural nouns that do not end in s to make them possessive.

Do not use apostrophes with nouns when used as descriptive terms.

Hyphenated compound terms: Use 's after the last word in a hyphenated compound term.

It's versus its: It's means it is. Do not use it's in a medical report. The word its is a singular possessive pronoun.

Whose versus who's: Whose is a relative pronoun that can function in various ways, including as a connector between a subordinate clause and a main clause. Who's is a contraction for the two words who is. Note the differences in use:

Eponyms: The AAMT style guidelines state not to use 's with eponymic terms (Alzheimer disease, not Alzheimer's disease). However, this has not been widely accepted. Therefore, defer to the wishes of your client or employer. It should be noted, though, that eponymic surgical terms generally do not require 's.

APPENDIX C

Common Drugs

Drugs, or pharmacologic agents, are medications or agents that are used therapeutically or for diagnostic purposes. Drugs have three nomenclatures: a chemical name, which describes the chemical structure and is written in small letters; a generic name, or the official name for the drug, written in small letters; and the brand (proprietary) name, which is capitalized. Following is a list of the drugs referenced in this text and other drugs that are commonly prescribed.

Name	Description
4-Way Nasal Spray (oxymetazoline)	decongestant
Accupril (quinapril)	angiotensin-converting enzyme (ACE) inhibitor; antihypertensive
Accutane (isotretinoin)	antiacne
acetaminophen	analgesic; antipyretic
acetaminophen and hydrocodone	narcotic; cough suppressant; analgesic
acetaminophen and oxycodone	narcotic analgesic
acetazolamide	anticonvulsant; antiglaucoma; diuretic
acetylcholine	neurotransmitter
acetylsalicylic acid (ASA)	analgesic
Achromycin-V (tetracycline)	antibiotic
acyclovir	antiviral
Adalat (nifedipine)	antianginal; antihypertensive
Adrenalin (epinephrine)	bronchodilator
Adriamycin (doxorubicin)	antibiotic; anticancer
Adrucil (fluorouracil)	anticancer
Advil (ibuprofen)	nonsteroidal anti-inflammatory drug (NSAID)
albumin (human)	human blood product
Albuminar (human albumin)	human blood product
albuterol	bronchodilator
Aldactazide (spironolactone with hydrochlorothiazide)	diuretic
Alka-Mints (calcium carbonate)	calcium antacid
allopurinol	antigout
alprazolam	tranquilizer
Alupent (metaproterenol)	bronchodilator
amantadine	antiparkinsonism; antiviral
Ambien (zolpidem)	sleeping drug
Amen (medroxyprogesterone)	female sex hormone
Amicar (aminocaproic acid)	promotes blood clotting
aminocaproic acid	promotes blood clotting
aminophylline	bronchodilator
Aminophylline (aminophylline)	bronchodilator
amitriptyline	antidepressant
amlodipine	antihypertensive
amoxicillin	antibiotic
amoxicillin and clavulanate	antibiotic
Amoxil (amoxicillin)	antibiotic
amphotericin B	antifungal
ampicillin	antibiotic
Anacin (acetylsalicylic acid)	analgesic
Ancef (cefazolin)	antibiotic
Ancobon (flucytosine)	antifungal
antihemophilic factor (human)	human blood product
antipyrine and benzocaine	analgesic (otic)
Aralen (chloroquine)	antimalarial
Aristocort (triamcinolone)	corticosteroid
Aromatic Cascara Fluidextract (cascara sagrada)	laxative
asparaginase	anticancer
aspirin (acetylsalicylic acid)	analgesic
atenolol	beta blocker
Ativan (lorazepam)	tranquilizer
Atropair Ophthalmic (atropine)	anticholinergic
atropine	anticholinergic

atropine and dephenoxylate	antidiarrheal
atropine, hyoscyamine, scopolamine, and phenobarbitol	anticholinergic; anticonvulsant
Atrovent (ipratropium)	bronchodilator
Augmentin (amoxicillin and clavulanate)	antibiotic
Auralgan (antipyrine and benzocaine)	analgesic (otic)
Aveeno Cleansing Bar (sulfur and salicylic acid)	topical antibacterial
Axid (nizatidine)	antiulcer
azathioprine	antirheumatic; immunosuppressant
azithromycin	antibiotic
Azmacort (triamcinolone)	corticosteroid
bacitracin, neomycin, and polymycin B sulfate	antibiotic
Bactrim (trimethoprim and sulfamethoxazole)	antibiotic
Bayer (acetylsalicylic acid)	analgesic
beclomethasone	corticosteroid
Beclovent (beclomethasone)	corticosteroid
Benadryl (diphenhydramine)	antiemetic; antihistamine; antiparkinsonism
benazepril	antihypertensive; angiotensin-converting enzyme (ACE) inhibitor
Benylin (diphenhydramine)	antiemetic; antihistamine; antiparkinsonism
Benzac W (benzoyl peroxide)	antiacne
benzocaine and antipyrine	analgesic (otic)
benzoyl peroxide	antiacne
Biaxin (clarithromycin)	antibiotic
BiCNU (carmustine)	anticancer
Blenoxane (bleomycin)	antibiotic; anticancer
bleomycin	antibiotic; anticancer
Bronkaid Mist (epinephrine)	bronchodilator
Bronkodyl (theophylline)	bronchodilator
Bronkosol (isoetharine)	bronchodilator
Bufferin (acetylsalicylic acid)	analgesic
Burow's solution	soothing mild astringent soak solution
Buspar (buspirone)	minor tranquilizer
buspirone	minor tranquilizer
busulfan	anticancer
Calan (verapamil)	antianginal; antiarrhythmic; antihypertensive
Calcijex (calcitriol)	vitamin D
Calcimar (calcitonin)	calcium regulator
Calciparine (heparin)	anticoagulant
calcitonin	calcium regulator
calcitriol	vitamin D
calcium carbonate	calcium antacid
calcium chloride	calcium supplement
Cal Plus (calcium chloride)	calcium supplement
Capoten (captopril)	angiotensin-converting enzyme (ACE) inhibitor
captopril	angiotensin-converting enzyme (ACE) inhibitor
carbamazepine	anticonvulsant
carboplatin	anticancer
Cardizem (diltiazem)	antianginal; calcium channel blocker
carmustine	anticancer
casanthranol and docusate	laxative
cascara sagrada	laxative
Catapres (clonidine)	antihypertensive
Ceclor (cefaclor)	antibiotic
cefaclor	antibiotic
cefadroxil	antibiotic
Cefadyl (cephapirin)	antibiotic
cefazolin	antibiotic
cefixime	antibiotic
Cefotan (cefotetan)	antibiotic
cefotaxime	antibiotic
cefotetan	antibiotic
cefoxitin	antibiotic
cefpodoxime	antibiotic
cefprozil	antibiotic
ceftazidime	antibiotic

Ceftin (cefuroxime)	antibiotic
ceftriaxone	antibiotic
cefuroxime	antibiotic
Cefzil (cefprozil)	antibiotic
cephalexin	antibiotic
cephalothin	antibiotic
cephapirin	antibiotic
Cerubidine (daunorubicin)	antibiotic; anticancer
chlorambucil	anticancer
chloramphenicol	antibiotic (otic)
Chloromycetin (chloramphenicol)	antibiotic (otic)
chloroquine	antimalarial
cilastatin and imipenem	antibiotic
cimetidine	antiulcer
cisplatin	anticancer
Claforan (cefotaxime)	antibiotic
clarithromycin	antibiotic
Claritin (loratadine)	antihistamine
clavanulate and amoxicillin	antibiotic
Clear Eyes (naphazoline)	decongestant
Cleocin (clindamycin)	antibiotic
clindamycin	antibiotic
clonazepam	anticonvulsant; tranquilizer
clonidine	antihypertensive
clotrimazole	antifungal
cocaine	stimulant
Cortaid (hydrocortisone)	corticosteroid
Cosmegen (dactinomycin)	anticancer
Cotazym (pancrelipase)	pancreatic enzyme replacement
Cotrim (trimethoprim and sulfamethoxazole)	antibiotic
Coumadin (warfarin)	anticoagulant
Creon (pancreatin)	pancreatic enzyme replacement
Crolom Ophthalmic Drops (cromolyn sodium)	antihistamine
cromolyn sodium	antihistamine
Curretab (medroxyprogesterone)	female sex hormone
Cyclogyl (cyclopentolate)	anticholenergic
cyclopentolate	anticholenergic
cyclophosphamide	anticancer
cytarabine	anticancer
Cytosar-U (cytarabine)	anticancer
Cytoxan (cyclophosphamide)	anticancer
dacarbazine	anticancer
dactinomycin	anticancer
Dalmane (flurazepam)	tranquilizer
Darvon (propoxyphene)	narcotic analgesic
daunorubicin	antibiotic; anticancer
Daypro (oxaprozin)	nonsteroidal anti-inflammatory drug (NSAID)
DDAVP (desmopressin)	antidiuretic hormone
Decadron (dexamethasone)	corticosteroid
deferoxamine	chelating agent
Deltasone (prednisone)	corticosteroid
Demerol (meperidine)	narcotic analgesic
dephenoxylate and atropine	antidiarrheal
Desferal (deferoxamine)	chelating agent
desmopressin	antidiuretic hormone
desogestrel and ethinyl estradiol	female sex hormone
dexamethasone	corticosteroid
dextromethorphan and guaifenesin	cough suppressant and expectorant
Diamox (acetazolamide)	anticonvulsant; antiglaucoma; diuretic
diazepam	tranquilizer; muscle relaxant; anticonvulsant
diazoxide	antihypertensive
diclofenac	analgesic; anti-inflammatory
digoxin	antiarrhythmic
Dilantin (phenytoin)	anticonvulsant

diltiazem	antianginal; calcium channel blocker
diphenhydramine	antiemetic; antihistamine; antiparkinsonism
dipivefrin	antiglaucoma
dipyridamole	anticlotting
Dizymes (pancreatin)	pancreatic enzyme replacement
dobutamine	stimulant
Dobutrex (dobutamine)	stimulant
docusate and casanthranol	laxative
Donnatal (hyoscyamine, atropine, scopolamine,	anticholinergic; anticonvulsant and phenobarbitol)
doxorubicin	antibiotic; anticancer
DTIC-Dome (dacarbazine)	anticancer
Duricef (cefadroxil)	antibiotic
Dyazide (triamterene with hydrochlorothiazide)	diuretic; antihypertensive
Dyrenium (triamterene)	diuretic
Elavil (amitriptyline)	antidepressant
Elixophyllin (theophylline)	bronchodilator
Elspar (asparaginase)	anticancer
E-Mycin (erythromycin)	antibiotic
enalapril	angiotensin-converting enzyme (ACE) inhibitor; vasodilator; antihypertensive
Endep (amitriptyline)	antidepressant
Engerix-B (hepatitis vaccine)	vaccine to prevent hepatitis B
epinephrine	bronchodilator; antiglaucoma
epoetin alfa	stimulates production of red blood cells
Epogen (epoetin alfa)	stimulates production of red blood cells
Ery-Tab (erythromycin)	antibiotic
Erythrocin (erythromycin)	antibiotic
erythromycin	antibiotic
Estrace (estradiol)	female sex hormone
Estraderm (estradiol)	female sex hormone
estradiol	female sex hormone
estrogens, conjugated	female sex hormone
ethambutol	antimycobacterial
ethinyl estradiol and desogestrel	female sex hormone
ethinyl estradiol and levonorgestrel	female sex hormone
etodolac	analgesic; nonsteroidal anti-inflammatory drug (NSAID)
etoposide	anticancer
factor IX complex (human)	antihemophilia; human blood product
famotidine	antiulcer
filgrastim (rhG-CSF)	stimulates neutrophil maturation
flucytosine (5-FC, f-flurocytosine)	antifungal
Fludara (fludarabine)	anticancer
fludarabine (FAMP, F-ara-AMP)	anticancer
fluoride	prevents tooth decay
fluorouracil (5-fluorouracil, 5-FU)	anticancer
fluoxetine	antidepressant
flurazepam	tranquilizer
folic acid	vitamin M
Fortaz (ceftazidime)	antibiotic
Fulvicin (griseofulvin)	antifungal
Fungizone (amphotericin B)	antifungal
furosemide	diuretic; antihypertensive
Gamimune N (immune globulin, human)	blood protein
Gammagard (immune globulin, human)	blood protein
Garamycin (gentamycin)	antibiotic
gentamycin	antibiotic
Glaucon (epinephrine)	antiglaucoma
Grifulvin (griseofulvin)	antifungal
Grisactin (griseofulvin)	antifungal
griseofulvin	antifungal
guaifenesin and dextromethorphan	expectorant and cough suppressant
Haltran (ibuprofen)	nonsteroidal anti-inflammatory drug (NSAID)
Hemofil-M (antihemophilic factor, human)	human blood product
heparin	anticoagulant

hepatitis vaccine	vaccine to prevent hepatitis B
Humate-P (antihemophilic factor, human)	human blood product
Hydrea (hydroxyurea)	anticancer
hydrochlorothiazide with spironolactone	diuretic
hydrochlorothiazide with triamterene	diuretic; antihypertensive
hydrocodone and acetaminophen	narcotic; cough suppressant; analgesic
hydrocortisone	corticosteroid
hydroxyurea	anticancer
hyoscyamine, atropine, scopolamine, and phenobarbitol	anticholinergic; anticonvulsant
Hyperstat (diazoxide)	antihypertensive
Hytrin (terazosin)	antihypertensive
ibuprofen	nonsteroidal anti-inflammatory drug (NSAID)
idoxuridine	antiviral
Ifex (ifosamide)	anticancer
ifosamide	anticancer
Ilosone (erythromycin)	antibiotic
imipenem and cilastatin	antibiotic
imipramine	antidepressant
immune globulin (human)	blood protein
Imuran (azathioprine)	antirheumatic; immunosuppressant
Indocin (indomethacin)	antigout; nonsteroidal anti-inflammatory drug (NSAID)
indomethacin	antigout; nonsteroidal anti-inflammatory drug (NSAID)
influenza vaccine	vaccine to prevent influenza
interferon	antiviral; anticancer
ipratropium	bronchodilator
isoetharine	bronchodilator
isoproterenol	bronchodilator
Isoptin (verapamil)	antianginal; antiarrhythmic; antihypertensive
Isopto Carpine (pilocarpine)	antiglaucoma
isotretinoin	antiacne
Isuprel (isoproterenol)	bronchodilator
Janimine (imipramine)	antidepressant
K-Dur (potassium chloride)	electrolyte replenisher
Keflex (cephalexin)	antibiotic
Keflin (cephalothin)	antibiotic
Kefzol (cefazolin)	antibiotic
Klonopin (clonazepam)	anticonvulsant; tranquilizer
Koate-HP (antihemophilic factor, human)	human blood product
Konyne (factor IX complex, human)	antihemophilia; human blood product
Lanoxin(digoxin)	antiarrhythmic
Larotid (amoxicillin)	antibiotic
Lasix (furosemide)	diuretic; antihypertensive
Leukeran (chlorambucil)	anticancer
levonorgestrel and ethinyl estradiol	female sex hormone
levothyroxine	thyroid hormone replacement
Liquifilm (idoxuridine)	antiviral
lisinopril	antihypertensive;.angiotensin-converting enzyme (ACE) inhibitor
Lodine (etodolac)	analgesic; nonsteroidal anti-inflammatory drug (NSAID)
Lomotil (dephenoxylate and atropine)	antidiarrheal
Lopressor (metoprolol)	beta blocker
loratadine	antihistamine
lorazepam	tranquilizer
Lortab (hydrocodone and acetaminophen)	narcotic; cough suppressant; analgesic
Lotensin (benazepril)	antihypertensive; angiotensin-converting enzyme (ACE) inhibitor
Lotrisone (clotrimazole)	antifungal
lovastatin	cholesterol reducer
Matulane (procarbazine)	anticancer
mechlorethamine	anticancer
medroxyprogesterone	female sex hormone
Mefoxin (cefoxitin)	antibiotic
meperidine	narcotic analgesic
Metaprel (metaproterenol)	bronchodilator
metaproterenol	bronchodilator
metoprolol	beta blocker

Mevacor (lovastatin)	cholesterol reducer
Micronor (norethindrone)	female sex hormone
Milk of MagnesiaóCascara (cascara sagrada)	laxative
Miochol (acetylcholine)	neurotransmitter
Motrin (ibuprofen)	nonsteroidal anti-inflammatory drug (NSAID)
Mustergen (mechlorethamine)	anticancer
Myambutol (ethambutol)	antimycobacterial
Mycostatin (nystatin)	antifungal
Mylanta (calcium carbonate)	calcium antacid
Myleran (busulfan)	anticancer
nabumetone	nonsteroidal anti-inflammatory drug (NSAID)
Nafcil (nafcillin)	antibiotic
nafcillin	antibiotic
naphazoline	decongestant
Nebcin (tobramycin)	antibiotic
neomycin, bacitracin, and polymyxin B sulfate	antibiotic
Neosar (cyclophosphamide)	anticancer
Neosporin (polymycin B sulfate, bacitracin, and neomycin)	antibiotic
Neupogen (filgrastim)	stimulates neutrophil maturation
nifedipine	antianginal; antihypertensive
Nitrogard (nitroglycerin)	antianginal
nitrogen mustard (mechlorethamine)	anticancer
nitroglycerin	antianginal
Nitrolingual Spray (nitroglycerin)	antianginal
Nitrong (nitroglycerin)	antianginal
Nitrostat (nitroglycerin)	antianginal
nizatidine	antiulcer
norethindrone	female sex hormone
normal saline	solution similar to the pH of blood
Norvasc (amlodipine)	antihypertensive
Nuprin (ibuprofen)	nonsteroidal anti-inflammatory drug (NSAID)
nystatin	antifungal
omeprazole	antiulcer
Omnipen (ampicillin)	antibiotic
Oncaspar (pegaspargase)	anticancer
Oncovin (vincristine)	anticancer
ondansetron	antiemetic
Ortho-Cept (desogestrel and ethinyl estradiol)	female sex hormone
Ortho-Novum (norethindrone)	female sex hormone
Os-Cal (calcium carbonate)	calcium supplement
oxaprozin	nonsteroidal anti-inflammatory drug (NSAID)
oxycodone and acetaminophen	narcotic analgesic
oxymetazoline	decongestant
Pancrease (pancrelipase)	pancreatic enzyme replacement
pancreatin	pancreatic enzyme replacement
pancrelipase	pancreatic enzyme replacement
Panoxyl (benzoyl peroxide)	antiacne
Panwarfin (warfarin)	anticoagulant
Paraplatin (carboplatin)	anticancer
paroxetine	antidepressant
Paxil (paroxetine)	antidepressant
PediaProfen (ibuprofen)	nonsteroidal anti-inflammatory drug (NSAID)
pegaspargase	anticancer
penicillin V potassium	antibiotic
Pentam 300 (pentamidine)	anti-infective
pentamidine	anti-infective
Pen-Vee-K (penicillin V potassium)	antibiotic
Pepcid (famotidine)	antiulcer
Percocet (oxycodone and acetaminophen)	narcotic analgesic
Peri-Colace (docusate and casanthranol)	laxative
Persantine (dipyridamole)	anticlotting
phenobarbitol, hyoscyamine, atropine, and scopolamine	anticholinergic; anticonvulsant
phenytoin	anticonvulsant
Phyllocontin (aminophylline)	bronchodilator

Pilocar (pilocarpine)	antiglaucoma
pilocarpine	antiglaucoma
Platinol (cisplatin)	anticancer
Pneumovax vaccine	vaccine to prevent pneumococcal pneumonia
Polycillin (ampicillin)	antibiotic
Polymox (amoxicillin)	antibiotic
polymycin B sulfate, bacitracin, and neomycin	antibiotic
potassium chloride	electrolyte replenisher
Poxicet (oxycodone and acetaminophen)	narcotic analgesic
Pravachol (pravastatin)	cholesterol reducer
pravastatin	cholesterol reducer
prednisone	corticosteroid
Premarin (estrogens, conjugated)	female sex hormone
Prilosec (omeprazole)	antiulcer
Primatene Mist (epinephrine)	bronchodilator
Primaxin (imipenem and cilastatin)	antibiotic
Principen (ampicillin)	antibiotic
Prinivil (lisinopril)	antihypertensive; angiotensin-converting enzyme (ACE) inhibitor
procarbazine	anticancer
Procardia (nifedipine)	antianginal; antihypertensive
Procrit (epoetin alfa)	stimulates the production of red blood cells
Profilnine (factor IX complex, human)	antihemophilia; human blood product
Proloprim (trimethoprim)	antibacterial
Propine (dipivefrin)	antiglaucoma
propoxyphene	narcotic analgesic
Proventil (albuterol)	bronchodilator
Provera (medroxyprogesterone)	female sex hormone
Prozac (fluoxetine)	antidepressant
pseudoephedrine	decongestant
quinapril	angiotensin-converting enzyme (ACE) inhibitor; antihypertensive
ranitidine	antiulcer
Relafen (nabumetone)	nonsteroidal anti-inflammatory drug (NSAID)
Retin-A (tretinoin)	antiacne
retinoic acid (tretinoin)	antiacne
Retrovir (zidovudine)	antiviral; antiAIDS
Rifadin (rifampin)	antimycobacterial
rifampin	antimycobacterial
Rimactane (rifampin)	antimycobacterial
Robitussin-DM (guaifenesin and dextromethorphan)	expectorant and cough suppressant
Rocaltrol (calcitriol)	vitamin D
Rocephin (ceftriaxone)	antibiotic
Roferon-A (interferon)	antiviral; anticancer
Rolaids (calcium carbonate)	calcium antacid
Roxicet (oxycodone and acetaminophen)	narcotic analgesic
Rufen (ibuprofen)	nonsteroidal anti-inflammatory drug (NSAID)
salicylic acid and sulfur	topical antibacterial
Sandoglobulin (immune globulin, human)	blood protein
scopolamine, hyoscyamine, atropine, and phenobarbitol	anticholinergic; anticonvulsant
Seldane (terfenadine)	antihistamine
senna	laxative
Senokot (senna)	laxative
Septra (trimethoprim and sulfamethoxazole)	antibiotic
sertraline	antidepressant
Silvadene (silver sulfadiazine)	topical antibacterial
silver nitrate	topical antibacterial
silver sulfadiazine	topical antibacterial
simvastatin	cholesterol reducer
Slo-Bid (theophylline)	bronchodilator
Slo-Phyllin (theophylline)	bronchodilator
Sodium Sulamyd (sulfacetamide)	antibacterial
Solu-Cortef (hydrocortisone)	corticosteroid
spironolactone with hydrochlorothiazide	diuretic
Sudafed (pseudoephedrine)	decongestant
sulfacetamide	antibacterial

sulfamethoxazole and trimethoprim	antibiotic
sulfur and salicylic acid	topical antibacterial
Suprax (cefixime)	antibiotic
Sus-Phrine (epinephrine)	bronchodilator
Symadine (amantadine)	antiparkinsonism; antiviral
Symmetrel (amantadine)	antiparkinsonism; antiviral
Synthroid (levothyroxine)	thyroid hormone replacement
Tagamet (cimetidine)	antiulcer
Tegretol (carbamazepine)	anticonvulsant
Tenormin (atenolol)	beta blocker
terazosin	antihypertensive
terfenadine	antihistamine
tetracycline	antibiotic
theophylline	bronchodilator
Ticar (ticarcillin)	antibiotic
ticarcillin	antibiotic
Timentin (ticarcillin)	antibiotic
tobramycin	antibiotic
Tobrex Ophthalmic (tobramycin)	antibiotic
Tofranil (imipramine)	antidepressant
tretinoin (retinoic acid)	antiacne
triamcinolone	corticosteroid
triamterene	diuretic
triamterene with hydrochlorothiazide	diuretic; antihypertensive
trimethoprim	antibacterial
trimethoprim and sulfamethoxazole	antibiotic
Trimox (amoxicillin)	antibiotic
Trimpex (trimethoprim)	antibacterial
Triphasil (levonorgestrel and ethinyl estradiol)	female sex hormone
Tums (calcium carbonate)	calcium antacid
Tylenol (acetaminophen)	analgesic; antipyretic
Tylox (oxycodone and acetaminophen)	narcotic analgesic
Unipen (nafcillin)	antibiotic
Valium (diazepam)	tranquilizer; muscle relaxant; anticonvulsant
Vancenase (beclomethasone)	corticosteroid
Vanceril (beclomethasone)	corticosteroid
Vantin (cefpodoxime)	antibiotic
Vasotec (enalapril)	angiotensin-converting enzyme (ACE) inhibitor; bronchodilator; antihypertensive
Vazepam (diazepam)	tranquilizer; muscle relaxant; anticonvulsant
V-Cillin-K (penicillin V potassium)	antibiotic
Veetids (penicillin V potassium)	antibiotic
Velban (vinblastine)	anticancer
Ventolin (albuterol)	bronchodilator
VePesid (etoposide)	anticancer
verapamil	antianginal; antiarrhythmic; antihypertensive
vinblastine	anticancer
vincristine	anticancer
Voltaren (diclofenac)	analgesic; anti-inflammatory
warfarin	anticoagulant
Xanax (alprazolam)	tranquilizer
Zantac (ranitidine)	antiulcer
Zestril (lisinopril)	antihypertensive; angiotensin-converting enzyme (ACE) inhibitor
zidovudine (AZT)	antiviral; antiAIDS
Zithromax (azithromycin)	antibiotic
Zocor (simvastatin)	cholesterol reducer
Zofran (ondansetron)	antiemetic
Zoloft (sertraline)	antidepressant
zolpidem	sleeping drug
Zovirax (acyclovir)	antiviral
Zyloprim (allopurinol)	antigout
Zymase (pancrelipase)	pancreatic enzyme replacement

APPENDIX D

Medical Abbreviations

A

AB or Ab	abortion
ABG	arterial blood gas
a.c.	before meals
AC	air conduction
ACC	accommodation
ACG	angiocardiography
ACS	American Cancer Society
ACTH	adrenocorticotropic hormone
AD	right ear (auris dextra)
ADH	antidiuretic hormone
ad lib	as desired
AE	above the elbow (amputation)
AFB	acid-fast bacillus (organism which causes tuberculosis)
AFP	alpha-fetoprotein (tumor marker for liver and germ cells)
A/G	albumin/globulin ratio
AGN	acute glomerulonephritis
AHF	antihemophilic factor VIII
AHG	antihemophilic globulin factor VIII
AICA	anterior inferior communicating artery
AIDS	acquired immunodeficiency syndrome; caused by HIV
AK	above the knee (amputation)
ALL	acute lymphoblastic leukemia
ALS	amyotrophic lateral sclerosis
a.m.	morning
AMA	American Medical Association
AML	acute myelogenous leukemia
ANC	absolute neutrophil count; antigen neutralizing capacity
ANLL	acute nonlymphoblastic leukemia
ANS	autonomic nervous system
AOM	acute otitis media
A&P	auscultation and percussion
AP	anterior posterior (used in radiology)
APL or APML	acute promyelocytic leukemia
ARDS	acute respiratory distress syndrome
AROM	active range of motion
AS	aortic stenosis; left ear (auris sinistra)
ASD	atrial septal defect
ASHD	arteriosclerotic heart disease
ATN	acute tubular necrosis
AV	atrioventricular; arteriovenous

B

BaE or BE	barium enema
baso	basophil
BBB	bundle-branch block
BBT	basal body temperature (temperature in the morning before doing anything muscular)
BCE	basal cell epithelioma
BCM	below costal margin
BE	barium enema (also BaE); below the elbow (amputation)
BFM	Berlin-Frankfurt-Munster (chemotherapy); biceps femoral muscle
BID or b.i.d.	twice a day
BiPAP	bilevel positive airway pressure
BK	below the knee (amputation)
BM	bowel movement; bone marrow (in oncology)
BMA	bone marrow aspiration
BMR	basal metabolic rate
BMT	bone marrow transplant
BOOP	bronchiolitis obliterans-organizing pneumonia
BP	blood pressure
BPH	benign prostatic hypertrophy
BSE	breast self-exam
BSO	bilateral salpingo-oophorectomy (removal of both ovaries and fallopian tubes)
BTL	bilateral tubal ligation (sterilization by cutting or cauterizing the fallopian tubes)
BUN	blood urea nitrogen (blood test)
BX or bx	biopsy

C

C	Celsius or centigrade
C-1, C-2, etc.	cervical vertebra (number)
CA	cancer or carcinoma
CA-125	ovarian carcinoma antigen (tumor marker for ovary)
CAD	coronary artery disease
CALLA or cALLa	common acute lymphocytic leukemia antigen
CAT scan	computerized axial tomography scan
CBC	complete blood count
CC	chief complaint; cardiac catheterization
cc	cubic centimeter
CCU	coronary care unit
CDC	Centers for Disease Control
CDH	congenital dislocation of the hip
CEA	carcinoembryonic antigen (tumor marker for colon, lung, breast, others)
CF	circumflex (artery)
cGy	centigray
CHF	congestive heart failure
CLL	chronic lymphoblastic leukemia
cm	centimeter
CML	chronic myelogenous leukemia
CMV	cytomegalovirus; one of a group of large species-specific herpes-type viruses with a wide variety of disease effects
CNS	central nervous system
C/O or c/o	complained of
CO2	carbon dioxide
COLD	chronic obstructive lung disease
contra	against
COPD	chronic obstructive pulmonary disease
CP	cerebral palsy
CPAP	continuous positive air pressure
CPD	cephalopelvic disproportion
CPR	cardiopulmonary resuscitation
C&S	culture and sensitivity
CS or C section	cesarean section
CSF	cerebrospinal fluid
CT scan	computerized tomography scan
CV	cardiovascular
CVA	cerebrovascular accident (stroke); costovertebral angle
CXR	chest radiograph; chest x-ray
cysto	cystoscopy; cystoscopic examination

D

D	diopter (strength of lens in eyeglass prescription)
d	day
db	decibel
D&C	dilatation (or dilation) and curettage (instrumental expansion of the cervix and scraping of the uterine cavity)
DC	discharge
DDS	Doctor of Dental Surgery
D&E	dilation and evacuation
derm	dermatology
DES	diethylstilbestrol
DI	diabetes insipidus
diff	differential (describes cells in the white blood count)
DIP	desquamative intersitial pneumonia
DIP joint	distal interphalangeal joint
DJD	degenerative joint disease
DM	diabetes mellitus
DNA	deoxyribonucleic acid
DNR	do not resuscitate
DO	Doctor of Osteopathy
DOA	date of admission; dead on arrival
DOB	date of birth
DOS	date of service
DPT	diphtheria-pertussis-tetanus (immunization)
DTR	deep tendon reflexes
DUB	dysfunctional uterine bleeding
DVM	Doctor of Veternary Medicin
DVT	deep vein thrombosis
DX or Dx	diagnosis

E

EAC	external ear canal
EBV	Epstein-Barr virus
ECG or EKG	electrocardiogram
EDC	estimated or expected date of confinement
EEG	electroencelphalogram or electroencephalography
EENT	eye, ear, nose, throat
EGD	esophagogastroduodenoscopy
ELISA	enzyme-linked immunoabsorbent assay (test to determine the amount of a given chemical in a mixture)
Em	emmetropia
EMG	electromyogram or electromyography
ENT	ear, nose, throat
EOM	extraocular movement
EOMI	extraocular muscle intact
eos or eosin	eosinophil (type of white blood cell)
ER	emergency room
ESR	erythrocyte sedimentation rate (blood test)
EST	electric shock therapy
ESWL	extracorporeal shock-wave lithotripsy
et al.	and others
EXT or ext	extremities

F	Fahrenheit
FAAP	Fellow of the Academy of Pediatrics
FAB L1	French-American-British Level 1
FACP	Fellow of the American College of Physicians
FACS	Fellow of the American College of Surgeons
FBS	fasting blood sugar
FDA	Food and Drug Administration
FEF	forced expiratory flow
FEF25-75%	forced midexpiratory flow
FEKG	fetal electrocardiogram
FEV	forced expiratory volume
FEV1	forced expiratory volume in one second
FEV3	forced expiratory volume in three seconds
FH	family history
FHR	fetal heart rate
FHT	fetal heart tone
FS	frozen section (pathology)
FSH	follicle stimulating hormone
FTI	free thyroxine index
FTND	full term normal delivery
FTNSVD	full term normal spontaneous delivery
FUO	fever of unknown origin
FVC	forced vital capacity
FVL	flow volume loop
FX or Fx	fracture

GB	gallbladder
GC	gonorrhea (gynococcal)
GERD	gastroesophageal reflux disease
GFR	glomerular filtration rate
GH	growth hormone
GI	gastrointestinal
gm	gram (measurement)
gr	grain (measurement)
GTT	glucose tolerance test
gtt or gtts	drop or drops (measurement)
GU	genitourinary
Gy	gray
GYN or Gyn	gynecology

h	hour
HAL	hyperalimentation
HCG or hCG	human chorionic gonadotropin (a hormone; tumor marker for germ cells)
HCl	hydrochloric acid
HCT or Hct or hct	hematocrit

HD	hip disarticulation; Hodgkinís disease
HDL	high-density lipoprotein (a type of cholesterol)
HEENT	head, eyes, ears, nose, throat
Hg	mercury
HGB or hgb or hb	hemoglobin
HIV	human immunodeficiency virus; causes deterioration of the immune system
HNP	herniated nucleus pulposus (disc); hemagglutinin neuroaminidase protein
HP	hemipelvectomy
HPI	history of present illness
HRT	hormone replacement therapy
h.s.	hour of sleep (at bedtime)
HSG	hysterosalpingography
HSV-1	herpes simplex virus Type 1
HSV-2	herpes simplex virus Type 2

I

ICA	internal carotid artery
ICP	intracranial pressure
ICU	intensive care unit
I&D	incision and drainage
ID	intradermal; infectious disease; internal development (ortho)
Ig	immunoglobulin
IICP	increased intracranial pressure
IM	intramuscular
IMA	internal mammary artery
I&O	intake and output
IOL	intraocular lens
IOP	intraocular pressure
IPPB	intermittent positive-pressure breathing
IQ or I.Q.	intelligence quotient
IS	intracostal space; incentive spirometry
ITP	immune thrombocytopenic purpura
IU	international unit
IUD	intrauterine device
IV or I.V.	intravenous (intravenously)
IVC	intravenous cholangiography
IVDA	intravenous drug abuser
IVIG	intravenous immunoglobulin
IVP	intravenous pyelogram

K

KD	knee disarticulation
kg	kilogram
KOH	potassium hydroxide
KUB	kidney, ureter, bladder (x-ray examination)

L

L or l	liter
L1, etc.	first lumbar vertebra, etc.
L&A	light and accommodation
LAD	left anterior descending coronary artery
LAT or lat	lateral
lb	pound
LCA	left coronary artery
LCF	left circumflex
LDH	lactic dehydrogenase (tumor marker germ cell and lymphoma)
LDL	low-density lipoprotein (a type of cholesterol)
LE	left eye
leuk	leukocytes (white blood cells)
LH	luteinizing hormone
LIMA	left internal mammary artery
LLQ	left lower quadrant
LMCA	left main coronary artery
LMP	last menstrual period
LOC	loss of consciousness; level of consciousness
LP	lumbar puncture (spinal tap)
LPA	left pulmonary artery
LPN	Licensed Practical Nurse
LRQ	lower right quadrant
LUQ	left upper quadrant
lymphs	lymphocytes (a type of white blood cell)

M

M or m	meter
mcg	microgram
MCH	mean corpuscular hemoglobin
MCHC	mean corpuscular hemoglobin concentration
MCP joint	metacarpophalangeal joint
MCV	mean corpuscular volume
MCL	midclavicular line
MD or M.D.	Medical Doctor or Doctor of Medicine
MDI	metered dose inhaler
mEq	milliequivalents
mets	metastases
mg	milligram
MI	myocardial infarction
ml	milliliter
mm	millimeter
mn or m	minum
mono	monocyte (a type of white blood cell)
MPA	main pulmonary artery
MRI	magnetic resonance imaging
MS	mitral (valve) stenosis; multiple sclerosis; musculoskeletal
MVP	mitral valve prolapse
MYOP or myop	myopia

N

NAD	no acute distress; no appreciable disease
NB	newborn
NB or N.B.	note well or notice (note bene)
neuts	neutrophils (a type of white blood cell)
NKDA	no known drug allergy
NL or N.L.	normal limits
NPH	neutral protamine Hegedron (a type of insulin)
NPO or n.p.o.	nothing by mouth
NSAID	nonsteroidal anti-inflammatory drug

O

O2	oxygen
OA	osteoarthritis
OB	obstetrics
OD	right eye (oculus dexter); doctor of optometry; overdose (drug)
od	once a day
OM	obtuse marginal coronary artery
OR	operating room
ortho	orthopedics
os	mouth
OS	left eye (oculus sinister)
Oto	otology
OU or ou	both eyes (oculi unitas)
oz	ounce

P

P	pulse
PA	physicianís assistant; posterior anterior view in an x-ray; pulmonary artery
P&A	percussion and auscultation
PAM	potential acuity meter
PAN	periodic alternating nystagmus; periarteritis nodosa
Pap	Papanicolaou smear
PAP	positive airway pressure
PAT	paroxysmal atrial tachycardia
Path	pathology
PBI	proteinbound iodine
PC or pc or P.C. or p.c.	after meals
PCP	Pneumocystis carinii pneumonia
PCV	packed cell volume
PD	patent ductus; peritoneal dialysis; postprandial (after meals)
PDA	posterior descending artery; patent ductus arteriosis
PE	physical examination
PE tubes	pressure-equalizing tubes
PEEP	positive end expiratory pressure
PEF	peak expiratory flow
per	through or by

PERRLA	pupils equal, round, and reactive to light and accommodation
pH	hydrogen ion concentration
PICA	posterior inferior communicating artery
PID	pelvic inflammatory disease
PIP joint	proximal interphalangeal joint
PKU	phenylketonuria (an amino acid)
plts	platelets
p.m.	afternoon or evening
PMD	primary medical doctor
PMH	past medical history
PMI	point of maximal impulse
PMN	polymorphonuclear neutrophil
PMP	previous menstrual period
PND	paroxysmal nocturnal dyspnea
PNH	paroxysmal nocturnal hematuria
PNS	peripheral nervous system
PO or po or P.O or p.o.	by mouth (per os)
poly	polymorphonuclear neutrophil
PP or pp	postprandial (after meals)
PROM	passive range of motion
prn or p.r.n.	as needed
PSA	prostate specific antigen (tumor marker for prostate)
PT	prothrombin time
PT or P/T	physical therapy
PTA	prior to admission
PTH	parathyroid hormone
PTT	partial thromboplastin time
PVC	premature ventricular contraction

q	every
qd or q.d.	every day
qh or q.h.	every hour
q. 2 h or q 2h	every 2 hours
QID or Q.I.D. or q.i.d.	four times a day
qns or q.n.s.	quantity not sufficient
q.o.d.	every other day

R	respiration
rad	radiation dose
RAI	radioactive iodine
RBC	red blood cell
RCA	right coronary artery
RDS	respiratory distress syndrome
RE	right eye
REM	rapid eye movement
Rh	rhesus blood factor (a factor within the blood)
RLQ	right lower quadrant
RN or R.N.	Registered Nurse
RNA	ribonucleic acid
ROJM	range of joint movement
ROM	range of motion
RP	retrograde pyelogram (a kidney test)
RPA	right pulmonary artery
RRR	regular rate and rhythm
RT or R/T	radiation therapy
RUQ	right upper quadrant
Rx or RX	prescription

S

S-1, etc.	first sacral vertebra, etc.
S-A	sinoätrial node
SAR	seasonal allergic rhinitis
SC or SQ or Subcu	subcutaneous
SD	shoulder disarticulation
sed rate	sedimentation rate
seg	segmented neutrophil
SFA	superficial femoral artery
SIDS	sudden infant death syndrome
SLE	systemic lupus erythematosus
SMR	submucosal resection
SNS	somatic nervous system
SOB	shortness of breath
sp. gr.	specific gravity
SQ or SC or Subcu	subcutaneous
ST	esotropia
staph	staphylococcus

Stat	immediately
STD	sexually transmitted disease
strep	streptococcus
Subcu or SC or SQ	subcutaneous

T	temperature
T1, etc.	first thoracic vertebra, etc.
T3	triiodothyronine
T4	thyroxine
T&A	tonsillectomy and adenoidectomy
tab	tablet
TAH	total abdominal hysterectomy
TAH/BSO	total abdominal hysterectomy with bilateral salpingo-oophorectomy
TB	tuberculosis
tbs or tblsp	tablespoonful
TENS	transcutaneous electric nerve stimulation
THA	total hip arthroplasty
TIA	transient ischemic attack
T.I.D. or tid or t.i.d.	three times a day
TM	tympanic membrane
TMJ	temporomandibular joint
TNM	tumor, nodes, metastasis (refers to tumor staging)
TPN	total parenteral nutrition
TPR	temperature, pulse, respiration
TSH	thyroid stimulating hormone
tsp	teaspoonful
TTH	thyrotrophic hormone
TUR; TURP	transurethral resection (prostatectomy)
Tx	treatment

UA or U/A	urinalysis
UC	uterine contractions
UGI	upper gastrointestinal
ULQ	upper left quadrant
ung	ointment
UPPP	uvulopalatophryngoplasty
URI	upper respiratory infection
URQ	upper right quadrant
USP	United States Pharmacopeia
UTI	urinary tract infection
UV	ultraviolet

VA	visual acuity
VAH	vaginal hysterectomy
VBAC	vaginal birth after cesarean section
VC	vital capacity
VD	venereal disease
VDRL	Venereal Disease Research Laboratory (test for syphilis)
VF	visual field
VH	vaginal hysterectomy
VHD	ventricular heart disese
VLDL	very lowdensity lipoprotein
VSD	ventricular septal defect

WBC	white blood cell
WDWN	well-developed, well-nourished
Wgt or wt	weight
WNL or W.N.L.	within normal limits

x	by (size as in 5 x 5 inches)
XRT	xray therapy or radiation therapy
XT	exotropia
XX	female sex chromosomes
XY	male sex chromosomes

APPENDIX E

Medical Symbols

Symbol	Meaning
p̄	after
α	alpha, is proportional to, particle
≈ or ≒	approximately equal to
@	at
↑↑	Babinski sign, extensor response (neurologic examination)
↓↓	Babinski sign, plantar response (neurologic examination)
ā	before
β	beta
Δ	change, prism diopter
✓c̄	check with
©	copyright
↓ or ↘	decrease, below, falling
°	degree
°C	degrees Centigrade
°F	degrees Fahrenheit
Λ	diastolic blood pressure
→ or ←	direction of reaction
Ⓧ	end of anesthesia (used in anesthesia records)
⊗	end of operation
=	equals
♀	female
f℥	fluid ounce
′	foot, minute, primary accent, univalent
γ	gamma
>	greater than; from which is derived
≥	greater than or equal to
″	inch, second, secondary accent, bivalent
↑ or ↗	increase, elevated, rising
(–)	insignificant
++++ or 4+	large amount or pronounced reaction
Ⓛ	left
<	less than; derived from
≤	less than or equal to
♂	male
μ	micron
–	minus, negative, alkaline reaction; deficiency
+++ or 3+	moderate amount of reaction
●	murmur
–	negative
≠	not equal to
≯	not greater than
≮	not less than
#	number, pound(s), gauge, weight, fracture
/	of, per
1×	once
i	one
℥	ounce
¶	paragraph
%	per cent
π	pi
+	plus, positive, acid reaction, excess
±	plus or minus
(±)	possibly significant
℞	prescription
1°	primary, first degree
●	pulse rate (used in anesthesia records)
?	questionable, possible
:	ratio, is to
○	respirations (used in anesthesia records)
®	right, registered trademark
2d	second
2ndry	secondary
2°	secondary, second degree
(+)	significant
∼	similar
+ or 1+	slight trace or reaction
X	start of anesthesia (used in anesthesia records)
⊙	start of operation
S	suction (used in anesthesia records)
V	systolic blood pressure
Δ	temperature (used in anesthesia records)
↓↓	testes descended
↑↑	testes undescended
∴	therefore
3°	third degree
iii	three
++ or 2+	trace or noticeable reaction
24°	24 hours
2× or ×2	twice
ii	two
™	trademark
⇡	up
±	very slight trace or reaction
c̄	with
s̄	without

APPENDIX F

Postal Abbreviations

TWO-LETTER ABBREVIATIONS FOR U.S. STATES AND DEPENDENCIES

Alabama	AL	Idaho	ID	Montana	MT	Rhode Island	RI
Alaska	AK	Illinois	IL	Nebraska	NE	South Carolina	SC
Arizona	AZ	Indiana	IN	Nevada	NV	South Dakota	SD
Arkansas	AR	Iowa	IA	New Hampshire	NH	Tennessee	TN
California	CA	Kansas	KS	New Jersey	NJ	Texas	TX
Canal Zone	CZ	Kentucky	KY	New Mexico	NM	Utah	UT
Colorado	CO	Louisiana	LA	New York	NY	Vermont	VT
Connecticut	CT	Maine	ME	North Carolina	NC	Virginia	VA
Delaware	DE	Maryland	MD	North Dakota	ND	Virgin Islands	VI
District of Columbia	DC	Massachusetts	MA	Ohio	OH	Washington	WA
Florida	FL	Michigan	MI	Oklahoma	OK	West Virginia	WV
Georgia	GA	Minnesota	MN	Oregon	OR	Wisconsin	WI
Guam	GU	Mississippi	MS	Pennsylvania	PA	Wyoming	WY
Hawaii	HI	Missouri	MO	Puerto Rico	PR		

TWO-LETTER ABBREVIATIONS FOR CANADIAN PROVINCES AND TERRITORIES

Alberta	AB	Nova Scotia	NS
British Columbia	BC	Ontario	ON
Labrador	LB	Prince Edward Island	PE
Manitoba	MB	Quebec	PQ
New Brunswick	NB	Saskatchewan	SK
Newfoundland	NF	Yukon Territory	Y
Northwest Territories	NT		

APPENDIX G

Lab Values

The following list includes the laboratory values that appear most frequently in dictation regarding test results and procedures. This information is based on data from a variety of sources, including *Clinical Laboratory Medicine: Clinical Application of Laboratory Data, Sixth Edition*, Mosby-Year Book, Inc., 1995; *Complete Guide to Medical Tests*, Fisher Books, 1988; *Everything You Need to Know about Medical Tests*, Springhouse Corporation, 1996; and *Saunders Manual of Medical Transcription*, W.B. Saunders Company, 1994.

Abbreviations

dl	deciliter	l	liter	mm^3	cubic millimeter
gm	gram	mEq	milli-equivalent	pg	picogram
Hg	mercury	mg	milligram	μl	microliter
IU	international	m	millimeter	μm^3	cubic micron

Blood Tests

	Normal Range	
Arterial blood gases		
Partial pressure of oxygen	75-100 mm Hg	
Partial pressure of carbon dioxide	35-45 mm Hg	
pH	7.35-7.42	
Oxygen content	15-23%	
Oxygen saturation	94-100%	
Bicarbonate	22-26 mEq/l	
Blood electrolytes		
Carbon dioxide	22-34 mEq/l	
Calcium	8.9-10.1 mg/dl	
Chloride	100-108 mEq/l	
Magnesium	1.7-2.1 mg/dl	
Phosphates	2.5-4.5 mg/dl	
Potassium	3.5-5.0 mEq/l	
Sodium	135-145 mEq/l	
Blood cell counts		
Erythrocytes		
Men	4.2-5.4 million/μl	
Women	3.6-5.0 million/μl	
Children	4.6-4.8 million/μl	
Erythrocyte sedimentation rate	0-20 mm/hour (increases with age)	
Leukocytes		
Total	4000-10,000 mm^3	
Differential	*Percentage*	*Absolute*
Myelocytes	0	0/mm^3
Band neutrophils	3-5	150-400/mm^3
Segmented neutrophils	54-62	3000-5800/mm^3
Lymphocytes	25-33	1500-3000/mm^3
Monocytes	3-7	300-500/mm^3
Eosinophils	1-3	50-250/mm^3
Basophils	0-0.75	15-50/mm^3

	Normal Range
Mean corpuscular volume (erythro.)	84-99 μm^3
Mean corpuscular hemoglobin (erythro.)	26-32 pg
Mean corpuscular hemoglobin concentration (erythro.)	30-36%
Hematocrit	
Men	40-54 ml/dl
Women	37-47 ml/dl
Newborns	49-54 ml/dl
Children (varies with age)	35-49 ml/dl
Hemoglobin	
Men	12.4-18 gm/dl
Women	11.7-16 gm/dl
Newborns	16.5-19.5 gm/dl
Children (varies with age)	11.2-16.5 gm/dl
Reticulocytes	0.5-2% of total erythrocyte count
Coagulation tests	
Bleeding time (template)	2-8 min
(modified template)	2-10 min
(Ivy method)	1-7 min
(Duke method)	1-3 min
Activated partial thromboplastin time (PTT)	25-36 sec
Prothrombin time (PT)	10-14 sec
Clotting factors II, V, VII, and X	50-150% of normal
Clotting factors VII, IX, XI, and XII	50-150% of normal
Thrombin time	10-15 sec
Fibrin split products (Thrombo-Welco test)	<10 μg/ml
Fibrinogen (Factor I)	195-365 mg/dl
Platelets	130,000-370,000/mm^3
Blood proteins and pigments	
Haptoglobin	38-270 mg/dl
Phenylalanine, serum	<3 mg/dl
Blood urea nitrogen	8-20 mg/dl
Creatinine	
Men	0.8-1.2 mg/dl
Women	0.6-0.9 mg/dl
Uric acid	
Men	4.3-8.0 mg/dl
Women	2.3-6.0 mg/dl
Bilirubin, serum	
Conjugated	0.1-0.4 mg/dl
Unconjugated	0.2-0.7 mg/dl
Total	0.3-1.1 mg/dl
Coombs' test	
Direct	Negative
Indirect	Negative

	Normal Range
Immune system components	
T-cell	68-75% of total white blood cell count
B-cell	10-20% of total white blood cell count
Null cells	5-20% of total white blood cell count
Immunoglobulins, serum	
IgG	700-1,800 mg/dl
IgA	70-443 mg/dl
IgM	60-290 mg/dl
IgD	0.5-3.0 mg/dl
IgE <500 ng/ml	
Blood enzymes	
Acid phosphatase (thymolphthalein monophosphate substrate), serum	0.5-1.9 IU/l
Alkaline phosphatase	
Men	90-239 IU/l
Women	
(under age 45)	76-196 IU/l
(over age 45)	87-250 IU/l
Blood fats and lipoproteins	
Cholesterol, serum	170-200 mg/dl
HDL	29-77 mg/dl
LDL	62-185 mg/dl
Triglycerides	
Men	40-160 mg/dl
Women	35-135 mg/dl
Plasma and serum values	
Adrenocorticotropin (ACTH), plasma	
6 a.m.	10-80 pg/ml
6 p.m.	<50 pg/ml
Alanine aminotransferase (ALT, SGPT), serum	5-30 U/l
Albumin, serum	3.5-5.5 gm/dl
Ammonia nitrogen, plasma	15-49 μg/dl
Aspartate aminotransferase (AST, SGOT), serum	10-30 U/l
Bile acids, serum	0.3-3.0 mg/dl
Cortisol, plasma	
8 a.m.	6-23 μg/dl
4 p.m.	3-15 μg/dl
10 p.m.	<50% of 8 a.m. value

	Normal Range
Follicle-stimulating hormone (FSH), plasma	
Men	4-25 mU/ml
Women	4-30 mU/ml
Postmenopausal	40-250 mU/ml
Glucose (fasting), plasma or serum	70-115 mg/dl
Growth hormone (hGH), plasma	0-10 ng/ml
Insulin (fasting), plasma	5-25 μU/ml
Iron binding capacity, serum	
Total	250-410 μg/dl
Saturation	20-55%
Lactate	
Venous blood	4.5-19.8 mg/dl
Arterial blood	4.5-14.4 mg/dl
Lactate dehydrogenase (LD, LDH), serum	100-190 U/l
Lipase, serum	10-140 U/l
Luteinizing (LH), serum	
Men	6-18 IU/l
Women	
Premenopausal	5-22 IU/l
Mid-cycle	3 times baseline
Postmenopausal	>30 IU/l
Protein, serum	
Total	6.0-8.0 gm/dl
Albumin	3.5-5.5 gm/dl
Alpha$_1$ globulin	0.2-0.4 gm/dl
Alpha$_2$ globulin	0.5-0.9 gm/dl
Beta globulin	0.6-1.1 gm/dl
Gamma globulin	0.7-1.7 gm/dl
Testosterone, plasma	
Men	275-875 ng/dl
Women	23-75 ng/dl
Pregnant	38-190 ng/dl
Thyroid-stimulating hormone (TSH), serum	0-7 μU/ml
Thyroxine, free (FT), serum	1.0-2.1 ng/dl
Thyroxine (T_4), serum	4.4-9.9 μg/dl
Triiodothyronine (T_3), serum	150-250 ng/dl
Triiodothyronine uptake, resin (T_3RU)	25-38% uptake
Urea, serum or plasma	24-49 mg/dl
Viscosity, serum	1.4-1.8 times water
Vitamin A, serum	20-80 μg/dl
Vitamin B_{12}, serum	180-900 pg/ml

Performance Comparison

PRE-TRANSCRIPTION PERFORMANCE COMPARISON

Copy this chart for each of your practice sessions. It will help you track and compare your progress from sight-keying to keying taped dictation.

Name_________________________Report Number_________Date__________

	Hard Copy Version		Transcription Version	
Error Categories	**No.**	**Description**	**No.**	**Description**
Transcription Errors				
Word omission				
Wrong word				
Spelling errors				
Format or Style Errors				
Capitalization Errors				
Usage/Grammar Errors				
Punctuation Errors				
Abbreviation Errors				
Errors with Numbers				
Transcription Blanks				
Speed Performance (WAM)				

Document Analysis:

Where did you make most of your errors when you keyed from hard copy? Where did you make most of your errors when you transcribed the document?________________

____

Analyze your transcription errors and list the kinds of listening errors you made: ______

____

____

What words or phrases caused you difficulty?_________________________

____

APPENDIX I

Answer Key

CHAPTER 2

Exercise 2.1: Recognizing Look-Alikes and Sound-Alikes

1. psoriasis
2. cirrhosis
3. discreet
4. discrete
5. perineum
6. patients
7. patience
8. glans
9. vesicles
10. wheals

Exercise 2.2: Matching Sound and Spelling

1. erythema
2. sebaceous
3. urticaria
4. desiccate
5. alopecia
6. confluent
7. petechia
8. comedo
9. perineum
10. excoriation
11. antecubital
12. cellulitis
13. apocrine
14. psoriasis
15. ecchymosis

Exercise 2.3: Choosing Words from Context

1. excoriations
2. pruritic
3. vesicle
4. integumentary
5. pustule or comedo or acne
6. maculopapular or erythematous
7. nevus
8. perineum
9. sebaceous
10. acne

Exercise 2.4: Pairing Words and Meanings

1. H or J 2. I 3. G 4. K 5. B 6. D 7. C 8. F 9. A 10. O

Exercise 2.5: Creating Terms from Word Forms

1. dermatology
2. hypertrophy
3. erythema
4. dermabrasion
5. cephalocaudal
6. erythroderma
7. dermatitis
8. seborrhea
9. erythrocyte
10. hematology

Exercise 2.6: Editing for Correct Punctuation

Note: Only corrections to run-ons and fragments have been made, since certain style conventions such as transcribing drug dosages in abbreviations may not have been introduced. Also, some sentences, for example, 6, 8, and 9, could be corrected differently. The suggested answers involve minimal editing, which is the general goal for editing transcription.

1. The patient's wife called 911, and the paramedics arrived some ten minutes later to find the patient in a semiconscious state with an irregular heart rhythm, the exact nature of which is unknown.
2. Strict sterile precautions must be taken, using only autoclaved instruments and adequate skin preparation.
3. Medications: Lasix 20 mg per morning, Micro-K 10 mEq twice per day, Cardizem 30 mg per day, Isordil 20 mg twice per day.
4. The patient was extubated and noted to have purulent sputum and purulent urine. Blood and urine cultures were positive for Klebsiella pneumoniae; therefore, the patient was started on gentamicin.
5. The patient was seen in routine followup six months since the last examination.
6. After informed consent was obtained, the patient was brought to the operating room, where general anesthesia was established. The lower abdomen was prepared and draped in the usual sterile fashion and an incision made just below the umbilicus.
7. The patient should apply the zinc oxide ointment directly to the lesions as often as needed to cool the burning sensation, making sure she washes her hands before and after the application.
8. The patient is a 17-year-old female, a known IV drug addict. She presents today to the emergency department. She has an infected area on her left arm. The area is red and tender.
9. On examination the head shows no deformities, the nose and throat are clear, the neck has no adenopathy, the chest is clear with normal breath sounds, the abdomen is soft and nontender, extremities are normal, and skin shows no rash or redness.
10. This 35-year-old Hispanic male presented today with a 1 cm laceration of the right hand at the web space between the middle and ring fingers.
    [No change is required.]

Exercise 2.7: Proofreading Review

Thank you for referring Kyle Sanderson to me. This baby is truly in pain with scrotal inflammation and excoriation of the perineum. I have instituted Burow soaks to the area q.i.d., with Mycostatin ointment after each soak. If this does not clear the rash, I would be concerned about a secondary infection. I would expect to see improvement within one week; otherwise, I feel the baby should be admitted to the hospital and more aggressive antifungal agents should be used to clear this rash.

CHAPTER 3

Exercise 3.1: Recognizing Look-Alikes and Sound-Alikes

1. superior
2. anterior
3. inferior
4. posterior
5. macule
6. hypothyroidism
7. hypertension
8. fundus
9. metastases
10. metastasis

Exercise 3.2: Matching Sound and Spelling

1. calcification
2. retinoblastoma
3. unilateral
4. pupillary
5. oblique
6. hydrocephalus
7. blepharitis
8. vitreous
9. photophobia
10. metastasis
11. nystagmus
12. exophthalmos
13. osteosarcoma
14. papillopathy
15. motility

Exercise 3.3: Choosing Words from Context

1. enucleation
2. optic
3. osteosarcoma
4. scotoma
5. strabismus
6. conjunctivitis
7. radiotherapy
8. esotropia
9. retinopathy
10. optic chiasm

Exercise 3.4: Pairing Words and Meanings

1.E 2.I 3.A 4.J 5.H 6.C 7.B 8.G 9.D 10.F

Exercise 3.5: Creating Terms from Word Forms

1. retinopathy
2. hypotropia
3. conjunctivitis
4. blepharectomy
5. retinoscopy
6. blepharoplasty
7. ophthalmoscopy
8. conjunctiva
9. blepharitis
10. keratoplasty

Exercise 3.6: Editing for Subject-Verb Agreement

SUBJECTIVE: The patient, a 56-year-old female with multiple medical problems, (present/presents) to the ophthalmology outpatient clinic with 24 hours of tearing and irritation of both eyes. Vision in both eyes (seems/seem) unimpaired. She has no history of allergies or URIs and (does/do) not wear contact lenses.

She has a thick mucous discharge in both eyes, which (causes/cause) the lashes to stick together. She denies any history of trauma to the eyes and no previous history of similar symptoms (is/are) noted.

OBJECTIVE: In each eye the conjunctiva (is/are) grossly inflamed and injected. There (is/are) moderate chemosis and some lid edema. Traces of mucopurulent discharge (is/are) noted on the eyelashes. Examination with Tetracaine and fluorescein (reveals/reveal) no corneal abrasion. Funduscopy and slit-lamp exam (is/are) entirely normal.

ASSESSMENT: Acute bacterial conjunctivitis OU.

PLAN: The patient, with her sister in attendance, (was/were) instructed to use sulfonamide ophthalmic solution two drops OU q.i.d. Techniques of careful handwashing and hygiene (was/were) explained to the patient. The patient will return if her symptoms (does/do) not improve.

Exercise 3.7: Proofreading Review

OBJECTIVE: On examination visual acuity at distance was 20/20 in both eyes. The intraocular pressure was 20 in both eyes. Motility was straight, with full versions, and the pupils were normal. External exam revealed fat protrusion on the lateral aspect of the upper and lower lids on both eyes. There was a firmness on the right eye.The contacts were centered well, with good movement; slit-lamp exam revealed a white conjunctiva, with a clear cornea. The lenses had some cortical changes. Dilated funduscopic exam revealed a .3 cup-to-disc ratio, with a normal macule, blood vessels, and peripheral retina.

CHAPTER 4

Exercise 4.1: Recognizing Look-Alikes and Sound-Alikes

1. aural
2. oral
3. auricle
4. shotty
5. passed
6. tinnitus
7. subtle
8. supple
9. assistants
10. assistance
11. serious, serous
12. malleus
13. malleolus
14. dysphagia
15. ostial

Exercise 4.2: Matching Sound and Spelling

1. neoadjuvant
2. purulent
3. eustachian
4. auricle
5. foramen
6. periauricular
7. naris
8. vertigo
9. tympanic membrane
10. symphysis
11. otalgia
12. malleus
13. tinnitus
14. lucency
15. epistaxis

Exercise 4.3: Choosing Words from Context

1. node
2. otitis
3. jugular
4. exudate
5. culture
6. palpable
7. erythematous
8. excision
9. purulent
10. buccal

Exercise 4.4: Pairing Words and Word Meanings

1. I
2. G
3. J
4. A
5. C
6. H
7. B
8. D
9. E
10. F

Exercise 4.5: Creating Terms from Word Forms

1. aphonia
2. dysphonia
3. excision
4. laryngostomy
5. neuroblastoma
6. ostectomy
7. otitis
8. oropharynx
9. periauricular
10. rhinitis

Exercise 4.6: Editing for Agreement of Pronouns and Antecedents

1. The patient and (I/me) have discussed the options for treatment.
2. (Whom/who) is my first patient today?
3. I will ask the nurse to arrange for my partner or (I/me) to see the child tomorrow.
4. A patient (who/whom) has a cholesteatoma may present with unilateral hearing loss.
5. The receptionist should always ask a new patient if (he or she/they) brought (his or her/their) records.
6. Do not assume that patients know how (his or her/their) medications are to be taken.
7. Both tympanic membranes were noted to be bulging, and (its/their) color was bright red.
8. This patient, (who/whom) I consider to be reliable, says that he was treated poorly by your department.
9. Please call if Dr. Adams or (I/me) can be of help.
10. A patient with chronic tonsillitis often has to have (their/his or her) throat cultured..

Exercise 4.7: Proofreading Review

CHIEF COMPLAINT: The patient had been well until about four weeks ago when he developed a runny nose, sore throat, and pain in both ears. He was seen by his pediatrician, who gave him an antibiotic for seven days. Two weeks later, the ear pain has not resolved.

PAST MEDICAL HISTORY: Noncontributory.

PHYSICAL EXAMINATION: Left TM is injected with whitish exudate. Palpable, shotty left submandibular lymph nodes and a 2 cm firm periauricular lymph node. Physical exam is otherwise within normal limits.

CHAPTER 5

Exercise 5.1: Recognizing Look-Alikes and Sound-Alikes

1. doses
2. dozed
3. presents
4. presence
5. inspiratory or expiratory
6. breath
7. breathe
8. course
9. profuse
10. lose

Exercise 5.2: Matching Sound and Spelling

1. tachycardia
2. pleural
3. anicteric
4. theophylline
5. bronchiectasis
6. pneumonitis
7. rhonchus
8. auscultation
9. tachypnea
10. thyromegaly
11. nasopharynx
12. hemoptysis
13. diffuse
14. trachea
15. organomegaly

Exercise 5.3: Choosing Words from Context

1. respiratory distress
2. auscultation
3. cyanotic
4. afebrile
5. effusion
6. hemoptysis
7. tachypneic
8. rhonchi
9. nebulizer
10. tachycardiac

Exercise 5.4: Pairing Words and Meanings

1. I
2. H
3. E
4. A
5. J
6. C
7. B
8. D
9. F
10. G or H

Exercise 5.5: Creating Terms from Word Forms

1. thyroidectomy
2. hypoxia
3. pneumonectomy or pulmonectomy
4. hyperplasia
5. hypercapnia
6. hypoplasia
7. hypercythemia
8. pulmonectomy or pneumonectomy
9. hypocapnia
10. bronchitis

Exercise 5.6: Editing for Correct Punctuation

1. Since the patient has improved with conservative management, we will not consider operative intervention at this time.
2. Our latest project, remodeling the waiting room, is going to be more expensive than we had planned.
3. Past surgeries include hysterectomy, cholecystectomy, and appendectomy.
4. Surprisingly, the patient's condition improved.
5. Laboratory tests to be ordered include a complete blood count, chemistry panel, and electrolytes.
6. The risks and benefits of the procedure were explained to the patient and his wife, and the patient signed the consent forms.
7. The planned surgery has a very high success rate; however, I explained to the patient that any surgery has an element of risk.
8. Abdomen is soft; no organomegaly is noted.
9. The patient is to return to the emergency department immediately if he develops nausea, fever over 100°, or dramatically increased pain.
10. The patient has a history of coronary artery disease, having undergone an angioplasty.
11. When testing, the students should refrain from speaking.
12. After the induction of general anesthesia, an endotracheal tube was placed.
13. The wound was then irrigated using normal saline, and the deep muscles were closed using chromic sutures.
14. The experimental drug studies were carried out in San Diego, California; Denver, Colorado; Minneapolis, Minnesota; and Atlanta, Georgia.
15. The patient is a young female college student.
16. Patients with AIDS, who generally are underweight, should receive nutritional counseling.
17. Thank you, Dr. Smith, for seeing this patient in pulmonary consultation.
18. Given the patient's overall debilitated condition and end-stage lung disease, he wishes to be made a DNR.

Exercise 5.7: Proofreading Review

PHYSICAL EXAMINATION: Pulse of 120, respiratory rate of 30, temperature of 99°, and weight 40.6 kg. She is a thin, pale, adolescent female in mild respiratory distress. Head is normocephalic and atraumatic. Pupils are equal, round, and reactive to light. Extraocular movements are full. Scleras are anicteric. Conjunctivae are not injected. Nose is without discharge. No flaring. Her mouth has pink and moist mucosa with no lesions. Her lips are cyanotic. Her face has a flush over the cheekbones. Her neck is supple, without palpable lymph nodes.

CHAPTER 6

Exercise 6.1: Recognizing Look-Alikes and Sound-Alikes

1. intraocular
2. recent
3. pulses
4. pedal
5. injection, intramuscularly
6. nitrites
7. palpation
8. palpitations
9. profusely
10. pericardial

Exercise 6.2: Matching Sound and Spelling

1. xiphoid
2. arrhythmia
3. anastomosis
4. nifedipine
5. Lisinopril
6. Lovastatin
7. lesion
8. occlusion
9. aneurysm
10. venous
11. terazosin
12. palpitations
13. angina
14. verapamil
15. captopril

Exercise 6.3: Choosing Words from Context

1. infarction
2. ambulating
3. intravenous
4. artery
5. oximetry
6. ventricular
7. hemodynamic
8. prolapse
9. attenuation
10. catheter

Exercise 6.4: Pairing Words and Meanings

1. H
2. J
3. L
4. A
5. B
6. G
7. K
8. D
9. C
10. E

Exercise 6.5: Creating Terms from Word Forms

1. tachycardia
2. sublingual
3. stenocardia
4. hemostasis
5. pericardial
6. dyspnea
7. diastolic
8. circumflex
9. bradycardia
10. diagram

Exercise 6.6: Editing for Correct Punctuation

1. CHIEF COMPLAINT: "I think I'm having a heart attack."
2. Gertrude "Trudy" Schmidt presented to my office today.
3. Because her chest pain did not resolve with sublingual nitroglycerin, she was transported to the emergency department by a family member (her son).
4. The patient states that his knee "doesn't feel right" when he walks.
5. The patient's history has been well documented on previous admissions—please see old records. [Parentheses around "please see old records" would also be acceptable.]
6. In accordance with his wishes, the patient was made a DNR (do not resuscitate).
7. Discharge Diagnosis: Acute bacterial endocarditis, resolving. [A dash is also acceptable.]
8. Please set up an appointment with Dr. Edwards (you can get his phone number from my secretary) at your earliest convenience. [Dashes instead of parentheses would also be correct.]
9. The patient has a history of (1) chronic obstructive pulmonary disease, (2) congestive heart failure, and (3) hypertension.
10. If the infection does not respond to amoxicillin, we may need to use one of the "big guns" like cephalexin.

Exercise 6.7: Proofreading Review

Left heart catheterization and coronary angiography were performed via Judkins technique using the right femoral artery. Hemodynamic recordings were made in the ascending aorta at rest.

Blood samples for oximetry were obtained from the pulmonary artery and ascending aorta. Repeat hemodynamic recordings were made on pullback. The catheter was then withdrawn, and direct pressure was applied to the right femoral artery. Both good hemostasis and pedal pulses were obtained. The patient tolerated the procedure well and left the laboratory in satisfactory condition.

CHAPTER 7

Exercise 7.1: Recognizing Look-Alikes and Sound-Alikes

1. anesthesia
2. anesthetic
3. hemostasis
4. ileum
5. mucus
6. mucous
7. cited
8. site
9. dysphagia
10. ileus

Exercise 7.2: Matching Sound and Spelling

1. cirrhosis
2. aphagia
3. eructation
4. polyp
5. albumin
6. aphthous stomatitis
7. intussusception
8. melena
9. sphincter
10. cachexia
11. malaise
12. flexure
13. hematemesis
14. bilirubin
15. diverticulosis
16. ileum or ilium

Exercise 7.3: Choosing Words from Context

1. biopsy
2. dehydration
3. supine
4. palpable
5. Crohn's disease
6. hyperemic
7. laparoscope
8. malignancy
9. cauterization
10. salivary glands

Exercise 7.4: Pairing Words and Meanings

1. F
2. G
3. J
4. I
5. E
6. C
7. D
8. A
9. B
10. H

Exercise 7.5: Creating Terms from Word Forms

1. percutaneous
2. carcinoma
3. cholecystitis
4. parotiditis
5. stomatitis
6. adenocarcinoma
7. glossitis
8. hematemesis
9. dyspeptic
10. hepatoma

Exercise 7.6: Editing for Placement of Modifiers

1. Because of increasing complaints of esophageal reflux, the patient was referred to a gastroenterologist, who ordered an upper GI.
2. The doctor performed the rectal examination in the left lateral Sims position.
3. She called about her husband's inflamed incision three weeks post appendectomy.
4. OK—no changes required.
5. Surgery was deferred because the patient improved on antibiotic therapy.
6. At 225 pounds, she was instructed to eat smaller meals and to exercise more often.
7. A curved incision of 3 cm was made just above the umbilicus.
8. Feeling very nauseous, the patient accepted an emesis basin from the nurse.
9. With a family history of colon polyps, the patient will require screening colonoscopy every two years.
10. The doctor arranged for Mr. Smith's admission. Had Mr. Smith notified the insurance company, reimbursement would have been greater.

Exercise 7.7: Proofreading Review

OPERATIVE PROCEDURE: The patient was placed on the operating table in the supine position. After satisfactory induction of general anesthesia, the abdominal wall was prepared and draped in the usual sterile fashion. Pneumoperitoneum was instilled through a small infraumbilical incision and a Veress needle.

Dissection of the hepatoduodenal ligament was then commenced with identification of the cystic artery and the cystic duct.

Earlier in the procedure, a percutaneous liver biopsy was performed to the right lobe of the liver, using a Tru-Cut needle under direct vision. No bleeding was found from this site later in the operation.

The abdomen was now copiously irrigated through the lateral ports. The ports were now removed under direct vision.

CHAPTER 8

Exercise 8.1: Recognizing Look-Alikes and Sound-Alikes

1. illicit
2. elicit
3. continuous
4. through
5. descent
6. dysmenorrhea
7. menorrhagia
8. imminent
9. menorrhalgia
10. menopause

Exercise 8.2: Matching Sound and Spelling

1. episiotomy
2. colposcopy
3. chromosome
4. amenorrhea
5. condyloma
6. graafian
7. gestation
8. hysterectomy
9. curettage
10. in situ
11. multipara
12. gonorrhea
13. menorrhagia
14. oligomenorrhea
15. perineum

Exercise 8.3: Choosing Words from Context

1. mammogram
2. menses
3. genital
4. introitus
5. lymphocyte
6. dysmenorrhea
7. carcinoma
8. gravida
9. uterine
10. peritoneum

Exercise 8.4: Pairing Words and Meanings

1. H
2. G
3. F
4. J
5. A
6. K
7. B
8. C
9. D
10. I

Exercise 8.5: Creating Terms from Word Forms

1. salpingectomy
2. thyromegaly
3. oophoritis
4. menses
5. leiomyoma
6. dysgerminoma
7. mammogram
8. leiomyoma
9. oophorectomy
10. hepatomegaly
11. mastectomy
12. sonogram

Exercise 8.6A: Editing for Correct Plural Forms

1. fossae
2. prognoses
3. appendices
4. labia
5. data
6. salpinges
7. uteri
8. ova
9. criteria
10. foramina

Exercise 8.6B: Editing for Correct Plural Forms

1. Colonoscopy revealed multiple (diverticulum/diverticula) in the ascending colon.
2. Hysterosalpingogram showed right (hydrosalpinx/hydrosalpinges).
3. Her history of intolerance to cold led to the diagnosis of Raynaud's (phenomenon/phenomena).
4. She was treated with ampicillin 500 (mg/mgs) q.i.d. times ten days.
5. Delivery of the infant was achieved using (forcep/forceps).
6. James was told by his doctor that he had a (herpe/herpes) infection.
7. Examination of her cervix revealed the presence of different (fungus/fungi).
8. Babinskis/Babinski's were negative.
9. Serial (CBC/CBCs/CBC's) were obtained.
10. (Ascitis/Ascites) is a common condition in people with liver disease.

Exercise 8.7: Proofreading Review

Bilateral mammograms were performed using film screen technique and compared to previous xeromammograms from June 1992 and February 1993. There appears to be a small and smoothly marginated, oval-shaped nodule in the upper quadrant of the right breast, not as clearly visualised on the previous xeromammograms.

Increased density is again seen in the upper outer quadrants bilaterally, unchanged and consistent with fibroglandular tissue. Neither breast demonstrates evidence of architectural distortion, clustered microcalcifications, skin thickening, or retraction.

The patient was placed on the operating table in the supine position under satisfactory general endotracheal anesthesia. A #14 Foley catheter was inserted. The abdomen was then prepped with Betadine scrub and solution and was draped in the usual sterile manner.

CHAPTER 9

Exercise 9.1: Recognizing Look-Alikes and Sound-Alikes

1. hole
2. too
3. farther
4. further
5. scene
6. too
7. status
8. to
9. addition
10. dilated

Exercise 9.2: Matching Sound and Spelling

1. dysuria
2. polyuria
3. lymphadenitis
4. nocturia
5. rhabdomyosarcoma
6. proteinuria
7. nephrolithotomy
8. epididymis
9. orchiectomy
10. calculus
11. proteinaceous
12. epithelium
13. nephrostomy
14. orchiocele
15. prostate

Exercise 9.3: Choosing Words from Context

1. renal failure
2. catheter
3. pendulous
4. proximal
5. vesicle
6. steroid
7. hematuria
8. neoplasm
9. genitalia
10. endoscope

Exercise 9.4: Pairing Words and Meanings

1. I
2. E
3. F
4. A
5. C
6. B
7. D
8. J
9. G
10. H

Exercise 9.5: Creating Terms from Word Forms

1. nephrectomy
2. dysuria
3. hepatic
4. hematuria
5. lymphadenopathy
6. nocturia
7. uremia
8. orchiectomy
9. nephritis
10. extrahepatic

Exercise 9.6: Editing for Correct Capitalization

HISTORY OF PRESENT ILLNESS: Willie Dayton is a 55-year-old African-American who speaks French and Chinese, presenting with a chief complaint of chest pain. He has been having mild chest pain since early autumn, but it has been increasing recently, especially over the holidays. He has been taking Dyazide for blood pressure and also uses ibuprofen occasionally. On Sunday, New Year's Day, he called his insurance company and was referred to South Side Hospital. The patient presented to the emergency department for evaluation and was noted to have T wave inversions on his ECG. Chest x-ray showed no pneumonia or pulmonary edema. He was given nitroglycerin sublingually times two, with resolution of his chest pain. CPK was shown to be elevated, and cardiology was called to evaluate this patient and assume his care. The patient was admitted to the intensive care unit at 0300.

PAST MEDICAL HISTORY: The patient has a diagnosis of early Parkinson's disease and is treated by a neurologist for this.

ALLERGIES: The patient is allergic to sulfa, which causes hives.

PHYSICAL EXAMINATION
VITAL SIGNS: Blood pressure 110/95, pulse 75, respirations 18.
HEENT: Normocephalic, atraumatic, pupils equal, round, reactive to light and accommodation. Fundi clear, no AV nicking. Ears, nose, and throat clear.
NECK: Supple, no JVD, no lymphadenopathy.
CHEST: Clear to percussion and auscultation
HEART: S1 and S2 normal. There was a grade 2/6 systolic ejection murmur heard best at the left lower sternal border.
ABDOMEN: Supple. No organomegaly or rebound tenderness.
GENITALIA: Deferred.
EXTREMETIES: No clubbing, cyanosis, or edema.

HOSPITAL COURSE: The patient was taken to the cardiac catheterization laboratory on the morning of admission. This study revealed no areas of stenosis of the coronary arterial system.

The patient was given nitroglycerin sublingually p.r.n. chest pain and was given Procardia for his hypertension. His ECG normalized, and on Tuesday he was subjected to a treadmill exercise test using the modified Bruce protocol. This test was interpreted by the cardiologist as showing no signs of ischemia.

The patient was discharged in excellent condition, to follow up in one week with Dr. Smith at the South Bay Regional Cardiac Center.

DISCHARGE MEDICATIONS
1. Procardia 10 mg q.d.
2. Aspirin one per day.
3. Nitroglycerin sublingual p.r.n. chest pain.

Exercise 9.7: Proofreading Review

S: 56-year-old Middle Eastern male who is seen in followup for an elevated PSA, recent pyelonephritis, and microscopic hematuria. He has been referred to urology and will see them in two weeks. Today, he says he has occasional mild burning with urination, but the dysuria has overall improved. He denies any flank or abdominal pain, nausea, or vomiting.

O: Routine laboratory was done at his last visit. His PSA was 14.3. He says that in the past his highest PSA was 6, and that was roughly six months ago. He had a transurethral resection of the prostate in 1992. Other laboratories: A CBC showed a platelet count of 124,000, hemoglobin 14.9, MCV 92. Chemistry profile within normal limits, including renal function.

A: 1. Resolved pyelonephritis.
2. Elevated PSA with a patient history of benign prostatic hypertrophy raises the question of possible prostate cancer.

P: 1. Will give another seven-day course of Bactrim to insure that the urinary tract infection is resolved by the time of his urology appointment in two weeks.
2. Patient is to call if he has any worsening of his symptoms.

CHAPTER 10

Exercise 10.1: Recognizing Look-Alikes and SoundAlikes

1. weak
2. week
3. affected
4. off
5. effective
6. accepted
7. osteal
8. affect
9. sprained
10. except

Exercise 10.2: Matching Sound and Spelling

1. osseous
2. chondromalacia
3. calcaneus
4. crepitus
5. trochanter
6. ankylosis
7. kyphosis
8. clavicula
9. diaphysis
10. chondritis
11. parietal
12. osteophyte
13. ischium
14. scoliosis
15. humerus
16. dactylomegaly
17. ankylotic
18. spondylitis
19. rheumatoid
20. ostealgia

Exercise 10.3: Choosing Words from Context

1. prosthesis
2. radiograph
3. residual
4. tibia
5. edematous
6. cervical
7. aseptic
8. kyphosis
9. neural
10. necrosis

Exercise 10.4: Pairing Words and Meanings

1. G
2. J
3. I
4. A
5. H
6. B
7. D
8. E
9. F
10. C

Exercise 10.5: Creating Terms from Word Forms

1. osteoporosis
2. epiphysis
3. spondylitis
4. necrosis
5. lordois
6. osteomyelitis
7. metatarsus
8. myelitis
9. diaphysis
10. kyphosis
11. metaphysis
12. osteophyte

Exercise 10.6: Editing for Correct Use of Numbers

DISCHARGE SUMMARY

PATIENT: Juarez, Juan
MR#: 12-34-56

DATE OF ADMISSION: (April 4 199_; 4/4/XX)
DATE OF DISCHARGE: (April 6 199_; 4/6/XX)

DISCHARGE DIAGNOSIS: Herniated nucleus pulposus, (L-5-S-1; L5-S1).

OPERATION PERFORMED: Right partial (L-4; L4) hemilaminectomy with excision of herniated disc.
HISTORY: This is a (fifty; 50)-year-old Hispanic male who presented with a (four; 4)-month history of progressive low back pain. Over the past (one; 1) month he has had worsening symptoms and now has numbness, tingling, and pain radiating down his right leg.

PAST MEDICAL HISTORY: His history is significant for (two; 2) episodes of pneumonia (five; 5) years ago, and he has chronic bronchitis.

SOCIAL HISTORY: The patient smokes (one; 1) pack of cigarettes per day and has done so for the past (20; twenty) years. He drinks (2 6-packs; two six-packs; two 6-packs; 2 six-packs) of beer per week.

ADMISSION MEDICATIONS

1. Theo-Dur (three hundred milligrams; 300 milligrams; 300 mg) (tid; t.i.d.; TID).
2. Proventil inhaler (two; 2) puffs (q12h; q. 12 h.; q.12h.)

DRUG ALLERGIES: CODEINE, which causes a rash.

PHYSICAL EXAMINATION
GENERAL APPEARANCE: This is a slightly obese Hispanic male appearing slightly older than his stated age of (50-years; fifty-years; 50 years).
VITAL SIGNS: Blood pressure (one hundred twenty over sixty; 120 over 60; 120/60), pulse (eighty; 80) and regular, respirations (twelve; 12), temperature (ninety-eight degrees; 98°).
HEENT: Pupils equal and reactive to light. The left tympanic membrane was (one plus/1+) injected. Nares were patent bilaterally.
NECK: Right shotty supraclavicular lymph node approximately (2, two) cm in size. Trachea midline.
LUNGS: Clear to percussion and auscultation.
HEART: Auscultation revealed a grade (two over six; 2 over 6; 2/6) systolic ejection murmur. PMI is at the (fifth; 5th) intercostal space.

DISCHARGE SUMMARY
PATIENT: Juarez, Juan
MR#: 12-34-56
Page 2

ABDOMEN: Slightly obese, (one plus; 1 plus; 1+) tenderness in the epigastrium. Bowel sounds were present, no hepatosplenomegaly.
SPINE: Negative CVA tenderness. There was (two plus; 2+) tenderness in the (L-4-L-5; L4-L5) area. Straight leg raising was negative on the left, positive on the right at (sixty; 60) degrees.
EXTREMITIES: No clubbing, cyanosis, or edema. Distal pulses were good.
NEUROLOGIC: Cranial nerves (two through twelve; II-XII; 2-12) were intact. The patient was alert and oriented (times three; x3).

LABORATORY DATA: Admission CBC revealed WBC of (5,800; 5800) with (seventy-one; 71) polys, (two; 2) bands, and (one; 1) eosinophil. Hemoglobin was (twelve; 12), hematocrit (thirty-nine percent; 39%; 39 percent). BUN was (eight; 8), creatinine (point nine; .9; 0.9).

HOSPITAL COURSE: Lumbar myelogram on day of admission revealed significant disc herniation at the (L-4-L-5; L4-L5) level. The patient was taken to the operating room, where right hemilaminectomy was performed.

Postoperatively the patient had a temperature spike to (101°; one-hundred one degrees) and was started on Ancef. He had no further temperature elevations and his chest x-ray remained clear. He had good resolution of his symptoms.

The patient was discharged to home to be followed in clinic in (five; 5) days. Instructions were given for no heavy lifting. It was suggested that a (thirty, 30)-minute walk be taken daily.

DISCHARGE MEDICATIONS

1. Vicodin (one; 1) p.o. (q.3-4h.; q three to four hours) p.r.n. pain.
2. Theo-Dur and Proventil as previously.

Exercise 10.7: Proofreading Review

DATE OF ADMISSION: 8/ 5/XX

Jonathan is status post right below-knee amputation for synovial sarcoma. He is without complaints and is ambulating with his below-knee prosthesis quite well. His abdomen is soft and nontender. There are no masses. The incision is well healed. The right thigh skin graph site is clean. There is no palpable mass and there is no open wound. If he experiences pain, he is to take one Vicodin p.o. q.4-6h.

CHAPTER 11

Exercise 11.1: Recognizing Look-Alikes and Sound-Alikes

1. recession
2. clenching
3. conscious
4. pair
5. pare
6. crises
7. radical
8. their
9. hemifocal
10. regression or remission

Exercise 11.2: Matching Sound and Spelling

1. syncope
2. radiculopathy
3. nausea
4. neuron
5. meninges
6. neurasthenia
7. aphasia
8. neuralgia
9. petit mal
10. psychosomatic
11. meningocele
12. pituitary
13. cerebrospinal
14. ataxia

Exercise 11.3: Choosing Words from Context

1. cranium
2. hemiparesis
3. parietal
4. plantar
5. funduscopic
6. cerebellar examination
7. atrophy
8. interictal
9. ventricle
10. cerebrovascular

Exercise 11.4: Pairing Words and Meanings

1. E
2. H
3. J
4. I
5. A
6. C
7. D
8. F
9. B
10. G

Exercise 11.5: Creating Terms from Word Forms

1. hemiparesis
2. encephalitis
3. somnipathy
4. paraplegia
5. interictal
6. meningitis
7. polyneuritis
8. postictal
9. hemiplegia
10. myelopathy

Exercise 11.6: Identifying Abbreviations

1. The patient was diagnosed with amyotrophic lateral sclerosis, a degenerative neurologic disease commonly known as Lou Gherig's disease.
2. Because of her symptoms of left hemiparesis and confusion, Mrs. Smith was felt to have suffered a cerebrovascular accident.
3. An electroencephalogram, a test showing the electrical activity of the brain, was performed to rule out seizure disorder.
4. Head, eyes, ears, nose, throat: Pupils equal, round, reactive to light and accommodation. Extraocular movements intact.
5. The patient suffers from weakness, paresthesias, and speech disturbances secondary to multiple sclerosis, a degenerative neurologic disorder.
6. The patient is alert and oriented, in no acute distress, resting comfortably.
7. The patient is nothing by mouth [or nil per os] in preparation for surgery; do not serve him breakfast.
8. The infant's phenylketonuria test was positive, so he will require a diet very low in phenylalanine to prevent mental retardation.
9. The patient has had several episodes of transient ischemic attacks with neurologic deficits.
10. Myelogram revealed herniated nucleus pulposus at the L3-L4 level, with a significant disc protrusion.

Exercise 11.7: Proofreading Review

DOB: 3/29/56

ADMISSION DIAGNOSIS: Loss of consciousness, drug overdose.

HISTORY OF PRESENT ILLNESS: The patient is a 40-year-old female who was found blue in the face and unconscious by family this a.m. This occurred approximately 10 to 15 minutes after she had injected a line of heroin IV. Reportedly her son started CPR and she gasped for breath. Fire department arrived and administered Narcan.

The patient now complains of headache. She reports that she has not used heroin for several months. The family reports that she does heroin four-five times per week.

PAST MEDICAL HISTORY: Seizure disorder, epilepsy since childhood. Intravenous drug addict for ten years.

MEDICATIONS: Percocet for migraine headaches, Dilantin and Phenobarbital.

ALLERGIES: No known drug allergies.

PHYSICAL EXAMINATION: A well-developed, well-nourished Caucasian female in no acute distress, awake, alert, oriented. HEENT: Pupils equal, round, and reactive to light and accommodation; extraocular muscles intact. Speech clear, respirations unlabored. Lungs clear to percussion and auscultation. HEART: Regular rate and rhythm. She follows instructions appropriately and moves all extremities. Deep tendon reflexes are symmetric.

EMERGENCY ROOM COURSE: The patient was examined as above. She will be observed for another hour, and if she maintains her present level of consciousness, plan to discharge to home with appropriate instructions.

ASSESSMENT: Heroin overdose.

PLAN: The patient is to be referred to the mental health unit for addiction counseling. She should continue with her Dilantin and Phenobarbital and follow up with her family M.D.

CHAPTER 12

Exercise 12.1: Recognizing Look-Alikes and Sound-Alikes

1. advised
2. generic
3. presents
4. advice
5. basal
6. energy
7. radical
8. acidic
9. prostate
10. prostrate

Exercise 12.2: Matching Sound and Spelling

1. ecchymosis
2. phagocytosis
3. sessile
4. palliative
5. lymphatic
6. metastasis
7. roentgenology
8. leukemia
9. agglutination
10. scirrhous
11. hemorrhage
12. squamous
13. lymphocyte
14. chromic
15. staphylococcemia

Exercise 12.3: Choosing Words from Context

1. leukemia
2. platelet
3. carcinoma
4. sclerosis
5. lumbar
6. embryo
7. ecchymoses
8. parenchyma
9. lymphadenopathy
10. pelvis

Exercise 12.4: Pairing Words and Meanings

1. G
2. I
3. H
4. A
5. J
6. B
7. C
8. D
9. F
10. E

Exercise 12.5: Creating Terms from Word Forms

1. anaplasia
2. reticulocyte
3. thrombocytosis
4. papilloma
5. thrombocyte
6. neutrophil
7. cytology
8. phagocytosis
9. immunology
10. macrocytes

Exercise 12.6: Editing for Correct Use of Apostrophes

1. B and C
2. B
3. A
4. C
5. C
6. A and B
7. A
8. B
9. B
10. C
11. C
12. C (assuming the correct spelling of the name is Simmons)

Exercise 12.7: Proofreading Review

Charlotte is a 30-year-old woman who first noted a fullness in the right lower anterior cervical region in the late winter. It had gradually grown in size. In early March she was treated with a one-week course of erythromycin without response. The mass "bothered" her slightly, but it was not painful. There has been no change in her usually good appetite. Her weight has remained stable.

The outside radiographic studies were reviewed with the radiologist. The chest x-ray reveals a relatively small anterior mediastinal mass (approximately one-fourth of the chest diameter). The chest CT scan confirms the presence of the mediastinal mass, without pulmonary parenchymal involvement.

CHAPTER 13

Exercise 13.1: Recognizing Look-Alikes and Sound-Alikes

1. in vitro
2. except
3. doze
4. allergen
5. costal
6. accept
7. weight-
8. course
9. coastal
10. except

Exercise 13.2: Matching Sound and Spelling

1. neutrophil
2. pathogen
3. prophylaxis
4. phagocyte
5. pyrexia
6. communicable
7. immunity
8. titer
9. lymphopenia
10. cefaclor

Exercise 13.3: Choosing Words from Context

1. prophylaxis
2. costal margin
3. in vitro
4. sinusitis
5. immunodeficiency
6. neutrophil count
7. titer
8. antigens
9. substernal
10. aerosolized

Exercise 13.4: Pairing Words and Meanings

1. H
2. F
3. E
4. A
5. C
6. G
7. J
8. D
9. B
10. I

Exercise 13.5: Creating Terms from Word Forms

1. bronchitis
2. immunoglobulin
3. splenomegaly
4. lymphadenitis
5. autoimmune
6. enterovirus
7. bacteremia
8. otitis
9. oxyhemoglobin
10. cytomegalovirus

Exercise 13.6: Editing for Correct Hyphen Use

HISTORY: This 30-year-old white male reported to clinic today for routine followup, with diagnosis of HIV disease.

He was initially diagnosed in mid-August 1993. Additional diagnoses include major depression, chronic serous otitis media, chronic active hepatitis, low back pain, and headaches.

Since his previous examination, the patient has continued to have active medical problems. With regard to his HIV infection, the patient continues to have a decreasing CD4 count. He is followed by a physician in Los Angeles, and his most recent CD4 count was an absolute value of 250. The patient notes a 10- to 12-week history of increasing night sweats. The patient at present is on no antiretroviral therapy, having discontinued AZT therapy two months ago.

The patient also had a long recovery complicated by infection following a scar revision of his lower lip earlier this year. He also continues to be followed for his diagnosis of chronic active hepatitis. He also is followed for chronic depression, for which he was recently tapered off Zoloft therapy. The patient continues to be affected by right-sided migrainelike headaches, for which he had a recent CT scan which was negative for any intracranial pathology.

FAMILY HISTORY: Noncontributory.

SOCIAL HISTORY: The patient continues to work but on a part-time basis. He works at home using his computer. He is a nondrinker. He was a one-pack-per-day smoker until two years ago, when he stopped.
PHYSICAL EXAMINATION: He is a slightly ill-appearing white male who just turned 30 years old. VITAL SIGNS: Temp. 97.6° F, P 80, R 20, BP 140/80. HEENT: Pupils equal and reactive. Extraocular movements are intact. NECK: Mild supraclavicular adenopathy. No jugular venous distention. LUNGS: Mild end-expiratory wheezes, worse on the left. HEART: Regular rate and rhythm. PMI is in the 5th left intercostal space at midclavicular line. Abdomen is soft, nontender on the left with some mild right-sided pain. Liver span is two fingerbreadths below the costal margin. Back reveals mild tenderness at the L4- L5 level. No costovertebral angle tenderness. GENITALIA: Normal male phallus with descended testes bilaterally. Rectal exam reveals normal anal sphincter tone with a few mild external and internal hemorrhoids. Pulses, including brachioradialis, femoral, popliteal, and dorsalis pedis, normal.

LABORATORY DATA: White blood cell count is 4.1, hematocrit 45.5, hemoglobin 15.6, platelet count 181,000. Differential shows 52% segs, 34% lymphocytes, 12% monocytes, 2% eosinophils. The urinalysis revealed 1-2 white cells per high power field, otherwise normal. The liver function tests are normal. The CD4 count is 210 with a CD4 percentage of 15%. Intradermal skin testing reveals the patient to be anergic. VDRL is nonreactive.

DIAGNOSES

1. Human immunodeficiency virus infection.
2. Chronic hepatitis B.
3. History of major depression.
4. Migraine-like headaches.
5. History of chronic middle ear infections.

PLAN: The patient will follow up in six months for clinic visit and repeat labs. We have discussed appropriate short- and long-term goals for this patient. He will continue to work part-time, as he enjoys this and is having no difficulty performing his job-related activities.

Exercise 13.7: Proofreading Review

This is a known severe asthmatic patient who has been admitted on numerous occasions. She developed her asthma approximately two years ago. She was well up until a week prior to admission when she developed a cold, which caused her to be short of breath and congested. The congestion continued, and she gave herself some injections
of Adrenalin.

Physical examination at the time of admission revealed a lady in moderate distress. There were wheezes, rales, and rhonchi throughout all lung fields.There were some substernal and intercostal retractions.The throat was somewhat inflamed.The rest of the physical examination at the time of admission was entirely within normal limits

Index